The Definitive
CARDIFF CITY F.C.

A statistical history

Richard Shepherd

Volume 17 in a series of club histories
A *SoccerData* Publication from Tony Brown

Published in Great Britain by Tony Brown,
4 Adrian Close, Beeston, Nottingham NG9 6FL.
Telephone 0115 973 6086. E-mail soccer@innotts.co.uk
First published 2002

Other volumes in this series are:

Rochdale
Northampton Town
Chesterfield
Portsmouth
Barnsley
Queen's Park Rangers
Scunthorpe United
Aldershot
Torquay United
Luton Town
Reading
Hartlepool United
Hull City
Barrow
Darlington
Newton Heath

Please write to the publisher for news of future volumes.

ISBN 1 899468 17 X

CARDIFF CITY RECORDS PAGE

PLAYERS:

Most Appearances   Phil Dwyer 531 (471 League, 23 FA Cup, 28 League Cup, 9 other)
(Phil also made 44 appearances in the Welsh Cup)
Don Murray 483 (406 + 23 + 21 + 33)

Most Goals   Len Davies 148 (128 + 19 + 0 + 1)

Most League Goals in a Season   Stan Richards, 30, 1946/47

Most International caps   Alf Sherwood, Wales 39 (plus two with Newport County)

THE CLUB:

Honours   Runners-up Division One, 1923/24
Champions Division Three (South) 1946/47
Champions Division Three 1992/93
F.A. Cup winners 1926/27
Charity Shield winners 1927
Welsh Cup winners on 22 occasions, 1912 to 1993
F.A.W. Premier Cup winners 2001/02

Best League performance   Second in Division One, 1923/24
Best F.A. Cup performance   Finalists 1924/25, winners 1926/27
Best League Cup performance Semi-finalists 1965/66
Best European performance   Semi-finalists, Cup Winners Cup, 1967/68
Most League points   86, 1982/83 (3 points for a win)
66, 1946/47 (2 points for a win)

Most League goals   95, 2000/01 Division Three
Most League wins in a season   30, 1946/47
Best League win   9-2 v. Thames 6 February 1932, Division Three (South)
Best League away win   7-1 v. Oldham Athletic, 16 March 2002
Best F.A. Cup win   8-0 v. Enfield, R1 28 November 1931
Best League run undefeated   21, 21 September 1946 to 1 March 1947
Undefeated League games, home 25, from 11 September 1982
Undefeated League games, away 10, from 28 September 1946
Best run of League wins   9, 26 October 1946 to 28 December 1946
Best run of home League wins 9, from 9 December 1922 and 29 September 1951
Longest run of League draws 6, 29 November 1980 to 17 January 1981

Most appearances; Phil Dwyer

Most goals; Len Davies

A SHORT HISTORY

The history of the Club began in 1899, when a football team known as Riverside was formed by a group of enthusiasts from Riverside Cricket Club. Games were first played in Sophia Gardens in almost the same area as the present Glamorgan Cricket Club have their headquarters. In 1902, the club joined forces with one of their local rivals to become "Riverside Albion" and six years later the name was changed to the present one of Cardiff City. Cardiff had become a city three years earlier and the South Wales Football Association were pleased to sanction the change. The Club turned professional in 1910, becoming a Limited Company and at the same time building its present home at Ninian Park. The ground was named after Lord Ninian Crichton-Stuart, second son of the 3rd Marquis of Bute.

The first match played at Ninian Park was a friendly, when an Aston Villa side provided the opposition on September 1 1910, with an estimated 7,000 spectators present. From 1910 to 1920, the club competed in The Southern League. In 1920, Cardiff City were elected to the Football League, taking their place in Division Two. Their first match was against Stockport County, which they duly won 5-2. They were so successful that promotion was gained to the First Division at the first attempt. They also reached the semi-final of the F.A. Cup that season.

More success was to follow; in 1924 they became the Football League Championship runners-up to Huddersfield Town, just missing the Championship on goal average. They would have finished first had they conceded just one goal fewer. In 1925, they reached the F.A. Cup Final, but lost to Sheffield United. However, in 1927, they became the first club to take the F.A. Cup out of England when they beat Arsenal 1-0. They then won the Charity Shield by beating Corinthians 2-1 at Stamford Bridge. The end of the 1920s however saw Cardiff City relegated, in 1929 to Division Two and again in 1931 to Division 3 South.

In 1947, Cardiff were promoted as champions from Division Three South, and in 1952 were back in the First Division, promoted as runners-up to Sheffield Wednesday. April 1953 saw a record League crowd packed into Ninian Park, when 57,893 spectators were present for the visit of Arsenal. City went down to Division Two in 1957, but returned to the top flight again in 1960. Meanwhile, another crowd record was being set for Ninian Park when 62,634 crammed in for the International match between Wales and England in October 1959.

In 1962, although back in Division Two, Cardiff gained their first taste of competitive European football by winning the Welsh Cup, going on to take part in the European Cup Winners Cup of 1964/65. The team that season could boast seven Welsh international players including both Charles brothers, John and Mel. In 1968, the Bluebirds came close to European glory, losing on aggregate by the odd goal in seven to SV Hamburg in the semi-final. In 1971, Cardiff beat Real Madrid 1-0 in the first leg of the European Cup Winners Cup quarter-final. A header from Brian Clark gave them the result, but the Bluebirds eventually lost the tie 2-1 on aggregate. Their first leg victory in front of 47,500 at Ninian Park rates as one of Cardiff City's greatest moments.

The last twenty years have seen the club yo-yo between the divisions, with six relegations and five promotions. A narrow defeat in the 2001/02 play-off games was disappointing, but leaves hope the club is once more on the way back to the top flight.

1911/12. Back: J McGill, J Burton, E Thompson, T Husbands, R Leah, D McDougall, Mr. L Nash, Mr. C Wall. Centre: J Evans, JS Bates, R Lawrie, Mr. W Empsall, A Waters (capt), Mr. SH Nicholls (Chairman), C Pinch, J Duffy, T Abley. Front: H Tracey, RF Hiftle, W Hardy, HW Featherstone.

August 1913. Back: R McKenzie, G West, J Evans, HJ Kneeshaw, P Cassidy, J Stephenson, E Milford, W Davidson, TW Witts, TH Robertson. Centre: T Doncaster, JK Bennett, A Holt, H Featherstone, JH Burton, H Harvey, W Hardy, H Ward, R Leah, J Clarke. Front: G Burton, H Tracey, W Devlin, H Keggans, WB Gaughan, J Henderson, FC Keenor.

August 1919. Players only: Back; FC Keenor (in suit), unknown, Jones, Dalton, A Layton, RC Brittan, P Cassidy, E Smith, H Harvey, J Evans, L Hopkins (in suit), G West. Centre; G Beare, Frampton, H Beadles, W Grimshaw, A Barnett, L Davies, C Jones, R Williams, W Davidson. Front; A Stewart, C Hewitt, HJ Kneeshaw, J Clarke.

March 23 1921, at Old Trafford for the FA Cup semi-final replay. George Beare, Billy Grimshaw, Fred Keenor, Bert Smith, Charlie Brittan, Ben Davies, Arthur Cashmore, Albert Barnett, Billy Hardy, Jack Evans, Jimmy Blair.

Taking the sea air at Southport, early 1923/24 season. George Latham (trainer), Jimmy Gill, Herbie Evans, Billy Hardy.

December 26 1925. Back; Sam Smith (travelling reserve), Billy Hardy, Jimmy Nelson, Tom Farquharson, Joe Nicholson, Tommy Watson. Front; Billy Davies, Len Davies, Hugh Ferguson, Joe Cassidy, George McLachlan, Tommy Sloan.

August 1926, a pre-season practice game. The players wore black armbands in sympathy with Tom Farquharson on the death of his father. Back; Tommy Watson, Tom Pirie, Percy Richards, George Blackburn, Jack Kneeshaw, Tommy Wainwright, A Pepper, George McLachlan, Jimmy Nelson, Hughie Ferguson. Centre; Billy Davies, Elvet Collins, Sam Smith, Fred Keenor, Ernie Curtis, Tommy Sloan, Harry Wake, Tom Potter Smith. Front; Jack Jennings, Jim Baillie, Len Davies, Fred Chard.

October 3 1927 at Celtic Park, Celtic (Scottish Cup winners) 4, Cardiff (FA Cup winners) 1. Players only: Back; P Connolly, W Thirlaway, P Wilson, T Farquharson, J Thomson, (T Dougray, referee), J Nelson, J MacFarlane, E Curtis. Centre; S Irving, J McGrory, J McStay, T Pirie, W McGonigle, G McLachlan, A Thomson, W Hardy. Front; H Ferguson, T McInally, F Keenor, W McStay, Len Davies, J McMenemy.

September 1 1928. Back; Tommy Sloan, George McLachlan, Tommy Farquharson, Stan Davies, Jack Jennings, Jimmy Nelson. Front; Billy Thirlaway, Len Davies, Fred Keenor, Hughie Ferguson, Billy Hardy.

August 29 1936. Back; Jack Kneeshaw (trainer), George Nicholson, Arthur Granville, Billy Fielding, Bill Scott, Bill Bassett, Harold Smith. Front; Reg Pugh, Les Talbot, Cliff Godfrey, Cecil Smith, Albert Pixton, Dai Ovenstone.

1938/39. Bill Corkhill, Arthur Granville, George Nicholson, George Ballsom, Reg Pugh, Len Ford, Jimmy Kelso, Albert Turner, Jack Kneeshaw (trainer), Ernie Blenkinsop, Bill Fielding, Jimmy Collins, Billy Main, George Gunn.

November 17 1945 at Ninian Park; Cardiff City 1, Moscow Dynamo 10. Dynamo captain Mikhail Semichastny presents City skipper Fred Stansfield with a bouquet of flowers. The City players each have a miner's lamp to present to the Dynamo team.

June 7 1947, champions of Division Three South. Back; Ken Hollyman, Bob Allison (trainer), Stan Richards, Dan Canning, Glyn Williams, Billy Rees, Bryn Allen, Roy Clarke. Centre; Colin Gibson, Arthur Lever, Fred Stansfield, Alf Sherwood, George Wardle. Front; Billy Baker, Bernard Ross.

December 1959. Back; Joe Bonson, Alec Milne, Graham Vearncombe, Derrick Sullivan, Colin Baker, Ron Stitfall. Front; Brian Walsh, Derek Tapscott, Danny Malloy, Graham Moore, Johnny Watkins.

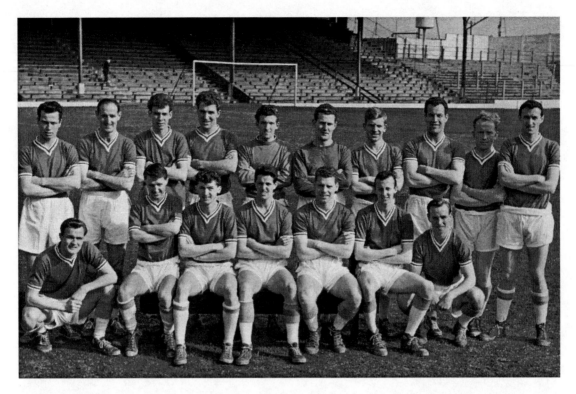

February 1962. Back; Derek Tapscott, Derek Hogg, Barry Hole, Frank Rankmore, Dilwyn John, Graham Vearncombe, Alan Durban, Mel Charles, Johnny King, Alec Milne. Front; Dai Ward, Danny McCarthy, Peter King, Alan Harrington, Colin Baker, Tony Pickrell, Trevor Edwards.

August 1964, pre-season training. Ivor Allchurch, Alan Harrington, Peter Rodrigues, Barry Hole, Derek Tapscott, Mel Charles, John Charles. Welsh internationals all!

INTRODUCTION TO THE STATISTICS PAGES

The season-by-season grids show the results of games in all major competitions, including European games, the Football League, F.A. Cup, Football League Cup, Third Division (South) Cup, the Associate Members' Cup and the Welsh Cup.

Home games are identified by the opponent's name in upper case, away games by the use of lower case. Cardiff's score is always given first. Attendances for League games are taken from the official Football League records since season 1925/26; before then, estimated attendances based on newspaper reports have been used.

Substitutes, from season 1965/66 onwards, have the numbers 12, 13 and 14. Number 12 is used if only one substitute was used (no matter what number was on the player's shirt).

A full player list is provided for every player who made a League appearance. Date and place of birth are shown, where known, and the year of death.

Players with the same name are given a (1) or (2) after their name to avoid confusion. The next two columns, "seasons played", act as an index to the season-by-season grids. The years shown are the "first year" of the season; for example, 1971 is season 1971/72. The two columns show the season in which the player made his first team debut; and the final season that he played. However, if he only played in one season, the second column is blank. An entry of "2001" in the second column does not imply that the player has left the club, but means that he appeared in the "final season" (2001/02) of the book. Countries for which a player made an international appearance are noted, though the cap may have been won at a club other than Cardiff City.

Note that some players also made F.A. Cup appearances before 1920/21 and in 1945/46. If a player also made a League appearance his F.A. Cup appearances from these seasons are included in the list. Previous and next clubs show where he was transferred from, and the club he moved to. Non-league club information is included when known.

The appearance columns have separate totals for the League, F.A. Cup, Football League Cup and the other tournaments including European games but excluding the Welsh Cup. "Goals scored" are also shown under the four headings. The Welsh Cup was a senior competition and forms a proper part of a player's career record. The appearance and goals totals in the Welsh Cup are omitted only for consistency with the other volumes in this series; the reader can extract the data from the line-ups if required.

If a player has had more than one spell at the club playing first team football, a consolidated set of appearance and goals are shown on the first line. Subsequent lines show the seasons involved on his return to the club, and his new pair of previous and next clubs.

A full record of meetings against all other League clubs (in the Football League) is included. Some clubs have played under different names, but the totals are consolidated under the present day name in this table. Final League tables will be found at the back of the book, with a list of club managers.

1910/11   4th in Southern League Division Two

Player columns (left→right): Abley T, Ball H, Cant J, Duffy J, Evans JH, Haggard, Husbands T, Latham G, Lawrie R, Malloch J, McDonald J, McDougall D, McKenzie J, Milford E, Mudie T, Nash L, Niblo T, Norton C, Peake R, Pinch, Powell F, Ramsay J, Stewart W, Watt W, Westall, White

#	Date		Opponent	Score	Scorers	Att	AbleyT	BallH	CantJ	DuffyJ	EvansJH	Hag	HusbT	LathG	LawR	MalJ	McDJ	McDoD	McKJ	MilE	MudT	NashL	NibT	NorC	PeakR	Pinch	PowF	RamJ	SteW	WatW	Wes	Whi
1	Sep	24	TON PENTRE	4-1	Peake 2, Watt, J Evans	8000	8			3	11		1		4		7	6	2						9			5		10		
2	Oct	8	Treharris	0-0		4500				3	11		1		5	8	7	6	2	9					10		4					
3	Nov	5	Aberdare	1-1	McDonals	4500	8		9	3	11				4		7	6	2				10					5				1
4		12	TREHARRIS	2-1	J Evans 2	6000	8			3	11				4		7	6	2				10		9			5				1
5	Dec	3	Salisbury City	4-1	J Evans 2, Cant, Pinch	4000			9	3	11		1		4		7	6	2				10			8		5				
6		7	ABERDARE	1-2	Pinch	6000			9	3	11		1		4				2				10		7	8		5	6			
7		24	Kettering	7-4	Peake 3, McDonald, J Evans, Pinch 2	5000				3	11		1		4		7	6	2						9	8		5		10		
8		26	Reading	0-0		8000			10	3	11		1		4		7	6	2						9	8		5				
9		27	Stoke	0-5		9000				3	11		1		4	9	7	6	2							8		5		10		
10	Jan	7	KETTERING	2-0	Peake, Ramsay	8000		10		3	11		1		4		7	6	2						9	8		5				
11		14	Chesham	7-1	Peake 4, J Evans 3	2500		10		3	11		1		4		7	6	2						9	8		5				
12		21	SALISBURY	3-1	Peake 2, Ball	4100		10		3	11		1		4		7	6	2						9	8		5				
13		28	CROYDON COMMON	1-0	Pinch	8500	10			3	11		1		4		7	6	2						9	8		5				
14	Feb	4	Croydon Common	3-1	Abley 2, Peake	6200	10			3	11		1		4		7	6	2						9	8		5				
15		11	Walsall	1-1	Pinch	4000	10			3	11		1		4		7	6					2		9	8		5				
16	Mar	4	WALSALL	2-1	Peake, Abley	6000	10				11		1		4		7	6	2	3					9	8		5				
17		11	Ton Pentre	2-4	Peake, Abley	14000	10						1	2	4		7	6		3					9	8		5			11	
18		18	MERTHYR TOWN	1-0	Peake	5000	8	10					1	5	4		7	6	2	3					9						11	
19		25	Merthyr Town	0-1		8000	8	10		3	11		1	5	4		7	6	2						9							
20	Apr	1	CHESHAM	6-0	Peake, J Evans 2, Pinch 2, Latham	4000	10			3	11		1	5	4		7	6	2						9	8						
21		17	READING	0-2		10000				3	11	9	1	5	4		7	6	2							8						
22		18	STOKE	1-2	Ramsay	6000	8			3	11		1		4	6	7		2						9			5		10		
			Apps				13	5	4	19	20	1	20	6	22	2	21	20	20	3	1	0	4	1	17	16	1	17	1	4	2	2
			Goals				4	1	1		11			1			2								17	7		2		1		

Glamorgan League

#	Date		Opponent	Score	Scorers	Att	AbleyT	BallH	CantJ	DuffyJ	EvansJH	Hag	HusbT	LathG	LawR	MalJ	McDJ	McDoD	McKJ	MilE	MudT	NashL	NibT	NorC	PeakR	Pinch	PowF	RamJ	SteW	WatW	Wes	Whi
1	Sep	5	Ton Pentre	3-2	Peake 2, Watt	4800	8			3	11		1		4		7	6	2						9			5		10		
2		10	MARDY	1-1	Ramsay	5000	8			3	11		1		4		7	6	2						9			5		10		
3		12	Aberdare	2-2	Peake 2	3000	8			3	11		1		4	9	7	6	2						10			5				
4		26	Cwm Albion	0-1		1200					11		1	8	4			3	2						9				5	10		
5	Oct	10	Merthyr Town	0-1		6000				3	11		1		5			6	2		9	8			10		4		7			
6		17	Cwmparc	2-2	Peake 2	1000	9			3	11				4	8	7		2						10			5				1
7	Nov	19	Barry	2-1	Niblo, J Evans (p)	4000	8		9	3	11		1		4			6	2				2		7			5				
8		26	CWM ALBION	5-0	Cant 2, Niblo 3	6000			9	3	11		1		4		7	6	2				10			8		5				
9	Dec	17	CWMPARC	3-0	Lawrie, Peake, Pinch	2500				3	11		1		5		7		2				10		9	8	4					
10		31	TREDEGAR	2-1	Ramsay, Peake	1500				3	11		1		4		7		2						9	8		5	6	10		
11	Jan	2	BARRY	5-1	Lawrie, Peake, Pinch, Ball 2	4000		10		2			1		4	7	11						3		9	8		5	6			
12	Feb	8	ABERDARE	1-1	J Evans (p)	5000	10			3	11		1		8		7	6	2						9			5	4			
13		25	Treharris	0-2		2500				3	11		1		4	8	7	6		10				2	9			5				
14	Mar	1	MERTHYR TOWN	1-1	J Evans	5500	10			3	11		1		4	8	7	6		2					9			5				
15	Apr	6	Mardy	1-1	Peake	2000																										
16		15	Tredegar	2-0	Watt, Cant	1000			8	2	11	4		5				6		3					9	7					10	1
17		19	TREHARRIS	2-1	Abley, Cant	3000	8		9	3	11		1		4				2						7			5		10		
18		28	TON PENTRE	0-0		4000	8				11		1												9			5		10		
			Apps				9	1	4	15	16	1	14	1	14	5	11	12	10	3	2	3	2		16	5	2	13	5	7	0	3
			Goals				1	2	4		3				2								4		10	2		2		2		

Some players unknown in Glamorgan League games 15, 17 and 18
Played at 6 in games 4 and 6: Wilson
Played at 6 in game 9: Pimlott
Played at 7 in game 4: H Evans

F.A. Cup

Rd	Date		Opponent	Score	Scorers	Att	AbleyT	DuffyJ	EvansJH	HusbT	LawR	McDJ	McDoD	McKJ	PeakR	RamJ	WatW
PR	Sep	17	BATH CITY	3-1	Peake 2, Watt	5000	8	3	11	1	4	7	6	2	9	5	10
Q1	Oct	1	MERTHYR TOWN	0-1		12800	8	3	11	1	4	7	6	2	9	5	10

Welsh Cup

Rd	Date		Opponent	Score	Scorers	Att	AbleyT	DuffyJ	EvansJH	HusbT	LawR	MalJ	McDJ	McDoD	McKJ	NibT	PeakR	Pinch	PowF	RamJ	SteW	WatW
R1	Oct	13	Mardy	1-0	Abley	3000	9	3	11	1	4	8		6	2		10			5	7	
R2		29	TREDEGAR	4-1	Malloch, Watt, J Evans, Stewart	4000		3	11	1	4	8	7	6	2					5	9	10
R3	Dec	10	TON PENTRE	2-2	Abley, Powell	5000	8	3	11	1	5		7	6	2	9			4			10
rep		15	Ton Pentre	0-1		8000		3	11	1	5		7	6	2	9		8	4			10

		p	w	d	l	f	a	pts
1	Reading	22	16	3	3	55	11	35
2	Stoke	22	17	1	4	72	21	35
3	Merthyr Town	22	15	3	4	52	22	33
4	CARDIFF CITY	22	12	4	6	48	29	28
5	Croydon Common	22	11	3	8	61	26	25
6	Treharris	22	10	3	9	38	31	23
7	Aberdare	22	9	5	8	38	33	23
8	Ton Pentre	22	10	3	9	44	40	23
9	Walsall	22	7	4	11	37	41	18
10	Kettering	22	6	1	15	34	68	13
11	Chesham	22	1	3	18	16	93	5
12	Salisbury City	22	0	3	19	16	92	3

1911/12   3rd in Southern League Division Two

#	Date	Opponent	Score	Scorers	Att	Abley T	Bates J	Burton G	Burton J	Douglas W	Duffy J	Evans JH	Featherstone H	Gaughan W	Germaine	Hardy W	Hiftle J	Husbands T	Latham G	Lawrie R	Leah R	Newton L	Pinch C	Thompson E	Tracey H	Waters A
1	Sep 2	KETTERING	3-1	Tracey, J Burton, Abley	6200	10			8			11	9			6		1		4	3			5	7	2
2	23	Pontypridd	2-3	J Burton 2	4000		10		9		3	11	8			6	7	1		4				5		2
3	Oct 7	CWM ALBION	5-1	Featherstone 4, J Burton	5000	10			8		3	11	9			6		1		4	2			5	7	
4	21	PORTSMOUTH	0-0		3500			9	8		3	11	10			6		1	5	4	2				7	
5	28	Cwm Albion	4-2	Evans 2, J Burton, G Burton	2000	4		9	8		2	11	10			6		1		5	3				7	
6	Nov 11	Ton Pentre	4-3	Featherstone 2, Evans	2200	4		8	10		3	11	9			6		1		5	2				7	
7	18	TREHARRIS	0-0		4000	4		8	10		3	11	9			6		1		5	2				7	
8	Dec 16	Chesham	4-0	Evans 2, J Burton, G Burton	3000	4		8	10		3	11	9			6		1		5	2				7	
9	23	Kettering	2-0	Featherstone, Evans	5000	4		8	10		3	11	9		1	6				5	2				7	
10	25	CROYDON COMMON	4-0	J Burton, Featherstone, Abley, G Burton	8000	4		8	10		3	11	9		1	6				5	2				7	
11	26	Croydon Common	0-2		2500	4		8	10		3	11	9		1	6								5	7	2
12	Jan 13	ABERDARE	3-1	Thompson, Featherstone, G Burton	5000	4		8	10		2	11	9		1					5				6	7	3
13	20	MARDY	1-1	Featherstone	6000	4		8	10		2	11	9		1	6				5					7	3
14	27	Aberdare	2-0	Evans, G Burton	4000	4		8	10		2	11	9		1	6				5					7	3
15	Feb 10	TON PENTRE	3-0	Lawrie, Tracey 2	7000	4		8	10		2	11	9		1	6				5					7	3
16	17	Portsmouth	2-3	Tracey, Evans	11000	4		8	10		2	11	9		1	6				5					7	3
17	24	MERTHYR TOWN	1-2	Evans	14000			8	10		2	11	9		1	6				5				4	7	3
18	29	Mardy	1-0	Douglas	2000	4		8	10	9	2	11				6		1		5					7	3
19	Mar 9	CHESHAM	5-0	Tracey, Abley, Douglas 3	2000	4		8	10	9	2	11				6		1		5					7	3
20	16	PONTYPRIDD	0-0		7100	4			10	9	2	11	8			6		1				5			7	3
21	18	Walsall	3-0	G Burton 2, Duffy	4000	4		8	10	9	2	11				6		1		5					7	3
22	Apr 5	SOUTHEND UNITED	0-2		10000	8		9	10	2		11						1		4	5			6	7	3
23	6	Merthyr Town	0-2		9000	4		9	10	3				11				1	2			5	8	6	7	
24	10	WALSALL	5-1	G Burton, Pinch 2, Tracey, J Burton	5000	4		9	10	2				11				1	3	5		8		6	7	
25	24	Southend United	1-0	Featherstone	2000	4		8	10	2		11	9			6		1						5	7	3
26	27	Treharris	0-2		2000	4		8	10	2			9	11	1	6								5	7	3
Apps						23	1	22	26	9	20	23	20	3	10	22	1	16	3	20	9	4	2	11	25	16
Goals						3		8	8	4	1	10	11							1				2	6	

F.A. Cup

	Date	Opponent	Score	Scorers	Att	Abley T	Bates J	Burton G	Burton J	Douglas W	Duffy J	Evans JH	Featherstone H	Gaughan W	Germaine	Hardy W	Hiftle J	Husbands T	Latham G	Lawrie R	Leah R	Newton L	Pinch C	Thompson E	Tracey H	Waters A
Q1	Sep 16	CARDIFF CORINTHIANS	3-0	Featherstone, Abley, Latham	3000	10			8		3	11	9			6		1	5	4					7	2
Q2	30	MARDY	2-0	Featherstone, Abley	2900	10			8		3	11	9			6		1		4	2			5	7	
Q3	Oct 14	Merthyr Town	1-1	Evans	8000	10			8		3	11	9			6		1		4	2			5	7	
rep	18	MERTHYR TOWN	1-2	Evans	5200	10			8		3	11	9			6		1	5	4	2				7	

Welsh Cup

	Date	Opponent	Score	Scorers	Att	Abley T	Bates J	Burton G	Burton J	Douglas W	Duffy J	Evans JH	Featherstone H	Gaughan W	Germaine	Hardy W	Hiftle J	Husbands T	Latham G	Lawrie R	Leah R	Newton L	Pinch C	Thompson E	Tracey H	Waters A
R3	Jan 10	TREHARRIS	1-0	Featherstone	3000	6		8	10		2	11	9		1	4				5					7	3
R4	Feb 3	Wrexham	2-1	J Burton, Featherstone	3500	4		8	10		2	11	9		1	6				5					7	3
SF	Mar 23	CHESTER	1-1	G Burton	3000	4		9	10			11				2		1		5			8	6	7	3
rep	27	Chester	2-1	G Burton, Tracey	3000	8		9	10	3		11				6		1		5				4	7	2
F	Apr 8	PONTYPRIDD	0-0		18000	4		9	10	2		11				3		1		5			8	6	7	
rep	18	Pontypridd	3-0	Tracey 2, Featherstone	6648	4		8	10			11	9			6		1	2					5	7	3

		p	w	d	l	f	a	pts
1	Merthyr Town	26	19	3	4	60	14	41
2	Portsmouth	26	19	3	4	73	20	41
3	CARDIFF CITY	26	15	4	7	55	26	34
4	Southend United	26	16	1	9	73	24	33
5	Pontypridd	26	13	6	7	39	24	32
6	Ton Pentre	26	12	3	11	56	45	27
7	Walsall	26	13	1	11	44	41	27
8	Treharris	26	11	5	10	44	47	27
9	Aberdare	26	10	3	13	39	44	23
10	Kettering	26	11	0	15	37	62	22
11	Croydon Common	26	8	2	15	43	45	18
12	Mardy	26	6	6	12	37	51	18
13	Cwm Albion	26	5	1	16	27	70	11
14	Chesham Town	26	1	0	25	18	131	2

1912/13 Champions of Southern League Division Two

#	Date	Opponent	Score	Scorers	Att	Abley T	Bennett J	Burton G	Burton J	Cassidy P	Clarke J	Croft R	Devlin W	Doncaster T	Douglas W	Evans JH	Featherstone H	Gaughan W	Hardy W	Harvey H	Holt A	Keggans H	Kneeshaw HJ	Latham G	Leah R	Lewis	McKechnie C	Saunders L	Tracey H
1	Sep 7	Swansea Town	1-1	J Burton	8000			8				2				11	9		6	4		10	1		3			5	7
2	12	Mid Rhondda	1-0	Keggans	4000			8	5					2		11	9		6	4		10	1		3				7
3	14	NEWPORT COUNTY	2-0	Tracey, Featherstone	8000			8	5					2		11	9		6	4		10	1		3				7
4	21	Ton Pentre	1-0	J Burton	6000			8	5					2	9		11		6	4		10	1		3				7
5	28	CROYDON COMMON	3-1	J Burton 2, Keggans	7000			8	5				9	2		11			6	4		10	1		3				7
6	Oct 5	Treharris	2-0	Keggans, Devlin	2000			8	5				9	2		11			6	4		10	1		3				7
7	19	MARDY	5-2	G Burton, J Burton, Cassidy, Evans, Devlin	6500	6		8	10	5			9	2		11				4			1		3				7
8	Nov 9	Croydon Common	2-1	G Burton, Evans	6000			8	10	5				2		11	9		6	4			1		3				7
9	Dec 7	TREHARRIS	2-1	Tracey, Cassidy	8000			8	10	5			9	2	1	11			6	4					3				7
10	21	SOUTHEND UNITED	1-0	Evans	8000			8	10	5			9	2		11			6	4					3				7
11	25	PONTYPRIDD	1-1	Featherstone	11000			8	10	5				2		11	9		6	4					3				7
12	26	Luton Town	0-2		6000			8	10	5				2		11	9		6	4					3				7
13	Jan 1	LLANELLY	5-0	J Burton 2, Featherstone 2, Devlin	3000				10	5			9	2		11	8		6	4					3				7
14	15	TON PENTRE	9-0	*See below	3000				10	5			9	2		11	8		6	4					3				7
15	Feb 8	Newport County	3-1	G Burton, Cassidy, Tracey	8000		10			5			9	2		11	9		6	4					3				7
16	12	ABERDARE	3-0	Harvey, Tracey, Devlin	4000				10	5			9	2		11	8		6	4					3				7
17	22	Southend United	1-1	G Burton	7000	7		8	10	5	9			2					6	4			1		3				11
18	Mar 1	MID RHONDDA	1-0	G Burton	6000			8	10	5	9			2		11			6	4			1		3				7
19	8	Mardy	2-1	G Burton, Clarke	3000			8	10	5	9			2		11			6		7		1		3		4		
20	15	SWANSEA TOWN	0-0		10000			8		5	10		9	2		11			6	4	7		1		3				
21	21	LUTON TOWN	3-0	J Burton 2, G Burton	22000			8	10	5			9	2		11			6	4			1		3				7
22	24	Pontypridd	1-1	Hardy	7500	7		8	10	5			9	2		11			6	4			1		3				
23	29	Llanelly	2-0	J Burton, Devlin	1500			8	10	5			9			11			6	4			1		3				7
24	Apr 5	Aberdare	3-2	Devlin, Evans, G Burton	2000			10	8	5			9	2		11			6	4			1		3				7
		Apps				1	2	15	22	23	4	1	14	22	2	22	10	1	23	23	2	6	23	2	23	0	1	1	21
		Goals						8	11	5	1		9			5	4		1	1		3							6

Scorers in game 14: Tracey 2, J Burton, Cassidy 2, Devlin 3, Evans

Southern Alliance — Bottom of the Southern Alliance

#	Date	Opponent	Score	Scorers	Att	Abley T	Bennett J	Burton G	Burton J	Cassidy P	Clarke J	Croft R	Devlin W	Doncaster T	Douglas W	Evans JH	Featherstone H	Gaughan W	Hardy W	Harvey H	Holt A	Keggans H	Kneeshaw HJ	Latham G	Leah R	Lewis	McKechnie C	Saunders L	Tracey H
1	Oct 3	Millwall	3-2	J Burton, Evans, Devlin		4		8	5				9	2		11			6			10	1		3				7
2	23	Brighton & Hove Albion	1-4	Evans		6		8	10	5			9	3	1	11				4			2						7
3	Nov 12	SOUTHAMPTON	1-2	J Burton				8	10	5				2		11	9		6	4			1		3				7
4	20	BRENTFORD	4-2	G Burton, Tracey, Featherstone, Hickleston (og)				8	10	5	3			2		11	9		6	4			1			1			7
5	Dec 11	Southampton	1-3	Devlin	500	4		8	10				9	2	1		5	11	6						3				7
6	Feb 1	PORTSMOUTH	1-1	Featherstone	3000				10				9	2		11	8		6	4			1		3				7
7	5	Croydon Common	0-3					8				3		2		11	9		6	4			1	5					7
8	26	BRIGHTON & HOVE ALB	0-1		3500	5	7	8	10		9			2				11	6				1		3		4		7
9	Mar 12	CROYDON COMMON	1-2	Holt	5000	4		8			10	3		2	9	11					7		1	5	3		6		7
10	22	SOUTHEND	1-1	J Burton				4	10		8		9	2		11							1	5	3		6		7
11	Apr 9	MILLWALL	3-2	Tracey 2, Clarke			7		10	5	9			2	1	11			6	4					3				8
12	12	Southend	0-1				7		10	5	9	3		2	1	11			6	4					1	5			8
13	14	Brentford	2-4	Bennett, Evans			7		10	5	9	3		2	1	11			6	4					1	5			8
14	19	Luton Town	0-2						10		8	3	9	2		11			6	4					5		1		7
15	23	Portsmouth	1-3	Devlin	2000				10		8	3	9	2	1	11			6	4					5				7
16	26	LUTON TOWN	5-2	Devlin 2, G Burton 2, Hardy				10		5	8	3	9	2		11			6	4			1						7
		Apps				5	4	9	13	7	9	8	8	16	6	14	5	2	13	11	1	1	9	6	7	2	3	0	14
		Goals					1	3	3		1		5			3	2		1					1					3

Played in game 7 at 10: L Nash
Played in games 6 and 9 at 5: L Newton
One own goal

F.A. Cup

#	Date	Opponent	Score	Scorers	Att	Abley T	Bennett J	Burton G	Burton J	Cassidy P	Clarke J	Croft R	Devlin W	Doncaster T	Douglas W	Evans JH	Featherstone H	Gaughan W	Hardy W	Harvey H	Holt A	Keggans H	Kneeshaw HJ	Latham G	Leah R	Lewis	McKechnie C	Saunders L	Tracey H
Q1	Oct 12	Merthyr Town	5-1	Harvey, J Burton, Devlin 3	11500			8	5				9	2		11			6	4		10	1		3				7
Q2	Nov 2	PONTYPRIDD	2-1	G Burton, J Burton	12000			8	10					2			9	11	6	4			1		3			5	7
Q3	16	Llanelly	4-1	G Burton, Tracey, Evans, Gough (og)	4000			8	10	5			9	2		11			6	4			1		3				7
Q4	30	EXETER CITY	5-1	Harvey, G Burton, J Burton, Devlin 2	14000			8	10	5			9	2	1	11			6	4					3				7
Q5	Dec 14	SOUTHEND	0-3		7000			8	10	5			9	2		11			6	4			1		3				7

Welsh Cup

#	Date	Opponent	Score	Scorers	Att	Abley T	Bennett J	Burton G	Burton J	Cassidy P	Clarke J	Croft R	Devlin W	Doncaster T	Douglas W	Evans JH	Featherstone H	Gaughan W	Hardy W	Harvey H	Holt A	Keggans H	Kneeshaw HJ	Latham G	Leah R	Lewis	McKechnie C	Saunders L	Tracey H
R3	Jan 4	TON PENTRE	4-2	G Burton, Douglas 2, Featherstone	2000		7	10						2	9		8	11	6	4			1	5	3				
R4	25	Bangor City	4-0	J Burton, Featherstone, Cassidy, Devlin					10	5			9	2		11	8		6	4			1		3				7
SF	Feb 15	SWANSEA TOWN	2-4	J Burton, Cassidy	12000				10	5			9	2		11	8		6	4			1		3				7

		p	w	d	l	f	a	pts
1	CARDIFF CITY	24	18	5	1	54	15	41
2	Southend United	24	14	6	4	43	23	34
3	Swansea Town	24	12	7	5	29	23	31
4	Croydon Common	24	13	4	7	51	29	30
5	Luton Town	24	13	4	7	52	39	30
6	Llanelly	24	9	6	9	33	39	24
7	Pontypridd	24	6	11	7	30	28	23
8	Mid Rhondda	24	9	4	11	33	31	22
9	Aberdare	24	8	6	10	38	40	22
10	Newport County	24	7	5	12	29	36	19
11	Mardy	24	6	3	15	38	38	15
12	Treharris	24	5	2	17	18	60	12
13	Ton Pentre	24	3	3	18	22	69	9

1913/14   10th in the Southern League Division One

#	Date	Opponent	Score	Scorers	Att	Bennett I	Brittan RC	Burton G	Burton J	Cassidy P	Clarke J	Davidson W	Devlin W	Doncaster T	Evans JH	Hardy W	Harvey H	Henderson J	Holt A	Hopkins L	Keenor FC	Keggans H	Kneeshaw HJ	Leah R	McKenzie K	Robertson T	Seymour T	Stephenson J	Tracey H	West G	West JF	Witts T
1	Sep 1	Bristol Rovers	0-1		7000			8	10	5			9	2	11	6	4		7				1	3								
2	6	Plymouth Argyle	1-2	Harvey	13463				10	5			9	2	11	6	4		7			8	1	3								
3	13	SOUTHAMPTON	1-2	Devlin	15000				10	5			9	2	11	6	4					8	1						7			
4	20	Reading	0-1		4000			8	10	5			9	2	11	6	4						1	3					7			
5	27	CRYSTAL PALACE	1-2	Devlin	12000			8	10	5			9	2	11	6	4		7				1	3								
6	Oct 4	Coventry City	2-2	Robertson 2	7000	7			10	5				2	11	6	4	8					1	3		9						
7	11	WATFORD	2-0	Robertson, Henderson	14000	7				5	11		10	2		6	4	8					1	3		9						
8	18	Norwich City	2-2	Robertson 2	7000	7			10	5				2	11	6	4	8					1	3		9						
9	25	GILLINGHAM	2-0	Henderson, Evans	13000	7			10	5				2	11	6	4	8					1	3		9						
10	Nov 1	Northampton Town	1-2	Burton	6000	7		9	10					2	11	6	4	8					1	3	5							
11	8	SOUTHEND UNITED	3-0	Hopkins 2, Harvey	14500	7			10					2	11	6	4	8		9			1	3	5							
12	15	Brighton & Hove Albion	1-2	Hopkins	7000	7			10					2	11	6	4	8		9			1	3	5							
13	22	PORTSMOUTH	1-3	Burton	15000	7			10	5				2	11	6	4	8		9			1									3
14	Dec 6	EXETER CITY	1-1	Hopkins	8000					5	11		7	2		3	4			9	6		1			8				10		
15	13	QUEEN'S PARK RANGERS	3-0	G West 3	12000					5			8	2	11	6	4			9			1			3			7	10		
16	20	Swindon Town	2-1	G West, Devlin	10000		2			5		4	9		11	6				8			1			3			7	10		
17	25	MERTHYR TOWN	1-1	Evans	20000		2			5			9		11	6	4			8						3		1	7	10		
18	26	Merthyr Town	2-2	Burton, Hopkins	12000		3		8	5		4		2	11	6				9								1	7	10		
19	27	PLYMOUTH ARGYLE	2-1	G West, Tracey	27000		3		8			4		2	11	5				9	6							1	7	10		
20	Jan 1	BRISTOL ROVERS	2-0	Burton, G West	16000		3		8	5	11	4		2		6				9								1	7	10		
21	3	Southampton	0-2		9000		3		8	5		4		2	11	6				9								1	7	10		
22	17	READING	1-0	G West	13000		3			5			8	2	11	6	4	7		9								1		10		
23	24	Crystal Palace	0-4		11000		3			5			8	2	11	6	4	7		9								1		10		
24	Feb 7	COVENTRY CITY	2-1	Harvey, G West	8500		3		8	5				2	11	6	4	7		9								1		10		
25	14	Watford	2-3	Cassidy, Hopkins	4000		2			5					11	6	4	8		9						3	7	1		10		
26	21	NORWICH CITY	3-0	Burton, Robertson, G West	14000		2		8	5					11	6	4			9						3	7	1		10		
27	21	Gillingham	0-0		8000		2			5	11	4	9			6				8						3	7	1		10		
28	Mar 7	NORTHAMPTON T	0-0		12000		2			5					11	6	4	8		9						3	7	1		10		
29	14	Southend United	1-2	G West	12000		2			5				3	11	6	4	8		9							7	1		10		
30	21	BRIGHTON & HOVE ALB.	0-0		12000		2			5			8	3	11	6	4			9							7	1		10		
31	28	Portsmouth	1-1	Evans	12470		2			5			8	3	11	6	4			9							7	1		10		
32	Apr 4	Millwall	0-3		9000		2			5			8	3	11	6	4			9							7	1		10		
33	10	WEST HAM UNITED	2-0	Devlin 2	20000		2			5			9	3	11	6	4										7	1		10	8	
34	11	Exeter City	1-0	Devlin	5000		2			5			9	3	11	6	4										7	1		10	8	
35	13	West Ham United	1-1	Doncaster	15000		2		8	5				3	11	6	4			9							7	1		10		
36	18	Queen's Park Rangers	2-0	Evans, JF West	10000		2			5				3	11	6	4			9							7	1		10	8	
37	25	SWINDON TOWN	0-0		25000		2			5			9	3	11	6	4										7	1		10	8	
38	29	MILLWALL	0-0		6500		2			5			9	3	11	6	4										7	1		10	8	
		Apps				8	22	5	18	33	4	6	19	31	34	38	32	12	3	21	3	3	16	20	3	11	14	22	9	25	5	1
		Goals							5	1			6	1	4		3	2		6						6			1	10	1	

Played in game 3 at 3: H Featherstone

F.A. Cup

	Date	Opponent	Score		Att	Bennett I			Burton J	Cassidy P				Doncaster T	Evans JH	Hardy W	Harvey H	Henderson J					Kneeshaw HJ			Robertson T					
Q4	Nov 29	Swansea Town	0-2		12000	7			10	5				2	11	6	4	8					1			9						

Played at 3: Dr. JL McBean

Welsh Cup

Fielded a reserve team, away to Oswestry Town on 3 January 1914. Lost 1-2.

Southern Alliance

Cardiff used their reserve team in this League, finishing in fourth place.

		p	w	d	l	f	a	w	d	l	f	a	pts
1	Swindon Town	38	14	3	2	57	11	7	5	7	24	30	50
2	Crystal Palace	38	12	5	2	41	13	5	11	3	19	19	50
3	Northampton Town	38	11	8	0	31	11	3	11	5	19	26	47
4	Reading	38	14	4	1	32	12	3	6	10	11	24	44
5	Plymouth Argyle	38	11	6	2	25	12	4	7	8	21	30	43
6	West Ham United	38	9	7	3	39	22	6	5	8	22	38	42
7	Brighton & Hove Alb.	38	12	5	2	30	16	3	7	9	13	29	42
8	Queen's Park Rangers	38	10	6	3	28	14	6	3	10	17	29	41
9	Portsmouth	38	10	7	2	31	13	4	5	10	26	35	40
10	CARDIFF CITY	38	10	6	3	27	11	3	6	10	19	31	38
11	Southampton	38	11	2	6	36	23	4	5	10	19	31	37
12	Exeter City	38	7	8	4	21	11	3	8	8	18	27	36
13	Gillingham	38	10	6	3	35	15	3	3	13	13	34	35
14	Norwich City	38	7	10	2	34	19	2	7	10	15	32	35
15	Millwall	38	10	6	3	34	20	1	6	12	17	36	34
16	Southend United	38	7	7	5	29	28	3	5	11	12	38	32
17	Bristol Rovers	38	10	5	4	32	25	0	6	13	13	42	31
18	Watford	38	9	4	6	37	20	1	5	13	13	36	29
19	Merthyr Town	38	7	7	5	23	18	2	3	14	15	43	28
20	Coventry City	38	4	8	7	28	28	2	6	11	15	40	26

17

1914/15　　　3rd in the Southern League Division One

#	Mon	Date	Opponent	Score	Scorers	Att	Barnett A	Beare G	Brittan RC	Burton G	Burton J	Cassidy P	Davidson W	Devlin W	Doncaster T	Evans JH	Goddard A	Hardy W	Harvey H	Henderson J	Hopkins L	Keenor F C	Kneeshaw HJ	Layton AED	Stephenson J	West G	West JF
1	Sep	2	Watford	1-2	Cassidy	8000		7	2			5				11		6	4		9		1	3		10	8
2		5	NORWICH CITY	1-0	Evans	8000		7	2			5				11		6	4	9	8		1	3			10
3		12	Gillingham	1-1	Burton	6000		7	2	9		5				11		6	4	8			1	3			10
4		19	BRIGHTON & HOVE ALB.	0-1		10000		7	2	9						11		6	4	8	5		1	3			10
5		26	Crystal Palace	2-0	Evans, Hopkins	9000		7	2			5				11	8	6			9	4	1	3			10
6	Oct	3	Exeter City	0-2		3000		7	2			5				11	8	6			9	4	1	3			10
7		10	LUTON TOWN	3-0	West, Hopkins, Cassidy	8000		7	2			5				11	8	6	4		9		1	3		10	
8		17	Portsmouth	1-0	West	16887		7	2			5				11	8	6	4		9		1	3		10	
9		24	SWINDON TOWN	3-0	West, Evans, Cassidy	16000		7	2			5				11	8	6	4		9		1	3		10	
10		31	Southend United	1-2	Beare	7000		7				5		9	2	11	8	6	4				1	3		10	
11	Nov	7	QUEEN'S PARK RANGERS	2-0	Beare, Evans	9000		7	2			5		9		11	8	6	4				1	3		10	
12		14	Millwall	1-2	Beare	6000		7	2			5				11	8	6	4		9		1	3		10	
13		21	BRISTOL ROVERS	7-0	Devlin 3, Evans, Goddard, West, Beare	10000		7	2			5		9		11	8	6	4				1	3		10	
14		28	Croydon Common	1-0	Cassidy	2000		7	2			5		9		11	8	6	4				1	3		10	
15	Dec	5	READING	3-2	Devlin 2, Crawford (og)	12000		7	2			5		9		11	8	6	4				1	3		10	
16		12	Southampton	1-1	West	8000		7	2			5		9		11	8	6	4				1	3		10	
17		19	NORTHAMPTON T	5-0	Devlin 2, Goddard 2, Beare	12000		7	2			5		9	3	11	8	6	4				1			10	
18		25	Plymouth Argyle	0-2		8000		7	2			5		9	3	11	8	6	4				1			10	
19		26	PLYMOUTH ARGYLE	2-0	Goddard, Beare	9000		7	2			5		9		11	8	6	4				1	3		10	
20	Jan	1	WATFORD	2-3	Evans, Beare	1900		7	2			5		9		11	8	6	4				1	3		10	
21		2	Norwich City	1-2	Beare	4000		7	2					9		11		6	4	8	5		1	3		10	
22		16	GILLINGHAM	3-1	West 2, Devlin	8000		7	2			5		9	3	11	8	6	4				1			10	
23		23	Brighton & Hove Albion	1-2	Evans	6000	10	7	2							11	8	6	4			5	1	3		9	
24		30	CRYSTAL PALACE	5-0	West 2, Barnett, Beare, Evans	10000	10	7	2							11	8	6	4			5	1	3		9	
25	Feb	6	EXETER CITY	1-0	Barnett	5000	10	7							2	11	8	6	4			5	1	3		9	
26		13	Luton Town	1-2	West	9000	10	7				5		8	2	11		6				4		3	1	9	
27		20	PORTSMOUTH	3-2	Barnett, Keenor, Evans	6000	10	7				5			2	11	8	6				4	1	3		9	
28		27	Swindon Town	0-0		5000	10	7	2			5				11	8	6	4		9		1	3			
29	Mar	6	SOUTHEND UNITED	3-0	Goddard, Keenor, Evans	10000	10	7	2			5				11	8	6	4		9		1	3			
30		13	Queen's Park Rangers	0-3		7000	10	7	2				5			11	8	6	4		9		1	3			
31		20	MILLWALL	4-1	Hopkins 3, Goddard	11000	10				7	5				11	8	2	4		9	6	1	3			
32		27	Bristol Rovers	1-0	Beare	11000	10	7	2							11	8	6	4		9	5	1	3			
33	Apr	2	West Ham United	1-2	Goddard	10000	10	7	2							11	8	6	4		9	5	1	3			
34		3	CROYDON COMMON	1-0	West	9000	10	7	2			5				11			4		9	6	1	3		8	
35		5	WEST HAM UNITED	2-1	Barnett, Goddard	13000	10	11	2		7	5					8		4			6	1	3		9	
36		10	Reading	2-1	Evans, West	6000	10	7	2							11	8	6	4			5	1	3		9	
37		17	SOUTHAMPTON	1-1	Barnett	12000	10	7	2							11	8	6	4			5	1	3		9	
38		24	Northampton Town	5-2	Barnett, Evans, West, Beare, Cassidy	5000	10	7	2			5				11	8	6	4				1	3		9	
			Apps				16	37	32	2	2	28	1	13	7	37	31	37	33	3	12	21	37	35	1	27	6
			Goals				6	11			1	5		8		12	8				5	2				13	

One own goal

F.A. Cup

	Mon	Date	Opponent	Score		Att	Barnett A	Beare G	Brittan RC	Burton G	Burton J	Cassidy P	Davidson W	Devlin W	Doncaster T	Evans JH	Goddard A	Hardy W	Harvey H	Henderson J	Hopkins L	Keenor F C	Kneeshaw HJ	Layton AED	Stephenson J	West G	West JF
R1	Jan	9	Bristol City	0-2		15000		7	2			5		9		11	8	6	4				1	3		10	

Welsh Cup

Withdrew

		p	w	d	l	f	a	w	d	l	f	a	pts
1	Watford	38	12	4	3	37	15	10	4	5	31	31	52
2	Reading	38	12	4	3	37	16	9	3	7	31	27	49
3	CARDIFF CITY	38	16	1	2	51	12	6	3	10	21	26	48
4	West Ham United	38	14	4	1	42	18	4	5	10	16	29	45
5	Northampton Town	38	11	5	3	37	22	5	6	8	19	29	43
6	Southampton	38	14	3	2	56	28	5	2	12	22	46	43
7	Portsmouth	38	10	5	4	26	14	6	5	8	28	28	42
8	Millwall	38	9	4	6	28	23	7	6	6	22	28	42
9	Swindon Town	38	11	5	3	55	21	4	6	9	22	38	41
10	Brighton & Hove Alb.	38	11	5	3	29	16	5	2	12	17	31	39
11	Exeter City	38	10	3	6	32	16	5	5	9	18	25	38
12	Queen's Park Rangers	38	8	4	7	30	28	5	8	6	25	28	38
13	Norwich City	38	10	6	3	33	16	1	8	10	20	40	36
14	Luton Town	38	6	3	10	27	34	7	5	7	34	39	34
15	Crystal Palace	38	8	4	7	24	25	5	4	10	23	36	34
16	Bristol Rover	38	12	2	5	42	28	2	1	16	11	47	31
17	Plymouth Argyle	38	8	7	4	34	25	0	7	12	17	36	30
18	Southend United	38	8	5	6	27	20	2	3	14	17	44	28
19	Croydon Common	38	7	6	6	28	18	2	3	14	19	45	27
20	Gillingham	38	6	7	6	32	29	0	1	18	11	54	20

Friendly Games pre-Football League

1910/11

Date	Opponent	Score	Scorers	Att	1	2	3	4	5	6	7	8	9	10	11
Sep 1	ASTON VILLA XI	1-2	Evans	7000	Husbands T	McKenzie J	Duffy J	Lawrie R	Ramsay J	McDougall D	McDonald J	Abley T	Malloch J	Watt W	Evans JH
Sep 3	BRISTOL LEAGUE	6-0	Watt, Peake 4, Woodman (og)	3000	Husbands T	McKenzie J	Milford E	Lawrie R	Ramsay J	McDougall D	Stewart W	Abley T	Peake R	Watt W	Evans JH
Oct 15	READING	0-1		1500	Husbands T	McKenzie J	Duffy J	Lawrie R	Ramsay J	Powell F	Stewart W	Abley T	Stallworthy	Watt W	Evans JH
Oct 19	SWINDON TOWN	1-4	Malloch	4000	Husbands T	McKenzie J	Duffy J	Lawrie R	Ramsay J	Wilson	McDonald J	Malloch J	Stallworthy	Peake R	Evans JH
Oct 22	NEWPORT LEAGUE	6-1	Ramsay, McDougall, Malloch, Evans, Stewart 2	2000	Husbands T	McKenzie J	Duffy J	Lawrie R	Ramsay J	McDougall D	Peake R	Pinch C	Evans, Harry	Watt W	Evans JH
Nov 10	Tredegar	3-0	J Evans 2, Pinch		White	Lawrie R	Nash L	Stewart W	Ramsay J	Pimcott	Peake R	Pinch C	Evans, Harry	Watt W	Evans JH
Nov 19	Barry District	2-1	Evans (p), Niblo	4000	White	Nash L	Duffy J	Lawrie R	Ramsay J	McDougall D	Peake R	Abley T	Cant J	Niblo T	Evans JH
Feb 18	CREWE ALEXANDRA	1-1	Malloch	2000	Husbands T	Norton C	Duffy J	Stewart W	Ramsay J	McDougall D	McDonald J	Malloch J	Abley T	Norton C	Watt W
Feb 23	Rhymney	3-2													
Apr 8	Merthyr Town	0-0		2000	Husbands T	McKenzie J	Duffy J	Lawrie R	Latham G	McDougall D	McDonald J	Pinch C	Evans ?	Watt W	Evans JH
Apr 14	EXETER CITY	1-0	J Evans	8000	Husbands T	McKenzie J	Duffy J	Lawrie R	Latham G	McDougall D	McDonald J	Pinch C	Evans ?	Abley T	Evans JH
Apr 27	Swindon League	1-0	Abley	2000	Husbands T	McKenzie J	Duffy J	Lawrie R	Ramsay J	McDougall D	McDonald J	Abley T	Pinch C	Watt W	Evans JH
Apr 29	NORTHAMPTON T	3-0	Abley 3	5000	Husbands T	McKenzie J	Duffy J	Lawrie R	Ramsay J	McDougall D	McDonald J	Abley T	Peake R	Watt W	Evans JH

1911/12

Date	Opponent	Score	Scorers	Att	1	2	3	4	5	6	7	8	9	10	11
Sep 4	Treharris	2-2	Thompson, Featherstone		Husbands T	Latham G	Duffy J	Lawrie R	Thompson E	Hardy W	Hiftle J	Pinch C	Featherstone H	Bates J	Evans JH
Sep 9	Pontypridd	1-1	Waters	4200	Husbands T	Waters A	Duffy J	Lawrie R	Thompson E	Hardy W	Tracey H	Burton J	Featherstone H	Abley T	Evans JH
Sep 20	PLYMOUTH ARGYLE	3-1	Burton, Featherstone, Bates		Husbands T	Duffy J	Leah R	Lawrie R	Thompson E	Hardy W	Hiftle J	Featherstone H	Burton J	Bates J	Evans JH
Oct 4	Exeter City	1-0	Abley		Husbands T	Leah R	Duffy J	Lawrie R	Thompson E	Hardy W	Tracey H	Burton J	Pinch C	Abley T	Burton G
Oct 11	Plymouth Argyle	0-6			Husbands T	Parr	Williams		Thompson E	McDougall D	Pinch C	Burton J	Tait J	Featherstone H	Evans JH
Oct 25	EXETER CITY	1-1	Evans		Husbands T	Duffy J	Waters A	Lawrie R	Latham G	Abley J	Latham G	Pinch C	Burton J	Bates J	Evans JH
Nov 1	Penarth	4-1	J Burton, Evans, Latham 2		Husbands T	Duffy J	Waters A	McDougall D	Lawrie R	Hardy W	Tracey H	Burton G	Featherstone H	Burton J	Evans JH
Nov 4	WEDNESBURY	4-0	Featherstone, Evans, G Burton 2		Husbands T	Leah R	Duffy J	Abley T	Lawrie R	Hardy W	Tracey H	Burton G	Featherstone H	Burton J	Evans JH
Nov 25	CHESTERFIELD	4-1	Featherstone 3, Pinch		Husbands T	Leah R	Duffy J	Abley T	Lawrie R	Hardy W	Tracey H	Pinch C	Featherstone H	Burton G	Evans JH
Dec 9	CHELSEA RESERVES	5-1	Featherstone 2, Evans 2, G Burton	4200	Husbands T	Latham G	Waters A	Tracey H	Thompson E	Hardy W	Hiftle J	Burton J	Evans JH	Bates J	McDonald J
Dec 27	CARDIFF & DIST. LGE	7-2	Hardy 2, Evans 4, Bates	7000	Germaine	Waters A	Duffy J	Abley T	Lawrie R	Hardy W	Latham G	Burton J	Featherstone H	Burton G	Tracey H
Jan 1	BRISTOL CITY	2-0	Tracey, Featherstone		Husbands T	Newton L	Waters A	Thompson E	Latham G	Hardy W	Hiftle J	Pinch C	Burton G	Gaughan W	Gaughan W
Mar 30	TREHARRIS	3-2	Pinch, G Burton, Gaughan								Gaughan W	Burton G		Clarke	Tracey H
Apr 20	CARDIFF & DIST. LGE	2-1	Tracey, G Burton		Husbands T	Douglas W	Waters A	Latham G	Thompson E	Hardy W	Briscoe	Burton J	Burton G	Bates J	Evans JH
Apr 30	Llanelly	3-0	J Burton, Bates, G Burton												

1912/13

Date	Opponent	Score	Scorers	Att	1	2	3	4	5	6	7	8	9	10	11
Sep 4	TREHARRIS	5-0	Douglas 2, Keggans 3		Kneeshaw	Croft R	Leah R	Harvey H	Saunders L	Hardy W	Bennett J	Burton G	Douglas W	Keggans H	Gaughan W
Nov 11	Cwm Albion	1-2	Bennett		Fearby	Milford E	Doncaster T	Abley T	Newton L	Hardy W	Bennett J	Latham G	Evans JH	Nash L	Nicholls S
Mar 25	Newport County	1-1	Devlin	3000							Bennett J				Devlin W
Apr 2	BRIDGEND YMCA	9-0	Bennett, Keggans 3, J Evans, D Evans 2, Keenor, Newton		Lewis	Latham G	Harvey H	Keenor F	Newton L	Woodman		Hardy W	Douglas W	Evans D	Devlin W
Apr 28	Pontypridd	1-1	Devlin								Bennett J				Devlin W
Apr 30	Mid Rhondda	1-1			Kneeshaw J	Doncaster T	Croft R	Keenor F	Newton L	Hardy W	Bennett J	Burton J	Douglas W	Devlin W	Evans JH

1913/14

Date	Opponent	Score	Scorers	Att	1	2	3	4	5	6	7	8	9	10	11
Nov 17	BLACKBURN ROVERS	1-2	Evans	15000	Kneeshaw J	Doncaster T	Leah R	Harvey H	McKenzie K	Hardy W	Bennett J	Henderson J	Burton G	Burton J	Evans JH
Jan 31	OLDHAM ATHLETIC	1-1	West	10000	Stephenson J	Doncaster T	Brittan C	Harvey H	Cassidy P	Hardy W	Henderson J	Devlin W	Hopkins L	West G	Evans JH

1914/15

Date	Opponent	Score	Scorers	Att	1	2	3	4	5	6	7	8	9	10	11
May 1	Ton Pentre	1-3													

1919/20

Date	Opponent	Score	Scorers	Att	1	2	3	4	5	6	7	8	9	10	11
Oct 6	SWANSEA TOWN	1-1	Devlin	4600	Kneeshaw J	Latham G	Layton A	Harvey H	Smith A	Bennett A	Beare G	Devlin W	Cox W	Jones C	Evans JH
Apr 27	BRISTOL CITY	1-3	Reed	6500	Kneeshaw J	Barnett A	Sayles B	Keenor F	Hopkins L	Anderson E	Beare G	Reed A	Jones C	Clarke	Evans JH
May 3	BRISTOL CITY	2-0	Beare, Hopkins	2400	Kneeshaw J	Sayles T	Sayles B	Keenor F	Smith A	Anderson E	Beare G	Griffiths	Hopkins L	Cashmore A	Evans JH

1915/16   War Time Competition

South-West Combination

	Date	Opponent	Score	Scorers	Att	1	2	3	4	5	6	7	8	9	10	11
1	Jan 8	Swindon Town	2-0	Beare, Coates		Kneeshaw	Dalton	Walton	Hewitt	Pinch	Smart	Beare	Jones E	Coates	Stone	Evans
2	15	SWINDON TOWN	1-0	Coates	2800	Kneeshaw	Dalton	Walton	Hewitt	Hardy	Smart	Beare	Jones E	Coates	Stone	Evans
3	22	BRISTOL CITY	1-0	E Jones	2500	Kneeshaw	Dalton	Walton	Hewitt	Pinch	Hardy	Beare	Jones E	Coates	Stone	Evans
4	29	BRISTOL ROVERS	1-2	Evans (p)		Kneeshaw	Dalton	Walton	Hewitt	Pinch	Hardy	Beare	Jones E	Coates	Stone	Evans
5	Feb 12	Southampton	3-6	Coates, E Jones, Stone		Holly	Hewitt	Dalton	Pinch	Mortimer	Jones C	Beare	Jones E	Coates	Stone	Evans
6	Mar 4	SOUTHAMPTON	2-0	Beare, Durham (og)	1500	Holly	Hewitt	Dalton	Pinch	Mortimer	Jones C	Beare	Jones E	Coates	Stone	Evans
7	11	Newport County	5-1	Jenkins 4, E Jones		Kneeshaw	Dalton	Walton	Hewitt	Pinch	Smart	Beare	Jones E	Coates	Jenkins	Evans
8	18	NEWPORT COUNTY	3-1	E Jones 2, Coates	1500	Kneeshaw	Dalton	Walton	Hewitt	Pinch	Smart	Beare	Jones E	Coates	Jenkins	Hardy
9	25	Portsmouth	0-4			Gibbons	Ordell	Dalton	Hewitt	Lee	Emerson	Beare	Quinn	Wood	Coates	Jenkins
10	Apr 1	Bristol Rovers	2-0	Beare, E Jones	600	Kneeshaw	Dalton	Walton	Hewitt	Pinch	Hardy	Beare	Jones E	Coates	Stone	Jenkins
11	8	Bristol City	0-2		2000	Kneeshaw	Dalton	Walton	Hewitt	Mortimer	Hardy	Beare	Jones E	Coates	Jenkins	Stone
12	15	PORTSMOUTH	1-2	Coates		Kneeshaw	Dalton	Walton	Hewitt	Mortimer	Hardy	Beare	Jones E	Coates	Jenkins	Stone

Cardiff City finished top on goal average.

Friendly Matches

	Date	Opponent	Score	Scorers	Att	1	2	3	4	5	6	7	8	9	10	11
Sep	4	BRISTOL ROVERS	4-1	Seymour, Stone, Beare 2	3000	Kneeshaw	Brittan	Hewitt	Jenkins	Pinch	Hardy	Beare	Seymour	Davies DW	Stone	Evans
	11	BRISTOL CITY	1-0	Seymour	4000	Kneeshaw	Hewitt	Brittan	Jenkins	Pinch	Hardy	Beare	Seymour	Davies DW	Doran	Evans
	18	Bristol City	1-1	Beare	2500	Kneeshaw	Hewitt	Brittan	Latham	Pinch	Hardy	Beare	Seymour	Davies DW	Stone	Evans
	25	PORTSMOUTH	2-0	Seymour, Stone, Beare 2	2500	Kneeshaw	Hewitt	Brittan	Jenkins	Pinch	Hardy	Beare	Seymour	Davies DW	Stone	Evans
Oct	2	FOOTBALLERS BATT.	0-1		500	Kneeshaw	Hewitt	Walton	Jenkins	Keenor	Hardy	Beare	Seymour	Davies DW	Stone	Evans
	9	Bristol Rovers	2-3	Millard, Beare		Kneeshaw	Brittan	Walton	Allden	Pinch	Hardy	Beare	Seymour	Millard	Davies DW	Evans
	16	BRISTOL LEAGUE	2-0	Davies, Seymour	200	Kneeshaw	Ford	Walton	Hewitt	Pinch	Hardy	Beare	Seymour	Millard	Stone	Evans
	23	Portsmouth	2-3	Millard, Beare	2000	Somers	Brittan	Walton	Fenwick	Doran	Hunter	Beare	Davies DW	Millard	Stone	Evans
Nov	6	BARRY TOWN	1-1	Evans		Kneeshaw	Brittan	Walton	Hewitt	Pinch	Hardy	Beare	Stone	Davies DW	Fish	Evans
	13	Southampton	2-2	Collier, Stone		Kneeshaw	Hewitt	Tinsley	Fish	Pinch	Hardy	Beare	Stone	Collier	Mitchell	Evans
	20	WELSH FIELD AMB. XI	6-1	Davies 4, Hardy, Stone	1000	Kneeshaw	Smart	Walton	Hewitt	Pinch	Tinsley	Seymour	Stone	Davies DW	Hardy	Evans
	27	MID RHONDDA	2-3	Hardy, Davies		Kneeshaw	Tinsley	Walton	Hewitt	Pinch	Smart	Beare	Stone	Davies DW	Hardy	Evans
Dec	11	WELSH REGIMENT XI	6-3	Hardy 2, Stone 2, Hewitt, Davies		Kneeshaw		Walton	Hewitt			Beare	Stone	Davies DW	Hardy	Evans
	18	Barry Town	0-1		2000	Kneeshaw	Dalton	Walton	Hewitt	Pinch	Hardy	Beare	Jones E	Davies DW	Stone	Evans
	25	Merthyr Town	2-1	Stone, Beare		Tinsley	Dalton	Walton	Smart	Pinch	Hardy	Beare	Jones E	Davies DW	Stone	Evans
	27	BARNSLEY	0-0		2000	Kneeshaw	Brittan	Walton	Smart	Bratley	Hardy	Beare	Jones E	Davies DW	Vizard	Evans
Jan	1	SOUTHAMPTON	1-0	Evans	250	Kneeshaw	Layton	Hewitt	Pinch	Pinch	Smart	Beare	Jones E	Hardy	Stone	Evans
Feb	5	Barry Town	0-3		3000	Kneeshaw	Dalton	Walton	Hewitt	Hardy	Smart	Beare	Jones E	Coates	Stone	Evans
	19	BARRY TOWN	0-1			Kneeshaw	Dalton	Walton	Hewitt	Mortimer	Hardy	Beare	Jones E	Coates	Stone	Evans
Apr	15	NOTTM. FOREST	2-1	Coates 2		Kneeshaw	Dalton	Walton	Hewitt	Hardy	Smart	Beare	Jones E	Coates	Jenkins	Evans
	22	SWINDON TOWN	3-2	Jones, Coates 2		Kneeshaw	Dalton	Walton	Hewitt	Pinch	Hardy	Beare	Jones E	Coates	Jenkins	Evans

Cardiff City played friendly games only in seasons 1916/17, 1917/18 and 1918/19

1919/20   4th in Southern League Division One

#		Date	Opponent	Result	Scorers	Att	Barnett A	Beare G	Brittan RC	Cashmore AA	Cassidy P	Clarke JW	Cox W	Davies LS	Devlin W	Evans JH	Grimshaw W	Hardy W	Harvey H	Hewitt C	Hopkins L	Jenkins ES	Jones C	Keenor FC	Kneeshaw HJ	Layton AED	Smith EE	Stewart A	West G
1	Aug	30	Reading	0-2		8000		7	2		5					11	8		4				10	6	1		3		9
2	Sep	1	Bristol Rovers	4-4	Grimshaw 2, Jones, Evans	6000		7	2							11	8		4		9		10	6	1	5	3		
3		6	SOUTHAMPTON	3-0	Keenor, West, Evans	11000		7	2							11	8	6	4					9	1	5	3		10
4		8	BRISTOL ROVERS	0-0		7500		7	2						8	11		6	4					9	1	5	3		10
5		13	Luton Town	2-2		10000	10		2					7	9	11	8		4					6	1	5	3		
6		20	GILLINGHAM	5-0	Grimshaw 2, Evans 2, Devlin	12500	10	7	2						9	11	8		4					6	1	5	3		
7		27	Swansea Town	1-2	Evans	15500	10	7	2						9	11	8		4					6	1	5	3		
8	Oct	4	EXETER CITY	1-0	Cox	12500	10	7	2				9			11	8		4					6	1	5	3		
9		11	Watford	0-0		8000	3	7	2			6	11		9	8	10		4						1	5			
10		18	Queen's Park Rangers	0-0		10000	3	7	2			6	9			11	10	8	4						1	5			
11		25	SWINDON TOWN	3-3	Clarke 2, Cox	13500	10	7	2			3	11			9	8		4					6	1	5			
12	Nov	1	Millwall	2-1	Grimshaw 2	12000	3	7	2				9			11	8		4					6	1	5			10
13		8	BRIGHTON & HOVE ALB.	2-0	Harvey, Grimshaw	14000	3	7	2				11		9		8		4					6	1	5			10
14		15	Newport County	3-1	West, Smith, Hopkins	10500	3	7	2							11	8		4		9			6	1	5			10
15		22	PORTSMOUTH	0-1		16000		7	2							11	8		4		9			6	1	5	3		10
16		29	Northampton Town	2-2	Grimshaw, West	7000		7	2				9			11	8		4					6	1	5	3		10
17	Dec	6	CRYSTAL PALACE	2-1	Evans, Cashmore	13000	3	7	2	9						8	11		4					6	1	5			10
18		13	Southend United	1-1	Cashmore	9000	3			9						8	11	7	4					6	1	5	2		10
19		25	Merthyr Town	1-1	Cashmore	10000		7	2	9						8	11		4					6	1	5	3		10
20		26	MERTHYR TOWN	3-2	Beare, Evans, Chamberlain (og)	18000	3	7		9						8	11		4					6	1	5	2		10
21		27	Brentford	2-1	Evans, Cashmore	10000	3	7		9						8	11	6	4						1	5	2		10
22	Jan	1	NORWICH CITY	1-0	Hardy	14000	3	7	2	9						8	11	6	4				10		1	5			
23		3	READING	4-0	Clarke 2, Cox 2	15000		7	2	9		10	8			11			4					6	1	5	3		
24		17	Southampton	2-2	Cashmore, Beare	10000	3	7	2	9		10	8			11			4					6	1	5			
25		24	LUTON TOWN	2-1	Cashmore, West	15000	3	7	2	9						11	8		4					6	1	5			10
26	Feb	7	SWANSEA TOWN	1-0	Beare	21371	3	7		9						8	11	2	4					6	1	5			10
27		14	Exeter City	1-1	Clarke	8000		7	2	9		11	8					6	4						1	5		3	10
28		28	QUEEN'S PARK RANGERS	4-0	Beare 2, Cashmore, West	17000	3	7		9						11	8		4					6	1	5	2		10
29	Mar	6	Swindon Town	2-2	Cashmore 2	9000	3	7		9						11	8		4					6	1	5	2		10
30		13	MILLWALL	4-2	Grimshaw 2, West, Clarke	12000	3	7	2			11	9			8		6	4						1	5			10
31		17	Gillingham	0-3		8000		7	2	9						11	8	6	4						1	5	3		10
32		20	Brighton & Hove Albion	1-1	Cashmore	13000	3	7	2	9		10				11	8	6	4						1	5			
33		27	NEWPORT COUNTY	0-0		20000	3	7		9		10	8			11		6	4	1						5	2		
34	Apr	2	Plymouth Argyle	0-1		19000		7	2	9						11	8	6	4						1	5	3		10
35		3	Portsmouth	0-0		24606		7	2	9						11	8	6	4						1	5	3		10
36		5	PLYMOUTH ARGYLE	0-2		25000	3	7	2	9			11				8	6	4						1	5			10
37		10	NORTHAMPTON T	6-1	* See below	12000			2							8	11	7	4	6	9				1	5	3		10
38		14	WATFORD	0-1		11000		7	2							8	11		4	6	9				1	5	3		10
39		17	Crystal Palace	1-1	Cashmore	16000		7	2	9			8				11	4	6						1	5	3		10
40		24	SOUTHEND UNITED	1-0	West	16000		7	2	9			8				11	6	4						1	5	3		10
41		29	Norwich City	1-1	West	5000			2	9							11	7	4	6	8				1	5	3		10
42	May	1	BRENTFORD	2-0	Evans, Cashmore	12000	3	7	2	9						11		6	4		8				1	5			10

Scorers in game 37: Hopkins 2, Grimshaw, West, Keenor, Evans

	Barnett A	Beare G	Brittan RC	Cashmore AA	Cassidy P	Clarke JW	Cox W	Davies LS	Devlin W	Evans JH	Grimshaw W	Hardy W	Harvey H	Hewitt C	Hopkins L	Jenkins ES	Jones C	Keenor FC	Kneeshaw HJ	Layton AED	Smith EE	Stewart A	West G
Apps	23	38	34	23	5	12	20	1	6	34	32	23	25	4	7	1	3	37	37	27	40	3	27
Goals		5		12		6	4		1	10	13	1	1		3		1	2			1		9

One own goal

F.A. Cup

		Date	Opponent	Result	Scorers	Att	Barnett A	Beare G	Cox W	Evans JH	Grimshaw W	Harvey H	Keenor FC	Kneeshaw HJ	Layton AED	Smith EE	West G
R1	Jan	10	OLDHAM ATHLETIC	2-0	West, Evans	21921	3	7	9	11	8	4	6	1	2	5	10
R2		31	Wolverhampton Wan.	2-1	Beare, Smith	36475	3	7	9	11	8	4	6	1	2	5	10
R3	Feb	21	Bristol City	1-2	Beare	32452	3	7	9	11	8	4	6	1	2	5	10

Welsh Cup

		Date	Opponent	Result	Scorers	Att	Barnett A	Beare G	Brittan RC	Cashmore AA	Cassidy P	Clarke JW	Cox W	Evans JH	Harvey H	Keenor FC	Kneeshaw HJ	Layton AED	Smith EE	Stewart A	West G
R3	Jan	14	MERTHYR TOWN	5-0	Harvey, Cox, Clarke 3	5500		7	2		5	10	8	11	4	6	1			3	
R4	Feb	11	CHESTER	5-0	Keenor, Evans, Smith, Cashmore 2	4000		7		9			8	11	2	6			5	3	10
SF	Mar	24	SWANSEA TOWN	2-1	West, Evans	7000	3	7	2	9			8	11	6	4	1		5		10
F	Apr	21	Wrexham	2-1	West 2	10000			2	9			8	11	4	6	1	3	5		10

Played at 9 in R3: J Johnstone
Played in R4: C Hewitt (at1), W Davidson (at 4)

		p	w	d	l	f	a	w	d	l	f	a	pts
1	Portsmouth	42	13	6	2	48	14	10	6	5	25	13	58
2	Watford	42	15	3	3	39	12	11	3	7	30	30	58
3	Crystal Palace	42	15	5	1	44	15	7	7	7	25	28	56
4	CARDIFF CITY	42	15	3	3	44	14	3	14	4	26	29	53
5	Plymouth Argyle	42	13	5	3	35	8	7	5	9	21	21	50
6	Queen's Park Rangers	42	12	7	2	39	13	6	3	12	23	37	46
7	Reading	42	11	5	5	30	14	5	8	8	21	29	45
8	Southampton	42	13	4	4	51	22	5	4	12	21	41	44
9	Swansea Town	42	11	4	6	28	14	5	7	9	25	31	43
10	Exeter City	42	14	3	4	44	22	3	6	12	13	30	43
11	Southend United	42	10	8	3	32	18	3	9	9	14	30	43
12	Norwich City	42	12	7	2	46	17	3	4	14	18	40	41
13	Swindon Town	42	13	4	4	45	25	4	3	14	20	42	41
14	Millwall	42	10	7	4	32	20	4	5	12	20	35	40
15	Brentford	42	11	5	5	35	21	4	5	12	18	38	40
16	Brighton & Hove Alb.	42	11	5	5	43	28	3	3	15	17	44	36
17	Bristol Rovers	42	10	7	4	43	29	1	6	14	19	49	35
18	Newport County	42	11	5	5	32	18	2	2	17	13	52	33
19	Northampton Town	42	8	9	4	35	40	4	5	12	29	63	33
20	Luton Town	42	7	7	7	29	28	3	3	15	22	48	30
21	Merthyr Town	42	7	6	8	30	32	2	5	14	17	47	29
22	Gillingham	42	7	5	9	24	23	3	2	16	10	51	27

1920/21   Second in Division Two: Promoted

#	Date	Opponent	Score	Scorers	Att	Abram RL	Barnett A	Beare G	Blair J	Brittan RC	Cashmore AA	Clark IW	Davies BE	Davies LS	Evans HP	Evans IH	Evans ST	Gault WE	Gill JJ	Grimshaw W	Hardy W	Jones C	Keenor FC	Kneeshaw HJ	Layton AED	Nash HE	Newton W	Page J	Pagnam F	Smith EE	West G
1	Aug 28	Stockport County	5-2	J Evans, Gill 2, Grimshaw, Keenor	13000					2	9					11			8	7	6		4	1	3					5	10
2	30	CLAPTON ORIENT	0-0		25000	6	3			2	9					11		8	10	7	4			1						5	
3	Sep 4	STOCKPORT COUNTY	3-0	Cashmore, Grimshaw 2	22000		3			2	9					11			8	7	6		4	1						5	10
4	6	Clapton Orient	0-2		12000		3			2	9					11			8	7	6		4	1						5	10
5	11	BIRMINGHAM	2-1	Gill, Cashmore	30000					2	9					11			8	7	6		4	1	3					5	10
6	18	Birmingham	1-1	Gill	45000		3			2	9					11			8	7	6		4	1						5	10
7	25	WEST HAM UNITED	0-0		30000		3			2	9					11	10		8	7	6		4	1						5	
8	Oct 2	West Ham United	1-1	Gill	26000		3	7		2	9					11			8		6		4	1						5	10
9	9	Fulham	3-0	Beare, Gill, West	28000		3	7		2	9					11			8		6		4	1						5	10
10	16	FULHAM	3-0	Cashmore 2, Keenor	25000		3	7		2	9					11			8		6		4	1						5	10
11	23	Notts County	2-1	Cashmore, Gill	22000		3	7		2	9					11			8		6		4	1						5	10
12	30	NOTTS COUNTY	1-1	Gill	30000		3	7		2	9					11			8		6		4	1						5	10
13	Nov 6	Leicester City	0-2		21000		3	7			9					11			8		6		4	1				2		5	10
14	13	LEICESTER CITY	2-0	Cashmore, Gill	20000		3	7		2	9					11			8		6		4	1						5	10
15	20	Blackpool	4-2	Gill, West, Cashmore, Baker (og)	10000			7	3	2	9					11			8		6		4	1						5	10
16	27	BLACKPOOL	0-0		28000			7	3	2	9					11			8		6		4	1						5	10
17	Dec 4	Sheffield Wednesday	1-0	West	12000			7	3	2	9					11			8		6		4	1						5	10
18	11	SHEFFIELD WEDNESDAY	1-0	West	28500			7	3	2	9					11			8		6		4	1						5	10
19	18	BURY	2-1	Gill, Cashmore	27500			7	3	2	9					11			8		6		4	1						5	10
20	25	Coventry City	4-2	Gill 2, Cashmore, Beare	22000			7	3	2	9					11			8		6		4	1						5	10
21	27	COVENTRY CITY	0-1		42000			7	3	2	9					11			8		6		4	1						5	10
22	Jan 1	Bury	1-3	Cashmore	25000			7	3	2	9					11			8		6		4	1						5	
23	15	Bristol City	0-0		35000	10		7	3	2	9					11			8		6		4	1						5	
24	22	BRISTOL CITY	1-0	Barnett	42000	10		7	3	2	9		1			11			8		6		4							5	
25	Feb 5	STOKE	0-1		27000				3	2	9		1			11			8	7	6	10	4							5	
26	12	Barnsley	2-0	Gill, Nash	17000				3	2		11	1	9					8	7	6					10			4	5	
27	14	Stoke	0-0		15000				3	2		11	1	9					8	7	6		4			10				5	
28	26	Nottingham Forest	2-1	Gill, Keenor	22000				3	2		11	1	9					8	7	6		5			10			4		
29	Mar 9	BARNSLEY	3-2	Gill, Beare, Pagnam	20000			7	3	2			1			11			8		6		4					10	9	5	
30	12	Rotherham County	0-2		18000		3	7		2			1			11					6		4					10	9	5	
31	26	PORT VALE	1-2	Grimshaw	30000				3	2	8		1			11				7	6		5					10	4		9
32	28	LEEDS UNITED	1-0	Pagnam	25000	10			3			11	1		8		7				6		4					2	9	5	
33	29	Leeds United	2-1	Pagnam, Keenor	20000			7	3			11	1		8						6		4			10		2	9	5	
34	Apr 2	Port Vale	0-0		18000			7	3			11	1		8						6		4			10		2	9	5	
35	4	NOTTM. FOREST	3-0	Pagnam 2, S Evans	27000				3	2		11	1		8		7				6		4			10			9	5	
36	9	SOUTH SHIELDS	1-0	Gill	30000					2		11	1				7		8		6					10	4	3	9	5	
37	11	ROTHERHAM COUNTY	1-0	Pagnam	30000				3			11	1		10		7		8		6		4					2	9	5	
38	16	South Shields	1-0	Hardy	17000			7	3			11	1						8		6		4			10		2	9	5	
39	23	HULL CITY	0-0		30000			7	3			11	1						8		6					10	4	2	9	5	
40	30	Hull City	0-2		10000				3	2			1			11			8	7	6		4						9	5	10
41	May 2	WOLVERHAMPTON W.	2-0	Gill, Pagnam	40000				3			11	1						8	7	6		4			10		2	9	5	
42	7	Wolverhampton Wan.	3-1	Pagnam, Nash, Gill	10000					2		11	1						8	7	6		4			10		3	9	5	
		Apps				1	16	23	25	35	26	13	19	3	5	29	4	2	37	15	42	1	38	23	2	14	5	9	14	40	21
		Goals				1	3				10					1	1		19	4	1		4			2			8		4

One own goal

F.A. Cup

	Date	Opponent	Score	Scorers	Att	Abram RL	Barnett A	Beare G	Blair J	Brittan RC	Cashmore AA	Clark IW	Davies BE	Davies LS	Evans HP	Evans IH	Evans ST	Gault WE	Gill JJ	Grimshaw W	Hardy W	Jones C	Keenor FC	Kneeshaw HJ	Layton AED	Nash HE	Newton W	Page J	Pagnam F	Smith EE	West G
R1	Jan 8	Sunderland	1-0	Beare	41923	10		7	3	2	9					11			8		6		4	1						5	
R2	29	Brighton & Hove Alb.	0-0		20260	10		7	3	2	9	1				11			8		6		4							5	
rep	Feb 2	BRIGHTON & HOVE ALB.	1-0	Cashmore	31000			7	3	2	9	1				11			8		6		4							5	10
R3	19	Southampton	1-0	Gill	21363	10			3	2	9	11	1						8	7	6		4							5	
R4	Mar 5	CHELSEA	1-0	Cashmore	50000	10		7	3	2	9					11			8		6		4							5	
SF	19	Wolverhampton Wan.	0-0		42000	10		7	3	2	9					11			8		6		4							5	
rep	23	Wolverhampton Wan.	1-3	Keenor (p)	45000	10		7	3	2	9					11				8	6		4							5	

SF at Anfield, Liverpool. SF replay at Old Trafford, Manchester

Welsh Cup

	Date	Opponent	Score	Scorers	Att	Abram RL	Barnett A	Beare G	Blair J	Brittan RC	Cashmore AA	Clark IW	Davies BE	Davies LS	Evans HP	Evans IH	Evans ST	Gault WE	Gill JJ	Grimshaw W	Hardy W	Jones C	Keenor FC	Kneeshaw HJ	Layton AED	Nash HE	Newton W	Page J	Pagnam F	Smith EE	West G
R3	Jan 15	Pontypridd	1-2	L Davies	2000	6				11	1			9		7							10			4	2				

Fielded the reserve team owing to a clash of fixtures.
Also played: T Sayles (at 3), T Wilmott (5), L Hopkins (8).

1921/22 4th in Division One

#	Date	Opponent	Score	Scorers	Att	Blair J	Brittan RC	Brown TH	Cashmore AA	Clark JW	Clennell J	Davies BE	Davies LS	Evans HP	Evans JH	Evans ST	Gill JJ	Grimshaw W	Hardy W	Jenkins ES	Keenor FC	Kneeshaw HI	McDonald K	Melville J	Nash HE	Nelson J	Newton W	Nock AJ	Page J	Pagnam F	Smith EE	West G
1	Aug 27	TOTTENHAM HOTSPUR	0-1		56000		2								11		8	7	6		4	1							3	9	5	10
2	29	Aston Villa	1-2	Smith	30000		2								11		8	7	6		4	1								9	5	10
3	Sep 3	Tottenham Hotspur	1-4	West	45000		2		8						11			7	6		4	1		3						9	5	10
4	5	ASTON VILLA	0-4		40000		2	11	9					8		7			6		4	1							3	10	5	
5	10	OLDHAM ATHLETIC	0-1		20000	3	2	11				1	9	8				7			4				10						5	
6	17	Oldham Athletic	1-2	Grimshaw	18000	3	2			10		1			11		8	7		5	4				6					9		
7	24	MIDDLESBROUGH	3-1	Gill 2, Nash	35000	3	2					1			11	4	8	7		6	5				10					9		
8	Oct 1	Middlesbrough	0-0		30000	3	2					1			11	4	8	7	6		5									9		10
9	8	BOLTON WANDERERS	1-2	Gill	40000	3	2					1			11	4	8	7	6		5				10					9		
10	15	Bolton Wanderers	2-1	Gill 2	25486	3	2					1			11	4	8	7		6	5				10					9		
11	22	West Bromwich Albion	2-2	Keenor, Gill	20000	3	2				10	1			11	4	8	7		6	5									9		
12	29	WEST BROMWICH ALB.	2-0	Gill 2	35000	3					10	1			11	4	8	7		6	5					2				9		
13	Nov 5	MANCHESTER CITY	0-2		38000	3					10	1			11	4	8	7		6	5					2				9		
14	12	Manchester City	1-1	Gill	25000	3					10	1			11	4	8	7		6	5									9		
15	19	EVERTON	2-1	L Davies 2	35000	3	2				10	1	9	4	11		8	7		6	5											
16	26	Everton	1-0	L Davies	30000	3	2				10	1	9	4	11		8	7	6												5	
17	Dec 3	SUNDERLAND	2-0	Gill, L Davies	35000		2				10	1	9	4	11		8	7	6										3		5	
18	10	Sunderland	1-4	Gill	20000		2				10	1	9	4	11		8	7	6										3		5	
19	17	HUDDERSFIELD T	0-0		25000	3	2				10	1	9	4	11	7	8		6												5	
20	24	Huddersfield Town	1-0	Grimshaw	20000	3					10	1	9	4	11		8	7	6										2		5	
21	26	Arsenal	0-0		35000	3					10	1	9	4	11		8	7	6										2		5	
22	27	ARSENAL	4-3	Clennell, Grimshaw, Gill, L Davies	41000	3					10	1	9	4	11		8	7	6										2		5	
23	31	Birmingham	1-0	L Davies	30000	3					10	1	9	4	11		8	7	6										2		5	
24	Jan 2	Blackburn Rovers	3-1	L Davies, Grimshaw	30000	3					10	1	9	4				7	6								11		2		5	
25	14	BIRMINGHAM	3-1	Clennel 2, Grimshaw	37000	3					10		9	4	11			7	6		8	1							2		5	
26	21	BRADFORD CITY	6-3	Gill 2, Clennell, L Davies 3	27000	3					10	1	9		11		8	7	6		4								2		5	
27	Feb 4	PRESTON NORTH END	3-0	McDonald, Grimshaw, Gill	27000	3	2				10	1			11		8	7	6		4		9								5	
28	8	CHELSEA	2-0	Clennell, Gill	25000	3	2				10	1	9		11		8	7	6		4										5	
29	11	Preston North End	1-1	L Davies	20000		2				10	1	9		11		8	7	6		4								3		5	
30	25	Chelsea	0-1		47000		2				10	1	9	4	11		8	7	6										3		5	
31	Mar 11	Sheffield United	2-0	McDonald, Clennell	35000	3	2				8	1		4	11			7	6		5		9		10							
32	15	Bradford City	0-1		15000	3	2				8	1			11			7	6		4		9		10						5	
33	18	Burnley	1-1	Hardy	30000		2				10	1	9	4	11	7	8		6		5								3			
34	25	BURNLEY	4-2	J Evans, Gill, L Davies 2	35000	3	2				10	1	9	4	11	7	8		6												5	
35	Apr 1	Newcastle United	0-0		25000	3				11	10	1					8	7	6		4		9						2		5	
36	8	NEWCASTLE UNITED	1-0	L Davies	25000		2				10	1	9		11		8	7	6		4								3		5	
37	15	Liverpool	1-5	Clennell	45000	3					10	1	9	4	11		8	7	6										2		5	
38	17	BLACKBURN ROVERS	1-3	Clennell	30000	3	2				10	1	9	4	11		8	7	6		5											
39	22	LIVERPOOL	2-0	Gill, L Davies	37000	3					10	1	9		11		8	7	6		4								2		5	
40	26	SHEFFIELD UNITED	1-1	Clennell	15000	3					10		9	4			8	7	6			1						11	2		5	
41	29	Manchester United	1-1	L Davies	15000	3					10		9		11		8	7	6		4	1							2		5	
42	May 6	MANCHESTER UNITED	3-1	Gill, Clennnell 2	19000	3					10		9	4			8	7	6									11	2		5	
		Apps				32	27	2	4	1	32	34	25	29	36	4	34	38	32	9	27	7	4	1	8	2	1	2	21	13	29	4
		Goals									10		17		1		20	6	1		1		2		1						1	1

Played in one game: G Latham (24, at 8), F Anderson (5, at 6),
A Barnett (2, at 3), TG Farquharson (42, at 1)

F.A. Cup

Rd	Date	Opponent	Score	Scorers	Att	Blair J	Brittan RC	Brown TH	Cashmore AA	Clark JW	Clennell J	Davies BE	Davies LS	Evans HP	Evans JH	Evans ST	Gill JJ	Grimshaw W	Hardy W	Jenkins ES	Keenor FC	Kneeshaw HI	McDonald K	Melville J	Nash HE	Nelson J	Newton W	Nock AJ	Page J	Pagnam F	Smith EE	West G
R1	Jan 7	Manchester United	4-1	L Davies 2, Nash, Clennell	25000	5	2			11	8	1	9	4				7	6						10				3			
R2	28	Southampton	1-1	Gill	19291	3					10	1	9	4	11		8	7	6										2		5	
rep	Feb 1	SOUTHAMPTON	2-0	Gill, Clennell	40000	3				11	10	1	9	4			8	7	6										2		5	
R3	18	NOTTM FOREST	4-1	L Davies 2, Gill, Clennell	50470	3					10	1	9	4	11		8	7	6										2		5	
R4	Mar 4	TOTTENHAM HOTSPUR	1-1	L Davies	51000	3					10	1	9	4	11		8	7	6										2		5	
rep	9	Tottenham Hotspur	1-2	Gill	53626	3					10	1	9	4	11		8	7	6		5								2			

Welsh Cup

Rd	Date	Opponent	Score	Scorers	Att	Blair J	Brittan RC	Brown TH	Cashmore AA	Clark JW	Clennell J	Davies BE	Davies LS	Evans HP	Evans JH	Evans ST	Gill JJ	Grimshaw W	Hardy W	Jenkins ES	Keenor FC	Kneeshaw HI	McDonald K	Melville J	Nash HE	Nelson J	Newton W	Nock AJ	Page J	Pagnam F	Smith EE	West G
R3	Jan 18	NEWPORT COUNTY	7-1	Keenor, Grimshaw 2, Davies 4	5500		2						9	4	11			7	6		8	1			10				3		5	
R4	Feb 22	MERTHYR TOWN	5-0	L Davies 3, Nash, Jackson (og)	5500	3	2						9	4	11	7	8		6						10						5	
SF	Apr 10	Pontypridd	3-0	Keenor, Gill, J Evans	12000	3	2				10	1	9	4	11		8	7			6										5	
F	May 4	Ton Pentre	2-0	Gill, L Davies	12000	3	2				10	1	9	4	11		8	7	6												5	

1922/23 — 9th in Division One

#	Date	Opponent	Score	Scorers	Att	Aitken FMcK	Blair J	Brittan RC	Clennell J	Davies BE	Davies LS	Evans HP	Evans JH	Evans ST	Farquharson TG	Gill JJ	Grimshaw W	Hardy W	Jones VW	Keenor FC	Kneeshaw HJ	Mason FO	McDonald K	Nash HE	Nelson J	Nock AJ	Page J	Reid GH	Smith EE	Taylor W	Turnbull WI
1	Aug 26	Tottenham Hotspur	1-1	Gill	40000		3	2	10	1	9		11			8	7	6		4									5		
2	28	ASTON VILLA	3-0	Clennell 2, Grimshaw	45000		3		10	1	9		11			8	7	6		4							2		5		
3	Sep 2	TOTTENHAM HOTSPUR	2-3	L Davies 2	50000		3		10	1	9	4	11			8	7			6							2		5		
4	4	Aston Villa	3-1	Nash, Grimshaw 2	25000		3			1	9	4	11			8	7			6				10			2		5		
5	9	ARSENAL	4-1	Grimshaw, Nash, L Davies 2	30000		3			1	9	4	11			8	7			6				10			2		5		
6	16	Arsenal	1-2	L Davies	45000			2		1	9		11			8	7	6		4				10			3		5		
7	23	EVERTON	0-2		30000		3		10	1	9		11			8	7	6		4							2		5		
8	30	Everton	1-3	Smith	35000		3		10	1	9		11			8	7	6		4							2		5		
9	Oct 7	SUNDERLAND	2-4	Clennell 2	37000		3		10	1	9	4	11				7	6					8		2				5		
10	14	Sunderland	1-2	McDonald	35000			2	8			4	11		1		7	6					5	10			3				
11	21	Liverpool	1-3	Clennell (p)	35000			2	8			4	11		1		7	6					5	10			3				
12	28	LIVERPOOL	3-0	Grimshaw, McDonald, Clennell	40000		3	2	10			4	11		1	8	7	6					5	9							
13	Nov 4	Birmingham	0-0		30000		3		10		8	4	11		1		7	6					5	9			2				
14	11	BIRMINGHAM	1-1	Gill	25000		3		10	1	9	4	11			8	7	6											5		
15	18	Huddersfield Town	0-1		15000		3		8	1		4	11				7	6		9			5	10		2					
16	25	HUDDERSFIELD T	0-1		27000		3	2	10	1	9	8	11				7	6		4									5		
17	Dec 2	STOKE	2-1	Gill, Clennell	27000			2	10	1		4	11			8	7	6					5	9			3				
18	9	Stoke	1-3	McDonald	15000			2	10			4	11		1	8	7	6					5	9			3				
19	16	MANCHESTER CITY	3-1	Gill, McDonald 2	20000	7		2					11		1	8		6		4			9	10			3		5		
20	23	Manchester City	1-5	Reid	16000	7	3	2					11		1	8		6		4				10				9	5		
21	26	WEST BROMWICH ALB.	3-0	Gill 2, Reid	35000		3		10				11		1	8	7	6		4							2	9	5		
22	27	West Bromwich Albion	0-3		14898		3						11		1	8	7	6		4				10			2	9	5		
23	30	Bolton Wanderers	0-0		15829		3		10				11		1	8	7	6		4					2			9	5		
24	Jan 6	BOLTON WANDERERS	1-0	Reid	25000		3		10				11		1	8	7	6		4					2			9	5		
25	20	Blackburn Rovers	1-3	Nash	20000			2		1			11			8	7	6		4				10			3	9	5		
26	27	BLACKBURN ROVERS	5-0	Gill 3, L Davies 2	25000		3		10	1	9	4	11			8	7	6									2		5		
27	Feb 10	NEWCASTLE UNITED	5-0	Grimshaw, L Davies 2, Gill 2	27000		3		10	1	9	4	11			8	7	6									2		5		
28	17	Nottingham Forest	2-3	L Davies, Gill	10000		3		10	1	9	4	11			8	7	6									2		5		
29	28	Newcastle United	1-3	L Davies	10000		3		10	1	9	4	11			8	7	6									2		5		
30	Mar 3	Chelsea	1-1	Gill	20000				10	1	9	4	11			8	7	6									2		5		
31	10	CHELSEA	6-1	L Davies 3, J Evans, Gill 2	25000		3		10	1	9	4	11			8	7	6									2		5		
32	17	MIDDLESBROUGH	2-0	Gill, Reid	22000				10			4	11		1	8	7	6							2		3	9	5		
33	24	Middlesbrough	1-0	Gill	15000		3		10		9		11		1	8	7	6		4							2		5		
34	30	Burnley	5-1	Clennell 3, Keenor, L Davies	22000		3		10		9	4	11		1		7	6		8							2		5		
35	31	PRESTON NORTH END	1-0	L Davies	20000		3		10		9	4	11		1		7	6		8							2		5		
36	Apr 2	BURNLEY	2-2	Keenor 2	35000		3		10			4	11		1		7	6		8			9				2		5		
37	7	Preston North End	0-3		20000		3		10		9	4	11		1		7	6		8							2		5		
38	14	SHEFFIELD UNITED	1-0	Clennell	15000				10				4	7		8		6	9		1	3					2		5		11
39	21	Sheffield United	0-0		20000		3		10	1	9		11			8	7	6		4							2		5		
40	25	NOTTM. FOREST	3-1	Clennell, L Davies 2	18000		3		10	1	9	4	11			8	7	6									2		5		
41	28	OLDHAM ATHLETIC	2-0	Clennell 2 (1p)	15000		3	2	10		9		11		1		7	6		4									5	8	
42	May 5	Oldham Athletic	1-3	L Davies	6000		3	2	10		9	4	11		1	8	7	6													
		Apps				2	32	13	35	20	27	27	41	1	21	31	40	34	1	38	1	1	7	8	17	1	23	7	32	1	1
		Goals							14		19		1			17	6			3			5	3				4	1		

F.A. Cup

Rd	Date	Opponent	Score	Scorers	Att	Blair J	Brittan RC	Clennell J	Davies BE	Davies LS	Evans HP	Evans JH	Farquharson TG	Gill JJ	Grimshaw W	Hardy W	Keenor FC	McDonald K	Nelson J	Page J	Smith EE
R1	Jan 13	WATFORD	1-1	J Evans (p)	34000	3		10				11	1	8	7	6	4	9		2	5
rep	17	Watford	2-2	L Davies, Clennell	12720	3	2	10		9	4	11		8	7	6					5
rep2	22	Watford	2-1	H Evans, L Davies	15000	3		10	1	9	4	11		8	7			6	2		5
R2	Feb 3	Leicester City	1-0	L Davies	35680	3		10	1	9	4	11		8	7			6	2		5
R3	24	TOTTENHAM HOTSPUR	2-3	Gill, J Evans (p)	54000	3		10	1	9	4	11		8	7			6	2		5

R1 replay a.e.t. Replay 2 at Villa Park.   Played at 5 in R3: ES Jenkins

Welsh Cup

Rd	Date	Opponent	Score	Scorers	Att	Blair J	Clennell J	Davies BE	Davies LS	Evans HP	Evans JH	Evans ST	Farquharson TG	Gill JJ	Grimshaw W	Hardy W	Keenor FC	McDonald K	Nelson J	Nock AJ	Page J	Reid GH	Smith EE
R4	Feb 7	RHYMNEY	7-0	Gill, L Davies, Nock, Keenor, S Evans	3000	3		1	9	4	11	7		8			6		2	10			5
R5	Mar 14	OSWESTRY	10-0	L Davies 3, Gill 3, Reid 3, Keenor	3000			1	10	4	11	7		8			6		2	3		9	5
SF	Apr 11	Swansea Town	3-2	Clennell 2, L Davies	12000	3	10		9	4	11		1		7	6		8			2		5
F	May 3	Aberdare Athletic	3-2	Grimshaw, Gill, L Davies	8000	3	10		9	4	11		1	8	7	6					2		5

League — Division One

#	Date	Opponent	Score	Scorers	Att	Blair J	Clennell J	Collins WE	Davies LS	Evans HP	Evans JH	Farquharson TG	Gill JJ	Grimshaw W	Hagan A	Hardy W	Jenkins ES	Jones J	Keenor FC	Kneeshaw HJ	Lawson D	Nelson J	Page J	Smith EE	Taylor W	Wake HW
1	Aug 25	BOLTON WANDERERS	3-2	Gill 2, Clennell	30000	3	10		9		11	1	8	7		6			4			2	5			
2	27	SUNDERLAND	2-1	Gill, J Evans (p)	25000	3	10		9	4	11	1	8	7		6			5			2				
3	Sep 1	Bolton Wanderers	2-2	Davies, Hardy	20013	3	10		9	4	11	1	8	7		6			5			2				
4	5	Sunderland	3-0	Gill, Clennell, Davies	30000	3	10		9	4	11	1	8	7		6			5			2				
5	8	West Ham United	0-0		30000	3	10		9	4	11	1	8	7		6			5			2				
6	15	WEST HAM UNITED	1-0	Davies	35000	3	10		9	4	11	1	8	7		6			5			2				
7	22	Newcastle United	1-1	Davies	40000	3	10		9	4	11	1	8	7		6			5			2				
8	29	NEWCASTLE UNITED	1-0	Davies	46000	3	10		9	4	11	1	8	7		6			5			2				
9	Oct 6	Chelsea	2-1	Clennell, Gill	40000	3	10		9	4	11	1	8	7		6			5			2				
10	13	CHELSEA	1-1	Davies	40000	3	10		9	4	11	1	8	7		6			5			2				
11	20	PRESTON NORTH END	1-1	Davies	35000	3	10		9	4	11		8	7		6			5	1		2				
12	27	Preston North End	1-3	Davies	20000	3	10		9	4	11	1	8	7		6			5			2				
13	Nov 3	WEST BROMWICH ALB.	3-0	Gill 2, H Evans	25000	3	8		9	4	11	1	10	7		6			5			2				
14	10	West Bromwich Albion	4-2	Davies 4	20000	3	8		9	4	11	1	10	7		6			5			2				
15	17	Manchester City	1-1	Grimshaw	20000	3	8		9	4	11	1	10	7		6						2		5		
16	24	MANCHESTER CITY	1-1	Davies	35000	3	8		9	4	11	1	10						6	7		2		5		
17	Dec 1	Nottingham Forest	1-0	J Evans	10000	3	10		9	4	11	1	8			6			5		7	2				
18	8	NOTTM. FOREST	4-1	Gill 2, Clennell, Davies	22000	3	10		9	4		1	8			6			5		7	2			11	
19	15	Liverpool	2-0	Clennell, Gill	40000	3	10		9	4	11	1	8			6			5		7	2				
20	22	LIVERPOOL	2-0	Davies 2	25000	3	10		9	4	11	1	8			6			5		7	2				
21	25	Sheffield United	1-1	Hardy	45000	3	10		9	4	11	1	8			6			5		7	2				
22	26	SHEFFIELD UNITED	3-1	Davies 2, Keenor	50000	3	10		9	4	11	1	8			6			5		7	2				
23	29	Aston Villa	1-2		52000	3			9	4		1	8		10	6					7	2		5	11	
24	Jan 1	Middlesbrough	1-0	Clennell	30000	3	10		9	4		1				6			5		8	2	7		11	
25	5	ASTON VILLA	0-2		40000	3	10		9	4		1	8			6			5			2	7		11	
26	19	Arsenal	2-1	Davies, Clennell	30000		10		9	4	11	1	8			6			5			2	7	3		
27	26	ARSENAL	4-0	Gill 3, Davies	35000		10		9	4	11	1	8			6			5			2	7	3		
28	Feb 9	BLACKBURN ROVERS	2-0	Gill, Hardy	20000	3	10		9	4	11	1	8			6			5			2	7			
29	16	Tottenham Hotspur	1-1	Hagan	35000		10				11	1			8	6	5	9			7	2		3		4
30	Mar 1	Huddersfield Town	0-2		25000	3	10		9	4	11		8			6			5	1	7	2				
31	15	NOTTS COUNTY	0-2		19800	3					11		8		10	6	5	9		1	7	2				4
32	20	Blackburn Rovers	1-2	Clennell	12000	3	10	7		4	11	1	8			6		9			5	2				
33	22	Notts County	0-1		20000	3	10	7			11	1	8			6		9			5	2				4
34	29	EVERTON	0-0		20000	3			9		11	1	8		10	6					5	2	7			4
35	Apr 5	Everton	0-0		45000	3	10		9		11	1	8			6	5					2	7			4
36	7	TOTTENHAM HOTSPUR	2-1	Jones, Clennell	25000		10		9		11	1	8			6			7		5	2	3			4
37	12	BURNLEY	2-0	J Evans, Davies	10000		10		9		11	1	8			6			7		5	2	3			4
38	14	HUDDERSFIELD T	0-0		30000		10		9		11	1	8			6			7		5	2	3			4
39	19	Burnley	2-1	Gill, Davies	15000	3	10		9		11	1	8			6			7		5	2				4
40	21	MIDDLESBROUGH	1-0	Clennell	30000	3	10		9		11	1	8			6			7		5	2				4
41	26	BIRMINGHAM	2-0	Jones, Clennell	18000	3	10				11	1	8			6		9	7		5	2				4
42	May 3	Birmingham	0-0		50000	3	10				11	1	8			6		9	7		5	2				4
		Apps				36	39	2	38	29	38	39	39	15	5	39	3	12	39	3	18	42	6	4	4	12
		Goals					11		23	1	3		15	1	1	3		2	1							

F.A. Cup

Rd	Date	Opponent	Score	Scorers	Att	Blair J	Clennell J	Collins WE	Davies LS	Evans HP	Evans JH	Farquharson TG	Gill JJ	Grimshaw W	Hagan A	Hardy W	Jenkins ES	Jones J	Keenor FC	Kneeshaw HJ	Lawson D	Nelson J	Page J	Smith EE	Taylor W	Wake HW
R1	Jan 12	GILLINGHAM	0-0		20000	3	10		9	4	11	1	8			6			5			2	7			
rep	16	Gillingham	2-0	Gill, Davies	19472	3	10		9	4	11	1	8			6			5			2	7			
R2	Feb 2	ARSENAL	1-0	Gill	35000		10		9	4	11	1	8			6			5			2	7	3		
R3	23	BRISTOL CITY	3-0	Gill 2, Clennell	50000	3	10		9	4	11	1	8			6			5			2	7			
R4	Mar 8	Manchester City	0-0		76166	3	10		9	4	11	1	8			6			5			2	7			
rep	12	MANCHESTER CITY	0-1	(aet)	50000	3	10		9	4	11	1	8			6			5			2	7			

Welsh Cup

Rd	Date	Opponent	Score	Scorers	Att	Blair J	Clennell J	Collins WE	Davies LS	Evans HP	Evans JH	Farquharson TG	Gill JJ	Grimshaw W	Hagan A	Hardy W	Jenkins ES	Jones J	Keenor FC	Kneeshaw HJ	Lawson D	Nelson J	Page J	Smith EE	Taylor W	Wake HW
R3	Feb 14	Shrewsbury Town	0-0		4000	3	10		9	4	11	1	8			6			5			2	7			
rep	27	SHREWSBURY TOWN	3-0	Clennell 2, Hardy	3500	3	10		9	4	11	1			8	6			5			2	7			
R4	Mar 17	Newport County	1-1	Jones	5500			7				1			8		5	9				2				4
rep	24	NEWPORT COUNTY	0-0		5000	3		7			11	1			10	6	5	9				2	8			
rep2	31	Newport County	0-0		4000	3		7	9			1			10	6						2			11	
rep3	Apr 10	Newport County	0-3		2000		10					1	7		8	6	5	9				2	3		11	

Played in R4: J Nock (10), A Barnett (3), J Lewis (6)
J Lewis also played at 4 in all three replays

1924/25   11th in Division One

#		Date	Opponent	Score	Scorers	Att	Beadles GH	Blair J	Clennell J	Collins WE	Davies LS	Davies W	Evans JH	Farquharson TG	Gill JJ	Hagan A	Hardy W	Hills JJ	Keenor FC	Lawson D	Lewis JJ	McIlvenny P	Nelson J	Nicholls JBL	Nicholson JR	Page J	Sloan TM	Taylor W	Wake HW
1	Aug	30	Burnley	0-0		17000		3	10		9		11	1	8		6		5	7			2						4
2	Sep	1	SHEFFIELD UNITED	1-1	L Davies	35000		3	10		9		11	1	8		6		5	7			2						4
3		6	LEEDS UNITED	3-0	L Davies 2, Lawson	30000		3	10		9		11	1	8		6		5	7			2		4				
4		8	Sheffield United	0-1		22000		3	10		9		11	1	8		6		5	7			2		4				
5		13	Birmingham	1-2	Gill	20000		3	10		9	11		1	8		6		5	7			2		4				
6		15	Preston North End	3-1	L Davies, Gill, Clennell	12000		3	10		9	11		1	8		6		5	7					4	2			
7		20	WEST BROMWICH ALB.	0-1		20000		3	10			11		1	8		6		5	7		9			4	2			
8		27	Tottenham Hotspur	1-1	McIlvenny	40000	10	3				7	11	1	8		6		5			9	2		4				
9	Oct	4	BOLTON WANDERERS	1-2	W Davies	30000		3	10			7	11	1	8		6					9	2		5				4
10		11	Notts County	0-3		20000		3	10		9	7	11	1	8		6		5				2		4				
11		18	EVERTON	2-1	L Davies 2	20000	10	3	8		9	7	11	1			6		5				2		4				
12		25	Newcastle United	2-1	L Davies 2	20000	10				9	7	11	1			6		5				2	8	4	3			
13	Nov	8	Nottingham Forest	1-2	Beadles	10000	10				9	7	11	1			6		5				2	8	4	3			
14		15	BURY	4-1	Beadles 2, L Davies 2	20000	10	3			9	8	11	1					5	7			2		6				4
15		22	Manchester City	2-2	Beadles, L Davies	15000	10	3			9	8	11	1					5	7			2		6				4
16		29	ARSENAL	1-1	Beadles	20000	10	3			9	8	11	1			6		5	7			2						4
17	Dec	6	Aston Villa	2-1	L Davies 2	30000	10	3			9	8	11	1			6		5	7			2						4
18		13	HUDDERSFIELD T	2-2	W Davies, Beadles	25000	10	3			9	8	11	1			6		5	7			2						4
19		15	LIVERPOOL	1-3	Gill	17000			10		9			1	8				5	7			2			6	3	11	4
20		20	Blackburn Rovers	1-3	Beadles	20000	10				9	8	11	1			3		5	7			2			6			4
21		25	West Ham United	2-3	W Davies, Beadles	27000	10	3			9	7	11	1	8				5				2			6			4
22		26	WEST HAM UNITED	2-1	Beadles, L Davies	31000	10	3			9	7	11	1	8				5				2			6			4
23	Jan	1	Sunderland	0-1		18000	10				9	7	11		8			1	5	7			2			6			4
24		3	Leeds United	0-0		13000	10				9	7	11		8	3		1	5				2			6			4
25		17	BIRMINGHAM	1-0	L Davies	16000	10	3			9	8	11	1			6		5	7			2						4
26		24	West Bromwich Albion	0-1		20000	10	3			9	7	11	1	8		6		5				2						4
27	Feb	7	Bolton Wanderers	0-3		17374	10	3			9	7	11	1	8		6		5				2						4
28		11	BURNLEY	4-0	Nelson (p), L Davies 2, Gill	8000	10	3			9	7	11	1	8		6		5				2						4
29		14	NOTTS COUNTY	1-1	Nicholson	20000		3	10				11	1	8		5			7					9	2	6		4
30		25	Everton	2-1	Beadles, W Davies	8000	10	3				11		1	8		6		5	7			2		9				4
31		28	NEWCASTLE UNITED	3-0	Nicholson 2, McIlvenny	25000		3					11		8		5	1		7		10	2		9		6		4
32	Mar	14	NOTTM. FOREST	2-0	Nelson (p), Gill	15000	10	3				11		1	8		6		5	7			2		9				4
33		18	TOTTENHAM HOTSPUR	0-2		27000		3			9	10	11	1	8		6		5	7			2						4
34		21	Bury	1-4	Nicholson	20000		3			9	7	11	1	8		5				4				10	2	6		
35	Apr	1	MANCHESTER CITY	0-2		15000	10					7	11	1	8		5					9	2				3		4
36		4	Arsenal	1-1	Beadles	25000	9	3					8	11		10	6	1	5	7			2						4
37		11	ASTON VILLA	2-1	Nicholson, Gill	18000	10	3					7	11	8		6	1	5						9				4
38		13	SUNDERLAND	2-0	L Davies 2	25000		3			11		7	1	8	10	6		5				2		9				4
39		15	BLACKBURN ROVERS	3-0	Gill, W Davies, Nicholson	12000		3				11		1	8	10	6		5	7			2		9				4
40		18	Huddersfield Town	0-0		16000		3		7				1	8	10	6					11	2		9			5	4
41		29	Liverpool	2-1	Beadles, Gill	20000	10	3			9		11	1	8		5			7			2		6				4
42	May	2	PRESTON NORTH END	0-0		17000	10	3			9		11	1	8		6		5	7			2						4
					Apps		25	36	12	1	30	31	33	37	32	3	36	5	36	26	1	5	37	2	29	9	4	1	31
					Goals		10		1		20	4			9	1				1		2	2		6				

F.A. Cup

		Date	Opponent	Score	Scorers	Att	Beadles GH	Blair J	Clennell J	Collins WE	Davies LS	Davies W	Evans JH	Farquharson TG	Gill JJ	Hagan A	Hardy W	Hills JJ	Keenor FC	Lawson D	Lewis JJ	McIlvenny P	Nelson J	Nicholls JBL	Nicholson JR	Page J	Sloan TM	Taylor W	Wake HW
R1	Jan	10	DARLINGTON	0-0		21150	10				9		11	1	8		3		5	7			2			6			4
rep		14	Darlington	0-0 (aet)		18808	10	3			9	8	11	1			6		5	7			2						4
rep2		19	Darlington	2-0	W Davies, L Davies	22465	10	3			9	8	11	1			6		5	7			2						4
R2		31	FULHAM	1-0	L Davies	20000	10	3			9	7	11	1	8		6		5				2						4
R3	Feb	21	Notts County	2-0	Nicholson, Gill	39000	10	3					11	1	8		6		5	7			2		9				4
R4	Mar	7	LEICESTER CITY	2-1	W Davies, Beadles	50272	10	3				11		1	8		6		5	7			2		9				4
SF		28	Blackburn Rovers	3-1	Beadles, Nicholson, Gill	20000	10	3				7	11	1	8		6		5				2		9				4
F	Apr	25	Sheffield United	0-1		91763	10	3				7	11	1	8		6		5				2		9				4

R1 replay 2 at Anfield, Liverpool. SF at Meadow Lane, Nottingham. Final at Wembley Stadium.

Welsh Cup

		Date	Opponent	Score	Scorers	Att	Beadles GH	Blair J	Clennell J	Collins WE	Davies LS	Davies W	Evans JH	Farquharson TG	Gill JJ	Hagan A	Hardy W	Hills JJ	Keenor FC	Lawson D	Lewis JJ	McIlvenny P	Nelson J	Nicholls JBL	Nicholson JR	Page J	Sloan TM	Taylor W	Wake HW
R5	Mar	2	Swansea Town	0-4		15000	10						8	11	1					7			2		9	3	6		4

Played at 5: G Whitcombe

1925/26   16th in Division One

#	Date	Opponent	Score	Scorers	Att	Beadles GH	Blair J	Cassidy J	Collins WE	Davies LS	Davies W	Evans HP	Evans JH	Farquharson TG	Ferguson H	Gill JJ	Hagan A	Hardy W	Hills JI	Jennings J	Keenor FC	Lawson D	McLachlan GH	Nelson J	Nicholson JR	Page J	Reed E	Sloan TM	Smith SJW	Smith TP	Wake HW	Watson T
1	Aug 29	Manchester City	2-3	Gill, Beadles	42529	10	3			9	11			1		8		6			5	7		2							4	
2	31	West Ham United	1-3	Nicholson	16129		3			9	11			1		8		6			5	7		2	10						4	
3	Sep 5	EVERTON	2-1	Gill, Beadles	13914	10	3			9	11			1		8		6			5	7		2							4	
4	7	WEST HAM UNITED	0-1		19462	10				9	11			1		8		6			5	7		2							4	3
5	12	Huddersfield Town	1-1	W Davies	19033		3			9	10	11		1		8		6			5	7		2							4	
6	14	Tottenham Hotspur	2-1	W Davies, Lawson	26716		3			9	10	11				8		6	1		5	7		2							4	
7	21	TOTTENHAM HOTSPUR	0-1		20698		3			9	10	11				8		6	1		5	7		2							4	
8	23	SUNDERLAND	0-1		18316		3			9	10		11			8		6	1		5	7				2					4	
9	26	Blackburn Rovers	3-6	Nicholson 2, Beadles	18042	10	3				11			1		8					5	7			9	2	6				4	
10	Oct 3	BURY	3-2	Nicholson, L Davies, Beadles	20281	10	3			11	8			1				6			5	7		2	9						4	
11	10	Birmingham	2-3	W Davies, Keenor	24335		3			11	8			1		10		4			5	7		2	9		6					
12	17	Arsenal	0-5		38130	10					11	7		1		8					5				9	2	6				4	3
13	24	MANCHESTER UNITED	0-2		15846			10		9			11	1		8		6			5	7		2							4	3
14	31	Aston Villa	2-0	Nicholson, Smith	33161			10		11				1				4				7		2	9			6	5	8		3
15	Nov 7	LEICESTER CITY	5-2	W Davies, Ferguson, Cassidy 3	25089			10		8	7			1	9			4			5		11	2				6				3
16	14	Leeds United	0-1		19360			10		8	7			1	9			4			5		11	2				6				3
17	21	NEWCASTLE UNITED	0-0		25539			10		8	7				9			4	1		5		11	2				6				3
18	28	Bolton Wanderers	1-0	Ferguson	21520			10		8	7			1	9			4			5		11	2				6				3
19	Dec 5	NOTTS COUNTY	2-1	Ferguson 2	17856			10		8	7			1	9			4			5		11	2				6				3
20	12	Liverpool	2-0	L Davies, Ferguson	31373			10		8	7			1	9			4			5		11	2				6				3
21	19	BURNLEY	2-3	L Davies, Ferguson	17678			10		8	7			1	9			4			5		11	2				6				3
22	25	WEST BROMWICH ALB.	3-2	L Davies, Ferguson 2	13683			10		8	7			1	9			4			5		11	2				6				3
23	26	West Bromwich Albion	0-3		35504			10		8	7			1	9			4			5		11	2				6				3
24	Jan 1	Sheffield United	2-1	W Davies, L Davies	21943		3	10		8	7			1	9			4			5		11	2				6				
25	2	MANCHESTER CITY	2-2	Cassidy 2	10242			10		8	7			1	9			4			5		11	2				6				3
26	16	Everton	1-1	McLachlan	26553		3	10		8					9			4	1		5	7	11	2				6				
27	23	HUDDERSFIELD T	1-2		13049		3	10		8					9			4	1		5	7	11	2				6				
28	Feb 6	BLACKBURN ROVERS	4-1	L Davies, Cassidy, McLachlan 2	16484			10	7	8			4		9			6	1				11	2				5				3
29	13	Bury	1-4	Ferguson	16777			10	7				4		9			6	1				11	2				5		8		3
30	20	BIRMINGHAM	2-0	L Davies, Ferguson	18862			10	7	8			4		9				1		5		11	2				6				3
31	27	ARSENAL	0-0		21684		3	10		8	7				9				1	4	5		11	2				6				
32	Mar 13	ASTON VILLA	2-0	Ferguson 2	21982					8	7				9				1	4	5		11	2				6		10		3
33	20	Leicester City	2-1	W Davies 2	24095			10		8	7				9			4	1		5		11	2				6				3
34	27	LEEDS UNITED	0-0		15300			10		8	11				9			4	1		5	7		2				6				3
35	31	Sunderland	3-1	W Davies, L Davies, Ferguson	4315					8	11				9			4	1		5	7		2				6		10		3
36	Apr 3	Newcastle United	1-0	Ferguson	26205					8	11				9			6	1		5	7		2						10	4	3
37	5	SHEFFIELD UNITED	0-1		22241		3	10		8			11		9			6	1		5	7		2							4	
38	10	BOLTON WANDERERS	0-1		13787		3	10	7				11		9			4	1		5			2				6	8			
39	17	Notts County	4-2	Ferguson 3, Keenor	8712				7	8	11				9			6	1		5			2						10	4	3
40	24	LIVERPOOL	2-2	Hardy, Ferguson	14868				7	8	11				9			4	1		5			2				6		10		3
41	28	Manchester United	0-1		9116				7	8	11				9			4	1		5			2				6		10		3
42	May 1	Burnley	1-4	L Davies	16381			10	7	9	11			1				6			5			2						8	4	3
		Apps				6	16	24	6	37	36	3	7	33	26	11	1	37	9	2	25	20	19	34	18	3	6	28	2	8	15	30
		Goals				4		6		8	9				19	2		1			2	1	2		6					1		

F.A. Cup

Rd	Date	Opponent	Score	Scorers	Att	Beadles GH	Blair J	Cassidy J	Collins WE	Davies LS	Davies W	Evans HP	Evans JH	Farquharson TG	Ferguson H	Gill JJ	Hagan A	Hardy W	Hills JI	Jennings J	Keenor FC	Lawson D	McLachlan GH	Nelson J	Nicholson JR	Page J	Reed E	Sloan TM	Smith SJW	Smith TP	Wake HW	Watson T
R3	Jan 9	BURNLEY	2-2	Cassidy, L Davies	30000			10		8	7			1	9			6	1		5		11	2	4							3
rep	13	Burnley	2-0	Ferguson 2	26811		5	10		8					9				1			7	11	2	4			6				3
R4	30	NEWCASTLE UNITED	0-2		42000			10							9			6	1			7	11	2	4			5	8			3

Welsh Cup

Rd	Date	Opponent	Score	Scorers	Att	Beadles GH	Blair J	Cassidy J	Collins WE	Davies LS	Davies W	Evans HP	Evans JH	Farquharson TG	Ferguson H	Gill JJ	Hagan A	Hardy W	Hills JI	Jennings J	Keenor FC	Lawson D	McLachlan GH	Nelson J	Nicholson JR	Page J	Reed E	Sloan TM	Smith SJW	Smith TP	Wake HW	Watson T
R5	Mar 3	Methyr Town	1-2	Ferrans (og)	4000		3	10		8				1								7	11	2	6			5			4	

Played at 9: H McCracken

1926/27　14th in Division One

No.	Date		Opponent	Score	Scorers	Att	Baillie J	Blackburn GF	Castle FR	Collins WE	Curtis ER	Davies LS	Davies W	Farquharson TG	Ferguson H	Hampson T	Hardy W	Irving SJ	Jennings J	Keenor FC	Matson FR	McLachlan GH	Nelson J	Pirie TS	Richards P	Sloan TM	Smith SJW	Smith TP	Thirlaway WI	Tysoe GF	Wake HW	Watson T
1	Aug	28	Burnley	3-4	Ferguson 2, L Davies	19985		6				8	7	1	9		2			5		11						10			4	3
2		30	Leeds United	0-0		14242		6				8	7	1	9		2	4		5		11						10				3
3	Sep	4	WEST BROMWICH ALB.	1-1	L Davies	19213		6				8	7	1	9		2	4		5		11						10				3
4		6	LEEDS UNITED	3-1	TP Smith, Ferguson, W Davies	13653		6				8	7	1	9		2	4		5		11						10				3
5		11	ASTON VILLA	2-3	Ferguson 2 (1p)	20081		6				8	7	1	9		3	4		5		11	2					10				
6		18	Bolton Wanderers	0-2		18737		6				8	7	1	9		3	4		5		11	2					10				
7		20	NEWCASTLE UNITED	1-1	W Davies	14048		6				8	7	1	9		3	4		5		11	2					10				
8		25	MANCHESTER UNITED	0-2		17267	4	6				10	11	7	1	8	3							2	9	5						
9	Oct	2	Derby County	3-6	L Davies, Ferguson, Curtis	21216					10	8	7	1	9		6	4		5		11	2									3
10		9	SHEFFIELD UNITED	3-0	W Davies, Irving, Ferguson	12282					10	8	7	1	9		6	4		5		11	2									3
11		16	Huddersfield Town	0-0		17705					10	8	7	1	9		6	4		5		11	2									3
12		23	SUNDERLAND	3-0	Ferguson 2, Curtis	15870	8				10		7	1	9		6	4		5		11	2									3
13		30	Bury	3-2	McLachlan, Ferguson 2	15182		6		7	10	8		1	9			4		5		11	2									3
14	Nov	6	BIRMINGHAM	1-0	McLachlan	10598		6			10	8	7	1	9			4		5		11	2									3
15		13	Tottenham Hotspur	1-4	Curtis	15350		6			10	8	7	1	9			4		5		11	2									3
16		20	WEST HAM UNITED	1-2	W Davies	10736					10	8	7	1	9		6			5		11	2								4	3
17		29	Sheffield Wednesday	0-3		16986	7	4			10	8		1	9		6			5		11	2									3
18	Dec	4	LEICESTER CITY	0-1		13627	4	6		7	10	8		1	9					5		11	2									3
19		11	Everton	1-0	Ferguson	27181				7	10			1	9		6	4				11	2			5	8					3
20		18	BLACKBURN ROVERS	0-1		12254					10			1	9		6	4		5	7	11	2				8					3
21		25	Newcastle United	0-5		36250			8		10			1	9		6	4			7	11	2		5							3
22		27	ARSENAL	2-0	Ferguson, Curtis	25387					10	9		1	7		6	4				11	2		5				8			3
23	Jan	1	Arsenal	2-3	Curtis, L Davies	31000					10	9		1	7		6	4				11	2		5				8			3
24		15	BURNLEY	0-0		14647					10	9		1	7		6	4				11	2		5				8			3
25		31	Aston Villa	0-0		10481					10	9		1	7		6	4				11	2			5			8			3
26	Feb	5	BOLTON WANDERERS	1-0	L Davies	12721					10	9		1			6	8		4		11	2			5						3
27		12	Manchester United	1-1	Ferguson	26213					10			1	9		6	8				11	2			5			7	4		3
28		21	West Bromwich Albion	2-1	McLachlan, Shaw (og)	12820					10	9		1			6	8		4		11	2			5						3
29		26	Sheffield United	1-3	L Davies	25658					10	8		1	9		6			5		11	2						7	4		3
30	Mar	12	Sunderland	2-2	Irving 2	17194					10			1	9		6	8		4		11	2			5			7			3
31		16	DERBY COUNTY	2-0	Ferguson 2	10057					10			1	9		6	8	3	4		11	2			5			7			
32		19	BURY	2-1	Ferguson, McLachlan	17594					10			1	9		6	8	3	4		11	2			5			7			
33		21	HUDDERSFIELD T	2-0	Ferguson 2	17051					10			1	9		6	8	3	4		11	2			5			7			
34	Apr	2	TOTTENHAM HOTSPUR	1-2	Skitt (og)	13384		6			10			1	9		4	8				11	2			5			7			3
35		7	Leicester City	1-3	Ferguson	10994					10			1	9		6	8	3	4		11	2			5			7			
36		9	West Ham United	2-2	Ferguson, Wake	14777		4			10			1	9		6		3			11	2	5					7		8	
37		15	Liverpool	0-5		35247			9		10			1			6	8		4		11	2			5			7			3
38		16	SHEFFIELD WEDNESDAY	3-2	Ferguson, Hooper (og), Wake	13426		6			10			1	9					4		11	2			5			7		8	3
39		18	LIVERPOOL	2-0	Irving, Ferguson	21668		4		7	10			1	9		6	8				11	2	5								3
40		27	Birmingham	2-1	Ferguson 2	23681					10			1	9		6	8		4		11	2	5					7			3
41		30	EVERTON	1-0	Keenor	18341		4			10			1			6			9	8	11	2	5					7			3
42	May	7	Blackburn Rovers	0-1		11786					10			1			6	8		4	9	11	2	5					7			3
			Apps				4	18	2	3	26	34	15	40	39	2	40	27	5	33	4	38	38	5	3	20	2	8	12	2	9	33
			Goals								5	7	3		26			3		1		5						2			2	

One own goal

F.A. Cup

	Date		Opponent	Score	Scorers	Att	Baillie J	Blackburn GF	Castle FR	Collins WE	Curtis ER	Davies LS	Davies W	Farquharson TG	Ferguson H	Hampson T	Hardy W	Irving SJ	Jennings J	Keenor FC	Matson FR	McLachlan GH	Nelson J	Pirie TS	Richards P	Sloan TM	Smith SJW	Smith TP	Thirlaway WI	Tysoe GF	Wake HW	Watson T
R3	Jan	8	ASTON VILLA	2-1	L Davies, Curtis	30000					10	9		1	7		6	4				11	2		5				8			3
R4		29	Darlington	2-0	McLachlan, Ferguson	12986					10	9		1	7		6	4				11	2			5			8			3
R5	Feb	19	Bolton Wanderers	2-0	Ferguson (p), L Davies	49463					10	9		1	7		6	8		4		11	2			5						3
R6	Mar	5	Chelsea	0-0		70184					10	9		1	7		6	8		4		11	2			5						3
rep		9	CHELSEA	3-2	Irving, L Davies, Ferguson (p)	47853					10	9		1	7		6	8		4		11	2			5						3
SF		26	Reading	3-0	Ferguson 2, Wake	39476					10			1	9		6	8		4		11	2			5			7			3
F	Apr	23	Arsenal	1-0	Ferguson	93206				7	10			1	9		6	8		4		11	2			5						3

SF at Molineux, Final at Wembley

Welsh Cup

	Date		Opponent	Score	Scorers	Att	Baillie J	Blackburn GF	Castle FR	Collins WE	Curtis ER	Davies LS	Davies W	Farquharson TG	Ferguson H	Hampson T	Hardy W	Irving SJ	Jennings J	Keenor FC	Matson FR	McLachlan GH	Nelson J	Pirie TS	Richards P	Sloan TM	Smith SJW	Smith TP	Thirlaway WI	Tysoe GF	Wake HW	Watson T
R6	Mar	29	Ebbw Vale	0-0		10000					10			1	9		6	8		4		11	2			5			7			3
rep	Apr	4	Ebbw Vale	6-1	* see below	8000		4	9	7	10			1			6	8				11	2	5								3
R7		28	BARRY TOWN	2-0	McLachlan, L Davies	5000					10	9		1			4	8			7	11	2	5			6					3
SF	May	2	Wrexham	2-1	L Davies 2	14600		4			10	9		1			6	8			7	11	2			5						3
F		5	Rhyl	2-0	L Davies, Irving	9600		4			10	9		1			6	8			7	11	2			5						3

Scorers in R6 replay: L Davies 2, Castle 2, McLachlan, Curtis

1927/28   6th in Division One

No	Date	Opponent	Score	Scorers	Att	Baillie J	Blackburn GF	Castle FR	Curtis ER	Davies LS	Davies W	Farquharson TG	Ferguson H	Hardy W	Hillier EIG	Irving SI	Jennings J	Keenor FC	Matson FR	McLachlan GH	Miles AE	Murphy J	Nelson J	Sloan TM	Smith TP	Thirlaway WI	Wake HW	Warren FW	Watson T
1	Aug 27	BOLTON WANDERERS	2-1	McLachlan, L Davies	24107				10	8		1	9	6			4	5		11			2			7			3
2	Sep 3	Sheffield Wednesday	3-3	Ferguson, Curtis, Thirlaway	19218				10	8		1	9	6			4	5		11			2			7			3
3	5	Blackburn Rovers	0-0		14343				10	8		1	9	6			4	5		11			2			7			3
4	10	MIDDLESBROUGH	1-1	McLachlan	23033				10	8		1	9	6			4	5		11			2			7			3
5	12	BLACKBURN ROVERS	1-1	L Davies	15955				10	8		1	9	6			4	5		11			2			7			3
6	17	Birmingham	3-1	Thirlaway, Ferguson 2	23723				10	8		1	9	6			4	5		11			2			7			3
7	24	NEWCASTLE UNITED	3-1	Curtis, L Davies, Ferguson	30590				10	8		1	9	6			4	5		11			2			7			3
8	Oct 1	Huddersfield Town	2-8	Ferguson 2	12975				10	8		1	9	6			4	5		11			2			7			3
9	8	TOTTENHAM HOTSPUR	2-1	L Davies, Ferguson	21811				10	8		1	9	6			4	5		11			2			7			3
10	15	Manchester United	2-2	Thirlaway, Curtis	31090		6		10	8		1	9	3			4	5		11			2			7			
11	22	PORTSMOUTH	3-1	Thirlaway, Ferguson, McLachlan	9060		6		10	8		1	9	3				5		11			2			7		4	
12	29	Leicester City	1-4	Smith	25634							1	9	6			4		8	11			2	5	10	7			3
13	Nov 5	Liverpool	1-1	Smith	12735							1	9	6			4	5		11			2		10	7			3
14	12	West Ham United	0-2		18189				10	8		1	9	6			4	5		11			2			7			3
15	19	DERBY COUNTY	4-4	L Davies 2, W Davies, Matson	6606					10	7	1	9	6			4	5	8	11			2						3
16	26	Sheffield United	4-3	McLachlan 2, L Davies, Ferguson	22999					10	8	1	9	6			4	5		11			2			7			3
17	Dec 3	ASTON VILLA	2-1	Ferguson 2	14264	4			10	8		1	9	6				5		11			2			7			3
18	10	Sunderland	2-0	Thirlaway, L Davies	16450				10	8		1	9	6			4	5		11			2			7			3
19	17	BURY	0-1		11961				10	8		1	9	6			4			11			2	5		7			3
20	24	Burnley	1-2	Thirlaway	13159				8	10		1	9	6			4	5		11			2			7			3
21	26	Everton	1-2	Wake	56305		6		8	10		1	9					5		11			2			7	4		
22	27	EVERTON	2-0	L Davies, Wake	25387		4			10				6	1	3				11	9		2	5		7	8		
23	31	Bolton Wanderers	1-2	Miles	15745		4			10				6	1	3				11	9		2	5		7	8		
24	Jan 7	SHEFFIELD WEDNESDAY	1-1	Ferguson	9208		4			10		1	9	3				5		11			2	6		7	8		
25	21	Middlesbrough	2-1	Thirlaway, Ferguson	21728					10		1	9	6		8		5		11			2			7	4		3
26	Feb 4	Newcastle United	0-2		26439		6		8			1	9	5		3				11			2		10	7	4		
27	11	HUDDERSFIELD T	4-0	L Davies, Wadsworth (og), Thirlaway 2	21073				10	9		1		6		8	3	5		11			2			7	4		
28	22	BIRMINGHAM	2-1	Ferguson, McLachlan	10758		4		8	10		1	9	6			3	5		11			2			7			
29	25	MANCHESTER UNITED	2-0	L Davies, Ferguson	15579				8	10		1	9	6			3	5		11			2			7	4		
30	Mar 3	Portsmouth	0-3		25157				8	10		1	9	6			3	5		11			2			7	4		
31	5	Tottenham Hotspur	0-1		6250				10	9		1		6			3	5	8	11			2			7	4		
32	10	LEICESTER CITY	3-0	Ferguson 2, McLachlan	13178					10		1	9	6			3	5		11			2		8	7	4		
33	17	Liverpool	2-1	L Davies, Thirlaway	34532			9		10		1		6			3	5		11			2		8	7	4		
34	24	WEST HAM UNITED	1-5	Ferguson	14529		4			10		1	9	6			3	5		11			2		8	7			
35	31	Derby County	1-7	Thirlaway	15565		4			10		1	9	6				5		11			2		8	7			3
36	Apr 6	Arsenal	0-3		36828		4							6	1	3				11	9	10	2	5	8	7			
37	7	SHEFFIELD UNITED	2-2	McLachlan 2	11283								9	6	1	3	4			11			2	5	10	7	8		
38	9	ARSENAL	2-2	Smith, Wake	17699								9	6	1	3	4		7	11			2	5	10		8		
39	14	Aston Villa	1-3	McLachlan	22428					10		1		6		3	4			9			2	5		7	8	11	
40	21	SUNDERLAND	3-1	Warren, L Davies, McLachlan	10268					10		1		6		3	4			9			2	5		7	8	11	
41	28	Bury	0-3		13375					10		1		6		3	4			9			2	5	8	7		11	
42	May 5	BURNLEY	3-2	L Davies 2, Warren	8663					10		1		6		3	4			9			2	5	8	7		11	
	Apps					1	11	1	20	37	5	37	32	41	5	20	19	36	4	42	3	1	41	12	12	40	17	4	21
	Goals								3	15	1		18						1	11	1				3	11	3	2	

One own goal

Charity Shield

Date	Opponent	Score	Scorers	Att	Blackburn GF	Curtis ER	Davies LS	Farquharson TG	Ferguson H	Hardy W	Jennings J	Keenor FC	McLachlan GH	Nelson J	Thirlaway WI
Oct 12	Corinthians	2-1	Ferguson, L Davies	10500	6	10	8	1	9	3	4	5	11	2	7

Played at Stamford Bridge

F.A. Cup

Rd	Date	Opponent	Score	Scorers	Att	Blackburn GF	Davies LS	Farquharson TG	Ferguson H	Hardy W	Irving SI	Jennings J	Keenor FC	McLachlan GH	Nelson J	Sloan TM	Thirlaway WI	Wake HW	Watson T
R3	Jan 14	SOUTHAMPTON	2-1	Ferguson, L Davies	23000	4	10	1	9	3			5	11	2	6	7	8	
R4	28	LIVERPOOL	2-1	McLachlan, Nelson	20000		10	1	9	6	8		5	11	2		7	4	3
R5	Feb 18	Nottingham Forest	1-2	Ferguson	30500		10	1	9	6	8	3	5	11	2		7	4	

Welsh Cup

Rd	Date	Opponent	Score	Scorers	Att	Blackburn GF	Castle FR	Curtis ER	Davies LS	Farquharson TG	Ferguson H	Hardy W	Irving SI	Jennings J	Keenor FC	McLachlan GH	Nelson J	Sloan TM	Smith TP	Thirlaway WI	Wake HW	Warren FW	Watson T
R5	Mar 15	Oswestry	7-1	L Davies 3, Castle 2, Smith 2	4000		9	10	11	1		6			5		2		8	7	4		3
R6	Apr 2	SWANSEA TOWN	1-0	Smith	10000	6			10	1	9		3	4		11	2	5	8	7			
SF	18	Rhyl	2-2	Ferguson 2	3000				10	1	9	6	3	4		11	2	5	8	7			
rep	25	Rhyl	2-0	Wake, L Davies	5000				10	1	9	6	3	4		11	2	5		7	8		
F	May 2	Bangor City	2-0	Ferguson 2	11000				10	1	9	6	3	4		11	2	5	8	7			

#	Date	Opponent	Res	Scorers	Att	Blackburn GF	Davies LS	Davies SC	Farquharson TG	Ferguson H	Hampson T	Hardy W	Harris F	Helsby T	Jennings J	John EJ	Keenor FC	Matson FR	McLachlan GH	Miles AE	Moss F	Munro JA	Nelson J	Robbins WW	Roberts WJ	Shaw W	Sloan TM	Smith TP	Thirlaway WJ	Wake HW	Warren FW	Watson T
1	Aug 25	Newcastle United	1-1	Ferguson (p)	36964			10	1	9		6			3		4		11			2					5		7	8		
2	Sep 1	BURNLEY	7-0	Ferguson 5, L Davies 2	20174		10	8	1	9		6			3		4		11			2					5		7			
3	Sep 8	Derby County	0-2		20462		10	8	1	9		6			3		4		11			2					5		7			
4	Sep 10	WEST HAM UNITED	3-2	Ferguson 2, Thirlaway	17189		10	8	1	9		6			3		4		11			2					5		7			
5	Sep 15	Sheffield United	1-3	S Davies	24207		10	8	1	9		6			3		4		11			2					5		7			
6	Sep 17	West Ham United	1-1	Ferguson	13750		10	8	1	9		6			3		4		11			2					5		7			
7	Sep 22	BURY	4-0	L Davies 2, Ferguson, Thirlaway	18739		10	8	1	9		6			3		4		11			2					5		7			
8	Sep 29	Aston Villa	0-1		30190		10		1	9		6	8		3		4		11			2					5		7			
9	Oct 6	LEICESTER CITY	1-2	Harris	19477		10		1			6	8		3		4		11			2		9			5		7			
10	Oct 13	Manchester United	1-1	McLachlan	26010	6	10		1				8		3		4		11			2		9			5		7			
11	Oct 20	SUNDERLAND	0-1		15361	6	10	8	1	9					3		4		11			2					5		7			
12	Oct 27	Sheffield Wednesday	0-1		20116	6		9	1						3		4		10			2					5	8	7			11
13	Nov 3	ARSENAL	1-1	Sloan	18757	6	10		1	9					3		4		11			2					5	8	7			
14	Nov 10	Everton	0-1		25994	6	10		1	9					3		4		11			2					5	8	7			
15	Nov 17	HUDDERSFIELD T	0-0		13845	6	10		1	9					3		4	5	11			2						8	7			
16	Nov 24	Manchester City	1-1	TP Smith	18778		10		1	9		6			3		4	5	11			2					5	8	7			
17	Dec 1	BIRMINGHAM	1-4	Thirlaway	13691	4	9	10	1			6			3				11			2					5	8	7			
18	Dec 8	Portsmouth	1-0	Miles	19649		10		1						3		4		11	9	6	2					5	8	7			
19	Dec 15	BOLTON WANDERERS	1-1	Robbins	11286		10		1						3		4		11		6	2		9			5	8	7			
20	Dec 22	Blackburn Rovers	0-2		11040	6	9		1						3		4		11			2			10		5	8	7			
21	Dec 25	Leeds United	0-3		28188	6	9		1						3		4		11			2			10		5	8	7			
22	Dec 26	LEEDS UNITED	2-1	Thirlaway, Wake	20439	6	9		1						3		4		11			2			10		5		7	8		
23	Dec 29	NEWCASTLE UNITED	2-0	Thirlaway, Wake	12254	6	9		1						3		4		11			2	5		10				7	8		
24	Jan 1	Bolton Wanderers	0-1		33651	6	9		1						3		4		11			2	5		10				7	8		
25	Jan 5	Burnley	0-3		10966	6	9		1						3		4		11			2	5		10				7	8		
26	Jan 19	DERBY COUNTY	3-0	Ferguson 2, McLachlan	14647			10	1	9							4		11		6	2	5		3			8	7			
27	Jan 26	SHEFFIELD UNITED	0-0		17334			10	1	9							4		11		6	2	5		3			8	7			
28	Feb 2	Bury	1-4	Ferguson	9954			10	1	9							4		11			2	5		3			8	7			
29	Feb 9	ASTON VILLA	0-2		15978		8	10	1	9							4		11		6	2			3		5		7			
30	Feb 21	Leicester City	0-2		12938			10	1	9							4		11		6	2	5		3			8	7			
31	Feb 23	MANCHESTER UNITED	2-2	Ferguson, S Davies	13070	6		10	1	9							4		11			2	5		3			8	7			
32	Mar 2	Sunderland	0-1		21546	6	10		1		8								11		9	2	5		3				7		4	
33	Mar 9	SHEFFIELD WEDNESDAY	3-1	Thirlaway, L Davies, Warren	18636	6	10		1		8								11		9	2	5		3				7		4	
34	Mar 16	Arsenal	1-2	L Davies	28393	6	10		1		8								11		9	2	5		3				7		4	
35	Mar 23	EVERTON	0-2		14681	6	10		1		8						4		11		9	2	5		3				7			
36	Mar 29	Liverpool	0-2		30927	6	10		1		8						4		11		9	2	5		3				7			
37	Mar 30	Huddersfield Town	1-1	L Davies	13332	6	9		1		8						4	7	10			2	5		3						11	
38	Apr 1	LIVERPOOL	1-2	Wake	16849	6	9		1					5			4	7	10			2			3					8	11	
39	Apr 6	MANCHESTER CITY	1-3	Munro	11392	6			1		8			5					10		9	2			3				7		4	11
40	Apr 13	Birmingham	0-0		12997	6	10	8	1					5			4				9	2			3				7		11	
41	Apr 20	PORTSMOUTH	1-1	Munro	10834	6	10	8						5			4				9	2			3				7		11	
42	May 4	BLACKBURN ROVERS	1-1	Harris	5738	6		10	1				8	5			4		9			2			3				7		11	

Played in one game: EJG Hillier (41, at 1), J McGrath (28, 6), M Robinson (41, 11)

| | | | | | Apps | 24 | 27 | 14 | 35 | 20 | 6 | 22 | 13 | 13 | 42 | 2 | 36 | 6 | 33 | 2 | 9 | 11 | 11 | 7 | 21 | 2 | 15 | 14 | 37 | 17 | 19 | 1 |
| | | | | | Goals | | 8 | 2 | | 14 | | | 2 | | | | 2 | 1 | | 2 | | 1 | | 2 | | | 1 | 1 | 5 | 3 | 1 | |

F.A. Cup

	Date	Opponent	Res	Scorers	Att	Blackburn GF	Davies LS	Davies SC	Farquharson TG	Ferguson H	Hampson T	Hardy W	Harris F	Helsby T	Jennings J	John EJ	Keenor FC	Matson FR	McLachlan GH	Miles AE	Moss F	Munro JA	Nelson J	Robbins WW	Roberts WJ	Shaw W	Sloan TM	Smith TP	Thirlaway WJ	Wake HW	Warren FW	Watson T
R3	Jan 12	Aston Villa	1-6	Hardy	51242		10		1			6			3		4		11			2		9			5		7	8		

Welsh Cup

	Date	Opponent	Res	Scorers	Att	Blackburn GF	Davies LS	Davies SC	Farquharson TG	Ferguson H	Hampson T	Hardy W	Harris F	Helsby T	Jennings J	John EJ	Keenor FC	Matson FR	McLachlan GH	Miles AE	Moss F	Munro JA	Nelson J	Robbins WW	Roberts WJ	Shaw W	Sloan TM	Smith TP	Thirlaway WJ	Wake HW	Warren FW	Watson T
R5	Feb 27	LOVELL'S ATHLETIC	3-1	Ferguson, Harris, L Davies	5000		10		1	9		6	8				4					2	5		3				7			11
R6	Mar 25	Newport County	1-0	Munro	4000	6	10	8	1										11		9	2	5		3				7		4	
SF	Apr 25	Rhyl	2-1	Blackburn, L Davies	7000	6	10		1	9								8	11			2	5		3				7		4	
F	May 1	Connah's Quay Nomads	0-3		10000	6	10		1	9								8	11			2	5		3				7		4	

1929/30   8th in Division Two

#	Date	Opponent	Res	Scorers	Att	Blackburn GF	Davies LS	Farquharson TG	Hardy W	Harris F	Helsby T	Hillier E|G	Jennings J	John EJ	Jones LJ	Keenor FC	Lievesley W	Matson FR	McGrath J	McClennett JJ	McLachlan GH	Miles AE	Munro JA	Nelson J	Robbins WW	Roberts WJ	Robinson M	Thirlaway WJ	Valentine AF	Wake HW	Warren FW	Williams RS
1	Aug 31	Charlton Athletic	1-4	Robbins	24173			1	6				3			4	8	7						2	10					9	11	
2	Sep 2	PRESTON NORTH END	2-0	Robbins 2	13510	6		1					2			5	8	7							10	3				9	4	11
3	7	HULL CITY	0-1		12664	6		1					2			5	8	7							10	3				9	4	11
4	9	Preston North End	3-2	Matson, Warren, Harris	5963		9	1	6	8			2			5		7							10	3					4	11
5	14	Stoke City	1-1	Davies	19065		9	1	6	8			2			5		7							10	3					4	11
6	16	NOTTS COUNTY	3-1	Harris, Matson, Warren	11533	6	9	1		8			2			5		7								3		10			4	11
7	21	WOLVERHAMPTON W.	0-0		13314		9	1	6	8			2			5		7								3		10			4	11
8	25	Notts County	1-2	Warren	7778	6	9	1		8			2			5		7								3		10			4	11
9	28	Bradford City	1-0	Warren	18886	10	9	1	6	8			2			5		7								3					4	11
10	Oct 5	SWANSEA TOWN	0-0		29093	6	9	1		8			2			5		7							10	3					4	11
11	12	Blackpool	0-3		15900	6	9	1		8			2			5		7							10	3					4	11
12	19	BARNSLEY	1-0	Harris	12058		9	1	6	8			2			5		7							10	3					4	11
13	26	Bradford Park Avenue	0-2		18455	6		1		8			2	5				7			11	9			10	3				4		
14	Nov 2	WEST BROMWICH ALB.	3-2	Davies, Miles, Thirlaway	11916	6	10	1		8			2			5					11	9				3		7		4		
15	9	Tottenham Hotspur	2-1	Miles, Robinson	23071	6	8	1					2			5					11	9				3	10	7		4		
16	16	SOUTHAMPTON	5-2	Roberts, Davies, Thirlaway 3	10969	6	8	1					2			5					11	9				3	10	7		4		
17	23	Millwall	0-2		14208	6				8		1	2			5					11	9				3	10	7		4		
18	30	OLDHAM ATHLETIC	5-0	McLachlan, Miles 3, Thirlaway	12112	6	8					1	2			5					11	9				3	10	7		4		
19	Dec 7	Nottingham Forest	1-3	McLachlan	4385	6	8					1	2			5					11	9				3	10	7		4		
20	14	CHELSEA	1-0	Davies	10536	6	8	1					2			5					11	9				3	10	7		4		
21	21	Bury	2-4	Thirlaway, Warren	9249	6	8	1					2			5						9			10	3		7		4		11
22	25	Bristol City	0-2		17140	6	8	1					2			5						9				3	10	7		4		
23	28	BRISTOL CITY	1-1	Wake	25244	11	8	1	6				3			5								2			10	7		9		
24	28	CHARLTON ATHLETIC	1-0	Miles	5793	6	8	1	4				2			5					11	9			10	3		7				
25	Jan 4	Hull City	2-2	Davies, Munro	11695	6	8	1					2			5					11		9			3	10	7		4		
26	18	STOKE CITY	1-2	Robinson	13888	6	8	1					3			5					11		9	2			10	7		4		
27	Feb 1	BRADFORD CITY	0-1		8287	6	8	1								5					11			2	10	3		7		4		9
28	8	Swansea Town	0-1		22121	6	8	1							10	5								2		3	11	7		4		9
29	15	BLACKPOOL	4-2	Williams, Blackburn, Davies, Harris	12730	6	7	1		8					10	5								2		3	11			4		9
30	22	Barnsley	2-2	Williams 2	7345	6	7	1		8					10	5								2		3	11			4		9
31	Mar 1	BRADFORD PARK AVE.	2-0	Williams, Jones	11442		7	1		8	6				10	5								2	11	3				4		9
32	8	West Bromwich Albion	2-0	Robbins, Harris	15310		7	1		8	6				10	5								2	11	3				4		9
33	15	TOTTENHAM HOTSPUR	1-0	Jones	15404	6	7	1		8					10	5								2	11	3				4		9
34	22	Southampton	1-1	Williams	13725	6	7	1		8					10	5								2	11	3				4		9
35	29	MILLWALL	3-1	Williams 2, Jones	12219	6	8	1							10	5								2	11	3		7		4		9
36	Apr 5	Oldham Athletic	1-4	Robbins	18596	6	8	1							10	5								2	11	3		7				9
37	12	NOTTM. FOREST	1-1	Davies	9328	6	8	1			4				10	5								2	11	3		7				9
38	14	Wolverhampton Wan.	0-4		5210	6	7	1		8					10	5								2	11	3				4		9
39	18	READING	2-1	Williams, Davies	12656	6	7	1		8					10	5								2	11	3				4		9
40	19	Chelsea	0-1		23100	6	7	1		8					10	5								2		3		11		4		9
41	21	Reading	0-2		18112	6	7	1		8					10	5					11			2		3				4		9
42	26	BURY	5-1	Williams 3, Bird, Davies	7136	6	7	1		8	4				10	5								2		3						9
				Apps		35	37	39	8	23	4	3	26	6	15	36	3	13	5	1	8	11	3	18	21	40	15	19	3	38	14	16
				Goals		1	9			5					3			2			2	6	1		5	1	2	6		1	5	11

Played in one game: DWC Bird (42, at 11, one goal), P Moore (game 1, at 5)

F.A. Cup

Rd	Date	Opponent	Res	Scorers	Att	Blackburn GF	Davies LS	Farquharson TG	Keenor FC	McLachlan GH	Miles AE	Nelson J	Roberts WJ	Robinson M	Thirlaway WJ	Wake HW
R3	Jan 11	Liverpool	2-1	Davies 2	50141	6	8	1	5	11	9	2	3	10	7	4
R4	25	Sunderland	1-2	Davies	49424	6	8	1	5	11	9	2	3	10	7	4

Welsh Cup

Rd	Date	Opponent	Res	Scorers	Att	Blackburn GF	Davies LS	Farquharson TG	Harris F	Helsby T	Jones LJ	Keenor FC	Lievesley W	McLachlan GH	Miles AE	Nelson J	Robbins WW	Roberts WJ	Wake HW
R5	Mar 17	Llanelly	4-1	Davies 2, Miles, Jones	5000	6	7	1	8		10	5			9	2	11	3	4
R6	Apr 2	SWANSEA TOWN	4-0	Thirlaway, Jones, Davies, Nelson	8000	6	8	1			10	5			9	2	11	3	4
SF	23	Wrexham	2-0	Miles, Jones	4000	6	7	1	8	4	10	5		11	9	2		3	
F	May 3	Rhyl	0-0		5000	6	11	1		4	10	5	7		9	2		3	8

Final replay played in season 1930/31

#	Mo	Day	Opponents	Score	Scorers	Att	Bird DWC	Blackburn GF	Davies LS	Emmerson GAH	Farquharson TG	Galbraith JMcD	Hardy W	Harris F	Helsby T	Jenkins EJ	John EJ	Jones LJ	Keenor FC	McCambridge J	McGrath J	Mclennett JJ	Merry W	Miles I	Robbins WW	Roberts WJ	Robinson M	Smith J	Valentine AF	Wake HW	Ware T	Weale RH	Williams RS
1	Aug	30	Swansea Town	2-3	Williams 2	20363		6		7	1			8				10	5			2			11	3					4		9
2	Sep	3	Bury	0-3		9488		6		7	1			8	4			10	5			2			11	3							9
3		6	WEST BROMWICH ALB.	3-6	Jones, Bird, Helsby	10987	11	6		7	1		2	8	4			10	5							3							9
4		8	EVERTON	1-2	Bird	11463	11	6		7	1				4		3	8	5						10	2							9
5		13	Port Vale	0-2		9693	11	6	7		1			8	4				5						10	3			2				9
6		17	Everton	1-1	Williams	17464	11	6		7	1			8		5									10	3			2		4		9
7		20	BRADFORD CITY	1-1	Bird	5839	11	3		7	1			8		5		6							10				2		4		9
8		22	PLYMOUTH ARGYLE	4-1	Robbins 2, Williams, Davies	6615	11	6	8	7	1				4		3		5						10				2				9
9		27	Charlton Athletic	1-4	Williams	12279	11		8	7	1				4		3		5		6				10				2				9
10	Oct	4	BARNSLEY	2-0	Hesby, Jones	9884		6	9	7	1				4		3	8	5						11				2				10
11		11	Bristol City	0-1		19447	11	6		7	1				4			8	5						10	3			2				9
12		18	Oldham Athletic	2-4	Harris, Emmerson	11663		6		7	1			9	8			10	4						11	3			2				
13		25	NOTTM. FOREST	1-1	Jones	8955	11	6		8	1				5			10						7		3			2		9	4	
14	Nov	1	Southampton	1-0	Keenor	12182	11	6		7	1			8				10	5							3			2		9	4	
15		8	READING	5-0	Robbins 2, Jones, Valentine 2	10902		6		7	1			8				11	5						10	3			2		9	4	
16		15	Stoke City	0-1		8666		6		7	1			8				11	5						10	3			2		9	4	
17		22	BRADFORD PARK AVE.	0-3		5475	11	6		7	1			8	5			10								3			2		9	4	
18		29	Wolverhampton Wan.	1-4	Valentine	6995		6		7	1		3	8				11	5						10				2		9	4	
19	Dec	6	MILLWALL	4-4	Emerson, Robbins 3	6400		6		7			3	4				10	5						11				2		9	8	
20		13	Preston North End	0-7		13457		6		8	1			4					5					7	11			10	2		9	3	
21		20	BURNLEY	4-0	Robbins 2, Jones, Emmerson	7485		6		7	1			4				10	5						11				2		8	3	9
22		26	Plymouth Argyle	1-5	Williams	31106		6		7	1			4				10	5						11				2		8	3	9
23		27	SWANSEA TOWN	1-0	Jones	24232		6		7	1			4				10	5						11				2		8	3	9
24	Jan	3	West Bromwich Albion	2-3	McCambridge 2	13792				7	1			4				10	5	9	6				11				2		8	3	
25		17	PORT VALE	2-1	Robbins 2	8028				7	1			4				8	5	10	6	2			9							3	11
26		31	CHARLTON ATHLETIC	0-2		4470		6		7	1			5				8	4	10					9				2			3	11
27	Feb	4	Bradford City	1-2	McCambridge	4799				7	1				4	5				9	6				11				2		8	3	
28		7	Barnsley	0-4		5399				7	1				4			10	5	9	6				11				2			3	
29		14	BRISTOL CITY	0-1		11780			10	7	1	5			4					6	9				11				2			3	
30		21	OLDHAM ATHLETIC	0-0		8911		6	9	7	1	5			4					10						2						3	11
31		28	Nottingham Forest	1-3	Davies	3565			9	7	1	5	6	4						10									2			3	11
32	Mar	7	SOUTHAMPTON	0-1		5555		6	11	7	1	5	3	9	4			10											2				
33		14	Reading	0-3		9555	11		8	7	1		3	4					5	9	6							10	2				
34		21	STOKE CITY	3-2	McCambridge 3	5372		6		7	1	5	2	4				10		9	11		8						3				
35		28	Bradford Park Avenue	0-3		6557				7	1	5	2	4			6	10		9	11		8						3				
36	Apr	3	Tottenham Hotspur	2-2	McCambridge 2	41547				7	1	5	2	4			6	10		9			8						3		11		
37		4	WOLVERHAMPTON W.	0-3		6659				7	1	5	2	4			6	10		9	11		8						3				
38		6	TOTTENHAM HOTSPUR	0-0		6666		6	9	7	1		3	4				10	5				8		11				2				
39		11	Millwall	0-0		14328				7	1	5	3	4			6	10		9	11		8						2				
40		18	PRESTON NORTH END	0-0		4082				7	1	5	3	4			6	10		9	11								2				
41		25	Burnley	0-1		4125				7		5	3	4			6	10		9	11								2				
42	May	2	BURY	1-3	Jones	3841						5		4			6	10		11									2				

Played in one game: TH Wilson (12, at 5), RG Blakemore (42, 3), AC Mayo (42, 9)
Played at 1 in three games, 19, 41 and 42: SJVL Evans
Played at 8 in 6 games, 28-30 and 40-42: AE Keating

							Bird DWC	Blackburn GF	Davies LS	Emmerson GAH	Farquharson TG	Galbraith JMcD	Hardy W	Harris F	Helsby T	Jenkins EJ	John EJ	Jones LJ	Keenor FC	McCambridge J	McGrath J	Mclennett JJ	Merry W	Miles I	Robbins WW	Roberts WJ	Robinson M	Smith J	Valentine AF	Wake HW	Ware T	Weale RH	Williams RS
Apps							12	27	10	40	39	12	14	19	29	8	6	32	27	16	14	3	8	3	25	17	2	33	13	10	12	5	14
Goals							3		2	3				1	2			7	1	8					11				3				6

F.A. Cup

	Mo	Day	Opponents	Score	Scorers	Att	Emmerson GAH	Farquharson TG	Harris F	Jones LJ	Keenor FC	McCambridge J	McGrath J	Robbins WW	Valentine AF	Ware T	Weale RH	Williams RS
R3	Jan	10	Brentford	2-2	Jones, Valentine	16500	7	1	4	10	5	6		11	2	8	3	9
rep		14	BRENTFORD	1-2	Robbins	25000	7	1	4	10	5	6	2	11		8	3	9

Welsh Cup (1929/30 Final replay)

	Mo	Day	Opponents	Score	Scorers	Att	Blackburn GF	Davies LS	Emmerson GAH	Farquharson TG	Hardy W	Helsby T	Jones LJ	Keenor FC	Robbins WW	Valentine AF	Ware T
rep	Oct	8	Rhyl	4-2	Davies 3, Jones	7000	6	9	7	1	3	4	10	5	11	2	8

Welsh Cup

	Mo	Day	Opponents	Score	Scorers	Att	Blackburn GF	Davies LS	Emmerson GAH	Farquharson TG	Galbraith JMcD	Hardy W	Harris F	John EJ	Jones LJ	McCambridge J	Merry W	Robinson M	Valentine AF	Williams RS
R5	Mar	4	BARRY TOWN	7-3	*see below	3000	6	9	7	1	5	3	4				8	10	2	11
R6		25	Chester	1-0	McCambridge	12000	6		7	1	5	2	4		10	9	8		3	
SF	Apr	13	Shrewsbury Town	0-1		4000			7	1	5	3	4	6	10	9	8		2	

Scorers in R5: Robinson 2, Davies 2, Merry 2, Emmerson

The column headings (player names) are, left to right:

Emmerson GAH · Evans AH · Evans SJVL · Farquharson TG · Galbraith JMcD · Hardy W · Harris F · Holt S · Jenkins EJJ · John EJ · Jones LJ · Keating AE · McCambridge J · McGrath J · McJennett JJ · McNally O · Morris EL · O'Neill H · Robbins WW · Roberts WJ · Ronan P · Smith J

#	Date		Opponent	Score	Scorers	Att	Emm	EvAH	EvSJ	Farq	Galb	Hdy	Har	Holt	Jen	Jhn	Jns	Kea	McC	McG	McJ	McN	Mor	ON	Rbb	Rbt	Rnn	Smi
1	Aug	29	Northampton Town	0-1		13448	7			1			4	5					10				8	9	11	3	6	2
2		31	BRIGHTON & HOVE ALB	1-1	O'Neill	10435	7			1	5		4						10				8	9	11	3	6	2
3	Sep	5	READING	5-1	Jones, Robbins 3, McCambridge	9562	7			1	5	6	4				10		9				8		11	3		2
4		7	Coventry City	1-2	McCambridge	11648	7		1		5	6	4						9				8	10	11	3		2
5		12	Southend United	1-1	French (og)	7494	7			1	5	6	4						10				9	11		3		2
6		14	COVENTRY CITY	6-1	Keating 2, Robbins 2, Jones, McCambridge	7105	7			1	5	6	4				10	8	9						11	3		2
7		19	FULHAM	0-3		13233	7			1	5	6	4				10	8	9						11	3		2
8		26	Thames	2-1	McCambridge, Keating	3538	7			1	5		4					8	10	6		9			11	3		2
9	Oct	3	BRENTFORD	3-2	Emmerson, Robbins, Keating	9521	7			1	5		4				10	8	9	6					11	3		2
10		10	Exeter City	1-3	Emmerson	8160	7	4	1		5		8						9	6					11	3		2
11		17	MANSFIELD TOWN	2-0	Emmerson, Robbins	7688	7		1		5		4				10	8		6				9	11	3		2
12		24	Watford	0-3		11526	7		1		5	2	4				10	8		6				9	11	3		
13		31	CRYSTAL PALACE	1-3	Emmerson	6757	7			1	5	2	4		6		10	8	9	11						3		
14	Nov	7	Bournemouth	0-3		6562	7			1	5	6	4					10		11					9	3		2
15		14	QUEEN'S PARK RANGERS	0-4		3491	7	8		1			4	5					10		2			9	11	3	6	
16		21	Bristol Rovers	2-2	O'Neill, Ronan (p)	9047	7	8		1	5		4						10					9	11	3	6	2
17	Dec	5	Clapton Orient	1-1	Keating	6524	7	8		1	5		4				11	10						9		3	6	2
18		19	Norwich City	0-2		7904	7			1	5		4					8	10					9	11	3	6	2
19		25	Luton Town	1-2	Keating	11609	7			1	5		4				10	8	9						11	3	6	2
20		26	LUTON TOWN	4-1	Robbins 2, Keating, McCambridge	13515	7			1	5		4				10	8	9						11	3	6	2
21	Jan	2	NORTHAMPTON T	5-0	Robbins, Emmerson, McCambridge 2, Harris	3917	7			1	5		4				10	8	9				2		11	3	6	
22		13	TORQUAY UNITED	5-2	Emmerson 2, McCambridge, Keating, Robbins	3890	7			1	5		4				10	8	9						11	3	6	2
23		16	Reading	1-5	McCambridge	7065	7			1	5				4		10	8	9				2		11	3	6	
24		23	SOUTHEND UNITED	2-3	French (og), Robbins	6831	7			1			4	5			10	8	9						11	3	6	2
25		30	Fulham	0-4		14690	7	8		1	5		4				10	9							11	3	6	2
26	Feb	6	THAMES	9-2	* see below	6698	7			1	5		4				9	8	10				2		11	3	6	
27		13	Brentford	3-2	McCambridge, Keating, Robbins	16239	7			1	5		4				9	8	10				2		11	3	6	
28		20	EXETER CITY	5-2	* see below	8817	7			1	5		4				9	8	10				2		11	3	6	
29		27	Mansfield Town	2-1	McCambridge 2	8316	7			1	5		4				9	8	10				2		11	3	6	
30	Mar	5	WATFORD	2-1	Robbins, Jones	10019	7			1	5		4				9	8	10				2		11	3	6	
31		12	Crystal Palace	0-5		13206	7			1	5		4				9	8	10				2		11	3	6	
32		19	BOURNEMOUTH	0-0		6863	7			1	5		4				9	8	10				2		11	3	6	
33		25	Gillingham	1-1	Keating	8015	7			1	5		4				9	8	10						11	3	6	2
34		26	Queen's Park Rangers	3-2	McCambridge 3	8324	7			1	5		4				9	8	10						11	3	6	2
35		28	GILLINGHAM	1-0	McCambridge	10455	7			1	5	4					9	8	10				2		11	3	6	
36	Apr	2	BRISTOL ROVERS	3-1	McCambridge, Keating 2	6773	7			1	5		4				9	8	10	6			2		11	3		
37		9	Torquay United	2-2	McCambridge 2	3437	7			1	5		4		6		11	8	10							3	10	2
38		13	SWINDON TOWN	3-0	Keating 2, Emmerson	4018	7			1	5		4		6		10	8	9	11						3		2
39		16	CLAPTON ORIENT	5-0	McCambridge 3, Keating 2	5290	7			1	5		4		6		10	8	9	11						3		2
40		23	Swindon Town	4-1	Keating 2, McCambridge 2	3728	7			1	5		4				10	8	9	11						3	6	2
41		30	NORWICH CITY	0-2		6487	7			1	5		4				10	8	9	11						3	6	2
42	May	7	Brighton & Hove Albion	0-0		5447	7	8		1	5		4					10		9	11					3	6	2
					Apps		42	7	4	38	39	9	40	2	5	1	35	32	38	13	1	6	11	9	33	42	27	28
					Goals		10						1				5	19	26					2	21		1	

Scorers in game 26: Jones, McCambridge, Emmerson, Keating, Robbins 5
Scorers in game 28: Robbins 2, Jones, Emmerson, McCambridge

Two own goals

F.A. Cup

R	Date		Opponent	Score	Scorers	Att	Emm	Far	Galb	Har	Jns	Kea	McC	Rbb	Rbt	Rnn	Smi	ON
R1	Nov	28	ENFIELD	8-0	* see below	6321	7	1	5	4	10	8		11	3	6	2	9
R2	Dec	12	CLAPTON ORIENT	4-0	* see below	10500	7	1	5	4	10	8	9	11	3	6	2	
R3	Jan	9	Bradford Park Avenue	0-2		18343	7	1	5	4	10	8	9	11	3	6	2	

Scorers in R1: Keating 3, O'Neill 2, Emmerson 2, Harris
Scorers in R2: McCambridge, Keating, Emmerson, Broadbent (og)

Welsh Cup

R	Date		Opponent	Score	Scorers	Att	Emm	Far	Galb	Hdy	Har	Jns	Kea	McC	Rbb	Rbt	Rnn
R5	Feb	8	Llanelly	5-3	Robbins 3, McCambridge	5000	7	1	5	3	4	10	8	9	11	2	6
R6	Mar	2	Chester	1-2	Emmerson	5000	7	1	5	2	4	10	8	9	11	3	6

#	Date	Opponent	Score	Scorers	Att	Adams RILM	Collins J	Cribb SR	Emmerson GAH	Evans AH	Evans R	Evans SIVL	Farquharson TG	Galbraith IMcD	Harris F	Henderson WJ	Hill FA	Horton R	Jenkins EIJ	Jones LI	Keating AE	Maidment T	McCambridge J	Morris EL	Paget WST	Pollard R	Richards LG	Roberts WJ	Ronan P	Russell GH	Tennant J
1	Aug 27	Reading	2-4	Cribb, McCambridge	13867			11	7	4			1	5			8			10			9			2			6	3	
2	29	BOURNEMOUTH	3-0	Keating, Cribb, Jones	8351			11	7	6			1	5	4					10	8		9			2				3	
3	Sep 3	NORWICH CITY	4-2	Emmerson, McCambridge 2, Cribb	9767			11	7	6			1	5	4		8			10			9			2				3	
4	7	Bournemouth	2-3	McCambridge 2	6264			11	7	6			1	5	4		8			10			9			2				3	
5	10	Brighton & Hove Albion	0-1		7790			11	7	8			1	5	4		9				6		10			2				3	
6	17	BRISTOL ROVERS	4-3	Keating, McCambridge 2, Cribb	9104			11	7	6			1	5	4		10				8		9			2				3	
7	24	Aldershot Town	0-1		7172			11	7	6			1	5	4		10				8		9			2				3	
8	Oct 1	QUEEN'S PARK RANGERS	2-5	Jones 2	7842			11	7	6			1	5	4					10	8		9			2				3	
9	8	Southend United	2-2	Keating, McCambridge	3590			11	7	6			1	5	4		10		3		8		9	2							
10	15	CRYSTAL PALACE	1-1	McCambridge	7144			11	7				1	5	4		10		2	6	8		9							3	
11	22	NEWPORT COUNTY	1-3	McCambridge	10163			11	7				1	5	4		10		2	6	8		9							3	
12	29	Luton Town	1-8	McCambridge	6002			11	7	6			1	5	4		8			10			9	2			3				
13	Nov 5	EXETER CITY	1-3	Emmerson	4881				7	6		1		5	4		10		3	11			9	2							
14	12	Torquay United	1-4	Cribb	3911			11	7	6			1	5	4		8		3	10			9	2							
15	19	BRENTFORD	2-1	Jones, Cribb	5274			11	7				1	5	4		8		3	10			9	2					6		
16	Dec 3	BRISTOL CITY	1-1	Jones	6115		11		7	6			1	5	4		8		3	10			9			2					
17	17	CLAPTON ORIENT	6-1	*see below	4433			11	7	6			1	5	4		8		3	10			9			2					
18	24	Swindon Town	2-6	McCambridge 2	6145			11	7	6			1	5	4		8		3	10			9			2					
19	26	GILLINGHAM	1-0	Jones	11178		11		7				1	5	4		8		6	10			9			2				3	
20	27	Gillingham	1-1	Jones	10449		11						1	5	4		8		6	10			9			2				3	7
21	31	READING	0-1		6773		11		7				1	5	4		8		6	10			9			2				3	
22	Jan 7	Norwich City	1-3	Jones (p)	9486		11						1	5	4		8		6	10			9			2				3	7
23	14	Coventry City	0-5		9752			11	7				1	5	4				6	10			9		8	2				3	
24	21	BRIGHTON & HOVE ALB	1-2	McCambridge	4185			11	7				1	5					4	10		8	9			2			6	3	
25	28	Bristol Rovers	0-0		6249		11						1	5	4		10		3	9	6	8			7	2					
26	Feb 4	ALDERSHOT TOWN	2-1	Maidment, Henderson	4287				7		6		1	5	4	9			3	11		8	10			2					
27	11	Queen's Park Rangers	1-5	Maidment	5347		11		7				1	5		9			3	6		8	10			4				2	
28	18	SOUTHEND UNITED	2-0	Jones 2	5275	1	11		7					5		9			6	10		8	4			2				3	
29	25	Crystal Palace	1-4	Maidment	5805	1	11		7					5		9			6	10		8	4			2				3	
30	Mar 4	Newport County	2-4	Emmerson, Henderson	7933		11		7				1	5		9			6	10		8	4			2				3	
31	11	LUTON TOWN	3-2	Jones, Cribb, Maidment	5919			11	7				1	5	4				6	10		8	9			2				3	
32	18	Exeter City	0-1		8146			11	7				1	5	4	9			6	10		8				2				3	
33	25	TORQUAY UNITED	2-1	Henderson 2	6630				7				1	5	4	9			6	10		8	11			2				3	
34	Apr 1	Brentford	3-7	Henderson 3	10831				7				1	5	4	9			6	10		8	11			2				3	
35	8	COVENTRY CITY	2-2	McCambridge, Henderson	5902			11	7				1	5	4	9			6	10			8			2				3	
36	10	Northampton Town	0-2		2304				7				1	5	4	9			6	10		8	11			2				3	
37	14	WATFORD	1-1	Maidment	9451				7				1	5	4	9			6	10		8	11			2				3	
38	15	Bristol City	1-3	Russell	7176	1			7					5	4	9		7	6	11		8	10			2				3	
39	17	Watford	1-2	Jones	7713				7				1	5		9		7	6	11		4	10		8	2				3	
40	22	NORTHAMPTON T	6-0	Henderson 5, Cribb	6631		11	7					1	5	4	9				8		6	10			2				3	
41	29	Clapton Orient	0-3		3739		11	7					1		4	9			5	8		6	10			2				3	
42	May 6	SWINDON TOWN	3-0	Maidment, Cribb 2	7871		11	7					1	5	4	9			3	8		6	10			2					
		Apps				3	7	27	38	15	1	1	38	41	35	16	21	1	33	38	7	18	41	5	3	31	1	10	3	25	2
		Goals						11	3					1	13	1				13	3	6	17							1	

Scorers in game 17: McCambridge 2, Hill, Harris, Jones, Cribb
Game 27 played at White City
Played in game 13 at 8: EF Carless

F.A. Cup

	Date	Opponent	Score	Scorers	Att	Adams RILM	Collins J	Cribb SR	Emmerson GAH	Evans AH	Evans R	Evans SIVL	Farquharson TG	Galbraith IMcD	Harris F	Henderson WJ	Hill FA	Horton R	Jenkins EIJ	Jones LI	Keating AE	Maidment T	McCambridge J	Morris EL	Paget WST	Pollard R	Richards LG	Roberts WJ	Ronan P	Russell GH	Tennant J
R1	Nov 26	BRISTOL ROVERS	1-1	Harris	11000			11	7				1	5	4		8		3	10			9	2					6		
rep	30	Bristol Rovers	1-4	McCambridge	9000			11	7				1	5	4		8		3	10			9	2					6		

Welsh Cup

	Date	Opponent	Score	Scorers	Att	Adams RILM	Collins J	Cribb SR	Emmerson GAH	Evans AH	Evans R	Evans SIVL	Farquharson TG	Galbraith IMcD	Harris F	Henderson WJ	Hill FA	Horton R	Jenkins EIJ	Jones LI	Keating AE	Maidment T	McCambridge J	Morris EL	Paget WST	Pollard R	Richards LG	Roberts WJ	Ronan P	Russell GH	Tennant J
R7	Feb 22	TRANMERE ROVERS	4-2	Jones 2, Henderson 2	4000	1	11		7							9			5	10		8	4			2			6	3	
R8	Mar 9	Swansea Town	1-1	Maidment	3000		11		7				1	5	4				6	10		8	9			2				3	
rep	15	SWANSEA TOWN	2-1	Maidment, Jones	5000		11		7				1	5	4				6	10		8	9			2				3	
SF	Apr 5	Chester	1-2	Henderson	10000				7				1	5	4	9			6	10		8	11			2				3	

1933/34 Bottom of Division Three (South)

#	Date	Opponent	Res	Scorers	Att	Adams RILM	Adlam LW	Calder R	Curtis ER	Durkan J	Duthie JF	Farquharson TG	Friend H	Galbraith JMcD	Henderson WJ	Hill FA	Hutchinson A	Jenkins EJ	Jones LJ	Keating RE	Lewis EG	Maidment T	Marcroft EH	Marshalsey WHG	Molloy P	Mort EF	Paget WST	Perks H	Postin EL	Rogers TW	Russell GH	West J
1	Aug 26	Watford	2-1	Hutchinson 2	11561			2				1		5	9		11	6	10			4	7						8		3	
2	28	READING	2-0	Henderson 2 (1p)	13824			2				1		5	9		11	6	10			4	7						8		3	
3	Sep 2	CHARLTON ATHLETIC	1-1	Postin	15513			2				1		5	9		11	6	10			4	7						8		3	
4	6	Reading	1-3	Maidment	9198			2			6	1		5	9	8			10			4	7				11				3	
5	9	Bournemouth	3-1	Postin, Henderson 2	9315			2				1		5	9			6	10			4	7				11		8		3	
6	16	TORQUAY UNITED	0-1		13666			2				1		5	9			6	10			4	7				11		8		3	
7	23	EXETER CITY	2-1	Marcroft, Hutchinson	10241			2				1		5	9		11	6	10			4	7						8		3	
8	30	Gillingham	2-6	Hutchinson, Henderson	8907			2				1		5	9		11	6	10			4	7						8		3	
9	Oct 7	CRYSTAL PALACE	4-0	Jones, Postin 2, Henderson	9022	1		2						5	11	9		6	10			4	7						8		3	
10	14	Bristol Rovers	1-3	Marcroft	11860	1		2						5	9	11			10			4	7	6					8		3	
11	21	Queen's Park Rangers	0-4		12169							1		5		11		6	10			8	7		4				9		2	
12	28	NEWPORT COUNTY	1-1	Jones	16175	1		2						5		11		6	10			8	7		4				9		3	
13	Nov 4	Norwich City	0-2		10698	1		2						5		11		6	10			8	7		4				9		3	
14	11	BRISTOL CITY	1-5	Galbraith	9090	1		2						5	9	11		6	10				7		4				8		3	
15	18	Clapton Orient	2-4	Hill, Henderson	8402			2				1		5	9	11		6	10			4	7						8		3	
16	Dec 2	Brighton & Hove Albion	0-4		5612	1		2	10		6			5	8							4	7					11			3	9
17	16	Luton Town	1-3	West	5984	1		2	10		6			5			11	8				4	7								3	9
18	23	NORTHAMPTON T	1-3	Curtis (p)	6168	1	6	2	10					5			11	8				4	7								3	9
19	25	Coventry City	1-4	Maidment	27589		4	2	10		6	1		5			11		8			9	7								3	
20	26	COVENTRY CITY	3-3	Curtis, Bisby (og), Postin	10729		4	2	11		6	1		5					10			8	7						9		3	
21	30	WATFORD	4-1	Postin, Rogers, Curtis, Jones	6010		4	2	11		6	1		5					10			8							9	7	3	
22	Jan 6	Charlton Athletic	0-2		11020			2	11		6	1		5				4	10				7					8	9		3	
23	17	SWINDON TOWN	0-1		2859			2	11		6	1		5	9			4		8		10	7								3	
24	20	BOURNEMOUTH	4-2	Henderson 2, West, Curtis	4261			2	10		6	1		5	9		11	4											8		3	7
25	27	Torquay United	1-3	Marshaley	3091			2	10		6	1		5	9		11							4					8		3	7
26	Feb 3	Exeter City	0-4		6091			2	10		6	1		5	9		11							4					8	7	3	
27	10	GILLINGHAM	1-3	Postin	5194			2	10		6	1		5	9		11					8		4					7		3	
28	17	Crystal Palace	2-3	Henderson, Curtis	6290			2	11	3		1					9		10	5		4	7		6				8			
29	24	BRISTOL ROVERS	1-5	Postin	6591			2	10	3		1					9		11	5		4	7		6				8			
30	Mar 3	QUEEN'S PARK RANGERS	3-1	Curtis, Henderson 2	6140			2	11			1			9					4	10		7		6	5			8		3	
31	10	Newport County	2-2	Postin 2	10438			2	11			1			9					4	10		7		6	5			8		3	
32	17	NORWICH CITY	0-2		8630			2				1			9		11			4	10		7		6	5			8		3	
33	24	Bristol City	0-3		7186			2				1		4	8		11			9	10		7			6		5			3	
34	30	SOUTHEND UNITED	1-1	Postin	7890			2				1		4			11	3		9	10		7			6		5	8			
35	31	CLAPTON ORIENT	1-2	Postin	5154			2				1	6	4			11	3		9	10		7					5	8			
36	Apr 2	Southend United	1-1	Postin	9303			2				1	6	4	10		11	3		9				7				5	8			
37	7	Swindon Town	3-6	Keating 2, Lewis	7163			2				1	6	4	10			3		9	7	11						5	8			
38	14	BRIGHTON & HOVE ALB	1-4	Keating	4237			2				1		4			11	3		9	10		7					5	8			
39	21	Aldershot Town	3-1	Keating 3	2484					2		1		4	8			3		9	6		7					5	11		10	
40	25	ALDERSHOT TOWN	1-2	Perks	2660					2		1		4	8			3		9	6			7				5	11		10	
41	28	LUTON TOWN	0-4		3080					2		1		4	8			3		9	6			7				5	11		10	
42	May 5	Northampton Town	0-2		2992					2		1		4	8			3			6		7					5	11		10	9
		Apps				8	4	37	16	6	13	34	3	36	27	8	23	31	22	12	14	26	28	7	9	13	3	9	33	2	31	6
		Goals							6					1	12	1	4		3	6	1	2	2	1				1	13	1		2

Played in game 11 at 3: JW Bartlett

One own goal

F.A. Cup

	Date	Opponent	Res	Scorers	Att	Adams RILM	Adlam LW	Calder R	Curtis ER	Durkan J	Duthie JF	Farquharson TG	Friend H	Galbraith JMcD	Henderson WJ	Hill FA	Hutchinson A	Jenkins EJ	Jones LJ	Keating RE	Lewis EG	Maidment T	Marcroft EH	Marshalsey WHG	Molloy P	Mort EF	Paget WST	Perks H	Postin EL	Rogers TW	Russell GH	West J
R1	Nov 25	ALDERSHOT	0-0		12000	1		2						5	9	11		6	10			4	7						8		3	
rep	29	Aldershot	1-3	Hill	6000	1		2			6			5	9	10	11					4	7						8		3	

Division Three (South) Cup

	Date	Opponent	Res	Scorers	Att	Adams RILM	Adlam LW	Calder R	Curtis ER	Durkan J	Duthie JF	Farquharson TG	Friend H	Galbraith JMcD	Henderson WJ	Hill FA	Hutchinson A	Jenkins EJ	Jones LJ	Keating RE	Lewis EG	Maidment T	Marcroft EH	Marshalsey WHG	Molloy P	Mort EF	Paget WST	Perks H	Postin EL	Rogers TW	Russell GH	West J
R1	Jan 1	ALDERSHOT	0-1		3000			2	11		6	1		5			8		10			4							9	7	3	

Welsh Cup

	Date	Opponent	Res	Scorers	Att	Adams RILM	Adlam LW	Calder R	Curtis ER	Durkan J	Duthie JF	Farquharson TG	Friend H	Galbraith JMcD	Henderson WJ	Hill FA	Hutchinson A	Jenkins EJ	Jones LJ	Keating RE	Lewis EG	Maidment T	Marcroft EH	Marshalsey WHG	Molloy P	Mort EF	Paget WST	Perks H	Postin EL	Rogers TW	Russell GH	West J
R6	Feb 14	BRISTOL CITY	2-2	Henderson, Curtis	1500			2	10		6	1			9		11			5		4	7						8		3	
rep	26	Bristol City	0-1		900			2	10		6	1		5	9	7	11					4							8		3	

1934/35   19th in Division Three (South)

#		Date	Opponent	Score	Scorers	Att	Attley L	Bassett WEG	Bland WH	Everest J	Farquharson TG	Fursland SA	Galbraith JMcD	Granville A	Griffiths PH	Griffiths S	Hill FA	Jackson W	Jennings WH	Jones DG	Jones G(1)	Keating RE	Lane E	Leckie JT	Lewis WL	Molloy P	Moore WA	Mort EF	Pugh R	Riley H	Taylor SG	Vaughan T	Whitlow FWI
1	Aug	25	CHARLTON ATHLETIC	2-1	Riley, Keating	17193	5	2		3	1		6		7			11	4			9								10		8	
2		27	LUTON TOWN	1-0	S Griffiths	18608	5	2		3	1		6			7		11	4			9								10		8	
3	Sep	1	Crystal Palace	1-6	Everest	17641	5	2		3	1		6		7			11	4			9								10			8
4		3	Luton Town	0-4		9392	5	4		3	1		6		11							8	2		9					10			7
5		8	QUEEN'S PARK RANGERS	2-1	Riley, Keating	12663	5	4		3	1		6				8		11			7	2							10			9
6		10	SOUTHEND UNITED	2-0	Riley, Keating	11922	5	4		3	1		6		7				11			8	2							10			9
7		15	Torquay United	2-5	Hill, Lewis	4309	5	4		3	1		6		7		11					8	2		9					10			
8		22	SWINDON TOWN	1-3	P Griffiths	7111	5			3	1	6			7			11	4			8	2		9					10			
9		29	Aldershot Town	0-2		4996	5			3		6						11	4			9	2	1	8					10	7		
10	Oct	6	BOURNEMOUTH	2-1	Riley, Bassett	5053	5			3			6		7			11	4			9	2	1	8					10			
11		13	BRIGHTON & HOVE ALB	0-0		8957	5	4		3			6		7			10		11		9	2	1	8								
12		20	Watford	3-1	Hill, Vaughan 2	7844	5			3							10	11				9	2	1		6		4	7			8	
13		27	NEWPORT COUNTY	3-4	Hill, Keating, Vaughan	16131	5			3							10	11				9	2	1		6		4	7			8	
14	Nov	3	Reading	1-1	Keating	8272	5			3							10	11				9	2	1		6		4	7			8	
15		10	NORTHAMPTON T	2-2	Riley, Hill	9378	5			3							10		2			9		1		6		4	7	11		8	
16		17	Millwall	2-2	Pugh, Keating	11047	5			3									4			9	2	1	10		6		7	11		8	
17	Dec	1	Clapton Orient	1-0	Whitlow	8145	5			3							8	11	4				2	1	10		6		7				9
18		8	GILLINGHAM	0-2		8463	5			3							8	11	4				2	1			6		7	10			9
19		15	Exeter City	1-2	Pugh	3439	5			3				4						11		9	2	1	10		6		7	8			
20		22	BRISTOL CITY	3-3	Riley, Bassett, Keating	7043	5			3				4							11	9	2	1	8		6		7	10			
21		26	Southend United	1-2	Galbraith	9438	5			3				4							11	9	2	1	8		6		7	10			
22		29	Charlton Athletic	1-3	Keating	12101	5			3			6								11	9	2	1	8				7	10			
23	Jan	5	CRYSTAL PALACE	2-0	Owens (og), Pugh	9648	5			3				4	2						11	9		1	10		6		7			8	
24		16	COVENTRY CITY	2-4	Keating 2	7235	5			3				4							11	9	2	1			6		7	10		8	
25		19	Queen's Park Rangers	2-2	Hill, Pugh	5548	5			3				4			8				11	9	2	1			6		7	10			
26		26	TORQUAY UNITED	1-1	Hill	8034	5			3							8				11	9	2	1	4	6			7	10			
27	Feb	2	Swindon Town	1-2	Everest	6043	5			3							8		4		11	9	2	1	10	6			7				
28		9	ALDERSHOT TOWN	1-1	Hill	6563				3							11		4			9	2	1		6	5		7	10		8	
29		16	Bournemouth	1-3	Everest (p)	4764	5			3				11			8		4				2	1	9	6			7	10			
30		23	Brighton & Hove Albion	1-3	Pugh	5828				3							8		4	11			2	1	9	6	5		7	10			
31	Mar	2	WATFORD	2-1	Riley, Lewis	9247		5		3				4			8			11			2	1	9	6			7	10			
32		9	Newport County	0-4		8461		5		3				4			8			11			2	1	9	6			7	10			
33		16	READING	1-1	S Griffiths	8684		5		3				4		11	8						2	1	9		6		7	10			
34		23	Northampton Town	0-3		3476		5		3				4			8	6					2	1		11			7	10			9
35		30	MILLWALL	3-1	Lewis 2, Attley	7282	10	5		3								4	6			9	2	1	8				7	11			
36	Apr	6	Coventry City	0-2		8176		5		3				11			8	2	6			9		1	10				7	4			
37		13	CLAPTON ORIENT	3-0	Keating, Lewis, Attley	7453	10	5		3	1			11				2	6			9			8				7	4			
38		19	BRISTOL ROVERS	4-1	Keating 2, Pugh, Hill	14392	10	5		3	1						11	2	6			9			8				7	4			
39		20	Gillingham	0-1		5820	10			3	1			11				2	6			9			8			5	7	4			
40		22	Bristol Rovers	2-3	Keating 2	10222		5		3	1		6				10	2				9							7	4	11	8	
41		27	EXETER CITY	5-0	Keating 4, Webb (og)	7016	10	5		3	1						11	2				9			8	6			7	4			
42	May	4	Bristol City	0-4		5558	10	5		3	1						11	2				9			8	6			7	4			
			Apps				6	39	8	42	14	2	15	5	12	2	23	12	26	9	11	34	30	28	26	14	11	7	31	35	1	12	7
			Goals				2	2		3			1		1	2	8					19			5				6	7		3	1

Two own goals

F.A. Cup

		Date	Opponent	Score	Scorers	Att	Attley L	Bassett WEG	Bland WH	Everest J	Farquharson TG	Fursland SA	Galbraith JMcD	Granville A	Griffiths PH	Griffiths S	Hill FA	Jackson W	Jennings WH	Jones DG	Jones G(1)	Keating RE	Lane E	Leckie JT	Lewis WL	Molloy P	Moore WA	Mort EF	Pugh R	Riley H	Taylor SG	Vaughan T	Whitlow FWI
R1	Nov	24	READING	1-2	Lewis	16733		5		3									4			9	2	1	10		6		7	11		8	

Division Three (South) Cup

		Date	Opponent	Score	Scorers		Attley L	Bassett WEG	Bland WH	Everest J	Farquharson TG	Fursland SA	Galbraith JMcD	Granville A	Griffiths PH	Griffiths S	Hill FA	Jackson W	Jennings WH	Jones DG	Jones G(1)	Keating RE	Lane E	Leckie JT	Lewis WL	Molloy P	Moore WA	Mort EF	Pugh R	Riley H	Taylor SG	Vaughan T	Whitlow FWI
R1	Oct	17	Crystal Palace	1-3	Vaughan					3			6			10	7			11			2	1		4	5					8	9

Welsh Cup

		Date	Opponent	Score	Scorers	Att	Attley L	Bassett WEG	Bland WH	Everest J	Farquharson TG	Fursland SA	Galbraith JMcD	Granville A	Griffiths PH	Griffiths S	Hill FA	Jackson W	Jennings WH	Jones DG	Jones G(1)	Keating RE	Lane E	Leckie JT	Lewis WL	Molloy P	Moore WA	Mort EF	Pugh R	Riley H	Taylor SG	Vaughan T	Whitlow FWI
R6	Feb	13	NEWPORT COUNTY	3-2	Riley 2, Lewis	2000				3						11	8		4				2	1	9		6	5	7	10			
R7	Mar	27	CHESTER	2-2	Burke (og), Everest	2000		5		3				4		11	8			6			2	1	9				7	10			
rep	Apr	10	Chester	0-3		5000		5		3						11	10			2	6	8		1	9				7	4			

1935/36   20th in Division Three (South)

#	Date	Opponent	Score	Scorers	Att	Attley L	Bassett WEG	Davies AB	Deighton J	Diamond JJ	Everest J	Godfrey C	Granville A	Hearty H	Hill FA	Jennings WH	Jones G(1)	Keating RE	Leckie JT	Lewis WL	McDonagh C	McKenzie JD	Mort EF	Poland G	Pugh R	Redwood DJ	Riley H	Roberts J	Roper H	Smith HR	Williams DJ
1	Aug 31	Crystal Palace	2-3	Riley, Hill	16694		5					3	4	2	11			9	1						7		10		8	6	
2	Sep 2	BRISTOL ROVERS	0-0		18774		5			9		3	4	2	11				1						7		10		8	6	
3	7	READING	2-3	Done (og), Roper	16850	10	5					3	4	2	11			9	1						7				8	6	
4	11	Bristol Rovers	1-1	Pugh	11209	10	2					3	4		11			9	1				5		7				8	6	
5	14	Newport County	0-0		15858		2	10				3	4		11			9	1				5		7				8	6	
6	16	CLAPTON ORIENT	4-1	Hill 2, Roper, Riley	7239		2					3	4		9				1				5		7		10	11	8	6	
7	21	Gillingham	0-3		5663		2					3	4		9				1				5		7		10	11	8	6	
8	28	BOURNEMOUTH	1-1	Smith	11844		2					3	4					9	1				5		7		10	11	8	6	
9	Oct 5	Luton Town	2-2	Diamond 2	12288		2			9		3	4						1				5		7		10	11	8	6	
10	12	NOTTS COUNTY	3-2	Hill, Diamond, Walker (og)	11458		2			9		3	4		10				1				5		7		11		8	6	
11	19	COVENTRY CITY	1-0	Roberts	12239		2			9		3	4		10				1				5		7			11	8	6	
12	26	Swindon Town	1-2	Pugh	8224		2			9		3	4		10				1				5		7			11	8	6	
13	Nov 2	ALDERSHOT TOWN	0-1		8506		2			9		3	4						1				5		7		10	11	8	6	
14	9	Exeter City	0-2		4590		2		1	9		3	4		8							10	5		7			11		6	
15	16	MILLWALL	3-1	Roberts 2, Diamond	8185				1	9		3	10		8	2							5		7		4	11		6	
16	23	Bristol City	2-0	Diamond, Roberts	10350				1	9		3	4		8	2							5		7		10	11		6	
17	Dec 7	Queen's Park Rangers	1-5	Diamond	5048		2		1	9		3	4										5		7		10	11	8	6	
18	25	Southend United	1-3	Everest	8478	10			1	9	2	3	4					8					5		7			11		6	
19	26	SOUTHEND UNITED	1-1	Diamond	11574					9	2	3	4					8	1				5		7		10	11		6	
20	28	CRYSTAL PALACE	1-1	Diamond	7411				1	9		6	2	3	11			8		10	4		5		7						
21	Jan 4	Reading	1-4	Keating	8713				1	9		6	2	3	11			8		10	4		5		7						
22	11	Torquay United	1-2	Keating	3560					9		6	2	3				8		10			5	1	7	11			4		
23	15	WATFORD	0-2		3765	10				9		6	2	3				8					5	1	7	11			4		
24	18	NEWPORT COUNTY	2-0	Smith, Riley	10981		5					4	2	3						10				1	7	11	8			6	9
25	25	GILLINGHAM	4-0	Williams 2, Riley, Roberts	5998		5					6	2	3				8						1	7		10	11		4	9
26	Feb 1	Bournemouth	4-4	Keating 2, Williams, Pugh	7058							6	2	3		5		8						1	7		10	11		4	9
27	8	LUTON TOWN	2-3	Williams 2	12142		5					6	2	3				8						1	7	11	10			4	9
28	15	Notts County	0-2		4639		5					6	2	3				8	1						7		10	11		4	9
29	22	Coventry City	1-5	Everest	11257		5				11	6	2	3				8	1			10			7				4		9
30	29	EXETER CITY	5-2	* see below	6390						11	3	5	2				8	1			10			7				4	6	9
31	Mar 7	Brighton & Hove Albion	0-1		8198						11	3	5	2				8	1			10			7				4	6	9
32	14	SWINDON TOWN	2-1	Keating 2	8637		5		1			3	6	2				8				10			7	11			4		9
33	18	BRIGHTON & HOVE ALB	1-0	Williams	4268		5		1			3	6	2			10	8							7			11	4		9
34	21	Millwall	4-2	Keating 3, Williams	11774				1			3	6	2				8							7		10	11	4	6	9
35	28	BRISTOL CITY	1-0	Keating	9755				1			3	6	2				8							7		10	11	4	6	9
36	Apr 4	Watford	0-4		5165				1			3	6	2				8							7		10	11	4	6	9
37	10	NORTHAMPTON T	0-0		11302				1			3	4	2				8					5		7		10	11	6		9
38	11	QUEEN'S PARK RANGERS	3-2	Riley 2, Pugh	8571		5	8	1			2	6	3											7		10	11	4		9
39	13	Northampton Town	0-2		7890		5	8	1			2	6	3								10			7			11	4		9
40	18	Aldershot Town	1-1	Williams	4271	11		8	1			2	5	3											7		10		4	6	9
41	25	TORQUAY UNITED	1-2	Pugh	4206	11		8	1			3	5	2											7		10		4	6	9
42	May 2	Clapton Orient	1-2	Hill	5460			8	1			3	5	2	11									9	7		10		4	6	

Scorers in game 30: Lewis, Pugh, Smith, Diamond, Williams

| | | | | | Apps | 6 | 25 | 6 | 18 | 18 | 31 | 42 | 21 | 18 | 15 | 4 | 1 | 24 | 18 | 9 | 2 | 1 | 20 | 6 | 42 | 6 | 26 | 22 | 27 | 36 | 18 |
| | | | | | Goals | | | | | 9 | 2 | | | | 5 | | | 10 | | 1 | | | | | 6 | | 6 | 5 | 2 | 3 | 9 |

Two own goals

F.A. Cup

	Date	Opponent	Score	Att	Deighton J	Diamond JJ	Godfrey C	Granville A	Hill FA	Jennings WH	Mort EF	Pugh R	Riley H	Roberts J	Smith HR
R1	Nov 30	DARTFORD	0-3	9000	1	9	3	4	8	2	5	7	10	11	6

Division Three (South) Cup

	Date	Opponent	Score	Scorers	Att	Bassett WEG	Diamond JJ	Godfrey C	Granville A	Hill FA	Leckie JT	Mort EF	Pugh R	Riley H	Roper H	Smith HR
R1	Sep 30	Crystal Palace	1-2	Diamond	8000	2	9	3	4	11	1	5	7	10	8	6

Welsh Cup

	Date	Opponent	Score	Scorers	Att	Bassett WEG	Everest J	Godfrey C	Granville A	Hearty H	Keating RE	Leckie JT	McKenzie JD	Poland G	Pugh R	Riley H	Roberts J	Roper H	Smith HR	Williams DJ
R6	Jan 29	BRISTOL CITY	2-1	Pugh, Keating	6000	5		6	2	3	8			1	7	10	11		4	9
R8	Mar 12	Rhyl	1-2	Pugh	7000		11	3	5	2	8	1	10		7			4	6	9

Bye in R7

37

Player columns (left → right): Bassett WEG · Davies AB · Fielding WJ · Ford L · Godfrey C · Granville A · MacAulay R · Main WG · McKenzie JD · Melaniphy EMJ · Mellor J · Nicholson G · Ovenstone DG · Pinxton AE · Poland G · Prescott JR · Pugh R · Redwood DJ · Roper H · Scott WJ · Smith FC · Smith HR · Smith JA · Talbot FL · Walton G · Welsby A · Williams DJ

#	Date	Opponent	Score	Scorers	Att	Bassett WEG	Davies AB	Fielding WJ	Ford L	Godfrey C	Granville A	MacAulay R	Main WG	McKenzie JD	Melaniphy EMJ	Mellor J	Nicholson G	Ovenstone DG	Pinxton AE	Poland G	Prescott JR	Pugh R	Redwood DJ	Roper H	Scott WJ	Smith FC	Smith HR	Smith JA	Talbot FL	Walton G	Welsby A	Williams DJ
1	Aug 29	Walsall	0-1		10268	5		1		6	2						4	11	10			7			3	9			8			
2	31	CLAPTON ORIENT	2-1	Pugh, C Smith	16698	5		1		6	2						4		10			7			3	9			8		11	
3	Sep 5	LUTON TOWN	3-0	C Smith 2, Pugh	17915	5		1		6	2						4	11	8			7			3	9			10			
4	10	Clapton Orient	1-0	Pugh	5471	5		1		6	2						4	11	8			7			3	9			10			
5	12	Newport County	3-2	Ovenstone, Talbot, C Smith	16732	5		1		6	2						4	11	8			7			3	9			10			
6	14	BRISTOL CITY	3-1	Pugh, Pinxton, Talbot	24936	5		1		6	2						4	11	8			7			3	9			10			
7	19	Crystal Palace	2-2	C Smith, Pugh	18348	5		1		6	2							11	8			7			3	9		4	10			
8	26	EXETER CITY	3-1	Ovenstone, Talbot, C Smith	21749	5		1		6	2						4	11	8			7			3	9			10			
9	28	SOUTHEND UNITED	1-1	Pinxton	26094	5		1		6	2						4	11	8			7			3	9			10			
10	Oct 3	Reading	0-3		13209	5		1		6	2						4	11	8			7			3	9			10			
11	10	QUEEN'S PARK RANGERS	2-0	Talbot, Williams	21897	5		1		6	2						4	11	8			7			3				10			9
12	24	Watford	0-2		14015	5		1		6	2						4	11	8			7			3				10			9
13	31	BRIGHTON & HOVE ALB	1-2	Granville (p)	17805	5		1			2						4	11				7			3	9	6		10	8		
14	Nov 7	Bournemouth	2-0	Talbot, Walton	9231	5		1		6	2						4	11	10			7			3				8	9		
15	14	NORTHAMPTON T	2-1	Pugh, Walton	18200	5		1		6	2						4	11	10			7			3				8	9		
16	21	Bristol Rovers	1-5	Talbot	17171	5		1		6	2						4	11	10			7			3				8	9		
17	Dec 5	Swindon Town	2-4	Prescott, C Smith	10532	5	8	1	2	6							4				11	7			3	9			10			
18	19	Gillingham	0-0		8361	5				6	2						4			1	9	7							8	10		11
19	25	Torquay United	0-1		4582					5	2			6	9		4			1	11	7							8	10		
20	26	WALSALL	2-2	Walton, Melaniphy	31594					5	2			6	9		4	11		1		7							8	10		
21	28	TORQUAY UNITED	0-2		12048				2	6					9		4			1		7	11					5	8	10		
22	Jan 2	Luton Town	1-8	Prescott	12368					6			3		9	2	4			1		7	11					5	8	10		
23	9	NEWPORT COUNTY	0-1		24681					6	2				9	3	4			1	11	7					5		8	10		
24	23	CRYSTAL PALACE	1-1	Talbot	9415					5	2				9	3	4	8		1		7					6		10	11		
25	Feb 3	Exeter City	1-3	Pinxton	2298					5	2			6	9	3	4	8		1			11						10		7	
26	6	READING	1-1	Walton	10569							2				3	4		10	1		7	11		6		5		8	9		
27	13	Queen's Park Rangers	0-6		11408		4					2				7	3	8		1					6	9		5	11	10		
28	20	Southend United	1-8	C Smith	7100			1				2		6		3	4					7	11			9			8	10		
29	27	WATFORD	2-2	Granville (p), Walton	6283						2				9	3	4			1		7	11				6	5	8	10		
30	Mar 6	Brighton & Hove Albion	2-7	McKenzie, Granville (p)	10632					6	3			9		2	4			1		7	11					5	8	10		
31	13	BOURNEMOUTH	2-1	McKenzie 2	8582			1		5	2			10		3	4				11	7		6					8	9		
32	20	Northampton Town	0-2		7334			1	2	5				10	8	3	4				11	7		6						9		
33	26	Notts County	0-4		17664				2	5				8		3	4		10	1	11	7						6		9		
34	27	BRISTOL ROVERS	3-1	McKenzie, Pugh, Granville (p)	9666					5	2			10		3	4			1	11	7				9		6	8			
35	29	NOTTS COUNTY	0-2		20245					5	2		4	10		3				1		7	11			9		6	8			
36	Apr 3	Millwall	1-3	Granville (p)	19489	5					9	6	2	10		3	4			1	11	7							8			
37	10	SWINDON TOWN	1-2	Walton	9066	5				6	2			10	9	3	4		11	1		7								8		
38	12	MILLWALL	0-1		6775				3	5	2			10	9		4		11	1		7						6		8		
39	17	Aldershot Town	1-0	Melaniphy	3084		1		3	5	2			10	9		4	11				7						6		8		
40	19	ALDERSHOT TOWN	4-1	Walton, Melaniphy 2, Ovenstone	5940		1		3	5	2			10	9		4	11				7						6		8		
41	24	GILLINGHAM	2-0	Melaniphy, Ovenstone	8358		1		2	5				10	9		4	11				7						6	3	8		
42	May 1	Bristol City	1-2	Hick (og)	4360		1		3	5				9			4						11					6	2			10
		Apps				20	2	24	10	37	32	4	5	13	15	16	39	21	20	18	11	39	7	4	17	16	14	7	29	30	3	2
		Goals									5			4	5			4	3		2	7				8			7	7		1

Played in game 42 only: H Campbell (7), AR Brown (8),
Played in game 20 (at 3) and 28 (5): C Turner
Played at 3 in games 18, 19 and 21: J Estor

One own goal

F.A. Cup

	Date	Opponent	Score	Scorers	Att	Bassett WEG	Davies AB	Fielding WJ	Ford L	Godfrey C	Granville A	McKenzie JD	Melaniphy EMJ	Mellor J	Nicholson G	Ovenstone DG	Pinxton AE	Poland G	Prescott JR	Pugh R	Scott WJ	Smith FC	Talbot FL	Walton G
R1	Nov 28	SOUTHALL	3-1	Walton, Talbot, Pugh	14000	5		1		6	2				4	10			11	7	3		8	9
R2	Dec 12	SWINDON TOWN	2-1	Granville (p), Prescott	18833	5	10			6	2				4			1	11	7	3		8	9
R3	Jan 16	GRIMSBY TOWN	1-3	Melaniphy	36245	5				6	2		9	3	4	8		1		7			10	11

Division Three (South) Cup

	Date	Opponent	Score	Bassett WEG	Fielding WJ	Ford L	Godfrey C	Nicholson G	Ovenstone DG	Pinxton AE	Pugh R	Scott WJ	Talbot FL	Walton G
R1	Oct 28	EXETER CITY	0-1	5	1	2	6	4	11	8	7	3	10	9

Att: 3000

Welsh Cup

	Date	Opponent	Score	Scorers	Att	Ford L	Godfrey C	Melaniphy EMJ	Mellor J	Ovenstone DG	Pugh R	Smith JA	Talbot FL	Walton G	Welsby A
R6	Mar 10	Barry Town	1-3	Walton	5000	2	6	9	3	8	7	5	4	10	11

Played at 1: Jack Deighton

#	Date	Opponent	Score	Scorers	Att	Bassett WEG	Blenkinsop E	Brown AR	Collins JH	Davies AB	Evans TJ	Finlay J	Ford L	Godfrey C	Granville A	Harrison J	Jones RH	McCaughey C	McKenzie JD	Melaniphy EMJP	Mellor J	Mitchell JW	Mort EF	Nicholson G	Prescott JR	Pugh R	Smith JA	Talbot FL	Turner A	Walton G	Williams TP
1	Aug 28	Clapton Orient	1-1	Collins	14598	5			9					6	2		1	4			3					7		10	11	8	
2	30	TORQUAY UNITED	5-2	Collins 3, Walton, Turner	20796	5			9					6	2		1	4			3					7		10	11	8	
3	Sep 4	SOUTHEND UNITED	5-0	* See below	22912	5			9					6	2		1	4			3					7		10	11	8	
4	8	Torquay United	1-0	Collins	5970	5			9					6	2		1	4			3					7		10	11	8	
5	11	Queen's Park Rangers	1-2	Turner	15300	5			9					6	2		1	4			3					7		10	11	8	
6	13	NORTHAMPTON T	4-1	Collins 2, Godfrey, Turner	20693	5			9					6			1	4			3					7	2	10	11	8	
7	18	BRIGHTON & HOVE ALB	4-1	Walton, Collins 2, Turner	28034	5			9					6	2		1	4			3	7						10	11	8	
8	25	Bournemouth	0-3		10320	5			9					6	2		1	4			3					7		10	11	8	
9	Oct 2	NOTTS COUNTY	2-2	Turner 2	35468	5			9					6	2		1	4			3					7		10	11	8	
10	9	WALSALL	3-1	Collins, Turner, Pugh	19086	5			9					6			1	4			2					7	3	10	11	8	
11	16	Newport County	1-1	Talbot	24268	5			9				2	6			1	4			3					7		10	11	8	
12	23	BRISTOL CITY	0-0		17858	5			9					6	2		1	4			3					7		10	11	8	
13	30	Watford	0-4		11183				9					6	2		1	4						5		7	3	10	11	8	
14	Nov 6	GILLINGHAM	4-0	Turner, Collins, Walton, Talbot	14818				9				3	5	2		1	4						6		7		10	11	8	
15	13	Exeter City	1-2	Collins	9541				9				3	6	2		1	4						5		7		10	11	8	
16	20	SWINDON TOWN	2-2	Collins, McCaughey	15404				9				3		2		1	4					5	6		7		10	11	8	
17	Dec 4	MILLWALL	3-2	Pugh, McCaughey, Walton	16160	5	3		9						2		1	4						6		7		10	11	8	
18	18	CRYSTAL PALACE	4-2	Turner 2 (1p), Collins, Talbot	18374	5			9				3		2		1	4						6		7		10	11	8	
19	25	Mansfield Town	0-3		12114	5			9				3		2		1	4						6		7		10	11	8	
20	27	MANSFIELD TOWN	4-1	Pugh, Collins, Turner 2 (1p)	37726	5			9				3		2		1	4						6		7		10	11	8	
21	Jan 1	CLAPTON ORIENT	2-0	Melaniphy 2	19580	5							3		2		1	4		9				6		7		10	11	8	
22	12	Aldershot	1-1	Collins	2711	5			9				3		2		1	4						6		7		10	11	8	
23	15	Southend United	1-3	Turner	6061	5			9				3		2		1	4						6		7		10	11	8	
24	22	QUEEN'S PARK RANGERS	2-2	Walton, Turner	26268	5			9				3		2		1	4						6		7		10	11	8	
25	29	Brighton & Hove Albion	1-2	Collins	9802	5			9				3	4	2		1	10						6		7			11	8	
26	Feb 5	BOURNEMOUTH	3-0	Walton, Melaniphy, Collins	17563	5	3		9						2		1	4		10				6	7				11	8	
27	12	Notts County	0-2		13278		3		9			7		5	2		1	4		10				6					11	8	
28	19	Walsall	0-1		4638				9	8			3		2		1	4					7	6					11	10	5
29	26	NEWPORT COUNTY	3-1	Turner 2 (1p), Pugh	25608	5			9				3		2		1	4						6		7		10	11	8	
30	Mar 5	Bristol City	1-0	Collins	38953	5			9				3		2		1	4						6		7		10	11	8	
31	12	WATFORD	1-1	McCaughey	25349	5	3		9						2		1	4	10					6		7		8	11		
32	19	Gillingham	0-1		6710	5	3		9						2		1	4	8					6	7			10	11		
33	26	EXETER CITY	1-1	Collins	12065	5	3		9						2		1	4	8				7	6				10	11		
34	Apr 2	Swindon Town	0-2		8797	5			9						2		1	4	8					6		7	3	10	11		4
35	9	ALDERSHOT	0-1		7761	5		10	9						2		1	4						6		7	3	8	11		
36	15	BRISTOL ROVERS	1-1	Collins	10384	5			9						2	10	1	4						6		7	3	8	11		
37	16	Millwall	0-1		25647	5							3	6	2		1	4		9					8	7		10	11		
38	18	Bristol Rovers	1-2	Prescott	9851	5			9				3	6	2		1	4	8						11	7		10			
39	23	READING	4-1	Turner 2, Collins 2	8281		3		9					6	2		1	4	8							7		10	11		5
40	30	Crystal Palace	0-1		9018	5	3		9						2		1	4	8					6		7		10	11		
41	May 4	Reading	0-0		4597	5	3		9						2		1	4	8					6		7		10	11		
42	7	Northampton Town	0-0		6410	5	3		9		11				2		1	4	8					6		7		10			
		Apps				35	10	1	40	1	1	1	21	25	30	1	42	41	9	5	12	2	3	25	4	36	6	38	40	30	3
		Goals							23					1	1			3		3					1	4		5	19	7	

Scorers in game 3: Talbot 2, Walton, Granville (p), Turner

F.A. Cup

#	Date	Opponent	Score	Scorers	Att	Bassett WEG	Blenkinsop E	Brown AR	Collins JH	Davies AB	Evans TJ	Finlay J	Ford L	Godfrey C	Granville A	Harrison J	Jones RH	McCaughey C	McKenzie JD	Melaniphy EMJP	Mellor J	Mitchell JW	Mort EF	Nicholson G	Prescott JR	Pugh R	Smith JA	Talbot FL	Turner A	Walton G	Williams TP
R1	Nov 27	Northampton Town	2-1	Collins 2	14000	5			9				3		2		1	4						6		7		10	11	8	
R2	Dec 11	BRISTOL CITY	1-1	Turner	25472	5	3		9						2		1	4						6		7		10	11	8	
rep	15	Bristol City	2-0	Collins 2	23050	5			9				3		2		1	4						6		7		10	11	8	
R3	Jan 8	Charlton Athletic	0-5		34637	5			9						2		1	4				3		6		7		10	11	8	

Division Three (South) Cup

#	Date	Opponent	Score	Scorers	Att	Bassett WEG	Blenkinsop E	Brown AR	Collins JH	Davies AB	Evans TJ	Finlay J	Ford L	Godfrey C	Granville A	Harrison J	Jones RH	McCaughey C	McKenzie JD	Melaniphy EMJP	Mellor J	Mitchell JW	Mort EF	Nicholson G	Prescott JR	Pugh R	Smith JA	Talbot FL	Turner A	Walton G	Williams TP
R1	Sep 27	Northampton Town	1-0	Turner	3689		10		9					6	2		1	4			3			5		7			11	8	
R2	Nov 10	Bristol City	1-2	Collins	2130				9				3	5	2		1	4						6		7		10	11	8	

Welsh Cup

#	Date	Opponent	Score	Scorers	Att	Bassett WEG	Blenkinsop E	Brown AR	Collins JH	Davies AB	Evans TJ	Finlay J	Ford L	Godfrey C	Granville A	Harrison J	Jones RH	McCaughey C	McKenzie JD	Melaniphy EMJP	Mellor J	Mitchell JW	Mort EF	Nicholson G	Prescott JR	Pugh R	Smith JA	Talbot FL	Turner A	Walton G	Williams TP
R6	Feb 16	CHELTENHAM TOWN	0-1		5000		3		9			7		5	2		1	4		10				6					11	8	

1938/39   13th in Division Three (South)

Note: in the tables below the 27 player columns are, in order:
Anderson RS, Baker WG, Ballsom WG, Bassett WEG, Collins JH, Corkhill WG, Egan H, Fielding WJ, Ford L, Granville A, Hill CJ, Jones RH, Kelso J, Main WG, McCaughey C, McKenzie JD, Mitchell JW, Nicholson G, Prescott JR, Pugh R, Rhodes A, Rickards CT, Smith R, Talbot FL, Turner A, Walton G, Williams TP.

#	Date	Opponent	Score	Scorers	Att	Anderson RS	Baker WG	Ballsom WG	Bassett WEG	Collins JH	Corkhill WG	Egan H	Fielding WJ	Ford L	Granville A	Hill CJ	Jones RH	Kelso J	Main WG	McCaughey C	McKenzie JD	Mitchell JW	Nicholson G	Prescott JR	Pugh R	Rhodes A	Rickards CT	Smith R	Talbot FL	Turner A	Walton G	Williams TP
1	Aug 27	EXETER CITY	1-2	Turner	24645		5			9	4												6		7				10	11	8	
2	31	Mansfield Town	2-2	Collins 2	6959		5			9	4				2		1	3					6				7	11	10		8	
3	Sep 3	Newport County	0-3		18387			2	5	9	4						1	3					6				7	11	10		8	
4	5	WALSALL	2-1	Collins 2	15697			2	5	9	4						1	3					6		7		8		10	11		
5	10	Ipswich Town	2-1	Rickards, Prescott	16179			2	5	9							1	3		4			6	11	7		8		10			
6	17	READING	0-1		15843			2	5	9							1	3		4			6	11	7		8				10	
7	24	Bristol Rovers	1-1	Talbot	10046			2	5	9							1	3		4			6	11	7		8		10			
8	Oct 1	BRIGHTON & HOVE ALB	4-1	Prescott, Collins 2, Rickards	17393			2	5	9							1	3		4			6	11	7		8		10			
9	8	Bournemouth	0-0		7211			2	5	9							1	3		4			6	11	7		8		10			
10	15	CLAPTON ORIENT	1-2	Talbot	16317			2	5	9							1	3		4			6	11	7		8		10			
11	22	Northampton Town	1-2	Prescott	10262				5	9					2	10	1	3		4			6	11	7		8					
12	29	SWINDON TOWN	2-1	Rickards, Collins	14313				5	9					2	10	1	3		4			6	11	7		8					
13	Nov 5	Port Vale	1-1	Collins	12521			2	5	9						10	1	3		4			6	11	7		8					
14	12	WATFORD	5-3	Collins 3, McCaughey, Hill	11646			2	5	9						10	1	3		4			6	11	7		8					
15	19	Crystal Palace	0-2		17898			2	5	9			1			10		3		4	11		6		7				8			
16	Dec 3	Aldershot	1-1	Collins	5699			2	5	9			1					3		4			6		7			8	10			
17	17	Torquay United	3-1	Talbot 2, Collins	2257			2	5	9	4		1					3					6		7			11	10		8	
18	24	Exeter City	1-1	Egan	4242			2	5	9	4	10	1					3					6		7		8	11				
19	26	QUEEN'S PARK RANGERS	1-0	Collins	26744				5	9		10	1		2			3		4			6		7		8	11				
20	27	Queen's Park Rangers	0-5		14799				5	9		10	1		2			3		4			6		7		8	11				
21	31	NEWPORT COUNTY	1-2	Smith	40187			2	5	9		10	1					3	6	4					7		8	11				
22	Jan 11	BRISTOL CITY	2-1	Smith, Walton	8645			2	5	9			1					3		4			6		7			11	10		8	
23	14	IPSWICH TOWN	2-1	Parry (og), Collins	15312			2	5	9	6	11	1					3		4					7		8		10			
24	28	BRISTOL ROVERS	0-2		12659			2	5	9			1					3		4			6		7			11	10		8	
25	Feb 1	Reading	0-0		3623			2	5	9	4	10	1					3					6		7		8					
26	4	Brighton & Hove Albion	2-1	Egan, Collins	9770			2	5	9	4	10	1					3			11		6		7		8					
27	11	BOURNEMOUTH	5-0	* See below	12309			2	5	9	4	10	1					3			11		6		7		8					
28	18	Clapton Orient	1-1	Egan	9035			2	5	9	4	10	1					3			11		6		7		8					
29	25	NORTHAMPTON T	2-0	Rickards, McCaughey	10282					9	4		1		2			3		6						7	8	11	10			
30	Mar 4	Swindon Town	1-4	Egan	8861			2	5	9	4	10	1					3		6	11				7		8					
31	11	PORT VALE	2-4	Egan, Talbot	9145			2	5	9	4	11	1					3		6						7	8		10			
32	18	Watford	0-1		6714				5	9	4	10	1		2			3			11		6			7			8			
33	25	CRYSTAL PALACE	0-1		11910				5	9	4		1	2				3			11		6		7							
34	Apr 1	Bristol City	1-1	Egan	10003				5	9	4	10	1		2			3			11		6		7		8					
35	7	Southend United	0-2		9299				5	9	4	10	1		2			3			11		6		7		8					
36	8	ALDERSHOT	2-4	Prescott, Egan	9060				5	9	4	10	1		2			3			11	8	6	7								
37	10	SOUTHEND UNITED	1-0	Pugh	8220					9	4	10	1		2			3			11		6		7		8					5
38	15	Notts County	1-1	McKenzie	7640	8		2	5		4	11	1					3		6	9				7				10			
39	17	NOTTS COUNTY	4-1	Talbot 2, Anderson, Pugh	5070	8		2	5		4	11	1					3		6	9				7				10			
40	22	TORQUAY UNITED	3-1	Collins, Talbot, Hill	7277			2	5	9	4		1			11		3					6		7		8		10			
41	29	MANSFIELD TOWN	0-0		5886			2		9	4		1			11		3					6		7				10		8	5
42	May 6	Walsall	3-6	Collins, Talbot, Hill	6246			2	5	9	4		1			11		3					6		7				10		8	

Scorers in game 27: Egan 2, Rickards, Walton, McKenzie
Played in game 33 at 8: HJ Court.
Played in game 16 at 11: WJ Davies

	Anderson RS	Baker WG	Ballsom WG	Bassett WEG	Collins JH	Corkhill WG	Egan H	Fielding WJ	Ford L	Granville A	Hill CJ	Jones RH	Kelso J	Main WG	McCaughey C	McKenzie JD	Mitchell JW	Nicholson G	Prescott JR	Pugh R	Rhodes A	Rickards CT	Smith R	Talbot FL	Turner A	Walton G	Williams TP
Apps	2	3	34	35	36	23	17	26	4	10	14	16	41	1	25	12	1	34	16	18	5	20	11	27	2	24	3
Goals	1				18		9				3				2	2			4	2		5	2	9	1	2	

One own goal

F.A. Cup

Rd	Date	Opponent	Score	Scorers	Att	Ballsom WG	Bassett WEG	Collins JH	Corkhill WG	Fielding WJ	Kelso J	McCaughey C	Nicholson G	Prescott JR	Pugh R	Rickards CT	Smith R	Talbot FL	Walton G
R1	Nov 26	Cheltenham Town	1-1	Prescott	8000	2	5	9		1	3	4	6	11	7			10	8
rep	30	CHELTENHAM TOWN	1-0	Prescott	8940	2	5	9		1	3	4	6	11	7			10	8
R2	Dec 10	CREWE ALEXANDRA	1-0	Talbot	19000	2	5	9		1	3	4	6		7		11	10	8
R3	Jan 7	CHARLTON ATHLETIC	1-0	Walton	22780	2	5	9		1	3	4	6		7		11	10	8
R4	21	NEWCASTLE UNITED	0-0		42060	2	5	9	11	1	3	4	6		7			10	8
rep	25	Newcastle United	1-4	Pugh	44649	2	5	9		1	3	4	6		7		11	10	8

Division Three (South) Cup

Rd	Date	Opponent	Score	Att	Bassett WEG	Collins JH	Corkhill WG	Granville A	Hill CJ	Jones RH	Kelso J	Main WG	McCaughey C	McKenzie JD	Talbot FL
R1	Nov 16	Bristol City	0-6	670	5	9	4	2	10	1	3	6	11	7	8

Welsh Cup

Rd	Date	Opponent	Score	Scorers	Att	Anderson RS	Baker WG	Ballsom WG	Bassett WEG	Collins JH	Corkhill WG	Egan H	Fielding WJ	Granville A	Hill CJ	Jones RH	Kelso J	McCaughey C	McKenzie JD	Mitchell JW	Nicholson G	Pugh R	Rhodes A	Rickards CT	Smith R	Talbot FL	Walton G	Williams TP
R5	Feb 8	SWANSEA TOWN	2-2	Mackenzie, McCaughey	4000			2		9	4		1		10		3	6	11					8			7	5
rep	23	Swansea Town	4-1	Egan 2, Rickards 2	1500	7	5			9	4		1	2			3	6						8	11	10		
R6	Mar 8	NEWPORT COUNTY	5-1	Egan 3, Rickards, Mackenzie	6000	7		2	5	9	4		1				3		11		6			8		10		
SF	30	Oswestry	1-1	Granville (p)	3000				5	9	4		1	2			3	6	11					8		10	7	
rep	Apr 13	Oswestry	2-2	Talbot, Collins	3000					9	4	10	1	2			3		11		6	7		8				5
rep2	26	Oswestry	2-1	Talbot, Collins	5000			2	5	9	4		1		11		3			8	6	7				10		
F	May 4	South Liverpool	1-2	Collins	5000			2		9	4		1		11		3				6	7				10	8	5

40

CARDIFF CITY IN WORLD WAR TWO

1939/40

Football League: Competition cancelled after 2 September 1939.

1 FL	Aug	26	Norwich City	2-1	Collins, Pugh	14000
2 FL		30	Swindon Town	1-0	Collins	10000
3 FL	Sep	2	NOTTS COUNTY	2-4	Collins 2	20000

The same line-up was used in all three matches. W Fielding; G Ballsom, E Sykes; W Corkhill, W Booth, J Cringan; R Pugh, E Marshall, J Collins, L McPhillips, J Myers.

Football League South West, League Cup, Welsh Cup

1 SW	Oct	21	Bristol City	1-1	Corkhill	6545
2 SW		28	SWANSEA TOWN	2-2	Court, Sabin	5000
3 SW	Nov	4	PLYMOUTH ARGYLE	1-0	Court	4000
4 SW		11	Swindon Town	2-2	Collins, Marshall	4161
5 SW		18	BRISTOL ROVERS	0-0		2000
6 SW		25	Newport County	1-3	Marshall	2228
7 SW	Dec	2	TORQUAY UNITED	2-2	Anderson, Court	1500
8 SW		9	BRISTOL CITY	7-3	Marshall 2, Court 2, Sabin 2, Egan	1195
9 SW		16	Swansea Town	0-4		2500
WC		16	Ebbw Vale	4-0	Court, Pugh 3	2000
10 SW		23	Plymouth Argyle	2-6	Egan, one og	2671
11 SW		10	SWINDON TOWN	1-1	James	3000
12 SW	Jan	6	Bristol Rovers	0-7		1012
13 SW		13	NEWPORT COUNTY	1-0	Court	4000
14 SW		20	Torquay United	0-5		1200
15 SW	Feb	10	PLYMOUTH ARGYLE	0-0		2000
16 SW		24	BRISTOL ROVERS	1-1	Pugh	3000
WC	Mar	2	NEWPORT COUNTY	1-1	Owen	3000
17 SW		9	TORQUAY UNITED	1-1	Pugh	3000
18 SW		16	BRISTOL CITY	3-2	Boulter 2, Pugh	4000
WC		18	Newport County	0-5		800
19 SW		22	Bristol City	2-3	Owen, Pugh	3343
20 SW		23	Swansea Town	0-1		3000
21 SW		10	Plymouth Argyle	1-4	Morris	3541
22 SW	Apr	6	SWINDON TOWN	1-1	Marshall	3000
LC		13	READING	1-1	Mitchell	3000
LC		17	Reading	0-1		2750
23 SW		20	Swindon Town	2-2	Collins 2	1665
24 SW	May	11	Torquay United	4-2	James, Marshall, Moore, Parker	1137
25 SW		13	NEWPORT COUNTY	4-1	Parker, Tobin, Pugh, Moore	3000
26 SW		18	SWANSEA TOWN	2-2	James, Tobin	2000
27 SW		25	Newport County	1-4	Baker	600
28 SW	Jun	1	Bristol Rovers	3-3	James, Meads 2	1210

SW = South West League
WC = Welsh Cup
LC = League Cup

League South West

		p	w	d	l	f	a	pts
1	Plymouth Argyle	28	16	4	8	72	41	36
2	Torquay United	28	14	6	8	73	62	34
3	Bristol Rovers	28	9	10	9	62	55	28
4	Newport County	28	12	4	12	70	63	28
5	Swindon Town	28	10	8	10	66	63	28
6	Swansea Town	28	10	6	12	54	60	26
7	CARDIFF CITY	28	6	13	9	45	63	25
8	Bristol City	28	7	5	16	57	92	19

1940/41

League South: League and League Cup

1 FL	Aug	31	Reading	0-2		2861
2 FL	Sep	7	READING	2-2	James, Moore	3000
3 FL		14	BIRMINGHAM CITY	5-2	Moore 3, James, Parker	2175
4 FL		21	Birmingham City	2-3	Pugh, James	3500
5 FL		28	BRISTOL CITY	2-2	James, Wrigglesworth	3500
6 FL	Oct	5	Bristol City	0-1		1546
7 FL		12	Coventry City	2-5	Parker 2	2700
8 FL		19	COVENTRY CITY	2-2	James, Hollyman	3000
9 FL		26	SWANSEA TOWN	8-0	James 3, Moore 3, Parker 2	4000
10 FL	Nov	9	Southampton	3-1	Moore 2, Parker	2000
11 FL		16	SOUTHAMPTON	1-1	Moore	1500
12 FL		23	Bristol City	1-4	James	2500
13 FL		30	BRISTOL CITY	5-1	James 2, Moore, Scott, Wood	2000
14 FL	Dec	7	Stoke Ciity	1-5	Steggles	1800
15 FL		14	STOKE CITY	4-0	Morris, James 3	1000
16 FL		21	Bournemouth	5-2	Moore 2, James, Baker, Parker	800
17 FL		25	Swansea Town	3-1	Moore, James 2	3000
18 FL		28	BOURNEMOUTH	1-3	T Jones	4000
19 FL	Jan	11	BRISTOL CITY	5-2	Moore 2, James 2, Joy	2000
20 FL		25	Swansea Town	3-2	Moore 2, James	1500
21 FL	Feb	8	Bristol City	7-4	Moore 4, Parker, Pugh, Williams	1500
LC		15	SWANSEA TOWN	3-2	Moore, Parker, James	4000
LC	Mar	1	SWANSEA TOWN	6-2	Moore 3, Parker 2, James	4000
LC		8	Reading	1-0	James	5000
LC		15	READING	4-1	James 2, Baker, Moore	10000
LC		22	Tottenham Hotspur	3-3	Moore 2, Barnes	5000
LC		29	TOTTENHAM HOTSPUR	2-3	James, Parker	21000
22 FL	May	17	WEST BROMWICH ALB.	4-4	Parker 2, James 2	3009
23 FL		24	PORTSMOUTH	4-1	Walker (og), Moore 2, Parker	2723
24 FL		31	WOLVERHAMPTON W.	5-1	James 2, Moore, T Jones, Parker	4204

Game 5 was a 'home game' for Bristol City

League South (top 6, determined on goal average)

		p	w	d	l	f	a	
1	Crystal Palace	27	16	4	7	86	44	1.954
2	West Ham United	25	14	6	5	70	39	1.794
3	Coventry City	10	5	3	2	28	16	1.750
4	Arsenal	19	10	5	4	66	38	1.736
5	CARDIFF CITY	24	12	5	7	75	50	1.500
6	Reading	26	14	5	7	73	51	1.431

Westerrn Regional League

1	Apr	5 Bath City	1-2	James	1500
2		12 LOVELL'S ATHLETIC	3-2	James 2, Parker	2500
3		14 Aberaman	2-2	Moore, Parker	750
4		19 Lovell's Athletic	1-2	Moore	2000
5		26 BATH CITY	5-2	James 3, Moore 2	1700
6	Jun	3 LOVELL'S ATHLETIC	1-6	Hollyman	

Game 6 was the Western League Cup Final

1941/42

Football League (Southern Section)

1 FL	Aug	30 West Bromwich Albion	3-6	Moore, James 2	4462
2 FL	Sep	6 WEST BROMWICH ALB.	1-1	Moore	4647
3 FL		27 SOUTHAMPTON	5-3	Parker 2, Moore, Hollyman, James	3930
4 FL	Oct	4 Southampton	3-1	Moore, Parker 2	2000
5 FL		11 Wolverhampton Wan.	3-0	Lewis, Moore, Perry	4612
6 FL		18 WOLVERHAMPTON W.	2-0	James, Parker	3217
7 FL		25 BOURNEMOUTH	0-2		2500
8 FL	Nov	1 Bournemouth	2-3	Moore, James	3000
9 FL		8 LUTON TOWN	6-1	James 3, Moore 2, Dare	2500
10 FL		15 Luton Town	0-2		2300
11 FL		22 SWANSEA TOWN	1-0	Parker	2000
12 FL		29 Swansea Town	1-4	Parker	2500
13 FL	Dec	6 BRISTOL CITY	8-2	Parker 3, Weir 3, Thomas, Steggles	3000
14 FL		13 Bristol City	6-2	Parker, Dare, Weir 2, Wood 2	4000
15 FL		25 SWANSEA TOWN	2-1	Moore, Parker	3750

Football League War Cup Qualifiers, Rounds Proper and League games

1 LCQ	Dec	27 Southampton	5-2	Parker 3, Morris, Butler	2500
2 LCQ	Jan	3 SOUTHAMPTON	9-1	Parker 5, Moore 2, Morgan, Wood	5000
3 LCQ		10 Swansea Town	1-1	Moore	4000
4 LCQ		17 SWANSEA TOWN	1-1	Parker	5000
5 LCQ		24 Bristol City	3-8	Moore 3	3312
6 LCQ		31 BRISTOL CITY	0-2		6000
7 LCQ	Feb	7 Bournemouth	1-2	Parker	2000
8 LCQ		14 BOURNEMOUTH	6-0	Parker 3, Moore 2, Wood	5300
9 LCQ		21 Swansea Town	5-1	Wright 3, Parker, Moore	5000
10 LCQ		28 SWANSEA TOWN	8-1	Wood 2, Weir 3, Parker 2, Moore	7000
L	Mar	14 LUTON TOWN	2-0	Fenton 2	5000
L		21 SWANSEA TOWN	4-1	Wright, Lewis, Moore 2	4320
R1/1	Apr	4 SOUTHAMPTON	3-1	Moore 2, Fenton	5000
R1/2		6 Southampton	1-1	Moore	3600
R2/1		11 WEST BROMWICH ALB.	1-1	Lewis	10781
R2/2		18 West Bromwich Albion	2-3	Shelley 2	10198
L	Apr	25 NORTHAMPTON T	0-1		3460
L	May	2 Northampton Town	1-6	Moore	2271
L		25 SWANSEA TOWN	4-1	Moore 3, Griffiths	3720
L		30 LUTON TOWN	2-4	Hollyman 2	2695

Football League South
(positions determined by points assuming each
club played 18 games)

		p	w	d	l	f	a	pts	
1	Leicester City	17	11	3	3	40	17	25	26.40
2	West Bromwich Alb.	13	9	1	3	62	26	19	26.30
3	CARDIFF CITY	15	9	1	5	43	28	19	22.80
4	Norwich City	8	4	2	2	20	13	10	22.50
5	Bournemouth	10	6	0	4	26	18	12	21.60
6	Bristol City	15	9	0	6	46	45	18	21.60
7	Walsall	18	9	1	8	49	45	19	19.00
8	Northampton T	16	7	2	7	39	38	16	18.00
9	Wolves	16	6	2	8	27	36	14	15.75
10	Southampton	10	4	0	6	27	32	8	14.40
11	Luton Town	18	5	1	12	34	73	11	11.00
12	Nottm. Forest	13	2	1	10	18	39	5	6.90
13	Swansea Town	9	1	0	8	18	39	2	4.00

League Cup Qualifying Competition (to March 28)

Cardiff City finished in 12th place with this record:

p	w	d	l	f	a	pts	
10	5	2	3	39	19	12	12.00

and qualified for the knock-out stages

1942/43

Football League West

1 FL	Aug	29 Bath City	0-3		2000
2 FL	Sep	5 BATH CITY	2-0	Moore, Clarke	2563
3 FL		12 Bristol City	1-9	Clarke	2743
4 FL		19 BRISTOL CITY	0-0		2500
5 FL		26 LOVELL'S ATHLETIC	4-8	Moore, McAulay, Griffiths, Pugh	2800
6 FL	Oct	3 Lovell's Athletic	3-1	Clarke, Moore, McAulay	3100
7 FL		10 Swansea Town	4-2	Clarke 2, K Griffiths 2	1200
8 FL		17 SWANSEA TOWN	5-0	Wright, Clarke 2, Moore, Parker	2500
9 FL		24 Aberaman	6-2	Moore 3, Clarke, Wright 2	500
10 FL		31 ABERAMAN	5-1	Grocott 2, Clarke 2, Moore	3000
11 FL	Nov	7 Lovell's Athletic	1-1	Moore	3000
12 FL		14 LOVELL'S ATHLETIC	0-1		3500
13 FL		21 ABERAMAN	1-1	Moroe	2500
14 FL		28 Aberaman	4-2	Morgan, Clarke 3	720
15 FL	Dec	5 BRISTOL CITY	4-3	Griffiths, Morgan 3	3000
16 FL		12 Bristol City	0-5		1800
17 FL		19 BATH CITY	1-3	Morgan	1000
18 FL		25 Swansea Town	1-3	Clarke	2426

Football League West (to 25 December)

		p	w	d	l	f	a	pts
1	Lovell's Ath.	18	14	2	2	59	21	30
2	Bath City	18	14	0	4	66	26	28
3	CARDIFF CITY	18	8	3	7	41	45	19
4	Bristol City	17	7	3	7	59	37	17
5	Swansea Town	18	3	1	14	27	77	7
6	Aberaman	17	2	1	14	29	75	5

League Cup North: Qualifying Competition, League Second Championship, League Cup (West)

1 LCQ	Dec	26	SWANSEA TOWN	2-2	K Griffiths, Wright	5000
2 LCQ	Jan	2	Bath City	1-2	Moore	2700
3 LCQ		9	ABERAMAN	0-1		2000
4 LCQ		16	Aberaman	1-3	Handford (og)	640
5 LCQ		23	Lovell's Athletic	0-4		5000
6 LCQ		30	LOVELL'S ATHLETIC	1-4	Moore	1800
7 LCQ	Feb	6	BRISTOL CITY	0-3		3000
8 LCQ		13	Bristol City	1-1	Clarke	3000
9 LCQ		20	Swansea Town	2-1	Clarke, Daly	2000
10 LCQ		27	BATH CITY	2-5	Parker, Daly	3000
L	Mar	6	SWANSEA TOWN	2-0	Sparshott 2	2000
L		13	Swansea Town	1-1	Moore	2000
L		20	LOVELL'S ATHLETIC	2-5	Nairn 2	3000
LCW	Apr	10	ABERAMAN	2-3	Clarke, Evans	2500
LCW		17	Bath City	3-4	Willicombe, Clarke 2	1500
LCW		24	SWANSEA TOWN	2-5	Murphy, Moore	2500
LCW	May	1	Bristol City	0-3		2500

League Cup North Qualifying Competition (to Feb 27)

Cardiff City finished in 49th place with this record:

p	w	d	l	f	a	pts
10	1	2	7	10	26	4

and did not qualify for the knock-out stage.

1943/44

Football League West

1 FL	Aug	28	LOVELL'S ATHLETIC	1-2	K Griffiths	3500
2 FL	Sep	4	Lovell's Athletic	1-3	Moore	4000
3 FL		11	BRISTOL CITY	4-1	Steggles 2, Williams, Sherwood	3000
4 FL		18	Bristol City	1-2	Raybould	3310
5 FL		25	Bath City	7-2	Court, Williams, Clarke 2, Moore 2, Raybould	3500
6 FL	Oct	2	BATH CITY	1-3	Moore	4000
7 FL		9	ABERAMAN	3-2	Moore 2, Williams	3000
8 FL		16	Aberaman	2-1	Wood, Clarke	450
9 FL		23	SWANSEA TOWN	5-0	williams 3, Moore, Clarke	4500
10 FL		30	Swansea Town	3-1	Moore 2, Raybould	2000
11 FL	Nov	6	BRISTOL CITY	1-0	Sherwood	3000
12 FL		13	Bristol City	1-1	Wood	4000
13 FL		20	BATH CITY	3-1	Clarke, Williams 2	3500
14 FL		27	Bath City	1-2	Williams	2300
15 FL	Dec	4	SWANSEA TOWN	1-0	Clarke	2500
16 FL		11	Swansea Town	4-2	Raybould 2, Williams, Moore	1000
17 FL		18	Lovell's Athletic	1-4	Raybould	2760
18 FL		25	LOVELL'S ATHLETIC	5-1	Moore 2, Williams 2, Clarke	3000

Football League West (to 25 December)

		p	w	d	l	f	a	pts
1	Lovell's Ath.	18	12	0	6	62	30	24
2	CARDIFF CITY	18	11	1	6	45	28	23
3	Bath City	18	9	1	8	41	42	19
4	Aberaman	18	8	2	8	32	35	18
5	Bristol City	18	8	1	9	32	36	17
6	Swansea Town	18	3	1	14	25	66	7

League Cup North Qualifying Competition, Rounds Proper, League (second competition)

1 LCQ	Dec	26	Bath City	2-3	Clarke, Steggles	6000
2 LCQ	Jan	1	BATH CITY	1-2	Sherwood	4000
3 LCQ		8	SWANSEA TOWN	7-1	Moore 3, Sherwood, Rees, Carless	2500
4 LCQ		15	Swansea Town	2-1	Rees, Wood	1200
5 LCQ		22	Aberaman	2-1	Rees, Carless	200
6 LCQ		29	ABERAMAN	4-1	Raybould, Williams 2, Rees	3000
7 LCQ	Feb	5	BRISTOL CITY	2-0	Moore, Rees	5000
8 LCQ		12	Bristol City	0-2		4000
9 LCQ		19	LOVELL'S ATHLETIC	2-0	Wood, Low (og)	6000
10 LCQ		26	Lovell's Athletic	1-2	Rees	7000
R1/1	Mar	4	Lovell's Athletic	0-2		6000
R1/2		11	LOVELL'S ATHLETIC	1-0	Rees	10000
1 L	Mar	18	ABERAMAN	6-0	Gibson, Moore 2, Rees 2, Clarke	2000
2 L		25	Aberaman	5-0	Rees 2, Clarke, Carless, Gibson	1000
3 L	Apr	1	BRISTOL CITY	6-0	Clarke, Preece (og), Rees 2, Carless, Gibson	1000
4 L		8	Bristol City	2-1	Rees, Rowe	2000
5 L		10	LOVELL'S ATHLETIC	1-1	Moore	3000
6 L		15	Lovell's Athletic	0-2		3000
7 L		22	Swansea Town	4-2	Gibson 3, Lester	4000
8 L		29	SWANSEA TOWN	3-1	Rees 2, Carless	2000

League Cup North Qualifying Competition (to Feb 26)

Cardiff City finished in 18th place with this record:

p	w	d	l	f	a	pts
10	6	0	4	23	13	12

and qualified for the knock-out stage.

League North second Championship (to May 6)

Cardiff City finished in 8th place with this record:

p	w	d	l	f	a	pts
21	13	1	7	53	28	27

League Cup West - Cup Final (Two legs)

F1	May	6	Bath City	2-4	Gibson, Clarke	5000
F2		13	BATH CITY	0-0		8000

1944/45

Football League West (Champions)

1 FL	Aug 26 BRISTOL CITY	4-1	Rees 3, Wood			6000
2 FL	Sep 2 Bristol City	0-3				3920
3 FL	9 BATH CITY	2-1	Wood, Rees			8000
4 FL	16 Bath City	2-2	Rees, Wood			3000
5 FL	23 ABERAMAN	8-2	Rees 3, Moore 2, Wood 2, Clarke			3500
6 FL	30 Aberaman	6-0	Rees, Moore, Wood 2, Clarke 2			700
7 FL	Oct 7 LOVELL'S ATHLETIC	1-1	Moore			9500
8 FL	14 Lovell's Athletic	1-1	Moore			5500
9 FL	21 SWANSEA TOWN	3-2	Wood, Clarke, Moore			7000
10 FL	28 Swansea Town	4-0	Clarke 2, Wood, Rees			5000
11 FL	Nov 4 Aberaman	3-0	Wood, Rees 2			800
12 FL	11 ABERAMAN	3-0	Wood 2, Moore			4000
13 FL	18 Bath City	2-4	Rees, Raybould			3000
14 FL	25 BATH CITY	6-2	Wood 2, Clarke 2, Rees 2			6000
15 FL	Dec 2 Swansea Town	3-1	Wood, B Moore, R Moore			3500
16 FL	9 SWANSEA TOWN	3-1	Clarke, Wood, Rees			4000
17 FL	16 Lovell's Athletic	3-2	Clarke, Moore, Rees			4800
18 FL	23 LOVELL'S ATHLETIC	0-1				10000

Football League West

		p	w	d	l	f	a	pts
1	CARDIFF CITY	18	12	3	3	54	24	27
2	Bristol City	18	13	1	4	59	30	27
3	Lovell's Ath.	18	10	3	5	40	31	23
4	Bath City	18	8	3	7	47	46	19
5	Aberaman	18	3	1	14	34	72	7
6	Swansea Town	18	2	1	15	32	63	5

League North Cup: Qualifying Competition, Rounds Proper, Second Championship

1 LCQ	Dec 25 SWANSEA TOWN	3-1	Lever, Clarke, Wood			4000
2 LCQ	30 Swansea Town	3-1	Clerke, Rees, Wood			4500
3 LCQ	Jan 6 Lovell's Athletic	0-1				7000
4 LCQ	13 LOVELL'S ATHLETIC	3-0	Moore, Rees 2			8000
5 LCQ	20 BATH CITY	4-2	Gibson, Clarke, Rees 2			3600
6 LCQ	Feb 3 Aberaman	5-2	Rees 4, Gibson			1000
7 LCQ	10 ABERAMAN	0-0				3500
8 LCQ	17 BRISTOL CITY	4-2	Gibson, Lester, Moore 2			11500
9 LCQ	24 Bristol City	0-1				11657
10 LCQ	Mar 3 Bath City	4-1	Clarke, Gibson, Rees 2			3000
1 L	10 Swansea Town	0-1				4000
2 L	17 SWANSEA TOWN	6-2	Gibson, Rees 4, Lester			10000
R1/1	24 LOVELL'S ATHLETIC	1-0	Rees			12000
R1/2	31 Lovell's Athletic	0-0				10000
3 L	Apr 2 BRISTOL CITY	3-2	Carless 2, Gibson			14000
R2/1	7 Bristol City	2-1	Carless, Lester			20714
R2/2	14 BRISTOL CITY	2-2	Hollyman, Rees			23161
R3/1	21 Wolverhampton Wan.	0-3				34927
R3/2	28 WOLVERHAMPTON W.	2-1	Hollyman, Carless			40283
4 L	May 12 LOVELL'S ATHLETIC	0-4				5000

R2/1 played to a finish, taking 3 hours, 22 minutes

League Cup North Qualifying Competition (to Mar 17)

Cardiff City finished in 6th place with this record:

p	w	d	l	f	a	pts
10	7	1	2	26	11	15

and qualified for the knock-out stages.

League North Second Championship

Cardiff City finished in 19th place with this record:

p	w	d	l	f	a	pts
20	12	2	6	41	27	26

FL - Football League West
LCQ - League Cup qualifying competition
L - Football League second competition (which included results from the League Cup)
R1/1 etc. - League Cup proper, played over two legs

Division Three South: Southern Section League and Cup

1 LS	Aug	25	BOURNEMOUTH	9-3	Rees 4, Clarke 2, Gibson 2, Carless	10000
2 LS	Sep	1	Bournemouth	5-1	Rees, Clarke 3, Wood	7000
3 LS		8	TORQUAY UNITED	6-0	Clarke, Wood, Carless, Rees 2, Gibson	12000
4 LS		12	Crystal Palace	0-3		5000
5 LS		15	Torquay United	7-0	Spencer (og), Lester, Rees 3, Clarke 2	5000
6 LS		22	ALDERSHOT	4-1	Rees 2, Carless, Wood	16000
7 LS		29	Albershot	5-1	Rees, Moore, Clarke, Carless, Hollyman	7000
8 LS	Oct	6	Bristoil City	2-3	Moore, Rees	18711
9 LS		13	BRISTOL CITY	2-4	Rees, Clarke	28000
10 LS		20	BRIGHTON & HOVE ALB.	4-0	Clarke, Rees 2, Reece (og)	22000
11 LS		27	Brighton & Hove Alb.	3-2	Moore, Gibson, Clarke	8500
12 LS	Nov	3	Exeter City	2-3	Gibson, Clarke	6341
13 LS		10	EXETER CITY	0-0		18000
14 LS	Dec	1	Swindon Town	2-1	Wood, Kelso (og)	11876
15 LS		8	SWINDON TOWN	3-0	Lever, Clarke, Wood	6000
16 LS		15	READING	2-1	Wood 2	8000
17 LS		22	Reading	1-3	Rees	5295
18 LS		25	Bristol Rovers	2-2	??	8000
19 LS		26	BRISTOL ROVERS	4-2	Allen, Hollyman, Clarke 2	18000
20 LS		29	CRYSTAL PALACE	6-2	Wright 2, Allen 2, Hollyman 2	25000
FAC	Jan	5	WEST BROMWICH ALB.	1-1	Allen	33000
FAC		9	West Bromwich Albion	0-4		18025
1 LC		12	Watford	7-1	Clarke 2, Wright 2, Allen 2, Tennant	7800
2 LC		19	WATFORD	0-2		14000
3 LC		26	Exeter City	1-2	Haddon	8000
4 LC	Feb	2	EXETER CITY	5-1	Rees 2, Wright, Lever, Clarke	15000
5 LC		9	Torquay United	0-1		4000
6 LC		16	TORQUAY UNITED	3-0	Allen, Rees 2	14700
7 LC		23	Bristol Rovers	0-1		11200
8 LC	Mar	2	BRISTOL ROVERS	3-0	Richards 3	18000
9 LC		9	Bristol City	2-3	Hollyman, Allen	17375
10 LC		16	BRISTOL CITY	3-2	Hill, Allen (p), Clarke	19000
11 LC		23	Swindon Town	2-3	Rees, Moore	11779
12 LC		30	SWINDON TOWN	2-0	Allen 2	19500
13 LC	Apr	6	Reading	2-3	Clarke, Richards	11000
14 LC		13	READING	5-2	Richards 2, Rees, Clarke, Gibson	21500
15 LC		20	Crystal Palace	1-1	Clarke	17500
16 LC		22	CRYSTAL PALACE	3-0	Allen, Hudghill (og), Rees	29000

LS   Division Three (South): South
LC   Division Three (South) Cup: Qualifying Competition, South Region
FAC   FA Cup Round Three

Third Division South, Southern Section
First half season; top 4 places:

		p	w	d	l	f	a	pts
1	Crystal Palace	20	14	4	2	50	15	32
2	CARDIFF CITY	20	11	4	5	54	31	26
3	Bristol City	20	9	6	5	34	25	24
4	Brighton & HA	20	10	2	8	42	47	22

Third Division South, Southern Section
Second half season, South Cup qualifying

Cardiff City finished in 5th place with this record:

p	w	d	l	f	a	pts
16	8	1	7	39	22	17

and did not qualify for the semi-finals.

FA Cup line-up 5 January 1946: K McLoughlin; A Sherwood, M Raybould; G Wright, F Stansfield, L Lester;
C Gibson, K Hollyman, B Allen, T Wood, R Clarke

FA Cup line-up 9 January 1946; K McLoughlin; A Sherwood, M Raybould; G Wright, F Stansfield, K Hollyman;
JFB Moore, B Allen, W Rees, T Wood, R Clarke

The FA Cup was played over two legs in 1945/46. No guest players were allowed.

Cardiff City met Moscow Dynamo in a friendly game on November 17, 1945, losing 1-10 before 31,000 spectators.
K McLoughlin; A Lever, M Raybould; K Hollyman, F Stansfield, L Lester; JFB Moore, E Carless, C Gibson, T Wood, R Clarke.
Moore scored Cardiff's goal.

Friendly games with Swansea Town were played in aid of the Football League's Jubilee Fund as pre-season matches
in 1938/39 and 1939/40.
August 20 1938, drew 3-3 at Swansea (Collins 2, Simmons (og)):
R Jones; J Kelso, A Granville; C McCaughey, W Bassett, W Corkhill; R Pugh, G Walton, J Collins, L Talbot, A Turner
August 19 1939, drew 1-1 at home (Marshall):
W Fielding; E Sykes, J Kelso; W Corkhill, W Booth, J Cringan; R Pugh, E Marshall, J Collins, H Egan, J Myers

1946/47 Champions of Division 3 (South): Promoted

#	Date	Opponent	Score	Scorers	Att	Allen BW	Baker WG	Canning LD	Clarke RJ	Gibson CH	Hill CJ	Hollyman KC	James WJ	Lever AR	Lewis W	Marshall E	Phillips JRW	Poland G	Rees W	Richards SV	Ross WB	Sherwood AT	Stansfield F	Wardle G	Williams GJ	Wood TL
1	Aug 31	Norwich City	1-2	Richards	20678	10			11	7		4		3				1	8	9		2	5			6
2	Sep 4	Swindon Town	2-3	Allen, Richards	14354	10			11	7		4		3				1	8	9		2	5			6
3	7	NOTTS COUNTY	2-1	James, Gibson	24779	10		1	11	7		4	8	2		6				9		3	5			
4	9	BOURNEMOUTH	2-0	Allen, James	19239	10		1	11	7		4	9	2					8			3	5			6
5	14	Northampton Town	2-0	Allen 2	8853	10	4	1	11	7	6			2					8	9		3	5			
6	18	Bournemouth	0-2		8926	8	6	1	11	7	10	4	9	2								3	5			
7	21	ALDERSHOT	2-1	Baker, Clarke	22475	8	6	1	11	7		4	9	2								3	5			10
8	23	SWINDON TOWN	5-0	Richards, Allen, Gibson 3	19172	10	6	1	11	7		4		2					8	9		3	5			
9	28	Brighton & Hove Albion	4-0	Rees, Richards 2, Allen	13193	10	6	1	11	7		4		2					8	9		3	5			
10	Oct 5	EXETER CITY	5-0	Allen, Richards 2, Baker, Clarke	27585	10	6	1	11	7		4		2					8	9		3	5			
11	12	Port Vale	4-0	Richards 2, Clarke, Rees	10724	10	6	1	11	7		4		2					8	9		3	5			
12	19	QUEEN'S PARK RANGERS	2-2	Clarke, Richards	44010	10	6	1	11	7		4		2			3		8	9			5			
13	26	Southend United	2-0	Gibson, Rees	12973	10	6	1	11	7		4		2					8	9		3	5			
14	Nov 2	BRISTOL ROVERS	4-0	Richards 2, Allen, Rees	28699	10	6	1	11	7		4		2					8	9		3	5			
15	9	Mansfield Town	3-1	Richards, Rees 2	9827	10	6	1	11	7		4		2					8	9		3	5			
16	16	TORQUAY UNITED	1-0	Rees	27259	10	6	1	11	7		4		2					8	9		3	5			
17	23	Crystal Palace	2-1	Richards 2	25296	10	6	1	11	7		4		2					8	9		3	5			
18	Dec 7	Walsall	3-2	Allen 2, Rees	16386	10	6	1	11	7		4		2					8	9		3	5			
19	21	Ipswich Town	1-0	Gibson	12398	10	6	1	11	7		4		2					8	9		3	5			
20	25	Leyton Orient	1-0	Rees	12947	10	6	1	11	7		4		2					8	9		3	5			
21	28	NORWICH CITY	6-1	Richards 3, Rees, Allen, Clarke	36285	10	6	1	11	7		4		2					8	9		3	5			
22	Jan 4	Notts County	1-1	Allen	28450	10	6	1	11	7		4		2					8	9		3	5			
23	18	NORTHAMPTON T	6-2	Allen 3, Rees 2, Richards	29426	10	6	1		7		4		2	11				8	9		3	5			
24	22	READING	3-0	Richards 2, Clarke	28534	10	6	1	11			4		2	7				8	9		3	5			
25	25	Aldershot	1-0	Richards	7239	10	6	1						2	7				8	9		3	5		4	
26	Feb 1	BRIGHTON & HOVE ALB	4-0	Richards 2, Rees, Clarke	20533	10	6	1	11					2	7				8	9		3	5		4	
27	Mar 1	SOUTHEND UNITED	3-1	Allen, Clarke 2	33698	10	6	1	11			4		2	7				8	9		3	5			
28	8	Bristol Rovers	0-1		30455	10	6	1	11	7		4		2					8	9		3	5			
29	15	MANSFIELD TOWN	5-0	Hollyman, Gibson, Richards 2, Clarke	9384	10	6	1	11	7		4		2					8	9		3	5			
30	22	Torquay United	0-0		9352	10	6	1	11	7		4	9	5			2		8			3				
31	29	CRYSTAL PALACE	0-0		24214	10	6	1	11	7		4		2					8	9		3	5			
32	Apr 4	Bristol City	1-2	Rees	32535	10	6	1	11	7		8		2					9			3	5		4	
33	5	Reading	0-0		21627	10	6	1	11	7		4		2	8							3	5		9	
34	7	BRISTOL CITY	1-1	Richards	49310	8	6	1	11	7	10	4		2						9		3	5			
35	12	WALSALL	3-0	Hill 2, Gibson	33195	8	6	1	11	7	10	4		2						9		3	5			
36	19	Watford	0-2		20030	10	6	1	9	8	11	4		2	7							3	5			
37	26	IPSWICH TOWN	3-2	Gibson, Richards, Allen	31219	10	6	1	11	7		4		2					8	9		3	5			
38	May 3	WATFORD	1-0	Richards	30368	10	6	1	11	7		4		2					8	9		3	5			
39	10	PORT VALE	1-0	Richards	36732	10	6	1	11	7		4		2					8	9		3	5			
40	17	Exeter City	2-0	Gibson, Rees	12031		6	1	11	7				2					8	9	10	3	5		4	
41	24	Queen's Park Rangers	3-2	Wardle, Ross 2	23272		6	1		7				2					8	9	10	3	5	11	4	
42	Jun 7	LEYTON ORIENT	1-0	Rees	24572		6	1		7				2					8	9	10	3	5	11	4	
		Apps				39	38	40	39	38	5	36	6	42	7	1	2	2	35	34	3	41	41	2	7	4
		Goals				17	2		10	10		1	3						17	30	2				1	

F.A. Cup

	Date	Opponent	Score	Scorers	Att	Allen BW	Baker WG	Canning LD	Clarke RJ	Gibson CH	Hill CJ	Hollyman KC	James WJ	Lever AR	Lewis W	Marshall E	Phillips JRW	Poland G	Rees W	Richards SV	Ross WB	Sherwood AT	Stansfield F	Wardle G	Williams GJ	Wood TL
R3	Jan 11	Brentford	0-1		32894	10	6	1	11	7		4		2					8	9		3	5			

Welsh Cup

	Date	Opponent	Score	Scorers	Att	Allen BW	Baker WG	Canning LD	Clarke RJ	Gibson CH	Hill CJ	Hollyman KC	James WJ	Lever AR	Lewis W	Marshall E	Phillips JRW	Poland G	Rees W	Richards SV	Ross WB	Sherwood AT	Stansfield F	Wardle G	Williams GJ	Wood TL
R5	Feb 6	Merthyr Tydfil	2-4	Rees, James	3000		6		11	7		4	9	2	10				8			3			5	

Played at 1: Wyn Griffiths

1947/48   5th in Division Two

No	Date	Opponent	Res	Scorers	Att	Allen BW	Ashton RW	Baker WG	Blair D	Canning LD	Gibson CH	Griffiths WR	Hollyman KC	Hullett WA	Lever AR	Lewis W	MacBennett SAC	Moore JFB	Parker RE	Rees W	Richards SV	Ross WB	Sherwood AT	Stansfield F	Stitfall RF	Sullivan D	Tobin R	Wardle G	Watson WT	Williams GJ
1	Aug 23	CHESTERFIELD	0-0		38028	10		6		1	7		4		2					8	9		3	5				11		
2	25	DONCASTER ROVERS	3-0	Wardle 2, Richards	44415			6	10	1			4		2		7			8	9		3	5				11		
3	30	Millwall	1-0	Wardle	28703			6	10	1			4		2				7	9		8	3	5				11		
4	Sep 4	Doncaster Rovers	2-2	Wardle, Blair	27760			6	10	1	7		4		2					9		8	3	5				11		
5	6	TOTTENHAM HOTSPUR	0-3		48894	8		6	10	1			4		2		7			9			3	5				11		
6	8	SOUTHAMPTON	5-1	Webber (og), Rees, Moore 2, Richards	39363			6	10	1					2			11		8	9		3	5				7		4
7	13	Sheffield Wednesday	1-2	Rees	36489			6	10	1			4		2		7			8	9		3	5				11		
8	17	Southampton	2-2	McBennett 2	16495			6	10	1			4		2		7			8	9		3	5				11		
9	20	PLYMOUTH ARGYLE	3-0	Blair, Lever (p), Rees	33060			6	10	1			4		2				7	8	9		3	5				11		
10	27	BRADFORD PARK AVE.	1-0	Rees	39796			6	10	1	7		4		2					8	9		3	5				11		
11	Oct 4	Nottingham Forest	2-1	Gibson 2	30618			6	10	1	7		4		2					8	9		3	5				11		
12	11	LUTON TOWN	1-0	Rees	39505			6	10	1	7		4		2					8	9		3	5				11		
13	18	Brentford	0-0		34483			6	10	1	7		4		2					8	9			5	3			11		
14	25	Leicester City	1-2	Frame (og)	36940			6	10	1	7		4		2					8	9		3	5				11		
15	Nov 1	LEEDS UNITED	0-0		36851				10	1	7		4		2					8	9		3	5				11		6
16	8	Fulham	1-4	Gibson	34778				10	1	7		4		2						9	8	3	5				11		6
17	15	COVENTRY CITY	1-1	Richards	35835				10	1	7		4		2					8	9		3	5				11	6	
18	22	Newcastle United	1-4	Lever (p)	56904			6	11	1	7		4		2					8	9		3	5				10		
19	29	BIRMINGHAM CITY	2-0	Richards 2	39646			6	11	1	7		4		2					8	9		3	5				10		
20	Dec 6	West Bromwich Albion	3-2	Blair 2, Gibson	38914			6	11	1	7		4		2					8	9			5	3			10		
21	13	BARNSLEY	1-0	Wardle	33538			6	11	1	7		4		2						9		3	5			8	10		
22	20	Chesterfield	2-2	Stitfall, Blair	18959			6	11	1	7		4		2					8			3	5	9			10		
23	26	BURY	2-2	Wardle, Gibson	43805			6	11	1	7		4		2					8			3	5	9			10		
24	Jan 1	Bury	2-1	Rees, Richards	12382			6	11	1	7		4		2					8	9		3	5				10		
25	3	MILLWALL	6-0	Rees 2, Blair, Gibson, Richards 2	29483			6	11	1	7		4		2					8	9		3	5				10		
26	17	Tottenham Hotspur	1-2	Rees	57386			6	8	1	7				5		11			9			3		2			10		4
27	31	SHEFFIELD WEDNESDAY	2-1	Richards, Rees	33147			6	11	1	7		4		2					8	9		3	5	10					
28	Feb 7	Plymouth Argyle	0-3		26396			6	11	1	7		4	9	2					8			3	5				10		
29	14	Bradford Park Avenue	1-0	Hullett	14756			6	11	1	7			9	2					8			3	5				10		
30	21	NOTTM. FOREST	4-1	Hullett 2, Wardle 2	28929			6		1	7			9	2					8			3	5	10			11		
31	28	Luton Town	1-1	Hullett	22112			6		1	7			9	2					8			3	5	10			11		
32	Mar 6	BRENTFORD	1-0	Hullett	41032			6		1	7			9	2					8			3	5	10			11		
33	13	LEICESTER CITY	3-0	Hullett 2, Wardle	39100			6	10	1	7			9	2					8			3	5	4			11		
34	20	Leeds United	0-4		34276			6	10	1	7			9	2					8			3	5	4			11		
35	26	WEST HAM UNITED	0-3		41700			6	10	1	7			9	2					8			3	5	4			11		
36	27	FULHAM	0-0		33786			6	11	1	7			9	2							10	3	5	4					
37	29	West Ham United	2-4	Hullett, Wardle	31667			6	11	1				9	2				8			10		5	3			7		
38	Apr 3	Coventry City	0-1		26175				11	1	7			9	2	6				8	10			5	3					4
39	10	NEWCASTLE UNITED	1-1	Lever (p)	49209				10	1	7				2	6				8	9			5	3	11				4
40	17	Birmingham City	0-2		52276				10	1				9	2	6				8				5				11		4
41	24	WEST BROMWICH ALB.	0-5		26179			6	11	1	7			9	5					8			2		3		10			4
42	May 1	Barnsley	2-1	Rees, Moore	14979		1	6			7				3			11		8	9		2	5	10					4
		Apps				2	1	36	37	40	33	1	25	13	42	3	4	4	2	38	23	5	39	40	19	1	2	36	1	15
		Goals						6			6			8	3		2	3		11	9				1			10		

Two own goals

F.A. Cup

| R3 | Jan 10 | SHEFFIELD WEDNESDAY | 1-2 | Rees | 48000 | | | 6 | 11 | 1 | 7 | | 4 | | 2 | | | | | 8 | 9 | | 3 | 5 | | | | 10 | | |

A.e.t.

Welsh Cup

| R5 | Jan 15 | Lovell's Athletic | 1-2 | Moore | 5000 | | | 6 | 11 | 1 | | | | | 3 | | | 4 | | | | | 2 | 5 | | | | 10 | | |

Also played: Billy Foulkes (at 7), Billy James (8), Davies (9)

1948/49   4th in Division Two

#	Date	Opponent	Score	Scorers	Att	Allen BW	Baker WG	Best TH	Blair D	Edwards G	Gorin ER	Hogg GS	Hollyman KC	Hullett WA	Joslin PJ	Lever AR	Montgomery SWJ	Moore JFB	Morris EC	Nibloe J	Price CA	Rees W	Rowland A	Sherwood AT	Stansfield F	Stevenson E	Stitfall AE	Stitfall RF	Sullivan D	Wardle G	Williams DR	Williams GJ
1	Aug 21	Bradford Park Avenue	0-3		15048	10	6		11				4		1	3						9		2	5				8			
2	23	LUTON TOWN	3-3	Hollyman, Hullett, Moore	35687	10	6						4	9	1	3		11				8		2	5				7			
3	28	SOUTHAMPTON	2-1	Hullett 2	37189	10	6						4	9	1	2						8		3	5			7	11			
4	30	Luton Town	0-3		20185	10	6						4	9	1	2						8		3	5			7	11			
5	Sep 4	Barnsley	1-1	Sullivan	18542				6				8	9	1	2								3	5			7	11	10		4
6	9	Queen's Park Rangers	0-0		25337		4		6				8	9	1	2						10		3	5			7	11			
7	11	GRIMSBY TOWN	3-0	Hollyman, Rees, Moody (og)	32156		4		6				8	9	1	2						10		3	5			7	11			
8	13	QUEEN'S PARK RANGERS	3-0	Rees 2, Hullett	36223		4		6				8	9	1	2						10		3	5			7	11			
9	18	Nottingham Forest	0-0		20417		4		6				8	9	1	2						10		3	5			7	11			
10	25	FULHAM	2-1	Hullett 2	38423		4		6				8	9	1	2						10		3	5			7	11			
11	Oct 2	Plymouth Argyle	1-0	Hollyman	27371		4		6				8	9	1	2						10		3	5			7				11
12	9	TOTTENHAM HOTSPUR	0-1		56018		4		6				8	9	1	2						10		3	5			7				11
13	16	West Ham United	1-3	Lever (p)	29433				6				8	9	1	2					11	10		3	5			7				4
14	30	West Bromwich Albion	0-2		46036		4	8	6					9	1	2		11						3	5	10		7				
15	Nov 6	CHESTERFIELD	3-4	Rees, Blair, Stansfield	36359		4	8	6				7		1	2						9		3	5	10		11				
16	13	Lincoln City	0-0		14438			8	6				7	9	1	2				11				3	5	10		4				
17	20	SHEFFIELD WEDNESDAY	1-1	Stevenson	30084		4	9	6				8		1	2								3	5	10	11	7				
18	27	Coventry City	1-0	Stevenson	22121		4	8	6		9		7		1	2								3	5	10	11					
19	Dec 4	LEEDS UNITED	2-1	Allen, Stevenson	31972	9	4		6				7		1	2						8		3	5	10			11			
20	11	Leicester City	2-2	Rees, Gorin	24343	8	4		6	11	7				1	2						9		3	5	10						
21	18	BRADFORD PARK AVE.	6-1	* see below	28002	8	4		6	11			7		1	2						9		3	5	10						
22	25	Brentford	1-1	Allen	22813	8	4		6	11			7		1	2						9		3	5	10						
23	27	BRENTFORD	2-0	Allen, Stevenson	49236	8	4		6	11			7		1	2						9		3	5	10						
24	Jan 1	Southampton	0-2		20937	8	4		6	11			7		1	2						9		3	5	10						
25	15	BARNSLEY	0-3		29116	8	4	10	6	11			7		1	2						9		3	5							
26	22	Grimsby Town	2-2	Rees, Montgomery	15210	8	4		6	11			7			2	5		1			9		3		10						
27	Feb 5	NOTTM. FOREST	1-0	Rees	31522	8	4		6	11			7		1	2	5					9		3		10						
28	19	Fulham	0-4		40795	8	4			11			7		1	2	6					9	5	3		10						
29	26	PLYMOUTH ARGYLE	1-0	Hollyman	29006	8	7			11			4		1	2	5					9		3		10						6
30	Mar 5	Tottenham Hotspur	1-0	Hollyman	51183	8	7	9		11			4		1	2	5							3		10						6
31	12	WEST HAM UNITED	4-0	Hollyman, Stevenson 2, Best	28271	8	7	9		11			4		1		5							2		10		3				6
32	19	Bury	3-1	Blair, Best, Edwards	15836			9	10	11		7	4		1		5							3				8				6
33	26	WEST BROMWICH ALB.	2-2	Blair, Best	47649		7	9	10	11			4		1		5							3				8				6
34	Apr 2	Chesterfield	2-0	Best, Edwards	14299			9	8	11			4		1		5					7		3		10						6
35	4	BURY	2-1	Blair, Best	34161			9	8	11			4		1		5					7		3		10						6
36	9	LINCOLN CITY	3-1	Stevenson 2, Edwards	32585		7	9	8	11			4		1	3	5									10		2				6
37	15	Blackburn Rovers	1-2	Edwards	23468		7	9	8	11			4		1		5							3		10		2				6
38	16	Sheffield Wednesday	1-1	Best	32297		7	9		11			4		1	3	5									10		2			8	6
39	18	BLACKBURN ROVERS	1-0	Lever	33325		7	9	6	11					1	3	5									10		2			8	4
40	23	COVENTRY CITY	3-0	Edwards, Stevenson 2	26441		7	9	6	11							5		1					3		10		2			8	4
41	30	Leeds United	0-0		19945			9	6	11							5		1					3		10	7	2			8	4
42	May 7	LEICESTER CITY	1-1	Baker	33496		7	9	6	11							5		1					3		10		2				4
		Apps				17	35	19	34	23	2	1	36	14	38	33	17	2	4	1	1	28	1	39	25	27	3	29	10	2	4	16
		Goals				4	1	6	4	6	1		7	7		3	1	1				6			1	12			1			

Scorers in game 21: Edwards, Allen, Stevenson 2, Lever (p), Hollyman
Played in game 1 at 7: A Gilchrist

One own goal

F.A. Cup

#	Date	Opponent	Score	Scorers	Att	Allen BW	Baker WG	Best TH	Blair D	Edwards G	Gorin ER	Hogg GS	Hollyman KC	Hullett WA	Joslin PJ	Lever AR	Montgomery SWJ	Moore JFB	Morris EC	Nibloe J	Price CA	Rees W	Rowland A	Sherwood AT	Stansfield F	Stevenson E	Stitfall AE	Stitfall RF	Sullivan D	Wardle G	Williams DR	Williams GJ
R3	Jan 8	Oldham Athletic	3-2	Hollyman 2, Allen	28991	8	4		6	11			7		1	2						9		3	5	10						
R4	29	Aston Villa	2-1	Hollyman, Rees	70718	8	4			11	6		7		1	2	5					9				10		3				
R5	Feb 12	Derby County	1-2	Stevenson	35746	8	4		6	11			7		1	2	5					9		3		10						

Welsh Cup

#	Date	Opponent	Score	Scorers	Att	Allen BW	Baker WG	Best TH	Blair D	Edwards G	Gorin ER	Hogg GS	Hollyman KC	Hullett WA	Joslin PJ	Lever AR	Montgomery SWJ	Moore JFB	Morris EC	Nibloe J	Price CA	Rees W	Rowland A	Sherwood AT	Stansfield F	Stevenson E	Stitfall AE	Stitfall RF	Sullivan D	Wardle G	Williams DR	Williams GJ
R6	Jan 12	TROEDYRHIW	3-1	Gorin, Wardle, Best	500		4	9	6		8		7			2			1					3	5					10		
R7	Mar 3	Milford United	2-1	Rowland, Edwards	7500	8	7	3		11			4		1	2	5						9			10						6
SF	Apr 7	Merthyr Tydfil	1-3	Stevenson	22000	8			11		7		4				5		1			9				10	3	2				6

SF at Swansea
Played at 11 in R6: Gordon Pembery

48

1949/50   10th in Division Two

#	Date	Opponent	Score	Scorers	Att	Baker WG	Best TH	Blair D	Edwards G	Evans EE	Gorin ER	Grant W	Hollyman KC	Joslin PJ	Lamie R	Lever AR	May H	McLaren R	Montgomery SWI	Morris EC	Pembery GD	Rowland A	Sherwood AT	Steel A	Stevenson E	Stitfall AE	Stitfall RF	Sullivan D	Taggart R	Williams DR	Williams GJ
1	Aug 20	Blackburn Rovers	0-1		28265		9	6	11				7	1		2						5	3		10					8	4
2	22	SHEFFIELD WEDNESDAY	1-0	Stevenson	37913	6	9	8	11				7	1		2			5				3		10						4
3	27	SWANSEA TOWN	1-0	Best	60855	6	9	8	11				7	1		2			5				3		10						4
4	29	Sheffield Wednesday	1-1	Stevenson (p)	32765	6	8		11	9			7	1		2			5				3		10						4
5	Sep 3	TOTTENHAM HOTSPUR	0-1		42649	6	9		11				7	1		2			5				3		10					8	4
6	5	HULL CITY	2-0	Best 2	40254	6	9	10	11					1		2			5				3		8					7	4
7	10	Bury	2-2	Best, R Williams	17371	6	9	10	11				8	1		2			5				3							7	4
8	17	LEICESTER CITY	2-4	Best, Edwards	32044	6	9	10	11				8	1		2			5				3							7	4
9	24	Bradford Park Avenue	3-3	Edwards, R Stitfall 2	13187	6		10	11				4			2			5	1			3		8		9			7	
10	Oct 1	CHESTERFIELD	2-0	Blair, Stevenson	29619	6		10	11				4	1		2			5				3		8		9			7	
11	8	Leeds United	0-2		25523	6		10	11				4	1		2					5		3		8		9			7	
12	22	Coventry City	1-2	Blair	23042	6		10	11				4	1		2			5				3		8		9			7	
13	29	LUTON TOWN	0-0		24011	10	9		11				8	1		2			5			6	3							7	4
14	Nov 5	Barnsley	0-1		18564			6		9				1	11	2			5				3		10		8			7	4
15	12	WEST HAM UNITED	0-1		21644			6		9				1	11	2			5				3		10		8			7	4
16	19	Sheffield United	0-2		24702			6	11				8	1		2			5				3		10		9			7	4
17	26	GRIMSBY TOWN	1-0	R Stitfall	22664	6			11				7	1		2			5				3		10		9			8	4
18	Dec 3	Queen's Park Rangers	1-0	R Stitfall	15954	4		6	11				7	1		2			5				3		10		9			8	
19	10	PRESTON NORTH END	3-2	R Stitfall, Edwards 2	21922	4		6	11				7	1		2			5				3		10		9			8	
20	17	BLACKBURN ROVERS	2-1	Edwards, R Stitfall	19882	4		6	11					1		2			5				3		10	7	9			8	
21	24	Swansea Town	1-5	R Stitfall	27264	4		6		11				1		2			5				3		10	7	9			8	
22	26	Plymouth Argyle	0-0		28585	4		6	11				7	1		2			5				3		10		9			8	
23	27	PLYMOUTH ARGYLE	1-0	Evans	32499	4		10		8		7		1		2			5				3				9	11			6
24	31	Tottenham Hotspur	0-2		59780	4		10				7		1		2			5				3			8	9	11			6
25	Jan 14	BURY	1-0	R Williams	27883	4		10	11					1	7	2			5				3				9			8	6
26	21	Leicester City	0-1		27300	4		10	11	8						2		9	5				3	1			7				6
27	Feb 4	BRADFORD PARK AVE.	1-2	Evans	25164	4		10	11	8			7	1		2			5				3				9				6
28	18	Chesterfield	1-0	Evans	15042	4			11	8			7	1		2			5				3		10		9				6
29	25	LEEDS UNITED	1-0	Evans	28423	4		10	11	9	6		7	1		2			5				3				8				
30	Mar 4	Southampton	1-3	Evans	23475	4		10	11	9	6		7	1		2			5				3				8				
31	11	COVENTRY CITY	1-0	Edwards	22875	4		10	11	9	6	7		1		2			5				3				8				
32	18	Luton Town	0-0		15071	4		10	11	9		7		1		2	8		5				3								6
33	25	BARNSLEY	3-0	Pallister (og), Evans, Grant	19987	4		10	11	8		7		1		2			5				3				9				6
34	Apr 1	Grimsby Town	0-0		14922	4		10	11	8		7							5				3	1			9		2		6
35	7	Brentford	0-1		24584	4		10	11	8		7							5				3	1			9		2		6
36	8	QUEEN'S PARK RANGERS	4-0	Sherwood (p), Evans 2, Lever	21102	4		10	11	8		7				2			5				3	1			9				6
37	10	BRENTFORD	0-0		16260	4		10	11	8		7				2			5				3	1			9				6
38	15	West Ham United	1-0	Lever	14109				11	8		7	4			2			5				3	1			9			10	6
39	17	SOUTHAMPTON	1-1	Edwards	21247	4			11	8		7	6			2							3	1			9			10	5
40	22	SHEFFIELD UNITED	1-2	Lever	33382	4			11	8		7				2			5				3	1			9			10	6
41	29	Preston North End	0-3		13799	4			11	8		7	6			2							3	1			9			10	5
42	May 6	Hull City	1-1	Gorin	18213	4			11	8	6	7				2							3	1			9			10	5
		Apps				37	9	33	36	20	4	12	30	31	3	37	1	1	37	1	1	2	42	10	23	3	33	2	2	26	26
		Goals					5	2	7	8	1	1				3							1		3		7			2	

One own goal

Game 3: the official Football League attendance, which is the number of tickets sold.
57510 were admitted up on the day.

F.A. Cup

Rnd	Date	Opponent	Score	Scorers	Att	Baker WG	Best TH	Blair D	Edwards G	Evans EE	Gorin ER	Grant W	Hollyman KC	Joslin PJ	Lamie R	Lever AR	May H	McLaren R	Montgomery SWI	Morris EC	Pembery GD	Rowland A	Sherwood AT	Steel A	Stevenson E	Stitfall AE	Stitfall RF	Sullivan D	Taggart R	Williams DR	Williams GJ
R3	Jan 7	WEST BROMWICH ALB.	2-2	Evans, G Williams	39980	4		10	11	8			7	1		2			5				3				9				6
rep	11	West Bromwich Albion	1-0	Edwards	37358	4		10	11	8			7	1		2			5				3				9				6
R4	28	Charlton Athletic	1-1	Evans	45829	4		10	11	8			7	1		2			5				3				9				6
rep	Feb 1	CHARLTON ATHLETIC	2-0	Evans 2	37000	4		10	11	8			7	1		2			5				3				9				6
R5	11	Leeds United	1-3	Sherwood (p)	53099	4		10	11	8			7	1		2			5				3				9				6

Welsh Cup

Rnd	Date	Opponent	Score	Scorers	Att	Baker WG	Best TH	Blair D	Edwards G	Evans EE	Gorin ER	Grant W	Hollyman KC	Joslin PJ	Lamie R	Lever AR	May H	McLaren R	Montgomery SWI	Morris EC	Pembery GD	Rowland A	Sherwood AT	Steel A	Stevenson E	Stitfall AE	Stitfall RF	Sullivan D	Taggart R	Williams DR	Williams GJ
R6	Jan 18	EBBW VALE	3-0	Edwards 2, Baker	2500	4			11	8	9					2			5							10	1			7	6
R7	Feb 23	Swansea Town	0-3		11000	6		9	11	8			4	1	7	2			5							10					

Played at 3 in both games: Ken Devonshire. Played at 1 in R6: Bob Stitfall.

49

1950/51   3rd in Division Two

No	Date	Opponent	Score	Scorers	Att	Baker WG	Blair D	Edwards G	Evans EE	Evans LN	Grant W	Hollyman KC	Joslin PJ	Lamie R	Lever AR	Marchant MG	McLaughlin R	Mills DG	Montgomery SWI	Morris EC	Oakley K	Rutter CF	Sherwood AT	Stitfall AE	Stitfall RF	Sullivan D	Tiddy MD	Williams DR	Williams GI
1	Aug 19	Grimsby Town	0-0		20083	6		11	10			4	1				8		5		9		3		2			7	
2	23	Manchester City	1-2	DR Williams	18242		6	11	10			4	1		5		8				9		3		2			7	
3	26	NOTTS COUNTY	2-0	Oakley, Edwards	36646	6		11				4	1				8				9		3		2		10	7	5
4	28	MANCHESTER CITY	1-1	E Evans	32817	6		11	8			4	1								9		3		2		10	7	5
5	Sep 2	Preston North End	1-1	Edwards	25900	6		11	8			4	1								9		3		2		10	7	5
6	4	WEST HAM UNITED	2-1	E Ecans, Blair	32292	6	10	11	9			4	1	7									3		2			8	5
7	9	BURY	2-2	Lamie, E Evans	29797	6	10	11	9			4	1	7									3		2			8	5
8	16	Queen's Park Rangers	2-3	E Evans, Nelson (og)	19236	6	10	11	9			4	1	7			8						3		2				5
9	23	CHESTERFIELD	1-0	Capel (og)	27754	6		11	9			4	1				8		5				3		2		10	7	
10	30	Leicester City	1-1	Blair	22696	6	9	11	10			4	1				8		5				3		2	7			
11	Oct 7	Blackburn Rovers	0-2		24831	6	9	11	8		7	4	1				10		5				3		2				
12	14	SOUTHAMPTON	2-2	Blair, Mallett (og)	26409	6	9		10		7	4	1				11		5				3		2				8
13	21	Doncaster Rovers	0-0		26356	6	10		9		7	4					11		5	1		2	3						8
14	28	BRENTFORD	1-1	Blair	22885	6	10		9		7	4					11		5	1			3		2				8
15	Nov 4	Swansea Town	0-1		26393	6					8	6					4		5	1			3		2			7	9
16	11	HULL CITY	2-1	DR Williams, Blair	25007		10	11			7	9	1				4		5				3		2			8	6
17	18	Barnsley	0-0		21818		10	11			9	4	1						5				3		2	7		8	6
18	25	SHEFFIELD UNITED	2-0	Edwards, DR Williams	25622		10	11			9	4	1						5			2	3			7		8	6
19	Dec 2	Luton Town	1-1	Grant	13062		10	11			9	4	1						5			2	3			7		8	6
20	9	LEEDS UNITED	1-0	Edwards	23716		10	11			9	4	1						5			2	3			7		8	6
21	16	GRIMSBY TOWN	5-2	Grant 3, DR Williams 2	15364		10	11			9	4	1						5			2	3			7		8	6
22	23	Notts County	2-1	Grant, DR Williams	27634		10	11			9	4	1						5			2	3			7		8	6
23	25	COVENTRY CITY	2-1	Edwards 2	32778		10	11			9	4	1						5			2	3			7		8	6
24	26	Coventry City	1-2	Grant	33194	6		11		10	9	4	1						5			2				7		8	3
25	30	PRESTON NORTH END	0-2		26717			11		10	9	4	1						5			2	3			7		8	6
26	Jan 13	Bury	2-1	Edwards, Griffiths (og)	10726	6		11		10	9	4	1				8		5				3			7			2
27	20	QUEEN'S PARK RANGERS	4-2	Grant 2, McLaughlin, Tiddy	21017	6		11			9	4	1				8		5				3			7			2
28	Feb 3	Chesterfield	3-0	Grant 2, Marchant	12998	6	10	11			9	4	1			8						2	3			7			5
29	17	LEICESTER CITY	2-2	Marchant, Baker	23583	6	10	11			9	4	1			8			5				3	2		7			
30	24	BLACKBURN ROVERS	1-0	Grant	32811	6	10	11			9	4	1			8			5				3						2
31	Mar 3	Southampton	1-1	Edwards	24233	6	10	11			9	4	1						5				3			7		8	2
32	10	DONCASTER ROVERS	0-0		27724	6	10	11			9	4	1			8			5				3			7			2
33	17	Brentford	0-4		19663	6	10	11			9	4	1			8			5				3			7			2
34	23	Birmingham City	0-0		15054	6		11			9	4	1			8	10		5				3			7			2
35	24	SWANSEA TOWN	1-0	Marchant	41074	6		11			9	4	1			8	10		5				3			7			2
36	26	BIRMINGHAM CITY	2-1	McLaughlin, Grant	36992	6		11			9	4	1			8	10		5				3			7			2
37	31	Hull City	0-2		20239	6		11			9	4	1			8	10		5				3			7			2
38	Apr 7	BARNSLEY	1-1	Grant	27631	6	10	11			9	4	1					8	5				3			7			2
39	14	Sheffield United	2-1	Tiddy, Edwards	20747	6		11			9	4	1			8	10		5				3			7			2
40	21	LUTON TOWN	2-1	Grant, Owen (og)	28022	6		11			9	4	1			8	10		5				3			7			2
41	28	Leeds United	0-2		14765	6		11		10	9	4	1			8			5				3			7			2
42	May 5	West Ham United	0-0		17942	6	10	11			9	4	1			8			5				3			7			2
		Apps				31	27	39	16	1	32	42	39	3	1	12	21	1	34	3	5	10	40	1	17	5	26	20	36
		Goals				1	5	9	4		14			1		3	2				1						2	6	

Five own goals

F.A. Cup

	Date	Opponent	Score	Scorers	Att	Baker WG	Blair D	Edwards G	Evans EE	Evans LN	Grant W	Hollyman KC	Joslin PJ	Lamie R	Lever AR	Marchant MG	McLaughlin R	Mills DG	Montgomery SWI	Morris EC	Oakley K	Rutter CF	Sherwood AT	Stitfall AE	Stitfall RF	Sullivan D	Tiddy MD	Williams DR	Williams GI
R3	Jan 6	West Ham United	1-2	Grant	30000	6		11		10	9	4	1						5				3			8	7		2

Welsh Cup

	Date	Opponent	Score	Scorers	Att	Baker WG	Blair D	Edwards G	Evans EE	Evans LN	Grant W	Hollyman KC	Joslin PJ	Lamie R	Lever AR	Marchant MG	McLaughlin R	Mills DG	Montgomery SWI	Morris EC	Oakley K	Rutter CF	Sherwood AT	Stitfall AE	Stitfall RF	Sullivan D	Tiddy MD	Williams DR	Williams GI
R5	Jan 31	BARRY TOWN	8-0	* see below	1500	6	10				7	9	4	1		8			5			2					11		3
R6	Mar 7	Bangor City	7-1	* see below	12000	6	10	11				9	4			8			5							5	7		3
SF	Apr 16	Wrexham	1-0	Edwards	5000	6		11				9	4	1		8	10		5			2					7		
F	May 7	Merthyr Tydfil	1-1	Grant	18000	6	10	11				9	4	1		8			5			2					7		2
rep	17	Merthyr Tydfil	2-3	Edwards, Tiddy	18000	6	10	11				9	4			8			5			2				5	7		3

Final and replay at Swansea
Scorers in R5: Marchant 2, L Evans 4, Grant, Kelly (og)
Scorers in R6: Edwards 3, Tiddy 2, Grant, Marchant

Played at 2 in R6 and 3 in SF: Crad Wilcox. Played at 1 in Final replay: Ron Howells

1951/52 — 2nd in Division Two: Promoted

#			Opponent	Score	Scorers	Att	Baker WG	Blair D	Chisholm KMcT	Edwards G	Evans EE	Evans LN	Grant W	Hollyman KC	Howells RG	Hughes I	McLaughlin R	Montgomery SWI	Norman AG	Nugent WC	Rutter CF	Sherwood AT	Stitfall RF	Sullivan D	Tiddy MD	Williams DR	Williams GJ
1	Aug	18	LEICESTER CITY	4-0	Edwards, Grant 2, DR Williams	28973	4	10		11			9			1					2	3		5	7	8	6
2		20	ROTHERHAM UNITED	2-4	Grant 2	32442	4	10		11			9			1					2	3		5	7	8	6
3		25	Nottingham Forest	3-2	Edwards 2, DR Williams	31776	6	10		11			9	4		1		5			2				7	8	3
4		27	Rotherham United	0-2		17062	6	10		11			9	4		1		5			2				7	8	3
5	Sep	1	BRENTFORD	2-0	Grant 2	27772	6	10		11	8		9	4		1		5				3			7		2
6		8	Doncaster Rovers	0-1		19676	6	10		11	8		9	4		1		5				3			7		2
7		12	Leeds United	1-2	E Evans	12680	6			11	10		9			1		5				3		4	7	8	2
8		15	EVERTON	3-1	Grant 2, E Evans	23923	4			11	10		9			1		5			2	3			7	8	6
9		17	SHEFFIELD UNITED	1-1	Grant	29176	4			11	10		9			1		5			2	3			7	8	6
10		22	Southampton	1-1	Tiddy	21672	4				10		9			1		5	11		2	3			7	8	6
11		29	SHEFFIELD WEDNESDAY	2-1	Grant 2	30352	4	10		11			9			1		5			2	3			7	8	6
12	Oct	6	COVENTRY CITY	4-1	Grant 2, Edwards, Tiddy	26277	4			11			9	8		1		5			2	3			7	10	6
13		13	West Ham United	1-1	McLaughlin	24103	4			11			9			1	8	5			2	3			7	10	6
14		27	Barnsley	0-2		11168	4			11			9			1	8				2	3		5	7	10	6
15	Nov	3	HULL CITY	1-0	Grant	23459	6			11			9	4		1	8	5		7	2	3				10	
16		10	Blackburn Rovers	1-0	Edwards	22477	6			11			9	4		1	8	5			2	3			7	10	
17		17	QUEEN'S PARK RANGERS	3-1	Blair 2, Sherwood (p)	21211	6	8		11			9	4		1		5			2	3			7	10	
18		24	Notts County	1-1	Montgomery	19452	6	8		11			9	4		1		5			2	3			7	10	
19	Dec	1	LUTON TOWN	3-0	Blair 2, Grant	26106	6	8		11			9	4		1		5			2	3			7	10	
20		8	Bury	1-1	Edwards	7887	6	8		11			9			1		5			2	3			7	10	4
21		15	Leicester City	0-3		26021	6	8		11			9			1		5			2	3			7	10	4
22		22	NOTTM. FOREST	4-1	Sherwood (p), Blair 2, Grant	19860	4	8		11			9			1	6	5				3			7	10	2
23		25	Swansea Town	1-1	Tiddy	19260	4	8		11			9			1	6	5				3			7	10	2
24		26	SWANSEA TOWN	3-0	Baker, Grant, Tiddy	46003	4	8		11			9		1		6	5			2				10	7	3
25		29	Brentford	1-1	Tiddy	27547		8		11			9		1		6	5			2	3			10	7	4
26	Jan	5	DONCASTER ROVERS	2-1	Sherwood 2	28404		8		11			9		1		6	5			2	3			10	7	4
27		19	Everton	0-3		49230	4	8					9		1		6	5			2	3			10	7	11
28		26	SOUTHAMPTON	1-0	Grant	23205	4			11			9			1	8	5			2	3			7	10	6
29	Feb	9	Sheffield Wednesday	2-4	E Evans 2	42867	4			11	10		9			1	6	5			2	3		8	7		
30		16	Coventry City	1-2	Sullivan	26410	4			11	10		9			1	6	5			2	3		8	7		
31	Mar	1	WEST HAM UNITED	1-1	Blair	29495		8	10		11		9			1		5				3	2	8	7		6
32		12	Sheffield United	1-6	Grant	16398	6	8	10				9	4		1		5			2			11	7		3
33		15	BARNSLEY	3-0	Chisholm 2, L Evans	24542		8	10			11	9			1	4	5			2	3			7		6
34		22	Hull City	0-0		27009		8	10			11	9			1	4	5			2	3			7		6
35	Apr	5	Queen's Park Rangers	1-1	Grant	17938	6		10	11			9			1		5				3	2		7	8	
36		11	Birmingham City	2-3	Grant, Chisholm	32941	6		10	11			9			1	4	5			2	3			7	8	
37		12	NOTTS COUNTY	1-0	Chisholm	24178	6	8	10				9			1	4	5			2	3		11	7		
38		14	BIRMINGHAM CITY	3-1	Chisholm 2, Grant	25470	6	8	10	11			9			1	4	5				3			7		2
39		19	Luton Town	2-2	Sherwood (p), DR Williams	14186	6	8	10	11			9			1	4	5				3	2		7		
40		21	BLACKBURN ROVERS	3-1	Grant, Chisholm, Sherwood (p)	31169	6	8	10	11			9			1	4	5				3			7		2
41		26	BURY	3-0	Blair 2, Grant	39907	6	8	10	11			9			1	4	5				3			7		2
42	May	3	LEEDS UNITED	3-1	Grant 2, Chisholm	45925	6	8	10	11			9			1	4	5				3			7		2
			Apps				38	28	11	36	8	2	42	11	16	26	23	39	1	1	30	38	3	13	35	31	30
			Goals				1	9	8	6	4	1	26				1	1				6		1	5	3	

F.A. Cup

			Opponent	Score	Scorers	Att	Baker WG	Blair D	Chisholm KMcT	Edwards G	Evans EE	Evans LN	Grant W	Hollyman KC	Howells RG	Hughes I	McLaughlin R	Montgomery SWI	Norman AG	Nugent WC	Rutter CF	Sherwood AT	Stitfall RF	Sullivan D	Tiddy MD	Williams DR	Williams GJ
R3	Jan	12	SWINDON TOWN	1-1	Grant	40000	4	8		11			9			1	6	5			2				7	10	
rep		15	Swindon Town	0-1	(aet)	24207	4			11	8		9			1	6	5			2	3		10	7		

Played at 3 in R3: C Wilcox

Welsh Cup

			Opponent	Score	Scorers	Att	Baker WG	Blair D	Chisholm KMcT	Edwards G	Evans EE	Evans LN	Grant W	Hollyman KC	Howells RG	Hughes I	McLaughlin R	Montgomery SWI	Norman AG	Nugent WC	Rutter CF	Sherwood AT	Stitfall RF	Sullivan D	Tiddy MD	Williams DR	Williams GJ
R5	Jan	3	Milford United	3-1	Wilcox 2, E Evans	2500				11	9					1		5		7	2			3	10		4
R6	Feb	2	Merthyr Tydfil	1-3	Edwards	13000		9		11					4	1	8			7	2	3		5		10	6

Played in R5: C Wilcox (8) and D Moss (6)

51

1952/53   12th in Divison One

#		Date	Opponent	Score	Scorers	Att	Baker WG	Blair D	Chisholm KMcT	Edwards G	Frowen J	Grant W	Harrington AC	Hazlett G	Hollyman KC	Howells RG	Mansell J	McLaughlin R	Montgomery SWI	Northcott TT	Sherwood AT	Stitfall RF	Sullivan D	Thomas WK	Tiddy MD	Vearncombe G	Williams DR	Williams GI
1	Aug	23	Wolverhampton Wan.	0-1		52309	6	8	10	11		9				1			5		3		4		7			2
2		27	Middlesbrough	0-3		42159	6	8	10	11		9		7		1		4	5		3	2						
3		30	SHEFFIELD WEDNESDAY	4-0	Hazlett, Chisholm 2, Grant	43478	4	8	10	11		9		7		1			5		3	2						6
4	Sep	3	MIDDLESBROUGH	1-1	Blair	51512	4	8	10	11		9		7		1			5		3	2						6
5		6	Tottenham Hotspur	1-2	Chisholm	62150	4	8	10	11		9		7		1			5		3	2						6
6		10	West Bromwich Albion	0-1		23343	4	10	9	11	2	7				1			5		3						8	6
7		13	BURNLEY	0-0		45182	4	8	10	11		9		7		1			5		3	2						6
8		17	WEST BROMWICH ALB.	1-2	Thomas	40338	4		10	11	2	9		7		1			5		3			8				6
9		20	Preston North End	3-2	Blair, DR Williams, Chisholm	29337	4	9	10	11						1			5		3	2			7		8	6
10		27	STOKE CITY	2-0	DR Williams 2	39223	4	9	10	11						1			5		3	2			7		8	6
11	Oct	4	Manchester City	2-2	Chisholm, Tiddy	33551	4	9	10	11						1			5		3	2			7		8	6
12		11	Charlton Athletic	1-3	Edwards	30583	4		10	11		9				1			5		3	2			7		8	6
13		25	Derby County	1-1	Chisholm	23208	4	8	10	11						1			5	9	3	2			7			6
14	Nov	1	BLACKPOOL	2-2	Northcott, Chisholm	43662	4		10	11						1			5	9	3	2	8		7			6
15		8	Chelsea	2-0	Edwards, Sherwood	52139	4		10	11						1			5	9	3	2	8		7			6
16		15	MANCHESTER UNITED	1-2	Chisholm	40096	4	6	10	11						1			5	9	3	2	8		7			
17		22	Portsmouth	2-0	Northcott, Grant	31258	4	6	10	11		8				1	3		5	9		2			7			
18	Dec	13	SUNDERLAND	4-1	Grant 2, Edwards, Chisholm	42518	4	6	10	11		8				1				9	3	2	5		7			
19		20	WOLVERHAMPTON W.	0-0		25598	4	6	10	11		8				1				9	3	2	5		7			
20		25	Newcastle United	0-3		36143	4	6	10	11		8				1				9	3	2	5		7			
21		27	NEWCASTLE UNITED	0-0		52202	4		10	11		8		7		1		6	5	9	3	2						
22	Jan	3	Sheffield Wednesday	0-2		39652	4	6	10	11		8				1			5	9	3	2			7			
23		17	TOTTENHAM HOTSPUR	0-0		36423		6	10	11					4	1			5	9	3	2	8		7			
24		24	Burnley	0-0		29491			10	11		8			4	1			5	9	3	2	6		7			
25	Feb	7	PRESTON NORTH END	0-2		32445	4	6	10			9		8		1			5	11	3	2			7			
26		14	Stoke City	0-0		21626		10		11		9			4	1		6	5		3	2	8		7			
27		21	MANCHESTER CITY	6-0	* See below	24886	4	10		11		9				1			5		3	2	6	7			8	
28		28	CHARLTON ATHLETIC	0-1		35248	4	10		11		9				1			5		3	2	6	7			8	
29	Mar	7	Arsenal	1-0	Blair	59780		10				9			4	1			5	11	3	2	6		7			8
30		11	BOLTON WANDERERS	1-0	Chisholm	31099			10			9			4	1			5	11	3	2	6		7			8
31		14	DERBY COUNTY	2-0	Northcott, DR Williams	33670			10			9			4	1	3		5	11		2	6		7			8
32		25	Blackpool	1-0	Northcott	15227	6		10			9			4	1	3		5	11		2			7			8
33		28	CHELSEA	3-3	Tiddy 2, Blair	19830		6	10		2	9	4			1	3		5	11					7			8
34	Apr	3	Liverpool	1-2	Northcott	52259	4	10				9				1			5	11	3	2	6		7			8
35		4	Manchester United	4-1	Grant 2, Tiddy, Chisholm	38987		6	10			9	4			1			5	11	3	2			7			8
36		6	LIVERPOOL	4-0	Grant 2, Chisholm 2	35419		6	10			9	4			1			5	11	3	2			7			8
37		11	PORTSMOUTH	0-1		35945		6	10			9	4			1			5	11	3	2			7			8
38		18	Bolton Wanderers	1-0	Sherwood	18037			10			9	4			1			5	11	3	2	6		7			8
39		22	ARSENAL	0-0		57893		11	10			9	4			1			5		3	2	6		7			8
40		25	ASTON VILLA	1-2	Grant	29917			10	11		9	4			1			5		3	2	6		7			8
41		27	Sunderland	2-4	Thomas, Tiddy	7469		10		5			4			1	3			9		2	6	11	7		8	
42		29	Aston Villa	0-2		18876		6	10		2		4						5	9	3			11	7	1	8	
					Apps		29	32	34	28	6	31	10	7	7	41	11	3	39	23	39	27	21	6	32	1	21	14
					Goals			4	13	4		11		1						5	2			4	5		5	

Scorers in game 27: DR Williams, Thomas 2, Grant 2, Edwards

F.A. Cup

		Date	Opponent	Score	Scorer	Att	Baker WG	Blair D	Chisholm KMcT	Edwards G	Frowen J	Grant W	Harrington AC	Hazlett G	Hollyman KC	Howells RG	Mansell J	McLaughlin R	Montgomery SWI	Northcott TT	Sherwood AT	Stitfall RF	Sullivan D	Thomas WK	Tiddy MD	Vearncombe G	Williams DR	Williams GI
R3	Jan	10	Halifax Town	1-3	Baker	25000	4	6	9	11		8				1	10		5		3	2						

Played at 7: WC Nugent

Welsh Cup

		Date	Opponent	Score	Scorers	Att	Baker WG	Blair D	Chisholm KMcT	Edwards G	Frowen J	Grant W	Harrington AC	Hazlett G	Hollyman KC	Howells RG	Mansell J	McLaughlin R	Montgomery SWI	Northcott TT	Sherwood AT	Stitfall RF	Sullivan D	Thomas WK	Tiddy MD	Vearncombe G	Williams DR	Williams GI
R6	Jan	15	Merthyr Tydfil	5-2	Chisholm 2, Hazlett, Northcott 2	8000			10		2			4	7			3	6	5	9					1	8	
R7		31	Barry Town	3-2	Tiddy, Northcott 2	9000			10		2	8				1	3	4	5	9			6		7		8	
SF	Mar	21	Rhyl	0-1		10000	6		10	11		9			4	1	3		5			2			7		8	

Played at 11 in R6 and R7: WC Nugent

#	Date	Opponent	Score	Scorers	Att	Baker WG	Blair D	Chisholm KMcT	Dudley FE	Edwards G	Ford T	Frowen J	Gale CM	Grant W	Harrington AC	Howells RG	Mansell J	Montgomery SWJ	Northcott TT	Nugent WC	Oakley K	Parfitt HE	Rainford JW	Rutter CF	Sherwood AT	Stitfall RF	Sullivan D	Thomas PJ	Thomas WK	Tiddy MD	Vearncombe G	Williams DR
1	Aug 19	Middlesbrough	0-0		33726	4								9		1		5		11			10		3	2	6			7		8
2	22	ASTON VILLA	2-1	Rainford, P Thomas	36671	4								9		1		5		11			10		3	2	6	7				8
3	26	Huddersfield Town	0-2		30089									9	4	1		5					10		3	2	6	7	11			8
4	29	Wolverhampton Wan.	1-3	Grant	33221			10				2		9	8	1		5							3		6					7
5	Sep 2	HUDDERSFIELD T	2-1	Grant, Chisholm	29446	6	8	10		11				9	4	1	3	5									2					7
6	5	SUNDERLAND	1-1	Chisholm, Edwards	42002	6	8	10		11				9	4	1	3	5									2					7
7	7	Sheffield United	1-0	Chisholm	34043	4	8	10		11				9		1	3	5								6	2					7
8	12	Manchester City	1-1	Edwards	31915	6	8	10		11				9	4	1	3	5									2					7
9	16	SHEFFIELD UNITED	2-0	Edwards, Grant	27350	4	8	10		11				9	6	1	3	5								2				7		
10	19	BOLTON WANDERERS	1-1	Chisholm	35788	6	8	10		11				9	4	1	3	5								2				7		
11	26	ARSENAL	0-3		49137	6	8	10		11				9	4	1	3	5							2				7			
12	Oct 3	Portsmouth	1-1	Sullivan	31766	6				11				8	4	1	3	5	9						2		10			7		
13	10	Preston North End	2-1	Chisholm 2	23500	4		10		11				8			3	5	9		7				2		6				1	
14	17	TOTTENHAM HOTSPUR	1-0	Grant (p)	41083	4		10		11				8		1	3	5	9						2		6			7		
15	24	Burnley	0-3		29539			10	9	11				8		1	3	5	7						2		6					
16	31	CHARLTON ATHLETIC	5-0	Dudley, Chisholm 3, Tiddy	25340	4		10	9	11						1	3	5	8						2		6			7		
17	Nov 7	Newcastle United	0-4		42355	4	10		9	11						1	3	5	8						2		6			7		
18	14	MANCHESTER UNITED	1-6	Chisholm	26844	4		10	9	11				7		1	3	5	8						2		6					
19	21	West Bromwich Albion	1-6	Chisholm	39444	4	6	10	8	11				9	2	1		5								3				7		
20	28	LIVERPOOL	3-1	Grant, Chisholm, Edwards	21284	6	8	10		11				9	4	1		5							2	3				7		
21	Dec 5	Sheffield Wednesday	1-2	Chisholm	26597	4		10		11	9			8		1		5							3	2	6			7		
22	12	MIDDLESBROUGH	1-0	Ford	31776	4		10		11	9					1		5	8						3	2	6			7		
23	19	Aston Villa	2-1	Northcott 2	27012	4	6			11	9					1		5	10	8					2	3				7		
24	26	Chelsea	0-2		61336	4	6			11	9					1		5	10	8					2	3				7		
25	28	CHELSEA	0-0		36958	4	6			11	9					1		5	10	8					2		3			7		
26	Jan 2	WOLVERHAMPTON W.	1-3	Nugent	42521	4				11	9					1		5	10	8					2	3	6			7		
27	16	Sunderland	0-5		40629					11	9		2	10	4	1		5							3					7		
28	23	MANCHESTER CITY	0-3		22516	4				11			3		8			5	10					9	2		6			7	1	
29	Feb 6	Bolton Wanderers	0-3		30777	4				11	9		10					5	8						2	3	6			7	1	
30	13	Arsenal	1-1	Ford	45497	4					9		2	11				5	10	8					3		6			7	1	
31	27	PRESTON NORTH END	2-1	Grant 2	30502	4					9		2	11				5	10	8					3		6			7	1	
32	Mar 3	PORTSMOUTH	3-2	Nugent, Tiddy, Grant	17842	4					9		2	11				5	10	8					3		6			7	1	
33	6	Tottenham Hotspur	1-0	Tiddy	45248	4					9		2	11				5	10	8					3		6			7	1	
34	13	BURNLEY	1-0	Sullivan	33413	4					9		2	11				5	10	8					3		6			7	1	
35	20	Charlton Athletic	2-3	Grant, Ford	20717	4					9	5	2	11					10	8					3		6			7	1	
36	27	NEWCASTLE UNITED	2-1	Nugent, Tiddy	26242	4				11				9		1		5		8					3	2	6			7		
37	Apr 3	Manchester United	3-2	Grant 2, Sullivan	24616	4				11				9		1		5		8				6	3	2	10			7		
38	10	WEST BROMWICH ALB.	2-0	Grant, Ford	43614	4					9			11		1		5	10	8					3	2	6			7		
39	16	Blackpool	1-4	Ford	26194	4					9			11		1		5	10	8					3	2	6			7		
40	17	Liverpool	1-0	Northcott	41340	4				11	9			7		1		5	10	8					3	2	6					
41	19	BLACKPOOL	0-1		44508	4					9			11				5	10	8				6	3	2				7	1	
42	24	SHEFFIELD WEDNESDAY	2-2	Sherwood, Ford	15777					11	9		5	4					8	7					3	2	10				1	

Played in one game: CW Baker (game 42, at 6), R McLaughlin (4, at 11).
Played at 4 in games 4 and 15: KC Hollyman

	Baker WG	Blair D	Chisholm KMcT	Dudley FE	Edwards G	Ford T	Frowen J	Gale CM	Grant W	Harrington AC	Howells RG	Mansell J	Montgomery SWJ	Northcott TT	Nugent WC	Oakley K	Parfitt HE	Rainford JW	Rutter CF	Sherwood AT	Stitfall RF	Sullivan D	Thomas PJ	Thomas WK	Tiddy MD	Vearncombe G	Williams DR
Apps	37	13	17	5	29	19	3	9	32	14	31	14	40	24	22	2	1	3	14	22	22	33	4	3	26	11	8
Goals			12	1	4	6			12					3	3				1		1	3	1		4		

F.A. Cup

	Date	Opponent	Score	Scorers	Att	Baker	Blair	Edwards	Ford	Frowen	Gale	Howells	Montgomery	Northcott	Nugent	Sherwood	Stitfall	Sullivan	Thomas PJ
R3	Jan 9	PETERBOROUGH UTD.	3-1	Ford 2, Northcott	34000	4	6	11	9			1	5	10	8	2		3	7
R4	30	PORT VALE	0-2		27000	4	10	11	9	5	8	1		7		2	3	6	

Welsh Cup

	Date	Opponent	Score	Scorers	Att
R5	Jan 20	Barry Town	1-1	Burder	2500
rep	Feb 10	BARRY TOWN	4-2	Nugent 2, Tiddy, Ford	4500
R7	20	Merthyr Tydfil	5-3	Grant 3, Nugent, Lowe (og)	7000
SF	Mar 24	Flint Town United	1-2	Northcott	10500

Bye in R6
SF at Wrexham

Played in R5: C Burder (at 11, one goal), T Bevan (6)
Played at 4 in R7 and SF: D Callan

1954/55   20th in Division One

#		Date	Opponent	Score	Scorers	Att	Baker CW	Baker WG	Dixon CH	Edwards G	Ford T	Frowen J	Gale CM	Grant W	Harrington AC	Hitchens GA	Howells RG	Jones I	Montgomery SWI	Northcott TT	Nugent WC	Nutt GE	Rutter CF	Sherwood AT	Stitfall RF	Stockin R	Sullivan D	Tiddy MD	Vearncombe G	Williams DR
1	Aug	21	Burnley	0-1		27836	4				9			11			1		5	10				3	2		6	7		8
2		25	PRESTON NORTH END	2-5	Tiddy, Ford	39448	4				9			11	6		1			10				3	2		5	7		8
3		28	LEICESTER CITY	2-1	Northcott, Ford	25938		6		11	9	5		4						10			2	3				7	1	8
4	Sep	1	Preston North End	1-7	Grant	29057		6		11		5	9	4						10			2	3				7	1	8
5		4	Chelsea	1-1	Tiddy	42688		6		11			9	4			1		5	10				3	2			7		8
6		8	SHEFFIELD UNITED	1-1	Tiddy	28511		6		11	9				4		1		5					3	2	10	8	7		
7		11	HUDDERSFIELD T	1-1	Sherwood (p)	21840		6			9	5			4		1			11				3	2	10	8	7		
8		13	Sheffield United	3-1	Sullivan, Ford, Stocklin	18090					9				4		1	6	5	11				3	2	10	8	7		
9		18	MANCHESTER CITY	3-0	Sherwood, Ewing (og), Stockin	28847					9				4		1	6	5		11			3	2	10	8	7		
10		25	Everton	1-1	Nugent	54248			7		9				4		1	6	5		11			3	2	10	8			
11	Oct	2	NEWCASTLE UNITED	4-2	Sullivan, Stockin, Ford 2	34760					9				4		1	6	5		11			3	2	10	8	7		
12		9	Manchester United	2-5	Ford, Stockin	41159					9				4		1	6	5		11			3	2	10	8	7		
13		16	Wolverhampton Wan.	1-1	Stockin	30166									4		1	6	5	9	11		3		2	10	8	7		
14		23	Charlton Athletic	1-4	Ford, Stockin	26376					9				4		1	6	5		11		2	3		10	8	7		
15		30	BOLTON WANDERERS	2-2	Wheeler (og), Nugent	31698			7		9						1	6	5	8	11			3	2	10	4			
16	Nov	6	Tottenham Hotspur	2-0	Stockin 2	38805					9				4		1		5	8	11		2	3		10	6	7		
17		13	SHEFFIELD WEDNESDAY	5-3	Nugent 2, Northcott, Sullivan, Tiddy	15998					9				4		1		5	10	11		2	3			6	7		8
18		20	Portsmouth	3-1	Northcott 2, Ford	31292					9						1	6	5	10	11		2	3			4	7		8
19		27	BLACKPOOL	1-2	Montgomery	19823			7		9							6	5		11		2	3		10	4		1	8
20	Dec	4	Aston Villa	2-0	Ford 2	25186					9						1	6	5	8	11		2	3		10	4	7		
21		11	SUNDERLAND	0-1		32098					9						1	6	5	8	11		2	3		10	4	7		
22		18	BURNLEY	0-3		22035					9				4		1		5	8	11		7	3	2	10	6			
23		25	WEST BROMWICH ALB.	3-2	Ford 2, Montgomery	22845					9						1	4	5		11		7	3	2	10	6			8
24		27	West Bromwich Albion	0-1		50885					9				6		1	4			11		7	3	2	10	5			8
25	Jan	1	Leicester City	1-2	Nutt	25408									6		1	4		9		11	7	3	2	10	5			8
26	Feb	5	Manchester City	1-4	Ford (p)	31922		4			9						1	6				11	7	3	2	10	5			8
27		12	EVERTON	4-3	Ford 2, Stockin 2	17108					9				4		1	6				11	7	3	2	10	5			8
28		26	MANCHESTER UNITED	3-0	Stockin 2, Nutt	16329					9	3			4		1		5	11		7			2	10	6			8
29	Mar	5	Sunderland	1-1	Stockin	41096		6			9				4		1		5	11			7	3	2	10				8
30		12	CHARLTON ATHLETIC	4-3	Nutt, Ford, Williams, Northcott	20261					9	5			4		1			11		7	2	3		10	6			8
31		19	Bolton Wanderers	0-0		25321					9	5			4		1			11	8	7	2	3		10	6			
32		23	CHELSEA	0-1		16649					9	5			4		1			11		7	2	3		10	6			8
33		26	TOTTENHAM HOTSPUR	1-2	Ford	14461					9	5			4		1			10	11	7	2	3			6			8
34	Apr	2	Sheffield Wednesday	1-1	Nutt	19541					9				4		1		5	10	11	7		3	2		6	8		
35		8	Arsenal	0-2		39052									4		1		5	9	11	7		3	2		6	8		10
36		9	ASTON VILLA	0-1		20720					9	5			4		1	6			11		2	3		10		7		8
37		11	ARSENAL	1-2	Harrington	29080					9	5			4		1				11	7		3	2	10	6			8
38		16	Blackpool	0-0		21832					9	5			4		1				11			3	2	10	6	7		8
39		23	PORTSMOUTH	1-1	Williams	21185					9	5			4		1				11			3	2	10	6	7		8
40		27	Newcastle United	0-3		19252					9	5			4						11		2	3		10	6	7	1	8
41		30	WOLVERHAMPTON W.	3-2	Ford 2, Hitchens	30903					9				4	8		6		11				3	2	10	5	7	1	
42	May	2	Huddersfield Town	0-2		10473		5							4	9		6		10	11		2	3				7	1	8
			Apps				2	8	3	4	36	11	2	5	34	2	36	20	24	29	24	16	22	34	26	30	36	27	6	25
			Goals								19			1	1	1			2	5	4	4		2		12	3	4		2

Two own goals

F.A. Cup

#		Date	Opponent	Score		Att	Ford T	Harrington AC	Howells RG	Jones I	Montgomery SWI	Northcott TT	Nugent WC	Rutter CF	Sherwood AT	Stockin R	Tiddy MD
R3	Jan	8	Arsenal	0-1		51298	9	6	1	4	5	11	8	2	3	10	7

Welsh Cup

#		Date	Opponent	Score	Scorers	Att	Baker CW	Dixon CH	Ford T	Harrington AC	Howells RG	Jones I	Montgomery SWI	Northcott TT	Nugent WC	Nutt GE	Rutter CF	Sherwood AT	Stitfall RF	Stockin R	Sullivan D	Tiddy MD	Williams DR
R5	Jan	12	Pembroke	7-0	Ford 4, Tiddy, Nugent, Stockin	4000	4		9		1	6		10	11	3	2			8	5	7	
R6	Feb	17	Newport County	3-1	Sullivan, Ford, Stockin	10223			9	4	1		5	11		7	2	3		10	6		8
SF	Apr	13	Chester	0-2		7961	4	11		9	1	6	5		8		7		2	10			

SF at Wrexham

Played at 3 in SF: H Parfitt

1955/56   17th in Division One

#	Date	Opponent	Score	Scorers	Att	Baker CW	Callan D	Davies RT	Dixon CH	Ford T	Frowen J	Gale CM	Harrington AC	Hitchens GA	Howells RG	Jones B	Jones I	Kirtley JH	Malloy D	McSeveney JH	Nugent WC	Nutt GE	O'Halloran N	Rutter CF	Sherwood AT	Stitfall RF	Stockin R	Sullivan D	Vearncombe G	Walsh JB	Williams DR
1	Aug 20	SUNDERLAND	3-1	McSeveney 2, Ford	36098				7	9			4		1		6	8		11					2	3	10	5			
2	23	Arsenal	1-3	Stockin	31361				7			5	4	9	1		6	8		11					2		10	3			
3	27	Aston Villa	0-2		32893				7	9			4		1		6	8		11					2	3	10	5			
4	31	BOLTON WANDERERS	1-0	Harrington	26973		2		7	9	5		4		1			8		11		10				3		6			
5	Sep 3	WOLVERHAMPTON W.	1-9	Stockin	42546				7	9	5		4		1			8		11					2	3	10	6			
6	7	Bolton Wanderers	0-4		25012			2	7	9			4		1		6	8		11					3			5			10
7	10	Manchester City	1-3	Williams	33240				7	9			4		1		6	10		11					2	3		5			8
8	17	SHEFFIELD UNITED	3-2	Harrington, Ford, Hitchens	23337				7	9			4	8	1		6	10		11					2	3		5			
9	24	HUDDERSFIELD T	1-2	Kirtley	25117			6	7	9			4	8	1			10		11					2	3		5			
10	Oct 1	Blackpool	1-2	Ford	33451				7	9			4		1			10		11				6	3	2		5			8
11	8	Preston North End	2-1	Ford, Stockin	19433					9			6		1			8		11				4	3	2	10	5		7	
12	15	BURNLEY	2-2	Ford 2	24338					9			6		1			8		11				4	3	2	10	5		7	
13	22	West Bromwich Albion	1-2	Kirtley	22131			2		9			6		1			8		11				4	3		10	5		7	
14	29	MANCHESTER UNITED	0-1		27795					9			6		1			8		11				4	3	2	10	5		7	
15	Nov 5	Tottenham Hotspur	1-1	Walsh	34368						5			9	1			8		11				4	3	2	10	6		7	
16	12	EVERTON	3-1	Walsh, McSeveney 2	22439						5			9	1			8		11				4	3	2	10	6		7	
17	19	Newcastle United	0-4		35603						5			9	1			8		11				4	3	2	10	6		7	
18	26	BIRMINGHAM CITY	2-1	Kirtley, Dixon	23638	6			11				4	9	1			8		10						3	2	5		7	
19	Dec 3	Luton Town	0-3		21827	6							4	9	1			8		11					2	3	10	5		7	
20	10	CHARLTON ATHLETIC	3-1	O'Halloran 3	23132	6							4	9	1			8	5	11			10			3	2			7	
21	17	Sunderland	1-1	Hedley (og)	29823	6							4	9	1			8	5	11			10			3	2			7	
22	24	ASTON VILLA	1-0	Hitchens	20384	6		2					4	9	1			8	5	11			10			3				7	
23	26	CHELSEA	1-1	Sherwood (p)	26794	6		2					4	9	1			8	5	11			10		3					7	
24	27	Chelsea	1-2	Hitchens	36740	6				9			4	8	1			7	5		11		10			3	2				
25	31	Wolverhampton Wan.	2-0	Hitchens, Ford	36772	6				9			4	10	1			8	5	11						3	2			7	
26	Jan 14	MANCHESTER CITY	4-1	Hitchens 2, McSeveney, Ford	26329	6				9			4	10	1			8	5	11						3	2			7	
27	21	Sheffield United	1-2	Sherwood	22921	6				9			4	10	1			8	5	11					2	3				7	
28	Feb 4	Huddersfield Town	2-1	Hitchens, Ford	12586	6				9			4	10				8	5	11						2		3	1	7	
29	11	BLACKPOOL	1-0	Ford	36019	6				9			4	10				8	5	11						2		3	1	7	
30	18	PRESTON NORTH END	3-1	Hitchens, Kirtley, Ford	25300	6				9			4	10				8	5	11						2		3	1	7	
31	25	Burnley	2-0	Hitchens 2, McSeveney, Ford	18549	6				9			4	10				8	5	11						2		3	1	7	
32	Mar 7	NEWCASTLE UNITED	1-1	Baker	31265	6				9				10				8	5	11				2		3		4	1	7	
33	10	Manchester United	1-1	Hitchens	44914	6				9			4	10				8	5	11						2		3	1	7	
34	24	Everton	0-2		29959	6				9			4	10				8	5	11						2		3	1	7	
35	30	Portsmouth	1-1	Ford	26443	6				9			4	10					5	11						2	8	3	1	7	
36	31	WEST BROMWICH ALB.	1-3	Hitchens	31641	6				9				10				8	5	11				4		2		3	1	7	
37	Apr 2	PORTSMOUTH	2-3	McSeveney, Ford	27018	6			7	9			4	10					5	11						2	8	3	1		
38	7	Birmingham City	1-2	Hitchens	37154	6		2		9			4	10				8	5	11								3	1	7	
39	14	LUTON TOWN	2-0	Hitchens, Walsh	16086					9			4	10				8	5	11						3	2	6	1	7	
40	21	Charlton Athletic	0-0		17726	6				9			4	8		10			5	11						2		3	1	7	
41	23	TOTTENHAM HOTSPUR	0-0		19684	6				9			4	8		10			5	11						2		3	1	7	
42	28	ARSENAL	1-2	Hitchens	23169	6				9			4	10				8	5	11						2		3	1	7	
		Apps				24	1	6	12	27	5	2	38	36	27	2	6	38	23	41	1	1	6	16	20	36	14	32	15	30	3
		Goals				1			1	13			2	15				4		6			3		2		3			3	1

One own goal

F.A. Cup

#	Date	Opponent	Score	Scorers	Att	Baker CW	Ford T	Harrington AC	Hitchens GA	Howells RG	Kirtley JH	Malloy D	McSeveney JH	Stitfall RF	Stockin R	Walsh JB
R3	Jan 7	Leeds United	2-1	Hitchens, McSeveney	40000	6	9	4	10	1	8	5	11	3	2	7
R4	28	West Ham United	1-2	Ford	35500	6	9	4	10	1	8	5	11	3	2	7

Welsh Cup

#	Date	Opponent	Score	Scorers	Att	Baker CW	Davies RT	Dixon CH	Ford T	Frowen J	Harrington AC	Hitchens GA	Howells RG	Kirtley JH	Malloy D	McSeveney JH	O'Halloran N	Stitfall RF	Stockin R	Sullivan D	Vearncombe G	Walsh JB
R5	Feb 1	Pembroke	2-2	Ford, Hitchens	5000	6	2		9			10	1	8	5	11		3		4		7
rep	8	PEMBROKE	9-0	Ford 4, Hitchens 3, Baker, McSeveney	4549	6		7	9			10		8	5	11		3	2	4	1	
R6	28	WREXHAM	5-3	Ford, McSeveney, Hitchens 3	5300	6	2		9	5	4	10		8		11				3	1	7
SF	Mar 17	Oswestry	7-0	Ford 2, Hitchens 5	11418	6			9	5	3	10		8		11	7	2		4	1	
F	Apr 30	SWANSEA TOWN	3-2	McSeveney, Walsh 2	37500	6			9		3	10		8	5	11		2		4	1	7

SF at Wrexham

1956/57   21st in Division One: Relegated

Results

#	Date	Opponent	Score	Scorers	Att
1	Aug 18	Arsenal	0-0		51069
2	22	NEWCASTLE UNITED	5-2	McSeveney, Ford 2, Nugent 2	35833
3	25	BURNLEY	3-3	McSeveney, Hitchens, Ford	30769
4	29	Newcastle United	0-1		34859
5	Sep 1	Preston North End	0-6		22102
6	5	SHEFFIELD WEDNESDAY	2-1	Hitchens, McSeveney	12983
7	8	CHELSEA	1-1	Armstrong (og)	26568
8	12	Sheffield Wednesday	3-5	McSeveney 2 (1p), Walsh	37235
9	15	Bolton Wanderers	0-2		28738
10	22	Birmingham City	1-2	O'Halloran	39931
11	29	WEST BROMWICH ALB.	0-0		22362
12	Oct 6	LEEDS UNITED	4-1	Hitchens 2, Ford, McSeveney	38333
13	13	Tottenham Hotspur	0-5		52429
14	27	Wolverhampton Wan.	1-3	Hitchens	34935
15	Nov 3	MANCHESTER CITY	1-1	Reynolds	23820
16	10	Charlton Athletic	2-0	Hitchens, Reynolds	17642
17	17	SUNDERLAND	1-0	Nugent	20017
18	24	Luton Town	0-3		13674
19	Dec 1	EVERTON	1-0	McSeveney	15600
20	8	Blackpool	1-3	Walsh	16623
21	15	ARSENAL	2-3	Hitchens 2	11302
22	22	Burnley	2-6	Hitchens 2	10118
23	26	Manchester United	1-3	Malloy (p)	28810
24	29	PRESTON NORTH END	2-3	Stockin, McSeveney	15474
25	Jan 12	Chelsea	2-1	McSeveney, Hitchens	28828
26	19	BOLTON WANDERERS	2-0	Hitchens, Walsh	12810
27	Feb 2	BIRMINGHAM CITY	1-2	McSeveney	16854
28	9	West Bromwich Albion	2-1	Hitchens, Baker	23522
29	16	Leeds United	0-3		21695
30	23	WOLVERHAMPTON W.	2-2	Hitchens, Baker	13879
31	Mar 9	BLACKPOOL	3-4	Hitchens 2, McSeveney (p)	15724
32	13	Aston Villa	1-4	Hitchens	12567
33	16	Manchester City	1-4	McSeveney (p)	26395
34	23	CHARLTON ATHLETIC	2-3	Baker, Hitchens	17047
35	30	Sunderland	1-1	Hitchens	40100
36	Apr 3	ASTON VILLA	1-0	McSeveney	18354
37	6	LUTON TOWN	0-0		18730
38	13	Everton	0-0		24397
39	19	Portsmouth	0-1		31223
40	20	TOTTENHAM HOTSPUR	0-3		25181
41	22	PORTSMOUTH	0-2		22197
42	27	MANCHESTER UNITED	2-3	Hitchens 2	17708

Appearances / shirt numbers

#	Vearncombe G	Rutter CF	Stitfall RF	Harrington AC	Malloy D	Baker CW	Walsh JB	McSeveney JH	Ford T	Hitchens GA	Nugent WC	Sullivan D	Davies RT	Frowen J	Dixon CH	O'Halloran N	Reynolds AB	Stockin R	Howells RG	Godwin DJ	Jones B	Tucker KJ	Jenkins B
1	1	2	3	4	5	6	7	8	9	10	11												
2	1	2	3	4	5		7	8	9	10	11	6											
3	1	2	3	4	5		7	8	9	10	11	6											
4	1		2	4	5	6	7	8	9	10	11	3											
5	1			4	5	6	7	8	9	10	11	3	2										
6	1		3	4			7	8	9	10	11	6	2	5									
7	1		3	4			7	8	9	10	11	6	2	5									
8	1		3	4			7	8	9	10	11	6	2	5									
9	1		3	4	5			8	9	10	11	6	2		7								
10	1		3	4	5			8	7	9	11	6	2			10							
11	1		3	4	5		7		9	8	11	6	2			10							
12	1		3	4	5		7	11	9	10		6	2				8						
13	1		3	4	5		7	11	9	10		6	2				8						
14	1		3	4	5		7	8		10	11	6	2		9								
15	1	2		4	5	6	7	11	9	10		3					8						
16	1	2		4	5	6	7	10		9		3					8						
17	1		3	4	5		7	10		9	11	6					8						
18	1		3	4	5		7	10		9	11	6					8						
19	1		3	4	5		7	11		10		6	2		9	8							
20	1		3	4	5		7	8		9		6	2				10						
21	1		3	2	5	4	7			9		6					10	8					
22	1		3	2	5	4	7			9		6					10	8					
23	1		2	4	5	6	7			9		3					10	8					
24	1		2	4	5	6			9		11	3			7		10	8					
25	1	2	3		5	4	7		8	9		6						10					
26	1	2	3		5	4	7		8	9		6						10					
27	1		3		5	4	7		8	9		6	2					10					
28			3		5	4	7			9		6	2				10	8			1	11	
29			3		5	4	7			9		6	2				10	8			1	11	
30			3		5	4				9	11	6	2		7		10	8			1		
31			3		5	4		8		9	11	6	2		7						1	10	
32	1		3		5	4		8		9	11	6	2		7							10	
33	1	2	3	4	5	6	7	8		9												10	11
34	1	2	3	8	4	6	7			9	11	5										10	
35	1	2	3	4	5	6		8		9	11				7	10							
36	1	2	3	4	5	6		8		9	7											11	10
37	1	2	3	4	5	6		8		9	7											11	10
38	1	2	3	4	5	6		8		9	7											11	10
39	1	2	3	4	5	6	7	8		9												11	10
40	1		3	4	5	6	7	8		9			2									10	11
41	1		3	4	5	6	7			9			2				8					10	11
42	1	2	3	4	5	6	7	8		9												10	11
Apps	38	15	39	33	42	27	32	34	14	41	28	31	17	9	6	4	14	13	4	2	7	8	4
Goals					1	3	3	13	4	21	3				1	2	1						

One own goal

F.A. Cup

Round	Date	Opponent	Score	Scorers	Att	Vearncombe G	Rutter CF	Stitfall RF	Malloy D	Baker CW	Walsh JB	McSeveney JH	Hitchens GA	Nugent WC	Sullivan D	Stockin R
R3	Jan 5	Leeds United	2-1	Stokin, McSeveney	34237	1	2	3	5	4	7	8	9	11	6	10
R4	26	BARNSLEY	0-1		32000	1	2	3	5	4	7	8	9	11	6	10

Welsh Cup

Round	Date	Opponent	Score	Scorers	Att	Vearncombe G	Rutter CF	Stitfall RF	Harrington AC	Malloy D	Baker CW	Walsh JB	Hitchens GA	Nugent WC	Sullivan D	Davies RT	Frowen J	Stockin R	Howells RG	Godwin DJ	Jones B	Tucker KJ
R5	Jan 31	Haverfordwest	3-3	Hitchens 2, Kirtley	1800	1		3		5	4	7	9	11	6	2		10				
rep	Feb 6	HAVERFORDWEST	8-1	* see below	3500			3			4	7	9		6	2	5	10			1	11
R6	27	CHESTER	0-2		5000		2	3	4	5	6		11		9			10		7	1	

Scorers in R5 replay: Hitchens 2, Walsh 2, Kirtley, Stokin, Sullivan, Williams (og)   Played at 8 in all three games: H Kirtley

1957/58   15th in Division Two

#	Date	Opponent	Score	Scorers	Att	Baker CW	Bonson J	Daniel WR	Davies RT	Harrington AC	Hewitt R	Hitchens GA	Hudson CAR	Jenkins B	Jones JA	Jones K	Malloy D	McGuckin GKW	Menzies AR	Milne AS	Nicholls J	Nugent WC	Reynolds AB	Rutter CF	Scott RJ	Stitfall RF	Sullivan D	Tucker KJ	Vearncombe G	Walsh JB
1	Aug 24	SWANSEA TOWN	0-0		42482					4	8	9	7				5				10			2		3	6	11	1	
2	27	Grimsby Town	1-1	Tucker (og)	18429					4	8	9	7				5				10			2		3	6	11	1	
3	31	Liverpool	0-3		45698				4	6	8	9	7				5				10			2		3		11	1	
4	Sep 4	GRIMSBY TOWN	1-3	Nicholls	13433	6			8	4		9	7				5				10	11		2		3			1	
5	7	MIDDLESBROUGH	0-2		14013	6			4			9	7							3	10	11		2					1	
6	11	HUDDERSFIELD T	1-0	Davies	10073	6			9	4	8						5			3	10					2		11	1	7
7	14	Leyton Orient	2-4	Davies, Nugent	16719	6			9	4	8						5			3	10					2		11	1	7
8	18	Huddersfield Town	1-1	Reynolds	9821	6				4	10	9					5			3	11		8			2			1	7
9	21	CHARLTON ATHLETIC	0-3		14439					6	4	10	9				5			3	11		8			2			1	7
10	28	Doncaster Rovers	1-0	Davies	9909				8	4	10	9					5			3	11					2	6		1	7
11	Oct 5	ROTHERHAM UNITED	2-2	Walsh, Hewitt (p)	14390				8	4	10	9					5			3	11					2	6		1	7
12	12	DERBY COUNTY	3-2	Hitchens, Hewitt, Walsh	15513	6				4	10	9					5			3	11		8	2					1	7
13	19	Bristol Rovers	2-0	Hitchens 2	23366	4		5				10	9							3			8				2	6		1	7
14	26	LINCOLN CITY	3-2	Hewitt, Nugent, Reynolds	14515	4		5				10	9							3			8	2			2	6		1	7
15	Nov 2	Notts County	2-5	Reynolds, Nicholls	14911			5		4		10									9	11	8	2		3	6		1	7
16	4	Stoke City	0-3		20016			5		4		10									9	11	8	2		3	6		1	7
17	9	IPSWICH TOWN	1-1	Bonson	16490		10	5		4		9	11				8			3						2	6		1	7
18	16	Blackburn Rovers	0-4		24642	6	9	5		4			10	11						3			8	2					1	7
19	23	SHEFFIELD UNITED	0-0		15215	6	9			4	8	10				1	5			3	11					2				7
20	30	West Ham United	1-1	Bonson	23954		9			4	8	10	11			1	5			3					6	2				7
21	Dec 7	BARNSLEY	7-0	Nugent 3, Hewitt 2 (1p), Bonson, Hudson	8941		9			4	8		11			1	5			3		10			6	2				7
22	14	Fulham	0-2		16024		10			4	8	9	11			1	5			3					6	2				7
23	21	Swansea Town	1-0	Hudson	19483	6	9			4	8		11			1	5			3		10				2				7
24	26	STOKE CITY	5-2	Hudson, Bonson 2, Reynolds, Walsh	23638	6	9			4			11			1	5			3		10	8			2				7
25	28	LIVERPOOL	6-1	Hudson, Reynolds 2, Hewitt, Bonson 2	30622	6	10			4	8		11			1	5			3			9			2				7
26	Jan 11	Middlesbrough	1-4	Walsh	23115	6	9			4	10		11			1	5			3			8			2				7
27	18	LEYTON ORIENT	1-1	Hewitt	13387	6	9			4	10		11			1	5			3			8			2				7
28	Feb 1	Charlton Athletic	1-3	Nugent	20556		9			4	8		11			1	5	6		3		10				2				7
29	8	DONCASTER ROVERS	3-1	Walsh, Nugent, Hewitt	13277				9	4	8		11			1	5					10				3	6			7
30	22	Sheffield United	0-3		19368		9			4	8		7			1	5					11	10			3	6			
31	Mar 15	NOTTS COUNTY	2-0	Bonson, Hewitt	11116	6	9			4	8		11			1	5						10			2	3			7
32	22	Ipswich Town	1-3	Bonson	13469	6	9			4			11			1	5					8	10			2	3			7
33	26	BRISTOL ROVERS	0-2		5867	6	9			4			11			1	5			2		8	10				3			7
34	29	BLACKBURN ROVERS	4-3	Hewitt 3 (1p), Bonson	10335	6	9			4	10		7				5					11	8			2	3		1	
35	Apr 4	BRISTOL CITY	2-3	Hewitt 2	15567	6	9			4	8		11			1	5					10				2	3			7
36	5	Derby County	2-0	Bonson, Jenkins	15529		9			4	8		7	11		1	5	6				10				2	3			
37	7	Bristol City	0-2		25723		9			4	8		7	11		1	5	6				10				2	3			
38	12	WEST HAM UNITED	0-3		17596	6	9			4	8		11			1	5					10		2		3				7
39	19	Barnsley	1-1	Hudson	8948		9						11			1	5	6				8	10	2		3	4			7
40	21	Rotherham United	1-3	Walsh	8147		9			4	8		11		1		5	6				10				2				7
41	26	FULHAM	3-0	Baker, Sullivan 2	11846	4	9						8			1	5			3		10				2	6			7
42	30	Lincoln City	1-3	Nugent	18001	4	9						8			1	5			3		10				2	6			7

Played in one game: J Frowen (game 5, at 5)

| | | | | | Apps | 23 | 25 | 6 | 9 | 36 | 36 | 16 | 28 | 4 | 1 | 22 | 36 | 4 | 1 | 27 | 8 | 31 | 17 | 11 | 3 | 37 | 23 | 5 | 19 | 33 |
| | | | | | Goals | 1 | 12 | | 3 | | 14 | 3 | 4 | 1 | | | | | | | 2 | 8 | 6 | | | | 2 | | | 6 |

One own goal

F.A. Cup

	Date	Opponent	Score	Scorers	Att	Baker CW	Bonson J	Daniel WR	Davies RT	Harrington AC	Hewitt R	Hitchens GA	Hudson CAR	Jenkins B	Jones JA	Jones K	Malloy D	McGuckin GKW	Menzies AR	Milne AS	Nicholls J	Nugent WC	Reynolds AB	Rutter CF	Scott RJ	Stitfall RF	Sullivan D	Tucker KJ	Vearncombe G	Walsh JB
R3	Jan 4	Leeds United	2-1	Harrington, Nugent	30374	6	9			4		10	11			1	5			3		8				2				7
R4	25	LEYTON ORIENT	4-1	Bishop (og), Walsh, Bonson 2	35849	6	9			4	8		11			1	5			3		10				2				7
R5	Feb 15	BLACKBURN ROVERS	0-0		45580	6	9			4	8		11			1	5			2		10				3				7
rep	20	Blackburn Rovers	1-2	Hewitt	27000	6	9			4	8		11			1	5			2		10				3				7

Welsh Cup

	Date	Opponent	Score	Scorers	Att	Baker CW	Bonson J	Daniel WR	Davies RT	Harrington AC	Hewitt R	Hitchens GA	Hudson CAR	Jenkins B	Jones JA	Jones K	Malloy D	McGuckin GKW	Menzies AR	Milne AS	Nicholls J	Nugent WC	Reynolds AB	Rutter CF	Scott RJ	Stitfall RF	Sullivan D	Tucker KJ	Vearncombe G	Walsh JB
R5	Jan 29	HEREFORD UNITED	0-2		1500		9	4				7				1	5					10	8	3		2	6	11		

1958/59

9th in Division Two

#	Date	Opponent	Result	Scorers	Att	Baker CW	Bonson J	Gammon SG	Gray AD	Harrington AC	Hewitt R	Hudson CAR	Hughes EM	Jenkins B	Jones K	Kelly GL	Knowles HF	Malloy D	Milne AS	Moore G	Nicholls RB	Nugent WC	Reynolds AB	Stitfall RF	Sullivan D	Tapscott DJR	Vearncombe G	Walsh JB
1	Aug 23	BARNSLEY	0-1		23731		9			4	8	11			1	10		5	3					2	6			7
2	27	Huddersfield Town	0-3		13267					4		11			1	8		5	3			10	9	2	6			7
3	30	Rotherham United	0-1		11474					4		11				8		5	3		1	10	9	2	6			7
4	Sep 3	HUDDERSFIELD T	3-2	Baker, Walsh (p), Nugent	13078	4								11		8		5	3		1	10	9	2	6			7
5	6	SHEFFIELD UNITED	3-1	Kelly 2, Reynolds	16079	4								11		8		5	3		1	10	9	2	6			7
6	8	Bristol Rovers	0-2		20579	4								11		8		5	3		1	10	9	2	6			7
7	13	Brighton & Hove Albion	2-2	Hewitt, Moore	26662	6	9			4	10	7		11				5	3	8	1			2				
8	17	BRISTOL ROVERS	2-4	Hudson, Moore	14495	6	9			4		7		11				5	3	8	1	10		2				
9	20	GRIMSBY TOWN	4-1	Hewitt 2, Bonson, Jenkins	15646	6	9	4			10			11				5	3		1			2	8			7
10	27	Liverpool	2-1	Bonson, Hewitt	41866	6	9	4			10			11				5	2		1			3	8			7
11	Oct 4	MIDDLESBROUGH	3-2	Jenkins, Hewitt, Walsh	20560	6	9	4			10			11				5	2		1			3	8			7
12	11	IPSWICH TOWN	1-2	Tapscott	20357	6	9	4			10			11				5	2		1			3	8			7
13	25	STOKE CITY	2-1	Stitfall, Tapscott	18359	6	9	4			10			11				5	2		1			3	8			7
14	Nov 1	Derby County	3-1	Reynolds, Hewitt (p), Walsh	17532	6		4			10			11				5	2		1		9	3	8			7
15	8	LINCOLN CITY	3-0	Hewitt, Jenkins, Walsh	15689	6					10			11				5	2		1		9	3	4	8		7
16	15	Fulham	1-2	Walsh	24078	6				2	10			11				5	3		1		9		4	8		7
17	22	SHEFFIELD WEDNESDAY	2-2	Jenkins, Tapscott	20195	6					10			11				5	2		1		9	3	4	8		7
18	Dec 6	LEYTON ORIENT	2-1	Hewitt 2 (1p)	15184	6					10			11				5	2		1		9	3	4	8		7
19	13	Sunderland	2-0	Tapscott, Bonson	30097	6	9				10							5	2		1		11	3	4	8		7
20	18	Scunthorpe United	0-1		10365	6	9				10							5	2		1		11	3	4	8		7
21	20	Barnsley	2-3	Hewitt, Walsh	7798	6	9		3		10							5	2		1		11		4	8		7
22	26	Bristol City	3-2	Bonson 2, Walsh	27570	6	9				10							5	2		1		11	3	4	8		7
23	27	BRISTOL CITY	1-0	Burden (og)	27146	6	9		3		10							5	2		1		11		4	8		7
24	Jan 3	ROTHERHAM UNITED	1-0	Reynolds	17115	6	9				10							5	3		1		11	2	4	8		7
25	31	BRIGHTON & HOVE ALB	3-1	Jenkins, Bonson	15891	6	9				10			11				5	2		1			3	4	8		7
26	Feb 7	Grimsby Town	1-5	Reynolds	9969	6					10			11			9	5	2		1		7	3	4	8		
27	14	LIVERPOOL	3-0	Tapscott 2, Reynolds	18313	4						11					9	5	2		1		10	3	6	8		7
28	21	Middlesbrough	1-1	Walsh	12986	4						11					9	5	2		1		10	3	6	8		7
29	28	Lincoln City	2-4	Reynolds, Jenkins	8736	6				2				11				5	3	10	1		9		6	8		7
30	Mar 7	SWANSEA TOWN	0-1		24450	4	10			2				11			9	5	3		1				6	8		7
31	14	Stoke City	1-0	Hewitt	11931	4	9			2	10	11						5	3		1				6	8		7
32	21	DERBY COUNTY	0-0		14011	6				2	10	11					9	5	3		1				4	8		7
33	28	Ipswich Town	3-3	Tapscott, Hewitt (p), Hudson	12159	4	9			2	10	11						5	3		1				6	8		7
34	30	Charlton Athletic	0-0		16344	4	9			2	10	11						5	3		1				6	8		7
35	31	CHARLTON ATHLETIC	1-2	Sullivan	16045	4	9			2	10	11						5	3		1				6	8		7
36	Apr 4	FULHAM	1-2	Walsh	23217	6				2	10			11				5	3	8	1				4	9		7
37	11	Sheffield Wednesday	1-3	Tapscott	22665	6				2	10			11				5	3		1		9		4	8		7
38	15	Swansea Town	3-1	Kelly 2, Nurse (og)	14893	6				4		11				8		5	2		1			3	10	9		7
39	18	SCUNTHORPE UNITED	0-2		13003	6				4		11				8		5	2		1			3	10	9		7
40	22	SUNDERLAND	2-1	Hewitt, Walsh	10734	6				4	10		8				9	5	2		1		11	3				7
41	25	Leyton Orient	0-3		11351	6				4	10						9	5	2		1		11	3		8		7
42	27	Sheffield United	1-1	Tapscott	12733	6	9	4		2								5	3	10			11			8	1	7
		Apps				39	21	7	2	20	29	16	1	19	2	8	7	42	42	5	39	6	24	25	35	33	1	39
		Goals				1	6				13	2		6		4						2	6	1	1	10		10

Two own goals

F.A. Cup

Rd	Date	Opponent	Result	Scorers	Att	Baker CW	Bonson J	Gammon SG	Gray AD	Harrington AC	Hewitt R	Hudson CAR	Hughes EM	Jenkins B	Jones K	Kelly GL	Knowles HF	Malloy D	Milne AS	Moore G	Nicholls RB	Nugent WC	Reynolds AB	Stitfall RF	Sullivan D	Tapscott DJR	Vearncombe G	Walsh JB
R3	Jan 10	Plymouth Argyle	3-0	Hewitt (p), Reynolds, Bonson	36247	6	9				10							5	2		1		11	3	4	8		7
R4	24	Norwich City	2-3	Hewitt, Bonson	38000	6	9				10							5	2		1		11	3	4	8		7

Welsh Cup

Rd	Date	Opponent	Result	Scorers	Att	Baker CW	Bonson J	Gammon SG	Gray AD	Harrington AC	Hewitt R	Hudson CAR	Hughes EM	Jenkins B	Jones K	Kelly GL	Knowles HF	Malloy D	Milne AS	Moore G	Nicholls RB	Nugent WC	Reynolds AB	Stitfall RF	Sullivan D	Tapscott DJR	Vearncombe G	Walsh JB
R5	Feb 5	Gloucester City	1-1	Hewitt	5000	6	9				10			11		8		5	2		1			3	4			7
rep	11	GLOUCESTER CITY	3-0	Milne, Bonson, Hudson	5000	4	9					7		11				5	2			10		3	6	8	1	
R6	25	RHYL	3-1	Reynolds, Tapscott, Knowles	4000	4								11			9	5	2		1		10	3	6	8		7
SF	Mar 19	Wrexham	6-0	Hewitt, Tapscott 2, Knowles 3	3621	4				2	10	11					9	5	3						6	8	1	7
F	Apr 30	Lovell's Athletic	2-0	Bonson, Hudson	8000	6	9	4				11						5	2	10				3		8	1	7

Final at Newport

1959/60   2nd in Division Two: Promoted

#	Date		Opponent	Score	Scorers	Att	Baker CW	Bonson I	Durban WA	Gammon SG	Harrington AC	Hole BG	Hudson CAR	Jenkins B	Knowles HF	Malloy D	Milne AS	Mokone SM	Moore G	Nicholls RB	Peck DT	Sittfall RF	Sullivan D	Tapscott DIR	Vearncombe G	Walsh IB	Watkins IV
1	Aug	22	LIVERPOOL	3-2	Mokone, Moore, Watkins	23744	6				2					5	3	10	9				4	8	1	7	11
2		26	MIDDLESBROUGH	2-0	Moore, Watkins	23052	6				2					5	3	10	9				4	8	1	7	11
3		29	Charlton Athletic	1-2	Moore	18513	6				2					5	3	10	9				4	8	1	7	11
4	Sep	2	Middlesbrough	1-1	Watkins	29122	6	10			2		7			5	3		9			8	4		1		11
5		5	BRISTOL CITY	4-2	Hudson 2, Watkins, Baker	22545	6	10		4	2		7			5	3		9			8			1		11
6		9	Derby County	2-1	Sullivan 2	17959	6		8	4	2		7			5	3		9				10		1		11
7		12	Scunthorpe United	2-1	Moore, Watkins	10933	6		8	4	2		7			5	3		9				10		1		11
8		16	DERBY COUNTY	2-0	Sullivan, Baker	21548	6		8	4	2		7			5	3		9				10		1		11
9		19	ROTHERHAM UNITED	1-4	Sullivan	24392	6			4	2		7			5	3		9				10	8	1		11
10		26	Lincoln City	3-2	Sullivan, Watkins, Harrington	8401	6		8	4	2		7			5			9			3	10		1		11
11	Oct	3	Hull City	0-0		14933	6		8	4	2		7			5			9			3	10		1		11
12		10	LEYTON ORIENT	5-1	Moore 2, Tapscott 2, Sullivan	18794	6			4	2					5			9			3	10	8	1	7	11
13		17	Huddersfield Town	1-0	Tapscott	18367	6	10		4					9	5	2					3		8	1	7	11
14		24	IPSWICH TOWN	3-2	Baker, Tapscot, Sullivan	20223	6			4	2					5	3		9				10	8	1	7	11
15		31	Bristol Rovers	1-1	Moore	27630	6			4	2					5			9			3	10	8	1	7	11
16	Nov	7	SWANSEA TOWN	2-1	Sullivan, Bonson	34881		10		4	2					5			9			3	6	8	1	7	11
17		14	Brighton & Hove Albion	2-2	Bonson 2	16253		10		4	2					5			9			3	6	8	1	7	11
18		21	STOKE CITY	4-4	Tapscott, Bonson 2, Gammon	21793		10		4	2					5			9			3	6	8	1	7	11
19		28	Portsmouth	1-1	Walsh	14018		10		4	2					5			9			3	6	8	1	7	11
20	Dec	5	SUNDERLAND	2-1	Watkins, Tapscott	20016		10		4	2					5			9			3	6	8	1	7	11
21		12	Aston Villa	0-2		50039		10		4						5	2		9			3	6	8	1	7	11
22		19	Liverpool	4-0	Tapscott 2, Watkins, Bonson	27291	6	10								5	2		9			3	4	8	1	7	11
23		26	SHEFFIELD UNITED	2-0	Bonson, Tapscott	29515	6	10								5	2		9			3	4	8	1	7	11
24		28	Sheffield United	1-2	Tapscott	18590	6	10								5	2		9			3	4	8	1	7	11
25	Jan	2	CHARLTON ATHLETIC	5-1	Baker 2, Tapscott, Bonson, Walsh	20619	6	10								5	2		9			3	4	8	1	7	11
26		16	Bristol City	3-0	Bonson, Moore, McCall (og)	18184	6	10								5	2		9			3	4	8	1	7	11
27		23	SCUNTHORPE UNITED	4-2	Watkins, Bonson, Tapscott, Moore	16759	6	10								5	2		9			3	4	8	1	7	11
28		30	Plymouth Argyle	1-1	Tapscott	21923	6	10								5	2		9			3	4	8	1	7	11
29	Feb	6	Rotherham United	2-2	Tapscott 2	16525	6	10								5	2		9			3	4	8	1	7	11
30		13	LINCOLN CITY	6-2	Bonson 2, Watkins 2, Tapscott, Walsh	16231	6	10								5	2		9			3	4	8	1	7	11
31		20	HULL CITY	3-2	Watkins, Bonson 2	21580	6	10								5	2		9			3	4	8	1	7	11
32		27	Leyton Orient	4-3	Tapscott 2, Bonson 2	22918	4	10				6				5	2		9			3		8	1	7	11
33	Mar	5	HUDDERSFIELD T	2-1	Moore, Watkins	32733	6	10				4				5	2		9			3		8	1	7	11
34		12	Ipswich Town	1-1	Bonson	18776	6	10				4				5	2		9			3		8	1	7	11
35		19	PORTSMOUTH	1-4	Tapscott	21011	6	10				4				5	2		9			3		8	1	7	11
36		26	Swansea Town	3-3	Bonson, Moore, Walsh	24004	6	10				4				5	2		9			3		8	1	7	11
37	Apr	2	BRIGHTON & HOVE ALB	1-4	Tapscott	19523	6	10		4						5	2		9	1		3		8		7	11
38		9	Stoke City	1-0	Watkins	9548				4							2		9	1	5	3	10	8		7	11
39		16	ASTON VILLA	1-0	Moore	52364	6			4					10	5	2		9	1		3		8		7	11
40		19	PLYMOUTH ARGYLE	0-1		28890	6			4					10	5	2		9	1		3		8		7	11
41		23	Sunderland	1-1	Baker	20663	6	10			2	4	7			5			9	1		3		8			11
42		30	BRISTOL ROVERS	2-2	Moore, Watkins	17624	6				2	4			11	5			9			3		8	1	7	10
			Apps				36	26	5	21	21	7	11	1	1	41	31	3	41	5	1	34	30	35	37	33	42
			Goals				6	18		1	1		2					1	13				8	20		4	15

One own goal

F.A. Cup

	Date		Opponent	Score		Att	Baker CW	Bonson I	Durban WA	Gammon SG	Harrington AC	Hole BG	Hudson CAR	Jenkins B	Knowles HF	Malloy D	Milne AS	Mokone SM	Moore G	Nicholls RB	Peck DT	Sittfall RF	Sullivan D	Tapscott DIR	Vearncombe G	Walsh IB	Watkins IV
R3	Jan	9	PORT VALE	0-2		25500		10		4						5	2		9			3	6	8	1	7	11

Welsh Cup

	Date		Opponent	Score	Scorers	Att	Baker CW	Bonson I	Durban WA	Gammon SG	Harrington AC	Hole BG	Hudson CAR	Jenkins B	Knowles HF	Malloy D	Milne AS	Mokone SM	Moore G	Nicholls RB	Peck DT	Sittfall RF	Sullivan D	Tapscott DIR	Vearncombe G	Walsh IB	Watkins IV
R5	Jan	20	LOVELL'S ATHLETIC	5-0	* see below	2000	6	10								5	2		9			3	4	8	1	7	11
R6	Feb	25	Swansea Town	2-1	Knowles, Woods (og)	11000				4	3	6	7	11	9			8		1	5						
SF	Mar	28	Bangor City	1-1	Moore	3600	6	10		4						5	2		9			3		8	1	7	11
rep	Apr	25	BANGOR CITY	4-1	Moore, Mokone, Jenkins 2 (1p)	2500	4		10	2		6		11		5		8	9			3			1	7	
F	May	2	WREXHAM	1-1	Jenkins	11172	4							11		5			9			3		8	1	7	10
rep		5	Wrexham	0-1		5800	6			4	2		7	10		5			9			3		8	1		11

Scorers in R5: Baker, Tapscott, Moore, Watkins, Bonson   Played in R6: A Monk (at 2), M Hughes (10)

1960/61   15th in Division One

#	Date	Opponent	Score	Scorers	Att	Baker CW	Donnelly P	Durban WA	Edgley BK	Edwards LT	Gammon SG	Harrington AC	Hogg D	Hole BG	Hudson CAR	Jenkins B	Malloy D	McMillan JS	Milne AS	Moore G	Nicholls RB	Pickrell AD	Sitfall RF	Sullivan D	Swan MMG	Tapscott DIR	Veamcombe G	Walsh JB	Ward D	Watkins IV
1	Aug 20	Fulham	2-2	Walsh, Moore	30911	6	10				4	2					5		3	9						8	1	7		11
2	24	SHEFFIELD WEDNESDAY	0-1		31335			10			4	2		6			5		3	9						8	1	7		11
3	27	PRESTON NORTH END	2-0	Tapscott 2	27213	6	8				4	2					5		3	9						10	1	7		11
4	31	Sheffield Wednesday	0-2		27537	6	10				4	2					5		3	9						8	1	7		11
5	Sep 3	Burnley	2-1	Tapscott, Watkins	19695	6	10		9		4	2					5		3							8	1	7		11
6	7	ASTON VILLA	1-1	Tapscott	34716	6	8		9		4	2					5		3							10	1	7		11
7	10	NOTTM. FOREST	1-3	Tapscott	24037	6	9				4	2					5		3	10						8	1	7		11
8	12	Aston Villa	1-2	Donnelly	32901	6	10				4	2					5		3	9						8	1	7		11
9	17	Manchester City	2-4	Tapscott, Durban	30932	6		9		3		2				11	5			10				4		8	1	7		
10	24	ARSENAL	1-0	Tapscott	32775	6	9			3	4	2			7		5			10						8	1			11
11	Oct 1	Newcastle United	0-5		17627	6	9			3		2		4	7		5			10						8	1			11
12	8	Wolverhampton Wan.	2-2	Hudson, Edwards	23800		10			9	4	2		6	7		5		3							8	1			11
13	15	BOLTON WANDERERS	0-1		22672		10			9	4	2		6	7		5		3							8	1			11
14	28	LEICESTER CITY	2-1	Donnelly, Hogg	19136	6	9			3	4	2	11				5							8		10	1	7		
15	Nov 2	Tottenham Hotspur	2-3	Donnelly 2	47605	6	12			3	4	2	11				5							8		9	1	7		
16	5	Blackpool	1-6	Tapscott	13457	6	10			3	4	2	11	8			5									9	1	7		
17	12	EVERTON	1-1	Watkins	19234	6	9				4	2	11				5						3			8	1	7		10
18	19	Blackburn Rovers	2-2	Tapscott, McEvoy (og)	15132	6			8		4	2	11				5						3			9	1	7		10
19	26	MANCHESTER UNITED	3-0	Hogg 2, Edgeley	21122	6			8		4	2	11				5						3			9	1	7		10
20	Dec 3	West Ham United	0-2		13967	6			8		4	2	11				5						3			9	1	7		10
21	10	CHELSEA	2-1	Walsh, Baker	21840	6			8		4	2	11				5						3			9	1	7		10
22	17	FULHAM	2-0	Baker, Tapscott	16807	6			8		4	2	11				5						3			9	1	7		10
23	26	WEST BROMWICH ALB.	3-1	Tapscott 3	25214	6			8		4	2	11				5						3			9	1	7		10
24	27	West Bromwich Albion	1-1	Baker	30131	6			8		4	2	11				5						3		1	9		7		10
25	31	Preston North End	1-1	Tapscott	11048	6					4	2	11				5				8		3		1	9		7		10
26	Jan 14	BURNLEY	2-1	Tapscott 2	25670	6					4	2	11				5				8		3		1	9		7		10
27	21	Nottingham Forest	1-2	Tapscott	19227	6	10				4	2	7				5				8		3		1	9				11
28	Feb 4	MANCHESTER CITY	3-3	Moore, Tapscott, Baker	15218	6	10			2	4		11				5				8		3		1	9		7		
29	11	Arsenal	3-2	Moore, Walsh, Donnelly	33534	6	10			2			11				5				8		3		1	9		7		
30	22	NEWCASTLE UNITED	3-2	Moore 2, Walsh	22502	6	10					2	11	4			5				8		3		1	9		7		
31	25	WOLVERHAMPTON W.	3-2	Walsh, Donnelly, Tapscott	24396	6	10					2	11	4			5				8	1	3			9		7		
32	Mar 4	Bolton Wanderers	0-3		21815	6	10					2	11	4			5				8	1	3			9		7		
33	11	TOTTENHAM HOTSPUR	3-2	Hogg, Walsh, Tapscott	45463	6	10					2	11	4			5				8	1	3			9		7		
34	24	Blackpool	0-2		19754	6	10					2	11	4			5				8	1	3			9		7		
35	31	BIRMINGHAM CITY	0-2		16339	6	10					2		4			5	3				11				9	1	7	8	
36	Apr 1	Chelsea	1-6	Durban	22697	4		8	9			2		6			5	3				11					1	7	10	
37	3	Birmingham City	1-2	Moore	20065	6	10		9				11	4			5	3		8				2			1	7		
38	8	BLACKBURN ROVERS	1-1	Edwards	16192	6	10			9		2	11	4			5			8			3				1	7		
39	10	Leicester City	0-3		32042	6	10			9		2	11	4			5	7	3	8							1			
40	15	Everton	1-5	Ward	34382	6						2	11	4			5	7	3	8						9	1		10	
41	22	WEST HAM UNITED	1-1	Donnelly	9549	6	10					2	11	4			5		3	8						9	1	7		
42	29	Manchester United	3-3	Hogg 2, Tapscott	30420	6	10					2	11	4			5		3	9						8	1	7		

	Baker CW	Donnelly P	Durban WA	Edgley BK	Edwards LT	Gammon SG	Harrington AC	Hogg D	Hole BG	Hudson CAR	Jenkins B	Malloy D	McMillan JS	Milne AS	Moore G	Nicholls RB	Pickrell AD	Sitfall RF	Sullivan D	Swan MMG	Tapscott DIR	Veamcombe G	Walsh JB	Ward D	Watkins IV
Apps	39	27	4	10	14	26	39	26	19	5	1	42	2	17	25	7	2	20	3	8	39	27	34	3	23
Goals	4	7	2	1	2			6		1					6						20		7	1	2

One own goal

F.A. Cup

	Date	Opponent	Score	Scorers	Att	Baker	Gammon	Harrington	Hogg	Malloy	Moore	Sitfall	Swan	Tapscott	Veamcombe	Walsh	Watkins
R3	Jan 7	MANCHESTER CITY	1-1	Tapscott	25640	6	4	2	11	5	8	3	1	9		7	10
rep	11	Manchester City	0-0	(aet)	40000	6	4	2	11	5	8	3	1	9		7	10
rep2	16	Manchester City	0-2	(aet)	24168	6	4	2	11	5	8	3	1	9		7	10

Replay 2 at Highbury

F.L. Cup

	Date	Opponent	Score	Notes	Att	Baker	Donnelly	Edwards	Gammon	Harrington	Hogg	Hudson	Jenkins	Malloy	McMillan	Milne	Tapscott	Veamcombe	Walsh
R1	Oct 3	Middlesbrough	4-3	* See below	15695	6	10	9		2		4	11	5		3	8	1	7
R2	24	BURNLEY	0-4		12000	6		9	4	2		10	11	5		3		1	7

Scorers in R1: Walsh, Donnelly, Hudson, Edwards(p)   Played at 8 in R2: PC King

Welsh Cup

	Date	Opponent	Score	Scorers	Att	Baker	Donnelly	Edgley	Harrington	Hogg	Hole	Malloy	Milne	Moore	Pickrell	Sitfall	Swan	Tapscott	Veamcombe	Walsh	Watkins
R5	Jan 28	KNIGHTON	16-0	* See below	1800	6	10			11		5		8		3	1	9		7	
R6	Feb 16	NEWPORT COUNTY	2-1	Moore, Hogg	12192	6	10	2		11	4	5		8		3	1	9		7	
SF	Mar 22	Swansea Town	1-1	Tapscott	10470	6	10		2	11	4	5		8	1	3		9		7	
rep	28	Swansea Town	1-2	Tapscott	20000	6	11	9	2	7	4	5	3					8	1		10

SF at Newport, replay at Llanelli
Scorers in R5: Tapscott 6, Moore 4, Malloy, Walsh 2, Donnelly 2, Hogg

1961/62   21st in Division One: Relegated

#	Date	Opponent	Result	Scorers	Att.	Baker CW	Charles M	Donnelly P	Durban WA	Edwards LT	Gammon SG	Harrington AC	Hogg D	Hole BG	John DJ	King JW	King PC	McCarthy DJA	McIntosh A	Milne AS	Moore G	Pickrell AD	Rankmore FEJ	Stitfall RF	Swan MMG	Tapscott DJR	Veamcombe G	Walsh JB	Ward D
1	Aug 19	Blackburn Rovers	0-0		18428	6						2	11	4		9				3	10		5				1	7	8
2	23	SHEFFIELD UNITED	1-1	J King	24662	6						2	11	4		9				3	10		5				1	7	8
3	26	BLACKPOOL	3-2	Ward 2, Hogg	22701	6						2	11	4		9				3	10		5				1	7	8
4	28	Sheffield United	0-1		19193	6						2	11	4		9				3	10		5				1	7	8
5	Sep 2	Tottenham Hotspur	2-3	J King, Ward	37834	6						2	11	4		9				3	10		5			7	1		8
6	6	CHELSEA	5-2	* see below	20853	6						2	11	4		9				3	10		5			7	1		8
7	9	BOLTON WANDERERS	1-2	Ward	22076	6						2		4		9				3	10	11	5			7	1		8
8	16	MANCHESTER UNITED	1-2	Ward	29251	6						2		4		9				3	10	11	5			7	1		8
9	20	Chelsea	3-2	Baker, Ward, Donnelly	15804	6		11	10			2		4	1	9				3			5			7			8
10	23	Wolverhampton Wan.	1-1	Harrington	26643	6		11	10			2		4	1	9				3			5			7			8
11	30	NOTTM. FOREST	2-2	Ward, J King	20502	6		11	10			2		4	1	9				3			5			7			8
12	Oct 7	Manchester City	2-1	Hole, J King	20143	6			10			2	11	4	1	9	7			3			5						8
13	18	WEST BROMWICH ALB.	2-2	Durban, Ward	16819	6			10			2		4	1	9			11	3			5					7	8
14	21	Burnley	1-2	Ward	22765	6			10			2	11	4	1	9	7			3			5						8
15	28	ARSENAL	1-1	Pickrell	25096	6						2		4	1	9	7			3	10	11	5						8
16	Nov 4	Fulham	1-0	Tapscott	20077	6						2		4	1	9	7			3	10	11	5			8			
17	11	SHEFFIELD WEDNESDAY	2-1	Tapscott 2	17987	6						2		4	1	9	7			3	10	11	5			8			
18	18	Leicester City	0-3		16992	6			10			2		4	1	9	7			3		11	5						8
19	25	IPSWICH TOWN	0-3		22823	6						2	11	4	1	9	7			3			5			8			10
20	Dec 2	Birmingham City	0-3		20959	5				9	4	2		6		11	7			3	10				1				8
21	9	EVERTON	0-0		15782	6						2		4	1	9	7			3	10	11	5			8			
22	16	BLACKBURN ROVERS	1-1	Moore	13799	6						2		4	1	9	7			3	10	11	5			8			
23	23	Blackpool	0-3		13961	4					6	2		10	1	9	7			3		11	5			8			
24	26	ASTON VILLA	1-0	Tapscott	18394	4					6	2		10	1		7			3		11	5			8			9
25	Jan 13	TOTTENHAM HOTSPUR	1-1	J King (p)	33606	6			8		4	2	11			9	7			3			5				1		10
26	23	Bolton Wanderers	1-1	Ward	11231	6			8		4	2	11			9	7			3			5				1		10
27	Feb 3	Manchester United	0-3		29200	6			10		4	2	11			9	7			3			5				1		8
28	9	WOLVERHAMPTON W.	2-3	Ward, Milne	18372	6			10			2		4	1	9	7		11	3			5						8
29	17	Nottingham Forest	1-2	J King	19227	6			10			2		4	1	9	7	11		3			5						8
30	24	MANCHESTER CITY	0-0		19347	6	9							4	1	10	7	11		3			5	2					
31	Mar 3	West Bromwich Albion	1-5	P King	13894	6	9		10			2	11	4	1		7			3			5			8			
32	14	BURNLEY	1-1	Charles	15416	6	9				2	5	11	4		10	7			3							1		8
33	17	Arsenal	1-1	Ward	25059	6	9				2	5		4		10	7	11		3							1		8
34	23	FULHAM	0-3		16758	6	9		10		2	5	11	4			7			3						8	1		
35	Apr 3	Sheffield Wednesday	0-2		17475	6	5				2			4		9	7	11		3							1		10
36	7	LEICESTER CITY	0-4		11058	6	9				2			4		10	7	11		3			5				1		
37	14	Ipswich Town	0-1		17693	6	9		10					6	1		8	7		3		11	5	2					
38	20	West Ham United	1-4	Pickrell	25459	4	9		10					6	1		8	7		3		11	5	2					
39	21	BIRMINGHAM CITY	3-2	Tapscott 3	8608	4	9		10	7				6	1					3		11	5	2		8			
40	23	WEST HAM UNITED	3-0	Ward 2, Tapscott	11274	6	9		10					4			7			3		11	5	2		8	1		9
41	28	Everton	3-8	Charles, Pickrell 2	31186	6	9		10					6			7			3		11	5	2		8	1		
42	May 1	Aston Villa	2-2	Ward, Charles	22174	6	9		8			2		4						3		11	5			7	1		10
				Apps		42	12	4	20	7	6	36	15	37	21	33	26	7	2	42	14	16	37	6	1	22	20	5	31
				Goals		1	3	1	1				1	1	1	6	1			1	2	4				9			17

Scorers in game 6: Ward 2, Tapscott, Moore, Mortimore (og)

One own goal

F.A. Cup

Round	Date	Opponent	Result	Att.	Baker CW	Harrington AC	Hole BG	John DJ	King JW	King PC	Milne AS	Pickrell AD	Rankmore FEJ	Tapscott DJR	Ward D
R3	Jan 10	Middlesbrough	0-1	29013	6	2	4	1	9	7	3	11	5	8	10

F.L. Cup

Round	Date	Opponent	Result	Scorers	Att.	Baker CW	Durban WA	Harrington AC	Hogg D	Hole BG	John DJ	King JW	King PC	McCarthy DJA	McIntosh A	Milne AS	Moore G	Pickrell AD	Rankmore FEJ	Tapscott DJR	Veamcombe G	Walsh JB	Ward D
R1	Sep 13	WREXHAM	2-0	Moore, Ward	6750	6		2	11	4		9				3	10		5		1	7	8
R2	Oct 5	Mansfield Town	1-1	J King	17100	6	10	2		4	1	9			11	3			5			7	8
rep	23	MANSFIELD TOWN	2-1	J King, Ward	4800	6	10	2		4	1	9	7	11		3			5				8
R3	Nov 15	Bournemouth	0-3		12857	6	10	2		4	1	9	7			3		11		8			

Played at 5 in R3: GC Williams

Welsh Cup

Round	Date	Opponent	Result	Scorers	Att.	Baker CW	Durban WA	Edwards LT	Gammon SG	Harrington AC	Hogg D	Hole BG	John DJ	King JW	King PC	McCarthy DJA	Milne AS	Pickrell AD	Rankmore FEJ	Stitfall RF	Tapscott DJR	Veamcombe G	Ward D
R5	Jan 30	NEWPORT COUNTY	4-1	J King 2, Durban, P King	5715	6	8		4	2	11			9	7		3		5			1	10
R6	Feb 20	Bristol City	2-0	Ward 2	13579	6						4	1	9	7	11	3		5	2	8		10
SF	Mar 20	Bangor City	0-2		5482	6		2		5		4		10	7	11	3				9	1	8

SF at Wrexham

Anglo-French Friendship Cup

Date	Opponent	Result	Scorers	Att.	Baker CW	Charles M	Gammon SG	Harrington AC	Hole BG	John DJ	King JW	King PC	Milne AS	Moore G	Pickrell AD	Rankmore FEJ	Tapscott DJR	Veamcombe G	Walsh JB	Ward D
Dec 13	RC Lensois	4-2	P King 2, J King, Moore	1500	6			2	4	1	9	7	3	10	11	5	8			
Mar 7	RC LENSOIS	2-0	Tapscott, Charles	3000	6	8	2		4		9	11	3				7	1		10

Played at 5 on March 7: DT Peck

1962/63   10th in Division Two

#	Date	Opponent	Score	Scorers	Att	Allchurch IJ	Baker CW	Brack AHB	Charles M	Durban WA	Edwards LT	Fraser G	Harrington AC	Hole BG	Hooper PJ	John DJ	King PC	McIntosh A	Milne AS	Murray DJ	Peck DT	Rankmore FEJ	Sittfall RF	Swan MMG	Tapscott DJR	Vearncombe G	Williams GC
1	Aug 18	NEWCASTLE UNITED	4-4	Hooper, Charles, Hole 2	27569	10	6		9	8			2	4	11	1		7	3			5					
2	22	Norwich City	0-0		25360	10	6			8		9	2	4	11	1		7	3			5					
3	25	Derby County	2-1	Hooper (p), Allchurch	14538	10	6			8		9	2	4	11	1		7				5	3				
4	29	NORWICH CITY	2-4	Hooper 2	26103	10	6		9	8			2	4	11	1		7	3			5					
5	Sep 1	MIDDLESBROUGH	1-2	Neal (og)	18940	10	6	2				9		4	11			7	3			5			8	1	
6	4	Swansea Town	1-2	Charles	24687	10	6		9				2	4	11			7				5	3		8	1	
7	8	Huddersfield Town	0-1		17573	10	6		9				2	4	11			7				5	3		8	1	
8	12	GRIMSBY TOWN	5-3	Hooper, McIntosh, Charles 2, Allchurch	14426	10	6		9				2	4	11			7				5	3		8		
9	15	SWANSEA TOWN	5-2	P.Davies (og), Charles 2, McIntosh, Hooper	23454	10	6		9					4	11	1		7	2			5	3		8		
10	18	Grimsby Town	2-1	Hooper 2	10962	10	6		9				2	4	11	1		7				5	3		8		
11	22	PORTSMOUTH	1-2	Tapscott	22302	10	6		9				2	4	11	1		7				5	3		8		
12	29	Preston North End	6-2	Tapscott, Hooper 2, Charles 2, Durban	11994		6		9	10			2	4	11			7				5	3		8	1	
13	Oct 6	Chelsea	0-6		25484	10	6		9				2	4	11			7				5	3		8	1	
14	13	LUTON TOWN	1-0	Hooper	15901		6		9	10			2	4	11			7				5	3		8	1	
15	27	SCUNTHORPE UNITED	4-0	McIntosh, Allchurch 2, Tapscott	12003	10	6		5	8	2			4	11			7					3		9	1	
16	31	Southampton	5-3	Hole, Allchurch 2, McIntosh, Durban	16616	10	6		5	8	3			4	11			7					2		9	1	
17	Nov 3	Bury	0-1		9915	10	6		4	8	3		2		11			7				5			9	1	
18	10	ROTHERHAM UNITED	4-1	Durban 2, Hooper 2	14199	10	6			8	3		2	4	11			7				5			9	1	
19	17	Charlton Athletic	4-2	Tapscott 3, Hooper	11509	10	6		5	8	3		2	4	11			7							9	1	
20	24	STOKE CITY	1-1	McIntosh	21543	10	6		5	8	3		2	4	11			7							9	1	
21	Dec 1	Sunderland	1-2	Allchurch	37603	10	6		5	8	3		2	4	11			7							9	1	
22	8	LEEDS UNITED	0-0		11334	10	6		9		3		2		11			7				5			8	1	4
23	15	Newcastle United	1-2	Hooper	27916	10	6		5	8	3		2		11			7							9	1	4
24	22	DERBY COUNTY	1-0	Hooper	12027	10	6		5	8	3		2		11			7							9	1	4
25	26	Plymouth Argyle	2-4	Durban 2	18992					8	3			4	11			7				5	2		9	1	6
26	Feb 23	CHELSEA	1-0	Harrington	16108	10	4		9		3		2	6	11			7				5			8	1	
27	Mar 9	SOUTHAMPTON	3-1	Allchurch, Tapscott, McIntosh	12427	10	4		9		3		2	6	11			7				5			8	1	
28	15	Scunthorpe United	2-2	Allchurch 2	8060	10	4		9	8	3		2	6	11			7				5				1	
29	23	BURY	3-1	Threlfall (og), Hooper, Charles	15565	10	4		9	8	3		2	6	11			7				5				1	
30	29	Rotherham United	1-2	Allchurch	9131	10	4		9	8	3		2	6	11			7				5				1	
31	Apr 6	CHARLTON ATHLETIC	1-2	Hole	12619	10	4		9	8	3		2	6	11			7				5				1	
32	13	Stoke City	0-1		30453		4		9	10	7		2	6	11	1						5	3		8		
33	15	WALSALL	2-2	Edwards, Tapscott	11257		4			8	3			6	11	1	10	7				5	2		9		
34	16	Walsall	1-2	King	10381				9		3			6	11	1	10	7				5	2		8		4
35	20	SUNDERLAND	5-2	Tapscott, Hooper 2, McIntosh, Charles	12293		6		9		3		2		11	1	10	7				5			8		4
36	24	Luton Town	3-2	Hooper 3	7237		6		9				2		11	1	10	7				5	3		8		4
37	27	Leeds United	0-3		19702	10	6		9		3		2		11	1		7				5			8		4
38	May 1	PLYMOUTH ARGYLE	2-1	Allchurch, Hole	9673	8	6		9	10			2		11	1		7			3	5					4
39	4	Portsmouth	0-2		10538	8	6		5	10			2		11	1		7			3				9		4
40	6	PRESTON NORTH END	1-1	Charles	8389	10	6		9				2		11	1		7			3	5			8		4
41	11	Middlesbrough	2-3	McIntosh 2	9628	10				8			2	6	11	1		7			3	5			9		4
42	18	HUDDERSFIELD T	3-0	King 2, Tapscott	8774	8	6						2		11	1	10	7			3	5			9		4
					Apps	35	39	1	33	23	22	4	39	33	40	18	3	41	5	1	8	30	17	6	33	18	13
					Goals	12			11	6	1		1	5	22		3	9							10		

Three own goals

F.A. Cup

R	Date	Opponent	Score	Att	Allchurch IJ	Baker CW	Brack AHB	Charles M	Durban WA	Edwards LT	Fraser G	Harrington AC	Hole BG	Hooper PJ	John DJ	King PC	McIntosh A	Milne AS	Murray DJ	Peck DT	Rankmore FEJ	Sittfall RF	Swan MMG	Tapscott DJR	Vearncombe G	Williams GC
R3	Feb 18	Charlton Athletic	0-1	13448	10	6		5	8	3		2	4	11			7							9	1	

F.L. Cup

R	Date	Opponent	Score	Scorers	Att	Allchurch IJ	Baker CW	Brack AHB	Charles M	Durban WA	Edwards LT	Fraser G	Harrington AC	Hole BG	Hooper PJ	John DJ	King PC	McIntosh A	Milne AS	Murray DJ	Peck DT	Rankmore FEJ	Sittfall RF	Swan MMG	Tapscott DJR	Vearncombe G	Williams GC
R2	Sep 26	READING	5-1	Durban 2, Charles, Hooper (p), Tapscott	4500		6		9	10			2	4	11			7				5	3		8	1	
R3	Oct 23	Bristol City	0-2		15000	10	6		9	8			2	4	11			7				5	3			1	

Welsh Cup

R	Date	Opponent	Score	Att	Allchurch IJ	Baker CW	Brack AHB	Charles M	Durban WA	Edwards LT	Fraser G	Harrington AC	Hole BG	Hooper PJ	John DJ	King PC	McIntosh A	Milne AS	Murray DJ	Peck DT	Rankmore FEJ	Sittfall RF	Swan MMG	Tapscott DJR	Vearncombe G	Williams GC
R5	Mar 26	ABERGAVENNY THURS	7-1 * see below	2200	10	4			8	3		2	6	11			7				5			9	1	
R6	Apr 11	Swansea Town	0-2	11500	10			9		3		4	6	11			7				5	2		8	1	

Scorers in R5: Allchurch 2, Durban 2, Tapscott (og), Hooper, Hole

1963/64   15th in Division Two

No.	Date	Opponent	Score	Scorers	Att	Allchurch II	Baker CW	Charles M	Charles WJ	Coldrick GG	Edwards LT	Farrell GIP	Gammon SG	Halliday T	Hole BG	John DJ	King PC	Lewis B	Mallory RJL	McIntosh A	Milne AS	Murray DJ	Peck DT	Rodrigues PJ	Scott RSA	Stitfall RF	Tapscott DJR	Upton JEG	Vearncombe G	Watkins PJ	Williams GC
1	Aug 24	NORWICH CITY	3-1	King, J Charles, Allchurch	21977	10		4	5		2				8		11				7				9	3				1	6
2	28	MANCHESTER CITY	2-2	Allchurch, J Charles	25134	10		8	5		2				6		11				7				9	3			1		4
3	30	Scunthorpe United	2-1	Williams, Tapscott	8366	10					2				6	1	11				7	5			9	3	8				4
4	Sep 4	Manchester City	0-4		22138	10		8			2				6	1	11				7	5			4	3					9
5	7	PORTSMOUTH	1-2	J Charles	17523	10		9	5		2				6	1	11				7				4	3	8				
6	11	BURY	2-1	Allchurch 2	15855	10		9			2				6		11				7	5			8	3		1			4
7	13	Rotherham United	0-1		11568	10		9			2				6		11					5			8		7	3	1		4
8	17	Bury	1-4	Allchurch	11918	10		9	8		2				6						7	5					11	3	1		4
9	21	LEEDS UNITED	0-0		16117	10			9		2				6	1	11				7	5					8	3			4
10	28	Sunderland	3-3	Allchurch 3	37287	10			9		2				8	1	11				7	5		3	6						4
11	Oct 2	GRIMSBY TOWN	0-0		10657	10	4		9		2					1	8		11		7	5		3	6						
12	5	NORTHAMPTON T	1-0	M Charles	10178	10	4		9							1	8		11		7	5		3	6	2					
13	19	SWANSEA TOWN	1-1	Scott (p)	21417	10	4		9		2			8	4	1	7		11			5			6	3					
14	26	Charlton Athletic	2-5	McIntosh, J Charles	26534	10	4		5		2			9	8	1	7			11					6			3			
15	Nov 2	MIDDLESBROUGH	1-1	J Charles	13455	10	4		9		2				8	1	7			11		5		3	6						
16	9	Newcastle United	4-0	King 2, Allchurch, J Charles	38495	10	4		9		2				8	1	7			11		5		3	6						
17	16	HUDDERSFIELD T	2-1	McIntosh, Baker	14398	10	4		9		2			9			7			11				3	6		8		1		
18	23	Derby County	1-2	J Charles	11852	10	4		9		2				8		7			11		5		3	6				1		
19	30	PLYMOUTH ARGYLE	3-1	J Charles 2, Allchurch	11193	10	4		9		2				8		7			11		5		3	6				1		
20	Dec 7	Southampton	2-3	Halliday, J Charles	17861	10	4		9		2			8			7			11		5		3	6				1		
21	14	Norwich City	1-4	Halliday	14130	10			9					7	8	4				11		5		3	6	2			1		
22	26	PRESTON NORTH END	0-4		18682	10			9		2				4		7			11		5		3			8		1		6
23	28	Preston North End	0-4		19458		6		9		3			8	10	1				11		2	5				7				4
24	Jan 11	Portsmouth	0-5		12046	11		5	9	10	7			8		1							2		3				6		4
25	17	ROTHERHAM UNITED	2-1	M Charles, Scott (p)	8773	10		9	5		2						11	7					3		6		8		1		4
26	Feb 1	Leeds United	1-1	M Charles	28056	10		9	5		2					1	11	7					3		6		8				4
27	8	SUNDERLAND	0-2		15600	10		9	5		2					1	11	7					3		6		8				4
28	15	Northampton Town	1-2	M Charles	11871	10		9	5		2				8	1	11	7					3		6						4
29	22	LEYTON ORIENT	2-1	Scott (p), M Charles	8690	10		9	5		3				8	1		7					2		6		11				4
30	29	Huddersfield Town	1-2	Scott	10580	10		9	5		3				6	1		7					2		8		11				4
31	Mar 7	CHARLTON ATHLETIC	1-1	J Charles	8066	10		9	5		3				6	1		7					2		8		11				4
32	20	NEWCASTLE UNITED	2-2	Allchurch, M Charles	9096	10		9	5		3	7			6	1		11					2		8						3
33	27	Swindon Town	2-1	King, Lewis	22318	10			5			7		9	6	1	8	11					2		3		4				
34	28	Swansea Town	0-3		18721	10		9	5			11		7	6	1	8						2		3		4				
35	30	SWINDON TOWN	1-0	M Charles	14033	10		9	5			11		7	6	1	8						2		3		4				
36	Apr 4	DERBY COUNTY	2-1	M Charles, King	8238	10		9				11		7	6	1	8					5	2		3		4				
37	8	SCUNTHORPE UNITED	3-1	Farrell 2, King	9618	10		9	5			11		7	6	1	8						2		3		4				
38	11	Plymouth Argyle	1-1	King	14993	10		9	5			11		7	6	1	8						2		3		4				
39	13	Leyton Orient	0-4		7278	10		9	5			11		7		1	8						2		3		4				6
40	15	Grimsby Town	2-0	Scott (p), M Charles	8914	10		9					4				11	7				5	2		3	6			1		8
41	18	SOUTHAMPTON	2-4	Knapp (og), Williams	10727	10			5				4		6		11	7					2		3	8			1		9
42	24	Middlesbrough	1-3	Allchurch	8472	10	2		9						6	1	11	7				5			3	4					8
	Apps					41	12	26	33	1	30	8	2	12	30	28	34	16	3	21	5	20	15	22	36	8	15	5	14	1	24
	Goals					12	1	9	11			2		2			7	1		2					5		1				2

One own goal

F.A. Cup

	Date	Opponent	Score		Att	Allchurch II	Baker CW	Charles M	Charles WJ	Coldrick GG	Edwards LT	Farrell GIP	Gammon SG	Halliday T	Hole BG	John DJ	King PC	Lewis B	Mallory RJL	McIntosh A	Milne AS	Murray DJ	Peck DT	Rodrigues PJ	Scott RSA	Stitfall RF	Tapscott DJR	Upton JEG	Vearncombe G	Watkins PJ	Williams GC
R3	Jan 4	LEEDS UNITED	0-1		14000	8	6	5	9		2					10	1		11			7			3						4

F.L. Cup

	Date	Opponent	Score	Scorers	Att	Allchurch II	Baker CW	Charles M	Charles WJ	Coldrick GG	Edwards LT	Farrell GIP	Gammon SG	Halliday T	Hole BG	John DJ	King PC	Lewis B	Mallory RJL	McIntosh A	Milne AS	Murray DJ	Peck DT	Rodrigues PJ	Scott RSA	Stitfall RF	Tapscott DJR	Upton JEG	Vearncombe G	Watkins PJ	Williams GC
R2	Sep 25	WREXHAM	2-2	Tapscott 2	4600	10			5		2				6	1	11				7	4					8	3			9
rep	Oct 7	Wrexham	1-1	King	11299	10	4	9								1	8		11		7	5		3	6	2					
rep2	21	Wrexham	0-3		8838	10	2								4	1	8					5			9			3		6	

Played in R2 replay: A Burns (at 7), AHB Brack (11)

Welsh Cup

	Date	Opponent	Score	Scorers	Att	Allchurch II	Baker CW	Charles M	Charles WJ	Coldrick GG	Edwards LT	Farrell GIP	Gammon SG	Halliday T	Hole BG	John DJ	King PC	Lewis B	Mallory RJL	McIntosh A	Milne AS	Murray DJ	Peck DT	Rodrigues PJ	Scott RSA	Stitfall RF	Tapscott DJR	Upton JEG	Vearncombe G	Watkins PJ	Williams GC
R5	Jan 25	Ebbw Vale	6-1	M Charles 2, King 2, Lewis 2	4000	10		9	5		2						11	7				3			6		8		1		4
R6	Feb 19	CHESTER	3-1	M Charles, Hole, Tapscott	3120	10		9	5						8	1		7					2	3	6		11				4
SF	Mar 11	Newport County	2-2	Allchurch, M Charles	5200	10		9	5		3				6	1		7					2		8		11				4
rep	25	NEWPORT COUNTY	1-0	M Charles	8400	10		9	5						6	1	11	7					2	3	8						4
F1	Apr 22	Bangor City	0-2		10000	10		9	5			11			6	1	8	7					2	3	4						
F2	29	BANGOR CITY	3-1	Lewis, Allchurch, M Charles	6000	10	2	8	9						6		11	7				5			3					1	4
PO	May 4	Bangor City	2-0	King 2	10014	10	2	8	9						6	1	11	7						5	3					1	4

SF at Swansea, Final play-off at Wrexham

1964/65   13th in Division Two

#	Date	Opponent	Result	Scorers	Att	Allchurch Il	Baker CW	Charles M	Charles WJ	Coldrick GG	Ellis KD	Farrell GJP	Gammon SG	Halliday T	Harrington AC	Harris GW	Hole BG	John DJ	Johnston G	King GH	King PC	Lewis B	Lloyd RC	Milne AS	Murray DJ	Peck DT	Rodrigues PJ	Scott RSA	Tapscott DJR	Williams GC	Wilson RJ
1	Aug 22	IPSWICH TOWN	0-0		16911	10		9	5			7	4				6				8	11			3		2				1
2	26	PRESTON NORTH END	3-3	Allchurch 2, Lewis	15805	10		9	5				4				6		11		8	7			3		2				1
3	29	Plymouth Argyle	1-3	Hole (p)	14585	10		9	5				4				6		11		8	7			3		2				1
4	31	Preston North End	1-1	Allchurch	23303	10		8	5					9			6				11	7			3		2			4	1
5	Sep 5	BOLTON WANDERERS	1-3	Allchurch	13501	10			5					9			6				11	7			3		2			4	1
6	12	Middlesbrough	0-0		22770	10		8	5					9			6				11	7			3		2			4	1
7	16	HUDDERSFIELD T	1-1	Hole (p)	9392	10		8	5			11		9			6				7				3		2			4	1
8	19	NEWCASTLE UNITED	1-1	Allchurch	11826	10			5	9		11					6				7		8		3		2			4	1
9	26	Northampton Town	0-1		12328	10			5								6			11	7		8		3		2		9	4	1
10	29	Huddersfield Town	1-3	Allchurch	5640	10			5		9						6				7	11			3		2		8	4	1
11	Oct 6	Rotherham United	1-3	Ellis	12601	10	8				9						6				7	11		5	3		2			4	1
12	10	DERBY COUNTY	2-1	P King Tapscott	8302	10					9						6				7	11		5	3		2		8	4	1
13	17	Swindon Town	3-3	Hole (p), M Charles 2	15937			10				7					6				8	11		5	3		2		9	4	1
14	24	PORTSMOUTH	1-0	Tapscott	8696						10	7					6				8	11			3	5	2		9	4	1
15	31	Manchester City	0-2		13146						10	7					6				8	11			3	5	2		9	4	1
16	Nov 7	CHARLTON ATHLETIC	2-1	Ellis 2	9616						10	7			2		6				8	11				5	3		9	4	1
17	14	Leyton Orient	3-1	Ellis 2 Lewis	6350						10	7			2		6				8	11				5	3		9	4	1
18	21	BURY	4-0	Tapscott 2, Ellis, Lewis	9883						10	7			2		6				8	11				5	3		9	4	1
19	28	Crystal Palace	0-0		18188						10	7			2		6				8	11				5	3		9	4	1
20	Dec 5	NORWICH CITY	1-3	Butler (og)	9877						10	7			2		6				8	11				5	3		9	4	1
21	12	Ipswich Town	1-1	Ellis	10010				4		9				2		6				10	11				5	3		7	8	1
22	19	PLYMOUTH ARGYLE	4-0	Tapscott 2 Neale (og), Rodrigues	9555						9	7			2		6	1			10	11				5	3		8	4	
23	26	Swansea Town	2-3	Ellis 2	17875				4		9	7	8		2		6	1			10	11				5	3				
24	Jan 15	MIDDLESBROUGH	6-1	P.King 3, Tapscott 2, Williams	9490				4			7			2		6				10	11				5	3		9	8	1
25	23	Newcastle United	0-2		37291						10	7			2		6				8	11				5	3		9	4	1
26	Feb 6	NORTHAMPTON T	0-2		7427			9				7			2		6				8	11				5	3		10	4	1
27	13	Southampton	1-1	Allchurch	14740	10			4		9	7					6					11			3	5	2			8	1
28	20	Derby County	0-1		10894	10					9	7					6		11		8				3	5	2			8	1
29	27	SWINDON TOWN	2-0	Ellis, Hole	9197	10			4		9	7					6				11				3	5	2			8	1
30	Mar 6	Norwich City	1-2	Allchurch	18036	10			4		9	7					6				11				3	5	2			8	1
31	12	MANCHESTER CITY	2-2	Allchurch, P King	9094	10			4		9	7					6				11				3	5	2			8	1
32	22	Charlton Athletic	2-2	Williams 2	7710	10			4		9	7				3	6				11						2			8	1
33	24	SOUTHAMPTON	2-2	Williams, J Charles	9642	10			4		9	7				3	6				11						2			8	1
34	27	LEYTON ORIENT	0-2		7627	10			4		9	7				3	6				11						2			8	1
35	Apr 3	Bury	2-1	King, Hole	4292	8			4							3	6			7	10	11				5	2			9	1
36	6	SWANSEA TOWN	5-0	Allchurch 3, J Charles 2	15896	8					9					3	6			7	10	11				5	2			4	1
37	10	CRYSTAL PALACE	0-0		9585	8	3				9						6			7	10	11				5	2			4	1
38	17	Portsmouth	0-1		13275	8	3			5	9						6			7	10	11					2			4	1
39	19	COVENTRY CITY	3-1	King, Allchurch 2	11228	8	3				9						6			7	10	11				5	2			4	1
40	20	Coventry City	2-0	Lewis, Hole	23913	8	3				9						6			7	10	11				5	2			4	1
41	24	ROTHERHAM UNITED	3-2	Allchurch, Rodrigues, King	9794	8	3				9						6			7	10	11				5	2			4	1
42	28	Bolton Wanderers	0-1		6498		3			9		8					6			7	10	11				5				4	1
		Apps				27	6	8	28	3	22	25	4	4	11	5	42	2	9	6	39	31	2	3	31	18	41	1	16	38	40
		Goals				15		2	3		9						6				8	4					2		9	4	

Two own goals

F.A. Cup

Rd	Date	Opponent	Result	Scorers	Att	Allchurch Il	Baker CW	Charles M	Charles WJ	Coldrick GG	Ellis KD	Farrell GJP	Gammon SG	Halliday T	Harrington AC	Harris GW	Hole BG	John DJ	Johnston G	King GH	King PC	Lewis B	Lloyd RC	Milne AS	Murray DJ	Peck DT	Rodrigues PJ	Scott RSA	Tapscott DJR	Williams GC	Wilson RJ
R3	Jan 9	CHARLTON ATHLETIC	1-2	Tapscott	13500						10	7			2		6				8	11				5	3		9	4	1

F.L. Cup

Rd	Date	Opponent	Result	Scorers	Att	Allchurch Il	Baker CW	Charles M	Charles WJ	Coldrick GG	Ellis KD	Farrell GJP	Gammon SG	Halliday T	Harrington AC	Harris GW	Hole BG	John DJ	Johnston G	King GH	King PC	Lewis B	Lloyd RC	Milne AS	Murray DJ	Peck DT	Rodrigues PJ	Scott RSA	Tapscott DJR	Williams GC	Wilson RJ
R2	Sep 23	Southampton	2-3	Lewis, P King	13076	10			5								6				7	11	8		3		2		9	4	1

European Cup Winners Cup

Rd	Date	Opponent	Result	Scorers	Att	Allchurch Il	Baker CW	Charles M	Charles WJ	Coldrick GG	Ellis KD	Farrell GJP	Gammon SG	Halliday T	Harrington AC	Harris GW	Hole BG	John DJ	Johnston G	King GH	King PC	Lewis B	Lloyd RC	Milne AS	Murray DJ	Peck DT	Rodrigues PJ	Scott RSA	Tapscott DJR	Williams GC	Wilson RJ
R1/1	Sep 9	Esbjerg	0-0		10000	10		8	5			11		9			6	1			7				3		2			4	
R1/2	Oct 13	ESBJERG	1-0	P King	8784	10						7					6	1			8	11			3	5	2		9	4	
R2/1	Dec 16	Sporting Lisbon	2-1	Farrell, Tapscott	20000				4			7			2		6	1			10	11				5	3		9	8	
R2/2	23	SPORTING LISBON	0-0		25000				4			7			2		6				10	11				5	3		9	8	1
QF1	Jan 20	Real Zaragoza	2-2	Williams, P King	35000				4			7			2		6				10	11				5	3		9	8	1
QF2	Feb 3	REAL ZARAGOZA	0-1		38458				4			7			2		6				10	11				5	3		9	8	1

Welsh Cup

Rd	Date	Opponent	Result	Scorers	Att	Allchurch Il	Baker CW	Charles M	Charles WJ	Coldrick GG	Ellis KD	Farrell GJP	Gammon SG	Halliday T	Harrington AC	Harris GW	Hole BG	John DJ	Johnston G	King GH	King PC	Lewis B	Lloyd RC	Milne AS	Murray DJ	Peck DT	Rodrigues PJ	Scott RSA	Tapscott DJR	Williams GC	Wilson RJ
R5	Jan 26	Merthyr Tydfil	3-1	P King 2, Tapscott	6000						10	7			2		6				8	11				5	3		9	4	1
R6	Feb 17	HEREFORD UNITED	3-1	Allchurch, Ellis, Farrell (p)	8000	10		8			9	7					6					11			3	5	2			4	1
SF	Mar 10	Swansea Town	1-0	Farrell (p)	7500	10			4		9	7					6					11			3	5	2		8		1
F1	Apr 12	WREXHAM	5-1	Johnston 2, Allchurch, P King 2	7000	8	3				9						6			7	10	11				5	2			4	1
F2	26	Wrexham	0-1		8000	8	3				9				2		6			7	10	11				5				4	1
PO	May 5	Wrexham	3-0	Allchurch 2, Mielczarek (og)	7840	8	3			9	2						6			7	10	11				5				4	1

Play Off at Shrewsbury

1965/66   20th in Division Two

#	Date	Opponent	Res	Scorers	Att	Andrews G	Baker CW	Bird RP	Carver DF	Charles WJ	Coldrick GG	Davies DL	Farrell GJP	Ferguson RB	Harkin JT	Harrington AC	Hole BG	Houston D	John DJ	Johnston G	King PC	Lewis B	Murphy P	Murray DJ	Rodrigues PJ	Summerhayes DM	Toshack JB	Williams GC	Wilson RJ
1	Aug 21	BURY	1-0	Charles	13392	4				9	5		7			3	6			10		11		2		12		8	1
2	25	DERBY COUNTY	2-1	Harkin, Charles	15260		3			9			7		10		6			8		11		5	2			4	1
3	28	Norwich City	2-3	Johnston (p), Harkin	13437		3			9			7		10		6			8		11		5	2			4	1
4	Sep 1	Derby County	5-1	Johnston 2 (1p), Charles 2, Harkin	10221					9	2		7		10		6			8		11		5	3			4	1
5	4	WOLVERHAMPTON W.	1-4	Johnston (p)	19827					9	2		7		10		6			8		11		5	3			4	1
6	11	Rotherham United	4-6	Farrell, Harkin 2, Johnston	9211					9			7		10	2	6			8		11		5	3			4	1
7	14	Charlton Athletic	2-5	Harkin, Johnston	13172								7		10	2	6			8	9	11		5	3			4	1
8	18	MANCHESTER CITY	4-3	Johnston 2, Hole, Harkin	11365		3				4				9		6		1	7	10	11		5	2			8	
9	25	Bristol City	1-1	Lewis	15300		3				4				10		6		1	7	8	11		5	2			9	
10	Oct 6	COVENTRY CITY	1-2	Williams	12469		3				4				10		6		1	7	8	11		5	2	12		9	
11	9	Plymouth Argyle	2-2	Farrell, Johnston	10740								7		9	3	6		1	8	10	11		5	2			4	
12	16	Portsmouth	1-2	Johnston	11781	9				5			7		10		6			12	8	11		2	3	4			1
13	23	Bolton Wanderers	1-2	Andrews	11088	9							7		12	2		6		8	10	11		5	3	4			1
14	30	IPSWICH TOWN	1-0	Farrell	8325	9							7		10	2	4	6		8	11			5	3	12			1
15	Nov 6	Birmingham City	2-4	Andrews 2	10744	9					5		7		10	2	4	6		8	11			3					1
16	10	CHARLTON ATHLETIC	3-1	Johnston 2 (2p), Andrews	8537	9					5		7			2	4	6		8	11			3					1
17	13	LEYTON ORIENT	3-1	Johnston, Andrews, Toshack	9017	9					5		7			2	4	6		10	11			3			12	8	1
18	20	Middlesbrough	4-3	Toshack 2, Davidson (og) Johnston (p)	11898	9	3						7			2	4	6		8	11						10	5	1
19	27	HUDDERSFIELD T	0-1		10898	9							7			2	4	6		8	11			3			10	5	1
20	Dec 4	Crystal Palace	0-0		11527	9							7			2	4	6		8	11			3			10	5	1
21	11	PRESTON NORTH END	1-3	Johnston	10754	9							7			2	4	6		8	10	11		3				5	1
22	18	Portsmouth	1-3	Andrews	8434	9							7			2	4	6		8	11			5	3		10		1
23	27	SOUTHAMPTON	3-5	Harkin, Andrews, Walker (og)	14768	9							7		10	2	6			8	11			5	3			4	1
24	Jan 1	PLYMOUTH ARGYLE	5-1	Andrews 2, Harkin 2, Hole	8890	9	12					1	7	3	10	2	8	6			11			5				4	
25	8	Leyton Orient	1-1	Andrews	5516	9						1	7	3	10	2	6			8	11		12	5				4	
26	29	Bury	1-1	Johnston	4677	9			2			1		3	10		6			8	11	7		5				4	
27	Feb 19	Wolverhampton Wan.	1-2	Andrews	24179	9	11	2				1		3			6			8	10	7		5				4	
28	26	ROTHERHAM UNITED	0-0		9184	9	11	2				1		3			6			10	8	7		5				4	
29	Mar 5	BOLTON WANDERERS	1-1	Farrell	8951	9		2				1	7	3			6			8	10	11		5				4	
30	12	Manchester City	2-2	Toshack, Johnston	29642	8		2				1	7	3			6			10	11			5			9	4	
31	18	BRISTOL CITY	2-1	King, Toshack	13405	8		2			6		7	3			5		1	10	11						9	4	
32	26	Coventry City	1-3	Andrews	20296	9		2			5		7	3			6		1	11	8						10	4	
33	Apr 2	BIRMINGHAM CITY	1-3	Hole	8150	9	11	2					7	3			6			8	10			5				4	
34	8	CARLISLE UNITED	1-1	Andrews	7844	9	11	2					7	3			6			8	10			5				4	
35	9	Ipswich Town	1-2	Toshack	10392	9		3			2	1	7				8	6			11			5			10	4	
36	12	Carlisle United	0-2		11252	9	11	2				1	7	3	10		6	12		8				5				4	
37	20	Southampton	2-3	King 2	18941	9		3			2		7				6	10	1	12	8	11		5				4	
38	23	Huddersfield Town	1-1	King	19138	9		3			2		7				6	10	1		8	11		5				4	
39	30	CRYSTAL PALACE	1-0	King	9420	9		3			2		7	12			6	8	1		10	11		5				4	
40	May 3	MIDDLESBROUGH	5-3	Hole, Farrell (p), Andrews 2, King	12935	9		3			2		7	8			6		1		10	11		5				4	
41	7	Preston North End	0-9		10018	8		2			4		7	3			10			9	11			5		6			
42	10	Norwich City	0-2		5934	9		3			2		7				6	1	8	10	11			5		4			

	Andrews G	Baker CW	Bird RP	Carver DF	Charles WJ	Coldrick GG	Davies DL	Farrell GJP	Ferguson RB	Harkin JT	Harrington AC	Hole BG	Houston D	John DJ	Johnston G	King PC	Lewis B	Murphy P	Murray DJ	Rodrigues PJ	Summerhayes DM	Toshack JB	Williams GC	Wilson RJ
Apps	31	8	5	17	7	18	11	36	15	20	17	40	17	12	36	35	24	1	32	22	7	8	35	19
Goals	15				4			5		10		4			17	6	1					6	1	

Two own goals

F.A. Cup

Rnd	Date	Opponent	Res	Scorers	Att	Andrews G	Bird RP	Coldrick GG	Davies DL	Farrell GJP	Ferguson RB	Harkin JT	Hole BG	Johnston G	King PC	Lewis B	Murray DJ	Williams GC
R3	Jan 26	PORT VALE	2-1	King, Hole	18898	2			1	7	3	10	6		8	9	11	5	4
R4	Feb 12	Southport	0-2		14230		2		9	1	7	3	10	6		8	11	5	4

F.L. Cup

Rnd	Date	Opponent	Res	Scorers	Att																								
R2	Sep 22	Crewe Alexandra	1-1	Lewis	5832	3			4		9	6	1	7	10	11	5	2	8
rep	29	CREWE ALEXANDRA	3-0	King 2, Harkin	6939	3			4	11	10	6	1	7	8	5	2	9
R3	13	PORTSMOUTH	2-0	King, Andrews	8803	9			5	7	10	6	8	11	2	3	4	1
R4	Nov 3	READING	5-1	Johnston 3, Harkin 2	6698	9			5	7	10	2	4	6	8	11	3	1
R5	17	IPSWICH TOWN	2-1	Hole, Andrews	8000	9			7	2	4	6	8	11	3	10	5	1
SF1	Dec 15	West Ham United	2-5	Andrews 2	19980	9			7	8	2	4	6	11	5	3	10	4
SF2	Feb 2	WEST HAM UNITED	1-5	Lewis	14313	9		2	1	11	6	8	10	7	5	4

Played at 3 in SF2: D Yorath

European Cup Winners Cup

Rnd	Date	Opponent	Res	Scorers	Att													
R1/1	Sep 8	STANDARD LIEGE	1-2	Johnston	12738	9	7	10	2	6	8	11	5	3	4	1
R1/2	Oct 20	Standard Liege	0-1		32000	9	7	10	2	6	8	11	5	3	4	1

Welsh Cup

Rnd	Date	Opponent	Res	Scorers	Att												
R5	Jan 4	Swansea Town	2-2	King, Andrews	10275	9	3	1	7	10	2	6	8	11	5	4
rep	Feb 8	SWANSEA TOWN	3-5	Johnston 2, Williams	9836	9	3	2	1	7	10	6	8	11	5	4

1966/67 20th in Division Two

#	Date	Opponent	Score	Scorers	Att	John DJ	Carver DF	Ferguson RB	Williams GC	Murray DJ	Coldrick GG	Farrell GP	King PC	Andrews G	Toshack JB	Lewis B	Johnston G	Bird RP	Davies DL	Bell G	Ryder DF	Houston D	Jones BH	Summerhayes DM	Brown RH	Harris B	Wilson RI	Winspear J	Jones BS	Dean N	Phillips L
1	Aug 20	IPSWICH TOWN	0-2		7628	1	2	3	4	5	6	7	8	9	10	11															
2	27	Bristol City	2-1	Toshack (p), Andrews	11952	1	2	3	6	5	4	7	8	9	10	11															
3	31	WOLVERHAMPTON W.	0-3		14208	1	2	3	4	5	6	7	8	9	10	11															
4	Sep 3	CARLISLE UNITED	4-2	King 2, Andrews, Toshack	6902	1	2	3	4	5	6	7	8	9	10	11															
5	7	HUDDERSFIELD T	1-1	Andrews	10344	1	2	3	4	5	6	7	8	9	10	11															
6	10	Blackburn Rovers	1-4	Toshack	12805	1	2	3	4	5	6	7	8	9	10	11															
7	17	BOLTON WANDERERS	2-5	Andrews, Toshack (p)	7594	1	2	3	4	5	6	7	8	9	10	11															
8	21	Wolverhampton Wan.	1-7	Andrews	19678			3	8	5	4	7	10	9	12	11				1	6										
9	24	Charlton Athletic	0-5		10182		2	3	4	5	6	7		9		10		8		1	11										
10	Oct 1	DERBY COUNTY	1-1	Sexton (og)	6244		2		4				10	9				7	8	1	11	3	6	12							
11	8	HULL CITY	2-4	Lewis, Andrews	9407		2		4				10	8		11	7			1		3			9	6					
12	15	Plymouth Argyle	1-7	Williams	14404		2		4	5		7	10	8				11		1		3			9	6	1				
13	29	Millwall	0-1		12856			3	4	5	2		10		8			11							9	6	1				
14	Nov 4	ROTHERHAM UNITED	0-0		5933			3	4	5	2	12	10		7	8		11							9	6	1				
15	12	Preston North End	0-4		11283			3	4	5	2	8	7	9				11								6	1	10			
16	19	BURY	3-0	Toshack 2, Brown	5910			3	4	5	2	7	10		8			11							9	6	1				
17	26	Coventry City	2-3	Toshack 2	19682			3	4	5	2	7			8		10	11							9	6	1				
18	Dec 3	NORWICH CITY	2-0	Farrall, Coldrick	5540			3	4	5	2	7	10		8			11							9	6	1				
19	10	Birmingham City	2-1	Coldrick, Brown	17046			3	4	5	2	7	10		8			11							9	6	1				
20	14	NORTHAMPTON T	4-2	G.Williams 2, Brown 2	7954			3	4	5	2	7	10		8	7		11							9	6	1				
21	17	Ipswich Town	0-0		11166			3	4	5	2		10		8	7		11						12	9	6	1				
22	26	CRYSTAL PALACE	1-2	G. Williams	17020			3	4	5	2	7	10		8			11							9	6	1				
23	27	Crystal Palace	1-3	Toshack	13553			3	4	5	2	7	10		8			11							9	6	1				
24	31	BRISTOL CITY	5-1	Brown 2, Low (og), Bird 2	12306			3	4	5	2	7	10			8		11						12	9	6	1				
25	Jan 7	Carlisle United	0-3		10295			3		5	2	7	10			8		11						4	9	6	1				
26	14	BLACKBURN ROVERS	1-1	Brown	11322			3		5	2	7	10			8		11						4	9	6	1				
27	21	Bolton Wanderers	1-3	Johnston	9071			3	4	5	2	11	10			7	8								9	6	1				
28	Feb 3	CHARLTON ATHLETIC	4-1	Bird, Johnston 2, King	10812			3	4	5	2		10			8		11							9	6	1	7			
29	11	Derby County	1-1	Brown	14573			3	4	5	2	7	10			8		11							9	6	1				
30	25	Hull City	0-1		23629			3	4	5	2		10	8				7			11				9	6	1				
31	Mar 4	MILLWALL	1-1	King	10845		2	3	4	5		7	10	9		8		11							9	6	1		7	8	
32	18	Northampton Town	0-2		11787		2	3	4	5			10					11							9	6	1		7	8	
33	22	PORTSMOUTH	0-0		11727			3	4	5	2		10					11							9	6	1		7	8	
34	25	PLYMOUTH ARGYLE	4-1	Toshack, Dean, Jones, Brown	11696		2	3	4	5	6		11		10										9		1		7	8	
35	27	Portsmouth	2-1	Williams, King	16363		2	3	4	5	6		10					11							9		1		7	8	
36	Apr 1	Rotherham United	1-4	Jones	8585		2	3	4	5	6		10					11							9		1		7	8	
37	8	PRESTON NORTH END	4-0	Jones, King, Ross (og), Brown	9630			3	4	5	2		8					11							9	6	1		7	10	
38	15	Bury	0-2		6234			3	4	5	2		10					11							8	6	1		7	9	
39	22	COVENTRY CITY	1-1	Brown	19739			3	4	5	2		10	9				11								6	1		7	9	
40	29	Norwich City	2-3	Williams, Dean	14264			3	4	5	2		10	8				11								6	1		7	9	12
41	May 6	BIRMINGHAM CITY	3-0	Brown 2, Jones	12678			3	4	5	2		10					11							8	6	1		7	9	
42	13	Huddersfield Town	1-3	Brown	3847			3	4	5	2		10					11							8	6	1		7	9	
	Apps					7	17	39	40	40	39	25	40	12	23	16	14	27	5	3	4	1	1	5	29	28	30	1	12	10	1
	Goals								6	2	1	6	6	10		1	3	3							14				4	2	

Three own goals

F.A. Cup

	Date	Opponent	Score	Scorers	Att	Ferguson	Williams	Murray	Coldrick	King	Johnston/Farrell	Toshack	Bird	Summerhayes	Brown	Harris	Wilson
R3	Jan 28	Barnsley	1-1	Bird	21464	3	4	5	2	10	7	8	11		9	6	1
rep	31	BARNSLEY	2-1	Johnston (p), King	21020	3	4	5	2	10	7	8	11	12	9	6	1
R4	Feb 18	MANCHESTER CITY	1-1	Williams	37205	3	4	5	2	7 10		8	11		9	6	1
rep	22	Manchester City	1-3	Johnson (p)	41616	3	4	5	2	7 10		8	11		9	6	1

F.L. Cup

	Date	Opponent	Score	Scorers	Att	John	Carver	Ferguson	Williams	Murray	Coldrick	Andrews	Toshack	Lewis	Johnston	Summerhayes
R1	Aug 24	BRISTOL ROVERS	1-0	Toshack	5574	1	2	3	4	5	6	9	10	11	7	
R2	Sep 14	EXETER CITY	0-1		5384	1	2	3	4	5	6	9	10	11	7	12

Played at 8 in both games (subbed in R2): JT Harkin

Welsh Cup

	Date	Opponent	Score	Scorers	Att	Carver	Ferguson	Williams	Murray	Coldrick	Farrell	King	Toshack	Lewis	Johnston	Bird	Summerhayes	Brown	Harris	Wilson	Jones BS	Dean
R5	Jan 17	Swansea Town	4-0	Lewis, Farrell, Johnston 2	11816		3	4	5	2	11	10	8		7			9	6	1		
R6	Feb 8	HEREFORD UNITED	6-3	*see below	11190		3	4	5	2	7	10	8			11		9	6	1		
SF	Mar 15	Newport County	2-1	Brown, King	8500	2	3	4	5			10	8			11	7	9	6	1		
F1	Apr 17	Wrexham	2-2	Brown, King	11437		3	4	5	2		10				11		8	6	1	7	9
F2	May 3	WREXHAM	2-1	Dean, Showell (og)	8299		3	4	5	2		10				11		8	6	1	7	9

Scorers in R6: King, Johnston 2, Coldrick, Ferguson, Brown

1967/68   13th in Division Two

#	Date	Opponent	Result	Scorers	Att	Allan AB	Bell G	Bird RP	Brown RH	Carver DF	Clark BD	Clarke MMcQ	Coldrick GG	Davies F	Dean N	Derrett SC	Ferguson RB	Harris B	Jones BH	Jones BS	King PC	Lea L	Lewis B	Morgan RL	Murray DJ	Phillips L	Summerhayes DM	Toshack JB	Williams GC	Wilson RI
1	Aug 19	PLYMOUTH ARGYLE	1-1	Brown (p)	17169	9			10	4			2				3	6		7	11				5				8	1
2	Aug 26	Bolton Wanderers	1-1	King	10654			11	9	4			2				3	6		7	10				5				8	1
3	Aug 30	CRYSTAL PALACE	4-2	Jones, Brown, Bird, King	14351			11	8				2	9			3	6		7	10				5				4	1
4	Sep 2	Portsmouth	1-3	Brown	17308			11	8	2		12		9			3	6		7	10				5				4	1
5	Sep 5	Charlton Athletic	1-1	Brown	8523			11	8	2		10					3	6		7	9				5				4	1
6	Sep 9	NORWICH CITY	3-1	King, Brown (p), Jones	14674			11	8				2				3	6		7	10				5			9	4	1
7	Sep 16	Rotherham United	2-3	King, Murray	5842			11	8			10	2				3	6		7	9				5			12	4	1
8	Sep 23	DERBY COUNTY	1-5	Bird (p)	15375	8		11				12	2				3	6		7	10				5				9	1
9	Sep 27	Crystal Palace	1-2	Jones	20424			11	8			10	2				3	6		7	9				5				4	1
10	Sep 30	Preston North End	0-3		13735			11				8	2				3	6		7	10				5			12	9	1
11 Oct	Oct 7	IPSWICH TOWN	1-1	Toshack	11261				8	3			2					6		7	10		11		5			9	4	1
12	Oct 14	Bristol City	1-1	Brown	15609			11	10			4	2				3	6		7	8				5			9		1
13	Oct 24	MIDDLESBROUGH	3-0	Toshack 2, King	10441			11	8			4	2				3	6		7	9				5			10		1
14	Oct 27	Hull City	2-1	Brown, Bird	18579			11	8			4	2				3	6		7	9				5			10		1
15 Nov	Nov 11	Blackpool	1-3	Clarke	11324			11	8	3		4	2					6		7	10				5			9		1
16	Nov 18	BIRMINGHAM CITY	1-3	Toshack	13673			11	8			4				2	3	6		7	10				5			9		1
17	Nov 25	Carlisle United	3-1	Toshack 2, Bell	10966		11		8			4				2	3	6		7	9				5			10		1
18 Dec	Dec 2	BLACKBURN ROVERS	3-2	King 2, Clarke	9829			11	8	3		4				2		6		7	10				5			9		1
19	Dec 5	MILLWALL	2-2	Toshack, Brown	11993			11	8	3		4				2		6		7	9				5			10		1
20	Dec 9	Huddersfield Town	0-1		8552				8	3		4			11	2		6		7	9				5			10		1
21	Dec 16	Plymouth Argyle	0-0		10736		11		8	3		4	2					6		7	9				5			10		1
22	Dec 23	BOLTON WANDERERS	1-3	Brown	11082				8	3		4	2					6		7	10	11			5			9		1
23	Dec 26	ASTON VILLA	3-0	Lea 2, Toshack	18180		12		8	3		4	2					6		7	9	11			5			10		1
24	Dec 30	Aston Villa	1-2	Dean	17667							4			8	2	3	6		7	10	11			5			9		1
25 Jan	Jan 6	PORTSMOUTH	3-0	Clarke, Bird, King	14925			11				4		1		2	3	6		7	9	8			5			10		
26	Jan 20	ROTHERHAM UNITED	2-2	Bird, Phillips	8748	3	11					4	2	1				6		7	9	8			5	12		10		
27 Feb	Feb 3	Derby County	4-3	Clark 2, King 2	18096	2					8		6	1		4	3			7	10	11			5			9		
28	Feb 10	PRESTON NORTH END	2-0	Clark, Toshack	12897						8	4		1		2	3	6		7	10	11			5			9		
29	Feb 24	Ipswich Town	2-4	Clark, Lea	15580						8	4		1		2	3	6		7	9	11			5			10		
30 Mar	Mar 2	BRISTOL CITY	0-1		15334						8	4		1		2	3	6		7	10	11			5			9		
31	Mar 9	Middlesbrough	3-2	Toshack, Clark, Jones	15582						8	4				2	3	6		7	10	11			5			9		1
32	Mar 22	HULL CITY	2-3	Clark, King	11975						8			1		4	2	3	6	7	9	11			5			10		
33	Mar 30	Millwall	1-3	Lea	7904						8	4	2	1		12	3	6		7	9	11			5			10		
34 Apr	Apr 6	BLACKPOOL	1-3	King	14416		11					4	2		8		3	6		7	10				5			9		1
35	Apr 12	Queen's Park Rangers	0-1		23043						8	4	2	1	12		3	6		7	9	11			5			10		
36	Apr 13	Birmingham City	0-0		29044						2	8	10	1	4		3	6	12	7	9	11			5					
37	Apr 16	QUEEN'S PARK RANGERS	1-0	Toshack	20021						2	8	4	1			3	6		7	10	11			5			9		
38	Apr 20	CARLISLE UNITED	1-0	Jones	13926						2	8	4	1			3	6		7	10	11			5			9		
39	Apr 27	Blackburn Rovers	1-1	Jones (p)	7195						2	8	4	1			3	6		7	10	11		5				9		
40 May	May 4	HUDDERSFIELD T	0-0		10647						8	4		1		2	3	6		7	10	11			5			9		
41	May 8	Norwich City	0-1		10177						2	4		1	9		3	6		7	8	11			5			10		
42	May 11	CHARLTON ATHLETIC	0-0		8396						2	4		1	8	12	3	6		7	9	11			5			10		
		Apps				2	5	20	21	19	14	36	20	16	10	17	32	39	1	42	42	20	1	2	40	2	1	35	11	26
		Goals					1	5	9		6	3			1					6	12	4			1	1		11		

F.A. Cup

#	Date	Opponent	Result	Scorers	Att	Allan AB	Bell G	Bird RP	Brown RH	Carver DF	Clark BD	Clarke MMcQ	Coldrick GG	Davies F	Dean N	Derrett SC	Ferguson RB	Harris B	Jones BH	Jones BS	King PC	Lea L	Lewis B	Morgan RL	Murray DJ	Phillips L	Summerhayes DM	Toshack JB	Williams GC	Wilson RI
R3 Jan	Jan 27	Stoke City	1-4	Jones	23563					12	8	4		1		2	3	6		7	10			11	5			9		

F.L. Cup

#	Date	Opponent	Result	Scorers	Att	Allan AB	Bell G	Bird RP	Brown RH	Carver DF	Clark BD	Clarke MMcQ	Coldrick GG	Davies F	Dean N	Derrett SC	Ferguson RB	Harris B	Jones BH	Jones BS	King PC	Lea L	Lewis B	Morgan RL	Murray DJ	Phillips L	Summerhayes DM	Toshack JB	Williams GC	Wilson RI
R1	Aug 23	Aldershot	3-2	Brown 2, King	5133			11	8				2	9			3	6		7	10				5				4	1
R2	Sep 12	Burnley	1-2	Coldrick	11631			11	8			10	2				3	6		7	9				5				4	1

European Cup Winners Cup

#	Date	Opponent	Result	Scorers	Att	Allan AB	Bell G	Bird RP	Brown RH	Carver DF	Clark BD	Clarke MMcQ	Coldrick GG	Davies F	Dean N	Derrett SC	Ferguson RB	Harris B	Jones BH	Jones BS	King PC	Lea L	Lewis B	Morgan RL	Murray DJ	Phillips L	Summerhayes DM	Toshack JB	Williams GC	Wilson RI
R1/1	Sep 20	Shamrock Rovers	1-1	King	21883			11				10	2				3	6		7	9				5			8	4	1
R1/2 Oct	Oct 4	SHAMROCK ROVERS	2-0	Brown (p), Toshack	14180			11	8	3			2					6		7	10				5			9	4	1
R2/1 Nov	Nov 15	NAC (Breda)	1-1	King	10000				7	8		4				2	3	6		11	9				5			10		1
R2/2	Nov 29	NAC (Breda)	4-1	Brown, Jones, Toshack, Clarke	16411		11		8			4	2				3	6		7	10				5			10		1
QF1 Mar	Mar 6	TORPEDO MOSCOW	1-0	BS Jones	30567			11				4				2	3	6	8	7	9				5			10		1
QF2	Mar 19	Torpedo Moscow	0-1		65000			11				4			8	2	3	6		7	9				5			10		1
rep Apr	Apr 3	Torpedo Moscow	1-0	Dean	31000			11				4	2		8		3	6		7	9			5				10		1
SF1	Apr 24	Hamburg	1-1	Dean	64410							2			8	4	3	6		7	9				5			10		1
SF2 May	May 1	HAMBURG	2-4	Dean, Harris	43070							2			8	4	3	6		7	9	11			5			10		1

QF2 played in Tashkent. QF replay at Augsberg, West Germany.

Welsh Cup

#	Date	Opponent	Result	Scorers	Att	Allan AB	Bell G	Bird RP	Brown RH	Carver DF	Clark BD	Clarke MMcQ	Coldrick GG	Davies F	Dean N	Derrett SC	Ferguson RB	Harris B	Jones BH	Jones BS	King PC	Lea L	Lewis B	Morgan RL	Murray DJ	Phillips L	Summerhayes DM	Toshack JB	Williams GC	Wilson RI
R5 Jan	Jan 16	EBBW VALE	8-0	Toshack 3, Bird 3 (1p), King, Lea	3542			11				4	2	1		12	3	6		7	9	8			5			10		
R6 Feb	Feb 12	Wrexham	3-1	Jones, Lea, Bird	7671		12	11				4		1		2	3	6		7	9	8			5			10		
SF Mar	Mar 27	Chester	3-0	King, Toshack, Lea	5488			11			8	4	2	1			3	6		9	7				5			10		
F1 May	May 6	Hereford United	2-0	Jones, King	5442						2	4		1	9		3	6		7	8	11			5			10		
F2	May 16	HEREFORD UNITED	4-1	Dean, Clarke, Lemsden (og), Lea	6036						2	4		1	8		3	6		7	9	11			5			10		

Played at 1 in R5: L Davies

1968/69   5th in Division Two

Player columns (left to right): Allan AB · Bell G · Bird RP · Carver DF · Clark BD · Clarke MMcQ · Coldrick GG · Davies F · Dean N · Derrett SC · Ferguson RB · Harris B · Jones BS · King PC · Lea L · Lewis TJ · Morgan RL · Murray DJ · Phillips L · Sharp F · Sutton MC · Toshack JB

#	Date	Opponent	Score	Scorers	Att	Allan AB	Bell G	Bird RP	Carver DF	Clark BD	Clarke MMcQ	Coldrick GG	Davies F	Dean N	Derrett SC	Ferguson RB	Harris B	Jones BS	King PC	Lea L	Lewis TJ	Morgan RL	Murray DJ	Phillips L	Sharp F	Sutton MC	Toshack JB
1	Aug 10	CRYSTAL PALACE	0-4		16373			11	2	8			1			3	6	7	9				5		4		10
2	14	CHARLTON ATHLETIC	0-1		11979			11	2	8			1			3	6	7	9				5			4	10
3	17	Norwich City	1-3	Bird	14476			11	2	8	10	3	1	4			6	7	9				5				
4	21	Bury	3-3	Clark, Jones, Toshack	7214		3	11		8		4	1		2		6	7	9				5				10
5	24	PRESTON NORTH END	1-0	King	10817		3	11		8		4	1		2		6	7	10				5				9
6	28	BIRMINGHAM CITY	4-0	Toshack 2, Bell, Clark	14967		3	11		8		4	1		2		6	7	9				5			12	10
7	31	Portsmouth	3-1	Clark, King, Toshack	21871		3			8	12	4	1		2		6	7	9				5			11	10
8	Sep 7	MIDDLESBROUGH	2-0	Gates (og), Clark	14225		11		2	8		4	1		3		6	7	10				5				9
9	14	Huddersfield Town	0-3		7523		3	11		8		4	1		2		6	7	9				5				10
10	21	CARLISLE UNITED	2-1	Clark, Jones	10809		3			8		12	1		2		6	7	9	11			5			4	10
11	28	Bristol City	3-0	King, Toshack, Jones	20632		3			8			1		2		6	7	10	11			5		12	4	9
12	Oct 5	ASTON VILLA	1-1	Toshack	17113		3			8			1		2			7	9	11	6		5			4	10
13	8	Birmingham City	0-2		28238		3	12		8			1		2			7		11	6		5		9		10
14	12	Millwall	0-2		13893		3			8			1		2		6	7		11			5		9	4	10
15	19	BOLTON WANDERERS	0-2		12026		3			8			1		2		6	7		11			5		10	4	9
16	26	Hull City	3-3	Toshack 2, Clark	17027		3	11	2	8			1				6	7	9				5			4	10
17	Nov 2	BLACKBURN ROVERS	2-1	Toshack, Bird	11672		6	11	2	8			1				3	7	9				5			4	10
18	9	Blackpool	2-1	Toshack 2	12085		3	11	2	8			1				6	7	9				5			4	10
19	16	DERBY COUNTY	1-1	Clark	17328		3	11	2	10			1				6	7	9				5		12	4	8
20	23	Oxford United	2-0	Clark, Toshack	9836			11	2	8			1		3		6	7	9				5			4	10
21	30	SHEFFIELD UNITED	4-1	Bird 2 (1p), Clark, Jones	14255		3	11	2	8			1				6	7	9				5			4	10
22	Dec 7	Fulham	5-1	Clark, Jones 2, Toshack, Lea	13191		3	11	2	8			1				6	7	9				5			4	10
23	14	MILLWALL	2-0	Toshack, Clark	22405		3	11	2	8			1				6	7	9				5			4	10
24	21	Bolton Wanderers	2-1	Bird, Jones	8895		3	11	2	8			1				6	7	9				5			4	10
25	26	Aston Villa	0-2		41296		3	11	2	8			1				6	7	9				5			4	10
26	28	HULL CITY	3-0	Clark, Bird, Toshack	24815		3	11	2	8			1				6	7	9				5			4	10
27	Jan 11	Blackburn Rovers	0-1		12100		3	11	2	8			1				6	7	9				5			4	10
28	25	BRISTOL CITY	3-0	Clark 2, King	26210		3		2	8			1				6	7	9	11			5			4	10
29	Feb 1	Derby County	0-2		34589		3		2	8			1				6	7	9	11			5			4	10
30	8	OXFORD UNITED	5-0	Bird, Clark 2, Toshack 2	16387		3	11	2	8			1				6	7	9				5			4	10
31	12	BLACKPOOL	1-0	Toshack	24206		3	11	2	8			1				6	7	10				5		12	4	9
32	Mar 1	Crystal Palace	1-3	Jones	19663		3	12	2				1				6	7	9	8			5	11		4	10
33	7	NORWICH CITY	3-1	Toshack, King, Bird	21389		3	12	2	8			1				6	7	9				5	11		4	10
34	11	Sheffield United	2-2	Clark, Jones	14508		3	11	2	8			1				6	7	9				5	12		4	10
35	15	Preston North End	1-0	Bird	10752			11	2	8			1		3		6	7	9				5	12		4	10
36	21	PORTSMOUTH	2-2	Toshack 2	21791		3		2	8			1		4		6	7	9				5			11	10
37	24	FULHAM	0-2		20723			12	2	8			1		3		6	7	9				5		11	4	10
38	29	Middlesbrough	0-0		24470			11	3	8	12		1		2		6	7					5			9	10
39	Apr 4	Charlton Athletic	1-4	Murray	21832		3	11	2	8	4		1			12	6	7					5			9	10
40	7	BURY	2-0	Toshack, Allan	13232	8		11	3				1		2		6	7	4				5			9	10
41	12	Carlisle United	0-1		5546	8		12	3				1		2			7	4		6	11	5			9	10
42	19	HUDDERSFIELD T	0-2		11549			11	3	12	7		1		2			9	4	8	6		5				10
		Apps				2	32	32	30	39	10	12	42	1	34	3	17	42	26	24	2	1	42	13	5	30	41
		Goals				1	1	9		17								9	5	1			1				22

One own goal

F.A. Cup

Rd	Date	Opponent	Score	Att	Allan AB	Bell G	Bird RP	Carver DF	Clark BD	Clarke MMcQ	Coldrick GG	Davies F	Dean N	Derrett SC	Ferguson RB	Harris B	Jones BS	King PC	Lea L	Lewis TJ	Morgan RL	Murray DJ	Phillips L	Sharp F	Sutton MC	Toshack JB
R3	Jan 4	ARSENAL	0-0	55136		3	11	2	8			1				6	7	9				5			4	10
rep	7	Arsenal	0-2	52681		3	11	2	8			1				6	7	9				5			4	10

F.L. Cup

Rd	Date	Opponent	Score	Att	Allan AB	Bell G	Bird RP	Carver DF	Clark BD	Clarke MMcQ	Coldrick GG	Davies F	Dean N	Derrett SC	Ferguson RB	Harris B	Jones BS	King PC	Lea L	Lewis TJ	Morgan RL	Murray DJ	Phillips L	Sharp F	Sutton MC	Toshack JB
R2	Sep 4	Carlisle United	0-2	7714					8		4	1		2	3	6	7	9				5			11	10

European Cup Winners Cup

Rd	Date	Opponent	Score	Scorers	Att	Allan AB	Bell G	Bird RP	Carver DF	Clark BD	Clarke MMcQ	Coldrick GG	Davies F	Dean N	Derrett SC	Ferguson RB	Harris B	Jones BS	King PC	Lea L	Lewis TJ	Morgan RL	Murray DJ	Phillips L	Sharp F	Sutton MC	Toshack JB
R1	Sep 18	PORTO	2-2	Toshack, Bird (p)	19202		3	11		8			1		2		6	7	9				5			4	10
R1s	Oct 2	Porto	1-2	Toshack	55000		3			8			1		2		6	7	9	11			5		12	4	10

Welsh Cup

Rd	Date	Opponent	Score	Scorers	Att	Allan AB	Bell G	Bird RP	Carver DF	Clark BD	Clarke MMcQ	Coldrick GG	Davies F	Dean N	Derrett SC	Ferguson RB	Harris B	Jones BS	King PC	Lea L	Lewis TJ	Morgan RL	Murray DJ	Phillips L	Sharp F	Sutton MC	Toshack JB
R5	Jan 15	Aberystwyth Town	3-0	Lea, Toshack, Jones	5000		3		2	8			1				6	9	11	7			5			4	10
R6	Feb 5	BETHESDA ATHLETIC	6-0	Clark 2, Lea, Jones, Bell, Toshack	6749		3		2	8			1				6	7	9	11			5			4	10
SF	Mar 19	Chester	2-0	Toshack 2	8404			12	2	8			1		3		6	7	9				5		11	4	10
F1	Apr 22	Swansea Town	3-1	Toshack 2, Nurse (og)	10207		3			8			1		2		6	11	4	9			5		7		10
F2	29	SWANSEA TOWN	2-0	Lea, Toshack	12617		3			8			1		2		6	11	4	9			5		7		10

68

1969/70   7th in Division Two

#	Date	Opponent	Score	Scorers	Att	Allan AB	Bell G	Bird RP	Carver DF	Clark BD	Coldrick GG	Davies F	Derrett SC	Eadie J	Harris B	Jones BS	King PC	Lea L	Lewis TJ	Murray DJ	Phillips L	Sharp F	Sutton MC	Toshack JB	Woodruff RW
1	Aug 9	Carlisle United	3-2	Clark, Toshack, King	10506		3		2	8		1			6	7	11	9		5			4	10	
2	13	SWINDON TOWN	2-2	King 2	27932		3		2	8		1			6	7	11	9		5			4	10	
3	16	BLACKBURN ROVERS	0-0		19745	12	3		2	8		1			6	7	11	9		5			_4_	10	
4	19	Swindon Town	1-2	Clark	21849		3	11	2	8		1			6	7	4	9		5				10	
5	23	Bristol City	2-0	Clark, Bird (p)	23237		3	11	2	8		1			6	7	4	9		5				10	
6	27	MIDDLESBROUGH	1-0	Toshack	21623		3		2	8		1			6	7	11	9		5			4	10	
7	30	BOLTON WANDERERS	2-1	Toshack, King	21048		3		2	8		1			6	7	11	9		5	12		_4_	10	
8	Sep 6	Charlton Athletic	0-0		13796		3		2	8		1			6	7	11	9		5	4			10	
9	13	LEICESTER CITY	1-1	Toshack	26947		3		2	8		1			6	_7_	11	9		5	4		12	10	
10	20	Sheffield United	0-1		17196			12	3	8	2	1			6	_7_	11			5	9		4	10	
11	27	QUEEN'S PARK RANGERS	4-2	Toshack 3, King	30048		3		2	8	12	1				7	9		6	5		_11_	4	10	
12	Oct 4	Blackpool	2-3	King 2	18115		3		2	8		1			6	_7_	9			5	12	11	4	10	
13	8	Blackburn Rovers	0-1		15062		3		2	8		1			6		11	9		5	7		4	10	
14	11	ASTON VILLA	4-0	Toshack 2, Bird 2 (1p)	25871		3	11	2	8		1			6		7	9		5			4	10	
15	18	NORWICH CITY	0-1		23596		3	_11_	2	8	12	1			6		7	9		5			4	10	
16	25	Birmingham City	1-1	Clark	28287	8	3		2	9		1			6		11	7		5			4	10	
17	Nov 1	HULL CITY	6-0	Sutton, Clark 2, King (p), Toshack 2	20419	9	3		2	8		1			6		11	7		5			4	10	
18	8	Portsmouth	0-3		17302	9	_3_		2	8		1		12	6		11	7		5			4	10	
19	15	Oxford United	1-1	Lea	11092	11	3		2	8		1			6		7	9		5			4	10	
20	22	PRESTON NORTH END	2-1	Clark, King	22653		3		2	8		1			6		11	9		5			4	10	7
21	Dec 6	WATFORD	3-1	Clark 2, Bird	15036		3	11	2	8		1			9		7			5			4	10	6
22	13	Leicester City	2-1	Clark, King	22590		3	11	2	8		1			9		7			5			4	10	6
23	15	Millwall	2-1	King, Bird (p)	9808		3	11	2	8		1			9		7			5			4	10	6
24	20	CHARLTON ATHLETIC	1-0	Clark	13906		3	11	2	8		1			9		7			5			4	10	6
25	29	BRISTOL CITY	1-0	Toshack	18479		3	11	2	8		1			9		7			5			4	10	6
26	Jan 10	SHEFFIELD UNITED	3-0	Clark 2, Bird	25111		3	11	2	8		1			9		7			5			4	10	6
27	17	Queen's Park Rangers	1-2	Toshack	22033		3	12	2	8		1			6		7			5	11		4	9	10
28	24	Huddersfield Town	0-1		21788		3	11	2	8		1			9		7			5			4	10	6
29	31	BLACKPOOL	2-2	Toshack 2	24586		3	11	2	8		1			9		_7_	12		5			4	10	6
30	Feb 7	Aston Villa	1-1	Clark	27024		3	12	2	8		1			9		11	_7_		5			4	10	6
31	14	CARLISLE UNITED	1-1	Woodruff	20120		3	11	2	8		1			6		7	9		5				10	4
32	21	BIRMINGHAM CITY	3-1	Clark, King, Bird (p)	21887		3	11	2	8		1			6		7	9		5				10	4
33	28	Norwich City	1-1	Clark	11290		3	11	2	8		1			6		7	9		5				10	4
34	Mar 14	HUDDERSFIELD T	0-1		25978		3		2	8		1			9		7	11		5			4	10	6
35	18	Bolton Wanderers	1-0	Woodruff	10434		3		2	10		1			6		7	8		5		11	4		9
36	21	Watford	1-2	Clark	17152		3		2	8		1		12	_6_		7	9		5		11	4		10
37	25	PORTSMOUTH	2-0	Sutton, Woodruff	17031		3		2	8			1		6			9		5		11	4	10	7
38	28	OXFORD UNITED	0-0		21097		3		2	8			1		6			9		5		11	4	10	7
39	31	Hull City	1-1	Sharp	13038		3		2	8		1			6		7	9		5		11	4	12	_10_
40	Apr 4	Middlesbrough	1-2	Clark	13859		3		2	8		1		12	_6_		7	10		5		11	4	9	
41	15	MILLWALL	0-0		8423		3		2	8		1					7	9		5	6	11	4	10	
42	20	Preston North End	2-1	Murray, Bird	8012		3	_11_	2	8		1					7	9		5	6	12	4		10
		Apps				5	41	19	42	42	3	40	3	2	39	12	39	32	1	42	9	10	36	39	21
		Goals						8		18							10	1		1		1	2	17	3

F.A. Cup

#	Date	Opponent	Score	Scorers	Att	Allan AB	Bell G	Bird RP	Carver DF	Clark BD	Coldrick GG	Davies F	Derrett SC	Eadie J	Harris B	Jones BS	King PC	Lea L	Lewis TJ	Murray DJ	Phillips L	Sharp F	Sutton MC	Toshack JB	Woodruff RW
R3	Jan 3	York City	1-1	Swallow (og)	8439		3	11	2	8		1			9		7			5			4	10	6
rep	Jan 12	YORK CITY	1-1	(aet) Toshack	21623		3	11	2	8		1			9		7			5			4	10	6
rep2	Jan 15	York City	1-3	(aet) King	7347	9	3		2	8	12	1	6				11			5			4	_10_	7

Replay 2 at St Andrews, Birmingham

F.L. Cup

#	Date	Opponent	Score	Scorers	Att	Allan AB	Bell G	Bird RP	Carver DF	Clark BD	Coldrick GG	Davies F	Derrett SC	Eadie J	Harris B	Jones BS	King PC	Lea L	Lewis TJ	Murray DJ	Phillips L	Sharp F	Sutton MC	Toshack JB	Woodruff RW
R2	Sep 3	Crystal Palace	1-3	Lea	18616		3		2	8		1			6	7	11	9		5			4	10	

European Cup Winners Cup

#	Date	Opponent	Score	Scorers	Att	Allan AB	Bell G	Bird RP	Carver DF	Clark BD	Coldrick GG	Davies F	Derrett SC	Eadie J	Harris B	Jones BS	King PC	Lea L	Lewis TJ	Murray DJ	Phillips L	Sharp F	Sutton MC	Toshack JB	Woodruff RW
R1/1	Sep 17	Mjondalen IF	7-1	Clark 2, Sutton, Lea, Toshack 2, King	8000			3		8		1	2		6	12	11	9		5		_7_	4	10	
R1/2	Oct 1	MJONDALEN IF	5-1	King 2, Allan 3	14753	9	3		2	8		1				7	11	12	6	5			4	_10_	
R2/1	Nov 12	Goztepe (Izmir)	0-3		24000		3		2	8		1			6		9	7		5		11	4	10	
R2/2	Nov 26	GOZTEPE (IZMIR)	1-0	Bird	17866	7	3	14	2	8	12	1			6		11	_9_		5			4	_10_	

Welsh Cup

#	Date	Opponent	Score	Scorers	Att	Allan AB	Bell G	Bird RP	Carver DF	Clark BD	Coldrick GG	Davies F	Derrett SC	Eadie J	Harris B	Jones BS	King PC	Lea L	Lewis TJ	Murray DJ	Phillips L	Sharp F	Sutton MC	Toshack JB	Woodruff RW
R5	Jan 21	BARMOUTH & DYFFRYN U	6-1	Clark 5, Toshack	4901		3	11	2	8		1			9		7			5			4	10	6
R6	Feb 4	WREXHAM	3-0	Clark 2, King	12332		3	12	2	8		1			9		11	7		5			4	_10_	6
SF	Mar 11	SWANSEA CITY	2-2	Woodruff, Toshack	18050		3		2	8		1			9		7	11		5			4	10	6
rep	May 2	Swansea City	2-0	Bird, King	16000		3	11	2	10		1			6		7	_9_		5			4	12	8
F1	8	Chester	1-0	Bird	3087		3	11	2	9		1			6		10	7		5			4		8
F2	13	CHESTER	4-0	Woodruff, King, Lea, Clark	5567		3	11	2	9		1			6		10	7		5			4		8

1970/71　　3rd in Division Two

#	Date	Opponent	Score	Scorers	Att	Bell G	Bird RP	Carver DF	Clark BD	Derrett SC	Eadie J	Gibson IS	Harris B	King PC	Murray DJ	Parsons FR	Parsons JS	Phillips L	Rees NR	Showers D	Sutton MC	Toshack JB	Warboys A	Woodruff RW
1	Aug 15	Leicester City	1-0	Clark	27578	3		2	7			8	6	11	5	1					4	10		9
2	22	MILLWALL	2-2	Toshack, King	25283	3		2	7			8	6	11	5	1					4	10		9
3	26	Sheffield Wednesday	2-1	Clark, Sutton	16896	3		2	7			8	6	11	5	1					4	10		9
4	29	Bristol City	0-1		24969	3		2	7			8	6	11	5	1					4	10		9
5	Sep 2	SHEFFIELD UNITED	1-1	Clark	21421	3	12	2	7			8	6	11	5	1					4	10		9
6	5	BIRMINGHAM CITY	2-0	Toshack 2	21690	3		2	8			7	6	11	5	1					4	10		9
7	12	Bolton Wanderers	2-0	Clark, Gibson	11086	3		2	8			7	6	11	5	1					4	10		9
8	19	NORWICH CITY	1-1	Clark	23745	3		2	8			7	6	11	5	1					4	10		9
9	26	Orient	0-0		11992	3		2	8			7	6	11	5	1					4	10		9
10	Oct 3	MIDDLESBROUGH	3-4	Clark, Woodruff, King	20925	3		2	8			7	6	11	5	1					4	10		9
11	10	Watford	1-0	Clark	16244	3		2	8		1	7	6	11	5						4	10		9
12	17	LEICESTER CITY	2-2	Gibson (p), Carver	25968	3		2	8		1	7	6	11	5						4	10		9
13	24	Carlisle United	1-1	Toshack	10955	3		2			1	7	6	11	5			9			4	10		8
14	28	PORTSMOUTH	1-0	Toshack	18510	3		2			1	7	6	11	5			9			4	10		8
15	31	HULL CITY	5-1	Toshack 3, Gibson, Phillips	21837	3		2			1	7	6	11	5			9			4	8		10
16	Nov 7	Queen's Park Rangers	1-0	Phillips	14268	3		2			1	7	6	11	5			9			4	8		10
17	14	BLACKBURN ROVERS	4-1	Clark 2, Woodruff, King	17213	3		2	8		1	7	6	11	5			9			4			10
18	21	Charlton Athletic	1-2	Woodruff	10788	3	12	2	8		1	7	6	11	5			9			4			10
19	28	LUTON TOWN	0-0		26666	3		2	8		1	7	6	11	5			9			4			10
20	Dec 5	Oxford United	0-1		12286	3		2	8	6	1	7		11	5			12	10		4			9
21	12	SUNDERLAND	3-1	Gibson, Phillips, Pitt (og)	15619	3		2	10	6	1	7		11	5			9			4			8
22	19	Millwall	1-2	Clark	8645	3		2	10		1	7	6	11	5			9			4			8
23	26	SWINDON TOWN	1-1	Sutton	24800	3		2	8		1	7	6	12	5			9			4		10	11
24	Jan 9	SHEFFIELD WEDNESDAY	4-0	Bell, King, Warboys 2	21464	3		2			1	8	6	7	5			10	11		4		9	
25	16	Portsmouth	3-1	Warboys 2, Murray	24747	3		2	12		1	8	6	7	5			10	11		4		9	
26	Feb 6	OXFORD UNITED	1-0	Parsons	14853	3		2	9		1	8	6	7	5		12	10	11		4			
27	13	Sunderland	4-0	Clark, Gibson, Parsons, Irwin (og)	11566	3		2	8		1	7		9	5		12	6	11				10	4
28	20	CHARLTON ATHLETIC	1-1	Gibson (p)	18009	3		2	10		1	7		9	5	8		6	11		4			
29	27	Hull City	1-1	Warboys	25091	3		2	8		1	7		9	5			6	11		4		10	12
30	Mar 6	CARLISLE UNITED	4-0	Warboys 4	22371	3		2	12		1	8		7	5			6	11		4		9	10
31	13	Blackburn Rovers	1-1	Clark	10458	3		2	7		1			8	5			6	11		4		9	10
32	20	QUEEN'S PARK RANGERS	1-0	Warboys	23309	3	11	2			1	8		7	5			6			4		9	10
33	27	Birmingham City	0-2		49025	3		2	12		1	8		7	5			6	11		4		9	10
34	Apr 3	BRISTOL CITY	1-0	Wimshurst (og)	24638	3	11	2			1	8	12	7	5			6			4		9	10
35	7	BOLTON WANDERERS	1-0	Clark	21282	3	11	2	8		1		12	7	5			6			4		10	9
36	10	Swindon Town	2-2	Warboys 2	21393	3		2	8		1	7		11	5			6			4		10	9
37	13	Middlesbrough	1-1	King	19559	3		2	8	12	1	7		11	5			6			4		10	9
38	17	WATFORD	0-1		26612	3		2	8		1	7		11	5			6			4		10	9
39	24	Norwich City	2-1	Warboys, Clark	15088	3		2	8	6	1	7		11	5			9			4		10	
40	27	Sheffield United	1-5	Derrett	42963	3		2	8	6	1	7		11	5			9			4		10	12
41	May 1	ORIENT	1-0	Clark	15750	3		2	8	6	1	7		11	5			9			4		10	12
42	4	Luton Town	0-3		10784	3		2	8	6	1	7		11	5			9			4		10	

| | | | | | Apps | 42 | 5 | 42 | 35 | 7 | 32 | 40 | 26 | 42 | 42 | 10 | 3 | 30 | 9 | 1 | 41 | 16 | 18 | 36 |
| | | | | | Goals | 1 | · | 1 | 15 | 1 | | 6 | | 5 | 1 | | 2 | 3 | | | 2 | 8 | 13 | 3 |

Three own goals

F.A. Cup

#	Date	Opponent	Score	Scorers	Att	Bell G	Bird RP	Carver DF	Clark BD	Derrett SC	Eadie J	Gibson IS	Harris B	King PC	Murray DJ	Parsons FR	Parsons JS	Phillips L	Rees NR	Showers D	Sutton MC	Toshack JB	Warboys A	Woodruff RW
R3	Jan 2	BRIGHTON & HOVE ALB.	1-0	King	19338	3		2	10		1	7	6	11	5			9	12		4			8
R4	Jan 23	BRENTFORD	0-2		23335	3		2	12		1		6	7	5			10	11		4		9	8

F.L. Cup

#	Date	Opponent	Score	Scorers	Att	Bell G	Bird RP	Carver DF	Clark BD	Derrett SC	Eadie J	Gibson IS	Harris B	King PC	Murray DJ	Parsons FR	Parsons JS	Phillips L	Rees NR	Showers D	Sutton MC	Toshack JB	Warboys A	Woodruff RW
R2	Sep 8	Queen's Park Rangers	0-4		15086	3	12	2	8			7	6	11	5	1					4	10		9

European Cup Winner's Cup

#	Date	Opponent	Score	Scorers	Att	Bell G	Bird RP	Carver DF	Clark BD	Derrett SC	Eadie J	Gibson IS	Harris B	King PC	Murray DJ	Parsons FR	Parsons JS	Phillips L	Rees NR	Showers D	Sutton MC	Toshack JB	Warboys A	Woodruff RW
R1/1	Sep 16	PEZOPORIKOS	8-0	* see below	12984	3		2	8			7	6	11	5	1					4	10		9
R1/2	30	Pezoporikos (Larnaca)	0-0		10000	3		2	8			7	6	11	5	1		12			4	10		9
R2/1	Oct 21	NANTES	5-1	Toshack 2, Gibson, King, Phillips	17905	3		2	8			7	6	11	5			12			4	10		9
R2/2	Nov 4	Nantes	2-1	Clark, Toshack	10000	3		2	12			7	6	11	5			9			4	8		10
QF1	Mar 10	REAL MADRID	1-0	Clark	47500	3		2	9		1	8		7	5			6	11		4			10
QF2	24	Real Madrid	0-2		70000	3		2	9		1	8	12	7	5			6	11		4			10

Scorers in R1/1: Clark 2, Sutton, Gibson, Woodruff, Toshack 2, King

Welsh Cup

#	Date	Opponent	Score	Scorers	Att	Bell G	Bird RP	Carver DF	Clark BD	Derrett SC	Eadie J	Gibson IS	Harris B	King PC	Murray DJ	Parsons FR	Parsons JS	Phillips L	Rees NR	Showers D	Sutton MC	Toshack JB	Warboys A	Woodruff RW
R5	Feb 2	Newport County	1-1	Clark	6162	3		2	9		1	8	6	7	5			12	10	11	4			
rep	10	NEWPORT COUNTY	4-0	Murray, Gibson, King, Parsons	10350	3	11	2	10		1	12	6	7	5			8	4					9
R6	17	BANGOR CITY	5-0	Clark, Gibson, King, Parsons, Rees	5019	3		2	10		1	7		9	5	8		6	11					4
SF	Mar 31	CHESTER	0-0		5522	3	11	2	8		1	7		12	5			6			4		10	9
rep	Apr 19	Chester	2-1	Clark, Derrett	7352	3		2	8	4	1	7		11	5			6					9	10
F1	May 10	Wrexham	1-0	Woodruff	14101	3	11	2			1	8		7	5			6			4		9	10
F2	12	WREXHAM	3-1	Gibson 2, Bird	4987	3	11	2	9		1	8		7	5			6			4			10

1971/72   19th in Division Two

League — Division Two

#	Date	Opponent	Score	Scorers	Att	Bell G	Carver DF	Clark BD	Couch A	Derrett SC	Eadie J	Foggon A	Gibson IS	Hoy RE	Irwin WJN	Jones K (2)	Kellock W	King PC	Morgan RL	Murray DJ	Parsons FR	Parsons JS	Pethard FJ	Phillips L	Rees NR	Sutton MC	Villars AK	Warboys A	Woodruff RW
1	Aug 14	BURNLEY	2-2	Clark 2	23004	3	2	8			1	11	7							5				6			4	10	9
2	Aug 16	Blackpool	0-3		19253	3	2	8		6	1	11	7							5		12					4	10	9
3	Aug 21	Orient	1-4	Mancini (og)	7824	3	2	10				7	6							5	1	8		11			4	9	
4	Aug 28	HULL CITY	1-1	Warboys	17110	3	2	8			1	11	7	9						5				6			4	10	
5	Aug 31	Bristol City	0-2		23525	3	2	8			1	11	7	9						5				6			4	10	
6	Sep 4	Watford	2-2	J Parsons, Clark	10233	3	2	8			1	11	7	4						5		12		6			9	10	
7	Sep 11	SHEFFIELD WEDNESDAY	3-2	Warboys 2, Clark	17067	3		8			1	11	7			2				5		12		6			4	10	9
8	Sep 18	Middlesbrough	0-1		18288	3		8			1					2		7		5				6	12	4		10	9
9	Sep 25	SWINDON TOWN	0-1		16275	3		8			1	12	7	11		2				5				6			4	10	9
10	Oct 2	Preston North End	2-1	King, Clark	13511	3		9			1	11	8	4		2		7		5				6				12	10
11	Oct 9	MILLWALL	1-2	Clark	17931	3		8				7	11	1		2				5				6			4	10	9
12	Oct 16	Burnley	0-3		12494	3		8				11				1	2	7		5		12		6			4	10	9
13	Oct 23	CHARLTON ATHLETIC	6-1	Clark 2, J Parsons, Gibson (p), Went (og)	13075	3	2	10				7	1							5		8		6	11	4			9
14	Oct 30	Norwich City	1-2	Clark	20546	3	2	10			12	7	1							5		8		6	11	4			9
15	Nov 6	QUEEN'S PARK RANGERS	0-0		16892	3	2	10				7	1							5		8		6	11	4		12	9
16	Nov 13	Fulham	3-4	Warboys, Clark 2	10700	3	2	8				11	1							5		12		6	4	7		10	9
17	Nov 20	Sunderland	1-2	Gibson	12718	3	2	8				11	1							5				6	4	7		10	9
18	Nov 27	Carlisle United	1-2	J Parsons	6845	3	2	10	9			11	1					5				8		6	7				4
19	Dec 1	PORTSMOUTH	3-2	Gibson (p), Clark, Woodruff	10143	3	2	8	9	6		11	1					5				4	12		7				10
20	Dec 11	Luton Town	2-2	Phillips, Clark	10606	3	2	8	9	6		11	1					5				4			7			10	12
21	Dec 18	Watford	2-0	King, Warboys	11092	3	2	8	6				1					7	5			4			11			10	9
22	Dec 27	Birmingham City	0-3		40793	3	2	8	6				7						5			4	11	12				10	9
23	Jan 1	MIDDLESBROUGH	1-0	Clark	12758		3	8					7		1		9	6	5			4	11	2				10	12
24	Jan 8	Hull City	0-0		12678	3	2	8					7		1				5			6	11	4				10	9
25	Jan 22	Portsmouth	0-2		11039	3	2	8				11	7		1		12		5			6		4				10	9
26	Jan 29	BLACKPOOL	3-4	Clark, Warboys, Gibson	11197	3	2	8				11	7		1		9		5			6						10	4
27	Feb 12	Charlton Athletic	2-2	Woodruff, Clark	7526	3	2	8					7		1	4	9	5				6	11				12	10
28	Feb 19	NORWICH CITY	0-0		17683	3	2	8					7		1	4	9	5				6	11		12	11	10
29	Mar 4	FULHAM	1-0	Clark	13122	3	2	8					7		1	4	9	5				6	11		12	10
30	Mar 11	Millwall	1-1	Warboys	13702	3	2	8					7		1	9	11	5				6	4			10
31	Mar 21	OXFORD UNITED	1-1	Clark	14477		2	8					7		1	9	11	5		3	6		4		10	9
32	Mar 25	Sheffield Wednesday	2-2	Warboys, Woodruff	12511		2	8					7		1	11	6	5		3			10	9
33	Mar 29	PRESTON NORTH END	5-2	Clark, Warboys 3, King	13241		2	8					7		1	11	5	3	6	4		10	9
34	Apr 1	BIRMINGHAM CITY	0-0		23667		2	8					7		1	11	5	3	6	4		10	9
35	Apr 4	Swindon Town	1-3	Clark	15641		2	8					7		1	12	11	5	3	6	4		10	9
36	Apr 8	Sunderland	1-1	Sutton	15224		2	8					7		1	11	5	3	6	4		10	9
37	Apr 12	ORIENT	1-0	Woodruff	16751		2	8				12	7		1	11	5	3	6	4		10	9
38	Apr 15	CARLISLE UNITED	3-1	King, Clark, Woodruff	17712		2	8					7		1	11	5	3	6	4		10	9
39	Apr 22	Oxford United	0-1		9092		2	8					7		1	11	5	3	6	12	4	10	9
40	Apr 26	BRISTOL CITY	2-3	Warboys, Woodruff	17227		2	8					7		1	11	5	3	6	4		10	9
41	Apr 29	LUTON TOWN	1-1	Warboys	12570		2	8					7		1	11	5	3	6	4		10	9
42	May 2	Queen's Park Rangers	0-3		8430	3	2	8					12			9		5	1		6	11	7	10	4
Apps						30	36	42	3	5	9	12	41	7	31	6	6	23	8	36	2	11	11	41	13	31	7	38	36
Goals								21					4					4				4		1		1		13	6

Game 42: Gibson (sub) played in goal

Two own goals

F.A. Cup

Rnd	Date	Opponent	Score	Scorers	Att	Bell G	Carver DF	Clark BD	Couch A	Derrett SC	Eadie J	Foggon A	Gibson IS	Hoy RE	Irwin WJN	Jones K (2)	Kellock W	King PC	Morgan RL	Murray DJ	Parsons FR	Parsons JS	Pethard FJ	Phillips L	Rees NR	Sutton MC	Villars AK	Warboys A	Woodruff RW
R3	Jan 15	Sheffield United	3-1	Murray, Carver, Woodruff	29342	3	2	8				11	7		1					5				6		4		10	9
R4	Feb 9	SUNDERLAND	1-1	King	27000	3	2	8				11	7		1		9	5					6		12	10	4
rep	Feb 14	Sunderland	1-1	(aet) Clark	39348	3	2	8	12				7		1	4	9	5				6			10
rep2	Feb 16	Sunderland	3-1	Clark, Woodruff, Kellock	8868	3	2	8				11	7		1	4	9	5				6		12	10
R5	Feb 26	LEEDS UNITED	0-2		49180	3	2	8				11	7		1	4	9	5				6		12	10

Replay 2 at Maine Road, Manchester
Played at 11 in R4 replay: Brian Rees (subbed)

F.L. Cup

Rnd	Date	Opponent	Score	Scorers	Att	Bell G	Carver DF	Clark BD	Couch A	Derrett SC	Eadie J	Foggon A	Gibson IS	Hoy RE	Irwin WJN	Jones K (2)	Kellock W	King PC	Morgan RL	Murray DJ	Parsons FR	Parsons JS	Pethard FJ	Phillips L	Rees NR	Sutton MC	Villars AK	Warboys A	Woodruff RW
R2	Sep 8	West Ham United	1-1	Foggon	24420	3		8			1	11	7			2				5		12		6			4	10	9
rep	Sep 22	WEST HAM UNITED	1-2	Clark	30109	3		8			1		7	11		2				5				6			4	10	9

European Cup Winners Cup

Rnd	Date	Opponent	Score	Scorers	Att	Bell G	Carver DF	Clark BD	Couch A	Derrett SC	Eadie J	Foggon A	Gibson IS	Hoy RE	Irwin WJN	Jones K (2)	Kellock W	King PC	Morgan RL	Murray DJ	Parsons FR	Parsons JS	Pethard FJ	Phillips L	Rees NR	Sutton MC	Villars AK	Warboys A	Woodruff RW
R1/1	Sep 15	Dynamo Berlin	1-1	Gibson	15000	3		8			1		11			2		7		5				6			4	10	9
R1/2	Sep 29	DYNAMO BERLIN	1-1	Clark	12676	3		8			1	12	11			2		7		5				6			4	10	9

Lost 4-5 on penalties a.e.t.

Welsh Cup

Rnd	Date	Opponent	Score	Scorers	Att	Bell G	Carver DF	Clark BD	Couch A	Derrett SC	Eadie J	Foggon A	Gibson IS	Hoy RE	Irwin WJN	Jones K (2)	Kellock W	King PC	Morgan RL	Murray DJ	Parsons FR	Parsons JS	Pethard FJ	Phillips L	Rees NR	Sutton MC	Villars AK	Warboys A	Woodruff RW
R5	Jan 3	Swansea City	2-0	Warboys, Clark	14391	3	2	8					7		1					5				6	11	4		10	9
R6	Feb 22	Llanelli	1-0	Foggon	6000	3	2	8				11	7		1	4	9	5				6			10
SF	Mar 14	Rhyl	2-1	Clark, Warboys	5000		2	8					7		1	9	11	5		3	6	12	4		10
F1	May 8	Wrexham	1-2	Woodruff	6984	3	2	8				9			1	4	11	5			6		7	10	12
F2	May 12	WREXHAM	1-1	Foggon	6508	3	2	8				7			1	9	5		6		4	11	10

1972/73   20th in Division Two

#	Date	Opponent	Score	Scorers	Att	Anderson WJ	Bell G	Carver DF	Clark BD	Couch A	Dwyer PJ	Foggon A	Gibson IS	Hoy RE	Irwin WJN	Kellock W	Larmour AAJ	McCulloch A	Morgan PW	Morgan RL	Murray DJ	Parsons FR	Pethard FJ	Phillips L	Powell D	Reece GI	Rees NR	Showers D	Villars AK	Vincent JV	Warboys A	Woodruff RW
1	Aug 12	LUTON TOWN	2-1	Bell (p), Warboys	16345		3	2	8			11	7		1	6					5			4					10	12	9	
2	19	Portsmouth	1-3	Showers	14067		3	2	8		4		7		1	6					5			9				11			10	12
3	26	BLACKPOOL	1-2	Bell (p)	12383		3		8							4	6				5			9	1	2		11	12		10	7
4	30	MILLWALL	1-0	Clark	9298		3		8		7					4					5			6	1	2				11	10	9
5	Sep 2	Oxford United	1-2	Rees	8300		3		8	12	7					4					5			6	1	2	11			10		9
6	9	ASTON VILLA	0-2		16707		3		8				7			4				5				6	1	2			12	11	10	9
7	16	Carlisle United	0-4		5911		3	2	8	12						4					5			6	1				10	11	7	9
8	19	Nottingham Forest	1-2	Gibson	6414		3	2	8	9			7		1	4					5			6					12	10		11
9	23	BRISTOL CITY	1-3	Bell (p)	14102		3	2	8				7		1	4					5			10	6	11						9
10	27	BRIGHTON & HOVE ALB	1-1	Foggon	8330		3	2	8			11	7		1						5			9	6	10						4
11	30	Queen's Park Rangers	0-3		11182		3	2	8			11	7		1	12					5			6	4	10						9
12	Oct 7	Orient	0-0		6284		3				2	7			1	4					5			10	6	11		8				9
13	14	MIDDLESBROUGH	2-0	Vincent, Bell (p)	10407		3				2				1	4					5			10	6	11		8		9		
14	21	Burnley	0-3		13442		3				2				1	4					5			7	6	11	12	10		8		9
15	28	PRESTON NORTH END	3-0	McCulloch, Woodruff 2	12087		3				2				1	4		9			5			7	6	11		10		8		12
16	Nov 4	Brighton & Hove Albion	2-2	Murray, Kellock	16387		3				2				1	4	12		6		5			7				10	11	8		9
17	11	NOTTM. FOREST	2-1	McCulloch, Woodruff	12765		3				2				1	4		10	6		5			7				11		8		9
18	18	Huddersfield Town	1-2	Reece	5886		3				2				1	4		10	6		5			7				11		8		9
19	25	FULHAM	3-1	McCulloch 2, Woodruff	9668		3				2				1	4		10	6	5				7				11		8		9
20	Dec 9	SHEFFIELD WEDNESDAY	4-1	Phillips 2, Woodruff 2	9890		3				2				1	4		10	6	5				7					11	8		9
21	16	Hull City	1-1	Kellock	5875		3		12		2				1	7		8	6	5				4				11		10		9
22	26	Bristol City	0-1		20490		3				2				1	7		8	6	5				4		11			12	10		9
23	29	PORTSMOUTH	0-2		12364		3		12		2				1	7		8		5				4		11				10		9
24	Jan 19	OXFORD UNITED	2-0	McCulloch 2	6991		3				2			9	1	7		8			5			4	6	11				10		
25	27	Aston Villa	0-2		28856		3				2			9	1	7		10			5			4	6	11				8		12
26	Feb 10	CARLISLE UNITED	1-0	McCulloch	7800		3				2				1	7	9	8	6		5			4					10	11		
27	17	Luton Town	1-1	Woodruff	10422						2				1	7		8	6		5		3	4					10	11		9
28	27	Swindon Town	0-3		10015	11	3				2				1			8			5			10	6				12	7		9
29	Mar 3	ORIENT	3-1	McCulloch 2, Bell (p)	8439	11	3				2				1			9			5			4	6				10	7		12
30	7	Blackpool	0-1		5303	11	3				2				1			8			5			4	6				9	10		7
31	10	Middlesbrough	0-2		7686	11	3				2				1			9			5	7	6	4					10	8		
32	17	BURNLEY	0-1		11343	11	3				2				1	8		9			5			4	6	7			12	10		
33	24	Preston North End	0-0		6889	11	3			10	2				1	7		8			5			4	6							9
34	31	Fulham	1-1	McCulloch	6262	11	3			8	2				1	6		10			5			4	7							9
35	Apr 7	SWINDON TOWN	1-1	McCulloch	9059	11	3			4	2				1	7		8			5			6						10		9
36	14	Sheffield Wednesday	0-1		10912	11	3				2			12	1		4	9	6		5			10		7				8		9
37	18	QUEEN'S PARK RANGERS	0-0		12033	11	3				2			12	1	8		6	5					4		7				10		9
38	21	HUDDERSFIELD T	4-1	McCulloch 2, Reece 2	12353	11	3				2			10	1	8		6			5			4		7						9
39	23	Sunderland	1-2	Phillips	27551	11	3				2			10	1	8		6			5			4		7						9
40	28	Millwall	1-1	McCulloch	7811	11	3				2			10	1	8		6			5			4		7				12		9
41	May 7	SUNDERLAND	1-1	Woodruff	21982	11	3				2			10	1	8		6			5			4		7				12		9
42	9	HULL CITY	0-2		6235	11	3				2			10	1			6			5			4		7			8			9

Played in one game: JE Impey (23, at 6), JS Parsons (13, at 7)
Played in game 19 and 30 at 12: JR McInch
Played in game 28 at 4 (subbed): PC King

		Anderson WJ	Bell G	Carver DF	Clark BD	Couch A	Dwyer PJ	Foggon A	Gibson IS	Hoy RE	Irwin WJN	Kellock W	Larmour AAJ	McCulloch A	Morgan PW	Morgan RL	Murray DJ	Parsons FR	Pethard FJ	Phillips L	Powell D	Reece GI	Rees NR	Showers D	Villars AK	Vincent JV	Warboys A	Woodruff RW
Apps		15	41	7	11	8	31	5	9	9	37	29	6	26	16	6	36	5	6	42	16	23	5	19	9	24	5	35
Goals			5		1			1	1			2		14			1			3		3	1	1		1	1	8

F.A. Cup

	Date	Opponent	Score	Scorers	Att	Bell G	Dwyer PJ	Irwin WJN	Kellock W	McCulloch A	Morgan PW	Morgan RL	Phillips L	Powell D	Reece GI	Rees NR	Vincent JV	Warboys A	Woodruff RW	Clark BD
R3	Jan 13	Scunthorpe United	3-2	Kellock. McCulloch, Phillips	6379	3	2	1	7	9		5	4	6	11	12	8		10	
R4	Feb 3	Bolton Wanderers	2-2	Kellock, Phillips	24729	3	2	1	7	9		5	4	6	11	10	8		9	
rep	7	BOLTON WANDERERS	1-1	(aet) McCulloch	14849	3	2	1	9	8	6	5	4		7	11	10			12
rep2	12	Bolton Wanderers	0-1		6609	3	2	1	7	8		5	4	6			10	11	12	

Replay 2 at The Hawthorns, West Bromwich   Played at 9 in R4 replay 2: PC King

F.L. Cup

	Date	Opponent	Score	Scorers	Att	Bell G	Carver DF	Clark BD	Dwyer PJ	Gibson IS	Irwin WJN	Kellock W	Murray DJ	Phillips L	Showers D	Warboys A
R1	Aug 16	BRISTOL ROVERS	2-2	Showers, Bell (p)	14540	3	2	8	4	7	1	6	5	9	11	10
rep	22	Bristol Rovers	1-3	Clark	14550	3	2	8	4	7	1	6	5	9	11	10

Welsh Cup

	Date	Opponent	Score	Scorers	Att	Anderson WJ	Bell G	Couch A	Dwyer PJ	Irwin WJN	Kellock W	Larmour AAJ	McCulloch A	Morgan PW	Murray DJ	Phillips L	Powell D	Reece GI	Villars AK	Vincent JV	Woodruff RW
R4	Jan 3	Aberystwyth Town	7-1	* see below	3500		3		2	1	7		8	6	5	4		11		10	9
R5	Feb 20	Newport County	3-1	Vincent, Phillips, Showers	11350		3		2	1	7		8	6	5	4			10	11	9
SF	Mar 21	Chester	1-0	McCulloch	2158	11	3	4	2	1	7		8		5	6			9	10	12
F1	Apr 4	Bangor City	0-1		5005	11	3	4	2	1	7		8		5	6	12			9	10
F2	11	BANGOR CITY	5-0	Reece 3, Phillips, Bell	4679	11	3		2	1		4	8		5	9	6	7		10	

Scorers in R4: McCulloch 2, Reece 2, Vincent, Woodruff 2

1973/74

#	Date	Opponent	Score	Scorers	Att	Anderson WJ	Bell G	Carlin W	Charles CM	Dwyer PJ	Farrington IR	Grotier PD	Healey R	Impey JE	Irwin WIN	King PC	Larmour AAJ	McCulloch A	McInch JR	Morgan RL	Murray DJ	Pethard FJ	Phillips L	Powell D	Reece GI	Sayer PA	Showers D	Smith G	Villars AK	Vincent IV	Whitham J	Woodruff RW
1	Aug 25	Carlisle United	1-1	Bell (p)	6830	11	3			2											5		4		8				10	6	7	9
2	Sep 1	PORTSMOUTH	1-1	McCulloch	10082	11	3			2					1	12		8			5		6						4	7	10	9
3	8	Sunderland	1-1	Vincent	29595	11	3			2					1			8			5		6						4	7	10	9
4	12	OXFORD UNITED	5-0	McCulloch 3, Villars, C Clark (og)	8529	11	3			2					1	12		8			5		6						4	7	10	9
5	15	FULHAM	0-0		11772		3			2					1	11		8			5		6						4	7	10	9
6	22	Crystal Palace	3-3	Blyth (og), Woodruff, Vincent	18290		3			2					1			8			5		6				11		4	7	10	9
7	29	HULL CITY	1-3	Bell (p)	10522		3			2					1			8			5		6				11		4	7	10	9
8	Oct 6	Aston Villa	0-5		24483		3			2					1	11	4	10			5		6		7			9				8
9	13	BLACKPOOL	1-0	Reece	8050		3			2					1	12		8	5				6		7			9	4		11	10
10	20	SHEFFIELD WEDNESDAY	0-1		7745		3			2					1	8		10			5		6		11		9		7			4
11	24	Oxford United	2-4	Anderson, Smith	6365	11	3			2					1			8			5		6		7		12	4		10		9
12	27	Preston North End	2-2	McCulloch, Reece	12050	11	3			2					1			8			5		6		7			4		10		9
13	Nov 3	WEST BROMWICH ALB.	0-1		10432	11	3			2	1							8			5		6		7			4	12	10		9
14	10	Millwall	0-2		8221	11	3			2	1							10			5		6		7			4	8			9
15	14	LUTON TOWN	0-0		5999		3			2				4	1				8		5		6		11		9		7	12		10
16	17	Middlesbrough	0-3		18034		3			2				4	1				8		5		6	7			10		11	12		9
17	24	BOLTON WANDERERS	1-0	Reece	9584		3	4		2	7				1			8			5			6	10			11				6
18	Dec 1	Orient	2-1	Woodruff, McCulloch	9564		3	8		2	7				1			10			5			4	11		12	9				6
19	8	NOTTM. FOREST	1-1	Reece	10312		3	8		2	7				1			10			5		12	4	9			11				6
20	12	Luton Town	0-1		7139		3	10		2	7				1			8			5		11	4	9		12					6
21	15	BRISTOL CITY	0-1		9368	12	3			2	7				1			8			5		10	6	11		4					9
22	22	Hull City	1-1	Farrington	6826	11	3	4		2	7			12	1			8			5		10	6								9
23	26	SWINDON TOWN	2-1	Farrington, Murray	10056	11	3	10		2	7				1			8			5		9	4				6				
24	29	SUNDERLAND	4-1	Farrington 3, Anderson	14979	11	3	10		2	7				1			8			5		9	4				6				
25	Jan 1	Portsmouth	0-1		20062	11	3	10		2	7			12	1			8			5		9	4				6				
26	12	Fulham	1-0	McCulloch	7413	11	3	10		2	7			4	1			8			5				9			6				
27	19	CARLISLE UNITED	2-2	McCulloch, Phillips	10674	11	3	10		2	7			4	1			8			5		9		12			6				
28	26	NOTTS COUNTY	1-0	Phillips	8432	11	3	10		2	7			4	1			8			5		9					6			12	
29	Feb 2	Bristol City	2-3	Phillips, McCulloch	24487	11	3	10		2	7			4	1			8			5		9					6				
30	16	Blackpool	1-2	Farrington	7410	11		10		2	7			4	1			8			5	3	6			12				9		
31	23	ASTON VILLA	0-1		12184	11		10		2	7			12	1			8			5	3		4	9			6				
32	Mar 2	Swindon Town	1-1	Powell	5319	12				2	7			4	1			9			5	3	8	6	11							10
33	9	PRESTON NORTH END	2-0	Dwyer, Whitham	7099	11				2	7				1			8			5	3	9	6						4		10
34	16	Sheffield Wednesday	0-5		13723	11				2	7				1			8			5	3	10	6			9	4				12
35	23	MILLWALL	1-3	McCulloch	7572			11		2	7				1		4	8			5	3	9					6				10
36	30	West Bromwich Albion	2-2	Vincent 2 (1p)	11528	11		8	6	2				1							5	3	4		9					7	10	
37	Apr 6	Bolton Wanderers	1-1	Reece	15148	11		8	6	2				1				4			3	5			9					7	10	
38	13	MIDDLESBROUGH	3-2	Reece, Carlin, Vincent	12861	11		8	4	2				1				5			3	6			9					7	10	
39	15	Notts County	1-1	Anderson, Smith	6975	11		10	4	2				1				5			3	9			7					6	8	
40	20	Nottingham Forest	1-2	Vincent	11138	11		8	4	2				1				6			3	5			9					7	10	
41	27	ORIENT	1-1	Reece	11613	11		10	4	2				1				5			3	9			7					6	8	
42	30	CRYSTAL PALACE	1-1	Villars	27139	11		10	4	2				1				5			3	9			7				12	6	8	
		Apps				29	29	22	7	42	19	2	7	11	33	6	2	32	2	7	35	13	38	14	25	1	11	16	32	19	6	22
		Goals				3	2	1		1	6							10			1		3	1	7			1	2	6	1	2

Two own goals

F.A. Cup

	Date	Opponent	Score	Scorers	Att	Anderson WJ	Bell G	Carlin W	Charles CM	Dwyer PJ	Farrington IR	Grotier PD	Healey R	Impey JE	Irwin WIN	King PC	Larmour AAJ	McCulloch A	McInch JR	Morgan RL	Murray DJ	Pethard FJ	Phillips L	Powell D	Reece GI	Sayer PA	Showers D	Smith G	Villars AK	Vincent IV	Whitham J	Woodruff RW
R3	Jan 5	Birmingham City	2-5	Impey, McCulloch	22435	11	3			2	7			9	1			8			5		4		12				6	10		

F.L. Cup

	Date	Opponent	Score	Scorers	Att	Anderson WJ	Bell G	Carlin W	Charles CM	Dwyer PJ	Farrington IR	Grotier PD	Healey R	Impey JE	Irwin WIN	King PC	Larmour AAJ	McCulloch A	McInch JR	Morgan RL	Murray DJ	Pethard FJ	Phillips L	Powell D	Reece GI	Sayer PA	Showers D	Smith G	Villars AK	Vincent IV	Whitham J	Woodruff RW
R1	Aug 29	HEREFORD UNITED	2-0	McCulloch 2	9821	11	3			2				12	1			8			5		6					9	4	7	10	
R2	Oct 10	BURNLEY	2-2	McCulloch, Vincent	8775		3			2					1			8	5				6		7			9	4		11	10
rep	16	Burnley	2-3 (aet)	Woodruff, Bell (p)	12313		3			2					1		4	8	5		6				12		7	9			10	11

European Cup Winners Cup

	Date	Opponent	Score	Scorers	Att	Anderson WJ	Bell G	Carlin W	Charles CM	Dwyer PJ	Farrington IR	Grotier PD	Healey R	Impey JE	Irwin WIN	King PC	Larmour AAJ	McCulloch A	McInch JR	Morgan RL	Murray DJ	Pethard FJ	Phillips L	Powell D	Reece GI	Sayer PA	Showers D	Smith G	Villars AK	Vincent IV	Whitham J	Woodruff RW
R1/1	Sep 19	SPORTING LISBON	0-0		13300		3			2					1	12		8			5		6				11		4	7	10	9
R1/2	Oct 3	Sporting Lisbon	1-2	Villars	40000		3			2					1	11		8			5		6		12		9		7	10		4

Welsh Cup

	Date	Opponent	Score	Scorers	Att	Anderson WJ	Bell G	Carlin W	Charles CM	Dwyer PJ	Farrington IR	Grotier PD	Healey R	Impey JE	Irwin WIN	King PC	Larmour AAJ	McCulloch A	McInch JR	Morgan RL	Murray DJ	Pethard FJ	Phillips L	Powell D	Reece GI	Sayer PA	Showers D	Smith G	Villars AK	Vincent IV	Whitham J	Woodruff RW
R4	Jan 9	TON PENTRE	1-0	Impey	856		3	8		2	7			4	1				12		5				9		6	11	10			
R5	Feb 21	Oswestry Town	3-1	Reece 2 (1p), Farrington	2500					2	7			4	1			8			5	3	9		6	11	12		10			
SF	Mar 13	Shrewsbury Town	2-1	Showers, Murray	1193			10		2	7				1						5	3	9	4			8		6		11	
F1	Apr 24	Stourbridge	1-0	Showers	5729				6		7			1			2				4	5	3				10	8			9	11
F2	May 6	STOURBRIDGE	1-0	Reece	4030	11		4	2			1		10							5	3	6		7		12		8	9		

1974/75 — 21st in Division Two: Relegated

#	Date	Opponent	Score	Scorers	Att	Anderson WI	Attley BR	Buchanan J	Charles CM	Dwyer PJ	Farrington JR	Finnieston SJ	Giles DC	Healey R	Impey JE	Irwin WJN	Larmour AAJ	McClelland J	McInch JR	Morgan RL	Murray DJ	Pethard FJ	Phillips L	Powell D	Reece GI	Sayer PA	Showers D	Smith G	Villars AK	Vincent IV	Witham J
1	Aug 17	OXFORD UNITED	1-1	Charles	10006	11			3					1					8		5	2	4		9			10	6	7	
2	24	Fulham	0-4		8110	11			3	2				1	6				8		5				9			12	4	7	10
3	27	York City	0-1		6321	11			8	2				1	12				10		5	3	6		9				4	7	
4	31	MANCHESTER UNITED	0-1		22344	11			8	2				1					7		5	3	6		9	12		4			10
5	Sep 7	Sheffield Wednesday	2-1	Anderson, Reece	9983	11			8					1			2		7		5	3	6		10		9		4		
6	14	BRISTOL CITY	0-1		8858	11	12		10					1			3		8		5	2	6		7		9		4		
7	21	Portsmouth	2-2	Showers, Vincent	9519				8		7			1	2				11		5	3		6	12		9		4	10	
8	24	Blackpool	0-4		5579			11			7			1	2				10		5	3		6	12		9		4	8	
9	28	HULL CITY	1-2	Rees	5648	11			12	2				1							5	3		6	10	8	9		7	4	
10	Oct 5	Bristol Rovers	0-1		10312	11				2	7						1				5		3	6			9		4	8	10
11	12	WEST BROMWICH ALB.	0-2		6737	11				2	7						1				5		3	6	12		9		4	8	10
12	16	YORK CITY	3-2	Vincent 2 (1p), Reece	5887	11		4		2			10				1				5		3	6	7		9	8		12	
13	19	Bolton Wanderers	1-2	Buchanan	9762	11		4		2			10				1				5		3		7		9	6		8	
14	26	OLDHAM ATHLETIC	3-1	Vincent, Buchanan, Finnieston	6727	11		4		2			10			1	12				5		3		7		9	6		8	
15	Nov 2	SUNDERLAND	2-0	Finnieston, Anderson (p)	9856	11		4		2			10		12	1	6				5		3		7		9	8			
16	9	Orient	1-1	Dwyer	6772	11		4		2			10			1	6				5		3		7		9	8			
17	16	NOTTM. FOREST	2-1	Dwyer, Showers	9279	11		4		2			10			1	6				5		3		7		9	8			
18	29	SOUTHAMPTON	2-2	Whitham, Showers	10640	11		4		2						1	6				5		3		7		9	8			10
19	Dec 7	Norwich City	1-1	Reece	17337	11		4		2			10			1	6				5		3		7		9	8			
20	11	FULHAM	0-0		8429	11		4		2			10			1	6				5		3		7		9	8		12	
21	14	Oxford United	0-1		8218	11		4		2			10			1	6				5		3		7		9	8			
22	21	NOTTS COUNTY	0-0		6646	11		4		2						1	6	12			5		3				9	8		7	10
23	26	Bristol City	0-0		12484	11		4		2						1	6				5		3		7		9	8			10
24	28	ASTON VILLA	3-1	Showers, Buchanan, Whitham	11060	11		4		2						1	6				5		3				9	8	7		10
25	Jan 11	NORWICH CITY	2-1	Reece 2	10951	11		4		2						1	6				5		3		10		9	8	7		
26	25	Millwall	1-5	Reece	8129	11		4		2						1	6				5		3		9		10	8	7		
27	Feb 1	ORIENT	0-0		7996	11		4		2						1	6				5		3		10		9	8	7		
28	8	Sunderland	1-3	Anderson	29315	11		4		2						1	6				5		3		9		10	7	12	8	
29	14	MILLWALL	0-1		6602	11		4		2						1	6				5		3			12	8	7	10	9	
30	22	Nottingham Forest	0-0		12806	11		4		2			8			1	6				5		3				9	7	10		
31	Mar 1	Manchester United	0-4		43601	11		4		2			8			1	6				5		3		7		9		10		
32	8	BLACKPOOL	1-1	Reece	7830	11	2	4		10						1	6				5		3		7		9		12		
33	15	Hull City	1-1	Showers	5248	11	2	4		8						1	6				5		3		9		12	7			
34	22	SHEFFIELD WEDNESDAY	0-0		6621	11	2	4		10	5					1	6						3		9		8	7		12	
35	29	Notts County	2-0	Dwyer, Charles	8105	7	2	4	8	10						1	6						3				11	9			
36	Apr 2	PORTSMOUTH	1-0	Sayer	9624	7	2	4	8	10						1	6				5		3			11	9				
37	5	Oldham Athletic	0-4		10243	7	2	4	8	10						1	6				5		3			11	9			12	
38	9	Aston Villa	0-2		32748		2	4	8	10					12	1	6				5		3			11				7	9
39	12	BRISTOL ROVERS	2-2	Dwyer, McClelland	13896		2	7		4				6		1	5	12	10				3		9		11			8	
40	19	West Bromwich Albion	0-2		10071		2		8	4						1	6	10			5		3		7		11	9		12	
41	22	Southampton	0-2		14273	11	2			4						1	6	12			5		3		9		7		8	10	
42	26	BOLTON WANDERERS	1-2	Reece	6376	11	2	4		7		12				1	6				5		3		9					8	10
		Apps				37	12	29	16	37	4	9	4	9	9	33	31	4	9	31	9	41	6	6	31	12	34	29	15	23	8
		Goals				3		3	2	4		2						1							9	1	5			4	2

F.A. Cup

Round	Date	Opponent	Score	Scorers	Att	Anderson WI	Buchanan J	Charles CM	Healey R	Impey JE	Murray DJ	Pethard FJ	Reece GI	Showers D	Smith G	Witham J
R3	Jan 4	Leeds United	1-4	Showers	31572	11	4	2	1	6	5	3	7	9	8	10

F.L. Cup

Round	Date	Opponent	Score	Scorers	Att	Anderson WI	Charles CM	Impey JE	Irwin WJN	McInch JR	Murray DJ	Pethard FJ	Powell D	Reece GI	Smith G	Villars AK	Vincent IV
R1	Aug 19	Bristol City	1-2	McInch	8813	11	3	12	1	10	5	2	6	9	8	4	7

European Cup Winners Cup

Round	Date	Opponent	Score	Scorers	Att	Anderson WI	Charles CM	Dwyer PJ	Farrington JR	Healey R	Impey JE	Larmour AAJ	McInch JR	Murray DJ	Pethard FJ	Powell D	Reece GI	Showers D	Smith G	Villars AK	Vincent IV
R1	Sep 18	Ferencvaros	0-2		26000	11	8		7	1	12	2	10	5	3	6	9			4	
R1s	Oct 2	FERENCVAROS	1-4	Dwyer	4229	7		2	12	1	14			5	3	6	10	9	8	4	11

Welsh Cup

Round	Date	Opponent	Score	Scorers	Att	Anderson WI	Attley BR	Buchanan J	Charles CM	Dwyer PJ	Finnieston SJ	Giles DC	Healey R	Impey JE	McClelland J	Murray DJ	Pethard FJ	Showers D	Smith G	Villars AK	Vincent IV	Witham J
R4	Jan 14	HEREFORD UNITED	2-0	Showers, Reece	3515	11		4	2				1	6		5	3	9	8	7		
R5	Feb 19	OWESTRY TOWN	4-0	Buchanan, Showers, Giles, Morgan (og)	1296	11		4	2			8	1	6		5	3	10	9	7		
SF	Mar 11	Newport County	1-0	Dwyer	3808	11	2	4		8	7		1	6		5	3	9				10
F1	May 5	Wrexham	1-2	Buchanan	6862	11	2	4		8	7		1	6	10		3	9			12	
F2	12	WREXHAM	1-3	Lamour	5280	11	2	4		8			1	6	10		3	12	9	7		

Played at 5 in F1 (subbed) and F2: K Pontin

1975/76   2nd in Division Three: Promoted

#	Date	Opponent	Res	Scorers	Att	Alston A	Anderson WJ	Attley BR	Buchanan I	Campbell AJ	Charles CM	Clark BD	Durrell JT	Dwyer PJ	England HM	Evans A	Giles DC	Healey R	Irwin WN	Larmour AAJ	Livermore DE	Morgan RL	Pethard FJ	Reece GI	Sayer PA	Showers D	Villars AK
1	Aug 16	Grimsby Town	0-2		6494			2	4		3		8	11	6			1		5				10	9		7
2	23	BURY	1-1	Villars	6833			4			3		10	11	2	5	12	1		6	7			9			8
3	30	Brighton & Hove Albion	1-0	Villars	11406			2			3		10	4	5	11		1		6	8					9	7
4	Sep 6	CRYSTAL PALACE	0-1		10454			2			3		8	4	5	11		1		6	10			12		9	7
5	13	Mansfield Town	4-1	Giles, Dwyer, Reece 2 (1p)	6684			2			3		10	4		11	8	1		6	7	5		9			
6	20	HALIFAX TOWN	0-0		8007			2			3		10	4	5	11	8	1		6	7			9			
7	22	Port Vale	1-2	Attley	5143			2			3		8	4	5	11		1		6	10			9			7
8	27	Preston North End	1-3	Evans	8103			2			3		10	4	5	11	12	1		6	8			9			7
9	Oct 4	WREXHAM	3-0	Dwyer 2, Evans	7730		11	2	8		3		9	4	5		10	1		6	7						
10	11	Rotherham United	0-1		4272		11	2	8		3		9	4	5		10	1		6	7						
11	18	SHEFFIELD WEDNESDAY	2-0	Evans, Quinn (og)	7911		11	2	8		3		12	4	5		10	1		6	7			9			
12	22	Aldershot	1-2	Anderson	3687		11	2	7		3		8	4	5		9	1		6	10		12				
13	25	Chester	1-1	Evans	5599		12	2	7		3		8	4	5		11	1		6	10			9			
14	31	CHESTERFIELD	4-3	Alston 2, Evans, Anderson	7456	10	11	2			3			4	5		9	1		6	8						7
15	Nov 4	WALSALL	0-0		9041	10	11	12			3			4	5		9		1	6	8		2				7
16	8	Gillingham	2-2	Anderson, Evans	5762	9	11				3			4	5	10	8		1	6	7		2	12			
17	15	COLCHESTER UNITED	2-0	Evans, Alston	7045	9	11		12		3			2	5	10	8		1	6	4						
18	29	SHREWSBURY TOWN	3-0	Anderson, Evans, Alston	8083	9	11		4		3			2	5	10			1	6	8						7
19	Dec 6	Millwall	3-1	Reece 2, Evans	6092	9	11		4		3			2	5	10			1	6	8			7			
20	22	SOUTHEND UNITED	3-1	Evans 2, Alston	9315	10	11		7		3			2	5	9	12		1	6	8			4			
21	26	Swindon Town	0-4		10202	10	11				3			2	5	9	7		1	6	8			4			
22	27	PETERBOROUGH UTD.	5-2	Anderson, Dwyer 2, Evans 2	16073	10	11		7		3			2	5	9			1	6	8			4			
23	Jan 10	BRIGHTON & HOVE ALB	0-1		17701	9	11		8		3			2	5	10			1	6	7			4			
24	17	Halifax Town	1-1	England	2399	10	11		4		3			2	5	9			1	6	8						7
25	20	MANSFIELD TOWN	1-0	Evans	9737	10	11		7		3			2	5	9			1	6	8			4			
26	31	ALDERSHOT	1-0	Alston	8913	10	11		7		3			2	5	9			1	6	8			4			
27	Feb 4	Hereford United	1-4	Buchanan	12962	10	11		7		3				5	9			1	6	8		2				4
28	7	Walsall	3-2	Alston 2, Dwyer	7109	10	11		8		3			2		9		1		6	7	5		4			
29	14	GILLINGHAM	4-1	Livermore, Buchanan, Evans, Alston	10912	10			8		3			2		9		1		6	7	5		4			11
30	21	Colchester United	2-3	Dwyer, Anderson (p)	3248		11				3			2		9	8	1		6	7	5		4			12
31	25	PORT VALE	1-1	Livermore	9109	10	11		7		3			2		9	12	1		6	8	5		4			
32	28	CHESTER	2-0	Alston, Buchanan	10000	10	11		4		3			2	5	9		1			8	6	12	7			
33	Mar 6	Chesterfield	1-1	Alston	4112	10			4	7	3	11		2	5	9		1		8	6						
34	8	Wrexham	1-1	Evans	5674	10			7	4	3	11		2	5	9		1		6	8						
35	13	ROTHERHAM UNITED	1-1	Alston	11698	10			4	7	3	11		2	5	9		1		8	6						
36	17	Sheffield Wednesday	3-1	Evans, Charles, Clark	9013	10			7	4	3	11		2	5	9		1		8	6						
37	20	Shrewsbury Town	1-3	Evans	7573	10			7	4	3	11		2	5	9		1		8	6		12				
38	27	MILLWALL	0-0		12185				6	3	11			4	5	9	7		1	8			2	12			
39	29	Southend United	2-0	Dwyer, Evans	4849				7	4	3	11		6	5	9		1		8			2				
40	Apr 3	GRIMSBY TOWN	2-1	Evans, Buchanan	9622	10	11		7	4	3			2	5	9		1		6	8						
41	7	PRESTON NORTH END	1-0	Evans	12408	10	11		7	4	3			2	5	9		1		6	8			12			
42	10	Crystal Palace	1-0	Alston	25863	10	11			4	3			2	5	9		1		6	8						
43	14	HEREFORD UNITED	2-0	Livermore, Campbell	35501	10	11			4	3			2	5	9		1		6	8		12	7			
44	17	SWINDON TOWN	0-0		23412	10				4	3			2	5	9	12	1		6	7		11	8			
45	19	Peterborough United	0-0		6846	10	11			4	3			2	5	9	7	1		6	8						
46	May 4	Bury	1-0	Alston	7133	10	11			4	3			2	5	9		1		6	8			7			
	Apps					33	29	15	28	14	39	21	2	45	40	45	11	33	13	39	45	10	20	21	9	2	10
	Goals					14	6	1	4	1	1	1		8	1	21	1				3			4			2

One own goal

F.A. Cup

R	Date	Opponent	Res	Scorers	Att	Als	And	Att	Buc	Cam	Cha	Cla	Dur	Dwy	Eng	Eva	Gil	Hea	Irw	Lar	Liv	Mor	Pet	Ree	Say	Sho	Vil
R1	Nov 22	EXETER CITY	6-2	Reece 2, Alston 3, Evans	7532	9	11		4		3			2	5	10			1	6	8			7			
R2	Dec 13	WYCOMBE WANDERERS	1-0	Evans	11607	9	11		4					2	5	10			1	6	8		3	7			
R3	Jan 3	Orient	1-0	Alston	8031	10	11				3			2		9			1	6	8	5		4			7
R4	Jan 24	Southend United	1-2	Evans	12863	10	11		7		3			2	5	9			1	6	8			4			

F.L. Cup

R	Date	Opponent	Res	Scorers	Att	Als	And	Att	Buc	Cam	Cha	Cla	Dur	Dwy	Eng	Eva	Gil	Hea	Irw	Lar	Liv	Mor	Pet	Ree	Say	Sho	Vil
R1/1	Aug 20	BRISTOL ROVERS	1-2	Reece (p)	6688				4		3		8	11	2	5	12	1		6				10	9		7
R1/2	26	Bristol Rovers	1-1	Clark	7220			2			3		8	4	5	11		1		6	10			9			7

Welsh Cup

R	Date	Opponent	Res	Scorers	Att	Als	And	Att	Buc	Cam	Cha	Cla	Dur	Dwy	Eng	Eva	Gil	Hea	Irw	Lar	Liv	Mor	Pet	Ree	Say	Sho	Vil
R4	Jan 14	SULLY	5-0	Evans 3, Livermore, Buchanan	3260	10	11		7		3			2	5				1	6	8			9	4		
R5	Feb 17	SWANSEA CITY	1-1	Bruton (og)	5812	10	11		7		3			2					1	6	8	5	4	9	12		
rep	Mar 2	Swansea City	3-0	Clark, Alston 2	10056	10			7		3	11		2	6				1		8	5	4	9			
SF	23	Chester	0-0		3743	10				4	3	11		6			7	1			8			2	9		
rep	Apr 1	CHESTER	1-0	Dunleavy (og)	4244	11			12	4	3	10		6	5				1		8			2	9	7	
F2	May 18	Hereford United	3-3	Evans, Dwyer 2	3709						3	11		5					4	1	6	8		2	9	7	10
Fr	19	HEREFORD UNITED	3-2	Pethard, Clark, Evans	2648	11					3	10		5					4	1	6	8		2	9	7	

First leg of final (Apr 29) drawn 2-2 but declared void since a Hereford player ineligible

Played at 5 in SF: K Pontin
Played at 12 in R4: M Morgan

1976/77   18th in Division Two

Division Two

No	Date	Opponent	Result	Scorers	Att	Alston A	Anderson WJ	Attley BR	Buchanan J	Campbell AJ	Charles CM	Dwyer PJ	Evans A	Friday R	Giles DC	Grapes SP	Healey R	Irwin WJN	Larmour AAJ	Livermore DE	Morgan RL	Pethard FJ	Pontin K	Sayer PA	Showers D	Went PF
1	Aug 21	Charlton Athletic	2-0	Showers 2	9762	10	11				4	3						1	6	8		2	5	7	9	
2	25	BRISTOL ROVERS	1-2	Charles (p)	12665	10	11		12		4	3						1	6	7		2	5	8	9	
3	28	BLACKBURN ROVERS	2-1	Showers, Alston	11845	12	11				4	3	10					1	6	8		2	5	7	9	
4	Sep 4	Oldham Athletic	2-3	Evans, Livermore	8511		11	3			4		10					1	6	7		2	5	8	9	
5	11	NOTTS COUNTY	2-3	Showers, Buchanan	11960		11		12		4	3	10					1	6	7	5	2		8	9	
6	18	Orient	0-3		5743	9	11		8		4	3	10					1	6	7	5	2		12		
7	24	MILLWALL	0-0		10325	10			4			3	2	9				1	6	8			5	12	7	11
8	Oct 2	Chelsea	1-2	Charles (p)	28409	10	11	2	4			3		9				1	6	8				7		5
9	9	BOLTON WANDERERS	3-2	Alston (p), Buchanan, Evans	10982	9	11		4			3	2	10				1	6	8				7		5
10	16	Plymouth Argyle	2-2	Evans, Dwyer	14198	9	11		4			3	2	10				1	6	8		12		7		5
11	23	BLACKPOOL	2-2	Evans 2	12148	9	11	12	4				2	10				1	6	7		3		8		5
12	30	SHEFFIELD UNITED	0-2		12031	10	11		4			12	2	9				1	6	8		3		7		5
13	Nov 6	Fulham	2-1	Buchanan, Evans	12366	12	11		4				2	9			1		6	8		3		7	10	5
14	10	SOUTHAMPTON	1-0	Dwyer	15160		11		4				2	9			1		6	8		3		7	10	5
15	20	Luton Town	1-2	Evans	8845	12	11		4				2	9			1		6	8		3		7	10	5
16	27	NOTTM. FOREST	0-3		12741	12	11		4				2	9			1		6	8		3		7	10	5
17	Dec 4	Burnley	0-0		8967	10		2	4	7		5		9		11	1		6	8		3		12		
18	11	HULL CITY	1-1	Buchanan	8270	10		2	4	7		5		9		11	1		6	8		3				
19	18	Carlisle United	3-4	Sayer, Buchanan, Evans	5934			2	4	7		5		9		11	1		6	8		3		12	10	
20	27	HEREFORD UNITED	3-1	Giles, Evans 2	14448			2	4			3	5	9	12	7	1		6	8				11	10	
21	Jan 1	FULHAM	3-0	Friday 2, Buchanan	20243				4			3	2	9	10	7	1		6	8				11		5
22	15	Bristol Rovers	1-1	Evans	9295	12		3					2	9	10	7	1		6	8				11		5
23	22	CHARLTON ATHLETIC	1-1	Went	11129			3	4				2	9	10	11	1		6	8				7		5
24	Feb 5	Blackburn Rovers	1-2	Sayer	9516			3	4				2	9	10	11	1		6	7				8		5
25	12	OLDHAM ATHLETIC	3-1	Friday, Evans, Sayer	12689			3	4			10	2	9		11	1		6	7				8		5
26	19	Notts County	0-1		9401			3	4			10	2	9		11	1		6	7				8		5
27	Mar 2	ORIENT	0-1		9336			3	12				2	9	10	7	1		6	8				11		5
28	5	Millwall	2-0	Evans 2	9479				12			3	2	9	10	7	1		6	8				11		5
29	8	Sheffield United	0-3		12907				12			3	2	9	10	7	1		6	8				11		5
30	12	CHELSEA	1-3	Dwyer	20168				4			3	2	9	10	7	1		6	8				11		5
31	26	PLYMOUTH ARGYLE	0-1		9567			3	11	4			2	9	10	7	1		6	8						5
32	Apr 2	Blackpool	0-1		7356			3	8	4			2	9	10	12	1		6	7				11		5
33	6	Hereford United	2-2	Sayer 2 (1p)	7670			3	7	4			2		10	12	1		6	8				11	9	5
34	9	WOLVERHAMPTON W.	2-2	Sayer, West	15422			3	8	4			2	9		12	1		6			7		11		5
35	11	Southampton	2-3	Friday, Evans	22674			3	7	4			2	9			1		6	8		12		11		5
36	16	LUTON TOWN	4-2	Sayer, Friday 2, Dwyer	10438			2		7		10	8	11			1		6	12		3		9		5
37	23	Nottingham Forest	1-0	Sayer	20646			2	4				8	11		7	1		6			3		9	10	5
38	26	Wolverhampton Wan.	1-4	Sayer	21324			2	4				8	11		7	1		6			3		9	10	5
39	30	BURNLEY	0-1		11247			2	7	4		10	8	11		12	1		6					9		5
40	May 7	Hull City	2-1	Buchanan 2 (1p)	3511				8	4			2	9	10	12	1		6	11		3		7		5
41	10	Bolton Wanderers	1-2	Buchanan (p)	23237				11	4			3	9	10		1		6	7		2		8		5
42	14	CARLISLE UNITED	1-1	Campbell	15775				8	4			2		10	11	1		6	7		3		9	12	5
	Apps					15	16	22	32	21	15	36	34	19	12	25	29	13	35	40	3	28	7	40	16	30
	Goals					2			9	1	2	4	15	6	1					1				9	4	2

F.A. Cup

Rd	Date	Opponent	Result	Scorers	Att	Alston A	Anderson WJ	Attley BR	Buchanan J	Campbell AJ	Charles CM	Dwyer PJ	Evans A	Friday R	Giles DC	Grapes SP	Healey R	Irwin WJN	Larmour AAJ	Livermore DE	Morgan RL	Pethard FJ	Pontin K	Sayer PA	Showers D	Went PF
R3	Jan 8	TOTTENHAM HOTSPUR	1-0	Sayer	27868			3	4				2	9	10	7	1		6	8				11		5
R4	29	WREXHAM	3-2	Giles, Sayer, Buchanan	28953			3	4	8			2	9		7	1		6	10				11		5
R5	Feb 26	EVERTON	1-2	Evans	35582			3	4				2	9	11	7	1		6	8				10		5

F.L. Cup

Rd	Date	Opponent	Result	Scorers	Att	Alston A	Anderson WJ	Attley BR	Buchanan J	Campbell AJ	Charles CM	Dwyer PJ	Evans A	Friday R	Giles DC	Grapes SP	Healey R	Irwin WJN	Larmour AAJ	Livermore DE	Morgan RL	Pethard FJ	Pontin K	Sayer PA	Showers D	Went PF
R1/1	Aug 14	BRISTOL ROVERS	2-1	Evans, Alston (p)	8496	9	11				4	3	10					1	6	8		2	5	7		
R1/2	17	Bristol Rovers	4-4	Evans 4	5592	10	11				4	3	9					1	6	8		2	5	7		
R2	Sep 1	QUEEN'S PARK RANGERS	1-3	Evans	23618	9	11	12			4		10					1	6	7		2	5	3	8	

European Cup Winners Cup

Rd	Date	Opponent	Result	Scorers	Att	Alston A	Anderson WJ	Attley BR	Buchanan J	Campbell AJ	Charles CM	Dwyer PJ	Evans A	Friday R	Giles DC	Grapes SP	Healey R	Irwin WJN	Larmour AAJ	Livermore DE	Morgan RL	Pethard FJ	Pontin K	Sayer PA	Showers D	Went PF
PR	Aug 4	SERVETTE	1-0	Evans	13266	9			7	4	3		10		12			1	6	8	5	2		11		
PRs	11	Servette (Geneva)	1-2	Showers	21500	9	14			4	3		10					1	6	8	5	2	12	7	11	
R1	Sep 15	DINAMO TBILISI	1-0	Alston	11181	10	11		7	4	3		9					1	6	8	5	2		14	12	
R1s	29	Dinamo Tbilisi	0-3		100000	9	14	3	7		6	5	11				1		4	8		2		12	10	

PR won on away goals

Welsh Cup

Rd	Date	Opponent	Result	Scorers	Att	Alston A	Anderson WJ	Attley BR	Buchanan J	Campbell AJ	Charles CM	Dwyer PJ	Evans A	Friday R	Giles DC	Grapes SP	Healey R	Irwin WJN	Larmour AAJ	Livermore DE	Morgan RL	Pethard FJ	Pontin K	Sayer PA	Showers D	Went PF
R4	Jan 19	STOURBRIDGE	2-0	Dwyer, Giles	1782		12	3					2	9	10	7	1		6	8				11		5
R5	Feb 16	Bangor City	2-0	Giles, Grapes	5000			3	4				2	9	10	12	1		6	8				11		5
SF	Mar 16	Bridgend Town	2-1	Sayer, Evans	2000				11			3	2	9	4	7	1		6	8				10		5
F1	May 16	SHREWSBURY TOWN	2-1	Pethard, Friday	2907				11	4			2		10	7	1		6	8		3	5	9	12	5
F2	18	Shrewsbury Town	0-3		3178				11	4			2		10	7	12	1	6			3	5	8	9	5

1977/78

19th in Division Two

Legend for shirt-number grid columns: Attley BR, Bishop RI, Buchanan I, Byrne G, Campbell AJ, Dwyer PJ, Evans A, Friday R, Giles DC, Grapes SP, Healey R, Irwin WJN, Larmour AAJ, Livermore DE, Pethard FJ, Pontin K, Robson K, Sayer PA, Thomas RJ, Went PF, Williams CR

#	Date	Opponent	Score	Scorers	Att	Att	Bis	Buc	Byr	Cam	Dwy	Eva	Fri	Gil	Gra	Hea	Irw	Lar	Liv	Pet	Pon	Rob	Say	Tho	Wen	Wil
1	Aug 20	BRISTOL ROVERS	1-1	Went	7581	3		4			2	9		11	7		1	6	8				10		5	
2	27	Blackburn Rovers	0-3		7088	3	8		12	7	2			11			1	6			4	9	10		5	
3	Sep 3	TOTTENHAM HOTSPUR	0-0		8880	3	12	8		7	4	2		11			1				6	9	10		5	
4	10	Notts County	1-1	Dwyer	7330	3		8		6	7	2		11			1				4	9	10		5	
5	17	MANSFIELD TOWN	1-1	Robson	6843	8		4		6	7	2	10	11	12		1				3	9			5	
6	24	FULHAM	3-1	Robson, Evans	8789	3		8		6	7	2	10	12			1				4	9	11		5	
7	Oct 1	Blackpool	0-3		8704	3		8		7	4	2	10				1		12		6	9	11		5	
8	4	Sunderland	1-1	Livermore	18484	3		11		7	4	2	9				1		8		6	10			5	
9	8	LUTON TOWN	1-4	Dwyer	8259	3		8		7	4	2	9				1				6	10	11		5	
10	15	Orient	1-2	Grapes	5444	3		8		7	2				11		1				6	4	9		10	
11	22	OLDHAM ATHLETIC	1-0	Went	6892	3		8	12	7	4				11		1				2	6	9		5	
12	29	Brighton & Hove Albion	0-4		22740	2		11		4			10	12	7		1				3	6	9		8	
13	Nov 5	STOKE CITY	2-0	Dwyer, Sayer	8577					4	8			11	7		1			6	3	9	10	2	5	
14	12	Hull City	1-4	Sayer (p)	5228	12				4	8			7	11		1			6		10	9	2	5	
15	19	BURNLEY	2-1	Dwyer, Sayer (p)	7069	2	12			6	3			4	11		1			10		9	7		5	8
16	26	Crystal Palace	0-2		16262	2		11	6	4	8			7			1				3	10	9		5	4
17	Dec 3	SHEFFIELD UNITED	1-6	Buchanan	6395	2		11		4	8			7	6		1				3	10	9		5	4
18	10	Bolton Wanderers	3-6	Robson, Sayer, Bishop	18072		12	11		4	2		9	7			1				3	6	10		8	
19	17	HULL CITY	0-0		5663		8	12		4	2			7	11		1	6			3	9	10		5	
20	26	Southampton	1-3	Robson	21861		10	12		4	2			7	11		1	6			3	9	8		5	
21	28	MILLWALL	4-1	Bishop, Buchanan 2, Robson	8253	11	10	8		4	2			7		1				6	3	5	9			
22	31	CHARLTON ATHLETIC	1-0	Berry (og)	8472	11	10	8		4	2			7		1				6	3	5				9
23	Jan 2	Bristol Rovers	2-3	Giles, Pontin	11957	11	10	8		4	2			7		1				6	3	5				9
24	14	BLACKBURN ROVERS	1-1	Bishop	7025	2	10			4	8			7	11	1				6	3	5	9		12	
25	21	Tottenham Hotspur	1-2	Went	29104		10	11		4	2			8	7	1				6	3	5		12	9	
26	28	SUNDERLAND	5-2	Buchanan 2 (1p), Went 2, Bishop	8436		10	11		4	2			8	7	1				6	3	5	12		9	
27	Feb 11	Mansfield Town	2-2	Bishop, Buchanan	6538		8	11		4	2			7		1				6	3	5	10		9	
28	25	BLACKPOOL	2-1	Went, Grapes	7304		8	11		4	2			10	7	1				6	3	5			9	
29	Mar 4	Luton Town	1-3	Buchanan	6029		10	11		4	2			8	7	1				6	3	5			9	
30	7	Fulham	0-1		6571		10	11	7	4	8			12		1				6	3	5		2	9	
31	18	Oldham Athletic	1-1	Went	7581		8	11		4	7			10		1				6	3	5		2	9	
32	24	BRIGHTON & HOVE ALB	1-0	Buchanan (p)	10308		12	11		4			9	8	7	1				6	3	5		2	10	
33	25	Millwall	1-1	Bishop	5941		9	11		4			12	8	7	1				6	3	5		2	10	
34	29	SOUTHAMPTON	1-0	Bishop	11332		9	11		4	8			7		1				6	3	5		2	10	
35	Apr 1	Stoke City	0-2		14804				12	4	8			11	7	1				6	3	5		2	10	9
36	4	Charlton Athletic	0-0		8395		9	11		4	8			7		1				6	3	5		2	10	
37	8	CRYSTAL PALACE	2-2	Dwyer 2	9314	9		11		4	8	12		7		1				6	3	5		2	10	
38	15	Burnley	2-4	Buchanan, Evans	11610		8	11	12	4		7	9			1				6	3	5		2	10	
39	22	BOLTON WANDERERS	1-0	Bishop	12538		12	11		4	8		9	7		1				6	3	5		2	10	
40	29	Sheffield United	1-0	Evans	13687		8	11		4	2	10		7		1				6	3	5			9	
41	May 3	NOTTS COUNTY	2-1	Buchanan, Went	9506		8	11		4	2		9	7		1				6	3	5		12	10	
42	9	Orient	0-1		8238		8	11		4	2		9	7		1				6	3	5			10	

	Att	Bis	Buc	Byr	Cam	Dwy	Eva	Fri	Gil	Gra	Hea	Irw	Lar	Liv	Pet	Pon	Rob	Say	Tho	Wen	Wil
Apps	20	26	37	13	41	39	14	2	28	27	22	20	26	3	33	36	21	20	16	39	3
Goals		8	10			6	4		1	2					1	1	5	4		8	

One own goal

F.A. Cup

Rd	Date	Opponent	Score	Att	Att	Bis	Cam	Dwy	Gil	Gra	Irw	Pet	Pon	Rob	Tho	Wen
R3	Jan 7	IPSWICH TOWN	0-2	13854	11	10	4	2	7	12	1	6	3	5	8	9

F.L. Cup

Rd	Date	Opponent	Score	Scorers	Att	Att	Buc	Cam	Dwy	Eva	Gil	Gra	Irw	Lar	Liv	Pet	Pon	Bis	Say	Wen
R1/1	Aug 13	Torquay United	0-1		3925	2	7	4	5	9	11		1	6	8				10	
R1/2	17	TORQUAY UNITED	3-2	Dwyer, Giles, Sayer	3500	2		4	5	9	11	7	1	6	8		12		10	
rep	24	TORQUAY UNITED	2-1	Sayer (p), Buchanan	1711	2	4	8		9	11	7	1			6	3		10	5
R2	30	Swindon Town	1-5	Buchanan	8919	3	8	7	4	2	11		1			6		12	9 / 10	5

Played at 3 in R1/1 and R1/2 (subbed): CM Charles

European Cup Winners Cup

Rd	Date	Opponent	Score	Att	Att	Bis	Buc	Byr	Cam	Dwy	Eva	Gil	Gra	Irw	Lar	Pet	Pon	Rob	Say	Wen
R1	Sep 14	AUSTRIA VIENNA	0-0	3631	2			3	4	10	9	11	12	1	7		6	8		5
R1s	28	Austria Vienna	0-1	8000	3	14	8	7	4	10	9			1		12	2	6	11	5

Welsh Cup

Rd	Date	Opponent	Score	Scorers	Att	Bis	Buc	Cam	Dwy	Eva	Gil	Gra	Hea	Irw	Pet	Pon	Rob	Say	Tho	Wen	Wil
R4	Dec 21	Worcester City	2-2	Went (p), Bishop	2915	10	8	4	2		7	11		1	6	3		9		5	
rep	Jan 11	WORCESTER CITY	3-0	Bishop, Robson, Barton (og)	963	10		4	2		8	7		1	6	3	5	9		11	
R5	Mar 1	KIDDERMINSTER HARR.	1-1	Buchanan	1639	10	11	4	2	12	8	7	1		6	3	5			9	
rep	15	Kidderminster Harriers	3-1	Giles 2, Buchanan (p)	3000	10	11	4	9		8	7	1		6	3	5		2	12	
SF	Apr 13	WREXHAM	0-2		8928	9	11	4	8		12		1		6	3	5		2	10	(Att 7)

1978/79 — 9th in Division Two

No		Date	Opponent	Result	Scorers	Att	Attley BR	Barber K	Bishop RJ	Buchanan J	Burns ME	Byrne G	Campbell AJ	Davies JG	Dwyer PJ	Evans A	Giles DC	Grapes SP	Harris GW (Gary)	Healey R	Jones L	Larmour AAl	Lewis J	Micallef C	Moore RD	Pethard FJ	Platt JA	Pontin K	Roberts DF	Stevens GM	Sullivan CJ	Thomas RJ	Went PF
1	Aug	19	PRESTON NORTH END	2-2	Went, Dwyer	7790			10	11	7		4		9		8			1						3			6			2	5
2		23	Stoke City	0-2		16007			10		7	11	4	1	9		8									3			6			2	5
3		26	OLDHAM ATHLETIC	1-3	Buchanan	6907	12			11	10		4	1	9		8	7								3			6			2	5
4	Sep	2	Bristol Rovers	2-4	Roberts, Buchanan (p)	6815				11	8		4	1	9			7	10							3			5	6		2	
5		9	CAMBRIDGE UNITED	1-0	Buchanan	6141		1	10	11	8		4		9			7								3			5	6	12	2	
6		16	Luton Town	1-7	Bishop	7752		1	12	9	8		7		11			6								5			3	4	10	2	
7		23	BLACKBURN ROVERS	2-0	Stevens, Bishop	6234	12		10	11			4		2			7		1	6	8				3			5	9			
8		30	Wrexham	2-1	Buchanan 2 (1p)	11766			10	8			4		2			7		1	6	11				3			5	9		12	
9	Oct	7	NOTTS COUNTY	2-3	Buchanan, Stevens	7952			10	8			4		2			7		1	6	11				3			5	9			
10		14	Orient	2-2	Buchanan, Stevens	6063				8			4		2	10		7		1	6	11				12		5	3	9			
11		21	LEICESTER CITY	1-0	Stevens	8758				8					3	10		7		1	6	11				12		2	5	9		4	
12		28	Newcastle United	0-3		23477				8		6	7		2	10				1		11				12		5	3	9		4	
13	Nov	4	CHARLTON ATHLETIC	1-4	Stevens	7772			12	8			4		2	10		7		1		11						5	3	9		6	
14		11	Preston North End	1-2	Evans	9268			12	7			4		2	10	8			1	6	11						5		9		3	
15		18	Oldham Athletic	1-2	Bishop	5357			8				4		2	10				1	6	11						5		9		3	
16		25	CRYSTAL PALACE	2-2	Evans, Dwyer	8723	8		11	7			4		2	10				1	6	12						5		9		3	
17	Dec	2	Millwall	0-2		5551	7		8	11			4		2	10					6				12		1	5		9		3	
18		9	SUNDERLAND	1-1	Evans (p)	7168	11		8	7			4		2	10					6				12		1			9		3	
19		16	Sheffield United	1-2	Evans (p)	11913				7			4		2	10					6	11			8		1			9		3	
20		23	FULHAM	2-0	Evans, Roberts	5542	7			8			4		9	10					6	11				3	1		5	12		2	
21		26	Brighton & Hove Albion	0-5		20127	7		12				4		10	9				1	6	11				3			5	8		2	
22		30	Burnley	0-0		9821	8		9				7		2	10				1	6	11				3			5			4	
23	Jan	13	Cambridge United	0-5		5344	2		10	9					11	8	7			1	6					3			5	4			
24	Feb	24	ORIENT	1-0	Buchanan	8239			12	9			4		5	10		7		1	2				11				6	8	3		
25		28	Blackburn Rovers	4-1	Stevens, Grapes, Buchanan, Evans	7158				11			4		6	10		7		1	2				9				5	8	3		
26	Mar	3	Leicester City	2-1	Dwyer, Stevens	12820			8	11			6		5			7		1					9				4	2	10	3	
27		10	NEWCASTLE UNITED	2-1	Bishop, Stevens	11089			8	11			6		5			7		1	2				9				4	10		3	
28		17	Charlton Athletic	1-1	Buchanan (p)	5658			8	11			4		6	12		7		1					9				5	2		3	
29		24	STOKE CITY	1-3	Buchanan (p)	14851			8	11			4	1	5	10		7					12		9				6	2		3	
30		27	Notts County	0-1		8211			8	11			4		6	9		7		1					10				5	2		3	
31		31	Crystal Palace	0-2		18511			8				4		6	9		7		1			12		10				5	2		3	
32	Apr	7	MILLWALL	2-1	Stevens, Kitchener (og)	7695			8				4			9				1	2		7	12	10				6	11	3		5
33		11	Fulham	2-2	Dwyer, Money (og)	6067			11	7			4		6	8				1	2				9				5	10	3		
34		14	BRIGHTON & HOVE ALB	3-1	Stevens, Evans, Moore	12686			8	7			4			9				1	2				10				6	11	3		5
35		16	West Ham United	1-1	Bishop	29058			7	11			4		6	8				1	2				9				5	10	3		
36		21	SHEFFIELD UNITED	4-0	Stevens, Buchanan 3 (1p)	10569			8	7			4		11	9				1	2								5	10	3	6	
37		25	LUTON TOWN	2-1	Moore, Stevens	10522			7	11			4			8		12		1	2				9				5	10	3	6	
38		28	Sunderland	2-1	Moore, Bishop	36526			8	7			4			9				1	2				10				5	11	3		
39	May	5	BURNLEY	1-1	Sullivan	10254			8	7			4			9		12		1	2				10				5	11	3		
40		7	BRISTOL ROVERS	2-0	Stevens, Buchanan (p)	10363				11			4		6	8		7		1	2				9				5	10	3		
41		11	WEST HAM UNITED	0-0		13124				11			4		6	8		7		1	2				9				5	10	3		
42		14	WREXHAM	1-0	Buchanan	11784				11			4		6	8		7		1	2				9				5	10	3		
			Apps				10	2	31	36	6	2	40	4	39	31	4	24	1	32	14	15	16	2	18	19	4	27	28	34	19	23	3
			Goals						6	16					4	7		1							3				2	13	1		1

Two own goals

F.A. Cup

		Date	Opponent	Result		Att	Attley	Bishop	Buchanan	Campbell	Dwyer	Evans	Healey	Jones	Larmour	Roberts	Stevens	Sullivan	Thomas
R3	Jan	9	Swindon Town	0-3		9983	7	8	12	4	2	9	1	6	11	5	3		10

F.L. Cup

		Date	Opponent	Result	Scorers	Att	Attley	Bishop	Buchanan	Burns	Campbell	Dwyer	Giles	Grapes	Healey	Roberts	Pethard	Thomas	Went
R1/1	Aug	12	OXFORD UNITED	1-2	Buchanan	4500		10	11	7	4	5	8	12	1	6	3	2	9
R1/2		16	Oxford United	1-2	Bishop	4760	2	12	11	9	4	5	8	7	1	6	3	10	

Anglo-Scottish Cup (Qualifying Round)

	Date	Opponent	Result	Scorers	Att	Bishop	Buchanan	Burns	Campbell	Davies	Dwyer	Giles	Grapes	Healey	Lewis	Pethard	Roberts	Thomas	Went
Aug	1	Bristol Rovers	0-1		5095	9	11		4	1	6	8	7			3	5	2	10
	5	FULHAM	1-0	Dwyer	4149	10	11	8	4	1	9		7		6	3	5	2	
	8	Bristol City	0-1		6916	10	11		4		8		7	1	6	3	5	2	9

Welsh Cup

		Date	Opponent	Result	Scorers	Att	Bishop	Buchanan	Dwyer	Evans	Giles	Grapes	Healey	Jones	Larmour	Lewis	Pethard	Roberts	Stevens	Sullivan	Thomas
R4	Jan	17	MERTHYR TYDFIL	2-1	Stevens, Evans (p)	694	8	11	2	9		7	1	6	4			5	10	3	
R5	Feb	12	Worcester City	2-3	Dwyer, Buchanan	2500	7	8	2	9	4		1			11	3	5	10		6

1979/80 — 15th in Division Two

#	Date		Opponent	Score	Scorers	Att	Bishop RJ	Buchanan J	Campbell AJ	Davies JG	Davies PA	Dwyer PJ	Elliott RM	Grapes SP	Grotier PD	Harris GW (Gary)	Healey R	Hughes BW	Jones L	Lewis J	Lloyd KIJ	Micallef C	Moore RD	Pontin K	Roberts DF	Ronson W	Stevens GM	Sullivan CJ	Thomas RJ
1	Aug	18	Notts County	1-4	Jones	7157	8	11	4			6					1		2		12		9		5	7	10	3	
2		22	QUEEN'S PARK RANGERS	1-0	Stevens	11577	7	11	4			6					1		2			12	9		5		10	8	3
3		25	BIRMINGHAM CITY	1-2	Stevens	11465		11	4			6		7			1		2				9		5		10	8	3
4	Sep	1	Wrexham	1-0	Stevens	9839	7	11	4			6					1		2				9		5		10	8	3
5		8	SHREWSBURY TOWN	1-0	Stevens	8651	7	11	4				12				1		2				9		5		10	8	3	6
6		15	Watford	1-1	Stevens	13741	7	12	4			6	11				1		2				9	5			10	8	3
7		22	CAMBRIDGE UNITED	0-0		8519		11	4			6	7				1		2				9	5			10	8	3
8		29	Bristol Rovers	1-1	Pontin	8974		11	4			6	7				1		2				9	5			10	8	3
9	Oct	6	LUTON TOWN	2-1	Bishop 2	9402	7	12	4			6					1	11	2				9	5			10	8	3
10		9	Queen's Park Rangers	0-3		12225	7		4			6					1	11	2				9	5			10	8	3
11		13	Burnley	2-0	Bishop, Ronson	6450	7	11	4			6					1		2				9	5			10	8	3
12		20	CHELSEA	1-2	Moore	15992	7	11	4			6					1		2				9	5			10	8	3
13		27	Charlton Athletic	2-3	Bishop, Hughes	6896	7	11	4			6					1	12	2				9	5			10	8	3
14	Nov	3	NOTTS COUNTY	3-2	Bishop 2, Buchanan	8316	7	8	4			6					1			11			9	5			10	12	3	2
15		10	Newcastle United	0-1		22867	7	8	4			6					1			11			9	5			10	12	3	2
16		17	ORIENT	0-0		8095		12	4					7			1			11		2	9	5			10	8	3	6
17		24	West Ham United	0-3		20292	7		4	1		8								11		2	9	5			10	12	3	6
18	Dec	1	OLDHAM ATHLETIC	1-0	Bishop	7048	8		4	1		2	7							11			9	5			10		3	6
19		8	Sunderland	1-2	Bishop	25370	8		4	1		2	7							11			9	5			10	12	3	6
20		15	PRESTON NORTH END	0-2		6711	7	12	4						1			11	2				8	5			10	9	3	6
21		21	Leicester City	0-0		12877	8		4			2			1			11		7			12	5			10	9	3	6
22		26	FULHAM	1-0	Pontin	8105	8		4			2			1			11		7			12	5			10	9	3	6
23		29	Birmingham City	1-2	Bishop	16682	8		4						1				2	7			11	5			10	9	3	6
24	Jan	1	Swansea City	1-2	Lewis	21306	8	11	4			2			1					7			9	5			10		3	6
25		12	WREXHAM	1-0	Moore	10803	8	11	4			2					1			7			9	5			10		3	6
26		19	Shrewsbury Town	2-1	Buchanan, Moore	6870	8	11	4			2		10			1			7			9	5			12	3	6
27	Feb	2	WATFORD	1-0	Lewis	7983	8	11	4			2					1	3		7			9	5			10	12	6
28		9	Cambridge United	0-2		5229	8	11	4					2			1	3		7			9	5			10	12	6
29		16	BRISTOL ROVERS	0-1		6918	8		4	12				2			1			3		7	9	5			10	11	6
30		23	BURNLEY	2-1	Pontin, Stevens	6342	8		4			2	7				1			3		11	9	5			10	12	6
31	Mar	1	Chelsea	0-1		18490			4			2	11				1			3		7	9	5			10	8	6
32		8	CHARLTON ATHLETIC	3-1	Stevens 2, Buchanan	6533	7	12	4			2	11				1			3			9	5			10	8	6
33		14	Luton Town	2-1	Buchanan, Stevens	9246		7	4			2	11				1			3			9	5			10	8	6
34		22	NEWCASTLE UNITED	1-1	Stevens	9284		7	4			2	11				1			3		12	9	5			10	8	6
35		29	Orient	1-1	Buchanan	4081		7	4			2	11				1			3			9	5			10	8	6
36	Apr	7	SWANSEA CITY	1-0	Ronson	14634		7	4			2	11				1			3			9	5			10	8	6
37		8	LEICESTER CITY	0-1		10193		7	4			2	11				1			3			9	5			10	8	12	6
38		12	Oldham Athletic	3-0	Buchanan, Stevens, Micallef	6339	8	7	4					2			1					11		12	5		10	9	3	6
39		15	Fulham	1-2	Bishop	5161	9	7	4					11			1			3		12		5			10	9	6
40		19	WEST HAM UNITED	0-1		12051	8	10	4					2	1	11				3				5		7	9	12	6
41		26	Preston North End	0-2		7493		7	4			12		2	11	1				3		8		5			10	9	6
42	May	3	SUNDERLAND	1-1	Bishop	19834	8		4					7	2	1	11			3				9	5		10		6
				Apps			31	31	42	3	1	32	7	18	7	3	32	8	17	28	1	8	38	37	5	41	38	30	30
				Goals			11	6										1	1	2		1	3	3		2	11		

F.A. Cup

Rnd	Date		Opponent	Score	Scorers	Att	Bishop RJ	Buchanan J	Campbell AJ	Davies JG	Davies PA	Dwyer PJ	Elliott RM	Grapes SP	Grotier PD	Harris GW (Gary)	Healey R	Hughes BW	Jones L	Lewis J	Lloyd KIJ	Micallef C	Moore RD	Pontin K	Roberts DF	Ronson W	Stevens GM	Sullivan CJ	Thomas RJ
R3	Jan	5	ARSENAL	0-0		21972	8	11	4			2					1			7			9	5			10	12	3	6
rep		8	Arsenal	1-2	Buchanan	36582	8	11	4			2					1			7			9	5			10	12	3	6

F.L. Cup

Rnd	Date		Opponent	Score	Scorers	Att	Bishop RJ	Buchanan J	Campbell AJ	Davies JG	Davies PA	Dwyer PJ	Elliott RM	Grapes SP	Grotier PD	Harris GW (Gary)	Healey R	Hughes BW	Jones L	Lewis J	Lloyd KIJ	Micallef C	Moore RD	Pontin K	Roberts DF	Ronson W	Stevens GM	Sullivan CJ	Thomas RJ
R2/1	Aug	28	Everton	0-2		18061		11	4			6	7				1		2				9		5		10	8	3
R2/2	Sep	5	EVERTON	1-0	Buchanan	9698	7	12	4			6	11				1		2				9		5		10	8	3

Welsh Cup

Rnd	Date		Opponent	Score	Scorers	Att	Bishop RJ	Buchanan J	Campbell AJ	Davies JG	Davies PA	Dwyer PJ	Elliott RM	Grapes SP	Grotier PD	Harris GW (Gary)	Healey R	Hughes BW	Jones L	Lewis J	Lloyd KIJ	Micallef C	Moore RD	Pontin K	Roberts DF	Ronson W	Stevens GM	Sullivan CJ	Thomas RJ
R4	Jan	22	Newport County	0-2		7709	8	11	4			2					1			7			9	5			10	3	6

1980/81   19th in Division Two

No.	Date	Opponent	Score	Scorers	Att	Bishop RI	Buchanan I	Campbell AI	Davies PA	Dwyer PI	Gilbert TH	Giles PA	Grapes SP	Grotier PD	Healey R	Hughes BW	Jones L	Kitchen MP	Lewis I	Maddy PM	Micallef C	Pontin K	Roberts DF	Ronson W	Stevens GM	Sullivan CJ	Thomas RI
1	Aug 16	BLACKBURN ROVERS	1-2	Stevens	6810	7	11	12		4			2	1					3		8	5		10	9		6
2	19	Wrexham	1-0	Bishop	7772	7	8	4		3			2	1					11			5		10	9		6
3	23	Oldham Athletic	0-2		5690	7	8	4		3			2	1				12	11			5		10	9		6
4	30	ORIENT	4-2	Stevens 2, Dwyer, Buchanan	5671	7	11	4		6			2	1				8	3			5		10	9		
5	Sep 6	Newcastle United	1-2	Kitchen	15787	7	11	4		6			2	1				8	3			5		10	9		
6	13	BOLTON WANDERERS	1-1	Stevens	6532	7	11	4		6			2	1				8	3			5		10	9		
7	20	BRISTOL ROVERS	2-1	Ronson, Pontin	6117	7	11	12		6			2	1				8	3		4	5		10	9		
8	27	Notts County	2-4	Dwyer, Kitchen	7229		11			6			2	1				8	3	4	7	5	12	10	9		
9	Oct 4	WATFORD	1-0	Micallef	6388		11			6			2	1				8	3	4	7	5	12	10	9		
10	7	West Ham United	0-1		20402		11						2	1		4		8			7	5	6	10	9		3
11	11	Sheffield Wednesday	0-2		15606	11		4		12			2	1				8			7	5	6	10	9		3
12	17	CAMBRIDGE UNITED	1-2	Smith (og)	4140			4		12			2	1			3	8	11		7	5	6	10	9		
13	22	QUEEN'S PARK RANGERS	1-0	Grapes	4453	7	10			6			4	1			2	9	3	11		5		8	12		
14	25	Shrewsbury Town	0-2		4466	7	9			6			4	1			2	8	3	11		5		10	12		
15	31	CHELSEA	0-1		8445	7	11			6			4	1			2	8	3		12	5		10	9		
16	Nov 8	Preston North End	1-3	Kitchen	5494	7	11			6				1		4	2	8	3			5		10	9		
17	12	WREXHAM	1-0	Kitchen (p)	4780		11			6			12		1	4	2	8	3		7	5		10	9		
18	15	Blackburn Rovers	3-2	Kitchen 2, Buchanan	7855		11			6		7			1	4	2	8				5		10	9		3
19	22	LUTON TOWN	1-0	Buchanan	6041		11			6		7			1	4	2	8		12		5		10	9		3
20	29	Derby County	1-1	Clark (og)	15581		11			6		7			1	4	2	8				5		10	9		3
21	Dec 6	GRIMSBY TOWN	1-1	Kitchen (p)	5936		11			6		7			1	4	2	8				5		10	9		3
22	26	Bristol City	0-0		15039		11			6					1	4	2	8	7			5	3	10	9		
23	27	SWANSEA CITY	3-3	Stevens, Kitchen, Buchanan	21198	7	11			6			12		1	4	2	8	3			5		10	9		
24	Jan 10	Luton Town	2-2	Kitchen, Giles	9013		11			6		7			1	4		8			12	5	2	10	9		3
25	17	Orient	2-2	Maddy 2	3838		11					7			1	4		8		6		5	2	10	9		3
26	31	OLDHAM ATHLETIC	0-2		5563		11		9	4		7			1	12		8		6		5		10			3
27	Feb 3	Queen's Park Rangers	0-2		9834		11			6		7			1	4	2	8			12	5		10	9		3
28	7	Bolton Wanderers	2-4	Buchanan 2	8115		11					7			1		2	8		6		5	4	10	9		3
29	20	NOTTS COUNTY	0-1		4958		11				3		4		1		2	8	7			5		10	9		6
30	25	NEWCASTLE UNITED	1-0	Kitchen	4226		11				3		4	1			2	8	7			5		10	9		6
31	28	Bristol Rovers	1-0	Grapes	7525		11				3		4	1			2	8	7			5		10	9		6
32	Mar 4	SHEFFIELD WEDNESDAY	0-0		6971		11				3		4	1			2	8	7			5		10	9		6
33	7	Watford	2-4	Kitchen, Jones	10114		11				3		4	1			2	8	7			5		10	9		6
34	21	Cambridge United	0-2		3719		11					3		1			2	8	7		4	5		10	9		6
35	28	SHREWSBURY TOWN	2-2	Lewis, Dwyer	5195		11					3		1			2	8	7		4	5		10	9		6
36	Apr 4	Chelsea	1-0	Stevens	11569		11			6			4	1			2	8	7			5		10	9	3	
37	11	PRESTON NORTH END	1-3	Dwyer	4987		11			6			4	1			2	8	7			5		10	9	3	
38	18	Swansea City	1-1	Kitchen	19038					6		11	4	1			2	8	7		12	5		10	9	3	
39	20	BRISTOL CITY	2-3	Grapes, Kitchen	5575					6			4	1			2	8	7		11	5		10	9	3	
40	25	Grimsby Town	1-0	Stevens	7377					6			4	1			2	8	7		11	5		10	9	3	
41	May 2	DERBY COUNTY	0-0		7577					6			4	1			2	8	7		11	5		10	9	3	
42	6	WEST HAM UNITED	0-0		10535					6			4	1			2	8	7		11	5		10	9	3	12
		Apps				13	35	9	1	34	5	11	28	22	20	14	29	40	32	8	18	42	8	42	40	7	23
		Goals				1	6			4		1	3				1	13	1	2	1	1			1		7

Two own goals

F.A. Cup

	Date	Opponent	Score	Scorers	Att	Bishop RI	Buchanan I	Campbell AI	Davies PA	Dwyer PI	Gilbert TH	Giles PA	Grapes SP	Grotier PD	Healey R	Hughes BW	Jones L	Kitchen MP	Lewis I	Maddy PM	Micallef C	Pontin K	Roberts DF	Ronson W	Stevens GM	Sullivan CJ	Thomas RI
R3	Jan 3	Leicester City	0-3		17527		11					7			1	4	2	8	3		12	5		10	9		6

F.L. Cup

	Date	Opponent	Score	Scorers	Att	Bishop RI	Buchanan I	Campbell AI	Davies PA	Dwyer PI	Gilbert TH	Giles PA	Grapes SP	Grotier PD	Healey R	Hughes BW	Jones L	Kitchen MP	Lewis I	Maddy PM	Micallef C	Pontin K	Roberts DF	Ronson W	Stevens GM	Sullivan CJ	Thomas RI
R1/1	Aug 9	Torquay United	0-0		3441	7	11						2	1		12	4		3		8	5	6	10	9		
R1/2	13	TORQUAY UNITED	2-1	Bishop, Stevens	3149	7	11			3			2	1			4				8	5	6	10	9		
R2/1	27	CHELSEA	1-0	Bishop	6549	7	11	4		6			2	1				8	3			5		10	9		12
R2/2	Sep 3	Chelsea	1-1	Kitchen	12959	7	11	4		6			2	1				8	3			5		10	9		
R3	23	Barnsley	2-3	Buchanan, Lewis	13135	7	11	4					2	1				8	3			5		10	9		6

Welsh Cup

	Date	Opponent	Score	Scorers	Att	Bishop RI	Buchanan I	Campbell AI	Davies PA	Dwyer PI	Gilbert TH	Giles PA	Grapes SP	Grotier PD	Healey R	Hughes BW	Jones L	Kitchen MP	Lewis I	Maddy PM	Micallef C	Pontin K	Roberts DF	Ronson W	Stevens GM	Sullivan CJ	Thomas RI
R3	Dec 3	CARDIFF CORINTHIANS	6-0	Kitchen 5, Hughes	1080	12	11			6		7			1	4	2	8	10			5			9		3
R4	Jan 27	Wrexham	0-3		4880		11					7			1	4	2	8		6		5		10	9		3

#	Date	Opponent	Score	Scorers	Att	Bennett DA	Bennett GE	Buchanan J	Dwyer PJ	Francombe P	Gilbert TH	Giles PA	Grapes SP	Grotier PD	Healey R	Henderson MR	Hughes BW	Jones L	Kitchen MP	Lewis J	Maddy PM	Micallef C	Mullen J	Polycarpou A	Pontin K	Ronson W	Sayer PA	Stevens GM	Sugrue PA	Sullivan CJ	Thomas RJ
1	Aug 29	Oldham Athletic	2-2	Stevens, Dwyer	4374			11	6				4		1			2	8	7					5	10		9		3	
2	Sep 5	CHELSEA	1-2	Kitchen	8884			11	6				4		1			2	8	7		12			5	10		9		3	
3	12	Rotherham United	0-1		7002			11	6				4		1			2	8	7					5	10		9		3	
4	19	BLACKBURN ROVERS	1-3	Ronson	4248				6						1			2	8	7	11	12			5	10	4	9		3	
5	22	Luton Town	3-2	Kitchen (p), Sayer, Stevens	9015				6						1			2	8	7		11			5	10	4	9		3	
6	26	Barnsley	1-0	Stevens	12114	7			6						1			2			11				5	10	4	9	8	3	
7	Oct 3	NEWCASTLE UNITED	0-4		5758	7			6						1			2	12	11					5	10	4	9	8	3	
8	10	Sheffield Wednesday	1-2	D Bennett	15839	7			6				3	12	1		10	2				11		8	5			9			4
9	17	BOLTON WANDERERS	2-1	Stevens, D Bennett	3874	7			6				3			1	10	2				11	4	8	5			9			12
10	24	SHREWSBURY TOWN	1-1	Stevens	4353	7			6				3	2	1		10					11	4	8	5			9			12
11	31	Cambridge United	1-2	Micallef	4041	7			6				3	2	1		10					11	4	8	5			9			
12	Nov 4	WREXHAM	3-2	Micallef, Stevens, Lewis	4618	7	5		6				3		1		10	2				11	4	8				9			
13	7	NORWICH CITY	1-0	D Bennett	5698	7	6						3		1		10	2				11	4	8				9			5
14	14	Watford	0-0		13982	7	6						3		1		10	2				11	4	8	5			9			
15	21	LEICESTER CITY	3-1	Micallef, D Bennett, Stevens	6656	7	6						3		1		10	2				11	4	8	5			9	12		
16	24	Wrexham	1-3	Dwyer	3625	7	6		12				3		1		10	2				11	4	8	5			9			
17	28	Queen's Park Rangers	0-2		10225	7	6		4				3	2	1		10					11		8	5			9	12		
18	Dec 4	DERBY COUNTY	1-0	Micallef	5506	7	6						3	2	1		10					11	4	8	5			9			
19	28	CHARLTON ATHLETIC	0-1		7879	8	6		3				2		1		10					11	4	7	5			9	12		
20	Jan 20	OLDHAM ATHLETIC	0-1		4108	7	6		10			3	11		1			2					4	8	5			9			
21	30	Blackburn Rovers	0-1		7001	7	6		9			3	11		1			2	10				4	8	5						
22	Feb 6	ROTHERHAM UNITED	1-2	Kitchen	3818	7	6		11	2		3	12		1				10				4	8	5			9			
23	13	Newcastle United	1-2	Stevens	15129	7	6		11			3			1			2	10				4	8	5			9			
24	17	Chelsea	0-1		9710	7	6		11			3			1			2	10				4	8	5			9			
25	20	Barnsley	0-0		4500	7	6		4			3			1		11	2	10		12	8			5			9			
26	27	SHEFFIELD WEDNESDAY	0-2		5767	7	6		4			3		12	1		11	2	10			8			5			9			
27	Mar 6	Bolton Wanderers	0-1		6269	7			4		3	12	8		1		6	2	10						5			9			
28	9	Crystal Palace	0-1		7202	7					12	3	11		1		6	2	10			8			5			9			
29	13	Shrewsbury Town	1-1	G Bennett	4089	7	6					3			1		11	2	10			8	12		5			9			
30	20	CAMBRIDGE UNITED	5-4	Stevens 3, Kitchen 2	3239	10	6					3	7		1		5	2	9			12	8		4			11			
31	27	Norwich City	1-2	Gilbert	11923	10					3	7			1	8	5	2	9			12	6		4			11			
32	30	GRIMSBY TOWN	2-1	Stevens, D Moore (og)	3920	10					3	7			1	8		2	9			5	6		4			11			
33	Apr 3	WATFORD	2-0	D Bennett, Micallef	6729	10					3	7			1	8		2	9			5	6		4			11			
34	10	ORIENT	2-1	D Bennett, Kitchen	5685	9						7			1	3		2	11		12	8	5	6	4			10			
35	13	Charlton Athletic	2-2	Stevens, Mullen	4186							7		8	1	12		2	9		10	5	6	3	4			11			
36	17	Leicester City	1-3	Kitchen	13650	12						7		8	1	10		2	9			5	6	3	4			11			
37	24	QUEEN'S PARK RANGERS	1-2	Micallef	5974	10						7		8	1	12		2	9		11	5	6	3	4						
38	28	Orient	1-1	Maddy	2527	10						7		8	1	5		2	9		11		6	3	4						
39	May 1	Derby County	0-0		10111	10						7		8	1	5		2	9		11		6	3	4						
40	8	CRYSTAL PALACE	0-1		5558	10						7	8					2	9		12	5	6	3	4			11			
41	15	Grimsby Town	1-0	Micallef	8148	11	9					7	8		1	3		2				5	6		4			10			
42	17	LUTON TOWN	2-3	Kitchen, Micallef	10277	11	9					7	8		1	3		2	12			5	6		4			10			

Played in games 23 (at 12) and 27 (at 11): AJ Sanders
Played at 1 in game 40: AG Dibble

	Bennett DA	Bennett GE	Buchanan J	Dwyer PJ	Francombe P	Gilbert TH	Giles PA	Grapes SP	Grotier PD	Healey R	Henderson MR	Hughes BW	Jones L	Kitchen MP	Lewis J	Maddy PM	Micallef C	Mullen J	Polycarpou A	Pontin K	Ronson W	Sayer PA	Stevens GM	Sugrue PA	Sullivan CJ	Thomas RJ
Apps	36	19	3	22	3	28	6	25	9	32	11	24	36	27	19	27	33	12	7	40	7	4	38	5	7	4
Goals	6	1		2		1								8	1	1	8	1			1	1	13			

F.A. Cup

	Date	Opponent	Score	Scorers	Att	Bennett DA	Bennett GE	Dwyer PJ	Grapes SP	Healey R	Hughes BW	Micallef C	Mullen J	Polycarpou A	Pontin K	Stevens GM	Sugrue PA
R3	Jan 2	Manchester City	1-3	Maddy	31547	7	6	3	2	1	10	11	4	8	5	9	12

F.L. Cup

	Date	Opponent	Score	Scorers	Att	Buchanan J	Dwyer PJ	Grapes SP	Healey R	Hughes BW	Jones L	Kitchen MP	Lewis J	Pontin K	Ronson W	Stevens GM	Sugrue PA	Sullivan CJ
R1/1	Sep 2	EXETER CIY	2-1	Stevens 2	2688	11	6	4	1		2	8	7	5	10	9		3
R1/2	16	Exeter City	1-3 (aet)	Sugrue	4449	11	6	4	1	12	2		7	5	10	9	8	3

Welsh Cup

	Date	Opponent	Score	Scorers	Att	Bennett DA	Bennett GE	Dwyer PJ	Francombe P	Gilbert TH	Grapes SP	Healey R	Henderson MR	Hughes BW	Jones L	Kitchen MP	Maddy PM	Micallef C	Mullen J	Polycarpou A	Pontin K	Ronson W	Sayer PA	Stevens GM	Sugrue PA
R3	Dec 6	Bridgend Town	4-1	Micallef 2, Lewis, Sugrue	1000		6	3			2	1		10				11	4	8	5			9	7
R4	Jan 15	NEWPORT COUNTY	3-1	D Bennett, Dwyer, Stevens	3915	7	6	3			2	1		10				11	4	8	5			9	
R5	Jan 9	WREXHAM	4-1	Stevens, Kitchen	2767	7	6	11	3		4	1			2	10				8	5			9	
SF1	Apr 8	Hereford United	0-0		4832	7	6				4	1	3		2	10	12	11		8	5			9	
SF2	19	HEREFORD UNITED	2-1	Micallef, Stevens	3635	10					7	1	8	6	2	9		5		3	4			11	
F1	May 11	SWANSEA CITY	0-0		11960	10	9				8		3		2			5	6		4			11	
F2	19	Swansea City	1-2	G Bennett	15828	10	9				8		3		2			5	6		4			12	

Played at 7 in F1 and F2: Lythgoe. Played at 12 in F1 and 11 in F2: McEwan
Played at 1 in F1 and F2: AG Dibble

1982/83   2nd in Division Three: Promoted

#	Date	Opponent	Result	Scorers	Att	Bennett DA	Bennett GE	Bodin PJ	Brown JG	Dibble AG	Dwyer PJ	Gibbins RG	Giles PA	Hatton RJ	Hemmerman JL	Humphries SR	Ingram GPA	Jones L	Lewis J	Maddy PM	Micallef C	Mullen J	Pontin K	Steele EG	Thomas MR	Tong DJ	Woof W
1	Aug 28	WREXHAM	1-2	D Bennett	5018	7	12	3			4	9			10	1		2		11	6	5				8	
2	Sep 5	Millwall	4-0	Lewis, D Bennett 2, Gibbins	5304	7	2	3			12	9			10				11	4	6	5			1	8	
3	8	Orient	0-4		1790	7	2	3				9			10		12		11	4	6	5			1	8	
4	11	WIGAN ATHLETIC	3-2	Lewis, G Bennett, Woof	3850	7	2	3				9					12		11	4	6	5			1	8	10
5	18	Walsall	2-1	Hemmerman, Dwyer	3161	7		3			5	9			10			2	11	4	6				1	8	
6	25	SHEFFIELD UNITED	2-0	D Bennett, Hemmerman	7147	7		3			5	9			10		12	2	11	4	6				1	8	
7	28	EXETER CITY	2-0	Hemmerman 2	4807	7		3			5	9			10		12	2	11	4	6				1	8	
8	Oct 2	Oxford United	2-2	Mullen, Gibbins	6205	7		3			5	9			10		12	2	11	4	6				1	8	
9	9	Bournemouth	1-3	Hemmerman	5818	7	12	3			5	9			10		4	2	11		6				1	8	
10	16	GILLINGHAM	1-0	Ingram	4828	7	6	3			5	9			10		4	2	11						1	8	
11	19	BRADFORD CITY	1-0	G Bennett	5007	7	6	3			5	9			10		4	2	11		12				1	8	
12	23	Huddersfield Town	0-4		6121	7	6	3			5	9			10		4	2	11		12				1	8	
13	30	PORTSMOUTH	1-0	Hemmerman	7082	7	6	3			5	9			10		8	2	11		4				1		
14	Nov 3	Reading	2-1	G Bennett, Dwyer	3217	7	6	3			5	9			10		8	2	11		4				1	12	
15	6	PRESTON NORTH END	3-1	Hemmerman, D Bennett, Ingram	5453	7	6	3			5	9			10		8	2	11		4				1		
16	13	Lincoln City	1-2	D Bennett	6585	7		3				9			10		12	2	11		4	6			1	8	
17	Dec 4	Doncaster Rovers	2-2	Micallef, Hemmerman	3078			3		1	5	9	12	7	10			2	11		4	6				8	
18	7	CHESTERFIELD	1-1	Hatton	3813	7		3		1		9		8				2	11			6				4	
19	17	Southend United	2-1	Hatton, Gibbins	3743	7		3		1	5	9		8	10			2	11			6				4	
20	27	NEWPORT COUNTY	3-2	Hemmerman 2, Hatton	15972	7	6			1	5	9		8	10			2	11			3				4	
21	28	Plymouth Argyle	2-3	Hatton, G Bennett	8631	7	6			1	5	9		8	10			2	11		12	3				4	
22	Jan 1	BRISTOL ROVERS	3-1	Hemmerman 2 (1p), G Bennett	11050	7	6			1	5	9		8	10			2	11			3				4	
23	3	Brentford	3-1	Gibbins, Hemmerman 2	7602		6	12		1	5	9	7	8	10			2	11			3				4	
24	15	Wrexham	0-0		3846	7	6			1	5	9		8	10			2	11			3				4	
25	22	WALSALL	3-1	G Bennett, Hemmerman (p), D Bennett	6115	7	6			1	5	9		8	10			2	11			3				4	
26	29	Exeter City	2-0	Hemmerman, Hatton	4019	7	6	2		1		9		8	10				11			3				4	
27	Feb 1	MILLWALL	3-0	G Bennett, D Bennett, Hemmerman	5643	7	6	2		1		9		8	10		12		11			3				4	
28	5	Sheffield United	0-2		11641	7	6	11		1		9		8	10			2			12	3				4	
29	12	OXFORD UNITED	3-0	Hemmerman (p), D Bennett, Hatton	6970	7		6		1		9		8	10			2				3				4	
30	16	Bradford City	2-4	Dwyer, Gibbins	3786			6		1	5	9		8	10			2	11		7	3				4	
31	19	BOURNEMOUTH	1-1	Gibbins	4878	7	6			1	5	9		8	10			2	11			3				4	
32	26	Gillingham	3-2	Hemmerman 2 (1p), Gibbins	4587	7	6			1	5	9		8	10			2	11			3				4	
33	Mar 1	READING	0-0		6173	7	6	6		1	5	9		8	10			2	11		12	3				4	
34	12	Portsmouth	0-0		24354	7	6				5	9		8	10			2	11			3		1		4	
35	15	HUDDERSFIELD T	1-1	Hatton	10379	7	6	5				9		8	10			2	11			3		1		4	
36	19	Preston North End	1-2	Hemmerman	4611	7	6					9		8	10			2			11	3		1		4	
37	26	LINCOLN CITY	1-0	G Bennett	8021	7	6					9		8	10			2			11	3		1		4	
38	Apr 2	PLYMOUTH ARGYLE	0-0		7146	7	6	12				9		8	10			2			11	3		1		4	
39	4	Newport County	0-1		16052		6					9	7	8	12			2	9		11	3		1		4	
40	9	DONCASTER ROVERS	3-0	Tong 2, Gibbins	5456		6	12				9		8	10			2	7		11	3		1		4	
41	16	Wigan Athletic	0-0		4383	12	6			1		9		8	10			2	7		11	3				4	
42	23	SOUTHEND UNITED	4-1	Hatton, Lewis 2, Hemmerman	6141	7	6	5		1		9		8	10			2	11			3				4	
43	30	Chesterfield	1-0	D Bennett	2797	7		5		1		9	6	8	10			2			11	3				4	
44	May 2	BRENTFORD	3-1	McNichol (og), Hatton, D Bennett	9112	7	6	3	1			9		8	10			2	11							4	
45	7	ORIENT	2-0	Lewis, D Bennett	11758	7	6		1			9		8	10			2	11			3				4	
46	14	Bristol Rovers	1-1	Gibbins	10731	7	6	12	1			9		8	10			2	11			3				4	
		Apps				41	36	31	3	20	41	46	7	30	44	1	11	43	39	8	20	39	4	7	15	44	1
		Goals				12	8				3	9		9	22		2		5		1	1				2	1

One own goal

F.A. Cup

#	Date	Opponent	Result	Scorers	Att	Bennett DA	Bennett GE	Bodin PJ	Brown JG	Dibble AG	Dwyer PJ	Gibbins RG	Giles PA	Hatton RJ	Hemmerman JL	Humphries SR	Ingram GPA	Jones L	Lewis J	Maddy PM	Micallef C	Mullen J	Pontin K	Steele EG	Thomas MR	Tong DJ	Woof W
R1	Nov 20	Wokingham Town	1-1	Tong	3000	7		3		1	5	9			10		12	2	11		4	6				8	
rep	23	WOKINGHAM TOWN	3-0	Jones, Hemmerman, Ingram	3755	7		3		1	5	9			10		4	2	11		12	6				8	
R2	Dec 11	WEYMOUTH	2-3	Gibbins, Hemmerman	4446	7	8	3		1	5	9	12		10			2	11			6				4	

F.L. Cup (Milk Cup)

#	Date	Opponent	Result	Scorers	Att	Bennett DA	Bennett GE	Bodin PJ	Brown JG	Dibble AG	Dwyer PJ	Gibbins RG	Giles PA	Hatton RJ	Hemmerman JL	Humphries SR	Ingram GPA	Jones L	Lewis J	Maddy PM	Micallef C	Mullen J	Pontin K	Steele EG	Thomas MR	Tong DJ	Woof W
R1/1	Aug 31	HEREFORD UNITED	2-1	D Bennett, Gibbins	?1808?	7	4	3				9			10			2	11		12	6	5		1	8	
R1/2	Sep 15	Hereford United	2-1	Gibbins, Hemmerman	3301	7	5	3				9			10			2	11		6	4			1	8	
R2/1	Oct 5	Arsenal	1-2	Gibbins	15115	7		3			5	9			10			2	11		4	6			1	8	
R2/2	26	ARSENAL	1-3	Hemmerman	11632	7	6	3			5	9			10		12	2	11		4				1	8	

Welsh Cup

#	Date	Opponent	Result	Scorers	Att	Bennett DA	Bennett GE	Bodin PJ	Brown JG	Dibble AG	Dwyer PJ	Gibbins RG	Giles PA	Hatton RJ	Hemmerman JL	Humphries SR	Ingram GPA	Jones L	Lewis J	Maddy PM	Micallef C	Mullen J	Pontin K	Steele EG	Thomas MR	Tong DJ	Woof W
R3	Nov 30	Newport County	0-1		7800	7		3		1	5	9	12		10			2	11		4	6				8	

1983/84   15th in Division Two

Player columns (left→right): Baird II, Bennett GE, Bodin PJ, Burke M, Crawford A, Dibble AG, Dwyer PJ, Elsey KW, Evans PA, Gibbins RG, Goldsmith MS, Grant D, Hemmerman IL, Jones L, Lee TC, Lewis J, Matthews WJ, Mullen J, Owen IG, Plumley GE, Rodon CP, Smith CR, Tong DJ, Townsend CG, Vaughan NM, Walker PA

#	Date	Opponent	Score	Scorers	Att	Bai	Ben	Bod	Bur	Cra	Dib	Dwy	Els	Eva	Gib	Gol	Gra	Hem	Jon	Lee	Lew	Mat	Mul	Owe	Plu	Rod	Smi	Ton	Twn	Vau	Wal
1	Aug 27	Charlton Athletic	0-2		4590		5	3		9	1	4			8				2	11		12		7		10		6			
2	29	MANCHESTER CITY	2-1	Boden 2	8895		5	3		9	1	4			8				2	11				7		10		6			
3	Sep 3	GRIMSBY TOWN	3-1	Owen 2 (1p), Crawford	5315		5	3		9	1	4			8				2	11		12		7		10		6			
4	6	Shrewsbury Town	0-1		4405		5	3		9	1	4			8				2	11		12		7		10		6			
5	10	Leeds United	0-1		12323		5	3		9	1	4			8				2	11		12	10	7				6			
6	17	PORTSMOUTH	0-0		9033		5	3		9	1	4			8				2	11		12	10	7				6			
7	Oct 1	BARNSLEY	0-3		6378	11		3			1	4		2	8							12	5	7				6		10	9
8	8	CARLISLE UNITED	2-0	Owen, Vaughan	4768			3			1	4		2	8					11			5	7				6	12	10	9
9	15	Chelsea	0-2		15459			3			1	4	11		8							12	5	7			2	6	9	10	
10	19	NEWCASTLE UNITED	0-2		9826			3			1	4	11		8							12	5	7			2	6	9	10	
11	31	Fulham	2-0	Bennett, Owen	5940	9		3			1	4	11		8							12	5	7			2	6		10	
12	Nov 5	Middlesbrough	0-2		7686	9		3			1	4	11		8							12	5	7			2	6		10	
13	8	Crystal Palace	0-1		5330	9		3			1	5	11		8							4		7			2	6	12	10	
14	12	CAMBRIDGE UNITED	5-0	Gibbins 2, Vaughan, Fallon (og), Owen	4730	9		3			1	5	11		8							4		7			2	6	12	10	
15	19	Oldham Athletic	1-2	Dwyer	3587	9	5	3			1	4	11		8							12		7			2	6		10	
16	26	HUDDERSFIELD T	3-1	Bodin, Laws (og), Owen	6013	9	5	3			1	4	11		8							12		7			2	6		10	
17	Dec 3	Brighton & Hove Albion	1-3	Baird	9905	9	5	3			1	4	11		8									7			2	6		10	
18	10	BLACKBURN ROVERS	0-1		5200	9	5	3				4			8		12				11			7	1		2	6		10	
19	17	Sheffield Wednesday	2-5	Baird 2	14793	9	5	3	11			4			8		12							7			2	6		10	
20	26	SWANSEA CITY	3-2	Gibbins, Vaughan, Lee	14580	9	5	3				4			8					11				7			2	6		10	
21	27	Derby County	3-2	Baird 2, Dwyer	16054	9	5	3	7			4			8					11							2	6		10	
22	31	Grimsby Town	0-1		7164	9	5	3	7			4			8					11								6	12		
23	Jan 21	Portsmouth	1-1	Lee	11938	9	5	3				4	2		8					11				7				6		10	
24	31	CHARLTON ATHLETIC	2-1	Owen, Bennett	4522	9	5				1	4	2		8					11				7			3	6			
25	Feb 4	Barnsley	3-2	Baird, Owen, May (og)	7107	9	5				1	4	2		8					11				7			3	6			
26	11	LEEDS UNITED	0-1		9407		5				1	4	2		8	11		10						7			3	6		9	
27	19	FULHAM	0-4		7149	11	5				1	4	2		8	12		10						7			3	6		9	
28	25	Newcastle United	1-3	Vaughan	27964		5				1	4	2		8			10		11				7			3	6		9	
29	Mar 3	MIDDLESBROUGH	2-1	Elsey, Goldsmith	4422		5				1	4	10		8	12	3			11				7			2	6		9	
30	10	Cambridge United	2-0	Smith, Vaughan	2512						1	4	2		8	11	3	12	10					7			5	6		9	
31	17	SHREWSBURY TOWN	2-0	Vaughan, Owen	3870						1	4	2		8		3	10		11				7			5	6		9	
32	24	Manchester City	1-2	Owen	20140						1	4	2		8		3	10		11				7			5	6		9	
33	31	CHELSEA	3-3	Gibbins, Owen (p), Vaughan	11060						1	4	2		8	12	3	10		11				7			5	6		9	
34	Apr 7	Carlisle United	1-1	Goldsmith	4704						1	4	2		8	12	3	10		11				7			5	6		9	
35	14	OLDHAM ATHLETIC	2-0	Owen (p), Lee	4637						1	4	2		8		3	10		11				7			5	6		9	
36	17	CRYSTAL PALACE	0-2		4901						1	4	2		8	12	3	10		11				7			5	6		9	
37	21	Swansea City	2-3	Smith, Owen	10275		10				1	4	2		8	12	3			11				7			5	6		9	
38	23	DERBY COUNTY	1-0	Owen	5156		3				1	4	2		8			10		11				7			5	6	12	9	
39	28	Huddersfield Town	0-4		5599		3	7			1	4	2		8			10		11							5	6	12	9	
40	May 5	BRIGHTON & HOVE ALB	2-2	Lee, Vaughan	4366		5				1	4	10		8		3			11				7			2	6		9	
41	7	Blackburn Rovers	1-1	Lee	3107	10	2				1	4			8		3			11	7							6		9	
42	12	SHEFFIELD WEDNESDAY	0-2		14176		5	10			1	4			8		3			11		7						6		9	
Apps						12	32	26	3	6	41	42	29	2	42	9	12	11	6	21	6	14	12	39	1	4	34	42	5	36	2
Goals						6	2	3		1		2	1		4	2				5				14					2	8	

Three own goals

F.A. Cup

Round	Date	Opponent	Score	Scorers	Att	Ben	Bod	Bur	Dib	Dwy	Els	Eva	Gib	Owe	Ton	Vau
R3	Jan 7	IPSWICH TOWN	0-3		10118	5	3	11	1	4	2	9	8	7	6	10

F.L. Cup (Milk Cup)

Round	Date	Opponent	Score	Scorers	Att	Ben	Bod	Cra	Dib	Dwy	Gib	Jon	Lee	Mat	Mul	Owe	Rod	Smi	Ton	Twn	Vau
R1/1	Aug 31	Exeter City	3-2	Dwyer, Owen, Crawford	4005	5	3	9	1	4	8	2	11	12		7	10		6		
R1/2	Sep 13	EXETER CITY	2-1	Crawford, Bennett	2721	5	3	9	1	4	8		11	12	10	7	2		6		
R2/1	Oct 4	NORWICH CITY	0-0		4425		3	10	1	4	8		11		5	7		2	6		9
R2/2	26	Norwich City	0-3		9887		3		1	4	7		11		5	10		2	6		12

Played at 8 in R2/2: Heycock

Welsh Cup

Round	Date	Opponent	Score	Scorers	Att	Bai	Ben	Bod	Bur	Dib	Dwy	Els	Gib	Lee	Mat	Owe	Plu	Smi	Ton	Twn	Vau
R3	Nov 22	TAFF'S WELL	5-0	* see below	894		5	3			4	11	8		9	7	1	2	6	12	10
R4	Jan 18	MAESTEG PARK ATH.	4-0	Owen 2 (2p), Baird, Lee	905	9	5	3			4	2	8	11		7	1	12	6		10
R5	Feb 7	HEREFORD UNITED	1-3	Vaughan	2033	9	5		11	1	4	2	8	12		7		3	6		10

Scorers in R3: Matthews, Owen, Gibbins, Vaughan, Townsend

1984/85   21st in Division Two: Relegated

#		Date	Opponent	Score	Scorers	Att.	Bannon PA	Bodin PJ	Dwyer PI	Elsey KW	Felgate DW	Flynn B	Ford MP	Francis GCJ	Gibbins RG	Grant D	Hamilton D	Jones V	King J	Martin MP	McLoughlin PB	Meacock KM	Micallef C	Mullen J	Plumley GE	Saunders DN	Seasman J	Smelt LA	Smith CR	Summerfield K	Tong DJ	Vaughan NM	Withey GA
1	Aug	25	CHARLTON ATHLETIC	0-3		5020		12	4	7					8	3		2									10	1	5	11	6	9	
2	Sep	1	Sheffield United	1-2	Gibbins	12133	12		4	7					8	3		2									10	1	5	11	6	9	
3		8	BRIGHTON & HOVE ALB	2-4	Elsey, Seasman (p)	4634	6	11	4	3				7	8												10		5		2	9	
4		12	LEEDS UNITED	2-1	Bodin, Dwyer	6802	8	11	4	9				7	12	3		2						1			10		5		6		
5		15	Barnsley	0-2		4692	8	11	4	9				7	12	3		2						1			10		5		6		
6		18	Blackburn Rovers	1-2	Summerfield	5922		11	4	2				7	8	3								1			10		5	6		9	
7		22	MANCHESTER CITY	0-3		6089		11	4	9				7	8	3		2						1			10		5	6		12	
8		29	Middlesbrough	2-3	Seasman, Vaughan	4259		11	4					7	8	3		2					12	1			10		5		6	9	
9	Oct	6	PORTSMOUTH	1-2	Elsey	6201			4	11				7	8	3		2					12				10	1	5		6	9	
10		14	Notts County	2-0	Vaughan 2	5893		10	4	11					8	3		2								7		1	5		6	9	
11		20	Fulham	2-3	Elsey, C Smith	5363		10	4	11					8	3		2								7		1	5		6	9	
12		27	GRIMSBY TOWN	2-4	Jones, Vaughan	3607		11	4	10					8	3		2					12				7	1	5		6	9	
13	Nov	3	Wolverhampton Wan.	0-3		7537			4	10					8	3		2			12	11						1	5	7	6	9	
14		10	OLDHAM ATHLETIC	2-2	Vaughan 2	3429			4	11			7		8	5					12	3						1	2	10	6	9	
15		17	CARLISLE UNITED	2-1	Tong, Vaughan	2855			4	11			7		8						5			3				1	2	10	6	9	
16		24	Huddersfield Town	1-2	Vaughan	6495			4	11			7		8			2		5		10		3				1			6	9	
17	Dec	1	BIRMINGHAM CITY	1-2	Elsey	5057		12	4	11	1		7		8			2		5				3						10	6	9	
18		9	Crystal Palace	1-1	Gibbins	6004			4	11	1		7		10			2	6				12	3						8	5	9	
19		15	WIMBLEDON	1-3	Dwyer	2976			4	11	1		7		6				5	12	8			3					2	10		9	
20		22	SHEFFIELD UNITED	1-3	Withey	3429			4	11	1		7		8			2	5	12				3							6	9	10
21		26	Oxford United	0-4		12224			4	11			7					2	5	12	8			3							6	9	10
22		29	Leeds United	1-1	Withey	11796			4	2		5	7		8					11	12			3							6	9	10
23	Jan	1	SHREWSBURY TOWN	0-0		4609			4	2		5	7		8					11				3							6	9	10
24	Feb	2	MIDDLESBROUGH	2-1	Meacock 2	2564			4	3			7		6			2		11	8			5	1						9	10	
25		9	Brighton & Hove Albion	0-1		7354			4	11	10				9			2		7	8	12		3	1						6		
26		16	Oldham Athletic	1-0	Vaughan	3592		12	4			5	7					2		11	8			3	1						6	9	10
27		23	WOLVERHAMPTON W.	0-0		4694			4			5	7		12			2		11	8			3	1						6	9	10
28	Mar	2	Grimsby Town	3-6	Gibbins, Mullen (p), Withey	4589			4			5	7		12			2		11	8			3	1						6	9	10
29		5	Charlton Athletic	4-1	Dwyer, Mullen (p), Withey 2	3930			4	6		5	7		9			2		11	8			3	1								10
30		9	FULHAM	0-2		4293			4	6		5	7		9			2		11	8			3	1					12			10
31		17	NOTTS COUNTY	1-4	Gibbins	3631			4	6		5	7		9			2		11	8			3	1					12			10
32		23	Portsmouth	0-0		13620		11				5	12		4			2		7	8			3	1						6	9	10
33		30	Manchester City	2-2	Gibbins, Withey	20047						5			4		11	2		7				3	1	8					6	9	10
34	Apr	6	OXFORD UNITED	0-2		6686						5	3		4		11	2		7	12				1	8					6	9	10
35		9	Shrewsbury Town	0-0		3919				3		5			4		11	2		7	12				1	8					6	9	10
36		13	BLACKBURN ROVERS	1-2	Vaughan	3387	3					5			4		11	2		7	8				1	12					6	9	10
37		20	Carlisle United	1-0	Vaughan	2651			3			5			4		11	2		7	8				1						6	9	10
38		23	Barnsley	3-0	M Ford, Vaughan 2	3044			3			5			4		11	2		7	8				1						6	9	10
39		27	HUDDERSFIELD T	3-0	Meacock, Vaughan 2	3414	7					5	6		4		11	2			8			3	1							9	10
40	May	4	Birmingham City	0-2		15868	7					5	6		4		11	2			8			3	1							9	10
41		6	CRYSTAL PALACE	0-3		5207	7					5			4		11	2		12	8			3	1						6	9	10
42		11	Wimbledon	1-2	Micallef	3252			7			5	2		4		11						8	3	1						6	10	9
			Apps				4	18	31	30	4	22	20	7	40	13	10	11	23	7	17	21	12	26	24	4	12	13	16	10	33	38	22
			Goals					1	3	4			1		5			1				3	1	2			2		1	1	1	15	6

Played in game 3 at 1, MJ Rees, and at 12, JP Woods
Played in games 32 at 12 and 34 at 3 (subbed): FM Ford

F.A. Cup

		Date	Opponent	Score	Scorers	Att.	Dwyer PI	Elsey KW	Ford MP	Flynn B	Gibbins RG	Martin MP	McLoughlin PB	Mullen J	Plumley GE	Tong DJ	Vaughan NM	Withey GA
R3	Jan	21	Gillingham	1-2	Withey	5452	4	2	7	5	8	11	12	3	1	6	9	10

F.L. Cup (Milk Cup)

		Date	Opponent	Score	Scorers	Att.
R1/1	Aug	29	Exeter City	0-1		3469
R1/2	Sep	4	EXETER CITY	2-0	Marker (og), Gibbins	2026
R2/1		25	Watford	1-3	Gibbins	12884
R2/2	Oct	9	WATFORD	1-0	Grant	4607

Appearances: R1/1 – Dwyer 4, Elsey 7, Gibbins 8, Grant 3, Jones 2, Seasman 10, Smelt 1, Smith 5, Summerfield 11, Tong 6, Vaughan 9. R1/2 – Bodin 11, Dwyer 4, Elsey 7, Gibbins 8, Grant 3, Jones 2, Seasman 10, Smelt 1, Smith 5, Tong 6, Vaughan 9. R2/1 – Bodin 11, Dwyer 4, Elsey 7, Gibbins 8, Grant 3, Jones 2, Mullen 1, Seasman 10, Smith 5, Tong 6, Vaughan 9. R2/2 – Bannon 3, Dwyer 4, Elsey 11, Gibbins 8, Grant 5, Jones 2, Micallef 12, Seasman 10, Tong 7, Vaughan 6, Withey 9.

Welsh Cup

		Date	Opponent	Score	Scorers	Att.
R3	Nov	27	MERTHYR TYDFIL	5-0	Tong, Micallef, Vaughan 2, Elsey	1399
R4	Jan	30	HEREFORD UNITED	0-4		2075

Appearances: R3 – Dwyer 4, Elsey 11, Ford 7, Gibbins 8, Jones 12, King 5, Micallef 10, Mullen 3, Smelt 1, Smith 2, Tong 6, Vaughan 9. R4 – Dwyer 4, Elsey 11, Ford 7, Flynn 5, Gibbins 6, King 2, McLoughlin 8, Mullen 3, Smelt 1, Vaughan 9, Withey 10.

1985/86   22nd in Division Three: Relegated

#	Date		Opponent	Result	Scorers	Att	Carver JW	Christie DHM	Curtis MW	Farrington MA	Flynn B	Foley W	Ford MP	Gibbins RG	Giles DC	Gummer JC	King J	Leonard CC	Marustik C	McLoughlin PB	Meacock KM	Micallef C	Mullen J	Nardiello G	Rees MI	Sander CA	Smelt LA	Stevenson NCA	Turner RP	Vaughan NM	Wheeler P	Withey GA
1	Aug	17	Notts County	4-1	* see below	3856	3			8	7		5		4		2			11			6			1			9	10		
2		24	CHESTERFIELD	0-2		3386	3			8	7		5		4		2			11			6			1			9	10		
3		26	Newport County	2-1	Mullen (p), Vaughan	5027	3			8	7		5		4		2			11		12	6			1			9	10		
4		31	READING	1-3	McLoughlin	3539	3			8	7		5		4					11		12	6			1			9	10		
5	Sep	7	York City	1-1	Ford	3760	3			8			5		4	11	7			2	10	12	6			1			9			
6		14	BRISTOL CITY	1-3	Withey	4412	3			8			5		4	11	7			2		12	6			1			9			10
7		17	BURY	0-0		2000	3			8	7		5		4					2	12	11	6			1			9			10
8		21	Blackpool	0-3		3783	3		12	8	7		5		4					2		11	6			1			9			10
9		28	DERBY COUNTY	0-2		3232	3		12	8	7		11		4					2			6			1			9			10
10	Oct	1	Rotherham United	0-3		2906	3		9	8	7		11		4					2		12	6			1				10		
11		5	BOURNEMOUTH	0-1		2156	3			8	7		4			2						12	6			1				10	11	9
12		12	Gillingham	0-2		3367				8	7		4				11	3		10		12	6			1			9			
13		19	WIGAN ATHLETIC	3-1	Marustik, Turner, Vaughan	1961							4				11		10	7	12		6			1			9	8		
14		22	Darlington	1-4	McLoughlin	2446	2		12				4			7			10	3	11		6			1			9	8		
15		26	BOLTON WANDERERS	0-1		2502		7		11			4					5	10	2			6			1		3	9	8		
16	Nov	2	Brentford	0-3		3934		7					4		10			5		2		11	6			1		3	9	8		
17		5	Walsall	3-6	Mullen (p), Christie, Vaughan	3282		7		10			4					2	3	11	12		6			1		5	9	8		
18		8	DONCASTER ROVERS	0-1		1894		7					4					2	3	11	10		6			1	5	9		8		
19		23	Bristol Rovers	1-2	Mullen (p)	4563		7	2	12					3				4			11	6			1	5			8		9
20		30	WOLVERHAMPTON W.	1-1	Curtis	2453		7	11	12					3		2		4				6			1	5		9	8	10	
21	Dec	14	Lincoln City	4-0	* see below	2127		7	2	12			11		3	4							6			1	5		9	8	10	
22		20	Chesterfield	4-3	Turner, Christie, Vaughan, Farrington	1773		7	2	12			10		3	4						11	6			1	5		9	8		
23		26	SWANSEA CITY	1-0	Vaughan	8375		7	2	10					3				4			11	6			1	5		9	8		
24		28	NEWPORT COUNTY	1-1	Ford	7450		7	2	10			4		3							11	6			1	5		9	8	12	
25	Jan	1	Plymouth Argyle	4-4	Turner, Ford, Vaughan, Mullen (p)	8520		7	2	10			4		3							11	6			1	5		9	8		
26		4	BRENTFORD	1-0	Vaughan	3398		7	2	12			4		3							11	6			1	5		9	8	10	
27		11	Reading	1-1	Ford	7004		7	2	12			4		3							11	6			1	5		9	8	10	
28		18	NOTTS COUNTY	1-3	Mullen (p)	2410		7	2	10			5		3				4			11	6			1			9	8	12	
29		25	Bristol City	1-2	Wheeler	7541		7		10			4		3				2	12		11	6			1	5		8	9		
30		31	YORK CITY	2-1	Vaughan, Wheeler	1988			2	7			5		3				4	12		11	6			1			9	8	10	
31	Feb	4	DARLINGTON	0-1		2222			2	7		5	11		3				4	12			6			1			9	8	10	
32		8	Wigan Athletic	0-2		3428	12		2	7		5	11		3				4				6			1			9	8	10	
33		22	BLACKPOOL	1-0	Curtis	2430		7	2			5	11		3				4				6			1			9	8	10	
34	Mar	1	Derby County	1-2	Vaughan	11014		7	2	12		5	11		3				4	6						1			9	8	10	
35		8	Bournemouth	1-1	Turner	2707			2	10					11				3			4	5	7		6		1		9	8	12
36		15	GILLINGHAM	1-1	Gummer	2579			2			5	9		3	10			4	7			6			1			8	11		
37		22	Bolton Wanderers	0-5		4114			2	10		12	4		3					7			6			1			9	8	11	
38		25	ROTHERHAM UNITED	2-3	McLoughlin, Mullen (p)	1663			2			8	11		3				4	7		10	6			1			9		12	
39		28	PLYMOUTH ARGYLE	1-2	Nardiello	3824						11	4		3				2	7		10	6	9		1			12	8		
40		31	Swansea City	0-2		6643			2				11		3				4	7		10	6	8		1			9	12		
41	Apr	5	WALSALL	1-1	Foley	1893						9	11		3				2	7		10	6	8		1			12	4		
42		8	Bury	0-3		1720						9	11		3				2	7		10	6	8		1			12	4		
43		12	Doncaster Rovers	2-0	Nardiello 2	2051		7	2				11		3				4	12		10		9		1				8		
44		19	BRISTOL ROVERS	2-0	Tanner (og), Vaughan	2735			2				11		3				4	7		10	6	9		1				8		
45		26	Wolverhampton Wan.	1-3	Nardiello	3353						12	11		3				4	2			6	9		1			10	8	7	
46	May	2	LINCOLN CITY	2-1	Turner 2	1904			2			9	11		3				4	12			6			1			10	8	7	

Played in one game: AJ Spring (game 12 at 2), DJ Tong (4, 2)
Played in games 19 at 10 (subbed) and 36 at 12: TD O'Connor
Played in six games 9-14 at 5: DE Corner
Played in ten games 37-46: PA Brignull
Played in games 13 (at 2, subbed) and 43 (at 6): AD Price
Scorers in game 1: McLoughlin, Farrington, Mullen(p), Vaughan
Scorers in game 21: Vaughan, Turner, Mullen (p), Farrington

	Carver JW	Christie DHM	Curtis MW	Farrington MA	Flynn B	Foley W	Ford MP	Gibbins RG	Giles DC	Gummer JC	King J	Leonard CC	Marustik C	McLoughlin PB	Meacock KM	Micallef C	Mullen J	Nardiello G	Rees MI	Sander CA	Smelt LA	Stevenson NCA	Turner RP	Vaughan NM	Wheeler P	Withey GA
Apps	13	19	27	31	10	12	44	11	34	5	7	4	26	32	4	28	44	7	9	13	24	14	34	43	21	5
Goals		2	2	3		1	4		1				1	4			8	4					7	12	2	1

One own goal

F.A. Cup

	Date		Opponent	Result	Scorers	Att	Christie	Ford	Leonard	Marustik	McLoughlin	Micallef	Mullen	Smelt	Stevenson	Turner	Vaughan
R1	Nov	16	Exeter City	1-2	Stevenson	2772	7	4	2	3	11	12	10	6	1	5	9	8

F.L. Cup (Milk Cup)

	Date		Opponent	Result	Scorers	Att	Carver	Farrington	Flynn	Ford	Giles	King	McLoughlin	Meacock	Micallef	Mullen	Sander	Turner	Vaughan
R1/1	Aug	20	SWANSEA CITY	2-1	Flynn 2	4218	3	8	7	5	4	2	11		12	6	1	9	10
R1/2	Sep	3	Swansea City	1-3	Farrington	4621	3	8	7	5	4	2	11	10	12	6	1		9

Associate Members Cup (Freight Rover Trophy)

	Date		Opponent	Result	Scorers	Att	Christie	Curtis	Farrington	Ford	Giles	Marustik	McLoughlin	Micallef	Mullen	Sander	Turner	Vaughan	Wheeler	Withey
R1	Jan	21	Newport County	0-1		1863			10	5	3	2	7	11	6	1	9	8	4	12
R1		28	SWANSEA CITY	0-2		1006	7	2		5	3	4	10	11	6	1	8	9		

Welsh Cup

	Date		Opponent	Result	Scorers	Att	Christie	Curtis	Farrington	Ford	Giles	Gummer	Marustik	McLoughlin	Meacock	Micallef	Mullen	Sander	Turner	Vaughan	Wheeler	Withey
R3	Nov	26	Caerleon	3-2	Vaughan 2, Marustik	500	7	2	12	10	3		4			11	6	1	5	8		9
R4	Jan	8	MOLD ALEXANDRA	4-1	Turner, Hemmerman, Vaughan 2	604	7	2		4	3	5		11		6		1	9	8	12	
R5	Mar	11	BARRY TOWN	0-0		2053	7	2		5	3		4	11		6		1	9	8	10	
rep		13	Barry Town	2-0	Hemmerman, Giles	1750	7	2	12	5	3		4	7		10	6	1	8	10		
SF1	Apr	15	Wrexham	1-4	Vaughan	1639		2		5	3		4	7		10	6	1	8	9		
SF2		22	WREXHAM	1-2	Marustik	1255		2		5	3	12	4	7		11	6	1	9	8		

Played at 11 in SF1: AD Price

1986/87   13th in Division Four

League — Division Four

No	Date	Opponent	Score	Scorers	Att	Bartlett KF	Boyle TDJ	Brignull PA	Curtis AT	Davies GR	Ford MP	Giles DC	Gummer JC	Horrix DV	Kerr AA	Mardenborough SA	Marustik C	Moseley G	Perry J	Pike C	Platnauer NR	Rees MJ	Rogers AJ	Sherlock SE	Simmons AJ	Turner RP	Vaughan NM	Wheeler P	Wimbleton PP
1	Aug 23	Hartlepool United	1-1	Turner	2804		6	5			12	7			2			1				11	3			8	10	9	4
2	30	ROCHDALE	0-0		3546		6	5	10			7			2			1				11	3			8		9	4
3	Sep 6	Wolverhampton Wan.	1-0	Wimbleton	5740		6	5	10			7			2			1				11	3			8		9	4
4	13	TRANMERE ROVERS	0-2		2868		6	5	10			7			2			1				11	3			12	8	9	4
5	16	LINCOLN CITY	1-1	Rogers	2406		6	5	8			7			2			1				11	3			12	10	9	4
6	20	Exeter City	0-0		3066		6	5	8			7			2			1				11	3				10	9	4
7	27	HEREFORD UNITED	4-1	Wheeler, Vaughan, Wimbleton (p), Curtis	3353		6	5	8			7			2			1				11	3				10	9	4
8	Oct 1	Peterborough United	2-1	Vaughan, Wheeler	2858		6	5	8			7			2			1			12	11	3				10	9	4
9	4	CREWE ALEXANDRA	1-1	Vaughan	3571		6	5	8			7			2			1			12	11	3				10	9	4
10	11	Wrexham	1-5	Vaughan	2926		6	5	8						2		7	1			12	11	3				10	9	4
11	17	Colchester United	1-3	Wheeler	3160		6	5	8						2		7				12	1	11				10	9	4
12	25	SCUNTHORPE UNITED	1-1	Boyle	2145		6	5	8		3	7			2						12	1	11				10	9	4
13	31	Halifax Town	1-1	Platnauer	1640	12	6	5	8		3				2		11				7	1					10	9	4
14	Nov 4	Preston North End	1-0	Ford	6636		6	5	8		3				2		11				7	1					10	9	4
15	8	SOUTHEND UNITED	0-2		2987	12	6	5	8		3				2		11				7	1					10	9	4
16	22	Stockport County	0-2		1674	12	6	5		8	3				2		11				7	1					10	9	4
17	29	CAMBRIDGE UNITED	3-0	Bartlett 2, Wimbleton (p)	2071	8	6	5	7		3				2		11					1		9			10		4
18	Dec 13	ALDERSHOT	2-0	Platnauer, Vaughan	2443	8	6	5			3				2		11	1		9	7						10	12	4
19	19	Burnley	3-1	Vaughan, Pike, Wimbleton	1717	8	6	5			3				2		11	1		9	7						10		4
20	26	SWANSEA CITY	0-0		11450	8	6	5	12		3				2		11	1		9	7						10		4
21	28	Northampton Town	1-4	Pike	11138	8	6	5	12		3				2		11	1		9	7						10		4
22	Jan 3	STOCKPORT COUNTY	1-1	Wheeler	3038		6	5	8		3				2		11	1			7		12				10	9	4
23	24	WOLVERHAMPTON W.	0-2		3331		6	5	10	12	3				2		11			9	7	1						8	4
24	Feb 7	Lincoln City	1-0	Wimbleton (p)	1954	8	6	5	10		3				2		11			9	7	1							4
25	21	Hereford United	2-0	Cegielski (og), Horrix	3969	12	6		10		3		9	5		2					7	1		8	11				
26	24	Tranmere Rovers	1-2	Simmons	1456	12	6		10		3		9	5		2					7	1		8	11				
27	28	PETERBOROUGH UTD.	0-1		2620	12	6	5	7		3		9		2						10	1		11	8				
28	Mar 3	HALIFAX TOWN	0-0		1785	12	6	5	7		3		9		2						10	1		11	8				
29	7	Scunthorpe United	3-1	Kerr, Horrix 2	1936		6	5	10		3		9		2						7	1		11				8	4
30	10	Rochdale	0-0		1386		6	5	10		3		9		2						7	1		11		12		8	4
31	14	COLCHESTER UNITED	0-2		2222		6	5	10		3	12	9		2	11					7	1						8	4
32	17	Orient	0-2		2411		6	5	10		3	11	9		2						7	1		12				8	4
33	21	WREXHAM	0-0		1556	12	6		10		3	11	9		2						7	1		5				8	4
34	24	ORIENT	1-1	Platnauer	1362	9	6		10		3	12			2						7	1		5			11	8	4
35	28	Crewe Alexandra	2-1	Wheeler 2	1762	9	6		10		3	5			2	12					7	1					11	8	4
36	31	EXETER CITY	0-0		1868	9	6	5	10		3	11					12		2		7	1						8	4
37	Apr 3	Southend United	0-2		3917		6	5	10		3	11			2	9					7	1					12	8	4
38	11	PRESTON NORTH END	1-1	Wimbleton	2528	12	6	5	10		3				2	9					7	1					11	8	4
39	18	TORQUAY UNITED	3-1	Mardenborough, Curtis, Wheeler	1840	12	6		10		3	5				9					7	1		11			2	8	4
40	20	Swansea City	0-2		6653		6	5	10		3	11				9					7	1		12			2	8	4
41	25	BURNLEY	1-0	Wimbleton (p)	2003		6		10		3	11				9					7	1		5			2	8	4
42	28	Torquay United	0-1		1440	8	6		10		3	11				9					7	1		5			2	12	4
43	May 1	Cambridge United	1-2	Gummer	1368	8	6		10		3	11	9								7	1		5			2	8	4
44	4	NORTHAMPTON T	1-1	Curtis	2682		6		10		3	11	9								7	1		5			2	8	4
45	7	HARTLEPOOL UNITED	4-0	Curtis, Gummer, Bartlett, Wimbleton	1334	12	6		10		3	11	9								7	1		5			2	8	4
46	9	Aldershot	2-1	Gummer, Bartlett	3680	9	6		10		3	11									7	1		5			2	8	4
		Apps				23	46	34	42	2	36	16	15	9	31	11	17	25	1	6	38	21	27	15	5	5	32	37	46
		Goals				4	1		4		1		3	3	1	1				2					1	1	6	7	8

One own goal

F.A. Cup

Rd	Date	Opponent	Score	Scorers	Att	Bartlett	Boyle	Brignull	Curtis	Davies	Ford	Giles	Gummer	Horrix	Kerr	Mardenb.	Marustik	Moseley	Perry	Pike	Platnauer	Rees	Rogers	Sherlock	Simmons	Turner	Vaughan	Wheeler	Wimbleton
R1	Nov 15	Ton Pentre	4-1	Marustik 2, Wimbleton, Wheeler	2700		6	5	8		3				2		11				7	1					10	9	4
R2	Dec 9	BRENTFORD	2-0	Wimbleton, Bartlett	2531	8	6	5			3	2	12				11	1			7						10	9	4
R3	Jan 10	Millwall	0-0		5615		6	5	8		3	2					11				7	1		4			10	9	
rep	20	MILLWALL	2-2 (aet)	Vaughan, Marustik	4585	8	6	5			3	2					11			9	7	1		4			10		12
rep2	26	MILLWALL	1-0	Pike	5012	8	6	5	10		3				2		11	1		9	7								4
R4	31	Stoke City	1-2	Wimbleton	20423	8	6	5	10	12	3				2		11	1		9	7								4

F.L. Cup (Littlewoods Challenge Cup)

Rd	Date	Opponent	Score	Scorers	Att	Bartlett	Boyle	Brignull	Curtis	Davies	Ford	Giles	Gummer	Horrix	Kerr	Mardenb.	Marustik	Moseley	Perry	Pike	Platnauer	Rees	Rogers	Sherlock	Simmons	Turner	Vaughan	Wheeler	Wimbleton
R1/1	Aug 26	PLYMOUTH ARGYLE	5-4	Vaughan 2, Boyle, Turner, Wheeler	2503		6	5	12			7			2			1				11	3			8	10	9	4
R1/2	Sep 2	Plymouth Argyle	1-0	Giles	5829		6	5	10			7			2			1				11	3			8		9	4
R3	Oct 28	CHELSEA	2-1	Platnauer 2	8018		6	5	8		11	12			2						7	1	3				10	9	4
R4	Nov 18	Shrewsbury Town	0-1		4673		6	5	8		3				2		11				7	1		12			10	9	4

Bye in R2 when drawn away to Luton Town

A.M. Cup (Freight Rover Trophy)

Rd	Date	Opponent	Score	Att	Bartlett	Boyle	Brignull	Curtis	Davies	Ford	Giles	Gummer	Horrix	Kerr	Mardenb.	Marustik	Moseley	Perry	Pike	Platnauer	Rees	Rogers	Sherlock	Simmons	Turner	Vaughan	Wheeler	Wimbleton
PR	Dec 2	WOLVERHAMPTON WAN.	0-1	1201	8	6	5	14		3	2	12					1			11	9					10	7	4
PR	Jan 6	Bournemouth	0-1	1482		6	5	8		3	9					2	1			11						10	12	4

Welsh Cup

Rd	Date	Opponent	Score	Scorers	Att	Bartlett	Boyle	Brignull	Curtis	Davies	Ford	Giles	Gummer	Horrix	Kerr	Mardenb.	Marustik	Moseley	Perry	Pike	Platnauer	Rees	Rogers	Sherlock	Simmons	Turner	Vaughan	Wheeler	Wimbleton
R3	Nov 25	TAFF'S WELL	4-0	Bartlett 2, Wheeler, Boyle	581	8	6				3				2		11				7	1		12			10	9	4
R4	Feb 3	Wrexham	0-1		1915	8	6	5	10		3				2		11	1		9	7							12	4

Played at 5 in R3: W Curtis

1987/88   2nd in Division Four: Promoted

No	Date	Opponent	Score	Scorers	Att	Abraham GI	Bartlett KF	Bater PT	Boyle TDJ	Curtis AT	Endersby SIG	Ford MP	Gilligan JM	Gummer JC	Judge AG	Kelly MD	Mardenborough SA	McDermott BJ	Moseley G	Perry J	Platnauer NR	Roberts JW	Sanderson PD	Stevenson NCA	Walsh IP	Wheeler P	Wimbleton PP	Wood G
1	Aug 15	LEYTON ORIENT	1-1	Gilligan	3357				6	7		3	9	4		11	12	10	1	2			8					
2	22	Bolton Wanderers	0-1		4530		14		6	7		3	9			11		10	1	2	4		8	5		12		
3	29	SWANSEA CITY	1-0	Gilligan	5790			2	6	7		3	9			11		10	1		4		8	5				
4	Sep 1	Cambridge United	0-0		2079		12	2	6	7		3	9			11		10	1		4		8	5				
5	5	WOLVERHAMPTON W.	3-2	McDermott, Bartlett, Boyle	2258		8		6	7		2	9			11	4	10	1	5	3		12					
6	12	Wrexham	0-3		2212	5	8	3	6	7		2	9			11	14	10	1				12				4	
7	15	DARLINGTON	3-1	Abrahams, Bartlett 2	2138	5	8		6	7		2	9			11		10	1								4	
8	19	CARLISLE UNITED	4-2	Wimbleton, Ford, Boyle, Gilligan	2659		8	2	6	7		3	9			11		10	1		5		12				4	
9	25	Tranmere Rovers	1-0	Wimbleton	2543		8	2	6	7		3	9			11		10	1		5					12	4	
10	29	HALIFAX TOWN	0-0		3566		8		6	7		2	9			11		10	1		3		12	5			4	
11	Oct 2	Stockport County	1-0	Bartlett	2332		8	2	6	7		3	9					10	1		11		12	5			4	
12	10	HEREFORD UNITED	0-1		4399		8	2	6	7		11	9			12		10	1		3		14	5			4	
13	17	Peterborough United	3-4	Ford 2, McDermott	3473		14	2	6	7		11	9			5	8	10	1		3		12				4	
14	20	TORQUAY UNITED	2-1	Ford, Gilligan	3455			2	6	7		11	9	14	1	5	8	10			3					12	4	
15	24	Scunthorpe United	1-2	Sanderson	2872			2	6			5	9		1	11	8	10			3		14	12	7		4	
16	31	ROCHDALE	1-0	Kelly	3046		12	2	6			4	9		1	11	8	10			3			5	7			
17	Nov 4	Scarborough	1-1	Wimbleton	2599			2	6	7		8	9		1	12		10			3		11	5			4	
18	7	EXETER CITY	3-2	Gilligan 2, Boyle	3474		12	2	6	7		8	9		1	5	14	10			3		11				4	
19	21	Newport County	2-1	Wimbleton, Platnauer	4158		11	2	6	7		8	9			5	12	10			3	1					4	
20	28	HARTLEPOOL UNITED	1-1	McDermott	3232		10	2	6	7		5	9		1	8	12	11			3		14				4	
21	Dec 12	Crewe Alexandra	0-0		2010			2	6			5	9		1		7	10			3			8		11	4	
22	19	BURNLEY	2-1	Gilligan 2	3401		14	2	6			8	9		1	12	7	10			3			5		11	4	
23	26	TRANMERE ROVERS	3-0	Gilligan 2, Wimbleton	5233			2	6	7	1	8	9			12		10			3		14	5		11	4	
24	28	Colchester United	1-2	Kelly	2599			2	6	7	1	8	9			11		10			3		14	5		12	4	
25	Jan 1	Swansea City	2-2	Ford, Gilligan	9560		14	2	6	7	1	8	9			12		10			3			5		11	4	
26	16	Carlisle United	0-0		2344		11	2	6	7	1	8	9					10			3		12	5			4	
27	30	CAMBRIDGE UNITED	4-0	Wimbleton (p), Bartlett, McDermott, Boyle	3940		11	2	6	7		8	9				14	10			3			5		12	4	1
28	Feb 2	Darlington	0-0		2332		11	2	6	7		8	9				12	10			3			5			4	1
29	6	Wolverhampton Wan.	4-1	Gilligan 2, Wimbleton 2	10077		11	2	6	7		8	9					10			3			5			4	1
30	13	COLCHESTER UNITED	1-0	Ford	5458		11	2	6	7		8	9				12	10			3			5			4	1
31	20	Leyton Orient	1-4	Bartlett	3523		11	2	6	7		8	9				12	10			3			5	14		4	1
32	27	STOCKPORT COUNTY	0-0		3937			2	6	7		8	9			3		10				1	12	5	11	14	4	
33	Mar 1	Halifax Town	1-0	Bartlett	1128		11	2	6			8	9			3		10				1	7	5			4	
34	4	PETERBOROUGH UTD.	0-0		4172		11	2	6			8	9			3	12	10				1	7	5		14	4	
35	13	Hereford United	2-1	Gilligan, Bartlett	3210		11	2	6	7		8	9			3		10				1		5			4	
36	16	WREXHAM	1-1	Gilligan	4083		11	2	6	7		8	9			3		10				1		5	12		4	
37	26	SCUNTHORPE UNITED	0-1		4527		11	2	6	7		8	9			14		10			3	1		5	12		4	
38	29	Rochdale	2-2	Bartlett, Bramhall (og)	1435		11	2	6	7		8	9					10			3	1		5	12		4	
39	Apr 2	Exeter City	2-0	Bartlett 2	2649		11	2	6	7		8	9			14		10			3			5	12		4	1
40	4	NEWPORT COUNTY	4-0	Stevenson, Wimbleton, McDermott, Ford	6536		11	2	6	7		8	9				12	10			3			5			4	1
41	9	Torquay United	0-2		3082		11	2	6	7		8	9			14	12	10			3			5			4	1
42	15	BOLTON WANDERERS	1-0	Gilligan	6703		11	2	6	7		8	9					10			3			5			4	1
43	23	SCARBOROUGH	2-0	Curtis, McDermott (p)	5751		11	2	6	7			9			10		8			3			5	12		4	1
44	30	Hartlepool United	1-0	Gilligan	1101		11	2	6	7		4	9			10		8			3			5				1
45	May 2	CREWE ALEXANDRA	2-0	Bartlett, McDermott	9852		11	2	6	7		4	9			10		8			3			5	12			1
46	7	Burnley	2-1	Curtis, Gilligan	8421		11	2	6	7		4	9			10		8			3			5	12			1
		Apps				2	37	40	46	40	4	45	46	2	8	36	21	45	13	3	38	8	21	36	6	16	37	13
		Goals				1	12		4	2		7	19			1		7			1						9	

One own goal

F.A. Cup

Rd	Date	Opponent	Score	Scorers	Att	Abraham GI	Bartlett KF	Bater PT	Boyle TDJ	Curtis AT	Endersby SIG	Ford MP	Gilligan JM	Gummer JC	Judge AG	Kelly MD	Mardenborough SA	McDermott BJ	Moseley G	Perry J	Platnauer NR	Roberts JW	Sanderson PD	Stevenson NCA	Walsh IP	Wheeler P	Wimbleton PP	Wood G
R1	Nov 14	Peterborough United	1-2	Bartlett	3600		11	2	6	7		8	9			5	14	10			3	1	12				4	

F.L. Cup (Littlewoods Challenge Cup)

Rd	Date	Opponent	Score	Scorers	Att	Abraham GI	Bartlett KF	Bater PT	Boyle TDJ	Curtis AT	Endersby SIG	Ford MP	Gilligan JM	Gummer JC	Judge AG	Kelly MD	Mardenborough SA	McDermott BJ	Moseley G	Perry J	Platnauer NR	Roberts JW	Sanderson PD	Stevenson NCA	Walsh IP	Wheeler P	Wimbleton PP	Wood G
R1/1	Aug 18	NEWPORT COUNTY	1-2	Curtiss	3383	5	12		6	7		3	9			11	4	10	1	2			8					
R1/2	25	NEWPORT COUNTY	2-2	Gilligan, Sanderson	3550		12		5	7		3	10			9		11	1	2	6		8	4				

R1/1 played at Ninian Park

A.M. Cup (Sherpa Van Trophy)

Rd	Date	Opponent	Score	Scorers	Att	Abraham GI	Bartlett KF	Bater PT	Boyle TDJ	Curtis AT	Endersby SIG	Ford MP	Gilligan JM	Gummer JC	Judge AG	Kelly MD	Mardenborough SA	McDermott BJ	Moseley G	Perry J	Platnauer NR	Roberts JW	Sanderson PD	Stevenson NCA	Walsh IP	Wheeler P	Wimbleton PP	Wood G
PR	Oct 13	WREXHAM	3-2	Wheeler, McDermott, Gilligan	1102		12	2				11	9	5		3	7	10	1		4		14	6		8		
PR	Nov 24	Walsall	1-3	Gilligan	2420		10	2	6	7		8	9		1	5	12				3	11					4	
R1	Jan 20	Notts County	0-2		2704		11		6	7		8	9			2		10			3	1	14	5		12	4	

Welsh Cup

Rd	Date	Opponent	Score	Scorers	Att	Abraham GI	Bartlett KF	Bater PT	Boyle TDJ	Curtis AT	Endersby SIG	Ford MP	Gilligan JM	Gummer JC	Judge AG	Kelly MD	Mardenborough SA	McDermott BJ	Moseley G	Perry J	Platnauer NR	Roberts JW	Sanderson PD	Stevenson NCA	Walsh IP	Wheeler P	Wimbleton PP	Wood G
R3	Nov 18	EBBW VALE	0-0		935		11	2	6	7		5	9			8	12	10			3	1	14				4	
rep	Dec 5	EBBW VALE	1-0	Bartlett	975		11	2	6	7		5	9		1	8	12	10			3						4	
R4	Jan 9	PORT TALBOT ATH.	3-0	Ford 2, Gilligan	1382		11	2	6	7	1	8	9			12	14	10			3			5			4	
R5	Feb 24	MERTHYR TYDFIL	3-1	Gilligan, Wimbleton 2	7213			2	6	7		8	9			12		10			3	1		5	11	14	4	
SF1	Apr 19	CAERNARFON TOWN	2-1	Wimbleton (p), Kelly	2750		11	2	6	7		8	9			10	12				3			5	14		4	1
SF2	27	Caernarfon Town	1-0	McDermott (p)	3000		11	2	6	7		4	9			10		8			3			5	12			1
F	May 17	Wrexham	2-0	Curtis, Gilligan	5645		11	2	6	7		4	9			10		8			3			5	12			1

R3 switched to Ninian Park
Final at Swansea

Player columns (left to right): Abraham GI, Bartlett KF, Bater PT, Boyle TDJ, Curtis AT, Fry CD, Gibbins RG, Gilligan JM, Gummer JC, Haig RN, Holmes MIE, Kelly MD, Ketteridge SJ, Lynex SC, McDermott BJ, Morgan JP, Platnauer NR, Roberts JW, Rodgerson I, Stevenson NCA, Tupling S, Walsh IP, Wheeler P, Wimbleton PP, Wood G

League – Division Three

#	Date	Opponent	Score	Scorers	Att	Abr	Bar	Bat	Boy	Cur	Fry	Gib	Gil	Gum	Hai	Hol	Kel	Ket	Lyn	McD	Mor	Pla	Rob	Rod	Ste	Tup	Wal	Whe	Wim	Woo
1	Aug 27	FULHAM	1-2	Walsh	6084		12	2	6	7			9				11		4	10		3		14	5		8			1
2	Sep 3	Bolton Wanderers	0-4		4831		12		6	7			9	10			11		14			3		2	5		8		4	1
3	10	HUDDERSFIELD T	3-0	Stevenson, Walsh 2	3891				6				9	10			11		7			3		2	5	12	8		4	1
4	17	Port Vale	1-6	Gilligan	4280			12	6	7			9	10					11	8		3		2	5				4	1
5	23	Southend United	0-0		3225			12	6	8			9	10			11		7			3		2	5				4	1
6	Oct 1	BRISTOL ROVERS	2-2	Gilligan, Bartlett	5023		12	10	6	8			9				11		7	14		3		2	5				4	1
7	8	READING	1-2	Curtis	4057		8	2	6	7			9				11		10	4		3			5			12		1
8	15	Chester City	0-0		2834	4	8	2	6				9					10	11				3		5			7		1
9	22	Mansfield Town	2-2	Ketteridge, McDermott	3566		8	2	6				9				4	10	11	7				3	5					1
10	29	Blackpool	0-1		3849	6	8						9				4	10	11	12		2		3	5			7		1
11	Nov 1	BURY	3-0	Gilligan, Bartlett, Ketteridge	2411	6	12						9				10	8	11					3	5				4	1
12	5	GILLINGHAM	1-0	Bartlett	3640	6	8						9				11		10			3		2	5				4	1
13	12	NORTHAMPTON T	1-0	Bartlett	3342	6	8	12					9				11		10			3		2	5				4	1
14	25	BRENTFORD	1-0	Gilligan	3405	5	8	12	6	7			9							11		3		2		10			4	1
15	Dec 3	Preston North End	3-3	Gilligan, Bartlett 2	4976	5	8	12	6	7			9							11		3		2		10			4	1
16	17	Bristol City	0-2		7493	5	8	12	6	7			9	10						11		3		2				14	4	1
17	26	SWANSEA CITY	2-2	Gilligan 2	10675	5	8		6	7			9	10			12			11				2	3				4	1
18	30	WIGAN ATHLETIC	2-2	Bartlett, Curtis	4621	5	8		6	7			9				10			11				2	3			12	4	1
19	Jan 2	Aldershot	1-0	Curtis	2768	5	8		6	7			9				10			11				2	3			12	4	1
20	10	Wolverhampton Wan.	0-2		14870	5	8		6	7			9				10			11				2	3			12	4	1
21	14	BOLTON WANDERERS	1-0	Bartlett	4212	5	8		6	14	7		9				10			11				2	3			12	4	1
22	21	Huddersfield Town	0-1		4869	5	8		6	14			9				10			11	7			2	3			12	4	1
23	28	PORT VALE	3-0	Gilligan 2, Bartlett	4507		8	3	5				9				10			11	12	7		2	6				4	1
24	Feb 4	Bristol Rovers	1-0	Gilligan	5815		8	3	5				9				10			11	14	7		2	6			12	4	1
25	11	SHEFFIELD UNITED	0-0		5826	7	8	6	5				9				10			11		3		2	6				4	1
26	18	Reading	1-3	Walsh	4359	6	8		5	7			9				12			11		3		2			14	10	4	1
27	28	Notts County	0-2		4266	6	8		5	7			9							11		3		2			12	10	4	1
28	Mar 4	MANSFIELD TOWN	0-0		3217	6	8		5	7			9				12			11		3		2			14	10	4	1
29	11	Gillingham	2-1	Boyle, Platnauer	2934	6	14		5	7			9				8			11	12	3		2				10	4	1
30	18	Fulham	0-2		4261	6	14		5	7			9				8			11	12	3		2				10	4	1
31	21	Chesterfield	0-4		2888	6	11		5	7			9				12			14	8	3		2				10	4	1
32	25	ALDERSHOT	3-2	Gilligan (p), Wheeler, Curtis	3251		8		5	7			9			12			11			3		2	6			10	4	1
33	27	Swansea City	1-1	Gilligan	9201		8		5	7			9						11			3		2	6			10	4	1
34	Apr 1	BRISTOL CITY	1-1	Platnauer	6358		8		5				9				7		11		4	3		2	6			12	10	1
35	4	WOLVERHAMPTON W.	1-1	Platnauer	7219				5	7		14	9						11		8	3		2	6		12	10	4	1
36	7	Wigan Athletic	0-1		2296		8		5	7		14	9						11			3		2	6		10	12	4	1
37	11	Sheffield United	1-0	Abraham	11618	5	8			7			9						11		4	3		2	6			10		1
38	15	Bury	0-1		2124	5	8		12	14	7		9						11		4	3		2	6			10		1
39	18	NOTTS COUNTY	0-1		3073	5	2			7	14	12	9						11		4	3			6			10	8	1
40	22	SOUTHEND UNITED	2-0	Abraham, Gilligan	3268	5	2			7		11	9	10							4	3			6			12	8	1
41	29	Northampton Town	0-3		3194	5	6			7	14		9	10					11		4	3		2	12				8	1
42	May 1	CHESTERFIELD	0-1		3244	5	8			7		11	9	10	14						4	3			6			12		1
43	5	PRESTON NORTH END	0-0		3196	5	8		6	7		11	9	10	14						4	3		2				12		1
44	9	CHESTER CITY	2-0	Boyle, Gilligan	2962	5	2		6	7		11	9	10			8				4	3						12	14	1
45	13	Brentford	1-1	Gummer	4865				6			11	9	10	14		8				12	3	1	2				7	4	
46	16	BLACKPOOL	0-0		3426	5	8		6	7	14	4	9	10					11		12	3		2						1
		Apps				31	22	36	36	35	9	12	46	11	1	1	28	6	36	6	19	39	1	40	32	4	11	27	36	45
		Goals				2	9		2	4			14	1			2		1			3			1		4	1		

F.A. Cup

Rd	Date	Opponent	Score	Scorers	Att	Abr	Bar	Bat	Boy	Cur	Fry	Gib	Gil	Gum	Hai	Hol	Kel	Ket	Lyn	McD	Mor	Pla	Rob	Rod	Ste	Tup	Wal	Whe	Wim	Woo
R1	Nov 19	HEREFORD UNITED	3-0	Bartlett, Tupling, Gilligan	4341	5	8		6	7			9						11			3		2		10			4	1
R2	Dec 11	Enfield	4-1	Wimbleton (p), Lynex, Gilligan 2	3604	5	8	12	6	7			9	10					11			3		2					4	1
R3	Jan 7	HULL CITY	1-2	Gilligan	7128	5	8		6	7			9				10		11					2	3	14		12	4	1

F.L. Cup (Littlewoods Challenge Cup)

Rd	Date	Opponent	Score	Scorers	Att	Abr	Bar	Bat	Boy	Cur	Fry	Gib	Gil	Gum	Hai	Hol	Kel	Ket	Lyn	McD	Mor	Pla	Rob	Rod	Ste	Tup	Wal	Whe	Wim	Woo
R1/1	Aug 30	SWANSEA CITY	0-1		6241		8		6	7			9	4			11		14	10		3		2	5	12				1
R1/2	Sep 20	Swansea City	2-0	Wheeler, Boyle	6987				6	8			9	10			11		7			3		2	5			12	4	1
R2/1	28	Queen's Park Rangers	0-3		6078			10	6	8			9				11		7	14		3		2	5			12		1
R2/2	Oct 11	QUEEN'S PARK RANGERS	1-4	Curtis	2692	3	8		6	7	11		9										4		5			10		1

Played in R2/2: J Perry (at 2), A Lewis (12)

A.M. Cup (Sherpa Van Trophy)

Rd	Date	Opponent	Score	Scorers	Att	Abr	Bar	Bat	Boy	Cur	Fry	Gib	Gil	Gum	Hai	Hol	Kel	Ket	Lyn	McD	Mor	Pla	Rob	Rod	Ste	Tup	Wal	Whe	Wim	Woo
PR	Dec 6	SWANSEA CITY	2-0	Curtis, Gilligan	2986	5	8	12	6	7			9	10			11					3		2					4	1
PR	20	Torquay United	1-3	Wimbleton (p)	1187	5	8	12	6	7			9	10			11					3		2					4	1
R1	Jan 24	Bristol Rovers	1-2	Wimbleton	4029	5	8		7				9				11	10			12	3		2	6				4	1

European Cup Winners Cup

Rd	Date	Opponent	Score	Scorers	Att	Abr	Bar	Bat	Boy	Cur	Fry	Gib	Gil	Gum	Hai	Hol	Kel	Ket	Lyn	McD	Mor	Pla	Rob	Rod	Ste	Tup	Wal	Whe	Wim	Woo
R1/1	Sep 7	Derry City	0-0		11000		14	2	6	7			9	10			11			12		3			5		8		4	1
R1/2	Oct 5	DERRY CITY	4-0	McDermott, Gilligan 3	6933		8	2	6	7			9				11			10	14	3			5				4	1
R2/1	26	AGF (AARHUS)	1-2	Gilligan	6155		8	2	6	14			9				10		11	7		3		12	5				4	1
R2/2	Nov 9	AGF (Aarhus)	0-4		3700	4	10		3	7			11				8			9				5	2				6	1

Played in R1/2: J Perry (at 12)

Welsh Cup

Rd	Date	Opponent	Score	Scorers	Att	Abr	Bar	Bat	Boy	Cur	Fry	Gib	Gil	Gum	Hai	Hol	Kel	Ket	Lyn	McD	Mor	Pla	Rob	Rod	Ste	Tup	Wal	Whe	Wim	Woo
R3	Nov 15	BATH CITY	3-0	Bartlett 2, Wimbleton	1517	5	8	12	6	7			9				11	10				3			2			14	4	1
R4	Jan 17	WORCESTER CITY	1-0	Kelly	1522	5	8	3			7		9				10		11					6	2			12	4	1
R5	Feb 8	Kidderminster Harriers	1-3	Bartlett	3012		8	3		5			9				10		11		6	7			2			12	4	1

1989/90 · 21st in Division Three: Relegated

No	Date	Opponent	Score	Scorers	Att
1	Aug 19	BOLTON WANDERERS	0-2		4681
2	26	Tranmere Rovers	0-3		5268
3	Sep 2	BRENTFORD	2-2	Gilligan, Fry	3499
4	9	Mansfield Town	0-1		2767
5	16	BRISTOL CITY	0-3		5970
6	23	Wigan Athletic	1-1	Lynex	2345
7	26	NORTHAMPTON T	2-3	Pike, Lynex	2801
8	30	Rotherham United	0-4		5013
9	Oct 7	Huddersfield Town	3-2	Griffith, Pike 2 (1p)	5835
10	13	CHESTER CITY	1-1	Barnard	3675
11	17	BRISTOL ROVERS	1-1	Kelly	6377
12	21	Blackpool	0-1		3502
13	28	LEYTON ORIENT	1-1	Griffith	2370
14	31	Birmingham City	1-1	Morgan	7468
15	Nov 3	BURY	3-1	Pike 2, Barnard	3437
16	11	Fulham	5-2	Pike 2, Griffith, Marshall (og), Morgan	4030
17	25	PRESTON NORTH END	3-0	Rodgerson, Pike, Griffith	3307
18	Dec 2	Crewe Alexandra	1-1	Morgan	3393
19	16	NOTTS COUNTY	1-3	Pike	3610
20	26	Swansea City	1-0	Barnard	12244
21	30	Walsall	2-0	Griffith, Pike	4256
22	Jan 13	TRANMERE ROVERS	0-0		4300
23	20	Bolton Wanderers	1-3	Griffith	7017
24	Feb 3	WIGAN ATHLETIC	1-1	Rodgerson	3218
25	10	Bristol City	0-1		11982
26	17	CREWE ALEXANDRA	0-0		2086
27	21	Brentford	1-0	Abraham	5174
28	24	Preston North End	0-4		5719
29	Mar 2	SHREWSBURY TOWN	0-1		2751
30	6	ROTHERHAM UNITED	2-0	Pike, Barnard	2570
31	10	Northampton Town	1-1	Pike	2574
32	13	Shrewsbury Town	0-0		2318
33	17	HUDDERSFIELD T	1-5	Pike	2628
34	20	Chester City	0-1		1874
35	24	Bristol Rovers	1-2	Rodgerson	4631
36	27	MANSFIELD TOWN	1-0	Barnard	2280
37	31	BLACKPOOL	2-2	Gibbins, Pike	2850
38	Apr 7	Leyton Orient	1-3	Pike	3411
39	10	BIRMINGHAM CITY	0-1		3322
40	14	Reading	1-0	Griffith	3198
41	16	SWANSEA CITY	0-2		8356
42	21	Notts County	1-2	Pike (p)	5532
43	24	WALSALL	3-1	Barnard, Pike, Griffith	2509
44	28	FULHAM	3-3	Daniel, Barnard, Rodgerson	3666
45	May 1	READING	3-2	Barnard, Pike (p), Griffith	3508
46	5	Bury	0-0		4224

Played in one game: S Tupling (game 12, at 14), EP Youds (23, 14), CG Powell (15, 12).

Appearances and Goals

Player	Apps	Goals
Abraham GI	37	1
Barnard LK	35	8
Blake NA	6	
Chandler IG	24	
Curtis AT	8	
Daniel RC	43	1
Fry CD	23	1
Gibbins RG	38	1
Gilligan JM	7	1
Griffith C	38	9
Gummer JC	1	
Haig RN	4	
Hansbury R	35	
Kelly MD	41	1
Kevan DJ	7	
Lewis A	11	
Love IJ	2	
Lynex SC	26	2
Morgan JP	32	3
Perry J	36	
Pike C	41	18
Rodgerson I	45	4
Scott MJ	9	
Sendall RA	4	
Thompson CD	2	
Ward GI	2	
Wood G	9	

One own goal

F.A. Cup

Round	Date	Opponent	Score	Scorers	Att
R1	Nov 18	HALESOWEN TOWN	1-0	Pike (p)	3972
R2	Dec 9	GLOUCESTER CITY	2-2	Scott 2	4531
rep	12	Gloucester City	1-0	Scott	3877
R3	Jan 6	QUEEN'S PARK RANGERS	0-0		13834
rep	10	Queen's Park Rangers	0-2		12226

Played at 12 in R3 replay: EP Youds

F.L. Cup (Littlewoods Challenge Cup)

Round	Date	Opponent	Score	Scorers	Att
R1/1	Aug 22	PLYMOUTH ARGYLE	0-3		2620
R1/2	29	Plymouth Argyle	2-0	Pike, Lynex	5728

A.M. Cup (Leyland DAF Cup)

Round	Date	Opponent	Score	Scorers	Att
PR	Nov 7	WALSALL	3-5	Griffith, Barnard, Abraham	1487
PR	Dec 19	Shrewsbury Town	0-4		1058

Played at 14 on Nov 7: CG Powell

Also played 19 Dec: DB Searle (at 3), JW Roberts (12), Miethig (8).

Welsh Cup

Round	Date	Opponent	Score	Scorers	Att
R3	Oct 25	NEWPORT AFC	1-0	Abraham	2929
R4	Jan 16	PORT TALBOT	4-1	Rodgerson, Pike 2, Barnard	1128
R5	Feb 6	ABERYSTWYTH TOWN	2-0	Rodgerson, Kelly	1319
SF1	Apr 2	HEREFORD UNITED	0-3		2393
SF2	4	Hereford United	3-1	Pike, Abraham, Griffith	2955

Played at 5 in R4: EP Youds.

1990/91   13th in Division Four

Player columns (left → right): Abraham GI, Baddeley LM, Barnard LK, Blake NA, Chandler JG, Daniel RC, De Mange KJPP, Fry CD, Gibbins RG, Griffith C, Hansbury R, Heard TP, Heath PA, Jones M, Lewis A, MacDonald KD, Matthews NP, Morgan JP, Perry J, Pike C, Rodgerson I, Russell KJ, Searle DB, Stephens LM, Summers, Taylor PMR, Toshack JC

#	Date	Opponent	Score	Scorers	Att	Abr	Bad	Bar	Bla	Cha	Dan	DeM	Fry	Gib	Gri	Han	Hea	Hth	Jon	Lew	Mac	Mat	Mor	Per	Pik	Rod	Rus	Sea	Ste	Sum	Tay	Tos
1	Aug 25	SCARBOROUGH	0-0		3819	5		4	12	14	3			9	8	1	11		7						6	10	2					
2	Sep 1	Hartlepool United	2-0	Griffith, Pike	2897	5		4	12		3			9	8	1	11		7						6	10	2					
3	8	TORQUAY UNITED	3-3	Griffith, Pike 2 (1p)	3656			4	5		3			9	8	1	11		7						6	10	2					
4	15	Lincoln City	0-0		3152			4	5		3			9	8	1	11		7	14		12			6	10	2					
5	18	Aldershot	0-0		2310			4	5		3			9	8	1	11		7			10			6		2					
6	22	STOCKPORT COUNTY	3-3	Giffith, Pike, Gibbins	3374			4	5		3			9	8	1	11					7			6	10	2					
7	29	Scunthorpe United	2-0	Pike 2 (1p)	2573			4	12		3			9	8	1	11		7			5			6	10	2					
8	Oct 2	ROCHDALE	0-1		3391			4	12		3			9	8	1	11		7	14		5			6	10	2					
9	5	WREXHAM	1-0	Pike	3452			4	12		3			9	8	1	11		7			5			6	10	2					
10	13	York City	2-1	Blake 2	2596			4	10		3		14	9	8	1	11		7			5			6		2	12				
11	20	Hereford United	1-1	Jones	5782			4	10		3			9	8	1	11		7			5			6	12	2					
12	23	DONCASTER ROVERS	0-2		3891			4	10		3		12	9	8	1	11		7			5			6		2					
13	27	PETERBOROUGH UTD.	1-1	Pike	2940			4	9		3		12		8	1			7			5	14		6	10	2	11				
14	Nov 3	Maidstone United	0-3		2010			4	12					9	8	1	11		7			5	2		6	10		3				
15	10	CHESTERFIELD	2-1	Gibbins, Pike	2019			4						9	8	1	11		7			2	5		6	10		3				
16	24	Gillingham	0-4		2821	5							12		8	1	11		7			2	5	4	6	9		3	10	14		
17	Dec 1	Burnley	0-2		6353								4	9	8	1	11		7			2	5	14	6	10		3	12			
18	15	WALSALL	0-2		2017				4			2		9	8	1	11					12	5		6	10		3			7	
19	21	Northampton Town	0-0		3033				2			4	12	9	8	1	11						5		6	10		3			7	
20	26	CARLISLE UNITED	3-1	Pike, Taylor 2	2281				4			6	2	9	8	1	11				12		5			10		3			7	
21	29	HALIFAX TOWN	1-0	Taylor	2903				4			6	2	9	8	1	11		12	14			5			10		3			7	
22	Jan 1	Darlington	1-4	Griffith	3151				4					9	8	1	11		2		12		5		6	10		3			7	
23	12	HARTLEPOOL UNITED	1-0	Griffith	2619				4				10	9	8	1			2		11		5		6			3			7	
24	26	LINCOLN CITY	0-1		2513				4				12	9	8	1			6		11		2		5	10	7	3				
25	Feb 1	ALDERSHOT	1-3	Gibbins	1629		6	4					10	9	8	1					11		2		5	12	7	3				
26	15	GILLINGHAM	2-0	Gibbins, Pike (p)	2170		6	4						9	8	1	11				14		2		5	10	7	3				
27	19	Scarborough	2-1	Grifith 2	1192		6	4					7	9	8	1	11				12		2		5	10		3				
28	23	Chesterfield	0-0		3065		6	4					7	9	8	1	11						2		5	10		3	12			
29	26	Stockport County	1-1	Blake	3376		6	4					7	9	8	1	11						2		5	10		3				
30	Mar 1	BURNLEY	3-0	Heard, Pike (p), Griffith	3591		6	4					7	9	8	1	11						2		5	10		3				
31	9	Walsall	0-0		3950		6	4					7	9	8	1	11						2		5	10		3				
32	12	Rochdale	0-0		1569		6	4					7	9	8	1	11						2		5	10		3				12
33	16	SCUNTHORPE UNITED	1-0	Pike (p)	2873		6	4					7	9	8	1	11				14		2		5	10		3				12
34	19	YORK CITY	2-1	Heard, Barnard	2620		6	4					7	9	8	1	11						2		5	10		3				12
35	22	Wrexham	0-1		1787			4					12	9	8	1	11				14		2		5	10		3				7
36	30	Carlisle United	2-3	Matthews, Blake	2263				4			6		9	8	1	11	7				10	2		5			3				
37	Apr 1	NORTHAMPTON T	1-0	Campbell (og)	4805				4			6		9	8	1	11	7				10	2		5			3				
38	6	Halifax Town	2-1	Pike, Heard	1364				12			4		9	8	1	11	7					6	2	5	10		3				
39	10	Torquay United	1-2	Gibbins	3341				12			4		9	8	1	11	7			14		6	2	5	10		3				
40	13	DARLINGTON	0-1		4544							4		9	8	1	11	7				5	6	2		10		3				
41	17	Blackpool	0-3		4813				8			4		9	12	1	11	7			14		6	2	5	10		3				
42	20	HEREFORD UNITED	0-2		2845				8			4		9	12	1	11	7			14		6	2	5	10		3				
43	27	Doncaster Rovers	1-1	Heath	2227				12			4		9	8	1		7				11	6	2	5	10		3				
44	May 2	BLACKPOOL	1-1	Griffith	1793				11			4	12	9	8	1		7					6	2	5	10		3			14	
45	4	Peterborough United	0-3		6642				11			4	12	9	8	1		7					6	2	5	10		3				
46	11	MAIDSTONE UNITED	0-0		2011		2		11					9	8	1		7	4		6				5	10		3				

Played in game 46: JJ Unsworth (at 12), GJ Ward (at 14)

| | | | | | Apps | 2 | 2 | 28 | 40 | 1 | 13 | 15 | 23 | 43 | 45 | 46 | 38 | 11 | 22 | | | 27 | 8 | 37 | 4 | 43 | 39 | 14 | 3 | 35 | 3 | 3 | 6 | 4 |
| | | | | | Goals | | | 1 | 4 | | | | | 5 | 9 | | 3 | 1 | 1 | | | 1 | | | 14 | | | | | | | 3 | |

One own goal

F.A. Cup

	Date	Opponent	Score	Scorers	Att	Bar	Bla	Fry	Gib	Gri	Han	Jon	Mat	Per	Pik	Rod	Rus	Sea
R1	Nov 17	HAYES	0-0		1844	4	10		9	8	1	7	2	5	6	11		3
rep	21	Hayes	0-1		4312	4	10	14	9	8	1	7	2	5	6	12	11	3

Replay at Brentford

F.L. Cup (Rumbelows Cup)

	Date	Opponent	Score	Scorers	Att	Abr	Bar	Bla	Cha	Dan	Gib	Gri	Han	Hea	Jon	Mat	Per	Pik	Rod	Rus
R1/1	Aug 28	Mansfield Town	1-1	Griffith	2091	5	4	12		3	9	8	1	11	7			6	10	2
R1/2	Sep 4	MANSFIELD TOWN	3-0	Griffith 2, Pike	2539		4	5	12	3	9	8	1	11	7			6	10	2
R2/1	25	PORTSMOUTH	1-1	Griffith	4224		4	12		3	9	8	1	11	7		5	6	10	2
R2/2	Oct 9	Portsmouth	1-3	(aet) Griffith	6174		4	10	12	3	9	8	1	11	7	2	5	6	14	

A.M. Cup (Leyland DAF Cup)

	Date	Opponent	Score	Scorers	Att	Bar	Bla	DeM	Fry	Gib	Gri	Han	Hea	Hth	Mat	Mor	Per	Pik	Rod	Sea	Tay	Tos
PR	Nov 13	EXETER CITY	0-1		1024	4	12			9	8	1	11		2		5	6	10	3	7	14
PR	Dec 11	Hereford United	1-1	Griffith	2007		4		14	9	8	1	11	7	2		5	6	12	3		

Welsh Cup

	Date	Opponent	Score	Scorers	Att	Bar	Bla	Gib	Gri	Han	Hea	Jon	Mat	Pik	Rod	Rus	Sea
R3	Nov 6	MERTHYR TYDFIL	1-4	Pike (p)	3204	4	12	9	8	1	11	7	5	6	10	2	3

1991/92 9th in Division Four

#	Date	Opponents	Res	Scorers	Att	Abraham GJ	Baddeley LM	Bellamy G	Blake NA	Dale C	Gibbins RG	Gill G	Gorman AD	Griffith C	Hansbury R	Harrison GR	Heard TP	Jones M	Lewis A	Matthews NP	Millar WP	Newton EJI	Perry J	Pike C	Ramsey PC	Searle DB	Semark RH	Toshack JC	Unsworth JJ	Walsh A	Ward GJ	Williams WJ
1	Aug 17	LINCOLN CITY	1-2	Pike (p)	5137	5	12				4			9	1		11	2	6	8				10		3	7					
2	24	Crewe Alexandra	1-1	Dale	3799	5				10	4			7	1			2	14	8	9		6		12	11	3					
3	31	CARLISLE UNITED	1-0	Jones (p)	4096	5			12	10	4					1	8	2			9		6		7	11	3					
4	Sep 4	Maidstone United	1-1	Dale	1019	5			7	10	4				12	1	8	2			9		6		14	11	3					
5	7	ROCHDALE	1-2	Pike	4029	5			7	10	4				12	1	8	2			9		6		14	11	3					
6	14	Blackpool	1-1	Davies (og)	3931	5				10	4				12			2	8		9		6		7	11	3				1	
7	17	Halifax Town	1-1	Dale	1041	5				10	4				12		14	2	8		9		6		7	11	3				1	
8	21	SCARBOROUGH	2-1	Heard, Dale	3227			5	9	10	4			8			11	2					6		7	3		12	14		1	
9	28	Barnet	1-3	Dale	4000			5	9	10	4			8			11	2	12				6		7	3					1	
10	Oct 5	WREXHAM	5-0	Dale, Blake, Pike 3	3652	5			11	10	4			8				2				12	6	9	7	3					1	
11	19	Mansfield Town	0-3		3180				11	10	4			8				5	2	12			6	9	7	3			14		1	
12	26	DONCASTER ROVERS	2-1	Pike 2 (2p)	2491				11	10	4			8				5					6	9		3	7	2			1	
13	Nov 2	SCUNTHORPE UNITED	2-2	Dale, Pike	2356			5	11	10	4			8	1			2	12				6	9	7	3						
14	5	Gillingham	0-0		2467				11	10	4			12	1			5	2				6	9	7	3	8					
15	23	NORTHAMPTON T	3-2	Gibbins, Dale 2	2922			5	11	10	4			8	1			6	2	12				9	7	3						
16	30	ROTHERHAM UNITED	1-0	Dale	3591			5	11	10	4			8				2	12					9	7	3		1				
17	Dec 14	York City	3-1	Pike, Dale 2	1904			7		10	4		11	8				2					6	9		3	12				1	5
18	26	Lincoln City	0-0		3162		11		12	10	4			8				2					6	9	7	3				1	5
19	28	Carlisle United	2-2	Pike (p), Ramsey	3080				11	10	4			8				2					6	9	7	3				1	5
20	Jan 1	MAIDSTONE UNITED	0-5		8023		12		11	10	4			8				2					6	9	7	3				1	5
21	11	HEREFORD UNITED	1-0	Dale	5305	6			11	10	4			8				2	12					9	7	3				1	5
22	18	Walsall	0-0		3654			5	11	10	4		2	8		6								9	7	3				1	
23	25	CHESTERFIELD	4-0	Pike 2, Dale, Blake	5131			5	12	10	4		2	8	11							6		9	7	3				1	
24	31	MANSFIELD TOWN	3-2	Blake, Pike (p), Newton	8265			5	11	10	4		2	8							6	12		9	7	3				1	
25	Feb 8	Doncaster Rovers	2-1	Dale, Douglas (og)	2094				11	10	4		2	12	8				14		6	5	9	7	3					1	
26	11	Rotherham United	2-1	Newton, Blake	3827	12			11	10	4		2	8							6	5	9	7	3				1	
27	15	YORK CITY	3-0	Pike 2 (1p), Dale	8067	5			11	10	4			8							6	2	9	7	3				1	
28	22	Hereford United	2-2	Ramsey, Harrison	5744	5			11	10	4		14	12	8						6	2	9	7	3				1	
29	29	BURNLEY	0-2		16030				11	10	4		14	12	8						6	2	9	7	3				1	
30	Mar 3	WALSALL	2-1	Dale, Searle	7517			5		10	4		12	11	8						6	2	9	7	3				1	
31	7	Chesterfield	2-2	Newton, Dale	3803	12	5			10	4			11	8						6	2	9	7	3				1	
32	10	GILLINGHAM	2-3	Griffith, Dale	8521	5	12			10	4			11	8					14		6	2	9	7	3				1	
33	14	Scunthorpe United	0-1		2766			5		10	4	8	14	12	1					2	11	6	9	7	3					
34	28	Northampton Town	0-0		2678			5		10	4	8		12	1						6	2	9	7	3			11		
35	31	BLACKPOOL	1-1	Burgess (og)	8430			5	12	10	4	8		11	1					14	6	2	9	7	3					
36	Apr 4	Rochdale	0-2		2651			5	11	10	4			8	1					12	6	2	9	7	3					
37	11	HALIFAX TOWN	4-0	Ramsey (p), Dale 2, Pike	5261			5	11	10	4	14	2		1					9	8	6	12	7	3					
38	14	Scarborough	2-2	Pike 2	935			5	11	10	4	14		12	1			2			8	6	9	7	3					
39	20	BARNET	3-1	Pike (p), Dale, Newton	7720		14	5	11	10	2			8	1			12			4	6	9	7	3					
40	22	Burnley	1-3	Blake, Pike (p), Newton	12400			5	11	10				8	1					2	9	4	6		7	3					
41	25	Wrexham	3-0	Pike 2, Gill	4002	6		5	11	10	4	14		8	1						12	2	9	7	3					
42	28	CREWE ALEXANDRA	1-1	Blake	10523	6		5	11	10	4			8	1					12		2	9	7	3					

Played in one game: P Marriott (game 10, at 14)

		Abraham GJ	Baddeley LM	Bellamy G	Blake NA	Dale C	Gibbins RG	Gill G	Gorman AD	Griffith C	Hansbury R	Harrison GR	Heard TP	Jones M	Lewis A	Matthews NP	Millar WP	Newton EJI	Perry J	Pike C	Ramsey PC	Searle DB	Semark RH	Toshack JC	Unsworth JJ	Walsh A	Ward GJ	Williams WJ
Apps		15	18	9	31	41	41	6	11	37	18	10	8	14	12	15	15	18	36	40	39	42	6	1	3	1	24	5
Goals					6	22	1	1		1			1	1	1			4		21	3	1						

Three own goals

F.A. Cup

| R1 | Nov 16 | Swansea City | 1-2 | Pike | 9315 | | | 5 | | 11 | 10 | 4 | | | 8 | 1 | | | 2 | 12 | | | 6 | 9 | 7 | 3 | | | | | | |

F.L. Cup (Rumbelows Cup)

| R1/1 | Aug 21 | BOURNEMOUTH | 3-2 | Millar, Gibbins, Searle | 3439 | 5 | | | | 10 | 4 | | | 7 | 1 | | 11 | 2 | 14 | 8 | 9 | | 6 | | 12 | 3 | | | | | | |
| R1/2 | 27 | Bournemouth | 1-4 | Jones (p) | 4489 | 5 | | | | 10 | 4 | | | 7 | 1 | | 8 | 2 | | | 9 | | 6 | | 12 | 11 | 3 | | | | | |

A.M. Cup (Autoglass Trophy)

PR	Nov 19	Swansea City	0-0		2955			5		11	10	4		14		1		8	2	12			6	9	7	3						
PR	Dec 10	BOURNEMOUTH	3-3	Pike, Dale 2	1337			5		11	10	4		8				12	2				6	9		3	7				1	
R1	Jan 14	Stoke City	0-3		4551			5		11	10	4		8				2			6			9	7	3		14	12		1	

Welsh Cup

R3	Oct 29	NEWPORT AFC	3-0	Pike, Griffith, Dale	2433					11	10	4		8	1			2	5				6	9		3	7		12			
R4	Dec 7	STOURBRIDGE	3-3	Pike 3 (1p)	1495			5		11	10	4		8		12					7			2	9	3	6	14				
rep	17	Stourbridge	2-1	dale, Griffith	1004			5			10	4		11	8		12	2					6	9	7	3					1	
R5	Feb 18	Swansea City	1-0	Pike	7303	5				11	10	4		12		8						6	2	9	7	3				1	
SF1	Mar 24	MAESTEG PARK ATH.	0-0		3308			5			10	4		8	12	1		11	2	14	6				7	3						
SF2	Apr 18	MAESTEG PARK ATH.	4-0	* see below	3578			5			10	4		12	11	1		2			8	6	9	7	3						
F	May 7	Hednesford Town	1-0	Dale	11000	6		5	11	10	4	12		8	1					14		2	9	7	3						

Scorers in SF2: Llewellyn (og), Dale, Searle, Jones
Played in SF1 (at 9) and SF2 (at 14): Bird
Final at the National Stadium, Cardiff

1992/93 Champions of (the new) Division Three: Promoted

#	Date	Opponent	Score	Scorers	Att	Baddeley LM	Bird A	Blake NA	Brazil DM	Dale C	Gibbins RG	Gorman AD	Grew MS	Griffith C	James RM	Kelly NAO	Matthews NP	Millar WP	Perry J	Pike C	Ramsey PC	Ratcliffe K	Richardson NJ	Searle DB	Stant PR	Ward GJ	Williams SD
1	Aug 15	DARLINGTON	0-0		8399			11	6	10			1	8	2			12	5	9	7		4	3			
2	22	Walsall	3-2	Searle, Dale 2	4611		12	11	6	10			1	8	2			4	5	9	7			3			
3	29	HALIFAX TOWN	2-1	James, Dale	7692			11	6	10			1	12	2			4	5	9	7		8	3			
4	Sep 1	NORTHAMPTON T	2-1	Ramsey (p), Dale	7494			11	6	10			1	8	2			9	5	12	7		4	3			
5	5	Torquay United	1-2	Pike	2939			11	6	10			1	8	2			10	5	9	7		4	3			14
6	8	CARLISLE UNITED	2-2	Pike (p), Perry	6954	5		11		10	12		1	8	2			4	6	9	7		14	3			
7	13	Hereford United	1-1	Blake	4039		14	11	6	10	12		1	8	2			7	5	9			4	3			
8	19	GILLINGHAM	3-1	Blake, Pike 2	6356	5		11	6	10			1		2			8		9	7		4	3			
9	Oct 3	ROCHDALE	1-1	Pike	6486	5		11	6	10			1	8	2			4		9	7		12	3			
10	10	Crewe Alexandra	0-2		3638	5		11		10	12			8	2			4	6	9	7			3		1	
11	24	Shrewsbury Town	2-3	Dale, Pike (p)	4161	5		11	6	10			1	8	2			12	14	9	7		4	3			
12	31	SCUNTHORPE UNITED	3-0	Blake, Kelly, Ramsey (p)	6027			9	6	10					2	8		11	5	12	7		4	3		1	
13	Nov 3	Chesterfield	1-2	James	2590			9	6	10					2	8	7	11	5	12			4	3		1	
14	7	COLCHESTER UNITED	3-1	Dale, Blake, English (og)	5505			9	6	10	2			4	8	5		11			7			3		1	
15	22	Barnet	1-2	Dale	4181			9	6	10	12				2	8		11	5		7		4	3		1	
16	28	BURY	3-0	Kearney (og), Blake, Griffith	4348			9	6	10				14	2	8		11	5	12	7		4	3		1	
17	Dec 11	Doncaster Rovers	1-0	Millar	2023			11	6	10					2			4	5		7		8	3	9	1	
18	18	WREXHAM	1-2	Blake	6832			11	6	10	12				2			4	5		7		8	3	9	1	
19	26	YORK CITY	3-3	Hall (og), Gorman, Stant	10411	12	10		6			11		14	2			4	5		7		8	3	9	1	
20	28	Lincoln City	2-3	Ramsey, Millar	4359	4	12		6					11	2			10	5		7		8	3	9	1	
21	Jan 2	HEREFORD UNITED	2-1	Stant, Richardson	6593	5			10					11	2			4			7	6	8	3	9	1	
22	9	Carlisle United	2-1	Bird, Radcliffe	3691		10							11	2			4	5		7	6	8	3	9	1	
23	23	Gillingham	1-0	Griffith	4066	12	10							11	2		4	7	5			6	8	3	9	1	
24	26	Halifax Town	1-0	Stant	1339		10							11	2		4	7	5			6	8	3	9	1	
25	30	WALSALL	2-1	Stant, Grifith	9012		10							11	2		4	7	5	12		6	8	3	9	1	
26	Feb 6	Darlington	2-0	Pike 2 (1p)	1775		10				14			11	2		4	7	5	12		6	8	3	9	1	
27	13	TORQUAY UNITED	4-0	Millar, Stant 2, Blake	7771		12							11	2		4	7	5	10		6	8	3	9	1	
28	19	Northampton Town	2-1	Stant, Pike	4522		12		4					11	2			7	5	10		6	8	3	9	1	
29	27	CREWE ALEXANDRA	1-1	Griffith	10012		12		4					11	2			7	5	10		6	8	3	9	1	
30	Mar 6	Rochdale	2-1	Blake, Griffith	2831			9	4					11	2			7	5	10		6	8	3		1	
31	9	SCARBOROUGH	1-0	Stant	8583		12	11	4						2			7	5	10		6	8	3	9	1	
32	12	Colchester United	4-2	Pike 2, Richardson, Matthews	4517				4					11	2		7		5	10		6	8	3	9	1	
33	20	CHESTERFIELD	2-1	Dale, Richardson	6756				4	10					2		11		5	12	7	6	8	3	9	1	
34	23	Bury	0-1		3574		12		4					10	2		11		5		7	6	8	3	9	1	
35	27	BARNET	1-1	Griffith	16073			11	4					14	2	8			5	10	7	6	12	3	9	1	
36	Apr 3	Scarborough	3-1	Pike (p), Richardson, Stant	2223				4		12			11	2		14		5	10	7	6	8	3	9	1	
37	6	DONCASTER ROVERS	1-1	Perry	9938			11	4						2	12	6		5	10	7		8	3	9	1	
38	10	York City	1-3	Griffith	6568		12		4					14	2				5	10	7		8	3	9	1	
39	12	LINCOLN CITY	3-1	Stant, Blake, Ramsey (p)	11257			10	4						2				5		7	6	8	3	9	1	
40	17	Wrexham	2-0	Griffith, Blake	10852			10	4		12				2				5		7	6	8	3	9	1	
41	May 1	SHREWSBURY TOWN	2-1	Perry, Blake	17253			9	4	10					2			14	5	12	7	6	8	3		1	
42	8	Scunthorpe United	3-0	Griffith 2, Stant	7407			10	4						2		6		5		7		8	3	9	1	
		Apps				8	9	34	34	20	8	1	10	34	42	5	14	33	39	28	30	19	39	42	24	32	1
		Goals					1	11		8		1		10	2	1	1	3	3	12	4	1	4	1	11		

Three own goals

F.A. Cup

R	Date	Opponent	Score	Scorers	Att	Baddeley LM	Bird A	Blake NA	Brazil DM	Dale C	Gibbins RG	Gorman AD	Grew MS	Griffith C	James RM	Kelly NAO	Matthews NP	Millar WP	Perry J	Pike C	Ramsey PC	Ratcliffe K	Richardson NJ	Searle DB	Stant PR	Ward GJ	Williams SD
R1	Nov 14	BATH CITY	2-3	Millar, Blake	4506			9	6	10	2			8	4			5	11	12	14	7		3		1	

F.L. Cup (Coca Cola Cup)

R	Date	Opponent	Score	Scorers	Att	Baddeley LM	Bird A	Blake NA	Brazil DM	Dale C	Gibbins RG	Gorman AD	Grew MS	Griffith C	James RM	Kelly NAO	Matthews NP	Millar WP	Perry J	Pike C	Ramsey PC	Ratcliffe K	Richardson NJ	Searle DB	Stant PR	Ward GJ	Williams SD
R1/1	Aug 18	BRISTOL CITY	1-0	Dale	4066			11	6	10	12		1	8	2			4	5	9	7			3			
R1/2	25	Bristol City	1-5	Dale	9801	12	9	11	6	10	7		1		2			4	5					3			

Played at 8 in R1/2: Callaway (subbed)

A.M. Cup (Autoglass Trophy)

R	Date	Opponent	Score	Scorers	Att	Baddeley LM	Bird A	Blake NA	Brazil DM	Dale C	Gibbins RG	Gorman AD	Grew MS	Griffith C	James RM	Kelly NAO	Matthews NP	Millar WP	Perry J	Pike C	Ramsey PC	Ratcliffe K	Richardson NJ	Searle DB	Stant PR	Ward GJ	Williams SD
R1	Dec 1	Shrewsbury Town	3-1	Millar, Richardson, Dale	936			11	6	10					2			4	5	9	7		8	3		1	
R1	8	HEREFORD UNITED	3-2	Ramsey (p), Stant, Dale	3246			11	6	10					2			4	5		7		8	3	9	1	
R2	Jan 18	SWANSEA CITY	1-2 (aet)	Blake	13516		14		10	12				11	2			4	5		7	6	8	3	9	1	

European Cup Winners Cup

R	Date	Opponent	Score	Scorers	Att	Baddeley LM	Bird A	Blake NA	Brazil DM	Dale C	Gibbins RG	Gorman AD	Grew MS	Griffith C	James RM	Kelly NAO	Matthews NP	Millar WP	Perry J	Pike C	Ramsey PC	Ratcliffe K	Richardson NJ	Searle DB	Stant PR	Ward GJ	Williams SD
R1/1	Sep 16	ADMIRA WACKER	1-1	Pike	9624	4	2	11	6	10	12		1	8						9	7			3			
R1/2	29	Admira Wacker	0-2		4700	4	12	11	6	10			1	8	2					9	7			3			

Played at 5 in both games: GJ Abraham (subbed in R1/2)

Welsh Cup

R	Date	Opponent	Score	Scorers	Att	Baddeley LM	Bird A	Blake NA	Brazil DM	Dale C	Gibbins RG	Gorman AD	Grew MS	Griffith C	James RM	Kelly NAO	Matthews NP	Millar WP	Perry J	Pike C	Ramsey PC	Ratcliffe K	Richardson NJ	Searle DB	Stant PR	Ward GJ	Williams SD
R3	Oct 27	Ton Pentre	2-0	Miller, Ramsey (p)	1700			11	6	10	12		1		2			8	5	9	7		4	3			
R4	Dec 5	Caerau	9-0	Richardson 3, Pike, Dale 4, Blake	2579			11	6	10	12			14	2			4	5	9	7		8	3		1	
R5	Jan 16	MAESTEG PARK ATH.	4-0	Stant 3, Ramsey	2867	10	4		6	12				11	2		14		5		7		8	3	9	1	
SF1	Mar 16	WREXHAM	2-0	Griffith, Dale	10251				4	12				11	2		7		5	10	14	6	8	3	9	1	
SF2	Apr 17	Wrexham	0-1		5735			10	4	12				11	2				5		7	6	8	3	9	1	
F	May 16	Rhyl	5-0	Stant 3, Griffith 2	16443			10	4	12				11	2		6		5	14	7		8	3	9	1	

Final at the National Stadium, Cardiff

1993/94   19th in Division Two

League (Division Two)

#	Date	Opponent	Score	Scorers	Att	Adams DS	Aizlewood M	Baddeley LM	Bird A	Blake NA	Brazil DM	Brock KS	Cornwell JA	Dale C	Evans T	Fereday W	Grew MS	Griffith C	James RM	Jones IM	Kite PD	Knill AR	Millar WP	Perry J	Ratcliffe K	Richardson NJ	Searle DB	Stant PR	Thompson GL	Wigg NM	Williams SD	Young S
1	Aug 14	LEYTON ORIENT	2-0	Blake, Griffith	9920				7	10	4						1	11	2		12		5	6		8	3		9			
2	21	Fulham	3-1	Blake 2, Thompson	5696			14	11	10	4		7						2		1		12	5	6	8	3		9			
3	28	BRIGHTON & HOVE ALB	2-2	Blake, Cornwell	7687			12	6	10	4		7					11	2		1			5		8	3		9	14		
4	31	Exeter City	2-2	Griffith, Cornwell	3049					10	4		7					11	2		1		6	5		8	3		9			
5	Sep 4	Port Vale	2-2	Blake, Griffith	8140			12		10			7					11	2		1		4	5	6	8	3		9			
6	11	HULL CITY	3-4	Thompson, Richardson 2 (1p)	7421					10			4					7	2		1		5	6		8	3	9	11			
7	18	Blackpool	0-1		4767			4	14									11	2	3	1		7	5	6	8	12	9	10			
8	25	PLYMOUTH ARGYLE	2-3	Stant, Millar	6362				7		8						1	11	2				5	11	4	6	3	9	10			
9	Oct 2	York City	0-5		3762			8		6								11	2	3			5	4			9	10	7	1		
10	10	Barnet	0-0		2084			6	7	10	4							11			1	5	12	2		3	9	8	14			
11	16	BRISTOL ROVERS	1-2	Richardson (p)	5676	6		14	10		4							11			1	5	7	2		8	3	12	9			
12	23	Wrexham	1-3	Bird	4245	6		5	14	10	4							11			1		7	2		8	3	12	9			
13	30	HARTLEPOOL UNITED	2-2	Bird, Blake (p)	3710	6		5	7	10	3							11			1		4	2			9	12				
14	Nov 2	Brentford	1-1	Blake	4756			5	7	10	2							11					4	6		8	3				1	
15	6	STOCKPORT COUNTY	3-1	Blake 3 (1p)	4738			5	7	10	2							11					4	6		8	3	9		12	1	14
16	19	Cambridge United	1-1	Bird	3076	4		5	7	10	2					1		11						6		8	3	9				
17	27	BRADFORD CITY	1-1	Stant	4213	4		5	7	10	2					1		11					12	6		8	3	9				
18	Dec 11	FULHAM	1-0	Blake	5120	4		5	7	10	2					1		11					12	6		8	3	9				
19	18	Leyton Orient	2-2	Stant, Thompson	3691	4		5	7		2					1		11					10	6		8	3	9	12			
20	22	SWANSEA CITY	1-0	Thompson	9815	4		5	14	10	2					1		11					12	6		8	3	9	7			
21	Jan 1	READING	3-0	Griffith, Aizlewood, Richardson	10257	4		5			2					1		11					10	6		8	3	9	7			
22	3	Rotherham United	2-5	Millar 2 (2p)	3405	4		5	12		2							11					10	6		8	3	9	7		1	
23	15	Bristol Rovers	1-2	Blake	5624				12	10	2				4		1	11					6	5		8	3	9	7	14		
24	22	BARNET	0-0		5698	14	4	12	11	10	2						1	9					6	5		8	3	7				
25	Feb 5	WREXHAM	5-1	Adams, Richardson, Bird, Blake 2	10847	9	4	5	7	10	2				14	12		11			1					8	3			6		
26	12	Burnley	0-2		11277	9		5	12	10	2				14		1	11					4	6		8	3		7			
27	Mar 1	BURNLEY	2-1	Thompson, Stant	5469			5	11		2	4			12								10	6		8	3	9	7			1
28	5	Hull City	0-1		4998			5	11		2	4			12								10	6		8	3	9	7			1
29	12	BLACKPOOL	0-2		5186			5			2	4			12	10							14	6		8	3	9	7			1
30	15	Bournemouth	2-3	Dale, Griffith	2385	12		5	9			4		10		2		11					7	6		8	3					1
31	19	Plymouth Argyle	2-1	Stant 2	9587			7				4		10		2		11						6		8	3	9		5	1	
32	22	Hartlepool United	0-3		1077	14		5	7			4		10		2		11						6		8	3			12	1	
33	26	YORK CITY	0-0		4806			4	5	14		7		10		2		11						6		8	3			12	1	
34	29	ROTHERHAM UNITED	1-0	Bird	3583			4	5	10	2	8				11		7					12	6			3	9			1	
35	Apr 2	Swansea City	0-1		3711			4	5	9	2	8				11		10					14	6	12		3			7	1	
36	4	HUDDERSFIELD T	2-2	Brock, Perry	5525	14		4	5	10	2	8				11		7					12	6			3				1	
37	9	Reading	1-1	Hopkins (og)	7129	10	4				2	7				11		12				1		6	5	8	3	9		14		
38	12	Brighton & Hove Albion	5-3	Millar 3 (2p), Stant, Fereday	7653	4					2	7				11		10				1		6	5	8	3	9		12		
39	16	BRENTFORD	1-1	Brock	5268	12						7				2						1		6	5	8	3	9	10	4		
40	19	Huddersfield Town	0-2		6267	7			12						14	2		11				1		6	5	8	3	9	10	4		
41	21	BOURNEMOUTH	2-1	Stant, Millar (p)	3838	10	4								14	2		11				1		6	5	8	3	9	7	12		
42	23	Stockport County	2-2	Stant, Flynn (og)	5455	4		14						10		2		11					6			8	3	9	7	12	1	5
43	26	EXETER CITY	2-0	Aizlewood, Dale	4631	5	4	12					8	10	2	3		11					6				9	7			1	14
44	30	CAMBRIDGE UNITED	2-7	Griffith, Dale	5175	11	4	8						10	2	3		12					6				9	7	14		1	5
45	May 3	PORT VALE	1-3	Stant	4705			4	5					12	2			11				1	6			8	3	9	7	10		14
46	7	Bradford City	0-2		6642	11			10						2							1	6			8	3	9		4	5

Played in game 46: DA Evans (14), B Graham (12), L Walker (7, subbed)

Apps	14	22	30	35	20	31	14	5	15	5	17	11	42	9	2	18	4	37	40	6	39	42	36	30	19	18	6
Goals	1	2		5	14		2	2	3		1		6					7	1		5		10	5			

Two own goals

F.A. Cup

#	Date	Opponent	Score	Scorers	Att	Adams DS	Aizlewood M	Baddeley LM	Bird A	Blake NA	Brazil DM	Dale C	Cornwell JA	Fereday W	Griffith C	James RM	Kite PD	Millar WP	Perry J	Ratcliffe K	Richardson NJ	Searle DB	Stant PR	Thompson GL	Wigg NM	Williams SD	Young S
R1	Nov 13	Enfield	0-0		2374	6		12		10	2				11			4	5		8	3		9			1
rep	30	ENFIELD	1-0	Blake	3232	4		5	7	10	2				11		1	8	6			3		9	14	12	
R2	Dec 4	Brentford	3-1	Westley (og), Stant, Bird	4845	4		5	7	10	2				11		1		6		8	3	9				
R3	Jan 8	MIDDLESBROUGH	2-2	Stant, Thompson	13750	4		5		10	2				12		1	11	6		8	3	7	9			
rep	19	Middlesbrough	2-1 (a.e.t.)	Stant, Blake	10769	4		11		10	2				12		1	6	5		8	3	7	9			
R4	29	MANCHESTER CITY	1-0	Blake	20486	4		5		10	2				11		1	9	6		8	3	7				
R5	Feb 20	LUTON TOWN	1-2	Stant	17296			5	7		2	10			11		1	6	4		8	3	14	9			

F.L. Cup (Coca Cola Cup)

#	Date	Opponent	Score	Scorers	Att	Baddeley LM	Bird A	Blake NA	Brazil DM	Cornwell JA	Griffith C	James RM	Kite PD	Millar WP	Perry J	Ratcliffe K	Richardson NJ	Searle DB	Thompson GL
R1/1	Aug 17	Bournemouth	1-3	Bird	3054	12	7	10	3		11	2	1	4	5	6	8		9
R1/2	24	BOURNEMOUTH	1-1	Morris (og)	4459	11		10	4	7		2	1	6	5		8	3	9

A.M. Cup (Autoglass Trophy)

#	Date	Opponent	Score	Scorers	Att	Adams DS	Baddeley LM	Bird A	Blake NA	Brazil DM	Dale C	Fereday W	Griffith C	Knill AR	Millar WP	Perry J	Richardson NJ	Searle DB	Thompson GL	Wigg NM
R1	Oct 20	Bristol Rovers	0-3		2035	6	5	12	10	4			11	1	7	2	8	3	9	
R1	Nov 9	TORQUAY UNITED	2-0	Thompson, Stant	1642	6	12	7	10	2			11		4	5	8	3	9	14
R2	Dec 14	Wycombe Wanderers	2-3 (aet)	Griffith, Stant	2703	4	5	7	10		2	1	11		12	6	8	3	9	14

European Cup Winners Cup

#	Date	Opponent	Score	Scorers	Att	Bird A	Blake NA	Brazil DM	Griffith C	James RM	Kite PD	Millar WP	Perry J	Ratcliffe K	Richardson NJ	Searle DB	Thompson GL	Wigg NM	Williams SD	Young S
R1/1	Sep 15	Standard Liege	2-5	Bird 2	25000	4	7	10	11	2	1	5	6		8	3	9			
R1/2	28	STANDARD LIEGE	1-3	James	6096	4	7		11	2		5	6		8	3	9	10	12	1

Played in R1/2 at 14: Bartley

Welsh Cup

#	Date	Opponent	Score	Scorers	Att	Adams DS	Aizlewood M	Baddeley LM	Bird A	Blake NA	Brazil DM	Brock KS	Dale C	Evans T	Fereday W	Griffith C	Knill AR	Millar WP	Perry J	Richardson NJ	Searle DB	Stant PR	Thompson GL	Wigg NM	Williams SD	Young S
R3	Oct 26	AFAN LIDO	2-0	Bird, Thompson	1451			5	7	10	3		2			11	1	4	6	8			9	12	14	
R4	Dec 7	Wrexham	2-0	Stant, Bird	2143		4	5	7	10	2				1	11			6	8	3	9	12			
R5	Feb 9	Ebbw Vale	1-1	Adams	3500	12	4	5		9	10	2		14	1	11				8	3	7			6	
rep	22	EBBW VALE	3-0	Thompson, Bird, Stant	1850	12		5	10		2			14		11		4	6	8	3	7	9			
SF1	Apr 14	Seansea City	2-1	Stant 2	3286	4						7	10	2		11		6	5	8	3	9	10		12	
SF2	28	SWANSEA CITY	4-1	Fereday, Bird, Miller (p), Stant	5606	11	4		8				10	2	3			6	5				9	7	12	14
F	May 15	Barry Town	1-2	Stant	14130	12	4		14			10		2		11		6	5	8	3	9		7		1

Final at the National Stadium, Cardiff

93

1994/95   22nd in Division Two: Relegated

#	Date	Opponent	Score	Scorers	Att	Adams DS	Aizlewood M	Baddeley LM	Bird A	Brazil DM	Dale C	Evans DA	Evans T	Fereday W	Griffith C	Honor CR	McLean I	Millar WP	Milsom PJ	Nicholls RR	Oatway APD	Pearson IS	Perry J	Ramsey PC	Richardson NJ	Scott AM	Searle DB	Stant PR	Thompson GL	Wigg NM	Williams DP	Williams SD	Young S
1	Aug 13	Stockport County	1-4	Stant	5139				10	12	14		2	11	7						6		5			8	3	9			1		
2	Aug 20	OXFORD UNITED	1-3	Stant	7281	12	4		10	3	14		2	11				7			6		5			8		9			1		
3	Aug 27	York City	1-1	Millar	2861			9		5	10		2	11	7			12			6					8	3				1		4
4	Aug 30	WREXHAM	0-0		4903				12	5	10		2	11	7			9			6					8	3				1		4
5	Sep 3	SWANSEA CITY	1-1	Richardson	5523		4		14	5	10		2		7			12			6				8		3	11		9	1		
6	Sep 10	Blackpool	1-2	Richardson	4189		4			6	10		2					11	5		12				7		3	9	14		1		
7	Sep 13	Chester City	2-0	Stant, Aizlewood	1671		4			12	2			10				11	5				7	6		8	3	9			1		
8	Sep 17	PLYMOUTH ARGYLE	0-1		5674		4	14		12	2			10				11	5		7		6			8	3	9			1		
9	Sep 24	Bournemouth	2-3	Scott, Griffith	3177		4	5						10				11			14		7	6		8	3	9			1		12
10	Oct 1	PETERBOROUGH UTD.	1-2	Fereday	4225		4	5	14		10			11	8				7		6		2		12		3	9			1		
11	Oct 8	CREWE ALEXANDRA	1-2	Stant	4126	10	4			2			12	11	7						6		5		8		3	9			1		
12	Oct 15	Bristol Rovers	2-2	Millar, Richardson	3933	10		5		2			12	11	7			14			4		6		8		3	9			1		
13	Oct 22	CAMBRIDGE UNITED	3-1	Stant 3	3580			5		2	10			11	7			8			4		6				3	9			1		
14	Oct 30	Bradford City	3-2	Millar 2 (1p), Stant	5937			5		2	10			11	7			8			4		6				3	9			1		
15	Nov 1	Leyton Orient	0-2		2559			5		2	10			11	7			8			4		6				3	9			1		
16	Nov 5	BRIGHTON & HOVE ALB	3-0	Baddeley, Stant 2	5004			5	12	2				11	8			10			4		6	7			3	9		14	1		2
17	Nov 19	Wycombe Wanderers	1-3	Stant	5391		4	5							12			11			8		6	7			3	9	10		1		2
18	Nov 25	HULL CITY	0-2		4226		4		14	5					12			11			6			7	8		3	9	10		1		2
19	Dec 10	Oxford United	0-1		6181			5		6	7			14	12			11			4				8		3	9	10		1		2
20	Dec 17	STOCKPORT COUNTY	1-1	Dale	3448		6	5			8			11				12			4			7			3	9	10		1		
21	Dec 26	Shrewsbury Town	1-0	Stant (p)	4933			5		8	10			11	12						4		6	7			3	9			1		14
22	Dec 28	BIRMINGHAM CITY	0-1		7420			5		8	10		2	11				12			4		6	7			3	9			1		7
23	Dec 31	Rotherham United	0-2		3064			5	14	8	10		2	12				11			4		6				3	9			1		14
24	Jan 2	BRENTFORD	2-3	Stant, Bird	5253			5	12	8			2								4		6	7	11		3	9	10		1		14
25	Jan 7	BLACKPOOL	0-1		3467			5		9	14		2	11					4	8	6		7				3		10		1		12
26	Jan 14	HUDDERSFIELD T	0-0		3808	9		5	14		11		2					12	4	8			6	7			3		10		1		
27	Jan 17	Cambridge United	0-2		2458	9		5	14		8				12			11			4		6	7			3		10		1		2
28	Feb 4	Hull City	0-4		3903		4	5			7			11		2				10		9		6	8		3		14		1		12
29	Feb 18	Huddersfield Town	1-5	Brazil	10035		4	5		6	8			2	7			12				9			10		3			11	1		
30	Feb 21	WYCOMBE WANDERERS	2-0	Dale, Richardson	3024		4	5			8			11	12	2					9	6			10		3			7	1		
31	Feb 25	Peterborough United	1-2	Dale	4226			5		4	8	9		11		2						6			10		3			7	1		
32	Mar 4	BOURNEMOUTH	1-1	Dale	3008		4	5		14	8	12		11		2					9	6			10		3			7	1		
33	Mar 7	Swansea City	1-4	Wigg	3942		4	5		12				11	8	2		14			9	6			10		3			7	1		
34	Mar 11	YORK CITY	1-2	Griffith	2689			5		12				3	4	2		11		14	9	6			10					7	1		12
35	Mar 15	Brighton & Hove Albion	0-0		6956			5						3	4	2		11		14	9	6			10					7	1		12
36	Mar 18	Wrexham	3-0	Nicholls, Griffith, Humes (og)	3106									4	2			11		8	9	6			10		3			7	1		5
37	Mar 25	Plymouth Argyle	0-0		5611			12		2				4				11	14	8	9	6			10		3			7	1		5
38	Mar 28	BRADFORD CITY	2-4	Perry, Millar	2560					2				4	2			11	12	8	9	6			10		3			7	1		5
39	Apr 1	CHESTER CITY	2-1	Dale, Millar	4405			5	12	2	10			11				7			14		9	6			8			4	1		
40	Apr 4	LEYTON ORIENT	2-1	Bird 2	4324			5	12	2	10			11				7			14		9	6			8			4	1		
41	Apr 8	ROTHERHAM UNITED	1-1	Griffith	6412			5	9	2	10	12		11				7					6				8			4	1		12
42	Apr 15	Birmingham City	1-2	Millar	17455			5	9	2	10			11				7					6				8			4	1	1	
43	Apr 17	SHREWSBURY TOWN	1-2	Bird	4677			5	9	2	10	12		11				7		14							8	3		4	1	1	6
44	Apr 22	Brentford	0-2		8268	14		5	9	2	10			11				7				12					8	3		4	1	1	6
45	Apr 29	Bristol Rovers	0-1		5462			5		2	8	14		11				7	9		12						10	3		4	1	1	6
46	May 6	Crewe Alexandra	0-0		4382			5		2	10	14		11				9			12						8	3		4	1	1	7
		Apps				6	17	36	19	30	35	12	7	27	38	10	4	35	3	12	30	12	34	11	33	13	32	19	13	19	40	6	22
		Goals					1	1	4	1	5			1	4			7		1			1		4	1		13		1			

One own goal

Played in games 34 at 8 and 35 at 8 (subbed): L Vick

F.A. Cup

Rnd	Date	Opponent	Score	Scorers	Att	Bird A	Brazil DM	Evans T	Fereday W	Griffith C	Millar WP	Oatway APD	Perry J	Ramsey PC	Searle DB	Stant PR	Thompson GL	Williams DP
R1	Nov 12	Enfield	0-1		2345	14	5	2	11	8	10	4	6	7	3	9	12	1

F.L. Cup (Coca Cola Cup)

Rnd	Date	Opponent	Score	Scorers	Att	Adams DS	Aizlewood M	Bird A	Brazil DM	Dale C	Evans T	Fereday W	Griffith C	Millar WP	Oatway APD	Perry J	Scott AM	Wigg NM	Williams DP	Young S
R1/1	Aug 16	TORQUAY UNITED	1-0	Oatway	2690		4	10	3	12	2	11	7	14	6	5	8	9	1	
R1/2	Aug 23	Torquay United	2-4	Stant 2	2709	12		7	5	10	2			11	6		8	9	1	4

Played in R1/2: Street (at 3, subbed)

A.M. Cup (Auto Windscreens Shield)

Rnd	Date	Opponent	Score	Scorers	Att	Adams DS	Aizlewood M	Baddeley LM	Bird A	Brazil DM	Dale C	Evans DA	Evans T	Fereday W	Griffith C	Millar WP	Oatway APD	Perry J	Ramsey PC	Richardson NJ	Scott AM	Searle DB	Stant PR	Thompson GL	Wigg NM	Williams DP	Williams SD	Young S
R1	Sep 27	PLYMOUTH ARGYLE	2-0	Griffith, Dale	1299	11	4	5	9		10				8	7	6	2		12		3				1		
R1	Nov 15	Exeter City	1-1	Young	1203	11	4	5							8	6			7			3	9	10	12	1		2
R2	Nov 29	Exeter City	0-1		1452			5		6	14		2	11	12		4		7	8		3	9	10		1		

94

1995/96 22nd in Division Three

#	Date	Opponent	Score	Scorers	Att	Adams DS	Baddeley LM	Bird A	Brazil DM	Dale C	Dobbs GF	Downing KG	Evans DA	Flack SR	Fleming HV	Gardner J	Harding PJ	Harper A	Haworth SO	Ingram CD	Jarman L	Johnson GP	McGorry BP	Oatway APD	Osman RC	Perry J	Philliskirk A	Rodgerson I	Scully ADT	Searle DB	Shaw P	Wigg NM	Williams DP	Young S
1	Aug 12	Rochdale	3-3	Bird 2, Dale	2321		5	11	2	10						4										6	8			3	9	7	1	
2	19	NORTHAMPTON T	0-1		7772		5	11	2	10						4			13							6	8			3	9	7	1	12
3	26	Doncaster Rovers	0-0		2186		5	11	2	10		12				4			13							6	8			3	9	7	1	
4	29	EXETER CITY	0-1		4444		5	11	2	10				8		4										6	7				9	12	1	
5	Sep 2	Darlington	1-0	Dale (p)	1895		5		2	10				8		4			12							6	7			3	9	11	1	13
6	9	TORQUAY UNITED	0-0		4318		5		2	10	11			8		4										6	7			3	9	12	1	
7	12	SCARBOROUGH	2-1	Todd (og), Dale	2390		5	11	2	10		7				4				9						6				3	8		1	12
8	16	Gillingham	0-1		5314	13	5	11	2	10		7					9									6	4			3	8		1	12
9	23	Hartlepool United	1-2	Dale (p)	2172	7	5	11		10						4	9	12								6	8			3			1	2
10	30	MANSFIELD TOWN	3-0	Ingram, Dale 2 (1p)	3468		5			10					11	4	9	7								6	8			3			1	2
11	Oct 7	Cambridge United	2-4	Adams, Bird	2648	13	5	10					9		11	4		7								6	8			3			1	2
12	14	BARNET	1-1	Dale	3342	12	5	8		10			13		11	4	9	7								6							1	3
13	21	Lincoln City	1-0	Gardner	2453				2	10					11	4			13				12	9						3		7	1	6
14	28	COLCHESTER UNITED	1-2	Adams	3207	8	5		2	10					11	4			13	12				9						3		7	1	6
15	31	SCUNTHORPE UNITED	0-1		2159	8		13	2	10					11				9	7	5								4	3			1	6
16	Nov 4	Plymouth Argyle	0-0		7434	8		12	2						7	11			9		5								4	3		10	1	6
17	18	BURY	0-1		3846	8			2	9					7	11			13		5								4	3		10	1	6
18	26	Hereford United	3-1	Dale 2, Adams	3521	8		13	12	9					7	11		10			5			2					4	3			1	6
19	Dec 9	HARTLEPOOL UNITED	2-0	Dale 2	2934					9					2	11	4	10			5						8	7		3			1	6
20	16	Mansfield Town	1-1	Searle	2212	12				9					2	11	4	10			5						8	7		3			1	6
21	19	Fulham	2-4	Dale, Rodgerson	2284					9					2	11	4	10			5						8	7		3			1	6
22	26	CHESTER CITY	0-0		6521	10				9					2	11	4			12	5						8	7		3			1	6
23	Jan 1	Preston North End	0-5		8346		13			9					2	11	4	8		12	5					10	7			3			1	6
24	6	LEYTON ORIENT	0-0		2873		13			9					2	11	4				5					10	7		8	3		12	1	6
25	13	Northampton Town	0-1		4454	4		11	9					12	2						5					10	13		8	3		7	1	6
26	20	ROCHDALE	1-0	Gardner	2248	7		12	9						2	11	4				5					10			8	3			1	6
27	Feb 3	DONCASTER ROVERS	3-2	Dale 3	2566	7			9					12	2	11	4				5					10			8	3			1	6
28	10	Leyton Orient	1-4	Philliskirk	3564			7	9					13	2	11					5					10	8			3		12	1	6
29	17	Scarborough	0-1		1414		11		9							12	4				5				7	10	2	8		3			1	6
30	20	DARLINGTON	0-2		2225		8		9					12			11				5				7	10	2	13	3				1	6
31	24	GILLINGHAM	2-0	Dale, Harris (og)	3028	7				10					2	11	4				5					9		8		3			1	6
32	27	Torquay United	0-0		2004	7				10					2	11	4				5					9		8		3		12	1	6
33	Mar 2	Chester City	0-4		2308			11		10					2	12	4				5					9		8		3		7	1	6
34	5	WIGAN ATHLETIC	3-0	Gardner 2, Philliskirk	1611		3		2	10						11	4				5				7	9	12	8					1	6
35	9	FULHAM	1-4	Dale	3489		3		2	10						11	4				5				7	9	8					12	1	6
36	12	Exeter City	0-2		2609		11		2	10				13							5				4	9	8	7		3		12	1	6
37	16	Wigan Athletic	1-3	Flack	2789		2			10				11	8	12	4				5				6	9	13	7		3			1	
38	23	PRESTON NORTH END	0-1		3642		2			10				11		7					5	8			6	9	12			3			1	4
39	30	CAMBRIDGE UNITED	1-1	Dale (p)	2440		5			10				9		11						13	8		12	7	2			3			1	6
40	Apr 2	Barnet	0-1		2107					10						11	4				5	12	8		7	9	2			3			1	6
41	6	Colchester United	0-1		3349					10				12		11	4				5	13	8		7	9	2			3			1	6
42	8	LINCOLN CITY	1-1	Dale	2788					10						11	4				5	7	8		2	9				3			1	6
43	13	Scunthorpe United	1-1	Dale	2044					10						11	4				5	12	8		7	9	2			3				6
44	20	PLYMOUTH ARGYLE	0-1		3489					10				12	3	11	4				5		8		7	9	2							6
45	27	HEREFORD UNITED	3-2	Dale, Philliskirk 2	3870					10				8	2	11					5				7	9				3		4		6
46	May 4	Bury	0-3		5658	14				10				8	2	11					5				7	9	12			3			4	6
				Apps		13	30	12	20	44	3	4	2	10	22	35	36	5	13	8	32	5	7	2	15	14	28	33	14	41	6	21	42	41
				Goals		3		3		21				1		4					1						4	1		1				

Played in one game: M Bolesan (15, at 12), IM Jones (4, at 3), AM Scott (35, 13)
Played in games 11 (at 12) and 12 (at 2): T Evans
Played at 13 in games 44 and 46: L Vick
Played in 4 games 43 to 46 at 1: SD Williams

Two own goals

F.A. Cup

#	Date	Opponent	Score	Scorers	Att	Adams DS	Baddeley LM	Bird A	Brazil DM	Dale C	Dobbs GF	Downing KG	Evans DA	Flack SR	Fleming HV	Gardner J	Harding PJ	Harper A	Haworth SO	Ingram CD	Jarman L	Johnson GP	McGorry BP	Oatway APD	Osman RC	Perry J	Philliskirk A	Rodgerson I	Scully ADT	Searle DB	Shaw P	Wigg NM	Williams DP	Young S
R1	Nov 11	Rushden & Diamonds	3-1	Dale 2, Jarman	4212	8			2	9		13			7	11					5		12						4	3		10	1	6
R2	Dec 2	Swindon Town	0-2		8274	10		2	13	9					7	11	4				5								8	3		12	1	6

F.L. Cup (Coca Cola Cup)

#	Date	Opponent	Score	Scorers	Att	Adams DS	Baddeley LM	Bird A	Brazil DM	Dale C	Dobbs GF	Downing KG	Evans DA	Flack SR	Fleming HV	Gardner J	Harding PJ	Harper A	Haworth SO	Ingram CD	Jarman L	Johnson GP	McGorry BP	Oatway APD	Osman RC	Perry J	Philliskirk A	Rodgerson I	Scully ADT	Searle DB	Shaw P	Wigg NM	Williams DP	Young S
R1/1	Aug 16	Portsmouth	2-0	Dale, Bird	4203		5	11	2	10			12			4			9							6	8			3		7	1	
R1/2	22	PORTSMOUTH	1-0	Dale	4347		5	11	2	10		12				4			9							6	8			3		7	1	13
R2/1	Sep 19	SOUTHAMPTON	0-3		9041	13	5	11		10	7					4			9							6	12			3	8		1	2
R2/2	Oct 4	Southampton	1-2	Rodgerson	12709	11	5			10						4			9	7						6	8			3			1	2

A.M. Cup (Auto Windscreens Shield)

#	Date	Opponent	Score	Scorers	Att	Adams DS	Baddeley LM	Bird A	Brazil DM	Dale C	Dobbs GF	Downing KG	Evans DA	Flack SR	Fleming HV	Gardner J	Harding PJ	Harper A	Haworth SO	Ingram CD	Jarman L	Johnson GP	McGorry BP	Oatway APD	Osman RC	Perry J	Philliskirk A	Rodgerson I	Scully ADT	Searle DB	Shaw P	Wigg NM	Williams DP	Young S
R1	Sep 26	Hereford United	3-3	Dale 2, Adams	1411	11	5			10						4			9	7						6	8			3			1	2
R1	Oct 17	GILLINGHAM	3-2	Dale 2, Adams	1034	13	5	8	6	10						11	4		9	14	12									3		7	1	2
R2	Nov 28	NORTHAMPTON T	1-2	Dale (p)	1450	8		2	12	9					7	11		10			5						4			3			1	6

Played at 13 on Sep 26: T Evans

95

1996/97   7th in Division Three

Player columns (left to right):
Baddeley LM · Bennett MR · Burton DJ · Coldicott S · Dale C · Davies GM · Eckhardt JE · Elliott AR · Fleming HV · Fowler IKG · Gardner J · Haworth SO · Jarman L · Lloyd KG · Middleton CD · Mountain PD · O'Halloran KJ · Partridge SM · Perry J · Phillskirk A · Rodgerson I · Rollo JS · Scott AM · Stoker G · Ware PD · White SJ · Williams SD · Young S

#	Date	Opponent	Score	Scorers	Att	Bad	Ben	Bur	Col	Dal	Dav	Eck	Ell	Fle	Fow	Gar	Haw	Jar	Llo	Mid	Mou	O'H	Par	Per	Phi	Rod	Rol	Sco	Sto	War	Whi	Wil	You
1	Aug 17	Scarborough	0-0		2455		7			10						8		5	3					4	11	2					9		6
2	24	BRIGHTON & HOVE ALB	1-0	Eckhardt	3897		7					10	1			8	12	5	3					4	11	2		13			9		6
3	27	WIGAN ATHLETIC	0-2		3845	12	7			10		6	1			8	13		3					4	11	2		5			9		
4	31	Cambridge United	2-0	White 2	2478		7		10			5	1			8	12	13	3	3				4	11	2					9		6
5	Sep 7	EXETER CITY	2-1	White 2	3659					8		10	1					5	3	7				4	11	2					9		6
6	10	Torquay United	0-2		2041				8		12	4	1		13			5	3	7					11	2					9		6
7	14	Scunthorpe United	1-0	Middleton	2121				8	10		4	1		13		12		3	7				5	11	2					9		6
8	21	NORTHAMPTON T	2-2	Phillskirk, Middleton	4124		12		8	10		4	1						3	7				5	11	2					9		6
9	28	Lincoln City	0-2		2925	12	13		8	10		4	1						3	7				5	11	2					9		6
10	Oct 12	BARNET	1-2	Middleton	2879		12			10		4	1			8	3	11	13	7				5		2					9		6
11	15	DARLINGTON	2-0	Dale, White	1667					10		4	1	2		8	3	11						5							9		6
12	19	Carlisle United	2-0	Dale, Fowler	4972	12				10		4	1	2		8	3	11	14	7				5	13						9		6
13	26	LEYTON ORIENT	3-0	White (p), Gardner, Dale	3647		13			10		4	1	2		8	3	5	12	7					11						9		6
14	29	Hull City	1-1	Middleton	2775	12	13			10		4	1	2		8		5	3	7					11						9		6
15	Nov 2	Colchester United	1-1	White (p)	3213	12	13			10		4	1	2		8	3	5		7					11						9		6
16	5	ROCHDALE	2-1	Bennett, Eckhardt	2835	6	8					10	4	1	2		3		12	7				5	11						9		
17	9	FULHAM	1-2	White	6144	6	12					10	4	1	2	8	3			7				5	11						9		
18	23	HEREFORD UNITED	2-0	White 2	3904					10		4	1			6	11			8				2	3	7					9		5
19	26	Chester City	1-0	Young	1540					10		4	1			6	11			8				2	3	7					9		5
20	30	Leyton Orient	0-3		4512		12			10		4	1			6	11			8			7	2	3						9		5
21	Dec 3	SWANSEA CITY	1-3	White	3721					10		4	1			6	11	12		8			7	2	3						9		5
22	7	MANSFIELD TOWN	1-2	Eckhardt	2238							4				6	11	12		8	1			2	10	7					9		3
23	26	TORQUAY UNITED	2-0	Burton 2	3651			10				4				5	11		12	8		1	6	2	3	7					9		
24	28	Exeter City	0-2		3585			10				4		13		5	11	12		8		1	6	2	3	7					9		
25	Jan 1	Northampton Town	0-4		4416	5		10				4		7			11	12	3	8		1	6	2							9		
26	11	LINCOLN CITY	1-3	Fowler	2033			10			9	4		5	7		11	12		8		1	6	2	3						13		
27	18	Rochdale	0-1		1704	5		10					1		7	11	9		3	4		8		2	12						13		6
28	25	HULL CITY	2-0	Haworth, Eckhardt	2328	13						4	1		5	11	10		3	7				2	12						9		6
29	31	Fulham	4-1	Fowler, White 2, Haworth	6459							4	1		5	10	2	3	7					14	12	13			8	11	9		6
30	Feb 8	COLCHESTER UNITED	1-2	Haworth	3912							4	1		5	13	10	2	3	7					12				8	11	9		6
31	11	Hartlepool United	3-2	Fowler, Eckhardt, Stoker	1120							4	1		5	10	2	3	7				9					8	11			
32	16	Hereford United	1-1	Stoker	5137							4	1		5	10	2	3	7	13				9	12			8	11			
33	22	HARTLEPOOL UNITED	2-0	Haworth, Davies	2971					14	5	4	1			10	2	3	7				6		9	12			8	11			
34	Mar 2	Swansea City	1-0	Haworth	4430					12	5	4	1		6		10	2		7				8	3	11		13				9	
35	8	Mansfield Town	3-1	Haworth, Stoker, Dale	2569					14	5	4	1		6		10	12		7				8	3	11		13	2			9	
36	14	DONCASTER ROVERS	0-2		5347					12	5		1		6		10	2	3	7				8	4			11				9	
37	18	SCARBOROUGH	1-1	Davies	2823					9	5		1		6	12	10	2	3	7				11	4			8					
38	22	Brighton & Hove Albion	0-2		9683					9	5		1		6	14	10		12				7	4	13	2		8			11	3
39	31	Wigan Athletic	1-0	Haworth	4634					9		4	1		6		10	2	3				7		11			8			12	5
40	Apr 5	CAMBRIDGE UNITED	0-0		3410					9			1		6	11	10	2	3	4			7					8			12	5
41	8	Doncaster Rovers	3-3	Haworth 2, Fowler	1989					9			1		6		10	2	3	11			7	4	12			8				5
42	12	CHESTER CITY	1-0	Dale	4079					9					6		10	2	3	11		1	7	4	12			8				5
43	15	SCUNTHORPE UNITED	0-0		4442					9					6		10	2	3	11		1	7	4	13			12				5
44	19	Barnet	1-3	Dale	2497					9				12	6		10	2	3	11		1	7	4				8		13		5
45	26	CARLISLE UNITED	2-0	Dale (p), Lloyd	5104					9					6		10	2	3	11		1	7	4	12			8		14		5
46	May 3	Darlington	1-2	Dale	3686					9	14				6		10	2	3	11		1	7	4	12			8		13		5

Played in one game: SR Flack (game 6 at 10, subbed), R McStay (22, 5), JD Michael (22, 13)
Played in games 31 and 32 (at 6) and 33 (at 12): L Phillips

Apps	9	14	5	6	33	6	35	36	10	37	28	24	32	31	41	5	8	15	35	33	21	10	2	17	5	38	5	32
Goals		1	2		8	2	5			5	1	9		1	4					1				3		13		1

Play Offs

	Date	Opponent	Score	Scorers	Att	Dal	Eck	Gar	Haw	Jar	Llo	Mid	Fow	Per	Phi	Rod	Sco	Sto	Wil	You
SF1	May 11	NORTHAMPTON T	0-1		11369	9	7	6		10	2	3	11	4			13	8	12	5
SF2	14	Northampton Town	2-3	Fowler, Haworth	7302	9	7	6	14	10	2	3	11	4	13			12	1	5

F.A. Cup

	Date	Opponent	Score	Scorers	Att	Ben	Dal	Eck	Ell	Fle	Gar	Haw	Jar	Mid	O'H	Per	Phi	Rod	Whi	You
R1	Nov 16	HENDON	2-0	White, Middleton	2592	11	10	4	1	2	6			8			3	7	9	5
R2	Dec 7	GILLINGHAM	0-2		3474	13	10	4			6	11	12	8	1	2	3	7	9	5

F.L. Cup (Coca Cola Cup)

	Date	Opponent	Score	Scorers	Att	Ben	Dal	Eck	Ell	Gar	Haw	Jar	Llo	Mid	Per	Phi	Rod	Sto	Whi	You
R1/1	Au 20	NORTHAMPTON T	1-0	Dale	2294	7	10		1	8		5	3		4	11	2	12	9	6
R1/2	Sep 3	Northampton Town	0-2		3567	7		10	1	8	12	5	3	13	4	11	2		9	6

A.M. Cup (Auto Windscreens Shield)

	Date	Opponent	Score	Scorers	Att	Bad	Ben	Bur	Dal	Dav	Eck	Fow	Gar	Haw	Jar	Llo	Mid	O'H	Par	Per	Phi	Rod	Whi	You
R1	Dec 10	Gillingham	2-1	Eckhardt, Dale	1193		12		10		4			11	13		8	1	6	2	3	7	9	5
R2	Jan 14	EXETER CITY	1-1	Dale	793	5		10		9	4	7		11		3	13	1	8	2	14		12	6

R1 won on golden goal rule in extra time. R2 lost on penalties a.e.t.

1997/98   21st in Division Three

#	Date	Opponent	Res	Scorers	Att	Beech C	Cadette ND	Carss AJ	Crowe GM	Dale C	Earnshaw R	Eckhardt JE	Elliott AR	Fowler JKG	Greenacre CM	Hallworth IG	Harris MA	Hill DRL	Jarman L	Lloyd KG	Middleton CD	Nugent KP	O'Sullivan WStJ	Partridge SM	Penney DM	Phillips L (2)	Roberts CJ	Rollo JS	Saville AV	Stoker G	White SI	Young S
1	Aug 9	Leyton Orient	1-0	Dale	5445	3		11		10				6		1	5		4		8	9		7						13	12	2
2	23	Mansfield Town	2-1	Partridge, Greenacre	2743	3		11						6	10	1	5		4		2		12	7	9					8	13	
3	30	NOTTS COUNTY	1-1	Young	6191	3		11						6	9	1	5		12		2			10	7					8	13	4
4	Sep 2	SHREWSBURY TOWN	2-2	Partridge, O'Sullivan	4271	3		11						6	9	1	5		2					10	7					8	12	4
5	9	Exeter City	1-1	Fowler	4843	3						14		6	9	1	5		2		12			7	11	8				13	10	4
6	13	ROCHDALE	2-1	White, Eckhardt	4389	3						12		6	9	1	5		2					7	11			13		8	10	4
7	16	CHESTER CITY	0-2		3949	3		12				2		6	9	1	5							7	11					8	10	4
8	20	Lincoln City	0-1		3134	3		10				2		6	9	1	5		12		14			7	11					8	13	4
9	27	Cambridge United	2-2	Greenacre, Eckhardt	2730	3		11				2	12	6	9	1	5				14			7	13					8	10	4
10 Oct	4	BARNET	1-1	Eckhardt	3941	3		11				2		6	9	1	5		10					7	12	8				14	13	4
11	18	Rotherham United	1-1	Penney (p)	3189	3		11						6	9	1	5		4		12			7		8		2		10		
12	21	Darlington	0-0		2278	3		11						6	9	1	5				12			7		8	4	2		10		
13	25	HARTLEPOOL UNITED	1-1	Crowe	3383	3		11	9	12				6		1	5							7	10	8	4	2				
14 Nov	2	SWANSEA CITY	0-1		6459	3		11	10					6		1	5				2			7	14	8			9	12	13	4
15	4	Doncaster Rovers	1-1	Saville	1004	3		14	10	13				6		1	5				2			7	12	8			9	11		4
16	8	TORQUAY UNITED	1-1	Stoker	2802	3			10	12				6		1	5				2			7		8			9	11		
17	11	SCUNTHORPE UNITED	0-0		2340	3		13	10	12				6		1	5				2			7		8			9	11		
18	18	HULL CITY	2-1	Saville, Penney	2509	3		11	10	12						1	5				2			7	6	8			9			
19	22	Brighton & Hove Albion	1-0	Allan (og)	2086	3		11	10	13		1					5							7	6	8			9		12	2
20	29	SCARBOROUGH	1-1	Dale	2615	3		11	13	10		1					5		12		2			7	6	8			9			
21 Dec	13	PETERBOROUGH UTD.	0-0		3488	3		11		10						1	5				2			7	6	8			9			4
22	20	Macclesfield Town	0-1		2403	3		11		10						1	5		12		2			7	6	8			9	13	14	4
23	26	EXETER CITY	1-1	Dale	6862	3		11		10				6		1	5				2			7		8			9			4
24	28	Shrewsbury Town	2-3	Fowler, Young	3238	3		11		10				6		1	5				2			7		8			9	12	13	4
25 Jan	10	LEYTON ORIENT	1-0	Penney (p)	4598	3		11		10				6		1	5				2	13	7		8			9	12		4
26	17	Notts County	1-3	Harris	6214	3		11		10		2		6		1	5					13	7		8			12	9	14	4
27	20	Colchester United	1-2	Dale	1924	3		11		10		2		6		1	5		14			9	7	13	8			12			4
28	27	Chester City	0-0		1757	3		11				6				1	5				2		7	10	8			9		12	4
29	31	Rochdale	0-0		1445	3		11		10		6				1	5				2		7		8			9	4	12	
30 Feb	7	LINCOLN CITY	0-1		2896	3		11		10				6		1	5		4		2		7	13				14	9	8	12
31	14	Barnet	2-2	Saville, Fowler	2406	3		11		10		8		6		1	5				2		7						9	12	13	4
32	17	MANSFIELD TOWN	4-1	* see below	2562	3		11		13		5				1	6				2		8		12				9		10	4
33	21	CAMBRIDGE UNITED	0-0		2683	3		11		10		5				1	6	8			2		13		14				9		12	4
34	24	ROTHERHAM UNITED	2-2	Saville, White	2731	3		11				4					5	8			2		12		6				9		10	
35	28	Scunthorpe United	3-3	Saville 3	2135	3		11				4				1	5	8			2				6				9		10	
36 Mar	3	Torquay United	0-1		3358	3		11				4				1		8			2			12	6				9		10	5
37	8	Swansea City	1-1	Fowler	5621	3						4		7		1		8	2					11	6		12		9		10	5
38	14	DONCASTER ROVERS	7-1	* see below	2931	3		12				4		7		1		8	2					11	6		10		9		13	5
39	21	Hull City	1-0	Roberts	3408	3		7		12		4				1		8	2					11	6		10		9			5
40	28	BRIGHTON & HOVE ALB	0-0		3519	3		7		12	13	4		8		1			2					11	6		10		9			5
41 Apr	3	Scarborough	1-3	Saville	2905	3	13	7		10		4		8		1			2		6			11			12	14	9			5
42	11	COLCHESTER UNITED	0-2		2809	3	13	7		10	12			8		1			2		6			11			4	14	9			
43	13	Peterborough United	0-2		4756	3	13	7		10	14			8		1			2		6			11			4	12	9			5
44	18	MACCLESFIELD TOWN	1-2	Roberts	2501	3	13	7				14		6		1	5		2	12				11			8	4	10	9		
45	25	Hartlepool United	0-2		2817	3		12				14		6		1	5		2	13	7			11			8	4	10	9		
46 May	2	DARLINGTON	0-0		2610	3		12						6		1	5		2		7			11			8	4	13	9		10

Scorers in game 38: Saville 2, O'Sullivan, Roberts, Beech, Penney, Young
Scorers in game 32: Saville (p), Fowler, Carss, Penney
Played in game 34 at 1: P Zois
Played in 5 games 16 to 20 at 4: S Paterson

Apps	45	4	41	8	24	5	21	3	37	11	42	37	7	22	2	32	3	43	21	34	8	11	5	33	19	28	30
Goals	1			1	1	4		3		5	2		1					2	2	5		3		11	1	2	3

One own goal

F.A. Cup

Rd	Date	Opponent	Res	Scorers	Att	Beech	Carss	Dale	Earnshaw	Fowler	Hallworth	Harris	Jarman	Middleton	Nugent	O'Sullivan	Partridge	Penney	Phillips	Roberts	Saville	Stoker	White	Young
R1 Nov 15	Slough Town	1-1	O'Sullivan	2262	3	12	10		6	1	5				2	7	8			9		11	4
rep 25	SLOUGH TOWN	3-2	(aet) Dale, Saville, White	2343	3	11	10	1			5	12	2			7	6	8	13	9		14	4
R2 Dec 6	HENDON	3-1	Dale 2, Saville	2578	3	11	10			1	5	13	2			7	6	8	12	9	14		4
R3 Jan 3	OLDHAM ATHLETIC	1-0	Fowler	6635	3	11	10	13	6	1	5		2			7	8			9	12		4
R4 Jan 24	READING	1-1	Nugent	10174	3	11	10	7	6	1	5		2	9			8			12			4
rep Feb 3	Reading	1-1	Dale	11808	3	11	10	6	14	1	5	13	2	9	7		8				12		4

R4 replay lost 3-4 on penalties

F.L. Cup (Coca Cola Cup)

Rd	Date	Opponent	Res	Scorers	Att	Beech	Carss	Fowler	Hallworth	Harris	Hill	Jarman	Middleton	Nugent	Partridge	Rollo	Stoker	White	Young
R1/1 Aug 12	SOUTHEND UNITED	1-1	Rollo	2804	3	11	6	1	5	4	14	8	10	7	12	13	9	2
R1/2 26	Southend United	1-2	Fowler	3002	3	11	6	1	5	13	14	2		12 7 9		8	10	4

A.M. Cup (Auto Windscreens Shield)

Rd	Date	Opponent	Res	Att	Carss	Crowe	Dale	Eckhardt	Harris	Partridge	Penney	Phillips	Rollo	Stoker	White	Young
R1 Dec 9	MILLWALL	0-2	1219	11	9	13	1	5	7	6	12	3	8	10	4

Played at 2: Harriott (subbed)

F.A. W. Invitation Cup

Rd	Date	Opponent	Res	Scorers	Att	Beech	Cadette	Carss	Crowe	Dale	Eckhardt	Elliott	Fowler	Greenacre	Hallworth	Harris	Hill	Jarman	Lloyd	Middleton	Nugent	O'Sullivan	Partridge	Penney	Phillips	Roberts	Saville	Stoker	White	Young
GP Oct 7	Wrexham	1-0	McGregor (og)	1181	3		11			4		6	9	1	5				12		7	10	8		2	13			
GP 27	WREXHAM	1-1	Partridge	1383	3		11	12	13			6		1	5				7		10			2	4	9			
GP Dec 16	Merthyr Tydfil	0-0		542		13	11			12	1				5		14		6	8	3	7		10	9	4		
GP 23	Newtown	1-1	Stoker	415		12				4	1			5		9		11		3	7		8	10			
GP Jan 14	NEWTOWN	3-2	White 2, Nugent p	951				12	4	1			5	2	9	7	6		3	11		8	10			
GP Feb 10	MERTHYR TYDFIL	1-0	Wager (og)	1055	3		11	10		7			1	5	4					8	2	12	9	6			
QF Mar 17	CONWY UNITED	4-0	Eckhardt, Roberts, Fowler 2	1328	3				4	7		1	12	8	2		11		6		10	9	14	13	5
SF1 Apr 17	Merthyr Tydfil	4-0	Middleton, Carss, Saville, Dale	1302	3	12	7		10	13		8		1		5		6	11		2	14	9		4
SF2 21	MERTHYR TYDFIL	3-1	Roberts, Williams (og), Earnshaw	825	3	14	7		13	6		1	5	2	12		11	8	4	10	9	
F May 17	Wrexham	1-2	Carss	3700			14		6	1	5	2		7	11	8	4	13	9	12

Played at 8 on Oct 27: Ramsey. Played at 6 on Dec 23: Osman
Played at 2 on Dec 16 and Dec 23 (subbed): Harriott

1998/99   Third in Division Three: Promoted

#		Date	Opponent	Score	Scorers	Att	Allen CA	Bonner M	Bowen JP	Brazier MR	Carpenter R	Delaney MA	Earnshaw R	Eckhardt JE	Ford MP	Fowler JKG	Hallworth IG	Hill DRL	Jarman L	Kelly S	Legg A	Middleton CD	Mitchell GL	Nugent KP	O'Sullivan WStJ	Phillips L(2)	Roberts CJ	Saville AV	Thomas DI	Williams JN	Young S
1	Aug	8	Hartlepool United	1-1	Earnshaw	2591		7			6	2	10		3	11	1						4	12				9		8	5
2		15	PETERBOROUGH UTD.	1-3	Saville	5629		7			6	2	13			11	1						4	10	12	3		9		8	5
3		21	Shrewsbury Town	3-0	Eckhardt, Thomas, Nugent	3003		7			6	2		3			1					12	4	11	9				10	13	5
4		29	ROTHERHAM UNITED	0-1		5356		7		8	6	2	14	3			1		12				13	4		11				9	10	5
5		31	Darlington	0-3		3925		7		8	6	2	12	3			1						4		11				9	10	5
6	Sep	5	PLYMOUTH ARGYLE	1-0	Wootton (og)	3939		7		8	6	2		3		12	1					13	4	10	11				9	14	5
7		8	BARNET	1-0	O'Sullivan	3742		7		8	6	2		3		13	1					12	4	10	11				9	14	5
8		11	Halifax Town	2-1	Fowler, Thomas	2814		7		8	6	2		3		13	1		5				4	10	11				9	12	
9		19	ROCHDALE	2-1	Brazier, Bonner	4643		7		8	6	2		3		12	1						4	10	11				9	13	5
10		26	Chester City	2-2	Jarman, Brazier	2842		7		8	6	2		3			1		12			13	4	10	11				9	14	5
11	Oct	3	BRIGHTON & HOVE ALB	2-0	Nugent, Williams	6143		7		8	6	2				12	1		3			13	4	10	11				9	14	5
12		9	Hull City	2-1	Thomas 2	8594		7		8	6			3	2	1							4	10	11				9	12	5
13		17	CAMBRIDGE UNITED	0-1		6886		7		8	6			3	2	1						12	4	10	11				9	13	5
14		20	LEYTON ORIENT	0-0		5001		7		8	6			3	2	1							4	10	11				9	12	5
15		31	EXETER CITY	1-0	Middleton	5411	8				6	2		3		7	1					12	4	10	11		13		9	14	5
16	Nov	7	Torquay United	0-0		3342	8				6	2		12	3		1					7	4	10	11		13		9	14	5
17		10	SCARBOROUGH	1-0	Williams	4422	8				6	2		12	3	7	1						11	4	10					9	5	
18		22	Swansea City	1-2	Williams	7757	12				6	2			3	7	1	13					11	4	10	8				9	5	
19		28	SOUTHEND UNITED	2-0	Middleton, Nugent	4638					6	2			3	7	1	13					11	4	10	8		12		9	5	
20	Dec	1	Carlisle United	1-0	Nugent (p)	2700					6	2			3	7	1	13					11	4	10	8				9	5	
21		12	Scunthorpe United	2-0	Williams 2	3200					6	2		13	3	7	1	12					11	4	10	8				9	5	
22		19	MANSFIELD TOWN	4-2	Williams 2, Nugent 2	9013					6	2			3		1	7				12	11	4	10	8				13	9	5
23		26	SHREWSBURY TOWN	3-0	Williams, Nugent, Hill	12452					6	2			3	11	1	7				13	12	4	10	8				14	9	5
24		28	Brentford	0-1		9535					6	2		12	3	11	1					13	7	4	10	8				9	5	
25	Jan	9	HARTLEPOOL UNITED	4-1	O'Sullivan, Nugent, Eckhardt, Middleton	7766					6	2		5	3		1	7				12	11	4	10	8				9		
26		16	Peterborough United	1-2	Nugent	5890					6	2		5	3	7	1	13				12	11	4	10	8				9		
27		23	DARLINGTON	3-2	Carpenter, Williams, Middleton	5803					6	2		5	3	7	1						11	4	10	8				12	9	
28		30	BRENTFORD	4-1	Williams, Eckhardt, Fowler, Nugent	11509					6	2		5	3	7	1	13				12	11	4	10	8				9		
29	Feb	6	Plymouth Argyle	1-1	Legg	6062			12		6			5		7	1	13			3	11		4	10	8				9	2	
30		13	Barnet	0-1		2234			13		6		14	5		7	1	11	12		3		4				8			10	9	2
31		19	HALIFAX TOWN	1-1	Eckhardt	8788			13		6	8		5		7	1	14			3	11	4	10	12					9	2
32		27	Rochdale	1-1	Legg	2431					6	8		5		7	1	11			3	13	4	10					12	9	2
33	Mar	5	CHESTER CITY	0-0		7528			13		6	2		5		7	1	12			3	11	4	10	14					9	8
34		9	Brighton & Hove Albion	2-0	Nugent, Young	2312	13		9		6			5		7	1	11			3		4	10	2				12		8
35		13	TORQUAY UNITED	2-2	Hill, Fowler	6956			9		6			5		7	1	11			3		4	10	2				12		8
36		16	Rotherham United	0-1		3663	13		9		6			5		7	1	11	12		3		4	10	2				14		8
37		20	Exeter City	2-0	Nugent 2	3653	7		9		6			5			1	11			3	12	4	10	2				14	13	8
38		27	CARLISLE UNITED	2-1	Nugent, Bowen	7094	13		9		6			5		7	1	11			3	12	4	10	2					9	8
39	Apr	3	Cambridge United	0-0		7787			9		6			5	8	7	1	11			3	13	4	10	2				12		
40		5	HULL CITY	1-1	Nugent (p)	8252	11		9		6			5	8	7	1	13			3	12	4	10	2				14		
41		10	Leyton Orient	1-1	Williams	5238	14		9		6			5	8	7	1	11			3	12	4		2				13	10	
42		13	Southend United	1-0	Williams	3923	6		9					5	8	7				1	3	11	4		2					10	
43		18	SWANSEA CITY	0-0		10809	6		13					5	8	7		12		1	3	11	4	10	2					9	
44		24	Scarborough	2-1	Eckhardt, Bowen	1834	6		12		13			5	8			7		1	3	11	4	10	2					9	
45	May	1	SCUNTHORPE UNITED	0-0		12455	6		12					5	8	7		13		1	3	11	4	10	2					9	
46		8	Mansfield Town	0-3		4032	6		9					5	8	7		2		1	3	11	4	10	12			14	13		

Played in one game: DM Penney (game 3, at 8 subbed)

	Allen CA	Bonner M	Bowen JP	Brazier MR	Carpenter R	Delaney MA	Earnshaw R	Eckhardt JE	Ford MP	Fowler JKG	Hallworth IG	Hill DRL	Jarman L	Kelly S	Legg A	Middleton CD	Mitchell GL	Nugent KP	O'Sullivan WStJ	Phillips L(2)	Roberts CJ	Saville AV	Thomas DI	Williams JN	Young S
Apps	4	25	17	11	42	28	5	35	25	37	41	26	6	5	24	35	46	41	42	2	4	2	24	43	33
Goals		1	2	2	1		1	5		3		2	1		2	4		15	2				1	4	12	1

One own goal

F.A. Cup

		Date	Opponent	Score	Scorers	Att	Carpenter R	Delaney MA	Eckhardt JE	Ford MP	Fowler JKG	Hallworth IG	Hill DRL	Middleton CD	Mitchell GL	Nugent KP	O'Sullivan WStJ	Phillips L(2)	Thomas DI	Williams JN	Young S
R1	Nov	14	CHESTER CITY	6-0	Fowler 2, Middleton, Williams 2, Delaney	4220	6	2		3	7	1		11	4	10	8		13	9	5
R2	Dec	5	HEDNESFORD TOWN	3-1	Middleton, Fowler, Williams	5638	6	2	13	3	7	1	12	11	4	10	8		14	9	5
R3	Jan	2	YEOVIL TOWN	1-1	Nugent	12561		2	5	3	6	1	7	12	11	4	10	8	13	9	
rep		12	Yeovil Town	2-1	(aet) Eckhardt, Nugent	8101	6	2	5	3	7	1		12	11	4	10	8	13	9	
R4	Jan	27	Sheffield United	1-4	Nugent	13296	6	2	5	3	7	1	14	12	11	4	10	8		9	

Played at 12 in R1: ND Cadette

F.L. Cup (Worthington Cup)

		Date	Opponent	Score	Scorers	Att	Bonner M	Carpenter R	Delaney MA	Earnshaw R	Fowler JKG	Hallworth IG	Middleton CD	Mitchell GL	Nugent KP	O'Sullivan WStJ	Phillips L(2)	Roberts CJ	Williams JN	Young S
R1/1	Aug	11	Fulham	1-2	Williams	4305	7	6	2		12	1		4	14	11	3	10	9	8	5
R1/2		18	FULHAM	1-2	Eckhardt	4768	7	6	2	13	12		11	1		4	10	14	3	9	8	5

A.M. Cup (Auto Windscreens Shield)

		Date	Opponent	Score	Att	Allen CA	Bonner M	Earnshaw R	Hill DRL	Jarman L	Middleton CD	Nugent KP	Thomas DI	Williams JN	Young S
R1	Dec	9	Millwall	0-2	1858	3	6		2		1	7	5	11	4	8	13	10	9

Played at 12: ND Cadette

F.A.W. Premier Cup

		Date	Opponent	Score	Scorers	Att	Allen CA	Bonner M	Bowen JP	Brazier MR	Carpenter R	Delaney MA	Earnshaw R	Eckhardt JE	Ford MP	Fowler JKG	Hill DRL	Jarman L	Kelly S	Legg A	Middleton CD	Mitchell GL	Nugent KP	O'Sullivan WStJ	Phillips L(2)	Roberts CJ	Saville AV	Thomas DI	Williams JN	Young S
Gp	Sep	14	BANGOR CITY	0-1		1100		13		8		12		3				5	1		7	4			11	2	14	9		10	
Gp	Oct	5	MERTHYR TYDFIL	2-2	Williams, Brazier	1191				8		2	14		5	6			3	1		7	4			11	12	9			10	
Gp		26	Bangor City	4-1	Thomas, Nugnt 2, Middleton	446	8				6	2			3	7	1				12	4	10	11				13	9	14	5
Gp	Nov	17	Merthyr Tydfil	0-0		945	8				6	2		4	3		1	7				11	10	12				13	9	5
Gp	Jan	5	Ryhl	4-0	Thomas 3, Earnshaw	302		7			6	12	13	5			11	8	1	3		4				2	10	9	
Gp	Feb	10	RHYL	3-2	Nugent, O'Sullivan, Middleton	832		7					9					4	1		11		10	8			12		
QF	Mar	2	SWANSEA CITY	3-2	Thomas, Eckhardt, Williams	2333		6						5				7	8	1	3	11	4		2			10	9	
SF1	Apr	27	Wrexham	1-3	Roberts	1509			10		8		13			7		11	5				2	4	12	9			
SF2	May	10	WREXHAM	2-1	Middleton, Nugent	1212			6	9				5		7		12		1	3	11	4	10	8	2		13		

Cadete played on Sep 14 (6, subbed), Oct 5 (13), Feb 10 (2, subbed), Apr 27 (3, subbed)
Played at 14 on Jan 5: Stoker
Also played on Feb 10: Skelly (at 3), Davies (5), Owen (6), P Kelly (13), Harris (14)
Skelly also played Apr 27 (at 6), and Loveless was at 1 in this match

1999/2000

21st in Division Two: Relgated

#		Date	Opponent	Score	Scorers	Att	Boland WJ	Bonner M	Bowen JP	Brayson P	Brazier MR	Carpenter R	Cornforth JM	Earnshaw R	Eckhardt IE	Faerber W	Ford MP	Fowler IKG	Hallworth JG	Hill DRL	Humphreys RJ	Kelly S	Legg A	Low JD	Middleton CD	Nogan K	Nugent KP	Perrett R	Roberts CJ	Schwinkendorf J	Thomas DJ	Vaughan AJ	Young S
1	Aug	7	MILLWALL	1-1	Boland (p)	10193	8	6	10		13				5	2		7		1	11		3				12	4			9		
2		14	Oxford United	3-2	Faerber, Nugent 2	6423	8	6	10		14		13		5	2	3	4		1	11		7				9						
3		20	WREXHAM	1-1	Bowen	11168	8	6	10				12		5	2	3	4		1	11		7				9						
4		28	Luton Town	0-1		5374			10		11	14	8		5	2	3	6		1			7		13		9						4
5		30	SCUNTHORPE UNITED	1-1	Hughes	8006	12		10		11	13	4		5	2	3	6		1			7		8		9						
6	Sep	11	Wycombe Wanderers	1-3	Bowen	4982	8		10		11	6			5	2	3			1			7				9		12				4
7		18	NOTTS COUNTY	2-1	Bowen, Eckhardt	6568	8		10				11	14	5	2	12	6		1			7				9					3	4
8		25	WIGAN ATHLETIC	0-0		7679	8		10				11		5	2		6	1	13			7				9				12	3	4
9		28	Brentford	1-2	Cornforth	5247	8		10				11		5	2	12	6	1	13			7				9					3	4
10	Oct	2	Bury	2-3	Nugent 2	3603	8		10				11		5	2		6		13		1	7				9				12	3	4
11		9	Bristol Rovers	1-1	Hill	7363	8				14	12	6		5	2	3			1	11		7		13		9				10	4	
12		16	OLDHAM ATHLETIC	1-1	Thomas	5650	8				13				5	2		6		1	11		7		12		9	4			10	3	
13		19	STOKE CITY	1-2	Legg	6146	8				12				5	2		6		1	11		7				9	4			10	3	
14		23	Wigan Athletic	0-2		5728	8				14		13		5	2		6		1	11		7				9	4			10	3	12
15	Nov	2	BLACKPOOL	1-1	Nugent	4523			10		8	14			5	2	3	6	1		11		7	12			9		13			4	
16		6	Bournemouth	0-1		4471	14		10		8	6			5	2	3		1		11		7	12			9	13				4	
17		12	CHESTERFIELD	2-1	Bowden 2	4863	12		10		8	6			5	2			1		11		7				4	9				3	
18		23	Colchester United	3-0	Hunphreys 2, Brazier	2512	12	8	10		11	6			5	2			1		9		7				4	13				3	
19		27	GILLINGHAM	1-2	Legg	7608		8	10		11	6			5	2	14		1	12	9		7				4	13				3	
20	Dec	4	Millwall	0-2		9044	12	8	10		11	6			5	2			1	13	9		7				4	14				3	
21		18	Burnley	1-2	Thomas (og)	9888	13	8	10		12	11				5	3	6	1		9		2	7		14			4				
22		26	READING	1-0	Nugent	9791					11			12	5	2		3	1		10			7	8		9	4		6			
23		28	Cambridge United	0-0		4250		6			11				5	2		3	1		10			7	8		9	4					
24	Jan	3	PRESTON NORTH END	0-4		10342		12	14		3	11			5	13		6	1		10			7	8		9	4		2			
25		9	Bristol City	0-0		10570		13	10			6			5			2	1	11			3	7	8		9	4	12				
26		15	OXFORD UNITED	1-1	Nugent	6914	8	6	10			11			5		4		1				3	7			9			2			
27		22	Wrexham	1-2	Low	4350	8	6	10		12	11			5		4		1	14	13		3	7			9			2			
28		30	LUTON TOWN	1-3	Bowen	6185	8	6	13			11			5	12	3		1		10		2	7			9	4					
29	Feb	5	Scunthorpe United	0-0		3614		6			8	11				3	10	1					2	7			9	4					5
30		12	BRENTFORD	1-1	Fowler	5478		6	12		8	11				3	10	1					2	7			9	4					5
31		22	BRISTOL CITY	0-0		6586		6	10		8	11		12		3	7	1					2				9	4					5
32		26	Notts County	1-2	Carpenter	5334	14	6	13		8	11		10	12	3	7	1					2				9	4					5
33	Mar	2	WYCOMBE WANDERERS	2-2	Nugent, Low	5011		6	13		8	11		10		3		1					2	12	7		9	4					5
34		7	BOURNEMOUTH	1-2	Earnshaw	4389	13	6	12		3			10	2			11	1	14				7	8		9	4					5
35		11	Blackpool	2-2	Nugent (p), Bowen	5015		6	12		8			10	2			11	1				3	7			9	4					5
36		17	COLCHESTER UNITED	3-2	Bowen 2, Nugent	5174		6	10		7	8	13			3		11	1	14			2	12			9	4					5
37		21	Chesterfield	1-1	Perrett	2348		6	10		9	8	11		12			3	7	1	13		2				4	14					5
38		25	Reading	1-0	Bowen	10044		8	10						5	2	3	6	1				7				9						
39	Apr	1	BURNLEY	1-2	Cox (og)	6457		8	10	12		11			5	2	3	6	1				7	13			9	4					
40		8	Preston North End	0-0		13794		6	10			11			5	2	3			1			12	7		8	9	4					
41		15	CAMBRIDGE UNITED	0-4		6592		6	10	12		11			5	2	3			1			7			8	9	4					13
42		22	Oldham Athletic	2-1	Bowen, Brayson	4549	8	6	10	7		11			5	2							1	3			9						4
43		24	BURY	0-2		6781	8	6	10	7	13	11			5	2				14			1	3		12	9						4
44		30	Stoke City	1-2	Young	14192	8	6	10	7	11				5	2							1	3			9						4
45	May	2	Gillingham	1-4	Bowen	9176	8	6	10	7	13	11			5	2				12			1	3		14	9						4
46		6	BRISTOL ROVERS	1-1	Young	6655	8	6	10	7					5	2				11			1	3			9						4

Played in games 5 (at 14, one goal) and 7 (at 13): JJ Hughes
Played in game 2 at 12: L Jarman

	Apps	28	31	39	9	30	33	10	6	41	33	26	28	39	23	9	8	42	17	10	6	39	27	8	5	7	14	22
	Goals	1		12	1	1	1	1	1	1	1		1		1	2		2	2			10	1			1		2

L Phillips played in three games at 12: games 4, 23, 46

Two own goals

F.A. Cup

		Date	Opponent	Score	Scorers	Att	Boland WJ	Bonner M	Bowen JP	Brazier MR	Carpenter R	Eckhardt IE	Faerber W	Ford MP	Fowler IKG	Hill DRL	Humphreys RJ	Legg A	Low JD	Middleton CD	Nugent KP	Perrett R	Schwinkendorf J	Young S
R1	Oct	30	Leyton Orient	1-1	Nugent (p)	3109	8		10	12			2	3	6	1	11	7			9	4		5
rep	Nov	9	LEYTON ORIENT	3-1	Brazier, Perrett, Nugent	3095	13		10	8	6	5	2	3		1	11	7			9	4	12	
R2		20	Bury	0-0		2603		8	10	11	6	5	2	3		1		7			4	9		
rep		30	BURY	1-0	(aet) Ford	4511	14	8	10	11	6	5	2	3	12	1		7			4	9	13	
R3	Dec	21	Bolton Wanderers	0-1		5734			10		11	5	12	3	6	1	14	2	7	13	4		8	

F.L. Cup (Worthington Cup)

		Date	Opponent	Score	Scorers	Att	Boland WJ	Bonner M	Bowen JP	Brazier MR	Carpenter R	Cornforth JM	Eckhardt IE	Faerber W	Ford MP	Fowler IKG	Hill DRL	Humphreys RJ	Legg A	Middleton CD	Nugent KP	Young S
R1/1	Aug	10	QUEEN'S PARK RANGERS	1-2	Bowen	5702	8	6	10	14		13	5	2	3	4	1	11	7		9	
R1/2		25	Queen's Park Rangers	2-1	Brazier, Hughes	6185		6	10	11		14	5	2	3		1		7	8	9	4
R2/1	Sep	14	WIMBLEDON	1-1	Nugent (p)	7613	8		10	12	11		5	2	3	6	1		7		9	4
R2/2		21	Wimbledon	1-3	Bowen	2772	8		10	12	14	11	5	2	3	6	1		7		9	4

R1 won 3-2 on penalties a.e.t. Played at 12 in R1/1 L Jarman and in R1/2 L Phillips. Played at 13 in R1/2, R2/1 and R2/2: JJ Hughes

A.M. Cup (Auto Windscreens Shield)

		Date	Opponent	Score	Att	Boland WJ	Bowen JP	Carpenter R	Cornforth JM	Faerber W	Hill DRL	Humphreys RJ	Legg A	Low JD	Middleton CD	Nogan K	Perrett R	Roberts CJ	Thomas DJ	Vaughan AJ	Young S
R1	Dec	7	Northampton Town	0-2	2431	7	9	11	6	2	1	8	10		12	13	4	14		5	3

F.A.W. Premier Cup

		Date	Opponent	Score	Scorers	Att	Boland WJ	Bonner M	Bowen JP	Brayson P	Brazier MR	Carpenter R	Cornforth JM	Earnshaw R	Eckhardt IE	Faerber W	Ford MP	Fowler IKG	Hallworth JG	Hill DRL	Humphreys RJ	Kelly S	Legg A	Low JD	Middleton CD	Nogan K	Nugent KP	Perrett R	Roberts CJ	Schwinkendorf J	Thomas DJ	Vaughan AJ	Young S
Gp	Sep	4	NEWTOWN	2-1	Legg, Bowen	1227	7		14		11	6	8			5				1	13			2							9		4
Gp	Oct	4	BARRY TOWN	2-2	Hill, Thomas	1030					8			11		6			10	1				3				5	7		9		
Gp		12	Newtown	1-0	Carpenter	700					11	8	7							1	3	9	6		4	2		10					
Gp		26	Barry Town	2-0	Roberts	1007		12	13	3		7	8							1			11					10			9	6	5
Gp	Dec	14	MERTHYR TYDFIL	3-1	Fowler 2, Bowen	753	13	7	9		11	8			4	2	6	12	1			10	3	14					5				
Gp	Jan	11	Merthyr Tydfil	0-0		607	7	8	10		11				4			6	1	12			3	2	13		9		14	5			
QF	Feb	15	ABERYSTWYTH TOWN	4-0	Legg, Bonner, Perrett, Nugent	903	12	8	9		11	2					6	7	1	13	14		3				10	5					4
SF1	Apr	11	Caernarfon Town	4-0	Hill, Young, Bowen, Nugent	646			13	8	11	12			5	2		7		6			3	14		9	10						4
SF2		18	CAERNARFON TOWN	4-1	Hill, Nugent 2, Brayson	946	7		9	8					5	2				6		1	3	11			10				12	13	4
F	May	14	Wrexham	0-2		3665	7	6	9	8	12				13	5	2			14		11	1	3			10						4

Also played Sep 4: Skelly (at 3), Cadette (12). Played at 10 on Sep 4, 14 and Oct 26: JJ Hughes
Played on Oct 4 (at 4), Oct 12 (at 5) and Oct 26 (at 4): L Jarman
L Phillips played at 2 on Oct 4 and 2 (subbed) on Oct 26

2000/01   2nd in Division Three: Promoted

Player columns (left→right): Boland WJ, Bonner M, Bowen JP, Brayson P, Brazier MR, Collins JM, Earnshaw R, Eckhardt IE, Evans K, Fortune-West LPO, Fowler JKG, Gabbidon DL, Giles MW, Gordon KG, Greene DM, Hill DRL, Hughes RD, Jordan AJ, Legg A, Low JD, McCulloch S, Nogan K, Nugent KP, Thompson AR, Walton MA, Weston RD, Young S

#	Date	Opponent	Score	Scorers	Att	Bol	Bon	Bow	Bra	Brz	Col	Ear	Eck	Eva	FW	Fow	Gab	Gil	Gor	Gre	Hil	Hug	Jor	Leg	Low	McC	Nog	Nug	Tho	Wal	Wes	You
1	Aug 12	Exeter City	2-1	Brayson, Low	3929	11	12	10	8	3					6					5				7				9	2	1		4
2	19	BLACKPOOL	1-1	Nugent	11019	6	8		10	11						12				5				2	7			9	3	1		4
3	26	Barnet	2-2	Low, Earnshaw	2266	6	8	10	3			14				12	2			5	13			11	7			9		1		4
4	28	SOUTHEND UNITED	2-2	Nugent, Brayson	7628		8	10	3			14	12		6		2			5	13			11	7			9		1		4
5	Sep 2	Rochdale	1-1	Brayson	2824		8	10	3					14	6		2			5	11			7		12	13	9		1		4
6	9	BRIGHTON & HOVE ALB	1-1	Hill	6741		8	10				12		13			2			5	11			3	7	6		9		1		4
7	12	HALIFAX TOWN	4-2	Young, Bowen, Earnshaw, F-West	5087	14		10				8		7	13		2			5	11			3	6			9		1		4
8	16	Scunthorpe United	2-0	Nugent, Earnshaw	3263			10	12	3		8	6	14			2			5	11			7		13		9		1		4
9	23	KIDDERMINSTER HARRIERS	0-0		8003	14		10	12	3		8		6	13		2			5	11			7				9		1		4
10	30	Hull City	0-2		5503	6	13	12	3			8			9		2			5	11			7	10					1		4
11	Oct 14	Leyton Orient	1-2	F-West	4649	8	10	12	3			14	5		9		2				11			7	13	6				1		4
12	17	Carlisle United	2-2	Legg, Nugent	1309	6	14	13	3			8		12	9		2				11			7	5			10		1		4
13	21	MANSFIELD TOWN	2-0	Earnshaw, Brayson	4625	11	10	13				8	5	6	12		2				3			7				9		1		4
14	24	DARLINGTON	2-0	Earnshaw, Evans	5440	11	10	13				8	5	6	12		2				3			7				9		1		4
15	28	Chesterfield	2-2	Evans, Bowen	5378	11	10					8	5	6	12		2				3			7	13			9		1		4
16	Nov 4	YORK CITY	4-0	Bowen 2, Young, Earnshaw	6101	11	10		13			8	5	6	14		2					12		3	7			9		1		4
17	22	LINCOLN CITY	3-2	Earnshaw, Brayson, Barnett (og)	4786	11	10	13				8		6	9		2			5				7			12			1	3	4
18	25	HARTLEPOOL UNITED	3-2	F-West, Bonner, Nogan	6251	11	10	14				8		6	9		2			5				7	12	13				1	3	4
19	Dec 2	Torquay United	4-1	Earnshaw 3, Brayson	2427	11	10	14		13		8		6	9		2							7	5	12				1	3	4
20	16	CHELTENHAM TOWN	3-1	F-West, Earnshaw, Brayson	6764	11	10	14				8	13		9		2							3	7	5			12	1	6	4
21	23	MACCLESFIELD TOWN	2-0	Young, Bowen	8088	11	10	13				8		14	9		2	12						3	7	5				1	6	4
22	26	Plymouth Argyle	1-2	F-West	8543	11		10				8	5	6	9		2	12						3	7	14				1	13	4
23	Jan 1	EXETER CITY	6-1	* see below	9038			10	14	3		8			2				9				12	11	13	5				1	6	4
24	13	Southend United	1-1	F-West	4601			10		3		14		6	9		2		8					11	13	12				1	5	4
25	20	PLYMOUTH ARGYLE	4-1	Earnshaw 2, F-West, McCulloch	9157	8		10	13	3		12			9		2							5	7	14				1	6	4
26	27	Macclesfield Town	5-2	Bowen, Young 2, Earnshaw 2	2376	11		10		3		8		7	9		2						6	5	12	14				1	13	4
27	Feb 2	ROCHDALE	0-0		11912	11		10	8	3				6	9	14	2		13					5	7					1	12	4
28	10	Brighton & Hove Albion	0-1		6922	11		10	8	3				12	9		2		13					5	7		14			1	6	4
29	13	Blackpool	0-1		4301	8		12	10	3				6	13		2		9				5	11	7		14			1	6	4
30	17	SCUNTHORPE UNITED	3-0	Gabbidon 2, Brazier	6057	11		10	8	13					9		2			5				3	7	12	14			1	6	4
31	20	Halifax Town	2-1	Brayson 2	1991	11		10	8						9		2	12		5				3	7					1	6	4
32	25	Kidderminster Harriers	4-2	* see below	4317	11		10	8			13					2			5				3	7		12			1	6	4
33	Mar 2	HULL CITY	2-0	Legg, Edwards (og)	10074	11		10	8	3		13					2	12		5					14					1	6	4
34	6	LEYTON ORIENT	1-1	Earnshaw	9022	11		10	8	3		14		7	9		2	12		5					13					1	6	4
35	10	Lincoln City	0-2		4451	11		13	10	3		8		7	9		2			5										1	6	4
36	13	Shrewsbury Town	4-0	Low, F-West, Boland (p), Bowen	3847	11		10	8	12				6	9		2			5				7	13	14				1	3	4
37	17	CARLISLE UNITED	4-1	Brayson 2, Bowen 2	7130	11		10	8						9		2			5				3	7	12				1	6	4
38	Apr 1	Cheltenham Town	1-3	Young	5139	11		10	14		13	8			9		2	12		5				3	7						6	4
39	4	BARNET	1-0	Low	6209	11		10				8		6	9		2	12	14				13	3	7						5	4
40	7	TORQUAY UNITED	2-1	Brayson, F-West	8210	11	13	10	8			12			14		2	9					5	3	7						6	4
41	14	Darlington	0-2		3863	11		10	8		14	12		13	9		2	6						3	7						5	4
42	16	CHESTERFIELD	3-3	Brayson 2 (1p), Evans	13602	11		10	8	6		12		4	9		2							7							3	5
43	21	York City	3-3	F-West 3	3881	11		10	8	3		13		6	9									7			12				2	5	4
44	24	Mansfield Town	1-2	Bowen	2304	11	13	10	8	3		14		6	9									7			12				2	4
45	28	SHREWSBURY TOWN	3-1	Young 2, Earnshaw	12188	11	12	10	8			14		6	9		2							7	13					1	3	4
46	May 5	Hartlepool United	1-3	Earnshaw	5324			13	12	10		8		6	9		2							11	7	5				14	1	3	4
		Apps				25	24	40	40	26	3	36	8	30	37	5	43	5	10	10	9	12	5	39	36	21	12	14	7	40	28	45
		Goals				1	1	12	15	2		19		3	12		3		1		1			3	4	1	1	4				10

Scorers game 23: Young, Gordon, Legg, Bowen, Brazier, Brayson. Scorers in game 32: Young, Bowen, Gabbidon, Earnshaw.
Played in games 6 (at 14) and 7 (at 12): G Jones
Played in games 44 (at 5) and 45 (5, subbed): R Perrett
JAJ Harper played at 7 (games 23 and 24) and at 11 (game 25). KL Lightbourne played at 9 (subbed) in games 32 and 33 and at 12 in game 35.
CD Muggleton played in 6 games 39 to 44 at 1

F.A. Cup

Rd	Date	Opponent	Score	Scorers	Att	Bol	Bon	Bow	Bra	Brz	Col	Ear	Eck	Eva	FW	Fow	Gab	Gil	Gor	Gre	Hil	Hug	Jor	Leg	Low	McC	Nog	Nug	Tho	Wal	Wes	You
R1	Nov 19	BRISTOL ROVERS	5-1	Earnshaw 3, Evans, F-West	8013			11	10	13	12	14		8	6		9			2				5	3	7				1		4
R2	Dec 9	CHELTENHAM TOWN	3-1	Earnshaw 2 (1p), Evans	9910	14	11	10	13			8		6	9		2							7		5			12	1	3	4
R3	Jan 6	CREWE ALEXANDRA	1-1	Young	13403	13		10		3		8		7	9		2							11	12	5	14			1	6	4
rep	16	Crewe Alexandra	1-2	Earnshaw	5785	11		10	12	3	13	8			9		2							7	14	5				1	6	4

F.L. Cup (Worthington Cup)

Rd	Date	Opponent	Score	Scorers	Att	Bol	Bon	Bow	Bra	Brz	Col	Ear	Eck	Eva	FW	Fow	Gab	Gil	Gor	Gre	Hil	Hug	Jor	Leg	Low	McC	Nog	Nug	Tho	Wal	Wes	You
R1/1	Aug 23	Crystal Palace	1-2	Young	5983	6	8		10	3							2			5				11	7			9		1		4
R1/2	Sep 5	CRYSTAL PALACE	0-0		4904		8					13		7			2			5	11			3		6	10	9		1		

Played in R1/2 at 4, G Jones, at 12: DJ Thomas

A.M. Cup (LDV Vans Trophy)

Rd	Date	Opponent	Score	Scorers	Att	Bol	Bon	Bow	Bra	Brz	Col	Ear	Eck	Eva	FW	Fow	Gab	Gil	Gor	Gre	Hil	Hug	Jor	Leg	Low	McC	Nog	Nug	Tho	Wal	Wes	You
R1	Dec 5	Brighton & Hove Alb.	0-2		2364	8		9	4					12						5	11			2	3	10			7	1	6	

F.A.W. Premier Cup

Rd	Date	Opponent	Score	Scorers	Att	Bol	Bon	Bow	Bra	Brz	Col	Ear	Eck	Eva	FW	Fow	Gab	Gil	Gor	Gre	Hil	Hug	Jor	Leg	Low	McC	Nog	Nug	Tho	Wal	Wes	You
Gp	Oct 3	CWMBRAN TOWN	1-0	Nogan	1503		4	7	10	12				13					6					11	2	3	9					
Gp	10	MERTHYR TYDFIL	2-1	Legg, Hill	1412		4	7	12	3	14		6		9				13	8				11	2	10					1	5
Gp	31	Llanelli	3-2	McCulloch (p), Nogan, F-West	650			9							10					4	7		5			6	11					
Gp	Nov 28	LLANELLI	2-1	Nogan, Davis (og)	1012	8			11		10									5	7					6	9					
Gp	Jan 9	Merthyr Tydfil	2-0	Nogan	630	7					10		6					13	3	4	8					5	9		2			
Gp	30	CWMBRAN TOWN	2-0	David (og), Gordon	1264			11		4		2			7		3	10	5	8							9					
QF	Mar 26	Merthyr Tydfil	0-1		486		7			3	14		5		13		12	9		8				6			11	10	2			

Jan 30 played at Ninian Park and Mar 26 played at Merthyr, by arrangement
Buttery played at 1 on Jan 9 and Jan 30
R Perrett played at 5 (Oct 3), 6 (Jan 30) and 4 (Mar 26)
JAJ Harper played at 11 (subbed) Jan 9
CD Muggleton played at 1 on Mar 26
Subs on Nov 28 were Busby (12), Mapes (13) and Heal (14)

Hallworth played at 1 on Oct 3, Oct 21 and Nov 28
Sheridan played at 8 on Oct 3, Oct 31
Lewis played at 2 on Oct 31, Nov 28 and at 12 on Jan 9
Skelly played at 3 on Oct 31
Hajgato played at 3 on Nov 28 (substituted)
Gray played at 4 on Nov 28

2001/02

4th in Division Two

	Date	Opponent	Result	Scorers	Att	Alexander N	Boland WJ	Bonner M	Bowen JP	Brayson P	Campbell A	Collins JM	Croft G	Earnshaw R	Fortune-West LPO	Gabbidon DL	Gordon D	Gordon KG	Hamilton D(2)	Hughes RD	Jeanne L	Jones G	Kavanagh G	Legg A	Low JD	Maxwell L	Nugent KP	Prior S	Simpkins M	Thorne P	Weston RD	Young S
1	Aug 11	WYCOMBE WANDERERS	1-0	Gabbidon	17403	1				14				10	13	6		9	4	12			8	11	7				3		2	5
2	18	Peterborough United	1-1	Kavanagh	6437	1	12			14				10	13	6		9	4	5			8	11	7				3		2	
3	25	BOURNEMOUTH	2-2	F-West, Earnshaw	13383	1	7			13				10	9	6			4				8	11	12			5	3		2	
4	Sep 8	Reading	2-1	F-West 2	13017	1		11		7				10	9	6			4				8	14	13	12		5	3		2	
5	15	Cambridge United	1-2	Legg	3454	1		11		10					9	6			4		13		8	12		7		5	3	14	2	
6	18	NORTHAMPTON T	2-0	Kavanagh, Brayson (p)	11232	1	12	7		10					13	6			4				8	11				5	3	9	2	
7	22	HUDDERSFIELD T	1-2	Thorne	12280	1	4		12	7					9	6							8	11				5	3	10	2	
8	25	Queen's Park Rangers	1-2	Kavanagh (p)	11667	1	7			13					9	6			4				8	11	12			5	3	10	2	
9	29	BRIGHTON & HOVE ALB	1-1	Brayson	12022	1	11		14	9						6			4		13		8	12	7			5	3	10	2	
10	Oct 9	Bristol City	1-1	Earnshaw (p)	13804	1	4	13	11	7				9		6			12				8					5	3	10	2	
11	12	WIGAN ATHLETIC	2-2	Brayson, Thorne	11072	1	4		11	7				9		6							8	13				5	3	10	2	12
12	21	Swindon Town	3-0	Bowen, Kavanagh, Earnshaw	8373	1	4		7	11				9		6		14					8	12	13			5	3	10	2	
13	24	Port Vale	2-0	Prior, Earnshaw	4552	1	4		7	11				9	14	6		10					8	3	13			5			2	12
14	27	TRANMERE ROVERS	1-1	Bowen	13070	1	4		7	11				9		6		10	12				8	3	13			5			2	
15	Nov 4	Wrexham	3-1	Kavanagh, G Gordon, F-West	5832	1	4		7	11				9	14	6		10	13				8	3				5			2	12
16	7	Bury	0-3		2549	1	4			11		14		10	9	6			7				8	3	12	13		5			2	
17	10	CHESTERFIELD	2-1	F-West, Earnshaw (p)	9516	1	4	12		11				10	9	2			7				8	3	13	14		5				6
18	20	COLCHESTER UNITED	1-1	Collins	8013	1	4	13				11		10	9	2			7				8	3		12		5				6
19	24	Notts County	0-0		6313	1	4	8	7			11		10	14	2	3							12		13	9	5				6
20	Dec 1	OLDHAM ATHLETIC	3-1	Kavanagh 2, Earnshaw	10004	1	4	11	7					10	13	2	3						8			12		5		9		6
21	4	BRENTFORD	3-1	Gabbison, Earnshaw, Thorne	10184	1	4	11	7					9	13	2	3						8			12		5		10		6
22	15	Blackpool	1-1	D Gordon	4880	1	4	11	7	12				10	13	2	3	9					8					5				6
23	19	Stoke City	1-1	D Gordon	14331	1	4	11	7	13				10	14	2	3	9					8					5			12	6
24	26	READING	2-2	Earnshaw 2	16708	1	4	11	7	14				9	13	2	3	10					8	12				5				6
25	29	BRISTOL CITY	1-3	Kavanagh	16149	1	4	11	7	14				9	13	2	3	10					8	12				5				6
26	Jan 12	PETERBOROUGH UTD.	0-2		11301	1	4	11		7				9	14	2		10					8	3	13			5			12	6
27	19	Wycombe Wanderers	1-0	Kavanagh	7165	1	7	11	13	14				9		4		10					8	3	2	12					5	6
28	22	STOKE CITY	2-0	Legg, Gudjonsson (og)	11771	1		11	7	13				9	14	6		10	2				8	3	12						4	5
29	31	Brighton & Hove Albion	0-1		6117	1	4	11	10						9	6			12				8	3	13	7					2	5
30	Feb 5	Bournemouth	3-1	Boland, Kavanagh, Earnshaw	4336	1	4	11	10	13				9		6		14	7				8	3					12		2	5
31	9	SWINDON TOWN	3-0	Earnshaw, Bowen 2	12045	1	11	7	10					9		6		14	2				8	3				12		13	4	5
32	12	Brentford	1-2	Bowen	6718	1	4	11	10	14					9	6							8		7	12			3	13	2	5
33	16	Wigan Athletic	0-4		5487	1	4	11	10	14		13				6							8	3	7			12		9	2	5
34	19	BURY	1-0	Kavanagh (p)	8273	1	4	11	10	12					13	6							8	3	7					9	2	5
35	23	CAMBRIDGE UNITED	2-0	Kavanagh 2 (1p)	10182	1	9	7	11							5							8	6	2	12				10	3	4
36	Mar 2	Northampton Town	2-1	Maxwell, Campbell	5495	1	7			8	11				14	3								5	9	6		12	13	10	2	4
37	5	QUEEN'S PARK RANGERS	1-1	Young	13425	1	8			6	11				13	4								5	9	7		12		10	2	3
38	9	BLACKPOOL	2-2	Campbell 2	11629	1	11			13	10				14	5			12				8	6	2	7		3		9		4
39	16	Oldham Athletic	7-1	* see below	6786	1	11				10	12			9	6						14	7	3				4	13	8	2	5
40	22	WREXHAM	3-2	Gabbison, Young, Thorne	15702	1	4			14	10	12			9	3							7	11				5	13	8	2	6
41	30	Chesterfield	2-0	F-West, Campbell	5442	1	4	13		14	10		12		9	3							7	11				5		8	2	6
42	Apr 1	PORT VALE	1-0	Thorne	15556	1	4	11		13	10		12	14	9	3							7					5		8	2	6
43	6	Colchester United	1-0	Prior	3970	1	4	11			10	12	3	13	9	6							7					5		8	2	
44	9	Huddersfield Town	2-2	Thorne 2	11660	1	4	11					12	10	9	3							7			13		5		8	2	6
45	13	NOTTS COUNTY	2-1	Young, F-West	17105	1	4	11					3	10	9								7					5		8	2	6
46	20	Tranmere Rovers	1-0	Croft	8375	1	4	11	14			12	3	10	9								7			13		5		8	2	6
					Apps	46	42	29	25	34	8	8	6	30	36	44	7	15	19	2	2	1	43	35	22	17	1	37	17	26	37	33
					Goals		1		5	3	7	1	1	11	9	3	2	1					13	2		1		2		8		4

Scorers in game 39: Campbell 3, F-West 2, Young, Thorne

One own goal

Play Offs

	Date	Opponent	Result	Scorers	Att	Alexander N	Boland WJ	Bonner M	Bowen JP	Brayson P	Campbell A	Collins JM	Croft G	Earnshaw R	Fortune-West LPO	Gabbidon DL	Gordon D	Gordon KG	Hamilton D(2)	Hughes RD	Jeanne L	Jones G	Kavanagh G	Legg A	Low JD	Maxwell L	Nugent KP	Prior S	Simpkins M	Thorne P	Weston RD	Young S
SF1	Apr 28	Stoke City	2-1	F-West, Earnshaw	21245	1	4	11			13	12	3	10	9								7					5		8	2	6
SF2	May 1	STOKE CITY	0-2	(aet)	19367	1	4	11	13		14		3	10	9								7			12		5		8	2	6

F.A. Cup

	Date	Opponent	Result	Scorers	Att	Alexander N	Boland WJ	Bonner M	Bowen JP	Brayson P	Campbell A	Collins JM	Croft G	Earnshaw R	Fortune-West LPO	Gabbidon DL	Gordon D	Gordon KG	Hamilton D(2)	Hughes RD	Jeanne L	Jones G	Kavanagh G	Legg A	Low JD	Maxwell L	Nugent KP	Prior S	Simpkins M	Thorne P	Weston RD	Young S
R1	Nov 17	TIVERTON TOWN	3-1	Hamilton, Earnshaw, Brayson	6648	1	4	14		11		13		10	9	6			7				8	3		12		5			2	
R2	Dec 8	PORT VALE	3-0	G Gordon, Earnshaw, F-West	9650	1	4	11	7	13				10	14	2		9					8	3				5			12	6
R3	Jan 6	LEEDS UNITED	2-1	Young, Kavanagh	22009	1	4	11		7				9	12	2		10					8	3				5				6
R4	27	Tranmere Rovers	1-3	Kavanagh (p)	9442	1	7	11	14	10		13			9	6			2				8	3	12						4	5

F.L. Cup (Worthington Cup)

	Date	Opponent	Result	Scorers	Att	Alexander N	Boland WJ	Bonner M	Bowen JP	Brayson P	Campbell A	Collins JM	Croft G	Earnshaw R	Fortune-West LPO	Gabbidon DL	Gordon D	Gordon KG	Hamilton D(2)	Hughes RD	Jeanne L	Jones G	Kavanagh G	Legg A	Low JD	Maxwell L	Nugent KP	Prior S	Simpkins M	Thorne P	Weston RD	Young S
R1	Aug 21	Millwall	1-2	Earnshaw	5516	1	4			7				10	9	6		13		5			8	11	12				3		2	

A.M. Cup (LDV Vans Trophy)

	Date	Opponent	Result	Scorers	Att	Alexander N	Boland WJ	Bonner M	Bowen JP	Brayson P	Campbell A	Collins JM	Croft G	Earnshaw R	Fortune-West LPO	Gabbidon DL	Gordon D	Gordon KG	Hamilton D(2)	Hughes RD	Jeanne L	Jones G	Kavanagh G	Legg A	Low JD	Maxwell L	Nugent KP	Prior S	Simpkins M	Thorne P	Weston RD	Young S
R1	Oct 16	RUSHDEN & DIAMONDS	7-1	G Gordon 5, Bonner, Giles	2052			8				14						9	4	6		12			7	11	10					5
R2	30	PETERBOROUGH U	1-3	Nugent (p)	2584			8				10			9				4	6		2			7	11	14					5

Played at 3: MR Brazier (R1) and S McCulloch (R2, subbed). Played at 1 in R1: Kendall
Played at 13 in R1 and 12 in R2: MW Giles. Played at 2 in R1 and 13 in R2: AR Thompson
Played at 1 in R2: MA Walton

F.A.W. Premier Cup

	Date	Opponent	Result	Scorers	Att	Alexander N	Boland WJ	Bonner M	Bowen JP	Brayson P	Campbell A	Collins JM	Croft G	Earnshaw R	Fortune-West LPO	Gabbidon DL	Gordon D	Gordon KG	Hamilton D(2)	Hughes RD	Jeanne L	Jones G	Kavanagh G	Legg A	Low JD	Maxwell L	Nugent KP	Prior S	Simpkins M	Thorne P	Weston RD	Young S
QF	Jan 16	Newtown	3-0	Jeanne, Collins, Wallis	848							9							4	6	7	5				11						
SF	Mar 12	Wrexham	1-1	Jones	826					10		6			9				7	4		8			2	11		5	3			
F	May 13	SWANSEA CITY	1-0	Kavanagh	6229		4		10			6			9					12	7		8	3		11		5			2	

SF won 4-3 on penalties a.e.t.

Played in QF: Hughes (at 12), Fish (at 13), Kendall (at 1), AR Thompson (at 2)
Played in QF (at 10) and SF (14): Wallis. Played at 3 in QF and 12 in SF: MW Giles
Played at 8 in QF and 13 in SF: K Evans
Played at 1 in SF and F: MA Walton

CARDIFF CITY AGAINST OTHER CLUBS (IN THE FOOTBALL LEAGUE)

	Home:						Away:					Totals:		
	p	w	d	l	f	a	w	d	l	f	a	f	a	% won
Aldershot	24	6	1	5	19	17	5	4	3	12	10	31	27	45.83
Arsenal	30	5	6	4	24	19	3	5	7	14	26	38	45	26.67
Aston Villa	44	12	2	8	30	23	5	3	14	20	39	50	62	38.64
Barnet	16	3	4	1	9	6	0	3	5	7	14	16	20	18.75
Barnsley	26	8	2	3	24	10	4	4	5	14	19	38	29	46.15
Birmingham City	54	16	2	9	44	30	4	8	15	23	42	67	72	37.04
Blackburn Rovers	54	14	7	6	48	29	4	6	17	26	49	74	78	33.33
Blackpool	56	7	12	9	37	41	3	4	21	20	60	57	101	17.86
Bolton Wanderers	64	15	5	12	37	39	6	6	20	25	61	62	100	32.81
Bournemouth	30	8	5	2	29	13	3	3	9	21	31	50	44	36.67
Bradford City	12	2	2	2	11	10	2	0	4	7	11	18	21	33.33
Bradford Park Ave.	10	3	0	2	10	6	1	1	3	4	11	14	17	40.00
Brentford	32	10	5	1	29	14	3	5	8	16	29	45	43	40.62
Brighton & Hove Alb.	48	10	8	6	40	29	6	5	13	26	45	66	74	33.33
Bristol City	60	11	7	12	41	43	7	8	15	26	38	67	81	30.00
Bristol Rovers	50	10	7	8	42	36	3	10	12	27	41	69	77	26.00
Burnley	56	14	8	6	53	32	7	5	16	31	51	84	83	37.50
Bury	54	19	4	4	57	22	6	4	17	29	60	86	82	46.30
Cambridge United	30	7	4	4	27	20	2	5	8	12	24	39	44	30.00
Carlisle Uunited	38	14	5	0	42	17	6	6	7	25	30	67	47	52.63
Charlton Athletic	58	14	5	10	51	38	4	9	16	37	65	88	103	31.03
Chelsea	34	6	6	5	29	22	5	2	10	15	30	44	52	32.35
Cheltenham Town	2	1	0	0	3	1	0	0	1	1	3	4	4	50.00
Chester City	16	4	3	1	8	4	2	4	2	6	8	14	12	37.50
Chesterfield	28	8	3	3	26	18	6	6	2	22	17	48	35	50.00
Colchester Utd.	18	4	1	4	12	12	3	1	5	14	14	26	26	38.89
Coventry City	28	7	4	3	30	18	3	0	11	16	33	46	51	35.71
Crewe Alexandra	12	1	4	1	6	5	1	4	1	4	5	10	10	16.67
Crystal Palace	42	5	8	8	25	29	2	5	14	18	45	43	74	16.67
Darlington	18	4	2	3	10	7	2	2	5	6	15	16	22	33.33
Derby Count	36	11	5	2	28	18	7	4	7	30	34	58	52	50.00
Doncaster Rovers	24	7	2	3	24	12	4	7	1	15	11	39	23	45.83
Everton	30	9	3	3	22	15	3	5	7	13	28	35	43	40.00
Exeter City	36	12	3	3	45	18	5	4	9	18	26	63	44	47.22
Fulham	48	11	4	9	31	30	9	3	12	41	47	72	77	41.67
Gateshead	2	1	0	0	1	0	1	0	0	1	0	2	0	100.00
Gillingham	32	11	1	4	30	13	3	5	8	13	29	43	42	43.75
Grimsby Town	24	8	2	2	29	17	4	4	4	13	18	42	35	50.00
Halifax Town	16	4	4	0	12	4	5	3	0	11	6	23	10	56.25
Hartlepool Utd.	18	6	3	0	20	7	3	2	4	10	14	30	21	50.00
Hereford United	18	7	0	2	17	8	3	5	1	15	13	32	21	55.56
Huddersfield Town	62	12	11	8	44	31	4	7	20	21	61	65	92	25.81
Hull City	46	10	5	8	40	29	4	12	7	20	31	60	60	30.43
Ipswich Town	20	4	3	3	12	14	2	4	4	12	16	24	30	30.00
Kidderminster H.	2	0	1	0	0	0	1	0	0	4	2	4	2	50.00
Leeds United	30	10	4	1	22	7	1	5	9	5	24	27	31	36.67
Leicester City	36	9	4	5	34	23	4	3	11	15	34	49	57	36.11
Leyton Orient	76	22	11	5	65	26	7	13	18	38	74	103	100	38.16
Lincoln City	28	8	2	4	28	18	4	3	7	15	19	43	37	42.86
Liverpool	26	9	2	2	33	12	7	0	6	18	23	51	35	61.54
Luton Town	50	14	6	5	41	30	3	8	14	26	67	67	97	34.00
Macclesfield Town	4	1	0	1	3	2	1	0	1	5	3	8	5	50.00
Maidstone United	4	0	1	1	0	5	0	1	1	1	4	1	9	0.00
Manchester City	38	6	8	5	35	31	1	8	10	24	46	59	77	18.42
Manchester Utd.	26	4	1	8	18	22	2	6	5	19	28	37	50	23.08
Mansfield Town	28	10	3	1	31	9	5	4	5	22	24	53	33	53.57

	Home:						Away:					Totals:		
	p	w	d	l	f	a	w	d	l	f	a	f	a	% won
Middlesbrough	44	16	3	3	46	22	5	7	10	21	35	67	57	47.73
Millwall	44	10	8	4	42	24	6	5	11	25	34	67	58	36.36
Newcastle Utd.	46	12	9	2	43	26	3	3	17	15	52	58	78	32.61
Newport County	20	4	2	4	19	15	3	3	4	12	19	31	34	35.00
Northampton Town	42	13	4	4	47	23	3	4	14	10	34	57	57	38.10
Norwich City	32	8	2	6	28	22	1	3	12	15	33	43	55	28.12
Nottingham Forest	30	9	4	2	31	17	5	2	8	18	23	49	40	46.67
Notts County	54	13	5	9	41	38	6	6	15	30	48	71	86	35.19
Oldham Athletic	30	8	3	4	24	13	4	2	9	25	31	49	44	40.00
Oxford United	22	5	4	2	20	8	2	2	7	11	19	31	27	31.82
Peterborough Utd.	16	1	3	4	8	11	1	2	5	8	15	16	26	12.50
Plymouth Argyle	38	11	2	6	36	16	2	10	7	22	39	58	55	34.21
Port Vale	16	4	1	3	12	11	2	3	3	11	13	23	24	37.50
Portsmouth	48	9	6	9	30	30	6	7	11	23	37	53	67	31.25
Preston North End	70	17	8	10	56	45	10	8	17	40	90	96	135	38.57
QPR	44	14	5	3	41	25	4	3	15	18	55	59	80	40.91
Reading	36	9	4	5	36	19	4	6	8	15	32	51	51	36.11
Rochdale	20	5	3	2	10	7	1	7	2	9	11	19	18	30.00
Rotherham United	40	8	7	5	29	26	1	2	17	17	48	46	74	22.50
Scarborough	16	5	3	0	10	4	3	3	2	11	10	21	14	50.00
Scunthorpe United	30	6	6	3	22	11	8	4	3	24	13	46	24	46.67
Sheffield United	54	12	10	5	43	27	7	4	16	28	58	71	85	35.19
Sheffield Wednesday	48	14	6	4	44	25	4	5	15	27	52	71	77	37.50
Shrewsbury Town	24	6	4	2	20	10	4	3	5	16	14	36	24	41.67
Southampton	28	7	4	3	30	22	2	5	7	20	28	50	50	32.14
Southend United	30	9	4	2	31	13	4	5	6	16	26	47	39	43.33
Stockport County	12	2	4	0	11	6	2	2	2	10	11	21	17	33.33
Stoke City	26	7	2	4	26	19	2	4	7	6	16	32	35	34.62
Sunderland	50	15	4	6	50	27	6	9	10	36	40	86	67	42.00
Swansea City	48	12	8	4	33	19	4	6	14	26	44	59	63	33.33
Swindon Town	36	9	5	4	31	16	3	3	12	29	49	60	65	33.33
Thames	2	1	0	0	9	2	1	0	0	2	1	11	3	100.00
Torquay United	36	10	5	3	37	21	3	4	11	17	29	54	50	36.11
Tottenham Hotspur	40	5	5	10	14	24	5	5	10	23	36	37	60	25.00
Tranmere Rovers	8	1	2	1	4	3	2	0	2	3	5	7	8	37.50
Walsall	24	7	4	1	23	13	5	2	5	20	23	43	36	50.00
Watford	30	10	3	2	27	14	3	3	9	13	29	40	43	43.33
West Bromwich Alb.	38	8	4	7	32	32	5	3	11	23	40	55	72	34.21
West Ham Utd.	36	6	5	7	19	22	1	8	9	15	32	34	54	19.44
Wigan Athletic	16	3	4	1	14	10	1	2	5	3	13	17	23	25.00
Wimbledon	2	0	0	1	1	3	0	0	1	1	2	2	5	0.00
Wolves	36	4	7	7	22	39	4	3	11	21	42	43	81	22.22
Wrexham	30	9	4	2	27	11	7	2	6	20	20	47	31	53.33
Wycombe Wan.	6	2	1	0	5	2	1	0	2	3	6	8	8	50.00
York City	16	5	2	1	18	9	2	3	3	11	16	29	25	43.75

TOTALS TO END 2001/02:

	p	w	d	l	f	a	w	d	l	f	a	f	a	pts
	3218	805	410	394	2720	1813	359	417	833	1718	2931	4438	4744	3489
Comprising:														
Old 1st	630	155	76	84	540	378	69	78	168	325	615	865	993	602
New 1st/Old 2nd	1344	347	160	165	1131	763	133	180	359	707	1231	1838	1994	1336
New 2nd/Old 3rd	414	86	66	55	291	230	53	53	101	234	347	525	577	514
New 3rd/Old 4th	452	110	71	45	345	205	71	67	88	255	307	600	512	681
Div 3 (S)	378	107	37	45	413	237	33	39	117	197	431	610	668	356

Name		D.O.B	Place of Birth	Died	First Season	Last Season	Int	Previous Club	Next Club	Appearances Lge	FAC	FLC	Oth.	Goals Lge	FAC	FLC	Oth.
Abraham GJ	Gareth	13/02/1969	Aberfan		1987	1992		YTS	Hereford Utd.	87	8	7	7	4	0	0	1
Abram RL	Lol	14/05/1889	Banks	1966	1920			Chelsea	Southport	1	0	0	0	0	0	0	0
Adams DS	Darren	12/01/1974	Bromley		1993	1995		Donson Furness	Aldershot Town	33	2	3	5	4	0	0	2
Adams RJLM	Bob	28/02/1917	Coleford	1970	1932	1933		Chepstow	Bristol Rovers	11	2	0	0	0	0	0	0
Adlam LW	Les	24/06/1897	Guildford		1933			QPR		4	0	0	0	0	0	0	0
Aitken FMcK	Fergie	05/06/1896	Glasgow	1989	1922			Blackburn Rovers	Birmingham City	2	0	0	0	0	0	0	0
Aizlewood M	Mark	01/10/1959	Newport		1993	1994	w	Bristol City	Methyr Town	39	7	1	5	3	0	0	0
Alexander N	Neil	10/03/1978	Edinburgh		2001			Livingston		46	4	1	2	0	0	0	0
Allan AB	Sandy	29/10/1947	Forfar		1967	1969		Rhyl	Bristol Rovers	9	1	0	2	1	0	0	3
Allchurch IJ	Ivor	16/10/1929	Swansea	1997	1962	1964	w	Newcastle United	Swansea Town	103	2	5	2	39	0	0	0
Allen BW	Bryn	28/03/1921	Gilfach Goch		1946	1947	w	Swansea Town	Newport County	58	6	0	0	21	2	0	0
					1948			Newport County	Reading								
Allen CA	Chris	18/11/1972	Oxford		1998			Nottm Forest (loan)		4	0	0	1	0	0	0	0
Alston A	Adrian	06/02/1949	Preston		1975	1976	au	Luton Town	Tampa Bay Rowdies	48	4	3	4	16	4	1	1
Anderson F	Frank 'Ernie'	1896	Scotland		1921			Stockport Co.	Aberdare Ath.	1	0	0	0	0	0	0	0
Anderson RS	Reginald	1914	London	1942	1938			Dulwich Hamlet	Killed in action	2	0	0	0	1	0	0	0
Anderson WJ	Willie	24/01/1947	Liverpool		1972	1976		Aston Villa	Portland Timbers	126	6	5	5	12	0	0	0
Andrews G	George	23/04/1942	Dudley		1965	1966		Luton Town	Southport	43	0	5	0	21	0	4	0
Ashton RW	Roger	16/08/1921	Llanidloes	1985	1947			Wrexham	Bath City	1	0	0	0	0	0	0	0
Attley BR	Brian	27/08/1955	Cardiff		1974	1978		App.	Swansea City	79	5	7	3	1	0	0	0
Attley L	Len	1910	Cardiff		1934	1935		Local	Yeovil & Petters	12	0	0	0	2	0	0	0
Baddeley LM	Lee	12/07/1974	Cardiff		1990	1996		YTS	Exeter City	133	8	6	17	1	0	0	0
Baillie J	Jim	08/06/1902	Hamilton		1926	1927		Wishaw	Dundee United	5	0	0	0	0	0	0	0
Baird IJ	Ian	01/04/1964	Rotherham		1983			Southampton (loan)		12	0	0	0	6	0	0	0
Baker CW	Colin	18/12/1934	Cardiff		1953	1965	w	Cardiff Nomads	Lottery manager	298	17	12	1	18	0	0	0
Baker WG	Billy	03/10/1920	Penrhiwceiber		1938	1954	w	Troedyrhiw	Ipswich Town	292	16	0	0	5	1	0	0
Ballsom WG	George	30/10/1912	Trealaw	1983	1938			Gillingham		34	6	0	1	0	0	0	0
Bannon PA	Paul	15/11/1956	Dublin		1984			Bristol Rovers (loan)		4	0	0	0	0	0	0	0
Barber K	Keith	21/09/1947	Luton		1978			Swansea City (loan)		2	0	0	0	0	0	0	0
Barnard LK	Leigh	29/10/1958	Worsley		1989	1990		Swindon Town	Swindon Comm Officer	63	7	4	3	9	0	0	1
Barnett A	Albert		Altrincham		1920	1921		Glossop	Aberdare Ath.	17	8	0	0	1	0	0	0
Bartlett JW	John		South Wales		1933			Local		1	0	0	0	0	0	0	0
Bartlett KF	Kevin	12/10/1962	Portsmouth		1986	1988		Fareham Town	West Bromwich A.	82	8	4	11	25	3	0	0
Bassett WEG	Billy	08/06/1912	Brithdir	1977	1934	1938		Aberaman	Crystal Palace	154	14	0	2	2	0	0	0
Bater PT	Phil	26/10/1955	Cardiff		1987	1988		Brentford	Gloucester City	76	2	1	8	0	0	0	0
Beadles GH	Harry	28/09/1897	Llanllwchaiarn	1958	1924	1925	w	Liverpool	Sheffield Wed.	31	8	0	0	14	2	0	0
Beare G	George	02/10/1885	Southampton	1970	1920			Everton	Bristol City	23	11	0	0	3	3	0	0
Beech C	Chris	05/11/1975	Congleton		1997			Manchester City	Rotherham Utd.	45	6	2	0	1	0	0	0
Bell G	Gary	04/04/1947	Stourbridge		1966	1973		Lower Gornal Ath.	Newport County	223	17	9	16	10	0	2	0
Bellamy G	Gary	04/07/1962	Worksop		1991			Wolves (loan)		9	0	0	0	0	0	0	0
Bennett DA	Dave	11/07/1959	Manchester		1981	1982		Manchester City	Coventry City	77	4	4	0	18	0	1	0
Bennett GE	Gary	04/12/1961	Manchester		1981	1983		Manchester City	Sunderland	87	3	6	0	11	0	1	0
Bennett MR	Mickey	27/07/1969	Camberwell		1996			Millwall	Cambridge City	14	2	2	1	1	0	0	0
Best TH	Tommy	23/12/1920	Milford Haven		1948	1949		Chester	QPR	28	0	0	0	11	0	0	0
Bird A	Tony	01/09/1974	Cardiff		1992	1995		YTS	Barry Town	75	6	8	11	13	1	2	2
Bird DWC	Don 'Dickie'	05/01/1908	Llandrindod Wells	1987	1929	1930		Llandridod Wells	Bury	13	0	0	0	4	0	0	0
Bird RP	Ronnie	27/12/1941	Erdington		1965	1970		Bury	Crewe Alexandra	108	8	4	8	25	1	0	2
Bishop RJ	Ray	24/11/1955	Hengoed		1977	1980		Cheltenham T	Newport County	101	4	9	4	26	0	3	0
Blackburn GF	George	08/03/1899	Willesden Green	1957	1926	1930	e	Aston Villa	Mansfield Town	115	3	0	1	1	0	0	0
Blair D	Dougie	26/06/1921	Ecclesfield		1947	1953		Blackpool	Hereford Utd.	204	12	0	0	30	0	0	0
Blair J	Jimmy	11/05/1888	Glenboig	1964	1920	1925	s	Sheffield Wed.	Bournemouth	177	31	0	0	0	0	0	0
Blake NA	Nathan	27/01/1972	Cardiff		1989	1993	w	Chelsea	Sheffield Utd.	131	10	8	15	35	4	0	1
Blakemore RG	Ralph				1930				Bradford City	1	0	0	0	0	0	0	0
Bland WH	Harry	12/01/1898	Leeds		1934			Plymouth Argyle		8	0	0	0	0	0	0	0
Blenkinsop E	Ernie	20/04/1902	Cudworth	1969	1937		e	Liverpool	Buxton	10	1	0	0	0	0	0	0
Bodin PJ	Paul	13/09/1964	Cardiff		1982	1984	w	Newport County	Bath City	75	4	11	0	4	0	0	0
Boland WJ	Willie	06/08/1975	Ennis		1999	2001		Coventry City		95	10	5	3	3	0	0	0
Bolesan M	Mirko	06/05/1975	Genoa, Italy		1995			Sestrese		1	0	0	0	0	0	0	0
Bonner M	Mark	07/06/1974	Ormskirk		1998	2001		Blackpool		109	8	6	6	2	0	0	1
Bonson J	Joe	19/06/1936	Barnsley	1991	1957	1959		Wolves	Scunthorpe Utd.	72	7	0	0	36	4	0	0
Bowen JP	Jason	24/08/1972	Merthyr Tydfil		1998	2001	w	Reading		121	12	4	2	31	0	2	0
Boyle TDJ	Terry	29/10/1958	Ammanford		1986	1988	w	Newport County	Swansea City	128	10	10	10	7	0	2	0
Brack AHB	Alistair	27/01/1940	Aberdeen		1962	1963			Worcester City	1	0	1	0	0	0	0	0
Brayson P	Paul	16/09/1977	Newcastle		1999	2001		Reading		83	7	2	1	19	1	0	0
Brazier MR	Matt	02/07/1976	Whipps Cross		1998			Fulham (loan)		67	6	5	2	5	1	0	0
					1999	2001		Fulham									
Brazil DM	Derek	14/12/1968	Dublin		1992	1995		Manchester Utd.	Newport AFC	115	9	8	9	1	0	0	0
Brignull PA	Phil	02/10/1960	Stratford		1985	1986		Bournemouth	Newport County	44	6	4	2	0	0	0	0
Brittan RC	Charlie	07/08/1887	Isle of Wight	1949	1920	1922		Tottenham H		75	10	0	0	0	0	0	0
Brock KS	Kevin	09/09/1962	Middleton Stoney		1993			Newcastle Utd (loan)		14	0	0	0	2	0	0	0
Brown AR	Andrew	20/02/1915	Coatbridge	1973	1936	1937		Cumbernauld Thistle	Torquay United	2	0	0	1	0	0	0	0
Brown JG	Jim	11/05/1952	Coatbridge		1982		s	Chicago Sting	Chesterfield	3	0	0	0	0	0	0	0
Brown RH	Bobby	02/05/1940	Streatham		1966	1967		Northampton Town	Retired - injury	50	4	2	3	23	0	2	2
Brown TH	Tommy	1896	Glasgow		1921			Brighton & Hove A.	Bristol City	2	0	0	0	0	0	0	0
Buchanan J	John	19/09/1951	Dingwall		1974	1981		Northampton Town	Northampton Town	231	11	15	7	54	2	5	0
Burke M	Marshall	26/03/1959	Glasgow		1983			Lincoln City (loan)		3	1	0	0	0	0	0	0
Burns ME	Micky	21/12/1946	Preston		1978			Newcastle United	Middlesbrough	6	0	2	1	0	0	0	0
Burton DJ	Deon	25/10/1976	Reading		1996		ja	Portsmouth (loan)		5	0	0	0	2	0	0	0
Byrne G	Gerry	10/04/1957	Glasgow		1977	1978		App.	Weymouth	15	0	1	2	0	0	0	0
Cadette ND	Nathan	06/01/1980	Cardiff		1997	1998		YTS	Inter Cardiff	4	1	0	1	0	0	0	0
Calder R	Bob	1909	Glasgow		1933			Glasgow Rangers	Bradford City	37	2	0	1	0	0	0	0
Callan D	Dennis	27/07/1932	Merthyr Tydfil		1955			Troedyrhiw	Exeter City	1	0	0	0	0	0	0	0
Campbell A	Andy	18/04/1979	Middlesbrough		2001			Middlesbrough		8	0	0	2	7	0	0	0

Name		D.O.B	Place of Birth	Died	First Season	Last Season	Int	Previous Club	Next Club	Appearances				Goals			
										Lge	FAC	FLC	Oth.	Lge	FAC	FLC	Oth.
Campbell AJ	Alan	21/01/1948	Arbroath		1975	1980		Birmingham City	Carlisle Utd.	167	4	14	8	2	0	0	0
Campbell H	Hugh		Glasgow		1936			Clapton Orient	Ballymena	1	0	0	0	0	0	0	0
Canning LD	Danny	21/02/1926	Pontypridd		1946	1947		Abercynon	Swansea Town	80	2	0	0	0	0	0	0
Carless EF	Ernie	09/09/1912	Barry	1987	1932			Wolves	Barry Town	1	0	0	0	0	0	0	0
Carlin W	Willie	06/10/1940	Liverpool		1973			Notts County	Retired	22	0	0	0	1	0	0	0
Carpenter R	Richard	30/09/1972	Sheerness		1998	1999		Fulham	Brighton & Hove A.	75	9	4	1	2	0	0	0
Carss AJ	Tony	31/03/1976	Alnwick		1997			Darlington	Chesterfield	41	6	2	1	1	0	0	0
Carver DF	David	16/04/1944	Wickersley		1965	1972		Rotherham Utd.	Hereford Utd.	210	14	6	13	1	1	0	0
Carver JW	John	16/01/1965	Newcastle		1985			Newcastle United	Newc. Blue Star	13	0	2	0	0	0	0	0
Cashmore AA	Arthur	30/10/1893	Birmingham		1920	1921		Darlaston	Notts County	30	7	0	0	10	2	0	0
Cassidy J	Joe	10/08/1896	Calder	1949	1925		s	Bolton Wanderers	Dundee	24	3	0	0	6	1	0	0
Castle FR	Fred	10/04/1902	Pen-y-graig	1982	1926	1927		Mid Rhondda	Chesterfield	3	0	0	0	0	0	0	0
Chandler JG	Jeff	19/06/1959	Hammersmith		1989	1990	r	Bolton Wanderers		25	3	2	1	0	0	0	0
Charles CM	Clive	03/10/1951	Bow		1973	1977		West Ham Utd.	Portland Timbers	77	4	7	5	5	0	0	0
Charles M	Mel	14/05/1935	Swansea		1961	1964	w	Arsenal	Porthmadog	79	2	3	2	25	0	1	1
Charles WJ	John	27/12/1931	Swansea		1963	1965	w	Roma	Hereford Utd.	68	1	3	7	18	0	0	0
Chisholm KMcT	Ken	12/04/1925	Glasgow	1990	1951	1953		Coventry City	Sunderland	62	1	0	0	33	0	0	0
Christie DHM	Derrick	15/03/1957	Bletchley		1985			Reading	Peterborough Utd.	19	1	0	1	2	0	0	0
Clark BD	Brian	13/01/1943	Bristol		1967 1975	1972		Huddersfield T Millwall	Bournemouth Newport County	204	13	9	14	79	2	3	7
Clark JW	Joe	15/02/1890	Willington Quay	1960	1920	1921		Hebburn Argyle	Aberaman	14	3	0	0	0	0	0	0
Clarke MMcQ	Malcolm	29/06/1944	Clydebank		1967	1968		Leicester City	Bristol City	46	1	2	8	3	0	0	1
Clarke RJ	Roy	01/06/1925	Newport		1946		w	Juniors	Manchester City	39	3	0	0	10	0	0	0
Clennell J	Joe	19/02/1889	New Silksworth	1965	1921	1924		Everton	Stoke City	118	17	0	0	36	5	0	0
Coldicott S	Stacy	29/04/1974	Redditch		1996			West Brom. A. (loan)		6	0	0	0	0	0	0	0
Coldrick GG	Graham	06/11/1945	Newport		1963	1969		App.	Newport County	96	7	9	6	2	0	1	0
Collins J	Jack		London		1932			Liverpool	Millwall	7	0	0	0	0	0	0	0
Collins JH	Jimmy	30/01/1911	Bermondsey	1983	1937	1938		Liverpool	Aberaman	76	10	0	3	41	4	0	1
Collins JM	James	23/08/1983	Newport		2000	2001		YTS		11	4	0	4	1	0	0	0
Collins WE	Elvet	16/10/1902	Bedwellty	1977	1923	1926	w	Rhymney Town	Clapton Orient	12	0	0	0	0	0	0	0
Corkhill WG	Billy	23/04/1910	Belfast	1978	1938			Notts County	Notts County	23	0	0	1	0	0	0	0
Corner DE	David	15/05/1966	Sunderland		1985			Sunderland (loan)		6	0	0	0	0	0	0	0
Cornforth JM	John	07/10/1967	Whitley Bay		1999		w	Wycombe Wan.	Scunthorpe Utd.	10	0	3	0	1	0	0	0
Cornwell JA	John	13/10/1964	Bethnal Green		1993			Southend Utd. (loan)		5	0	1	0	2	0	0	0
Couch A	Alan	15/03/1953	Neath		1971	1972		Juniors	Barry Town	11	1	0	0	0	0	0	0
Court HJ	Jack	13/06/1917	Tir Phil		1938			Llanbradach	Dundee	1	0	0	0	0	0	0	0
Crawford A	Andy	30/01/1959	Filey		1983			Bournemouth	Middlesbrough	6	0	3	0	1	0	2	0
Cribb SR	Stan	11/05/1905	Gosport	1989	1932			QPR	Gosport Boro (mgr)	27	2	0	0	11	0	0	0
Croft G	Gary	17/02/1974	Burton on Trent		2001			Ipswich T (loan)		6	0	0	2	1	0	0	0
Crowe GM	Glen	25/12/1972	Dublin		1997			Wolves	Wolves	8	0	0	1	1	0	0	0
Curtis AT	Alan	16/04/1954	Ton Pentre		1986	1989	w	Southampton	Swansea City	125	8	12	9	10	0	2	1
Curtis ER	Ernie	10/06/1907	Cardiff	1992	1926 1933	1927	w	Cadiff Corries Birmingham	Birmingham Coventry City	62	6	0	2	14	1	0	0
Curtis MW	Wayne	22/02/1967	Neath		1985			Swansea City	Brecon Corries	27	0	0	1	2	0	0	0
Dale C	Carl	29/04/1966	Colwyn Bay		1991	1997		Chester City	Yeovil Town	212	14	11	16	71	6	5	12
Daniel RC	Ray	10/12/1964	Luton		1989	1990		Hull City	Portsmouth	56	5	5	1	1	0	0	0
Daniel WR	Ray	02/11/1928	Swansea	1997	1957		w	Sunderland	Swansea City	6	0	0	0	0	0	0	0
Davies AB	Bryn		Cardiff		1935	1937		Army	Ipswich Town	9	1	0	0	0	0	0	0
Davies BE	Ben		Middlesbrough	1970	1920	1922		Middlesbrough	Leicester City	73	16	0	0	0	0	0	0
Davies DL	Lyn	29/09/1947	Neath		1965	1966		App.	Llanelli	16	2	1	0	0	0	0	0
Davies F	Fred	22/08/1939	Liverpool		1967	1969		Wolves	Bournemouth	98	5	2	6	0	0	0	0
Davies GM	Gareth	11/12/1973	Hereford		1996			Crystal Palace (loan)		6	0	0	0	2	0	0	0
Davies GR	Gareth	06/10/1959	Cardiff		1986			Sully		2	1	0	2	0	0	0	0
Davies JG	John	18/11/1959	Llandyssil		1978	1979		App.	Hull City	7	0	0	2	0	0	0	0
Davies LS	Len	28/04/1899	Splott	1945	1920	1930	w	Victoria Athletic	Thames	305	33	0	0	128	19	0	1
Davies PA	Paul	09/10/1960	Kidderminster		1979	1980		Oldswinford	Trowbridge Town	2	0	0	0	0	0	0	0
Davies RT	Ron	21/09/1932	Merthyr Tydfil		1955	1957		Merthyr Tydfil	Southampton	32	0	0	0	3	0	0	0
Davies SC	Stan	24/03/1898	Chirk	1972	1928		w	Birmingham	Rotherham Utd.	14	0	0	0	2	0	0	0
Davies W	Willie	16/02/1900	Troedyrhiwfuwch	1953	1924	1927	w	Swansea Town	Notts County	87	9	0	0	17	2	0	0
Davies WJ	Jim		South Wales		1938			Troedyrhiw		1	0	0	0	0	0	0	0
Dean N	Norman	13/09/1944	Corby		1966	1968		Southampton	Barnsley	21	0	1	4	3	0	0	3
Deighton J	Jack				1935			Everton		18	1	0	0	0	0	0	0
Delaney MA	Mark	13/05/1976	Haverfordwest		1998		w		Aston Villa	28	5	2	0	0	1	0	0
De Mange KJPP	Ken	03/09/1964	Dublin		1990		r	Liverpool (loan)		15	0	0	0	0	0	0	0
Derrett SC	Steve	16/10/1947	Cardiff		1967	1971	w	App.	Carlisle Utd.	66	5	1	6	1	0	0	0
Diamond JJ	Jack	30/10/1910	Middlesbrough	1961	1935			Barnsley	Bury	18	1	0	1	9	0	0	1
Dibble AG	Andy	08/05/1965	Cwmbran		1981	1983	w	App.	Luton Town	62	4	4	0	0	0	0	0
Dixon CH	Cecil	28/03/1935	Trowbridge		1954	1956		Trowbridge Town	Newport County	21	0	0	0	1	0	0	0
Dobbs GF	Gerald	24/01/1971	Lambeth		1995			Wimbledon (loan)		3	0	1	0	0	0	0	0
Donnelly P	Peter	22/09/1936	Hull		1960	1961		Scunthorpe Utd.	Swansea Town	31	0	1	0	8	0	1	0
Downing KG	Keith	23/07/1965	Oldbury		1995			Stoke City	Hereford Utd.	4	0	1	0	0	0	0	0
Dudley FE	Frank	09/05/1925	Southend-on-Sea		1953			Southampton	Brentford	5	0	0	0	1	0	0	0
Durban WA	Alan	07/07/1941	Bridgend		1959	1962	w	Juniors	Derby County	52	1	5	0	9	0	2	0
Durkan J	Jack	14/07/1915	Bannockburn		1933				Bristol Rovers	6	0	0	0	0	0	0	0
Durrell JT	Joe	15/03/1953	Stepney		1975			Bristol City (loan)		2	0	1	0	0	0	0	0
Duthie JF	John	07/01/1903	Fraserburgh	1969	1933			Aberdeen	Caerau	13	1	0	1	0	0	0	0
Dwyer PJ	Phil	28/10/1953	Cardiff		1972	1984	w	Juniors	South Wales Police	471	23	28	9	41	0	2	2
Eadie J	Jim	04/02/1947	Alexandria		1969	1971		Kirkintilloch Rob Roy	Bristol Rovers	43	2	2	6	0	0	0	0
Earnshaw R	Robert	06/04/1981	Zambia		1997	2001		YTS		82	8	3	3	32	8	1	1
Eckhardt JE	Jeff	07/10/1965	Sheffield		1996	2000		Stockport Co.		140	12	7	5	14	1	1	1
Edgley BK	Brian	26/08/1937	Shrewsbury		1960			Shrewsbury Town	Brentford	10	0	0	0	1	0	0	0
Edwards G	George	02/12/1920	Treherbert		1948	1954	w	Birmingham City	Retired	195	14	0	0	36	1	0	0
Edwards LT	Trevor	24/01/1937	Rhondda		1960	1963	w	Charlton Ath.	Hakoah (Aust.)	73	2	3	1	3	0	1	0

Name		D.O.B	Place of Birth	Died	First Season	Last Season	Int	Previous Club	Next Club	Appearances				Goals			
										Lge	FAC	FLC	Oth.	Lge	FAC	FLC	Oth.
Egan H	Harry	23/02/1912	Tibshelf	1979	1938			Aldershot	Retired	17	1	0	0	9	0	0	0
Elliott AR	Tony	30/11/1969	Nuneaton		1996	1997		Carlisle Utd.	Scarborough	39	2	2	1	0	0	0	0
Elliott RM	Mark	20/03/1959	Rhondda		1979			Brighton & Hove A.	Ton Pentre	7	0	1	0	0	0	0	0
Ellis KD	Keith	06/11/1935	Sheffield		1964			Scunthorpe Utd.	Lincoln City	22	1	0	0	9	0	0	0
Elsey KW	Karl	20/11/1958	Swansea		1983	1984		Newport County	Gillingham	59	2	4	0	5	0	0	0
Emmerson GAH	George	15/05/1906	Bishop Auckland	1966	1930	1932		Middlesbrough	QPR	120	7	0	0	16	3	0	0
Endersby SIG	Scott	20/02/1962	Lewisham		1987			York City (loan)		4	0	0	0	0	0	0	0
England HM	Mike	02/12/1941	Holywell		1975		w	Tottenham H	New England Teamen	40	3	2	0	1	0	0	0
Eslor J	Jack		Scotland		1936			Hearts	Workington	3	0	0	0	0	0	0	0
Evans A	Tony	11/01/1954	Liverpool		1975	1978		Blackpool	Birmingham City	124	8	7	6	47	4	6	1
Evans AH	Albert		South Wales		1931	1932			Dundalk	22	0	0	0	0	0	0	0
Evans DA	Andy	25/11/1975	Aberystwyth		1994	1995		YTS	Merthyr Tydfil	15	1	2	1	0	0	0	0
Evans EE	Elfed	28/08/1926	Ferndale	1988	1949	1951		Treharris	West Bromwich A.	44	7	0	0	16	4	0	0
Evans HP	Herbie	30/08/1894	Llandaff	1982	1920	1925	w	Cardiff Corries	Tranmere Rovers	93	16	0	0	1	1	0	0
Evans JH	Jack	31/01/1889	Bala	1971	1920	1925	w	Wrexham	Bristol Rovers	184	42	0	0	6	6	0	0
Evans K	Kevin	16/12/1980	Carmarthen		2000			Leeds United		30	3	1	1	3	2	0	0
Evans LN	Leslie	13/10/1929	Kingswinford		1950	1951		Brierley Hill	Plymouth Argyle	3	0	0	0	1	0	0	0
Evans PA	Paul	14/09/1964	Brentwood		1983			Juniors	Brecon Corries	2	1	0	0	0	0	0	0
Evans R	Rollo		Cardiff		1932				Bristol Rovers	1	0	0	0	0	0	0	0
Evans SJVL	Len	20/05/1903	Llandaff	1977	1930	1932	w	Barry	Birmingham	8	0	0	0	0	0	0	0
Evans ST	Sid		Darlaston		1920	1922		Darlaston	Manchester Utd.	9	0	0	0	1	0	0	0
Evans T	Terry	08/01/1976	Pontypridd		1993	1995		YTS	Barry Town	14	1	2	3	0	0	0	0
Evans TJ	Trevor		South Wales		1937			Caerau Ath.	Brighton & Hove A.	1	0	0	0	0	0	0	0
Everest J	Jack	20/07/1908	Kilcullen	1979	1934	1935		Blackpool	Southend Utd.	73	2	0	2	5	0	0	0
Faerber W	Winston	23/07/1971	Surinam		1999			Ado Den Haag	FC Den Bosch	33	5	4	1	1	0	0	0
Farquharson TG	Tom		Dublin	1974	1921	1934	ir	Abertillery	Retired	445	34	0	2	0	0	0	0
Farrell GJP	Greg	19/03/1944	Motherwell		1963	1966		Birmingham City	Bury	94	5	6	8	8	0	0	1
Farrington JR	John	19/06/1947	Lynemouth		1973	1974		Leicester City	Northampton Town	23	1	0	2	6	0	0	0
Farrington MA	Mark	15/06/1965	Liverpool		1985			Norwich City	Willem II (Ned.)	31	0	2	1	3	0	1	0
Felgate DW	David	04/03/1960	Blaenau Ffestiniog		1984		w	Lincoln City (loan)		4	0	0	0	0	0	0	0
Fereday W	Wayne	16/06/1963	Warley		1993	1994		West Bromwich A.	Merthyr Tydfil	44	0	1	1	2	0	0	0
Ferguson H	Hughie	02/03/1898	Motherwell	1930	1925	1928		Motherwell	Dundee	117	13	0	1	77	9	0	1
Ferguson RB	Bobby	08/01/1938	Dudley, Northumberland		1965	1968		Derby County	Barry Town	89	7	4	8	0	0	0	0
Fielding WJ	Bill	17/06/1915	Broadhurst		1936	1938		Hurst	Bolton Wanderers	50	7	0	1	0	0	0	0
Finlay J	Jim		Scotland		1937			Bute Athletic		1	0	0	0	0	0	0	0
Finnieston SJ	Steve	30/11/1954	Edinburgh		1974			Chelsea (loan)		9	0	0	0	2	0	0	0
Flack SR	Steve	29/05/1971	Cambridge		1995	1996		Cambridge City	Exeter City	11	0	0	0	1	0	0	0
Fleming HV	Hayden	14/03/1978	Islington		1995	1996		YTS	Merthyr Tydfil	32	2	0	1	0	0	0	0
Flynn B	Brian	12/10/1955	Port Talbot		1984	1985	w	Burnley	Doncaster Rovers	32	1	2	0	0	0	2	0
Foggon A	Alan	23/02/1950	West Pelton		1971	1972		Newcastle United	Middlesbrough	17	4	3	1	1	0	1	0
Foley W	Will	25/06/1960	Bellshill		1985			Frickley Ath.	Frickley Ath.	12	0	0	0	1	0	0	0
Ford FM	Francis	03/02/1967	Bridgend		1984			YTS	Exeter City	2	0	0	0	0	0	0	0
Ford L	Louis	18/05/1914	Cardiff	1980	1936	1938		Local	Retired	35	2	0	2	0	0	0	0
Ford MP	Mike	09/02/1966	Bristol		1984	1987		Devizes Town	Oxford United	196	19	10	7	13	1	0	0
					1998	1999		Oxford United	Oxford United								
Ford T	Trevor	01/10/1923	Swansea		1953	1956	w	Sunderland	PSV Eindhoven	96	5	0	0	42	3	0	0
Fortune-West LPO	Leo	09/04/1971	Stratford		2000	2001		Rotherham Utd.		73	8	1	3	21	2	0	1
Fowler JKG	Jason	20/08/1974	Bristol		1996	2000		Bristol City		144	14	8	3	14	4	1	1
Francis GCJ	Gerry	06/12/1951	Chiswick		1984		e	Exeter City	Swansea City	7	0	0	0	0	0	0	0
Francombe P	Peter	04/08/1963	Cardiff		1981			Crystal Palace	Bridgend	3	0	0	0	0	0	0	0
Fraser G	Gordon	27/11/1943	Elgin		1962			Forres Mechanics	Millwall	4	0	0	0	0	0	0	0
Friday R	Robin	27/07/1952	Hammersmith	1991	1976	1977		Reading		21	0	0	0	6	0	0	0
Friend H	Harold		Cardiff		1933			Cardiff Corries		3	0	0	0	0	0	0	0
Frowen J	John	11/10/1931	Trelewis		1952	1957		Nelson	Bristol Rovers	35	0	0	0	0	0	0	0
Fry CD	Chris	23/10/1969	Cardiff		1988	1990		YTS	Hereford Utd.	55	2	3	2	1	0	0	0
Fursland SA	Syd	31/07/1914	Llwynypia		1934				Stoke City	2	0	0	0	0	0	0	0
Gabbidon DL	Daniel	08/08/1979	Cwmbran		2000	2001		West Bromwich A.		87	8	3	0	6	0	0	0
Galbraith JMcD	Jack		Renton		1930	1934		Clapton Orient	Milford United	143	7	0	2	2	0	0	0
Gale CM	Colin	31/08/1932	Pontypridd		1953	1955		Juniors	Northampton Town	13	1	0	0	0	0	0	0
Gammon SG	Steve	24/09/1939	Swansea		1958	1964		Juniors	Kettering Town	66	3	1	1	1	0	0	0
Gardner J	Jimmy	27/09/1967	Dunfermline		1995	1996		Scarborough	Exeter City	63	3	1	5	5	0	0	0
Gault WE	Ernie	20/09/1889	Wallsend	1980	1920			Everton	Stockport Co.	2	0	0	0	0	0	0	0
Gibbins RG	Roger	06/09/1955	Enfield		1982	1985		Cambridge Utd.	Swansea City	281	14	23	6	25	1	6	0
					1988	1992		Newport County	Coach								
Gibson CH	Colin	16/09/1923	Normanby	1992	1946	1947		Penarth Pontoons	Newcastle United	71	3	0	0	16	0	0	0
Gibson IS	Ian	30/03/1943	Newton Stewart		1970	1972		Coventry City	Bournemouth	90	6	5	8	11	0	0	3
Gilbert TH	Tim	28/08/1958	South Shields	1995	1980	1981		Sunderland	Darlington	33	0	0	0	1	0	0	0
Gilchrist A	Alex	28/09/1923	Holytown	1989	1948				Barry Town	1	0	0	0	0	0	0	0
Giles DC	David	21/09/1956	Cardiff		1974	1978	w	App.	Wrexham	109	6	8	8	3	1	2	0
					1985	1986		Newport County	Barry Town								
Giles MW	Martin	01/01/1979	Shrewsbury		2000	2001		Chester City		5	0	0	2	0	0	0	1
Giles PA	Paul	21/02/1961	Cardiff		1980	1982		Juniors	Excelsior (Ned.)	24	2	0	0	1	0	0	0
Gill G	Gary	28/11/1964	Middlesbrough		1991			Darlington		6	0	0	0	1	0	0	0
Gill JJ	Jimmy	09/11/1894	Sheffield		1920	1925		Sheffield Wed.	Blackpool	184	28	0	0	82	12	0	0
Gilligan JM	Jimmy	24/01/1964	Hammersmith		1987	1989		Lincoln City	Portsmouth	99	4	8	10	34	4	1	7
Godfrey C	Cliff	17/02/1909	Baildon		1935	1937		Bradford	Walsall	104	6	0	2	1	0	0	0
Godwin DJ	Don	05/07/1932	Aberbargoed		1956			Bargoed	Merthyr Tydfil	2	0	0	0	0	0	0	0
Goldsmith MS	Martin	25/05/1962	Carmarthen		1983			Cambridge Utd.	Merthyr Tydfil	9	0	0	0	2	0	0	0
Gordon DD	Dean	13/02/1973	Croydon		2001			Middlesbro' (loan)		7	0	0	0	2	0	0	0
Gordon KG	Gavin	24/06/1979	Manchester		2000	2001		Lincoln City		25	2	1	1	2	1	0	5
Gorin ER	Ted	02/02/1924	Cardiff		1948	1949		Grange Ath.	Scunthorpe Utd.	6	0	0	0	2	0	0	0
Gorman AD	Andy	13/09/1974	Cardiff		1991	1992		YTS	Yeovil Town	12	0	0	2	1	0	0	0
Graham B	Ben	23/09/1975	Pontypool		1993			YTS	Bath City	1	0	0	0	0	0	0	0

Name		D.O.B	Place of Birth	Died	First Season	Last Season	Int	Previous Club	Next Club	Appearances				Goals			
										Lge	FAC	FLC	Oth.	Lge	FAC	FLC	Oth.
Grant D	David	02/06/1960	Sheffield		1983	1984		Oxford United	Rochdale	25	0	4	0	0	0	1	0
Grant W	Wilf	03/08/1920	Ashington	1990	1949	1954		Southampton	Ipswich Town	154	5	0	0	65	2	0	0
Granville A	Arthur	1912	Llwynypia	1987	1934	1938		Porth United	Retired	98	5	0	3	6	1	0	0
Grapes SP	Steve	25/02/1953	Norwich		1976	1981		Norwich City	Torquay United	147	5	12	2	6	0	0	0
Gray AD	Alick	07/11/1936	Arbroath		1958			Arbroath	Worcester City	2	0	0	0	0	0	0	0
Greenacre CM	Chris	23/12/1977	Wakefield		1997			Manchester C (loan)		11	0	0	0	2	0	0	0
Greene DM	David	26/10/1973	Luton		2000			Colchester Utd.	Cambridge Utd.	10	0	2	1	0	0	0	0
Grew MS	Mark	15/02/1958	Bilston		1992	1993		Port Vale	Hednesford Town	21	6	2	3	0	0	0	0
Griffith C	Cohen	26/12/1962	Georgetown, Guyana		1989	1994		Kettering Town	Barry Town	234	16	9	16	39	0	5	4
Griffiths PH	Phil	25/10/1908	Tylorstown	1978	1934		w	West Bromwich A.	Folkestone	12	0	0	0	1	0	0	0
Griffiths S	Stan	1911	Pentre		1934			Gillingham	Dundalk	2	0	0	0	2	0	0	0
Griffiths WR	Wyn	17/10/1919	Blaengwynfi		1947			Newport County	Newport County	1	0	0	0	0	0	0	0
Grimshaw W	Billy		Burnley		1920	1923		Bradford City	Sunderland	108	16	0	0	17	0	0	0
Grotier PD	Peter	18/10/1950	Stratford		1973			West Ham Utd. (loan)		40	0	5	0	0	0	0	0
					1979	1981		Lincoln City	Grimsby Town								
Gummer JC	Jason	27/10/1967	Tredegar		1985	1989		YTS		34	1	4	4	5	0	0	0
Hagan A	Alfie	10/11/1895	Usworth	1980	1923	1925		Newcastle United	Tranmere Rovers	9	0	0	0	2	0	0	0
Haig RN	Richard	29/12/1970	Pontypridd		1988	1989		YTS	Merthyr Tydfil	5	1	0	1	0	0	0	0
Halliday T	Tom	28/04/1940	Ayr		1963	1964		Dumbarton	Dumbarton	16	0	0	1	2	0	0	0
Hallworth JG	Jon	26/10/1965	Stockport		1997	1999		Oldham Athletic		122	15	8	2	0	0	0	0
Hamilton D	David	07/11/1960	South Shields		1984	2001		Blackburn Rovers		29	2	0	2	0	1	0	0
Hampson T	Tommy	02/05/1898	Bury		1926	1928		Darlington	Notts County	8	1	0	0	0	0	0	0
Hansbury R	Roger	26/01/1955	Barnsley		1989	1991		Birmingham City	Retired	99	5	6	3	0	0	0	0
Harding PJ	Paul	06/03/1964	Mitcham		1995			Birmingham City	Worcester City	36	1	4	2	0	0	0	0
Hardy W	Billy	18/04/1891	Bedlington	1981	1920	1931		Stockport Co.	Bradford (mgr)	354	53	0	1	6	0	0	0
Harkin JT	Terry	14/09/1941	Derry		1965	1966	n	Crewe Alexandra	Notts County	20	2	7	2	10	0	3	0
Harper A	Alan	01/11/1960	Liverpool		1995			Burnley		5	0	0	1	0	0	0	0
Harper JAJ	James	09/11/1980	Chelmsford		2000			Arsenal		3	0	0	0	0	0	0	0
Harrington AC	Alan	17/11/1933	Cardiff		1952	1965	w	Cardiff Nomads	Sully (mgr)	348	14	11	8	6	1	0	0
Harris B	Brian	16/05/1935	Bebington		1966	1970		Everton	Newport County	149	9	5	18	0	0	0	1
Harris F	Frank	05/04/1908	Catshill		1928	1932		Bromsgrove Rovers	Charlton Ath.	130	5	0	0	10	2	0	0
Harris GW	Gordon	19/02/1943	Campmuir		1964			Forfar Ath.		5	0	0	0	0	0	0	0
Harris GW	Gary	31/05/1959	Birmingham		1978	1979		App.	Trowbridge Town	4	0	0	1	0	0	0	0
Harris MA	Mark	15/07/1963	Reading		1997			Gillingham	Kingstonian	37	6	2	0	1	0	0	0
Harrison GR	Gerry	15/04/1972	Lambeth		1991			Bristol City		10	0	0	0	1	0	0	0
Harrison J	James		Bolton		1937			Hibernian	Chorley	1	0	0	0	0	0	0	0
Hatton RJ	Bob	10/04/1947	Hull		1982			Sheffield Utd.	Retired	30	0	0	0	9	0	0	0
Haworth SO	Simon	30/03/1977	Cardiff		1995	1996	w	YTS	Coventry City	37	1	4	4	9	0	0	1
Hazlett G	George	10/03/1923	Glasgow		1952			Bury	Millwall	7	0	0	0	1	0	0	0
Healey R	Ron	30/08/1952	Manchester		1973	1981	r	Manchester City	Retired - injury	216	9	12	4	0	0	0	0
Heard TP	Pat	17/03/1960	Hull		1990	1991		Rotherham Utd.	Hull City	46	0	6	2	4	0	0	0
Hearty H	Hugh	1912	Scotland		1935			Hearts	Clapton Orient	18	0	0	0	0	0	0	0
Heath PA	Phil	24/11/1964	Stoke-on-Trent		1990			Oxford United	Aldershot	11	0	0	0	1	0	0	0
Helsby T	Tom	1904	Runcorn	1961	1928	1930		Runcorn	Bradford City	46	3	0	0	2	1	0	0
Hemmerman JL	Jeff	25/02/1955	Hull		1982	1983		Portsmouth	Merthyr Tydfil	55	3	4	0	22	2	2	0
Henderson MR	Mick	31/03/1956	Gosforth		1981			Watford	Sheffield Utd.	11	0	0	0	0	0	0	0
Henderson WJ	Jim		Kilbirnie		1932	1933		Penicuick Ath.		43	2	0	1	25	0	0	0
Hewitt R	Ron	21/06/1928	Flint		1957	1958	w	Wrexham	Wrexham	65	6	0	0	27	3	0	0
Hill CJ	Charlie'Midge'	06/09/1918	Cardiff	1998	1938	1946		Local	Torquay United	19	0	0	1	3	0	0	0
Hill DRL	Danny	01/10/1974	Enfield		1997			Tottenham H (loan)		65	6	2	3	4	0	0	0
					1998	2000		Oxford United									
Hill FA	Freddie	1914	Cardiff		1932	1935		Local		67	5	0	1	15	1	0	0
Hillier EJG	Ernest 'Joe'	10/04/1907	Bridgend		1927	1929		Bridgend	Middlesbrough	9	0	0	0	0	0	0	0
Hills JJ	Joe	14/10/1897	Plumstead	1969	1924	1925		Northfleet	Swansea Town	14	3	0	0	0	0	0	0
Hitchens GA	Gerry	08/10/1934	Kidderminster	1983	1954	1957	e	Kidderminster H.	Aston Villa	95	4	0	0	40	1	0	0
Hogg D	Derek	04/11/1930	Stockton		1960	1961		West Bromwich A.	Kettering Town	41	3	1	0	7	0	0	0
Hogg GS	Graham	15/01/1922	Neath		1948			Cardiff Corries	Scunthorpe Utd.	1	1	0	0	0	0	0	0
Hole BG	Barry	16/09/1942	Swansea		1959	1965	w	Juniors	Blackburn Rovers	208	6	18	9	16	1	1	0
Hollyman KC	Ken	18/11/1922	Cardiff		1946	1953		Cardiff Nomads	Newport County	189	13	0	0	8	3	0	0
Holmes MJE	Matty	01/08/1969	Luton		1988			Bournemouth (loan)		1	0	0	0	0	0	0	0
Holt S	Stan				1931			Macclesfield Town	Berne (Swiz.)	2	0	0	0	0	0	0	0
Honor CR	Chris	05/06/1968	Bristol		1994			Airdrie (loan)		10	0	0	0	0	0	0	0
Hooper PJ	Peter	02/02/1933	Teignmouth		1962			Bristol Rovers	Bristol City	40	1	2	0	22	0	1	0
Horrix DV	Dean	21/11/1961	Taplow	1990	1986			Reading (loan)		9	0	0	0	3	0	0	0
Horton R	Ralph		South Wales		1932			Lovells Ath.		1	0	0	0	0	0	0	0
Houston D	David	07/09/1948	Glasgow		1965	1966		Juniors	Crystal Palace	18	0	3	0	0	0	0	0
Howells RG	Ron	12/01/1927	Ponthenry		1951	1956	w	Barry Town	Worcester City	155	8	0	0	0	0	0	0
Hoy RE	Roger	06/12/1946	Poplar		1971	1972		Luton Town	Dagenham	16	0	1	0	0	0	0	0
Hudson CAR	Colin	05/10/1935	Undy		1957	1960		Newport County	Brighton & Hove A.	60	4	2	0	9	0	1	0
Hughes BW	Wayne	08/03/1958	Port Talbot		1979	1981		Tulsa Roughnecks	Bath City	46	2	2	0	1	0	0	0
Hughes EM	Mike 'Blodwyn'	03/09/1940	Llanidloes		1958			Juniors	Exeter City	1	0	0	0	0	0	0	0
Hughes I	Iorrie	26/05/1925	Llandulas	1993	1951		w	Luton Town	Worcester City	26	0	0	0	0	0	0	0
Hughes JJ	Jamie	05/04/1977	Liverpool		1999			Tranmere Rovers	Bangor City	2	0	3	0	1	0	1	0
Hughes RD	David	01/02/1978	Wrexham		2000	2001		Shrewsbury Town		14	0	1	2	0	0	0	0
Hullett WA	Bill	19/11/1915	Liverpool	1982	1947	1948		Merthyr Tydfil	Nottm. Forest	27	0	0	0	15	0	0	0
Humphreys RJ	Richie	30/11/1977	Sheffield		1999			Sheffield Wed. (loan)		9	1	0	1	2	0	0	0
Humphries SR	Steve	29/05/1961	Hull		1982			Doncaster Rovers	Wrexham	1	0	0	0	0	0	0	0
Hutchinson A	Alex	1908	Musselburgh		1933			Bo'ness	Bo'ness	23	1	0	0	4	0	0	0
Impey JE	John	11/08/1954	Minehead		1972	1974		App.	Bournemouth	21	1	2	2	0	1	0	0
Ingram CD	Chris	05/12/1976	Cardiff		1995			YTS	Merthyr Tydfil	8	0	1	2	1	0	0	0
Ingram GPA	Godfrey	26/10/1959	Luton		1982			San Jose Earthquakes	San Jose Earthquakes	11	2	1	0	2	1	0	0
Irving SJ	Sam	28/08/1894	Belfast	1969	1926	1927	in	Dundee	Chelsea	47	9	0	1	3	1	0	0
Irwin WJN	Billy	23/07/1951	Newtownards		1971	1977		Bangor City	Washington Diplomats	180	15	9	6	0	0	0	0

Name		D.O.B	Place of Birth	Died	First Season	Last Season	Int	Previous Club	Next Club	Appearances				Goals			
										Lge	FAC	FLC	Oth.	Lge	FAC	FLC	Oth.
Jackson W	Billy	15/07/1902	Farnworth	1974	1934			Bristol Rovers	Watford	12	0	0	1	0	0	0	0
James RM	Robbie	23/03/1957	Gorseinon	1998	1992	1993	w	Bradford City	Merthyr Tydfil	51	1	4	6	2	0	0	1
James WJ	Billy	18/10/1921	Cardiff	1980	1946			Cardiff Corries	Retired	6	0	0	0	3	0	0	0
Jarman L	Lee	16/12/1977	Cardiff		1995	1999		YTS	Exeter City	93	6	5	7	1	1	0	0
Jeanne LC	Leon	17/01/1980	Cardiff		2001			Queen's Park Rangers		2	0	0	0	0	0	0	0
Jenkins B	Brian	01/08/1935	Treherbert		1956	1960		Cwmparc	Exeter City	29	0	0	0	7	0	0	0
Jenkins EJJ	Eddie	16/07/1909	Cardiff		1930	1933		Cardiff East	Bristol City	77	3	0	0	0	0	0	0
Jenkins ES	Eddie	06/07/1895	Cardiff	1976	1921	1923	w	Cardiff Corries	Lovells Ath.	12	1	0	0	0	0	0	0
Jennings J	Jack	27/08/1902	Platt Bridge	1997	1925	1929		Wigan Borough	Middlesbrough	94	3	0	0	0	0	0	0
Jennings WH	Wally	01/04/1909	Bristol	1993	1934	1935		Cheltenham T	Bristol St George	30	2	0	1	0	0	0	0
John DJ	Dilwyn	03/06/1944	Tonypandy		1961	1966		Juniors	Swansea Town	88	1	10	5	0	0	0	0
John EJ	Emlyn	1907	Tonypandy		1928	1931		Mid Rhondda	Newport County	15	0	0	0	0	0	0	0
Johnson GP	Glenn	16/07/1972	Sydney, Australia		1995			Blacktown City (Aust.)	Blacktown City (Aust.)	5	0	0	0	0	0	0	0
Johnston G	George	21/03/1947	Glasgow		1964	1966		Juniors	Arsenal	59	6	7	2	20	2	3	1
Jones B	Bernard	10/04/1934	Coventry		1955	1956		Northampton Town	Shrewsbury Town	9	0	0	0	0	0	0	0
Jones BH	Bryn	08/02/1948	Llandrindod Wells		1966	1967		App.	Bristol Rovers	2	0	0	1	0	0	0	0
Jones BS	Barrie	10/10/1941	Swansea		1966	1969	w	Plymouth Argyle	Yeovil Town	108	3	4	13	19	1	0	2
Jones C	Charlie	12/12/1899	Troedyrhiw	1966	1920		w	Troedyrhiw	Stockport Co.	1	0	0	0	0	0	0	0
Jones DG	Dai	10/06/1914	Ynysddu	1988	1934			Tottenham H	Fulham	9	0	0	0	0	0	0	0
Jones G	Gethin	08/08/1981	Carmarthen		2000	2001		Carmarthen Town		3	0	1	2	0	0	0	0
Jones G	Glyn	1916	South Wales		1934	1935		Local		12	0	0	0	0	0	0	0
Jones I	Islwyn	08/04/1935	Merthyr Tydfil		1954	1955		Juniors		26	1	0	0	0	0	0	0
Jones IM	Ian	26/08/1976	Germany		1993	1995		YTS	Merthyr Tydfil	3	0	0	0	0	0	0	0
Jones J	Jimmy	1901	Treorchy	1977	1923		w	Ton Pentre	Wrexham	12	0	0	0	2	0	0	0
Jones JA	Alan	12/09/1939	Cefn Mawr		1957			Druids	Exeter City	1	0	0	0	0	0	0	0
Jones K	Ken	02/01/1936	Aberdare		1957	1958		Juniors	Scunthorpe Utd.	24	4	0	0	0	0	0	0
Jones K	Ken	26/06/1944	Havercroft		1971			Southampton	Bath City	6	0	2	2	0	0	0	0
Jones L	Linden	05/03/1961	New Tredegar		1978	1983		App.	Newport County	145	4	11	2	2	1	0	0
Jones LJ	Les	01/07/1911	Aberdare	1981	1929	1933	w	Aberdare Ath.	Coventry City	142	6	0	1	31	1	0	0
Jones M	Mark	26/09/1961	Berinsfield		1990	1991		Swindon Town	Farnborough T	36	2	6	2	2	0	1	0
Jones RH	Bob	09/01/1902	Everton	1989	1937	1938		Bolton Wanderers	Southport (ass. trainer)	58	4	0	3	0	0	0	0
Jones V	Vaughan	02/09/1959	Tonyrefail		1984			Newport County	Bristol Rovers	11	0	4	0	1	0	0	0
Jones VW	Vince	1900	Carmarthen	1950	1922			Local	Merthyr Town	1	0	0	0	0	0	0	0
Jordan AJ	Andrew	14/12/1979	Manchester		2000			Bristol City		5	1	0	0	0	0	0	0
Joslin PJ	Phil	01/09/1916	Kingsteignton	1981	1948	1950		Torquay United	Retired - injury	108	9	0	0	0	0	0	0
Judge AG	Alan	14/05/1960	Kingsbury		1987			Oxford United (loan)		8	0	0	1	0	0	0	0
Kavanagh GA	Graham	02/12/1973	Dublin		2001		r	Stoke City		43	4	1	2	13	2	0	0
Keating AE	Albert	28/06/1902	Swillington Common	1984	1930	1932		Blackburn Rovers	Bristol City	45	3	0	0	22	4	0	0
Keating RE	Reg	14/05/1904	Halton	1961	1933	1935		Bath City	Doncaster Rovers	70	1	0	1	35	0	0	0
Keenor FC	Fred	31/07/1894	Cardiff	1972	1920	1930	w	Roath Wednesday	Crewe Alexandra	371	42	0	1	13	1	0	0
Kellock W	Billy	07/02/1954	Glasgow		1971	1972		Aston Villa	Norwich City	35	7	0	0	2	3	0	0
Kelly GL	George	29/06/1933	Aberdeen		1958			Stoke City	Stockport Co.	8	0	0	0	4	0	0	0
Kelly MD	Mark	07/10/1966	Blackpool		1987	1989		Shrewsbury Town	Fulham	105	7	7	9	2	0	0	0
Kelly NAO	Tony	14/02/1966	Meriden		1992			Stoke City (loan)		5	0	0	0	1	0	0	0
Kelly S	Seamus	06/05/1974	Tullamore		1998	1999		UCD Dublin	St Patricks Ath.	13	0	0	0	0	0	0	0
Kelso J	Jimmy	08/12/1910	Cardross	1987	1938			Newport County	Swindon Town	41	6	0	1	0	0	0	0
Kerr AA	Andy	07/04/1966	West Bromwich		1986			Shrewsbury Town	Telford United	31	4	4	1	1	0	0	0
Ketteridge SJ	Steve	07/11/1959	Stevenage		1988			Leyton Orient (loan)		6	0	0	0	2	0	0	0
Kevan DJ	David	31/08/1968	Wigtown		1989			Notts County (loan)		7	0	0	0	0	0	0	0
King GH	Gerry	09/04/1947	Radnor		1964			Juniors	Torquay United	6	0	0	0	0	0	0	0
King J	Jake	29/01/1955	Glasgow		1984	1985		Wrexham	Limerick City	30	1	1	0	0	0	0	0
King JW	Johnny	09/08/1932	Wrenbury		1961			Stoke City	Crewe Alexandra	33	1	4	2	6	0	2	1
King PC	Peter	03/04/1943	Worcester		1960	1973		Worcester City	Retired - injury	356	20	22	33	67	5	6	11
Kirtley JH	Harry	23/05/1930	Washington		1955			Sunderland	Gateshead	38	2	0	0	4	0	0	0
Kitchen MP	Peter	16/02/1952	Mexborough		1980	1981		Fulham	Happy Valley (HK)	67	1	4	0	21	0	1	0
Kite PD	Phil	26/10/1962	Bristol		1993			Sheffield Utd.	Bristol City	18	1	2	2	0	0	0	0
Kneeshaw HJ	Justin 'Jack'	1883	Beckhill	1955	1920	1923		Bradford City	Ass. trainer	34	7	0	0	0	0	0	0
Knill AR	Alan	08/10/1964	Slough		1993		w	Bury (loan)		4	0	0	0	0	0	0	0
Knowles HF	Harry	06/09/1932	Hednesford		1958	1959		Worcester City	Worcester City	8	0	0	0	0	0	0	0
Lamie R	Bob	28/12/1928	Newarthill		1949	1950		Stonehouse Violet	Swansea Town	6	0	0	0	1	0	0	0
Lane E	Edward	1908			1934			Notts County		30	1	0	1	0	0	0	0
Larmour AAJ	Albert	27/05/1951	Belfast		1972	1978		Linfield	Torquay United	154	10	11	5	0	0	0	0
Lathom G	George	01/01/1881	Newtown	1939	1921		w	Southport Central	Trainer	1	0	0	0	0	0	0	0
Lawson D	Denis	11/12/1897	Lennoxtown		1923	1925	s	St. Mirren	Springfield Providence	64	13	0	0	2	0	0	0
Layton AED	Arthur	1885	Gornal	1959	1920			Middlesbrough	Stockport Co.	2	4	0	0	0	0	0	0
Lea L	Les	05/10/1942	Manchester		1967	1969		Blackpool	Barnsley	76	2	1	7	6	0	1	1
Leckie JT	Jock	1909	Alva		1934	1935		Stockport Co.	Walsall	46	1	0	2	0	0	0	0
Lee TC	Trevor	03/07/1954	Lewisham		1983			Bournemouth	Northampton Town	21	0	0	0	5	0	0	0
Legg A	Andy	28/07/1966	Neath		1998	2001	w	Reading		140	16	7	0	9	0	0	0
Leonard CC	Carleton	03/02/1958	Oswestry		1985			Hereford Utd.	Oswestry Town	4	1	1	0	0	0	0	0
Lever AR	Arthur	25/03/1920	Cardiff		1946	1950	w	Juniors	Leicester City	155	10	0	0	9	0	0	0
Lewis A	Allan	31/05/1971	Pontypridd		1988	1991		YTS		50	2	3	6	0	0	0	0
Lewis B	Bernie	12/03/1945	Aberfan		1963	1967		Juniors	Watford	88	4	6	7	7	0	3	0
Lewis DB	David		South Wales					Local									
Lewis EG	Ernest		South Wales		1933			Local		14	0	0	0	1	0	0	0
Lewis J	John	15/10/1955	Tredegar		1978	1983		Pontllanfraith	Newport County	140	8	12	0	9	0	1	0
Lewis JJ	Jack 'Ginger'	1902	Newport		1924		w	Newport County	Tranmere Rovers	1	0	0	0	0	0	0	0
Lewis TJ	Terry	22/10/1950	Newport		1968	1969		App.	Retired	3	0	0	1	0	0	0	0
Lewis W	Billy	04/07/1923	Cardiff		1946	1947		Juniors	Newport County	10	0	0	0	0	0	0	0
Lewis WL	Wilf	01/07/1903	Swansea	1976	1934	1935	w	Bath City	Haverfordwest Co.	35	1	0	0	6	1	0	0
Lievesley W	Wilf	06/10/1902	Staveley		1929			Wigan Borough	Retired	3	0	0	0	0	0	0	0
Lightbourne KL	Kyle	29/09/1968	Bermuda		2000		bm	Coventry City (loan)		3	0	0	0	0	0	0	0
Livermore DE	Doug	27/12/1947	Liverpool		1975	1977		Norwich City	Chester	88	7	6	6	5	0	0	0

Name		D.O.B	Place of Birth	Died	First Season	Last Season	Int	Previous Club	Next Club	Appearances				Goals			
										Lge	FAC	FLC	Oth.	Lge	FAC	FLC	Oth.
Lloyd KG	Kevin	26/09/1970	Llanidloes		1996	1997		Hereford Utd.	Oldham Athletic	33	0	4	3	1	0	0	0
Lloyd KJJ	Kevin	12/06/1958	Wolverhampton		1979			Darlaston	Gillingham	1	0	0	0	0	0	0	0
Lloyd RC	Clive	04/09/1945	Merthyr Tydfil		1964			Norwich City	Swindon Town	2	0	1	0	0	0	0	0
Love IJ	Ian	01/03/1958	Cardiff		1989			Torquay United	Barry Town	2	0	0	0	0	0	0	0
Low JD	Josh	15/02/1979	Bristol		1999	2001		Leyton Orient (loan)		75	5	2	4	6	0	0	0
Lynex SC	Steve	23/01/1958	West Bromwich		1988	1989		West Bromwich A.	Telford United	62	6	5	5	2	1	1	0
MacAulay R	Bob	28/08/1904	Wishaw	1994	1936		s	Chelsea	Sligo Rovers	4	0	0	0	0	0	0	0
MacBennett JC	Seamus	16/11/1925	Newcastle, Co Down	1995	1947			Belfast Celtic	Tranmere Rovers	4	0	0	0	2	0	0	0
McCambridge J	Jimmy	1905	Larne		1930	1932	n	Everton	Bristol Rovers	95	5	0	0	51	2	0	0
McCarthy DJA	Danny	26/09/1942	Abergavenny		1961			Abergavenny Thistle	Merthyr Tydfil	7	0	2	0	0	0	0	0
McCaughey C	Cecil	1909	Bootle		1937	1938		Coventry City	Southport	66	10	0	2	5	0	0	0
McClelland J	John	07/12/1955	Belfast		1974		n	Portadown	Bangor City	4	0	0	0	1	0	0	0
McCulloch A	Andy	03/01/1950	Northampton		1972	1973		QPR	Oxford United	58	5	3	2	24	3	3	0
McCulloch S	Scott	29/11/1975	Cumnock		2000	2001		Dundee United		21	3	1	2	1	0	0	0
McDermott BJ	Brian	08/04/1961	Slough		1987	1988		Oxford United	Exeter City	51	1	3	6	8	0	0	2
McDonagh C	Charles				1935			Kidderminster H.	Peterborough Utd.	2	0	0	0	0	0	0	0
McDonald K	Ken	24/04/1898	Llanrwst		1921	1922		Caerau	Manchester Utd.	11	1	0	0	7	0	0	0
MacDonald KD	Kevin	22/12/1960	Inverness		1990			Coventry City (loan)		8	0	0	0	0	0	0	0
McGorry BP	Brian	16/04/1970	Liverpool		1995			Wycombe Wan. (loan)		7	0	0	0	0	0	0	0
McGrath J	Jimmy	04/03/1907	Washington		1928	1931		Washington Colliery	Port Vale	33	4	0	0	0	0	0	0
McGuckin GKW	George	11/08/1938	Dundee		1957			Dundee Shamrock		4	0	0	0	0	0	0	0
McIlvenny P	Paddy	1900	Belfast		1924		i	Distillery	Sheffield Wed.	5	0	0	0	2	0	0	0
McInch JR	Jim	27/06/1953	Glasgow		1972	1974		Juniors	Bath City	13	0	1	1	0	0	1	0
McIntosh A	Alan	29/07/1939	Llandudno		1961	1963		Llandudno	Retired - injury	64	2	4	0	11	0	0	0
McJennett JJ	Jack	1906	Cardiff		1929	1931		Local	Exeter City	5	2	0	0	0	0	0	0
McKenzie JD	James	1914	Sudbrook		1935	1938		Leicester City	Notts County	35	1	0	1	6	0	0	0
McLachlan GH	George	21/09/1902	Glasgow		1925	1929		Clyde	Manchester Utd.	140	13	0	1	22	2	0	0
McLaren R	Bobby	05/08/1929	Chryston		1949			Barry Town	Barry Town	1	0	0	0	0	0	0	0
McLaughlin R	Bobby	06/12/1925	Belfast		1950	1953		Wrexham	Southampton	48	2	0	0	3	0	0	0
McLean I	Ian	13/08/1966	Paisley		1994		ca	Bristol Rovers (loan)		4	0	0	0	0	0	0	0
McLoughlin PB	Paul	23/12/1963	Bristol		1984	1985		Gisborne (NZ)	Oster Vaxjo (Swe)	49	1	2	2	4	0	0	0
McMillan JS	John	14/04/1937	Renton		1960			Dumbarton	Exeter City	2	0	0	0	0	0	0	0
McNally O	Owen	20/06/1906	Denny	1973	1931			Bray Unknowns	Bray Unknowns	6	0	0	0	0	0	0	0
McSeveney JH	John	08/02/1931	Shotts		1955	1956		Sunderland	Newport County	75	4	0	0	19	2	0	0
McStay R	Ray	16/05/1970	Hamilton		1996			Hamilton Acad.		1	0	0	0	0	0	0	0
Maddy PM	Paul	17/08/1962	Cwmcarn		1980	1982		App.	Swansea City	43	1	0	0	3	1	0	0
Maidment T	Tom	04/11/1905	Monkwearmouth	1971	1932	1933		Workington	Blyth Spartans	44	2	0	0	8	0	0	0
Main WG	Walter 'Bill'	30/11/1915	St Monance	1969	1936	1938		Raith Rovers	Colchester United	6	0	0	2	0	0	0	0
Mallory RJL	Dick	10/08/1942	Bermuda		1963			Bermuda	Bermuda	3	0	1	0	0	0	0	0
Malloy D	Danny	06/11/1930	Dennyloanhead		1955	1960		Dundee	Doncaster Rovers	226	14	2	0	1	0	0	0
Mansell J	Jack	22/08/1927	Salford		1952	1953		Brighton & Hove A.	Portsmouth	25	1	0	0	0	0	0	0
Marchant MG	Marwood	19/06/1922	Milford Haven	1972	1950			Milford United	Torquay United	12	0	0	0	3	0	0	0
Marcroft EH	Ted	1910	Rochdale		1933			QPR	Accrington Stanley	28	2	0	0	2	0	0	0
Mardenborough SA	Steve	11/09/1964	Selly Oak		1986	1987		Newport County	Hereford Utd.	32	1	1	2	1	0	0	0
Marriott PW	Paul	26/09/1973	Liverpool		1991			YTS		1	0	0	0	0	0	0	0
Marshall E	Ernie	23/05/1918	Dinnington	1983	1946			Sheffield Utd.	Yeovil Town	1	0	0	0	0	0	0	0
Marshalsey WHG	Bill	18/04/1910	Fife	1977	1933			Hearts		7	0	0	1	1	0	0	0
Martin MP	Mick	09/07/1951	Dublin		1984		r	Vancouver Whitecaps	Peterborough Utd.	7	0	0	0	0	0	0	0
Marustik C	Chris	10/08/1961	Swansea		1985	1986	w	Swansea City	Barry Town	43	7	1	3	1	3	0	0
Mason FO	Frank	01/08/1901	Solihull		1922			Coventry City	Rochdale	1	0	0	0	0	0	0	0
Matson FR	Frank	21/11/1905	Reading	1985	1926	1929		Reading	Newport County	27	0	0	0	3	0	0	0
Matthews NP	Neil	03/12/1967	Manchester		1990	1992		Blackpool	Rochdale	66	4	3	5	2	0	0	0
Matthews WJ	Wayne	11/09/1964	Cardiff		1983			Juniors	Ton Pentre	14	0	3	0	0	0	0	0
Maxwell LJ	Leyton	03/10/1979	Rhyl		2001			Liverpool		17	1	0	3	1	0	0	0
May H	Harry	15/10/1928	Glasgow		1949			Thorniewood Utd.	Swindon Town	1	0	0	0	0	0	0	0
Mayo AC	Alfred				1930			Local		1	0	0	0	0	0	0	0
Meacock KM	Kevin	16/09/1963	Bristol		1984	1985		Devizes Town	Gisborne City (NZ)	25	1	1	0	3	0	0	0
Melaniphy EMJP	Eugene 'Ted'	05/02/1913	Westport		1936	1937		Plymouth Argyle	Worcester City	20	1	0	0	8	1	0	0
Mellor J	John		Oldham		1936	1937		Manchester Utd.	Retired	28	2	0	1	0	0	0	0
Melville J	James		Dykehead		1921			Clyde	East Stirling	1	0	0	0	0	0	0	0
Menzies AR	Ross	31/10/1934	Rutherglen		1957			Glasgow Rangers		1	0	0	0	0	0	0	0
Merry W	Bill	14/12/1910	Fishguard		1930			Fishguard Sports	Drumcondra	8	0	0	0	0	0	0	0
Micallef C	Tarki	24/01/1961	Cardiff		1978	1982		App.	Newport County	121	6	9	2	12	0	0	0
					1984	1985		Gillingham	Bristol Rovers								
Michael JD	Jamie	22/10/1978	Pontypridd		1996			YTS	Newport AFC	1	0	0	0	0	0	0	0
Middleton CD	Craig	10/09/1970	Nuneaton		1996	1999		Cambridge Utd.	Halifax Town	118	14	4	6	8	3	0	0
Miles AE	Albert	1903	Treorchy		1927	1929		Derby County	Crystal Palace	16	1	0	0	8	0	0	0
Miles I	Idris	02/08/1908	Neath	1983	1930			Local	Yeovil & Petters	3	0	0	0	0	0	0	0
Millar WP	Paul	16/11/1966	Belfast		1991	1994		Port Vale		120	9	8	9	17	1	1	1
Mills DG	Don	17/08/1926	Maltby	1994	1950			QPR	Leeds United	1	0	0	0	0	0	0	0
Milne AS	Alec	04/06/1937	Dundee		1957	1964		Arbroath	Barry Town	172	8	6	2	1	0	0	0
Milsom PJ	Paul	05/10/1974	Bristol		1994			Bristol City	Oxford United	3	0	0	0	0	0	0	0
Mitchell GL	Graham	16/02/1968	Shipley		1998			Bradford City	Halifax Town	46	5	2	1	0	0	0	0
Mitchell JW	Jimmy	01/09/1918	Barry		1937	1938		Local	Barry Town	3	0	0	1	0	0	0	0
Mokone SM	Steve	23/03/1932	Pretoria, South Africa		1959		sa	PSV Eindhoven	Barnsley	3	0	0	0	1	0	0	0
Molloy P	Paddy	20/04/1909	Haslingden	1993	1933	1934		Bristol Rovers	QPR	23	0	0	1	0	0	0	0
Montgomery SWJ	Stan	07/07/1920	West Ham	2000	1948	1954		Southend Utd.	Worcester City	230	13	0	0	4	0	0	0
Moore G	Graham	07/03/1941	Hengoed		1958	1961	w	Juniors	Chelsea	85	4	1	1	23	0	1	1
Moore JFB	Beriah	25/12/1919	Cardiff		1947	1948		Bangor City	Bangor City	6	1	0	0	4	0	0	0
Moore P	Paddy	1909	Ballybough	1951	1929		nr	Shamrock Rovers	Tranmere Rovers	1	0	0	0	0	0	0	0
Moore RD	Ronnie	29/01/1953	Liverpool		1978	1979		Tranmere Rovers	Rotherham Utd.	56	2	2	0	6	0	0	0
Moore WA	Billy	14/10/1912	Llanbradach		1934			Local	Southampton	11	1	0	0	0	0	0	0
Morgan JP	Jon	10/07/1970	Cardiff		1988	1990		YTS	Merthyr Tydfil	55	5	5	5	3	0	0	0

Name		D.O.B	Place of Birth	Died	First Season	Last Season	Int	Previous Club	Next Club	Appearances Lge	FAC	FLC	Oth.	Goals Lge	FAC	FLC	Oth.
Morgan PW	Peter	28/10/1951	Cardiff		1972			Juniors	Hereford Utd.	16	1	0	0	0	0	0	0
Morgan RL	Richie	03/10/1946	Cardiff		1967	1976		Cardiff Corries	Manager	68	5	2	4	0	0	0	0
Morris EC	Ted	06/05/1921	Pontypool		1948	1950		Bewdley	Barry Town	8	0	0	0	0	0	0	0
Morris EL	Eric		Cardiff		1931	1932		Local		16	2	0	0	0	0	0	0
Mort EF	Enoch	1912	Ogmore Vale		1933	1937		Gilfach Goch	Carlisle Utd.	43	1	0	3	0	0	0	0
Moseley G	Graham	16/11/1953	Manchester		1986	1987		Brighton & Hove A.	Retired - injury	38	3	4	3	0	0	0	0
Moss F	Frank	17/04/1895	Aston	1965	1928		e	Aston Villa	Bromsgrove Rovers	9	0	0	0	0	0	0	0
Mountain PD	Pat	01/08/1976	Pontypridd		1996			YTS	Barry Town	5	1	0	2	0	0	0	0
Muggleton CD	Carl	13/09/1968	Leicester		2000			Leicester City (loan)		6	0	0	0	0	0	0	0
Mullen J	Jimmy	08/11/1952	Jarrow		1981	1985		Rotherham Utd.	Newport County	133	5	9	2	12	0	0	0
Munro JA	Jim	20/05/1905	Glasgow	1978	1928	1929		St. Johnstone	Millwall	14	2	0	0	3	0	0	0
Murphy J	Jerry	1907	Dowlais		1927			Merthyr Town	Fulham	1	0	0	0	0	0	0	0
Murphy P	Pat	19/12/1947	Merthyr Tydfil		1965			App.	Methyr Tydfil	1	0	0	0	0	0	0	0
Murray DJ	Don	18/01/1946	Duffus		1962	1974		Juniors	Hearts	406	23	21	33	6	1	0	0
Nardiello G	Gerry	05/05/1966	Warley		1985			Shrewsbury Town (loan)		7	0	0	0	4	0	0	0
Nash HE	Harry	10/04/1892	Fishponds	1970	1920	1922		Coventry City	Merthyr Town	30	1	0	0	6	1	0	0
Nelson J	Jimmy	07/01/1901	Greenock	1965	1921	1929	s	Crusaders	Newcastle United	240	30	0	1	2	1	0	0
Newton EJI	Eddie	13/12/1971	Hammersmith		1991			Chelsea (loan)		18	0	0	0	4	0	0	0
Newton W	Billy	14/05/1893	Cramlington	1973	1920	1921		Newcastle United	Leicester City	6	0	0	0	0	0	0	0
Nibloe J	Joe	10/12/1926	Glasgow		1948			Clydebank Juniors		1	0	0	0	0	0	0	0
Nicholls J	Johnny	03/04/1931	Wolverhampton	1995	1957		e	West Bromwich A.	Exeter City	8	0	0	0	2	0	0	0
Nicholls JBL	Jack	14/02/1898	Cardiff	1970	1924		w	Newport County	Swansea Town	2	0	0	0	0	0	0	0
Nicholls RB	Ron	04/12/1933	Sharpness	1994	1958	1960		Bristol Rovers	Bristol City	51	2	1	0	0	0	0	0
Nicholls RR	Ryan	10/05/1973	Cardiff		1994			Leeds United	Merthyr Tydfil	12	0	0	0	1	0	0	0
Nicholson G	George	12/05/1905	Pelaw		1936	1938		Bolton Wanderers	Oldham Athletic	98	13	0	2	0	0	0	0
Nicholson JR	Joe	04/06/1898	Ryhope	1974	1924	1925		Clapton Orient	Aston Villa	47	8	0	0	12	2	0	0
Nock AJ	Jack	1899	Stourbridge		1921	1922		Cradley Heath	Wrexham	3	0	0	0	0	0	0	0
Nogan K	Kurt	09/09/1970	Cardiff		1999	2000		Preston NE		18	1	1	1	1	0	0	0
Norman AG	Griff	20/02/1926	Cardiff		1951			Local	Torquay United	1	0	0	0	0	0	0	0
Northcott TT	Tommy	05/12/1931	Torquay		1952	1954		Torquay United	Lincoln City	76	3	0	0	13	1	0	0
Nugent KP	Kevin	10/04/1969	Edmonton		1997	2001		Bristol City		98	9	9	2	29	6	1	1
Nugent WC	Cliff	03/03/1929	Islington		1951	1958		Headington Utd.	Mansfield Town	113	9	0	0	19	1	0	0
Nutt GE	Gordon	08/11/1932	South Yardley		1954	1955		Coventry City	Arsenal	17	0	0	0	4	0	0	0
Oakley K	Ken	09/05/1929	Rhymney		1950	1953		Ebbw Vale	Northampton Town	7	0	0	0	1	0	0	0
Oatway APD	Charlie	28/11/1973	Hammersmith		1994	1995		Yeading	Torquay United	32	2	2	2	0	0	1	0
O'Connor TD	Tim	03/10/1967	Neath		1985			Afan Lido	Afan Lido	2	0	0	0	0	0	0	0
O'Halloran KJ	Keith	10/11/1975	Dublin		1996			Middlesbrough		8	0	0	2	0	0	0	0
O'Halloran N	Neil	21/06/1933	Cardiff	1995	1955	1956		Juniors	Newport County	10	0	0	0	4	0	0	0
O'Neill H	Harry	1894	Castle Ward, Newcastle		1931			Runcorn	Berne (Swiz.)	9	2	0	0	2	2	0	0
Osman RC	Russell	14/02/1959	Repton		1995		e	Brighton & Hove A.	Manager	15	0	0	0	0	0	0	0
O'Sullivan WStJ	Wayne	25/02/1974	Akrotiri, Cyprus		1997	1998		Swindon Town	Plymouth Argyle	85	10	3	2	4	1	0	0
Ovenstone DG	Davie	17/06/1913	St Monance	1983	1936			QPR	Watford	21	0	0	1	4	0	0	0
Owen JG	Gordon	14/06/1959	Barnsley		1983			Sheffield Wed.	Barnsley	39	1	4	0	14	0	1	0
Page J	Jack	24/03/1886	Liverpool	1951	1920	1925		Everton	Merthyr Town	71	8	0	0	0	0	0	0
Paget WST	Tommy	1909	Cardiff		1932	1933		Local	Newport County	6	0	0	0	0	0	0	0
Pagnam F	Fred	04/09/1891	Poulton-le-Fylde	1962	1920	1921		Arsenal	Watford	27	0	0	0	8	0	0	0
Parfitt HE	Harry	26/09/1929	Cardiff		1953			Local	Worcester City	1	0	0	0	0	0	0	0
Parker REA	Reg	10/06/1921	Pontyclun		1947			Local	Newport County	2	0	0	0	0	0	0	0
Parsons FR	Frank	29/10/1947	Amersham		1970	1972		Crystal Palace	Fulham	17	0	1	2	0	0	0	0
Parsons JS	John	10/12/1950	Cardiff		1970	1972		App.	Bournemouth	15	0	1	0	6	0	0	0
Partridge SM	Scott	13/10/1974	Grimsby		1996	1997		Bristol City	Torquay United	36	2	2	1	2	0	0	0
Paterson S	Scott	13/05/1972	Aberdeen		1997			Bristol City		5	0	0	0	0	0	0	0
Pearson JS	John	01/09/1963	Sheffield		1994			Mansfield Town	Merthyr Tydfil	12	0	0	0	0	0	0	0
Peck DT	Trevor	25/05/1938	Llanelli		1959	1964		Llanelli	Worcester City	42	0	1	3	0	0	0	0
Pembery GD	Gordon	10/10/1926	Cardiff		1949			Norwich City	Torquay United	1	0	0	0	0	0	0	0
Penney DM	David	17/08/1964	Wakefield		1997	1998		Swansea City	Doncaster Rovers	35	6	2	0	5	0	0	0
Perks H	Harry	1912	Cardiff		1933			Local	Newport County	9	0	0	0	1	0	0	0
Perrett R	Russell	18/06/1973	Barton-on-Sea		1999	2000		Portsmouth		29	5	0	1	1	1	0	0
Perry J	Jason	02/04/1970	Newport		1986	1996	w	Juniors	Bristol Rovers	281	15	22	20	5	0	0	0
Pethard FJ	Freddie	07/10/1950	Glasgow		1971	1978		Celtic	Torquay United	171	3	7	10	0	0	0	0
Phillips JRW	Joe	08/07/1923	Cardiff		1946			Cardiff Corries		2	0	0	0	0	0	0	0
Phillips L	Leighton	25/09/1949	Briton Ferry		1966	1974	w	App.	Aston Villa	182	12	8	11	11	2	0	1
Phillips L	Lee	18/03/1979	Aberdare		1996	1999		YTS	Barry Town	16	0	3	1	0	0	0	0
Philliskirk A	Tony	10/02/1965	Sunderland		1995	1996		Burnley	Oldham Athletic	61	2	2	2	5	0	0	0
Pickrell AD	Tony	03/11/1942	Neath		1960	1961		Juniors	Retired - illness	18	1	1	1	4	0	0	0
Pike C	Chris	19/10/1961	Cardiff		1986			Fulham (loan)		154	10	8	9	67	3	2	2
					1989	1992		Fulham	Hereford Utd.								
Pinxton AE	Albert	1912	Shelton		1936			Blackburn Rovers	Torquay United	20	2	0	1	3	0	0	0
Pirie TS	Tom	09/12/1900	Aberdeen		1926			Aberdeen	Bristol Rovers	5	0	0	0	0	0	0	0
Platnauer NR	Nicky	10/06/1961	Leicester		1986	1988		Birmingham City	Notts County	115	9	6	12	7	0	2	0
Platt JA	Jim	26/01/1952	Ballymoney		1978		n	Middlesbrough (loan)		4	0	0	0	0	0	0	0
Plumley GE	Gary	24/03/1956	Birmingham		1983	1984		Happy Valley	Ebbw Vale	25	0	1	0	0	0	0	0
Poland G	George	21/09/1913	Penarth	1988	1935	1936	w	Swindon Town	Wrexham	26	2	0	0	0	0	0	0
					1946			Liverpool	Lovells Ath.								
Pollard R	Bob	25/08/1899	Platt Bridge		1932			QPR	St. Etienne (Fra)	31	0	0	0	0	0	0	0
Polycarpou A	Andy	15/08/1958	Islington		1981			Cambridge Utd.	Greece	7	0	0	0	0	0	0	0
Pontin K	Keith	14/06/1956	Pontyclun		1976	1982	w	App.	Merthyr Tydfil	193	6	14	6	5	0	0	0
Postin EL	Eli	03/06/1905	Dudley	1991	1933			Dudley Town	Bristol Rovers	33	2	0	1	13	0	0	0
Powell CG	Cliff	21/02/1968	Watford		1989			Sheffield Utd. (loan)		1	0	0	1	0	0	0	0
Powell D	David	15/10/1944	Dolgarrog		1972	1974	w	Sheffield Utd.	Sth Wales Police	36	3	1	2	1	0	0	0
Prescott JR	James		Waterloo, Lancashire		1936	1938		Liverpool	Hull City	31	4	0	0	7	3	0	0
Price AD	Allen	24/03/1968	Gelligaer		1985			Newport County		2	0	0	0	0	0	0	0
Price CA	Cecil	02/12/1919	Cardiff		1948			Local	Bradford City	1	0	0	0	0	0	0	0

Name		D.O.B	Place of Birth	Died	First Season	Last Season	Int	Previous Club	Next Club	Appearances Lge	FAC	FLC	Oth.	Goals Lge	FAC	FLC	Oth.
Prior SJ	Spencer	22/04/1971	Rochford		2001			Manchester City	.	37	3	0	2	2	0	0	0
Pugh R	Reg	1917	Aberaman		1934	1938		Aberaman	Retired	166	12	0	4	25	2	0	0
Rainford JW	Johnny	11/12/1930	Camden Town	2001	1953			Crystal Palace	Brentford	3	0	0	0	1	0	0	0
Ramsey PC	Paul	03/09/1962	Derry		1991 1994	1992	n	Leicester City St. Johnstone (loan)	St. Johnstone	80	3	2	9	7	0	0	1
Rankmore FEJ	Frank	21/07/1939	Cardiff		1961	1962	w	Cardiff Corries	Peterborough Utd.	67	1	5	1	0	0	0	0
Ratcliffe K	Kevin	12/11/1960	Mancot		1992	1993	w	Everton	Nottm. Forest	25	0	1	3	1	0	0	0
Redwood DJ	Doug	1918	Ebbw Vale		1935	1936		Ebbw Vale	Walsall	13	0	0	0	0	0	0	0
Reece GI	Gil	02/07/1942	Cardiff		1972	1975	w	Sheffield Utd.	Swansea City	100	9	5	2	23	2	1	0
Reed E	Ebor	30/11/1899	Spennymoor	1971	1925			Newcastle United	Nottm. Forest	6	0	0	0	0	0	0	0
Rees MJ	Mel	25/01/1967	Cardiff	1993	1984	1986		YTS	Watford	31	3	3	0	0	0	0	0
Rees NR	Nigel	11/07/1953	Bridgend		1970	1972		Juniors	Bridgend	27	5	0	2	1	0	0	0
Rees W	Billy	10/03/1924	Blaengarw	1996	1946	1948	w	Carn Rovers	Tottenham H	101	6	0	0	34	2	0	0
Reid GH	George 'Paddy'	1896	Belfast		1922		i	Walsall	Fulham	7	0	0	0	4	0	0	0
Reynolds AB	Brayley	30/05/1935	Blackwood		1956	1958		Lovells Ath.	Swansea Town	55	2	0	0	14	1	0	0
Rhodes A	Arthur	1920	Devon		1938			Torquay United		5	0	0	0	0	0	0	0
Richards LG	Len	13/04/1911	Barry	1985	1932			Tottenham H	Dundalk	1	0	0	0	0	0	0	0
Richards P	Percy	1907	Merthyr Tydfil		1926			Merthyr Vale	Chesterfield	3	1	0	0	0	0	0	0
Richards SV	Stan	21/01/1917	Cardiff	1987	1946	1947	w	Tufnell Park	Swansea Town	57	2	0	0	39	0	0	0
Richardson NJ	Nick	11/04/1967	Halifax		1992	1994		Halifax Town	Bury	111	6	4	9	13	0	0	1
Rickards CT	Tom 'Tex'	19/02/1915	Giltbrook	1980	1938			Notts County	Scunthorpe Utd.	20	2	0	0	5	0	0	0
Riley H	Harry	22/11/1909	Hollinwood	1982	1934	1935		Notts County	Northampton Town	61	2	0	1	13	0	0	0
Robbins WW	Walter	24/11/1910	Cardiff	1979	1928	1931	w	Ely United	West Bromwich A.	86	6	0	0	38	1	0	0
Roberts CJ	Chris	22/10/1979	Cardiff		1997	1999		YTS	Exeter City	23	5	2	2	3	0	0	0
Roberts DF	David	26/01/1949	Southampton		1978	1980	w	Hull City	Barry Town	41	1	4	0	2	0	0	0
Roberts J	Joe	02/10/1900	Birkenhead	1984	1935			Luton Town	Dartford	22	1	0	0	5	0	0	0
Roberts JW	Jon	30/12/1968	Llwynypia		1987	1989		YTS	Barry Town	9	1	0	2	0	0	0	0
Roberts WJ	Bill		Birmingham		1928	1932		Flint Town Utd.		130	5	0	0	1	0	0	0
Robinson M	Matthew		Felling		1928	1930		Pelaw	Manchester Utd.	18	2	0	0	2	0	0	0
Robson K	Keith	15/11/1953	Hetton-le-Hole		1977			West Ham Utd.	Norwich City	21	0	1	0	5	0	0	0
Rodgerson I	Ian	09/04/1966	Hereford		1988 1995	1990 1996		Hereford Utd. Sunderland	Birmingham City Hereford Utd.	153	14	14	10	5	0	1	0
Rodon CP	Chris	09/06/1963	Swansea		1983			Brighton & Hove A.		4	0	2	0	0	0	0	0
Rodrigues PJ	Peter	21/04/1944	Cardiff		1963	1965	w	Juniors	Leicester City	85	2	8	8	2	0	0	0
Rogers AJ	Alan	06/07/1954	Plymouth		1986			Southend Utd.	Saltash Utd.	27	2	3	2	1	0	0	0
Rogers TW	Thomas		South Wales		1933			Local		2	0	0	1	1	0	0	0
Rollo JS	Jimmy	22/05/1976	Wisbech		1996	1997		Bath City	Forest Green Rovers	15	2	1	2	0	0	1	0
Ronan P	Peter		Dysart		1931	1932		Roslyn Juniors	East Fife	30	5	0	0	1	0	0	0
Ronson W	Billy	22/01/1957	Fleetwood		1979	1981		Blackpool	Wrexham	90	3	9	0	4	0	0	0
Roper H	Harry	13/04/1910	Romiley	1983	1935	1936		Leeds United	Stockport Co.	31	0	0	1	2	0	0	0
Ross WB	Bernard	08/11/1924	Swansea		1946	1947		Towey United	Sheffield Utd.	8	0	0	0	2	0	0	0
Rowland A	Alf	02/09/1920	Stokesley	1997	1948	1949		Aldershot	Stockton	3	0	0	0	0	0	0	0
Russell GH	George	1902	Atherstone		1932	1933		Bristol Rovers	Newport County	56	2	0	1	1	0	0	0
Russell KJ	Kevin	06/12/1966	Portsmouth		1990			Leicester City (loan)		3	0	0	0	0	0	0	0
Rutter CF	Charlie	22/12/1927	Poplar		1950	1957		Taunton Town	Exeter City	118	7	0	0	0	0	0	0
Ryder DF	Derek	18/02/1947	Leeds		1966			Leeds United	Rochdale	4	0	0	0	0	0	0	0
Sander CA	Chris	11/11/1962	Swansea		1985			Swansea City	Barry Town	13	0	1	0	0	0	0	0
Sanders AJ	Alan	29/10/1963	Newport		1981			Juniors		2	0	0	0	0	0	0	0
Sanderson PD	Paul	16/12/1966	Blackpool		1987			Halifax Town	Walsall	21	1	2	3	1	0	1	0
Saunders DN	Dean	21/06/1964	Swansea		1984		w	Swansea City (loan)		4	0	0	0	0	0	0	0
Saville AV	Andy	12/12/1964	Hull		1997	1998		Wigan Ath.	Scarborough	35	5	1	0	12	2	0	0
Sayer PA	Peter	02/05/1955	Cardiff		1973	1981	w	Juniors	Brighton & Hove A.	86	4	7	5	15	2	2	0
Schwinkendorf J	Jorn	27/01/1971	Hamburg, Germany		1999			SV Waldhof	Osnabruck (Ger)	5	1	0	0	0	0	0	0
Scott AM	Andy	27/06/1975	Manchester		1994	1996		Blackburn Rovers	Rochdale	16	1	1	0	1	0	0	0
Scott MJ	Morrys	17/12/1970	Swansea		1989			YTS	Colchester United	9	2	0	1	0	3	0	0
Scott RJ	Bob	16/03/1937	Dundee		1957			Dundee Violet	Swindon Town	3	0	0	0	0	0	0	0
Scott RSA	Dick	26/10/1941	Thetford		1963	1964		Norwich City	Scunthorpe Utd.	37	0	2	0	5	0	0	0
Scott WJ	Bill		Ireland		1936			Stockport Co.	Wigan Athletic	17	2	0	1	0	0	0	0
Scully ADT	Tony	12/06/1976	Dublin		1995			Crystal Palace (loan)		14	0	0	0	0	0	0	0
Searle DB	Damon	26/10/1971	Cardiff		1989	1995		YTS	Stockport Co.	234	13	9	22	3	0	1	0
Seasman J	John	21/02/1955	Liverpool		1984			Rotherham Utd.	Chesterfield	12	0	4	0	2	0	0	0
Semark RH	Robin	05/09/1972	Portsmouth		1991			YTS	Havant Town	6	0	0	1	0	0	0	0
Sendall RA	Richard	10/07/1967	Stamford		1989			Carlisle Utd.		4	0	0	0	0	0	0	0
Sharp F	Frank	28/05/1947	Edinburgh		1968	1969		Carlisle Utd.	Barnsley	15	0	0	1	1	0	0	0
Shaw P	Paul	04/09/1973	Burnham		1995			Arsenal		6	0	0	0	0	0	0	0
Shaw W	William	03/10/1897	Kilnhurst		1928			Gainsborough Trin.	Gainsborough Trin.	2	0	0	0	0	0	0	0
Sherlock SE	Steve	10/05/1959	Birmingham		1986			Stockport Co.	Newport County	15	0	3	0	0	0	0	0
Sherwood AT	Alf	13/11/1923	Aberaman	1990	1946	1955	w	Aberaman	Newport County	354	18	0	0	14	1	0	0
Showers D	Derek	28/01/1953	Merthyr Tydfil		1970	1976	w	Juniors	Bournemouth	83	2	7	8	10	1	1	1
Simmons AJ	Tony	09/02/1965	Stocksbridge		1986			Lincoln City (loan)		5	0	0	0	1	0	0	0
Simpkins MJ	Mike	28/11/1978	Sheffield		2001			Chesterfield		17	0	1	0	0	0	0	0
Sloan TM	Tom	11/09/1900	Portadown		1924	1928	in	Linfield	Linfield	79	11	0	0	1	0	0	0
Smelt LA	Lee	13/03/1958	Edmonton		1984	1985		Halifax Town	Welling United	37	2	3	2	0	0	0	0
Smith CR	Colin	03/11/1958	Ruddington		1983	1984		Caroline Hill (HK)	Aldershot	50	0	5	0	3	0	0	0
Smith EE	Bert		Donegal		1920	1923	i	Army	Middlesbrough	105	18	0	0	2	1	0	0
Smith FC	Cecil	30/10/1904	Marchwiel	1977	1936			Burnley		16	0	0	0	8	0	0	0
Smith G	George	07/10/1945	Newcastle		1973	1974		Birmingham City	Swansea City	45	1	3	2	1	0	0	0
Smith HR	Harold		Wealdstone		1935	1936		Notts County		50	1	0	1	3	0	0	0
Smith J	Jock	07/12/1898	Dalbeattie		1930	1931	s	Middlesbrough	Distillery	61	4	0	0	0	0	0	0
Smith JA	James		Worcester		1936	1937		Army	Wrexham	13	0	0	0	0	0	0	0
Smith R	Ritchie		Aberdeen		1938			Aberdeen	Clyde	11	5	0	0	2	0	0	0
Smith SJW	Sam	07/09/1904	Stafford	1988	1925	1926		Cradley Heath	Port Vale	4	1	0	0	0	0	0	0
Smith TP	Thomas	1901	Newcastle	1978	1925	1928		Merthyr Town	Brighton & Hove A.	42	0	0	0	7	0	0	0

111

Name		D.O.B	Place of Birth	Died	First Season	Last Season	Int	Previous Club	Next Club	Appearances				Goals			
										Lge	FAC	FLC	Oth.	Lge	FAC	FLC	Oth.
Spring AJ	Andy	17/11/1965	Gateshead		1985			Bristol Rovers (loan)		1	0	0	0	0	0	0	0
Stansfield F	Fred	12/12/1917	Cardiff		1946	1948	w	Grange Ath.	Newport County	106	5	0	0	1	0	0	0
Stant PR	Phil	13/10/1962	Bolton		1992	1994		Mansfield Town	Bury	79	7	2	8	34	4	2	3
Steel A	Alf	15/08/1925	Glasgow		1949			Walsall		10	0	0	0	0	0	0	0
Steele EG	Eric	14/05/1954	Wallsend		1982			Watford (loan)		7	0	0	0	0	0	0	0
Stephens LM	Lee	30/09/1971	Cardiff		1990			YTS		3	0	0	1	0	0	0	0
Stevens GM	Gary	30/08/1954	Birmingham		1978	1981		Evesham	Shrewsbury Town	150	4	9	0	44	0	3	0
Stevenson E	Ernie	28/12/1923	Rotherham	1970	1948	1949		Wolves	Southampton	50	3	0	0	15	1	0	0
Stevenson NCA	Nigel	02/11/1958	Swansea		1985 / 1987	1988	w	Swansea City (loan) / Swansea City		82	2	5	6	2	1	0	0
Stitfall AE	Albert	07/07/1924	Cardiff		1948	1950		Juniors	Torquay United	7	0	0	0	1	0	0	0
Stitfall RF	Ron	14/12/1925	Cardiff		1947	1963	w	Juniors	Retired	398	20	3	0	8	0	0	0
Stockin R	Ron	27/06/1931	Birmingham		1954	1956		Wolves	Grimsby Town	57	3	0	0	16	1	0	0
Stoker G	Gareth	22/02/1973	Bishop Auckland		1996	1997		Hereford Utd.	Rochdale	36	4	2	3	4	0	0	0
Sugrue PA	Paul	06/11/1960	Coventry		1981			Manchester City	Kansas City (USA)	5	1	1	0	0	0	1	0
Sullivan CJ	Colin	24/06/1951	Saltash		1978	1981		Norwich City	Hereford Utd.	63	2	4	0	1	0	0	0
Sullivan D	Derrick	10/08/1930	Newport	1983	1947	1960	w	Juniors	Exeter City	275	10	0	0	19	0	0	0
Summerfield K	Kevin	07/01/1959	Walsall		1984			Walsall	Plymouth Argyle	10	0	2	0	1	0	0	0
Summerhayes DM	David	21/03/1947	Cardiff		1965	1967		App.	Hereford Utd.	13	0	1	1	0	0	0	0
Summers C	Chris	06/01/1972	Cardiff		1990			YTS		3	0	0	1	0	0	0	0
Sutton MC	Mel	13/02/1946	Birmingham		1968	1971		Aston Villa	Wrexham	138	8	5	14	5	0	0	2
Swan MMG	Maurice	27/09/1938	Drumcondra		1960	1962	r	Drumcondra	Hull City	15	3	1	0	0	0	0	0
Taggart R	Bobby	10/03/1927	Newmains		1949			Coltness Utd.	Torquay United	2	0	0	0	0	0	0	0
Talbot FL	Les	03/08/1910	Hednesford		1936	1938		Blackburn Rovers	Walsall	94	13	0	3	21	2	0	0
Tapscott DJR	Derek	30/06/1932	Barry		1958	1964	w	Arsenal	Newport County	193	9	5	7	79	2	3	2
Taylor PMR	Mark	20/11/1964	Hartlepool		1990			Blackpool (loan)		6	0	0	0	3	0	0	0
Taylor SG	Sidney				1934					1	0	0	0	0	0	0	0
Taylor W	Billy	05/06/1898	Langley Green		1922	1924		Stourbridge	Aberdare Ath.	6	0	0	0	0	0	0	0
Tennant J	Jim		Canada		1932				St. Johnstone	2	0	0	0	0	0	0	0
Thirlaway WJ	Billy	10/10/1896	New Washington	1983	1926	1929		Birmingham	Tunbridge Wells	108	6	0	1	22	0	0	0
Thomas DJ	Dai	26/09/1975	Caerphilly		1998	2000		Watford	Merthyr Tydfil	31	3	1	1	5	0	0	0
Thomas MR	Martin	28/11/1959	Senghenydd		1982		w	Bristol Rovers (loan)		15	0	4	0	0	0	0	0
Thomas PJ	Peter	18/10/1932	Treforest		1953			Juniors	Exeter City	4	1	0	0	1	0	0	0
Thomas RJ	Rod	11/01/1947	Glyncorrwg		1977	1981	w	Derby County	Gloucester City	96	4	4	3	0	0	0	0
Thomas WK	Keith	28/07/1929	Oswestry		1952	1953		Sheffield Wed.	Plymouth Argyle	9	0	0	0	4	0	0	0
Thompson AR	Andy	09/11/1967	Cannock		2000	2001		Tranmere Rovers		7	1	0	3	0	0	0	0
Thompson CD	Chris	24/01/1960	Walsall		1989			Blackpool	Walsall	2	0	0	0	0	0	0	0
Thompson GL	Garry	07/10/1959	Birmingham		1993	1994		QPR	Northampton Town	43	7	2	6	5	1	0	1
Thorne PL	Peter	21/06/1973	Manchester		2001			Stoke City		26	0	0	2	8	0	0	0
Tiddy MD	Mike	04/04/1929	Helston		1950	1954		Torquay United	Arsenal	146	4	0	0	20	0	0	0
Tobin R	Bobby	29/03/1921	Cardiff		1947			Cardiff Corries	Barry Town	2	0	0	0	0	0	0	0
Tong DJ	David	21/09/1955	Blackpool		1982	1985		Shrewsbury Town	Bristol City	120	5	12	0	3	1	0	0
Toshack JB	John	22/03/1949	Cardiff		1965	1970	w	App.	Liverpool	162	6	6	19	74	1	1	11
Toshack JC	Cameron	07/03/1970	Cardiff		1990	1991		Bristol City	Dundee	5	0	0	1	0	0	0	0
Townsend CG	Chris	30/03/1966	Caerleon		1983			Juniors	Southampton	5	0	2	0	0	0	0	0
Tucker KJ	Ken	15/07/1935	Merthyr Tydfil		1956	1957		Aston Villa	Shrewsbury Town	13	0	0	0	0	0	0	0
Tupling S	Steve	11/07/1964	Wensleydale		1988	1989		Newport County	Hartlepool Utd.	5	2	0	0	0	1	0	0
Turnbull WJ	Billy	21/12/1900	Blyth		1922			West Stanley	Newport County	1	0	0	0	0	0	0	0
Turner A	Bert	03/09/1907	Sheffield		1937	1938		Doncaster Rovers	Bristol Rovers	42	4	0	2	20	1	0	1
Turner C	Charles				1936			Bangor City		2	0	0	0	0	0	0	0
Turner RP	Robbie	18/09/1966	Littlethorpe		1985	1986		Huddersfield T	Bristol Rovers	39	1	3	1	8	0	1	0
Tysoe GF	Frank	13/11/1902	Northampton		1926			Birmingham Trams	Charlton Ath.	2	0	0	0	0	0	0	0
Unsworth JJ	Jamie	01/05/1973	Bury		1990	1991		YTS	Radcliffe Borough	4	0	0	1	0	0	0	0
Upton JE	Jim	03/06/1940	Coatbridge		1963			Celtic	Bath City	5	0	2	0	0	0	0	0
Valentine AF	Arthur	03/06/1907	Higher Ince	1990	1929	1930		Southport	Wigan Borough	16	2	0	0	3	1	0	0
Vaughan AJ	Tony	11/10/1975	Manchester		1999			Manchester City (loan)		14	0	0	1	0	0	0	0
Vaughan NM	Nigel	20/05/1959	Caerleon		1983	1986	w	Newport County	Wolves	149	7	9	4	41	1	2	0
Vaughan T	Tommy		Cardiff		1934			Chester	Folkestone	12	1	0	1	3	0	0	1
Vearncombe G	Graham	28/03/1934	Cardiff		1952	1963	w	Juniors	Merthyr Tydfil	207	5	3	1	0	0	0	0
Vick L	Leigh	08/01/1978	Cardiff		1994	1995		YTS		4	0	0	0	0	0	0	0
Villars AK	Tony	24/01/1952	Cwmbran		1971	1975	w	Cwmbran Town	Newport County	73	3	4	4	4	0	0	1
Vincent JV	Johnny	08/02/1947	West Bromwich		1972	1974		Middlesbrough	Atherstone Town	66	5	3	3	11	0	1	0
Wake HW	Harry	21/01/1901	Seaton Delaval	1978	1923	1930		Newcastle United	Mansfield Town	149	17	0	0	9	1	0	0
Walker L	Lee	27/06/1976	Pontypool		1993			YTS		1	0	0	0	0	0	0	0
Walker PA	Phil	27/01/1957	Kirkby-in-Ashfield		1983			Rotherham Utd. (loan)		2	0	0	0	0	0	0	0
Walsh A	Alan	09/12/1956	Hartlepool		1991			Shrewsbury Town	Southampton	1	0	0	0	0	0	0	0
Walsh IP	Ian	04/09/1958	St Davids		1987	1988	w	Grimsby Town		17	0	1	1	4	0	0	0
Walsh JB	Brian	26/03/1932	Aldershot	2001	1955	1961		Arsenal	Newport County	206	14	4	0	33	1	1	0
Walton G	George	1911	Burnley		1936	1938		Bolton Wanderers	Walsall	84	11	0	3	16	2	0	0
Walton MA	Mark	01/06/1969	Merthyr Tydfil		2000	2001		Brighton & Hove A.		40	4	2	2	0	0	0	0
Warboys A	Alan	18/04/1949	Goldthorpe		1970	1972		Sheffield Wed.	Sheffield Utd.	61	5	4	2	27	0	0	0
Ward D	Dai	16/07/1934	Barry	1996	1960	1961	w	Bristol Rovers	Watford	34	1	3	1	18	0	2	0
Ward GJ	Gavin	30/06/1970	Sutton Coldfield		1989	1992		West Bromwich A.	Leicester City	59	1	0	7	0	0	0	0
Wardle G	George	24/09/1919	Kimblesworth	1991	1948			Exeter City	QPR	40	1	0	0	11	0	0	0
Ware PD	Paul	07/11/1970	Congleton		1996			Stockport Co. (loan)		5	0	0	0	0	0	0	0
Ware T	Tom		Cardiff		1930			Local		12	2	0	0	0	0	0	0
Warren FW	Freddie	23/12/1907	Cardiff	1986	1927	1929	w	Local	Middlesbrough	37	1	0	0	8	0	0	0
Watkins JV	Johnny	09/04/1933	Bristol		1959	1960		Bristol City	Bristol Rovers	65	4	0	0	17	0	0	0
Watkins PJ	Phil	02/01/1945	Caerphilly		1963			Juniors	Barry Town	1	0	1	0	0	0	0	0
Watson T	Tom	04/10/1902	Belfast		1925	1928	i	Crusaders	Linfield	85	11	0	0	0	0	0	0
Watson WT	Bill	11/06/1918	Swansea	1978	1947			Preston NE		1	0	0	0	0	0	0	0
Weale RH	Bobby	09/11/1903	Troedyrhiw	1970	1930			Southampton	Guildford City	5	0	0	0	0	0	0	0
Welsby A	Arthur	17/11/1902	Downall Green	1980	1936			Southport	Mossley	3	0	0	0	0	0	0	0

Name		D.O.B	Place of Birth	Died	First Season	Last Season	Int	Previous Club	Next Club	Appearances				Goals			
										Lge	FAC	FLC	Oth.	Lge	FAC	FLC	Oth.
Went PF	Paul	12/10/1949	Bromley-by-Bow		1976	1978		Portsmouth	Orient	72	4	4	4	11	0	0	0
West G	George		Wardley		1920	1921		Wallsend	Stockport Co.	25	5	0	0	5	1	0	0
West J	Joe	1910	Walker	1965	1933			Newcastle United	Darlington	6	0	0	0	2	0	0	0
Weston RD	Rhys	27/10/1980	Kingston		2000	2001		Arsenal		65	6	1	3	0	0	0	0
Wheeler P	Paul	03/01/1965	Caerphilly		1985	1988		Aberaman	Hull City	101	4	7	6	10	1	2	1
White SJ	Steve	02/01/1959	Chipping Sodbury		1996	1997		Hereford Utd.	Bath City	66	3	4	5	15	2	0	0
Whitham J	Jack	08/12/1946	Burnley		1973	1974		Liverpool	Reading	14	1	0	0	3	0	0	0
Whitlow FWJ	Fred	03/09/1904	Bristol	1978	1934			Exeter City	Barry	7	0	0	1	1	0	0	0
Wigg NM	Nathan	27/09/1974	Cardiff		1993	1995		YTS	Dundalk	59	3	3	3	1	0	0	0
Williams CR	Chris	25/12/1955	Brecon		1977			Talgarth	Bridgend	3	0	0	0	0	0	0	0
Williams DJ	Daniel		Cardiff		1935	1936		Local		20	0	0	0	10	0	0	0
Williams DP	David	18/09/1968	Liverpool		1994	1995		Burnley	Linfield	82	3	6	5	0	0	0	0
Williams DR	Roley	10/07/1927	Swansea		1948	1955		Milford United	Northampton Town	138	1	0	0	19	0	0	0
Williams GC	Gareth	30/10/1941	Hendon		1961	1967		Juniors	Bolton Wanderers	161	8	12	9	13	1	0	1
Williams GJJ	Glyn	03/11/1918	Maesteg		1946	1952	w	Caerau	Aberystwyth	144	6	0	0	0	1	0	0
Williams JN	John	11/05/1968	Birmingham		1998			Exeter City	York City	43	5	2	1	12	3	1	0
Williams RS	Ralph	02/10/1905	Aberaman	1985	1929	1930		Colwyn Bay	Crewe Alexandra	30	2	0	0	17	0	0	0
Williams SD	Steve	16/10/1974	Aberystwyth		1992	1996		Coventry City	Dundalk	34	1	0	5	0	0	0	0
Williams TP	Thomas	1915	Cardiff		1937	1938		Local		6	0	0	0	0	0	0	0
Williams WJ	John	03/10/1960	Liverpool		1991			Bournemouth	Commercial Officer	5	0	0	0	0	0	0	0
Wilson RJ	Bob	23/05/1943	Birmingham		1964	1967		Aston Villa	Exeter City	115	5	7	13	0	0	0	0
Wilson TH	Tom	09/12/1902	Walthamstow		1930			Wigan Borough	Charlton Ath.	1	0	0	0	0	0	0	0
Wimbleton PP	Paul	13/11/1964	Havant		1986	1988		Portsmouth	Bristol City	119	9	6	11	17	4	0	2
Winspear J	Jack	24/12/1946	Leeds		1966			Leeds United	Rochdale	1	0	0	0	0	0	0	0
Withey GA	Graham	11/06/1960	Bristol		1984	1985		Coventry City	Bath City	27	1	0	1	7	1	0	0
Wood G	George	26/09/1952	Douglas		1987	1989	s	Crystal Palace	Hereford Utd.	67	6	6	7	0	0	0	0
Wood TL	Terry	03/09/1920	Newport		1946			Newport Docks		4	2	0	0	0	0	0	0
Woodruff RW	Bobby	09/11/1940	Highworth		1969	1973		Crystal Palace	Newport County	150	12	5	10	22	2	1	1
Woods JP	Jonathan	05/10/1966	Blackwood		1984			Juniors	Ebbw Vale	1	0	0	0	0	0	0	0
Woof W	Billy	16/08/1956	Gateshead		1982			Blyth Spartans	Gateshead	1	0	0	0	1	0	0	0
Youds EP	Eddie	03/05/1970	Liverpool		1989			Everton		1	1	0	0	0	0	0	0
Young S	Scott	14/01/1976	Pontypridd		1993	2001		YTS		264	20	14	14	21	2	1	1
Zois P	Peter	21/04/1978	Australia		1997			Purfleet		1	0	0	0	0	0	0	0

Played in FA Cup Only

Name		D.O.B	Place of Birth	Died	First Season	Last Season	Int	Previous Club	Next Club	Lge	FAC	FLC	Oth.	Lge	FAC	FLC	Oth.
Wilcox C	Crad	08/11/1923	Treharris		1951			Treharris	Newport County	0	1	0	0	0	0	0	0
Rees B	Brian				1971					0	1	0	0	0	0	0	0

Played in League Cup Only

Name		D.O.B	Place of Birth	Died	First Season	Last Season	Int	Previous Club	Next Club	Lge	FAC	FLC	Oth.	Lge	FAC	FLC	Oth.
Burns A	Albert				1963					0	0	1	0	0	0	0	0
Callaway NAD	Nilsson				1992			YTS		0	0	1	0	0	0	0	0
Heycock R	Russell				1983			YTS		0	0	1	0	0	0	0	0
Street DC					1994					0	0	1	0	0	0	0	0
Yorath D	David				1965			Local	Margate	0	0	1	0	0	0	0	0

Played in Miscellaneous Games Only

Name		D.O.B	Place of Birth	Died	First Season	Last Season	Int	Previous Club	Next Club	Lge	FAC	FLC	Oth.	Lge	FAC	FLC	Oth.
Bartley KD	Kevin				1993			YTS		0	0	0	1	0	0	0	0
Harriott ML	Marvin	20/04/1974	Dulwich		1997			Gloucester C (trial)		0	0	0	1	0	0	0	0
Kendall LM	Lee	08/01/1981	Newport		2001			Crystal Palace	Shrewsbury T	0	0	0	1	0	0	0	0
Miethig M	Mario				1989			FC Spandau		0	0	0	1	0	0	0	0

Played in 1939/40 season only

Name		D.O.B	Place of Birth	Died	First Season	Last Season	Int	Previous Club	Next Club
Cringan JA	Jimmy	1918	Douglas Water					Wolves	Retired - injury
McPhillips L	Laurence		Bathgate					Albion Rovers	
Myers JH	Jim	05/03/1920	Barnsley					Wolves	
Sykes EA	Ernest	27/12/1912	Temple Normanton					Birmingham	Retired

1920/21 Division 2

1	Birmingham	42	16	4	1	55	13	8	6	7	24	25	58
2	CARDIFF CITY	42	13	5	3	27	9	11	5	5	32	23	58
3	Bristol City	42	14	3	4	35	12	5	10	6	14	17	51
4	Blackpool	42	12	3	6	32	19	8	7	6	22	23	50
5	West Ham United	42	13	5	3	38	11	6	5	10	13	19	48
6	Notts County	42	12	5	4	36	17	6	6	9	19	23	47
7	Clapton Orient	42	13	6	2	31	9	3	7	11	12	33	45
8	South Shields	42	13	4	4	41	16	4	6	11	20	30	44
9	Fulham	42	14	4	3	33	12	2	6	13	10	35	42
10	Sheffield Wed.	42	9	7	5	31	14	6	4	11	17	34	41
11	Bury	42	10	8	3	29	13	5	2	14	16	36	40
12	Leicester City	42	10	8	3	26	11	2	8	11	13	35	40
13	Hull City	42	7	10	4	24	18	3	10	8	19	35	40
14	Leeds United	42	11	5	5	30	14	3	5	13	10	31	38
15	Wolverhampton Wan.	42	11	4	6	34	24	5	2	14	15	42	38
16	Barnsley	42	9	10	2	31	17	1	6	14	17	33	36
17	Port Vale	42	7	6	8	28	19	4	8	9	15	30	36
18	Nottingham Forest	42	9	6	6	37	26	3	6	12	11	29	36
19	Rotherham County	42	8	9	4	23	21	4	3	14	14	32	36
20	Stoke	42	9	5	7	26	16	3	6	12	20	40	35
21	Coventry City	42	8	6	7	24	25	4	5	12	15	45	35
22	Stockport County	42	8	6	7	30	24	1	6	14	12	51	30

1921/22 Division 1

1	Liverpool	42	15	4	2	43	15	7	9	5	20	21	57
2	Tottenham Hotspur	42	15	3	3	43	17	6	6	9	22	22	51
3	Burnley	42	16	3	2	49	18	6	2	13	23	36	49
4	CARDIFF CITY	42	13	2	6	40	26	6	8	7	21	27	48
5	Aston Villa	42	16	3	2	50	19	6	0	15	24	36	47
6	Bolton Wanderers	42	12	4	5	40	24	8	3	10	28	35	47
7	Newcastle United	42	11	5	5	36	19	7	5	9	23	26	46
8	Middlesbrough	42	12	6	3	46	19	4	8	9	33	50	46
9	Chelsea	42	9	6	6	17	16	8	6	7	23	27	46
10	Manchester City	42	13	7	1	44	21	5	2	14	21	49	45
11	Sheffield United	42	11	3	7	32	17	4	7	10	27	37	40
12	Sunderland	42	13	4	4	46	23	3	4	14	14	39	40
13	West Bromwich Alb.	42	8	6	7	26	23	7	4	10	25	40	40
14	Huddersfield Town	42	12	3	6	33	14	3	6	12	20	40	39
15	Blackburn Rovers	42	7	6	8	35	31	6	6	9	19	26	38
16	Preston North End	42	12	7	2	33	20	1	5	15	9	45	38
17	Arsenal	42	10	6	5	27	19	5	1	15	20	37	37
18	Birmingham	42	9	2	10	25	29	6	5	10	23	31	37
19	Oldham Athletic	42	8	7	6	21	15	5	4	12	17	35	37
20	Everton	42	10	7	4	42	22	2	5	14	15	33	36
21	Bradford City	42	8	5	8	28	30	3	5	13	20	42	32
22	Manchester United	42	7	7	7	25	26	1	5	15	16	47	28

1922/23 Division 1

1	Liverpool	42	17	3	1	50	13	9	5	7	20	18	60
2	Sunderland	42	15	5	1	50	25	7	5	9	22	29	54
3	Huddersfield Town	42	14	2	5	35	15	7	9	5	25	17	53
4	Newcastle United	42	13	6	2	31	11	5	6	10	14	26	48
5	Everton	42	14	4	3	41	20	6	3	12	22	39	47
6	Aston Villa	42	15	3	3	42	11	3	7	11	22	40	46
7	West Bromwich Alb.	42	12	7	2	38	10	5	4	12	20	39	45
8	Manchester City	42	14	6	1	38	16	3	5	13	12	33	45
9	CARDIFF CITY	42	15	2	4	51	18	3	5	13	22	41	43
10	Sheffield United	42	11	7	3	41	20	5	3	13	27	44	42
11	Arsenal	42	13	4	4	38	16	3	6	12	23	46	42
12	Tottenham Hotspur	42	11	3	7	34	22	6	4	11	16	28	41
13	Bolton Wanderers	42	11	8	2	36	17	3	4	14	14	41	40
14	Blackburn Rovers	42	12	7	2	32	19	2	5	14	15	43	40
15	Burnley	42	12	3	6	39	24	4	3	14	19	35	38
16	Preston North End	42	12	3	6	41	26	1	8	12	19	38	37
17	Birmingham	42	10	4	7	25	19	3	7	11	16	38	37
18	Middlesbrough	42	11	4	6	41	25	2	6	13	16	38	36
19	Chelsea	42	5	13	3	29	20	4	5	12	16	33	36
20	Nottingham Forest	42	12	2	7	25	23	1	6	14	16	47	34
21	Stoke	42	7	9	5	28	19	3	1	17	19	48	30
22	Oldham Athletic	42	9	6	6	21	20	1	4	16	14	45	30

1923/24 Division 1

1	Huddersfield Town	42	15	5	1	35	9	8	6	7	25	24	57
2	CARDIFF CITY	42	14	5	2	35	13	8	8	5	26	21	57
3	Sunderland	42	12	7	2	38	20	10	2	9	33	34	53
4	Bolton Wanderers	42	13	6	2	45	13	5	8	8	23	21	50
5	Sheffield United	42	12	5	4	39	16	7	7	7	30	33	50
6	Aston Villa	42	10	10	1	33	11	8	3	10	19	26	49
7	Everton	42	13	7	1	43	18	5	6	10	19	35	49
8	Blackburn Rovers	42	14	5	2	40	13	3	6	12	14	37	45
9	Newcastle United	42	13	5	3	40	21	4	5	12	20	33	44
10	Notts County	42	9	7	5	21	15	5	7	9	23	34	42
11	Manchester City	42	11	7	3	34	24	4	5	12	20	47	42
12	Liverpool	42	11	5	5	35	20	4	6	11	14	28	41
13	West Ham United	42	10	6	5	26	17	3	9	9	14	26	41
14	Birmingham	42	10	4	7	25	19	3	9	9	16	30	39
15	Tottenham Hotspur	42	9	6	6	30	22	3	8	10	20	34	38
16	West Bromwich Alb.	42	10	6	5	43	30	2	8	11	8	32	38
17	Burnley	42	10	5	6	39	27	2	7	12	16	33	36
18	Preston North End	42	8	4	9	34	27	4	6	11	18	40	34
19	Arsenal	42	8	5	8	25	24	4	4	13	15	39	33
20	Nottingham Forest	42	7	9	5	19	15	3	3	15	23	49	32
21	Chelsea	42	7	9	5	23	21	2	5	14	8	32	32
22	Middlesbrough	42	6	4	11	23	23	1	4	16	14	37	22

1924/25 Division 1

1	Huddersfield Town	42	10	8	3	31	10	11	8	2	38	18	58
2	West Bromwich Alb.	42	13	6	2	40	17	10	4	7	18	17	56
3	Bolton Wanderers	42	18	2	1	61	13	4	9	8	15	21	55
4	Liverpool	42	13	5	3	43	20	7	5	9	20	35	50
5	Bury	42	13	4	4	35	20	4	11	6	19	31	49
6	Newcastle United	42	11	6	4	43	18	5	10	6	18	24	48
7	Sunderland	42	13	6	2	39	14	6	4	11	25	37	48
8	Birmingham	42	10	8	3	27	17	7	4	10	22	36	46
9	Notts County	42	11	6	4	29	12	5	7	9	13	19	45
10	Manchester City	42	11	7	3	44	29	6	2	13	32	39	43
11	CARDIFF CITY	42	11	5	5	35	19	5	6	10	21	32	43
12	Tottenham Hotspur	42	9	8	4	32	16	6	4	11	20	27	42
13	West Ham United	42	12	7	2	37	12	3	5	13	25	48	42
14	Sheffield United	42	10	5	6	34	25	3	8	10	21	38	39
15	Aston Villa	42	10	7	4	34	25	3	6	12	24	46	39
16	Blackburn Rovers	42	7	6	8	31	26	4	7	10	22	40	35
17	Everton	42	11	4	6	25	20	1	7	13	15	40	35
18	Leeds United	42	9	8	4	29	17	2	4	15	17	42	34
19	Burnley	42	7	8	6	28	31	4	4	13	18	44	34
20	Arsenal	42	12	3	6	33	17	2	2	17	13	41	33
21	Preston North End	42	8	2	11	29	35	2	4	15	8	39	26
22	Nottingham Forest	42	5	6	10	17	23	1	6	14	12	42	24

1925/26 Division 1

1	Huddersfield Town	42	14	6	1	50	17	9	5	7	42	43	57
2	Arsenal	42	16	2	3	57	19	6	6	9	30	44	52
3	Sunderland	42	17	2	2	67	30	4	4	13	29	50	48
4	Bury	42	12	4	5	55	34	8	3	10	30	43	47
5	Sheffield United	42	15	3	3	72	29	4	5	12	30	53	46
6	Aston Villa	42	12	7	2	56	25	4	5	12	30	51	44
7	Liverpool	42	9	8	4	43	27	5	8	8	27	36	44
8	Bolton Wanderers	42	11	6	4	46	31	6	4	11	29	45	44
9	Manchester United	42	12	4	5	40	26	7	2	12	26	47	44
10	Newcastle United	42	13	3	5	59	33	3	7	11	25	42	42
11	Everton	42	9	9	3	42	26	3	9	9	30	44	42
12	Blackburn Rovers	42	11	6	4	59	33	4	5	12	32	47	41
13	West Bromwich Alb.	42	13	5	3	59	29	3	3	15	20	49	40
14	Birmingham	42	14	2	5	35	25	2	6	13	31	56	40
15	Tottenham Hotspur	42	11	4	6	45	36	4	5	12	21	43	39
16	CARDIFF CITY	42	8	5	8	30	25	8	2	11	31	51	39
17	Leicester City	42	11	3	7	42	32	3	7	11	28	48	38
18	West Ham United	42	14	2	5	45	27	1	5	15	18	49	37
19	Leeds United	42	11	5	5	38	28	3	3	15	26	48	36
20	Burnley	42	7	7	7	43	35	6	3	12	42	73	36
21	Manchester City	42	8	7	6	48	42	4	4	13	41	58	35
22	Notts County	42	11	4	6	37	26	2	3	16	17	48	33

1926/27 Division 1

1	Newcastle United	42	19	1	1	64	20	6	5	10	32	38	56
2	Huddersfield Town	42	13	6	2	41	19	4	11	6	35	41	51
3	Sunderland	42	15	3	3	70	28	6	4	11	28	42	49
4	Bolton Wanderers	42	15	5	1	54	19	4	5	12	30	43	48
5	Burnley	42	15	4	2	55	30	4	5	12	36	50	47
6	West Ham United	42	9	6	6	50	36	10	2	9	36	34	46
7	Leicester City	42	13	4	4	58	33	4	8	9	27	37	46
8	Sheffield United	42	12	6	3	46	33	5	4	12	28	53	44
9	Liverpool	42	13	4	4	47	27	5	3	13	22	34	43
10	Aston Villa	42	11	4	6	51	34	7	3	11	30	49	43
11	Arsenal	42	12	5	4	47	30	5	4	12	30	56	43
12	Derby County	42	14	4	3	60	28	3	3	15	26	45	41
13	Tottenham Hotspur	42	11	4	6	48	33	5	5	11	28	45	41
14	CARDIFF CITY	42	12	3	6	31	17	4	6	11	24	48	41
15	Manchester United	42	9	8	4	29	19	4	6	11	23	45	40
16	Sheffield Wed.	42	15	3	3	49	29	0	6	15	26	63	39
17	Birmingham	42	13	3	5	36	17	4	1	16	28	56	38
18	Blackburn Rovers	42	9	5	7	40	40	6	3	12	37	56	38
19	Bury	42	8	5	8	43	38	4	7	10	25	39	36
20	Everton	42	10	6	5	35	30	2	4	15	29	60	34
21	Leeds United	42	9	7	5	43	31	2	1	18	26	57	30
22	West Bromwich Alb.	42	10	4	7	47	33	1	4	16	18	53	30

1927/28 Division 1

1	Everton	42	11	8	2	60	28	9	5	7	42	38	53
2	Huddersfield Town	42	15	1	5	57	31	7	6	8	34	37	51
3	Leicester City	42	14	5	2	66	25	4	7	10	30	47	48
4	Derby County	42	12	4	5	59	30	5	6	10	37	53	44
5	Bury	42	13	1	7	53	35	7	3	11	27	45	44
6	CARDIFF CITY	42	12	7	2	44	27	5	3	13	26	53	44
7	Bolton Wanderers	42	12	5	4	47	26	4	6	11	34	40	43
8	Aston Villa	42	13	3	5	52	30	4	6	11	26	43	43
9	Newcastle United	42	9	7	5	49	41	6	6	9	30	40	43
10	Arsenal	42	10	6	5	49	33	3	9	9	33	53	41
11	Birmingham	42	10	7	4	36	25	3	8	10	34	50	41
12	Blackburn Rovers	42	13	5	3	41	22	3	4	14	25	56	41
13	Sheffield United	42	12	4	5	56	42	3	6	12	23	44	40
14	Sheffield Wed.	42	9	6	6	45	29	4	7	10	36	49	39
15	Sunderland	42	9	5	7	37	29	6	4	11	37	47	39
16	Liverpool	42	10	6	5	54	36	3	7	11	30	51	39
17	West Ham United	42	9	7	5	48	34	5	4	12	33	54	39
18	Manchester United	42	12	6	3	51	27	4	1	16	21	53	39
19	Burnley	42	12	5	4	55	31	4	2	15	27	67	39
20	Portsmouth	42	13	4	4	40	23	3	3	15	26	67	39
21	Tottenham Hotspur	42	12	3	6	47	34	3	5	13	27	52	38
22	Middlesbrough	42	7	9	5	46	35	4	6	11	35	53	37

1928/29 Division 1

1	Sheffield Wed.	42	18	3	0	55	16	3	7	11	31	46	52
2	Leicester City	42	16	5	0	67	22	5	4	12	29	45	51
3	Aston Villa	42	16	2	3	62	30	7	2	12	36	51	50
4	Sunderland	42	16	2	3	67	30	4	5	12	26	45	47
5	Liverpool	42	11	4	6	53	28	6	8	7	37	36	46
6	Derby County	42	12	5	4	56	24	6	5	10	30	47	46
7	Blackburn Rovers	42	11	6	4	42	26	6	5	10	30	37	45
8	Manchester City	42	12	3	6	63	40	6	6	9	32	46	45
9	Arsenal	42	11	6	4	43	25	5	7	9	34	47	45
10	Newcastle United	42	15	2	4	48	29	4	4	13	22	43	44
11	Sheffield United	42	12	5	4	57	30	3	6	12	29	55	41
12	Manchester United	42	8	8	5	32	23	6	5	10	34	53	41
13	Leeds United	42	11	5	5	42	28	5	4	12	29	56	41
14	Bolton Wanderers	42	10	6	5	44	25	4	6	11	29	55	40
15	Birmingham	42	8	7	6	37	32	7	3	11	31	45	40
16	Huddersfield Town	42	9	6	6	45	23	5	5	11	25	38	39
17	West Ham United	42	11	6	4	55	31	4	3	14	31	65	39
18	Everton	42	11	2	8	38	31	6	2	13	25	44	38
19	Burnley	42	12	5	4	55	32	3	3	15	26	71	38
20	Portsmouth	42	13	2	6	43	26	2	4	15	13	54	36
21	Bury	42	9	5	7	38	35	3	2	16	24	64	31
22	CARDIFF CITY	42	7	7	7	34	26	1	6	14	9	33	29

1929/30 Division 2

1	Blackpool	42	17	1	3	63	22	10	3	8	35	45	58
2	Chelsea	42	17	3	1	49	14	5	8	8	25	32	55
3	Oldham Athletic	42	14	5	2	60	21	7	6	8	30	30	53
4	Bradford Park Ave.	42	14	5	2	65	28	5	7	9	26	42	50
5	Bury	42	14	2	5	45	27	8	3	10	33	40	49
6	West Bromwich Alb.	42	16	1	4	73	31	5	4	12	32	42	47
7	Southampton	42	14	6	1	46	22	3	5	13	31	54	45
8	CARDIFF CITY	42	14	4	3	41	16	4	4	13	20	43	44
9	Wolverhampton Wan.	42	14	3	4	53	24	2	6	13	24	55	41
10	Nottingham Forest	42	9	6	6	36	28	4	9	8	19	41	41
11	Stoke City	42	12	4	5	41	20	4	4	13	33	52	40
12	Tottenham Hotspur	42	11	8	2	43	24	4	1	16	16	37	39
13	Charlton Athletic	42	10	6	5	39	23	4	5	12	20	40	39
14	Millwall	42	10	7	4	36	26	2	8	11	21	47	39
15	Swansea Town	42	11	5	5	42	23	3	4	14	15	38	37
16	Preston North End	42	7	7	7	42	36	6	4	11	23	44	37
17	Barnsley	42	12	7	2	39	22	2	1	18	17	49	36
18	Bradford City	42	7	7	7	33	30	5	5	11	27	47	36
19	Reading	42	10	7	4	31	20	2	4	15	23	47	35
20	Bristol City	42	11	4	6	36	30	2	5	14	25	53	35
21	Hull City	42	11	3	7	30	24	3	4	14	21	54	35
22	Notts County	42	8	7	6	33	26	1	8	12	21	44	33

1930/31 Division 2

1	Everton	42	18	1	2	76	31	10	4	7	45	35	61
2	West Bromwich Alb.	42	14	3	4	40	16	8	7	6	43	33	54
3	Tottenham Hotspur	42	15	5	1	64	20	7	2	12	24	35	51
4	Wolverhampton Wan.	42	15	2	4	56	25	6	3	12	28	42	47
5	Port Vale	42	15	3	3	39	16	6	2	13	28	45	47
6	Bradford Park Ave.	42	15	4	2	71	24	3	6	12	26	42	46
7	Preston North End	42	12	5	4	55	31	5	6	10	28	42	45
8	Burnley	42	13	5	3	55	30	4	6	11	26	47	45
9	Southampton	42	13	4	4	46	22	6	2	13	28	40	44
10	Bradford City	42	12	5	4	39	26	5	5	11	22	37	44
11	Stoke City	42	11	6	4	34	17	6	4	11	30	54	44
12	Oldham Athletic	42	13	5	3	45	28	3	5	13	16	44	42
13	Bury	42	14	3	4	44	20	5	0	16	31	62	41
14	Millwall	42	12	4	5	47	25	4	3	14	24	55	39
15	Charlton Athletic	42	11	4	6	35	33	4	5	12	24	53	39
16	Bristol City	42	11	5	5	29	23	4	3	14	25	59	38
17	Nottingham Forest	42	12	6	3	54	35	2	3	16	26	50	37
18	Plymouth Argyle	42	10	3	8	47	33	4	5	12	29	51	36
19	Barnsley	42	13	3	5	42	23	0	6	15	17	56	35
20	Swansea Town	42	11	5	5	40	29	1	5	15	11	45	34
21	Reading	42	11	2	8	47	33	1	4	16	25	63	30
22	CARDIFF CITY	42	7	6	8	32	31	1	3	17	15	56	25

1931/32 Division 3 (South)

1	Fulham	42	15	3	3	72	27	9	6	6	39	35	57
2	Reading	42	19	1	1	65	21	4	8	9	32	46	55
3	Southend United	42	12	5	4	41	18	9	6	6	36	35	53
4	Crystal Palace	42	14	7	0	48	12	6	4	11	26	51	51
5	Brentford	42	11	6	4	40	22	8	4	9	28	30	48
6	Luton Town	42	16	1	4	62	25	4	6	11	33	45	47
7	Exeter City	42	16	3	2	53	16	4	4	13	24	46	47
8	Brighton & Hove A.	42	12	4	5	42	21	5	8	8	31	37	46
9	CARDIFF CITY	42	14	2	5	62	29	5	6	10	25	44	46
10	Norwich City	42	12	7	2	51	22	5	5	11	25	45	46
11	Watford	42	14	4	3	49	27	5	4	12	32	52	46
12	Coventry City	42	17	2	2	74	28	1	6	14	34	69	44
13	Queen's Park Rgs.	42	11	6	4	50	30	4	6	11	29	43	42
14	Northampton Town	42	12	3	6	48	26	4	4	13	21	43	39
15	Bournemouth	42	8	8	5	42	32	5	4	12	28	46	38
16	Clapton Orient	42	7	8	6	41	35	5	3	13	36	55	35
17	Swindon Town	42	12	2	7	47	31	2	4	15	23	53	34
18	Bristol Rovers	42	11	6	4	46	30	2	2	17	19	62	34
19	Torquay United	42	9	6	6	49	39	3	3	15	23	67	33
20	Mansfield Town	42	11	5	5	54	45	0	5	16	21	63	32
21	Gillingham	42	8	6	7	26	26	2	2	17	14	56	28
22	Thames	42	6	7	8	35	35	1	2	18	18	74	23

1932/33 Division 3 (South)

1	Brentford	42	15	4	2	45	19	11	6	4	45	30	62
2	Exeter City	42	17	2	2	57	13	7	8	6	31	35	58
3	Norwich City	42	16	3	2	49	17	6	10	5	39	38	57
4	Reading	42	14	5	2	68	30	5	8	8	35	41	51
5	Crystal Palace	42	14	4	3	51	21	5	4	12	27	43	46
6	Coventry City	42	16	1	4	75	24	3	5	13	31	53	44
7	Gillingham	42	14	4	3	54	24	4	4	13	18	37	44
8	Northampton Town	42	16	5	0	54	11	2	3	16	22	55	44
9	Bristol Rovers	42	13	5	3	38	22	2	9	10	23	34	44
10	Torquay United	42	12	7	2	51	26	4	5	12	21	41	44
11	Watford	42	11	8	2	37	22	5	4	12	29	41	44
12	Brighton & Hove A.	42	13	3	5	42	20	4	5	12	24	45	42
13	Southend United	42	11	5	5	39	27	4	6	11	26	55	41
14	Luton Town	42	12	8	1	60	32	1	5	15	18	46	39
15	Bristol City	42	11	5	5	59	37	1	8	12	24	53	37
16	Queen's Park Rgs.	42	9	8	4	48	32	4	3	14	24	55	37
17	Aldershot Town	42	11	6	4	37	21	2	4	15	24	51	36
18	Bournemouth	42	10	7	4	44	27	2	5	14	16	54	36
19	CARDIFF CITY	42	12	4	5	48	30	0	3	18	21	69	31
20	Clapton Orient	42	7	8	6	39	35	1	5	15	20	58	29
21	Newport County	42	9	4	8	42	42	2	3	16	19	63	29
22	Swindon Town	42	7	9	5	36	29	2	2	17	24	76	29

1933/34 Division 3 (South)

1	Norwich City	42	16	4	1	55	19	9	7	5	33	30	61
2	Coventry City	42	16	3	2	70	22	5	9	7	30	32	54
3	Reading	42	17	4	0	60	13	4	8	9	22	37	54
4	Queen's Park Rgs.	42	17	2	2	42	12	7	4	10	28	39	54
5	Charlton Athletic	42	14	5	2	53	27	8	3	10	30	29	52
6	Luton Town	42	14	3	4	55	28	7	7	7	28	33	52
7	Bristol Rovers	42	14	4	3	49	21	6	7	8	28	26	51
8	Swindon Town	42	13	5	3	42	25	4	6	11	22	43	45
9	Exeter City	42	12	5	4	43	19	4	6	11	25	38	43
10	Brighton & Hove A.	42	12	7	2	47	18	3	6	12	21	42	43
11	Clapton Orient	42	14	4	3	60	25	2	6	13	15	44	42
12	Crystal Palace	42	11	6	4	40	25	5	3	13	31	42	41
13	Northampton Town	42	10	6	5	45	32	4	6	11	26	46	40
14	Aldershot Town	42	8	6	7	28	27	5	6	10	24	44	38
15	Watford	42	12	4	5	43	16	3	3	15	28	47	37
16	Southend United	42	9	6	6	32	27	3	4	14	19	47	34
17	Gillingham	42	8	8	5	49	41	3	3	15	26	55	33
18	Newport County	42	6	9	6	25	23	2	8	11	24	47	33
19	Bristol City	42	7	8	6	33	22	3	5	13	25	63	33
20	Torquay United	42	10	4	7	32	28	3	3	15	21	65	33
21	Bournemouth	42	7	7	7	41	37	2	2	17	19	65	27
22	CARDIFF CITY	42	6	4	11	32	43	3	2	16	25	62	24

1934/35 Division 3 (South)

1	Charlton Athletic	42	17	2	2	62	20	10	5	6	41	32	61
2	Reading	42	16	5	0	59	23	5	6	10	30	42	53
3	Coventry City	42	14	5	2	56	14	7	4	10	30	36	51
4	Luton Town	42	12	7	2	60	23	7	5	9	32	37	50
5	Crystal Palace	42	15	3	3	51	14	4	7	10	35	50	48
6	Watford	42	14	2	5	53	19	5	7	9	23	30	47
7	Northampton Town	42	14	4	3	40	21	5	4	12	25	46	46
8	Bristol Rovers	42	14	6	1	54	27	3	4	14	19	50	44
9	Brighton & Hove A.	42	15	4	2	51	16	2	5	14	18	46	43
10	Torquay United	42	15	2	4	60	22	3	4	14	21	53	42
11	Exeter City	42	11	5	5	48	29	5	4	12	22	46	41
12	Millwall	42	11	4	6	33	26	6	3	12	24	36	41
13	Queen's Park Rgs.	42	14	6	1	49	22	2	3	16	14	50	41
14	Clapton Orient	42	13	3	5	47	21	2	7	12	18	44	40
15	Bristol City	42	14	3	4	37	18	1	6	14	15	50	39
16	Swindon Town	42	11	7	3	45	22	2	5	14	22	56	38
17	Bournemouth	42	10	5	6	36	26	5	2	14	18	45	37
18	Aldershot Town	42	12	6	3	35	20	1	4	16	15	55	36
19	CARDIFF CITY	42	11	6	4	42	27	2	3	16	20	55	35
20	Gillingham	42	10	7	4	36	25	1	6	14	19	50	35
21	Southend United	42	10	4	7	40	29	1	5	15	25	49	31
22	Newport County	42	7	4	10	36	40	3	1	17	18	72	25

1935/36 Division 3 (South)

1	Coventry City	42	19	1	1	75	12	5	8	8	27	33	57
2	Luton Town	42	13	6	2	56	20	9	6	6	25	25	56
3	Reading	42	18	0	3	52	20	8	2	11	35	42	54
4	Queen's Park Rgs.	42	14	4	3	55	19	8	5	8	29	34	53
5	Watford	42	12	3	6	47	29	8	6	7	33	25	49
6	Crystal Palace	42	15	4	2	64	20	7	1	13	32	54	49
7	Brighton & Hove A.	42	13	4	4	48	25	5	4	12	22	38	44
8	Bournemouth	42	9	6	6	36	26	7	5	9	24	30	43
9	Notts County	42	10	5	6	40	25	5	7	9	20	32	42
10	Torquay United	42	14	4	3	41	27	2	5	14	21	35	41
11	Aldershot Town	42	9	6	6	29	21	5	6	10	24	40	40
12	Millwall	42	9	8	4	33	21	5	4	12	25	50	40
13	Bristol City	42	11	5	5	32	21	4	5	12	16	38	40
14	Clapton Orient	42	13	2	6	34	15	3	4	14	21	46	38
15	Northampton Town	42	12	5	4	38	24	3	3	15	24	66	38
16	Gillingham	42	9	5	7	34	25	5	4	12	32	52	37
17	Bristol Rovers	42	11	6	4	48	31	3	3	15	21	64	37
18	Southend United	42	8	7	6	38	21	5	3	13	23	41	36
19	Swindon Town	42	10	5	6	43	33	4	3	14	21	40	36
20	CARDIFF CITY	42	11	5	5	37	23	2	5	14	23	50	36
21	Newport County	42	8	4	9	36	44	3	5	13	24	67	31
22	Exeter City	42	7	5	9	38	41	1	6	14	21	52	27

1936/37 Division 3 (South)

1 Luton Town	42	19	1	1	69	16	8	3	10	34	37	58
2 Notts County	42	15	3	3	44	23	8	7	6	30	29	56
3 Brighton & Hove A.	42	15	5	1	49	16	9	0	12	25	27	53
4 Watford	42	14	4	3	53	21	5	7	9	32	39	49
5 Reading	42	14	5	2	53	23	5	6	10	23	37	49
6 Bournemouth	42	17	3	1	45	20	3	6	12	20	39	49
7 Northampton Town	42	15	4	2	56	22	5	2	14	29	46	46
8 Millwall	42	12	4	5	43	24	6	6	9	21	30	46
9 Queen's Park Rgs.	42	12	2	7	51	24	6	7	8	22	28	45
10 Southend United	42	10	8	3	49	23	7	3	11	29	44	45
11 Gillingham	42	14	5	2	36	18	4	3	14	16	48	44
12 Clapton Orient	42	10	8	3	29	17	4	7	10	23	35	43
13 Swindon Town	42	12	4	5	52	24	2	7	12	23	49	39
14 Crystal Palace	42	11	7	3	45	20	2	5	14	17	41	38
15 Bristol Rovers	42	14	3	4	49	20	2	1	18	22	60	36
16 Bristol City	42	13	3	5	42	20	2	3	16	16	50	36
17 Walsall	42	11	3	7	38	34	2	7	12	25	51	36
18 CARDIFF CITY	42	10	5	6	35	24	4	2	15	19	63	35
19 Newport County	42	7	7	7	37	28	5	3	13	30	70	34
20 Torquay United	42	9	5	7	42	32	2	5	14	15	48	32
21 Exeter City	42	9	5	7	36	37	1	7	13	23	51	32
22 Aldershot Town	42	5	6	10	29	29	2	3	16	21	60	23

1937/38 Division 3 (South)

1 Millwall	42	15	3	3	53	15	8	7	6	30	22	56
2 Bristol City	42	14	6	1	37	13	7	7	7	31	27	55
3 Queen's Park Rgs.	42	15	3	3	44	17	7	6	8	36	30	53
4 Watford	42	14	4	3	50	15	7	7	7	23	28	53
5 Brighton & Hove A.	42	15	3	3	40	16	6	6	9	24	28	51
6 Reading	42	17	2	2	44	21	3	9	9	27	42	51
7 Crystal Palace	42	14	4	3	45	17	4	8	9	22	30	48
8 Swindon Town	42	12	4	5	33	19	5	6	10	16	30	44
9 Northampton Town	42	12	4	5	30	19	5	5	11	21	38	43
10 CARDIFF CITY	42	13	7	1	57	22	2	5	14	10	32	42
11 Notts County	42	10	6	5	29	17	6	3	12	21	33	41
12 Southend United	42	12	5	4	43	23	3	5	13	27	45	40
13 Bournemouth	42	8	10	3	36	20	6	2	13	20	37	40
14 Mansfield Town	42	12	5	4	46	26	3	4	14	16	41	39
15 Bristol Rovers	42	10	7	4	28	20	3	6	12	18	41	39
16 Newport County	42	9	10	2	31	15	2	6	13	12	37	38
17 Exeter City	42	10	4	7	37	32	3	8	10	20	38	38
18 Aldershot	42	11	4	6	23	14	4	1	16	16	45	35
19 Clapton Orient	42	10	7	4	27	19	3	0	18	15	42	33
20 Torquay United	42	7	5	9	22	28	2	7	12	16	45	30
21 Walsall	42	10	4	7	34	37	1	3	17	18	51	29
22 Gillingham	42	9	5	7	25	25	1	1	19	11	52	26

1938/39 Division 3 (South)

1 Newport County	42	15	4	2	37	16	7	7	7	21	29	55
2 Crystal Palace	42	15	4	2	49	18	5	8	8	22	34	52
3 Brighton & Hove A.	42	14	5	2	43	14	5	6	10	25	35	49
4 Watford	42	14	6	1	44	15	3	6	12	18	36	46
5 Reading	42	12	6	3	46	23	4	8	9	23	36	46
6 Queen's Park Rgs.	42	10	8	3	44	15	5	6	10	24	34	44
7 Ipswich Town	42	14	3	4	46	21	2	9	10	16	31	44
8 Bristol City	42	14	5	2	42	19	2	7	12	19	44	44
9 Swindon Town	42	15	4	2	53	25	3	4	14	19	52	44
10 Aldershot	42	13	6	2	31	15	3	6	12	22	51	44
11 Notts County	42	12	6	3	36	16	5	3	13	23	38	43
12 Southend United	42	14	5	2	38	13	2	4	15	23	51	41
13 CARDIFF CITY	42	12	1	8	40	28	3	10	8	21	37	41
14 Exeter City	42	9	9	3	40	32	4	5	12	25	50	40
15 Bournemouth	42	10	8	3	38	22	3	5	13	14	36	39
16 Mansfield Town	42	10	8	3	33	19	2	7	12	11	43	39
17 Northampton Town	42	13	5	3	41	20	2	3	16	10	38	38
18 Port Vale	42	10	5	6	36	23	4	4	13	16	35	37
19 Torquay United	42	7	5	9	27	28	7	4	10	27	42	37
20 Clapton Orient	42	10	9	2	40	16	1	4	16	13	39	35
21 Walsall	42	9	6	6	47	23	2	5	14	21	46	33
22 Bristol Rovers	42	8	8	5	30	17	2	5	14	25	44	33

1946/47 Division 3 (South)

1 CARDIFF CITY	42	18	3	0	60	11	12	3	6	33	19	66
2 Queen's Park Rgs.	42	15	2	4	42	15	8	9	4	32	25	57
3 Bristol City	42	13	4	4	56	20	7	7	7	38	36	51
4 Swindon Town	42	15	4	2	56	25	4	7	10	28	48	49
5 Walsall	42	11	6	4	42	25	6	6	9	32	34	46
6 Ipswich Town	42	11	5	5	33	21	5	9	7	28	32	46
7 Bournemouth	42	12	4	5	43	20	6	4	11	29	34	44
8 Southend United	42	9	7	5	38	22	8	3	10	33	38	44
9 Reading	42	11	6	4	53	30	5	5	11	30	44	43
10 Port Vale	42	14	4	3	51	28	3	5	13	17	35	43
11 Torquay United	42	11	5	5	33	23	4	7	10	19	38	42
12 Notts County	42	11	4	6	35	19	4	6	11	28	44	40
13 Northampton Town	42	11	5	5	46	33	4	5	12	26	42	40
14 Bristol Rovers	42	9	6	6	34	26	7	2	12	25	43	40
15 Exeter City	42	11	6	4	37	27	4	3	14	23	42	39
16 Watford	42	11	4	6	39	27	6	1	14	22	49	39
17 Brighton & Hove A.	42	8	7	6	31	35	5	5	11	23	37	38
18 Crystal Palace	42	9	7	5	29	19	4	4	13	20	43	37
19 Leyton Orient	42	10	5	6	40	28	2	3	16	14	47	32
20 Aldershot	42	6	7	8	25	26	4	5	12	23	52	32
21 Norwich City	42	6	3	12	38	48	4	5	12	26	52	28
22 Mansfield Town	42	8	5	8	31	38	1	5	15	17	58	28

1947/48 Division 2

1 Birmingham City	42	12	7	2	34	13	10	8	3	21	11	59
2 Newcastle United	42	18	1	2	46	13	6	7	8	26	28	56
3 Southampton	42	15	3	3	53	23	6	7	8	18	30	52
4 Sheffield Wed.	42	13	6	2	39	21	7	5	9	27	32	51
5 CARDIFF CITY	42	12	6	3	36	18	6	5	10	25	40	47
6 West Ham United	42	10	7	4	29	19	6	7	8	26	34	46
7 West Bromwich Alb.	42	11	4	6	37	29	7	5	9	26	29	45
8 Tottenham Hotspur	42	10	6	5	36	24	5	8	8	20	19	44
9 Leicester City	42	10	5	6	36	29	6	6	9	24	28	43
10 Coventry City	42	10	5	6	33	16	4	8	9	26	36	41
11 Fulham	42	6	9	6	24	19	9	1	11	23	27	40
12 Barnsley	42	10	5	6	31	22	5	5	11	31	42	40
13 Luton Town	42	8	8	5	31	25	6	4	11	25	34	40
14 Bradford Park Ave.	42	11	3	7	45	30	5	5	11	23	42	40
15 Brentford	42	10	6	5	31	26	3	8	10	13	35	40
16 Chesterfield	42	8	4	9	32	26	8	3	10	22	29	39
17 Plymouth Argyle	42	8	9	4	27	22	1	11	9	13	36	38
18 Leeds United	42	12	5	4	44	20	2	3	16	18	52	36
19 Nottingham Forest	42	10	5	6	32	23	2	6	13	22	37	35
20 Bury	42	6	8	7	27	28	3	8	10	31	40	34
21 Doncaster Rovers	42	7	8	6	23	20	2	3	16	17	46	29
22 Millwall	42	7	7	7	27	28	2	4	15	17	46	29

1948/49 Division 2

1 Fulham	42	16	4	1	52	14	8	5	8	25	23	57
2 West Bromwich Alb.	42	16	3	2	47	16	8	5	8	22	23	56
3 Southampton	42	16	4	1	48	10	7	5	9	21	26	55
4 CARDIFF CITY	42	14	4	3	45	21	5	9	7	17	26	51
5 Tottenham Hotspur	42	14	4	3	50	18	3	12	6	22	26	50
6 Chesterfield	42	9	7	5	24	18	6	10	5	27	27	47
7 West Ham United	42	13	5	3	38	23	5	5	11	18	35	46
8 Sheffield Wed.	42	12	6	3	36	17	3	7	11	27	39	43
9 Barnsley	42	10	7	4	40	18	4	5	12	22	43	40
10 Luton Town	42	11	6	4	32	16	3	6	12	23	41	40
11 Grimsby Town	42	10	5	6	44	28	5	5	11	28	48	40
12 Bury	42	12	5	4	41	23	5	1	15	26	53	40
13 Queen's Park Rgs.	42	11	4	6	31	26	3	7	11	13	36	39
14 Blackburn Rovers	42	12	5	4	41	23	3	3	15	12	40	38
15 Leeds United	42	11	6	4	36	21	1	7	13	19	42	37
16 Coventry City	42	12	3	6	35	20	3	4	14	20	44	37
17 Bradford Park Ave.	42	8	8	5	37	26	5	3	13	28	52	37
18 Brentford	42	7	10	4	28	21	4	4	13	14	32	36
19 Leicester City	42	6	10	5	41	38	4	6	11	21	41	36
20 Plymouth Argyle	42	11	4	6	33	25	1	8	12	16	39	36
21 Nottingham Forest	42	9	6	6	22	14	5	1	15	28	40	35
22 Lincoln City	42	6	7	8	31	35	2	5	14	22	56	28

1949/50 Division 2

1 Tottenham Hotspur	42	15	3	3	51	15	12	4	5	30	20	61
2 Sheffield Wed.	42	12	7	2	46	23	6	9	6	21	25	52
3 Sheffield United	42	9	10	2	36	19	10	4	7	32	30	52
4 Southampton	42	13	4	4	44	25	6	10	5	20	23	52
5 Leeds United	42	11	8	2	33	16	6	5	10	21	29	47
6 Preston North End	42	12	5	4	37	21	6	4	11	23	28	45
7 Hull City	42	11	8	2	39	25	6	3	12	25	47	45
8 Swansea Town	42	11	3	7	34	18	6	6	9	19	31	43
9 Brentford	42	11	5	5	21	12	4	8	9	23	37	43
10 CARDIFF CITY	42	13	3	5	28	14	3	7	11	13	30	42
11 Grimsby Town	42	13	5	3	53	25	3	3	15	21	48	40
12 Coventry City	42	8	6	7	32	24	5	7	9	23	31	39
13 Barnsley	42	11	6	4	45	28	2	7	12	19	39	39
14 Chesterfield	42	12	3	6	28	16	3	6	12	15	31	39
15 Leicester City	42	8	9	4	30	25	4	6	11	25	40	39
16 Blackburn Rovers	42	10	5	6	30	15	4	5	12	25	45	38
17 Luton Town	42	8	9	4	28	22	2	9	10	13	29	38
18 Bury	42	10	8	3	37	19	4	1	16	23	46	37
19 West Ham United	42	8	7	6	30	25	4	5	12	23	36	36
20 Queen's Park Rgs.	42	6	5	10	21	30	5	7	9	19	27	34
21 Plymouth Argyle	42	6	6	9	19	24	2	10	9	25	41	32
22 Bradford Park Ave.	42	7	6	8	34	34	3	5	13	17	43	31

1950/51 Division 2

1 Preston North End	42	16	3	2	53	18	10	2	9	38	31	57
2 Manchester City	42	12	6	3	53	25	7	8	6	36	36	52
3 CARDIFF CITY	42	13	7	1	36	20	4	9	8	17	25	50
4 Birmingham City	42	12	6	3	37	20	8	3	10	27	33	49
5 Leeds United	42	14	4	3	36	17	6	4	11	27	38	48
6 Blackburn Rovers	42	13	3	5	39	27	6	5	10	26	39	46
7 Coventry City	42	15	3	3	51	25	4	4	13	24	34	45
8 Sheffield United	42	11	4	6	44	27	5	8	8	28	35	44
9 Brentford	42	13	3	5	44	25	5	5	11	31	49	44
10 Hull City	42	12	5	4	47	28	4	6	11	27	42	43
11 Doncaster Rovers	42	9	6	6	37	32	6	7	8	27	36	43
12 Southampton	42	10	9	2	38	27	5	4	12	28	46	43
13 West Ham United	42	10	5	6	44	33	6	5	10	24	36	42
14 Leicester City	42	10	4	7	42	28	5	7	9	26	30	41
15 Barnsley	42	9	5	7	42	22	6	5	10	32	46	40
16 Queen's Park Rgs.	42	13	5	3	47	25	2	5	14	24	57	40
17 Notts County	42	7	7	7	37	34	6	6	9	24	26	39
18 Swansea Town	42	14	1	6	34	25	2	3	16	20	52	36
19 Luton Town	42	7	9	5	34	23	2	5	14	23	47	32
20 Bury	42	9	4	8	33	27	3	4	14	27	59	32
21 Chesterfield	42	7	7	7	30	28	2	5	14	14	41	30
22 Grimsby Town	42	6	8	7	37	38	2	4	15	24	57	28

1951/52 Division 2

1	Sheffield Wed.	42	14	4	3	54	23	7	7	7	46	43	53
2	CARDIFF CITY	42	18	2	1	52	15	2	9	10	20	39	51
3	Birmingham City	42	11	6	4	36	21	10	3	8	31	35	51
4	Nottingham Forest	42	12	6	3	41	22	6	7	8	36	40	49
5	Leicester City	42	12	6	3	48	24	7	3	11	30	40	47
6	Leeds United	42	13	7	1	35	15	5	4	12	24	42	47
7	Everton	42	12	5	4	42	25	5	5	11	22	33	44
8	Luton Town	42	9	7	5	46	35	7	5	9	31	43	44
9	Rotherham United	42	11	4	6	40	25	6	4	11	33	46	42
10	Brentford	42	11	7	3	34	20	4	5	12	20	35	42
11	Sheffield United	42	13	2	6	57	28	5	3	13	33	48	41
12	West Ham United	42	13	5	3	48	29	2	6	13	19	48	41
13	Southampton	42	11	6	4	40	25	4	5	12	21	48	41
14	Blackburn Rovers	42	11	3	7	35	30	6	3	12	19	33	40
15	Notts County	42	11	5	5	45	27	5	2	14	26	41	39
16	Doncaster Rovers	42	9	4	8	29	28	4	8	9	26	32	38
17	Bury	42	13	2	6	43	22	2	5	14	24	47	37
18	Hull City	42	11	5	5	44	23	2	6	13	16	47	37
19	Swansea Town	42	10	4	7	45	26	2	8	11	27	50	36
20	Barnsley	42	8	7	6	39	33	3	7	11	20	39	36
21	Coventry City	42	9	5	7	36	33	5	1	15	23	49	34
22	Queen's Park Rgs.	42	8	8	5	35	35	3	4	14	17	46	34

1952/53 Division 1

1	Arsenal	42	15	3	3	60	30	6	9	6	37	34	54
2	Preston North End	42	15	3	3	46	25	6	9	6	39	35	54
3	Wolverhampton Wan.	42	13	5	3	54	27	6	8	7	32	36	51
4	West Bromwich Alb.	42	13	3	5	35	19	8	5	8	31	41	50
5	Charlton Athletic	42	12	8	1	47	22	7	3	11	30	41	49
6	Burnley	42	11	6	4	36	20	7	6	8	31	32	48
7	Blackpool	42	13	5	3	45	22	6	4	11	26	48	47
8	Manchester United	42	11	5	5	35	30	7	5	9	34	42	46
9	Sunderland	42	11	9	1	42	27	4	4	13	26	55	43
10	Tottenham Hotspur	42	11	6	4	55	37	4	5	12	23	32	41
11	Aston Villa	42	9	7	5	36	23	5	6	10	27	38	41
12	CARDIFF CITY	42	7	8	6	32	17	7	4	10	22	29	40
13	Middlesbrough	42	12	5	4	46	27	2	6	13	24	50	39
14	Bolton Wanderers	42	9	4	8	39	35	6	5	10	22	34	39
15	Portsmouth	42	10	6	5	44	34	4	4	13	30	49	38
16	Newcastle United	42	9	5	7	34	33	5	4	12	25	37	37
17	Liverpool	42	10	6	5	36	28	4	2	15	25	54	36
18	Sheffield Wed.	42	8	6	7	35	32	4	5	12	27	40	35
19	Chelsea	42	10	4	7	35	24	2	7	12	21	42	35
20	Manchester City	42	12	2	7	45	28	2	5	14	27	59	35
21	Stoke City	42	10	4	7	35	26	2	6	13	18	40	34
22	Derby County	42	9	6	6	41	29	2	4	15	18	45	32

1953/54 Division 1

1	Wolverhampton Wan.	42	16	1	4	61	25	9	6	6	35	31	57
2	West Bromwich Alb.	42	13	5	3	51	24	9	4	8	35	39	53
3	Huddersfield Town	42	13	6	2	45	24	7	5	9	33	37	51
4	Manchester United	42	11	6	4	41	27	7	6	8	32	31	48
5	Bolton Wanderers	42	14	6	1	45	20	4	6	11	30	40	48
6	Blackpool	42	13	6	2	43	19	6	4	11	37	50	48
7	Burnley	42	16	2	3	51	23	5	2	14	27	44	46
8	Chelsea	42	12	3	6	45	26	4	9	8	29	42	44
9	Charlton Athletic	42	14	4	3	51	26	5	2	14	24	51	44
10	CARDIFF CITY	42	12	4	5	32	27	6	4	11	19	44	44
11	Preston North End	42	12	2	7	43	24	7	3	11	44	34	43
12	Arsenal	42	8	8	5	42	37	7	5	9	33	36	43
13	Aston Villa	42	12	5	4	50	28	4	4	13	20	40	41
14	Portsmouth	42	13	5	3	53	31	1	6	14	28	58	39
15	Newcastle United	42	9	2	10	43	40	5	8	8	29	37	38
16	Tottenham Hotspur	42	11	3	7	38	33	5	2	14	27	43	37
17	Manchester City	42	10	4	7	35	31	4	5	12	27	46	37
18	Sunderland	42	11	4	6	50	37	3	4	14	31	52	36
19	Sheffield Wed.	42	12	4	5	43	30	3	2	16	27	61	36
20	Sheffield United	42	9	5	7	43	38	2	6	13	26	52	33
21	Middlesbrough	42	6	6	9	29	35	4	4	13	31	56	30
22	Liverpool	42	7	8	6	49	38	2	2	17	19	59	28

1954/55 Division 1

1	Chelsea	42	11	5	5	43	29	9	7	5	38	28	52
2	Wolverhampton Wan.	42	13	5	3	58	30	6	5	10	31	40	48
3	Portsmouth	42	13	5	3	44	21	5	7	9	30	41	48
4	Sunderland	42	8	11	2	39	27	7	7	7	25	27	48
5	Manchester United	42	12	4	5	44	30	8	3	10	40	44	47
6	Aston Villa	42	11	3	7	38	31	9	4	8	34	42	47
7	Manchester City	42	11	5	5	45	36	7	5	9	31	33	46
8	Newcastle United	42	12	5	4	53	27	5	4	12	36	50	43
9	Arsenal	42	12	3	6	44	25	5	6	10	25	38	43
10	Burnley	42	11	3	7	29	19	6	6	9	22	29	43
11	Everton	42	9	6	6	32	24	7	4	10	30	44	42
12	Huddersfield Town	42	10	4	7	28	23	4	9	8	35	45	41
13	Sheffield United	42	10	3	8	41	34	7	4	10	29	52	41
14	Preston North End	42	8	5	8	47	33	8	3	10	36	31	40
15	Charlton Athletic	42	8	6	7	43	34	7	4	10	33	41	40
16	Tottenham Hotspur	42	9	4	8	42	35	7	4	10	30	38	40
17	West Bromwich Alb.	42	11	5	5	44	33	5	3	13	32	63	40
18	Bolton Wanderers	42	11	6	4	45	29	2	7	12	17	40	39
19	Blackpool	42	8	6	7	33	26	6	4	11	27	38	38
20	CARDIFF CITY	42	9	4	8	41	38	4	7	10	21	38	37
21	Leicester City	42	9	6	6	43	32	3	5	13	31	54	35
22	Sheffield Wed.	42	7	7	7	42	38	1	3	17	21	62	26

1955/56 Division 1

1	Manchester United	42	18	3	0	51	20	7	7	7	32	31	60
2	Blackpool	42	13	4	4	56	27	7	5	9	30	35	49
3	Wolverhampton Wan.	42	15	2	4	51	27	5	7	9	38	38	49
4	Manchester City	42	11	5	5	40	27	7	5	9	42	42	46
5	Arsenal	42	13	4	4	38	22	5	6	10	22	39	46
6	Birmingham City	42	12	4	5	51	26	6	5	10	24	31	45
7	Burnley	42	11	3	7	37	20	7	5	9	27	34	44
8	Bolton Wanderers	42	13	3	5	50	24	5	4	12	21	34	43
9	Sunderland	42	10	8	3	44	36	7	1	13	36	59	43
10	Luton Town	42	12	4	5	44	27	5	4	12	22	37	42
11	Newcastle United	42	12	4	5	49	24	5	3	13	36	46	41
12	Portsmouth	42	9	8	4	46	38	7	1	13	32	47	41
13	West Bromwich Alb.	42	13	3	5	37	25	5	2	14	21	45	41
14	Charlton Athletic	42	13	2	6	47	26	4	4	13	28	55	40
15	Everton	42	11	5	5	37	29	4	5	12	18	40	40
16	Chelsea	42	10	4	7	32	26	4	7	10	32	51	39
17	CARDIFF CITY	42	11	4	6	36	32	4	5	12	19	37	39
18	Tottenham Hotspur	42	9	4	8	37	33	6	3	12	24	38	37
19	Preston North End	42	6	5	10	32	36	8	3	10	41	36	36
20	Aston Villa	42	9	6	6	32	29	2	7	12	20	40	35
21	Huddersfield Town	42	9	4	8	32	30	5	3	13	22	53	35
22	Sheffield United	42	8	6	7	31	35	4	3	14	32	42	33

1956/57 Division 1

1	Manchester United	42	14	4	3	55	25	14	4	3	48	29	64
2	Tottenham Hotspur	42	15	4	2	70	24	7	8	6	34	32	56
3	Preston North End	42	15	4	2	50	19	8	6	7	34	37	56
4	Blackpool	42	14	3	4	55	26	8	6	7	38	39	53
5	Arsenal	42	12	5	4	45	21	9	3	9	40	48	50
6	Wolverhampton Wan.	42	17	2	2	70	29	3	6	12	24	41	48
7	Burnley	42	14	5	2	41	21	4	5	12	15	29	46
8	Leeds United	42	10	8	3	42	18	5	6	10	30	45	44
9	Bolton Wanderers	42	13	6	2	42	23	3	6	12	23	42	44
10	Aston Villa	42	10	8	3	45	25	4	7	10	20	30	43
11	West Bromwich Alb.	42	8	8	5	31	25	6	6	9	28	36	42
12	Chelsea	42	7	8	6	43	36	6	5	10	30	37	39
12	Birmingham City	42	12	5	4	52	25	3	4	14	17	44	39
14	Sheffield Wed.	42	14	3	4	55	29	2	3	16	27	59	38
15	Everton	42	10	5	6	34	28	4	5	12	27	51	38
16	Luton Town	42	10	4	7	32	26	4	5	12	26	50	37
17	Newcastle United	42	10	5	6	43	31	4	3	14	24	56	36
18	Manchester City	42	10	2	9	48	42	3	7	11	30	46	35
19	Portsmouth	42	8	6	7	37	35	2	7	12	25	57	33
20	Sunderland	42	9	5	7	40	30	3	3	15	27	58	32
21	CARDIFF CITY	42	7	6	8	35	34	3	3	15	18	54	29
22	Charlton Athletic	42	7	3	11	31	44	2	1	18	31	76	22

1957/58 Division 2

1	West Ham United	42	12	8	1	56	25	11	3	7	45	29	57
2	Blackburn Rovers	42	13	7	1	50	18	9	5	7	43	39	56
3	Charlton Athletic	42	15	3	3	65	33	9	4	8	42	36	55
4	Liverpool	42	17	3	1	50	13	5	7	9	29	41	54
5	Fulham	42	13	5	3	53	24	7	7	7	44	35	52
6	Sheffield United	42	12	5	4	38	22	9	5	7	37	28	52
7	Middlesbrough	42	13	3	5	52	29	6	4	11	31	45	45
8	Ipswich Town	42	13	4	4	45	29	3	8	10	23	40	44
9	Huddersfield Town	42	9	8	4	28	24	5	8	8	35	42	44
10	Bristol Rovers	42	12	5	4	52	31	5	3	13	33	49	42
11	Stoke City	42	9	4	8	49	36	9	2	10	26	37	42
12	Leyton Orient	42	14	2	5	53	27	4	3	14	24	52	41
13	Grimsby Town	42	13	4	4	54	30	4	2	15	32	53	40
14	Barnsley	42	10	6	5	40	25	4	6	11	30	49	40
15	CARDIFF CITY	42	10	5	6	44	31	4	4	13	19	46	37
16	Derby County	42	11	3	7	37	36	3	5	13	23	45	36
17	Bristol City	42	9	5	7	35	31	4	4	13	28	57	35
18	Rotherham United	42	8	3	10	38	44	6	2	13	27	57	33
19	Swansea Town	42	8	3	10	48	45	3	6	12	24	54	31
20	Lincoln City	42	6	6	9	33	35	5	3	13	22	47	31
21	Notts County	42	9	3	9	24	31	3	3	15	20	49	30
22	Doncaster Rovers	42	7	5	9	34	40	1	6	14	22	48	27

1958/59 Division 2

1	Sheffield Wed.	42	18	2	1	68	13	10	4	7	38	35	62
2	Fulham	42	18	1	2	65	26	9	5	7	31	35	60
3	Sheffield United	42	16	2	3	54	15	7	5	9	28	33	53
4	Liverpool	42	15	3	3	57	25	9	2	10	30	37	53
5	Stoke City	42	16	2	3	48	19	5	5	11	24	39	49
6	Bristol Rovers	42	13	5	3	46	23	5	7	9	34	41	48
7	Derby County	42	15	1	5	46	29	5	7	9	28	42	48
8	Charlton Athletic	42	13	3	5	53	33	5	4	12	39	57	43
9	CARDIFF CITY	42	12	2	7	37	26	6	5	10	28	39	43
10	Bristol City	42	11	3	7	43	27	6	4	11	31	43	41
11	Swansea Town	42	12	5	4	52	30	4	4	13	27	51	41
12	Brighton & Hove A.	42	10	9	2	46	29	5	2	14	28	61	41
13	Middlesbrough	42	9	7	5	51	26	6	3	12	36	45	40
14	Huddersfield Town	42	12	3	6	39	20	4	5	12	23	35	40
15	Sunderland	42	13	4	4	42	23	3	4	14	22	52	40
16	Ipswich Town	42	12	4	5	37	27	5	2	14	25	50	40
17	Leyton Orient	42	9	4	8	43	30	5	4	12	28	48	36
18	Scunthorpe United	42	7	6	8	32	37	5	3	13	23	47	33
19	Lincoln City	42	10	5	6	45	37	1	2	18	18	56	29
20	Rotherham United	42	9	5	7	32	28	1	4	16	10	54	29
21	Grimsby Town	42	7	7	7	41	36	2	3	16	21	54	28
22	Barnsley	42	8	4	9	34	34	2	3	16	21	57	27

1959/60 Division 2

1	Aston Villa	42	17	3	1	62	19	8	6	7	27	24	59
2	CARDIFF CITY	42	15	2	4	55	36	8	10	3	35	26	58
3	Liverpool	42	15	3	3	59	28	5	7	9	31	38	50
4	Sheffield United	42	12	5	4	43	22	7	7	7	25	29	50
5	Middlesbrough	42	14	5	2	56	21	5	5	11	34	43	48
6	Huddersfield Town	42	13	3	5	44	20	6	6	9	29	32	47
7	Charlton Athletic	42	12	7	2	55	28	5	6	10	35	59	47
8	Rotherham United	42	9	9	3	31	23	8	4	9	30	37	47
9	Bristol Rovers	42	12	6	3	42	28	6	5	10	30	50	47
10	Leyton Orient	42	12	4	5	47	25	3	10	8	29	36	44
11	Ipswich Town	42	12	5	4	48	24	7	1	13	30	44	44
12	Swansea Town	42	12	6	3	54	32	3	4	14	28	52	40
13	Lincoln City	42	11	3	7	41	25	5	4	12	34	53	39
14	Brighton & Hove A.	42	7	8	6	35	32	6	4	11	32	44	38
15	Scunthorpe United	42	9	7	5	38	26	4	3	14	19	45	36
16	Sunderland	42	8	6	7	35	29	4	6	11	17	36	36
17	Stoke City	42	8	3	10	40	38	6	4	11	26	45	35
18	Derby County	42	9	4	8	31	28	5	3	13	30	49	35
19	Plymouth Argyle	42	10	6	5	42	36	3	3	15	19	53	35
20	Portsmouth	42	6	6	9	36	36	4	6	11	23	41	32
21	Hull City	42	7	6	8	27	30	3	4	14	21	46	30
22	Bristol City	42	8	3	10	27	31	3	2	16	33	66	27

1960/61 Division 1

1	Tottenham Hotspur	42	15	3	3	65	28	16	1	4	50	27	66
2	Sheffield Wed.	42	15	4	2	45	17	8	8	5	33	30	58
3	Wolverhampton Wan.	42	17	2	2	61	32	8	5	8	42	43	57
4	Burnley	42	11	4	6	58	40	11	3	7	44	37	51
5	Everton	42	13	4	4	47	23	9	2	10	40	46	50
6	Leicester City	42	12	4	5	54	31	6	5	10	33	39	45
7	Manchester United	42	14	5	2	58	20	4	4	13	30	56	45
8	Blackburn Rovers	42	12	3	6	48	34	3	10	8	29	42	43
9	Aston Villa	42	13	3	5	48	28	4	6	11	30	49	43
10	West Bromwich Alb.	42	10	3	8	43	32	8	2	11	24	39	41
11	Arsenal	42	12	3	6	44	35	3	8	10	33	50	41
12	Chelsea	42	10	5	6	61	48	5	2	14	37	52	37
13	Manchester City	42	10	5	6	41	30	3	6	12	38	60	37
14	Nottingham Forest	42	8	7	6	34	33	6	2	13	28	45	37
15	CARDIFF CITY	42	11	5	5	34	26	2	6	13	26	59	37
16	West Ham United	42	12	4	5	53	31	1	6	14	24	57	36
17	Fulham	42	8	8	5	39	39	6	0	15	33	56	36
18	Bolton Wanderers	42	9	5	7	38	29	3	6	12	20	44	35
19	Birmingham City	42	10	4	7	35	31	4	2	15	27	53	34
20	Blackpool	42	9	3	9	44	34	3	6	12	24	39	33
21	Newcastle United	42	7	7	7	51	49	4	3	14	35	60	32
22	Preston North End	42	7	6	8	28	25	3	4	14	15	46	30

1961/62 Division 1

1	Ipswich Town	42	17	2	2	58	28	7	6	8	35	39	56
2	Burnley	42	14	4	3	57	26	7	7	7	44	41	53
3	Tottenham Hotspur	42	14	4	3	59	34	7	6	8	29	35	52
4	Everton	42	17	2	2	64	21	3	9	9	24	33	51
5	Sheffield United	42	13	5	3	37	23	6	4	11	24	46	47
6	Sheffield Wed.	42	14	4	3	47	23	6	2	13	25	35	46
7	Aston Villa	42	13	5	3	45	20	5	3	13	20	36	44
8	West Ham United	42	11	6	4	49	37	6	4	11	27	45	44
9	West Bromwich Alb.	42	10	7	4	50	23	5	6	10	33	44	43
10	Arsenal	42	9	6	6	39	31	7	5	9	32	41	43
11	Bolton Wanderers	42	11	7	3	35	22	5	3	13	27	44	42
12	Manchester City	42	11	3	7	46	38	6	4	11	32	43	41
13	Blackpool	42	10	4	7	41	30	5	7	9	29	45	41
14	Leicester City	42	12	2	7	38	27	5	4	12	34	44	40
15	Manchester United	42	10	3	8	44	31	5	6	10	28	44	39
16	Blackburn Rovers	42	10	6	5	33	22	4	5	12	17	36	39
17	Birmingham City	42	9	6	6	37	35	5	4	12	28	46	38
18	Wolverhampton Wan.	42	8	7	6	38	34	5	3	13	35	52	36
19	Nottingham Forest	42	12	4	5	39	23	1	6	14	24	56	36
20	Fulham	42	8	3	10	38	34	5	4	12	28	40	33
21	CARDIFF CITY	42	6	9	6	30	33	3	5	13	20	48	32
22	Chelsea	42	7	7	7	34	29	2	3	16	29	65	28

1962/63 Division 2

1	Stoke City	42	15	3	3	49	20	5	10	6	24	30	53
2	Chelsea	42	15	3	3	54	16	9	1	11	27	26	52
3	Sunderland	42	14	5	2	46	13	6	7	8	38	42	52
4	Middlesbrough	42	12	4	5	48	35	8	5	8	38	50	49
5	Leeds United	42	15	2	4	55	19	4	8	9	24	34	48
6	Huddersfield Town	42	11	6	4	34	21	6	8	7	29	29	48
7	Newcastle United	42	11	8	2	48	23	7	3	11	31	36	47
8	Bury	42	11	6	4	28	20	7	5	9	23	27	47
9	Scunthorpe United	42	12	7	2	35	18	4	5	12	22	41	44
10	CARDIFF CITY	42	12	5	4	50	29	6	2	13	33	44	43
11	Southampton	42	15	3	3	52	23	2	5	14	20	44	42
12	Plymouth Argyle	42	13	4	4	48	24	2	8	11	28	49	42
13	Norwich City	42	11	6	4	53	33	6	2	13	27	46	42
14	Rotherham United	42	11	3	7	34	30	6	3	12	33	44	40
15	Swansea Town	42	13	5	3	33	17	2	4	15	18	55	39
16	Portsmouth	42	9	5	7	33	27	4	6	11	30	52	37
17	Preston North End	42	11	6	4	43	30	2	5	14	16	44	37
18	Derby County	42	10	5	6	40	29	2	7	12	21	43	36
19	Grimsby Town	42	8	6	7	34	26	3	7	11	21	40	35
20	Charlton Athletic	42	8	4	9	33	38	5	1	15	29	56	31
21	Walsall	42	7	7	7	33	37	4	2	15	20	52	31
22	Luton Town	42	10	4	7	45	40	1	3	17	16	44	29

1963/64 Division 2

1	Leeds United	42	12	9	0	35	16	12	6	3	36	18	63
2	Sunderland	42	16	3	2	47	13	9	8	4	34	24	61
3	Preston North End	42	13	7	1	37	14	10	3	8	42	40	56
4	Charlton Athletic	42	11	4	6	44	30	8	6	7	32	40	48
5	Southampton	42	13	3	5	69	32	6	6	9	31	41	47
6	Manchester City	42	12	4	5	50	27	6	6	9	34	39	46
7	Rotherham United	42	14	3	4	52	26	5	4	12	38	52	45
8	Newcastle United	42	14	2	5	49	26	6	3	12	25	43	45
9	Portsmouth	42	9	7	5	46	34	7	4	10	33	36	43
10	Middlesbrough	42	14	4	3	47	16	1	7	13	20	36	41
11	Northampton Town	42	10	2	9	35	31	6	7	8	23	29	41
12	Huddersfield Town	42	11	4	6	31	25	4	6	11	26	39	40
13	Derby County	42	10	6	5	34	27	4	5	12	22	40	39
14	Swindon Town	42	11	5	5	39	24	3	5	13	18	45	38
15	CARDIFF CITY	42	10	7	4	31	27	4	3	14	25	54	38
16	Leyton Orient	42	8	6	7	32	32	5	4	12	22	40	36
17	Norwich City	42	9	7	5	43	30	2	6	13	21	50	35
18	Bury	42	8	5	8	35	36	5	4	12	22	37	35
19	Swansea Town	42	11	4	6	44	26	1	5	15	19	48	33
20	Plymouth Argyle	42	6	8	7	26	32	2	8	11	19	35	32
21	Grimsby Town	42	6	7	8	28	34	3	7	11	19	41	32
22	Scunthorpe United	42	8	8	5	30	25	2	2	17	22	57	30

1964/65 Division 2

1	Newcastle United	42	16	4	1	50	16	8	5	8	31	29	57
2	Northampton Town	42	14	7	0	37	16	6	9	6	29	34	56
3	Bolton Wanderers	42	13	6	2	46	17	7	4	10	34	41	50
4	Southampton	42	12	6	3	49	25	5	8	8	34	38	48
5	Ipswich Town	42	11	7	3	48	30	4	10	7	26	37	47
6	Norwich City	42	15	4	2	47	21	5	3	13	14	36	47
7	Crystal Palace	42	11	6	4	37	24	5	7	9	18	27	45
8	Huddersfield Town	42	12	4	5	28	15	5	6	10	25	36	44
9	Derby County	42	11	5	5	48	35	5	6	10	36	44	43
10	Coventry City	42	10	5	6	41	29	7	4	10	31	41	43
11	Manchester City	42	12	3	6	40	24	4	6	11	23	38	41
12	Preston North End	42	11	8	2	46	29	3	5	13	30	52	41
13	CARDIFF CITY	42	10	7	4	43	25	3	7	11	21	32	40
14	Rotherham United	42	10	7	4	39	25	4	5	12	31	44	40
15	Plymouth Argyle	42	10	7	4	36	28	6	1	14	27	51	40
16	Bury	42	9	4	8	36	30	5	6	10	24	36	38
17	Middlesbrough	42	8	5	8	40	31	5	4	12	30	45	35
18	Charlton Athletic	42	8	5	8	35	34	5	4	12	29	41	35
19	Leyton Orient	42	10	4	7	36	34	2	7	12	14	38	35
20	Portsmouth	42	11	4	6	36	22	1	6	14	20	55	34
21	Swindon Town	42	12	3	6	43	30	2	2	17	20	51	33
22	Swansea Town	42	9	7	5	40	29	2	3	16	22	55	32

1965/66 Division 2

1	Manchester City	42	14	7	0	40	14	8	8	5	36	30	59
2	Southampton	42	13	4	4	51	25	9	6	6	34	31	54
3	Coventry City	42	14	5	2	54	31	6	8	7	19	22	53
4	Huddersfield Town	42	12	7	2	35	12	7	6	8	27	24	51
5	Bristol City	42	9	10	2	27	15	8	7	6	36	33	51
6	Wolverhampton Wan.	42	15	4	2	52	18	5	6	10	35	43	50
7	Rotherham United	42	12	6	3	48	29	4	8	9	27	45	46
8	Derby County	42	13	2	6	48	31	3	9	9	23	37	43
9	Bolton Wanderers	42	12	2	7	43	25	4	7	10	19	34	41
10	Birmingham City	42	10	6	5	41	29	6	3	12	29	46	41
11	Crystal Palace	42	11	7	3	29	16	3	6	12	18	36	41
12	Portsmouth	42	13	4	4	47	26	3	4	14	27	52	40
13	Norwich City	42	8	7	6	33	27	4	8	9	19	25	39
14	Carlisle United	42	16	2	3	43	19	1	3	17	17	44	39
15	Ipswich Town	42	12	6	3	38	23	3	3	15	20	43	39
16	Charlton Athletic	42	10	6	5	39	29	2	8	11	22	41	38
17	Preston North End	42	7	10	4	37	23	4	5	12	25	47	37
18	Plymouth Argyle	42	7	8	6	37	26	5	5	11	17	37	37
19	Bury	42	12	5	4	45	25	2	2	17	17	51	35
20	CARDIFF CITY	42	10	3	8	37	35	2	7	12	34	56	34
21	Middlesbrough	42	8	8	5	36	28	2	5	14	22	58	33
22	Leyton Orient	42	3	9	9	19	36	2	4	15	19	44	23

1966/67 Division 2

1	Coventry City	42	17	3	1	46	16	6	10	5	28	27	59
2	Wolverhampton Wan.	42	15	4	2	53	20	10	4	7	35	28	58
3	Carlisle United	42	15	3	3	42	16	8	3	10	29	38	52
4	Blackburn Rovers	42	13	6	2	33	11	6	7	8	23	35	51
5	Ipswich Town	42	11	8	2	45	25	6	8	7	25	29	50
6	Huddersfield Town	42	14	3	4	36	17	6	6	9	22	29	49
7	Crystal Palace	42	14	4	3	42	23	5	6	10	19	32	48
8	Millwall	42	14	5	2	33	17	4	4	13	16	41	45
9	Bolton Wanderers	42	10	7	4	36	19	4	7	10	28	39	42
10	Birmingham City	42	11	5	5	42	23	5	3	13	28	43	40
11	Norwich City	42	10	7	4	31	21	3	7	11	18	34	40
12	Hull City	42	11	5	5	46	25	5	2	14	31	47	39
13	Preston North End	42	14	3	4	44	23	2	4	15	21	44	39
14	Portsmouth	42	7	5	9	34	37	6	8	7	25	33	39
15	Bristol City	42	10	8	3	38	22	2	6	13	18	40	38
16	Plymouth Argyle	42	12	4	5	42	21	2	5	14	17	37	37
17	Derby County	42	8	6	7	40	32	4	6	11	28	40	36
18	Rotherham United	42	10	5	6	39	28	3	5	13	22	42	36
19	Charlton Athletic	42	11	4	6	34	16	2	5	14	15	37	35
20	CARDIFF CITY	42	9	7	5	43	28	3	2	16	18	59	33
21	Northampton Town	42	8	6	7	28	33	4	0	17	19	51	30
22	Bury	42	9	3	9	31	30	2	3	16	18	53	28

1967/68 Division 2

1	Ipswich Town	42	12	7	2	45	20	10	8	3	34	24	59
2	Queen's Park Rgs.	42	18	2	1	45	9	7	6	8	22	27	58
3	Blackpool	42	12	6	3	33	16	12	4	5	38	27	58
4	Birmingham City	42	12	6	3	54	21	7	8	6	29	30	52
5	Portsmouth	42	13	6	2	43	18	5	7	9	25	37	49
6	Middlesbrough	42	10	7	4	39	19	7	5	9	21	35	46
7	Millwall	42	9	10	2	35	16	5	7	9	27	34	45
8	Blackburn Rovers	42	13	5	3	34	16	3	6	12	22	33	43
9	Norwich City	42	12	4	5	40	30	4	7	10	20	35	43
10	Carlisle United	42	9	9	3	38	22	5	4	12	20	30	41
11	Crystal Palace	42	11	4	6	34	19	3	7	11	22	37	39
12	Bolton Wanderers	42	8	6	7	37	28	5	7	9	23	35	39
13	CARDIFF CITY	42	9	6	6	35	29	4	6	11	25	37	38
14	Huddersfield Town	42	10	6	5	29	23	3	6	12	17	38	38
15	Charlton Athletic	42	10	6	5	43	25	2	7	12	20	43	37
16	Aston Villa	42	10	3	8	35	30	5	4	12	19	34	37
17	Hull City	42	6	8	7	25	23	6	5	10	33	50	37
18	Derby County	42	8	5	8	40	35	5	5	11	31	43	36
19	Bristol City	42	7	7	7	26	25	6	3	12	22	37	36
20	Preston North End	42	8	7	6	29	24	4	4	13	14	41	35
21	Rotherham United	42	7	4	10	22	32	3	7	11	20	44	31
22	Plymouth Argyle	42	5	4	12	26	36	4	5	12	12	36	27

1968/69 Division 2

1	Derby County	42	16	4	1	43	16	10	7	4	22	16	63
2	Crystal Palace	42	14	4	3	45	24	8	8	5	25	23	56
3	Charlton Athletic	42	11	8	2	39	21	7	6	8	22	31	50
4	Middlesbrough	42	13	7	1	36	13	6	4	11	22	36	49
5	CARDIFF CITY	42	13	3	5	38	19	7	4	10	29	35	47
6	Huddersfield Town	42	13	6	2	37	14	4	6	11	16	32	46
7	Birmingham City	42	13	3	5	52	24	5	5	11	21	35	44
8	Blackpool	42	9	8	4	33	20	5	7	9	18	21	43
9	Sheffield United	42	14	4	3	41	15	2	7	12	20	35	43
10	Millwall	42	10	5	6	33	23	7	4	10	24	26	43
11	Hull City	42	10	7	4	38	20	3	9	9	21	32	42
12	Carlisle United	42	10	5	6	25	17	6	5	10	21	32	42
13	Norwich City	42	7	6	8	24	25	8	4	9	29	31	40
14	Preston North End	42	8	8	5	23	19	4	7	10	15	25	39
15	Portsmouth	42	11	5	5	39	22	1	9	11	19	36	38
16	Bristol City	42	9	9	3	30	15	2	7	12	16	38	38
17	Bolton Wanderers	42	8	7	6	29	26	4	7	10	26	41	38
18	Aston Villa	42	10	8	3	22	11	2	6	13	15	37	38
19	Blackburn Rovers	42	9	6	6	30	24	4	5	12	22	39	37
20	Oxford United	42	8	5	8	21	23	4	4	13	13	32	33
21	Bury	42	8	4	9	35	33	3	4	14	16	47	30
22	Fulham	42	6	7	8	20	28	1	4	16	20	53	25

1969/70 Division 2

1	Huddersfield Town	42	14	6	1	36	10	10	6	5	32	27	60
2	Blackpool	42	10	9	2	25	16	10	4	7	31	29	53
3	Leicester City	42	12	6	3	37	22	7	7	7	27	28	51
4	Middlesbrough	42	15	4	2	36	14	5	6	10	19	31	50
5	Swindon Town	42	13	7	1	35	17	4	9	8	22	30	50
6	Sheffield United	42	16	2	3	50	10	6	3	12	23	28	49
7	CARDIFF CITY	42	12	7	2	38	14	6	6	9	23	27	49
8	Blackburn Rovers	42	15	2	4	42	19	5	5	11	12	31	47
9	Queen's Park Rgs.	42	13	5	3	47	24	4	6	11	19	33	45
10	Millwall	42	14	4	3	38	18	1	10	10	18	38	44
11	Norwich City	42	13	5	3	37	14	3	6	12	12	32	43
12	Carlisle United	42	10	6	5	39	28	4	7	10	19	28	41
13	Hull City	42	11	6	4	43	28	4	5	12	29	42	41
14	Bristol City	42	11	7	3	37	13	2	6	13	17	37	39
15	Oxford United	42	9	9	3	23	13	3	6	12	12	29	39
16	Bolton Wanderers	42	9	6	6	31	23	3	6	12	23	38	36
17	Portsmouth	42	8	4	9	39	35	5	5	11	27	45	35
18	Birmingham City	42	9	7	5	33	22	2	4	15	18	56	33
19	Watford	42	6	8	7	26	21	3	5	13	18	36	31
20	Charlton Athletic	42	7	8	6	23	28	0	9	12	12	48	31
21	Aston Villa	42	7	8	6	23	21	1	5	15	13	41	29
22	Preston North End	42	7	6	8	31	28	1	6	14	12	35	28

1970/71 Division 2

1	Leicester City	42	12	7	2	30	14	11	6	4	27	16	59
2	Sheffield United	42	14	6	1	49	18	7	8	6	24	21	56
3	CARDIFF CITY	42	12	7	2	39	16	8	6	7	25	25	53
4	Carlisle United	42	16	3	2	39	13	4	10	7	26	30	53
5	Hull City	42	11	5	5	31	16	8	8	5	23	25	51
6	Luton Town	42	12	7	2	40	18	6	6	9	22	25	49
7	Middlesbrough	42	13	6	2	37	16	4	8	9	23	27	48
8	Millwall	42	13	5	3	36	12	6	4	11	23	30	47
9	Birmingham City	42	12	7	2	30	12	5	5	11	28	36	46
10	Norwich City	42	11	8	2	34	20	4	6	11	20	32	44
11	Queen's Park Rgs.	42	11	5	5	39	22	5	6	10	19	31	43
12	Swindon Town	42	12	7	2	38	14	3	5	13	23	37	42
13	Sunderland	42	11	6	4	34	21	4	6	11	18	33	42
14	Oxford United	42	8	8	5	23	23	6	6	9	18	25	42
15	Sheffield Wed.	42	10	7	4	32	27	2	5	14	19	42	36
16	Portsmouth	42	9	4	8	32	28	1	10	10	14	33	34
17	Leyton Orient	42	5	11	5	16	15	4	5	12	13	36	34
18	Watford	42	6	7	8	18	22	4	6	11	20	38	33
19	Bristol City	42	9	6	6	30	28	1	5	15	16	36	31
20	Charlton Athletic	42	7	6	8	28	30	1	8	12	13	35	30
21	Blackburn Rovers	42	5	8	8	20	28	1	7	13	17	41	27
22	Bolton Wanderers	42	6	5	10	22	31	1	5	15	13	43	24

1971/72 Division 2

1	Norwich City	42	13	8	0	40	16	8	7	6	20	20	57
2	Birmingham City	42	15	6	0	46	14	4	12	5	14	17	56
3	Millwall	42	14	7	0	38	17	5	10	6	26	29	55
4	Queen's Park Rgs.	42	16	4	1	39	9	4	10	7	18	19	54
5	Sunderland	42	11	7	3	42	24	6	9	6	25	33	50
6	Blackpool	42	12	6	3	43	16	8	1	12	27	34	47
7	Burnley	42	13	4	4	43	22	7	2	12	27	33	46
8	Bristol City	42	14	3	4	43	22	4	7	10	18	27	46
9	Middlesbrough	42	16	4	1	31	11	3	4	14	19	37	46
10	Carlisle United	42	12	6	3	38	22	5	3	13	23	35	43
11	Swindon Town	42	10	6	5	29	16	5	6	10	18	31	42
12	Hull City	42	10	6	5	33	21	4	4	13	16	32	38
13	Luton Town	42	7	8	6	25	24	3	10	8	18	24	38
14	Sheffield Wed.	42	11	7	3	33	22	2	5	14	18	36	38
15	Oxford United	42	10	8	3	28	17	2	6	13	15	38	38
16	Portsmouth	42	9	7	5	31	26	3	6	12	28	42	37
17	Leyton Orient	42	12	4	5	32	19	2	5	14	18	42	37
18	Preston North End	42	11	4	6	32	21	1	8	12	20	37	36
19	CARDIFF CITY	42	9	7	5	37	25	1	7	13	19	44	34
20	Fulham	42	10	7	4	29	20	2	3	16	16	48	34
21	Charlton Athletic	42	9	7	5	33	25	3	2	16	22	52	33
22	Watford	42	5	5	11	15	25	0	4	17	9	50	19

1972/73 Division 2

1	Burnley	42	13	6	2	44	18	11	8	2	28	17	62
2	Queen's Park Rgs.	42	16	4	1	54	13	8	9	4	27	24	61
3	Aston Villa	42	12	5	4	27	17	6	9	6	24	30	50
4	Middlesbrough	42	12	6	3	29	15	5	7	9	17	28	47
5	Bristol City	42	10	7	4	34	18	7	5	9	29	33	46
6	Sunderland	42	12	6	3	35	17	5	6	10	24	32	46
7	Blackpool	42	12	6	3	37	17	6	4	11	19	34	46
8	Oxford United	42	14	2	5	36	18	5	5	11	16	25	45
9	Fulham	42	11	6	4	32	16	5	6	10	26	33	44
10	Sheffield Wed.	42	14	4	3	40	20	3	6	12	19	35	44
11	Millwall	42	12	5	4	33	18	4	5	12	22	29	42
12	Luton Town	42	6	9	6	24	23	9	2	10	20	30	41
13	Hull City	42	9	7	5	39	22	5	5	11	25	37	40
14	Nottingham Forest	42	12	5	4	32	18	2	7	12	15	34	40
15	Leyton Orient	42	11	6	4	33	18	1	6	14	16	35	36
16	Swindon Town	42	8	9	4	28	23	2	7	12	18	37	36
17	Portsmouth	42	7	6	8	21	22	5	5	11	21	37	35
18	Carlisle United	42	10	5	6	40	24	1	7	13	10	28	34
19	Preston North End	42	6	8	7	19	25	5	4	12	18	39	34
20	CARDIFF CITY	42	11	4	6	32	21	0	7	14	11	37	33
21	Huddersfield Town	42	7	9	5	21	20	1	8	12	15	36	33
22	Brighton & Hove A.	42	7	8	6	32	31	1	5	15	14	52	29

1973/74 Division 2

1	Middlesbrough	42	16	4	1	40	8	11	7	3	37	22	65
2	Luton Town	42	12	5	4	42	25	7	7	7	22	26	50
3	Carlisle United	42	13	5	3	40	17	7	4	10	21	31	49
4	Leyton Orient	42	9	8	4	28	17	6	10	5	27	25	48
5	Blackpool	42	11	5	5	35	17	6	8	7	22	23	47
6	Sunderland	42	11	6	4	32	15	8	3	10	26	29	47
7	Nottingham Forest	42	12	6	3	40	19	3	9	9	17	24	45
8	West Bromwich Alb.	42	8	9	4	28	24	6	7	8	20	21	44
9	Hull City	42	9	9	3	25	15	4	8	9	21	32	43
10	Notts County	42	8	6	7	30	35	7	7	7	25	25	43
11	Bolton Wanderers	42	12	5	4	30	17	3	7	11	14	23	42
12	Millwall	42	10	6	5	28	16	4	8	9	23	35	42
13	Fulham	42	11	4	6	26	20	5	6	10	13	23	42
14	Aston Villa	42	8	9	4	33	21	5	6	10	15	24	41
15	Portsmouth	42	9	8	4	26	16	5	4	12	19	46	40
16	Bristol City	42	9	5	7	25	20	5	5	11	22	34	38
17	CARDIFF CITY	42	8	7	6	27	20	2	9	10	22	42	36
18	Oxford United	42	8	8	5	27	21	2	8	11	8	25	36
19	Sheffield Wed.	42	9	6	6	33	24	3	5	13	18	39	35
20	Crystal Palace	42	6	7	8	24	24	5	5	11	19	32	34
21	Preston North End	42	7	8	6	24	23	2	6	13	16	39	31
22	Swindon Town	42	6	7	8	22	27	1	4	16	14	45	25

1974/75 Division 2

1	Manchester United	42	17	3	1	45	12	9	6	6	21	18	61
2	Aston Villa	42	16	4	1	47	6	9	4	8	32	26	58
3	Norwich City	42	14	3	4	34	17	6	10	5	24	20	53
4	Sunderland	42	14	6	1	41	8	5	7	9	24	27	51
5	Bristol City	42	14	5	2	31	10	7	3	11	16	23	50
6	West Bromwich Alb.	42	13	4	4	33	15	5	5	11	21	27	45
7	Blackpool	42	12	6	3	31	17	2	11	8	7	16	45
8	Hull City	42	12	8	1	25	10	3	6	12	15	43	44
9	Fulham	42	9	8	4	29	17	4	8	9	15	22	42
10	Bolton Wanderers	42	9	7	5	27	16	6	5	10	18	25	42
11	Oxford United	42	14	3	4	30	19	1	9	11	11	32	42
12	Leyton Orient	42	8	9	4	17	16	3	11	7	11	23	42
13	Southampton	42	10	6	5	29	20	5	5	11	24	34	41
14	Notts County	42	7	11	3	34	26	5	5	11	15	33	40
15	York City	42	9	7	5	28	18	5	3	13	23	37	38
16	Nottingham Forest	42	7	7	7	24	23	5	7	9	19	32	38
17	Portsmouth	42	9	7	5	28	20	3	6	12	16	34	37
18	Oldham Athletic	42	10	7	4	28	16	0	8	13	12	32	35
19	Bristol Rovers	42	10	4	7	25	23	2	7	12	17	41	35
20	Millwall	42	8	9	4	31	19	2	3	16	13	37	32
21	CARDIFF CITY	42	7	8	6	24	21	2	6	13	12	41	32
22	Sheffield Wed.	42	3	7	11	17	29	2	4	15	12	35	21

1975/76 Division 3

1	Hereford United	46	14	6	3	45	24	12	5	6	41	31	63
2	CARDIFF CITY	46	14	7	2	38	13	8	6	9	31	35	57
3	Millwall	46	16	6	1	35	14	4	10	9	19	29	56
4	Brighton & Hove A.	46	18	3	2	58	15	4	6	13	20	38	53
5	Crystal Palace	46	7	12	4	30	20	11	5	7	31	26	53
6	Wrexham	46	13	6	4	38	21	7	6	10	28	34	52
7	Walsall	46	11	8	4	43	22	7	6	10	31	39	50
8	Preston North End	46	15	4	4	45	23	4	6	13	17	34	48
9	Shrewsbury Town	46	14	2	7	36	25	5	8	10	25	34	48
10	Peterborough Utd.	46	12	7	4	37	23	3	11	9	26	40	48
11	Mansfield Town	46	8	11	4	31	22	8	4	11	27	30	47
12	Port Vale	46	10	10	3	33	21	5	6	12	22	33	46
13	Bury	46	11	7	5	33	16	3	9	11	18	30	44
14	Chesterfield	46	11	5	7	45	30	6	4	13	24	39	43
15	Gillingham	46	10	8	5	38	27	2	11	10	20	41	43
16	Rotherham United	46	11	6	6	35	22	4	6	13	19	43	42
17	Chester City	46	13	7	3	34	19	2	5	16	9	43	42
18	Grimsby Town	46	13	7	3	39	21	2	3	18	23	53	40
19	Swindon Town	46	11	4	8	42	31	5	4	14	20	44	40
20	Sheffield Wed.	46	12	6	5	34	25	0	10	13	14	34	40
21	Aldershot	46	10	8	5	34	26	3	5	15	25	49	39
22	Colchester United	46	9	6	8	25	27	3	8	12	16	38	38
23	Southend United	46	9	7	7	40	31	3	6	14	25	44	37
24	Halifax Town	46	6	5	12	22	32	5	8	10	19	29	35

1976/77 Division 2

1	Wolverhampton Wan.	42	15	3	3	48	21	7	10	4	36	24	57
2	Chelsea	42	15	6	0	51	22	6	7	8	22	31	55
3	Nottingham Forest	42	14	3	4	53	22	7	7	7	24	21	52
4	Bolton Wanderers	42	15	2	4	46	21	5	9	7	29	33	51
5	Blackpool	42	11	7	3	29	17	6	10	5	29	25	51
6	Luton Town	42	13	5	3	39	17	8	1	12	28	31	48
7	Charlton Athletic	42	14	5	2	52	27	2	11	8	19	31	48
8	Notts County	42	11	5	5	29	20	8	5	8	36	40	48
9	Southampton	42	12	6	3	40	24	5	4	12	32	43	44
10	Millwall	42	9	6	6	31	22	6	7	8	26	31	43
11	Sheffield United	42	9	8	4	32	25	5	4	12	22	38	40
12	Blackburn Rovers	42	12	4	5	31	18	3	5	13	11	36	39
13	Oldham Athletic	42	11	6	4	37	23	3	4	14	15	41	38
14	Hull City	42	9	8	4	31	17	1	9	11	14	36	37
15	Bristol Rovers	42	8	9	4	32	27	4	4	13	21	41	37
16	Burnley	42	8	9	4	27	20	3	5	13	19	44	36
17	Fulham	42	9	7	5	39	25	2	6	13	15	36	35
18	CARDIFF CITY	42	7	6	8	30	30	5	4	12	26	37	34
19	Leyton Orient	42	4	8	9	18	23	5	8	8	19	32	34
20	Carlisle United	42	7	7	7	31	33	4	5	12	18	42	34
21	Plymouth Argyle	42	5	9	7	27	25	3	7	11	19	40	32
22	Hereford United	42	6	9	6	28	30	2	6	13	29	48	31

1977/78 Division 2

1	Bolton Wanderers	42	16	4	1	39	14	8	6	7	24	19	58
2	Southampton	42	15	4	2	44	16	7	9	5	26	23	57
3	Tottenham Hotspur	42	13	7	1	50	19	7	9	5	33	30	56
4	Brighton & Hove A.	42	15	5	1	43	21	7	7	7	20	17	56
5	Blackburn Rovers	42	12	4	5	33	16	4	9	8	23	44	45
6	Sunderland	42	11	6	4	36	17	3	10	8	31	42	44
7	Stoke City	42	13	5	3	38	16	3	5	13	15	33	42
8	Oldham Athletic	42	9	10	2	32	20	4	6	11	22	38	42
9	Crystal Palace	42	9	7	5	31	20	4	8	9	19	27	41
10	Fulham	42	9	8	4	32	19	5	5	11	17	30	41
11	Burnley	42	11	6	4	35	20	4	4	13	21	44	40
12	Sheffield United	42	13	4	4	38	22	3	4	14	24	51	40
13	Luton Town	42	11	4	6	35	20	3	6	12	19	32	38
14	Leyton Orient	42	8	11	2	30	20	2	7	12	13	29	38
15	Notts County	42	10	9	2	36	22	1	7	13	18	40	38
16	Millwall	42	8	8	5	23	20	4	6	11	26	37	38
17	Charlton Athletic	42	11	6	4	38	27	2	6	13	17	41	38
18	Bristol Rovers	42	10	7	4	40	26	3	5	13	21	51	38
19	CARDIFF CITY	42	12	6	3	32	23	1	6	14	19	48	38
20	Blackpool	42	7	8	6	35	25	5	5	11	24	35	37
21	Mansfield Town	42	6	6	9	30	34	4	5	12	19	35	31
22	Hull City	42	6	6	9	23	25	2	6	13	11	27	28

1978/79 Division 2

1	Crystal Palace	42	12	7	2	30	11	7	12	2	21	13	57
2	Brighton & Hove A.	42	16	3	2	44	11	7	7	7	28	28	56
3	Stoke City	42	11	7	3	35	15	9	9	3	23	16	56
4	Sunderland	42	13	3	5	39	19	9	8	4	31	25	55
5	West Ham United	42	12	7	2	46	15	6	7	8	24	24	50
6	Notts County	42	8	10	3	23	15	6	6	9	25	45	44
7	Preston North End	42	7	11	3	36	23	5	7	9	23	34	42
8	Newcastle United	42	13	3	5	35	24	4	5	12	16	31	42
9	CARDIFF CITY	42	12	5	4	34	23	4	5	12	22	47	42
10	Fulham	42	10	7	4	35	19	3	8	10	15	28	41
11	Leyton Orient	42	11	5	5	32	18	4	5	12	19	33	40
12	Cambridge United	42	7	10	4	22	15	5	6	10	22	37	40
13	Burnley	42	11	6	4	31	22	3	6	12	20	40	40
14	Oldham Athletic	42	10	7	4	36	23	3	6	12	16	38	39
15	Wrexham	42	10	6	5	31	16	2	8	11	14	26	38
16	Bristol Rovers	42	10	6	5	34	23	4	4	13	14	37	38
17	Leicester City	42	7	8	6	28	23	3	9	9	15	29	37
18	Luton Town	42	11	5	5	46	24	2	5	14	14	33	36
19	Charlton Athletic	42	6	8	7	28	28	5	5	11	32	41	35
20	Sheffield United	42	9	6	6	34	24	2	6	13	18	45	34
21	Millwall	42	7	4	10	22	29	4	6	11	20	32	32
22	Blackburn Rovers	42	5	8	8	24	29	5	2	14	17	43	30

1979/80 Division 2

1	Leicester City	42	12	5	4	32	19	9	8	4	26	19	55
2	Sunderland	42	16	5	0	47	13	5	7	9	22	29	54
3	Birmingham City	42	14	5	2	37	16	7	6	8	21	22	53
4	Chelsea	42	14	3	4	34	16	9	4	8	32	36	53
5	Queen's Park Rgs.	42	10	9	2	46	25	8	4	9	29	28	49
6	Luton Town	42	9	10	2	36	17	7	7	7	30	28	49
7	West Ham United	42	13	2	6	37	21	7	5	9	17	22	47
8	Cambridge United	42	11	6	4	40	23	3	10	8	21	30	44
9	Newcastle United	42	13	6	2	35	19	2	8	11	18	30	44
10	Preston North End	42	8	10	3	30	23	4	9	8	26	29	43
11	Oldham Athletic	42	12	5	4	30	21	4	6	11	19	32	43
12	Swansea City	42	13	1	7	31	20	4	8	9	17	33	43
13	Shrewsbury Town	42	12	3	6	41	23	6	2	13	19	30	41
14	Leyton Orient	42	7	9	5	29	31	5	8	8	19	23	41
15	CARDIFF CITY	42	11	4	6	21	16	5	4	12	20	32	40
16	Wrexham	42	13	2	6	26	15	3	4	14	14	34	38
17	Notts County	42	4	11	6	24	22	7	4	10	27	30	37
18	Watford	42	9	6	6	27	18	3	7	11	12	28	37
19	Bristol Rovers	42	9	8	4	33	23	2	5	14	17	41	35
20	Fulham	42	6	4	11	19	28	5	3	13	23	46	29
21	Burnley	42	5	9	7	19	23	1	6	14	20	50	27
22	Charlton Athletic	42	6	6	9	25	31	0	4	17	14	47	22

1980/81 Division 2

1	West Ham United	42	19	1	1	53	12	9	9	3	26	17	66
2	Notts County	42	10	8	3	26	15	8	9	4	23	23	53
3	Swansea City	42	12	5	4	39	19	6	9	6	25	25	50
4	Blackburn Rovers	42	12	8	1	28	7	4	10	7	14	22	50
5	Luton Town	42	10	6	5	35	23	8	6	7	26	23	48
6	Derby County	42	9	8	4	34	26	6	7	8	23	26	45
7	Grimsby Town	42	10	8	3	21	10	5	7	9	23	32	45
8	Queen's Park Rgs.	42	11	7	3	36	12	4	6	11	20	34	43
9	Watford	42	13	5	3	34	18	3	6	12	16	27	43
10	Sheffield Wed.	42	14	4	3	38	14	3	4	14	15	37	42
11	Newcastle United	42	11	7	3	22	13	3	7	11	8	32	42
12	Chelsea	42	8	6	7	27	15	6	6	9	19	26	40
13	Cambridge United	42	13	1	7	36	23	4	5	12	17	42	40
14	Shrewsbury Town	42	9	7	5	33	22	2	10	9	13	25	39
15	Oldham Athletic	42	7	9	5	19	16	5	6	10	20	32	39
16	Wrexham	42	5	8	8	22	24	7	6	8	21	21	38
17	Leyton Orient	42	9	8	4	34	20	4	4	13	18	36	38
18	Bolton Wanderers	42	10	5	6	40	27	4	5	12	21	39	38
19	CARDIFF CITY	42	7	7	7	23	24	5	5	11	21	36	36
20	Preston North End	42	8	7	6	28	26	3	7	11	13	36	36
21	Bristol City	42	6	10	5	19	15	1	6	14	10	36	30
22	Bristol Rovers	42	4	9	8	21	24	1	4	16	13	41	23

1981/82 Division 2

1	Luton Town	42	16	3	2	48	19	9	10	2	38	27	88
2	Watford	42	13	6	2	46	16	10	5	6	30	26	80
3	Norwich City	42	14	3	4	41	19	8	2	11	23	31	71
4	Sheffield Wed.	42	10	8	3	31	23	10	2	9	24	28	70
5	Queen's Park Rgs.	42	15	4	2	40	9	6	2	13	25	34	69
6	Barnsley	42	13	4	4	33	14	6	6	9	26	27	67
7	Rotherham United	42	13	5	3	42	19	7	2	12	24	35	67
8	Leicester City	42	12	5	4	31	19	6	7	8	25	29	66
9	Newcastle United	42	14	4	3	30	14	4	4	13	22	36	62
10	Blackburn Rovers	42	11	4	6	26	15	5	7	9	21	28	59
11	Oldham Athletic	42	9	9	3	28	23	6	5	10	22	28	59
12	Chelsea	42	10	5	6	37	30	5	7	9	23	30	57
13	Charlton Athletic	42	11	5	5	33	22	2	7	12	17	43	51
14	Cambridge United	42	11	4	6	31	19	2	5	14	17	34	48
15	Crystal Palace	42	9	2	10	25	26	4	7	10	9	19	48
16	Derby County	42	9	8	4	32	23	3	4	14	21	45	48
17	Grimsby Town	42	5	8	8	29	30	6	5	10	24	35	46
18	Shrewsbury Town	42	10	6	5	26	19	1	7	13	11	38	46
19	Bolton Wanderers	42	10	4	7	28	24	3	3	15	11	37	46
20	CARDIFF CITY	42	9	2	10	28	32	3	6	12	17	29	44
21	Wrexham	42	9	4	8	22	22	2	7	12	18	34	44
22	Leyton Orient	42	6	8	7	23	24	4	1	16	13	37	39

1982/83 Division 3

1	Portsmouth	46	16	4	3	43	19	11	6	6	31	22	91
2	CARDIFF CITY	46	17	5	1	45	14	8	6	9	31	36	86
3	Huddersfield Town	46	15	8	0	56	18	8	5	10	28	31	82
4	Newport County	46	13	7	3	40	20	10	2	11	36	34	78
5	Oxford United	46	12	9	2	41	23	10	3	10	30	30	78
6	Lincoln City	46	17	1	5	55	22	6	6	11	22	29	76
7	Bristol Rovers	46	16	4	3	55	21	6	5	12	29	37	75
8	Plymouth Argyle	46	15	2	6	37	23	4	6	13	24	43	65
9	Brentford	46	14	4	5	50	28	4	6	13	38	49	64
10	Walsall	46	14	5	4	38	19	3	8	12	26	44	64
11	Sheffield United	46	16	3	4	44	20	3	4	16	18	44	64
12	Bradford City	46	11	7	5	41	27	5	6	12	27	42	61
13	Gillingham	46	12	4	7	37	29	4	9	10	21	30	61
14	Bournemouth	46	11	7	5	35	20	5	6	12	24	48	61
15	Southend United	46	10	8	5	41	28	5	6	12	25	37	59
16	Preston North End	46	11	10	2	35	17	4	3	16	25	52	58
17	Millwall	46	12	7	4	41	24	2	6	15	23	53	55
18	Wigan Athletic	46	10	4	9	35	33	5	5	13	25	39	54
19	Exeter City	46	12	4	7	49	43	2	8	13	32	61	54
20	Leyton Orient	46	10	6	7	44	38	5	3	15	20	50	54
21	Reading	46	10	8	5	37	28	2	9	12	27	51	53
22	Wrexham	46	11	6	6	40	26	1	9	13	16	50	51
23	Doncaster Rovers	46	6	8	9	38	44	3	3	17	19	53	38
24	Chesterfield	46	6	6	11	28	28	2	7	14	15	40	37

1983/84 Division 2

1 Chelsea	42	15	4	2	55	17	10	9	2	35	23	88
2 Sheffield Wed.	42	16	4	1	47	16	10	6	5	25	18	88
3 Newcastle United	42	16	2	3	51	18	8	6	7	34	35	80
4 Manchester City	42	13	3	5	43	21	7	7	7	23	27	70
5 Grimsby Town	42	13	6	2	36	15	6	7	8	24	32	70
6 Blackburn Rovers	42	9	11	1	35	19	8	5	8	22	27	67
7 Carlisle United	42	10	9	2	29	13	6	7	8	19	28	64
8 Shrewsbury Town	42	13	5	3	34	18	4	5	12	15	35	61
9 Brighton & Hove A.	42	11	6	4	42	17	6	3	12	27	43	60
10 Leeds United	42	13	4	4	33	16	3	8	10	22	40	60
11 Fulham	42	9	6	6	35	24	6	6	9	25	29	57
12 Huddersfield Town	42	8	6	7	27	20	6	9	6	29	29	57
13 Charlton Athletic	42	13	4	4	40	26	3	5	13	13	38	57
14 Barnsley	42	9	6	6	33	23	6	1	14	24	30	52
15 CARDIFF CITY	42	11	3	7	32	27	4	3	14	21	39	51
16 Portsmouth	42	8	3	10	46	32	6	4	11	27	32	49
17 Middlesbrough	42	9	8	4	26	18	3	5	13	15	29	49
18 Crystal Palace	42	8	5	8	18	18	4	6	11	24	34	47
19 Oldham Athletic	42	10	6	5	33	27	3	2	16	14	46	47
20 Derby County	42	9	5	7	26	26	2	4	15	10	46	42
21 Swansea City	42	7	4	10	20	28	0	4	17	16	57	29
22 Cambridge United	42	4	7	10	20	33	0	5	16	8	44	24

1984/85 Division 2

1 Oxford United	42	18	2	1	62	15	7	7	7	22	21	84
2 Birmingham City	42	12	6	3	30	15	13	1	7	29	18	82
3 Manchester City	42	14	4	3	42	16	7	7	7	24	24	74
4 Portsmouth	42	11	6	4	39	25	9	8	4	30	25	74
5 Blackburn Rovers	42	14	3	4	38	15	7	7	7	28	26	73
6 Brighton & Hove A.	42	13	6	2	31	11	7	6	8	23	23	72
7 Leeds United	42	12	7	2	37	11	7	5	9	29	32	69
8 Shrewsbury Town	42	12	6	3	45	22	6	5	10	21	31	65
9 Fulham	42	13	3	5	35	26	6	5	10	33	38	65
10 Grimsby Town	42	13	1	7	47	32	5	7	9	25	32	62
11 Barnsley	42	11	7	3	27	12	3	9	9	15	30	58
12 Wimbledon	42	9	8	4	40	29	7	2	12	31	46	58
13 Huddersfield Town	42	9	5	7	28	29	6	5	10	24	35	55
14 Oldham Athletic	42	10	4	7	27	23	5	4	12	22	44	53
15 Crystal Palace	42	8	7	6	25	27	4	5	12	21	38	48
16 Carlisle United	42	8	5	8	27	23	5	3	13	23	44	47
17 Charlton Athletic	42	8	7	6	34	30	3	5	13	17	33	45
18 Sheffield United	42	7	6	8	31	28	3	8	10	23	38	44
19 Middlesbrough	42	6	8	7	22	26	4	2	15	19	31	40
20 Notts County	42	6	5	10	25	32	4	2	15	20	41	37
21 CARDIFF CITY	42	5	3	13	24	42	4	5	12	23	37	35
22 Wolverhampton Wan.	42	5	4	12	18	32	3	5	13	19	47	33

1985/86 Division 3

1 Reading	46	16	3	4	39	22	13	4	6	28	29	94
2 Plymouth Argyle	46	17	3	3	56	20	9	6	8	32	33	87
3 Derby County	46	13	7	3	45	20	10	8	5	35	21	84
4 Wigan Athletic	46	17	4	2	54	17	6	10	7	28	31	83
5 Gillingham	46	14	5	4	48	17	8	8	7	33	37	79
6 Walsall	46	15	7	1	59	23	7	2	14	31	41	75
7 York City	46	16	4	3	49	17	4	7	12	28	41	71
8 Notts County	46	12	6	5	42	26	7	8	8	29	34	71
9 Bristol City	46	14	5	4	43	19	4	9	10	26	41	68
10 Brentford	46	8	8	7	29	29	10	4	9	29	32	66
11 Doncaster Rovers	46	7	10	6	20	21	9	6	8	25	31	64
12 Blackpool	46	11	6	6	38	19	6	6	11	28	36	63
13 Darlington	46	10	7	6	39	33	5	6	12	22	45	58
14 Rotherham United	46	13	5	5	44	18	2	7	14	17	41	57
15 Bournemouth	46	9	6	8	41	31	6	3	14	24	41	54
16 Bristol Rovers	46	9	8	6	27	21	5	4	14	24	54	54
17 Chesterfield	46	10	6	7	41	30	3	8	12	20	34	53
18 Bolton Wanderers	46	10	4	9	35	30	5	4	14	19	38	53
19 Newport County	46	7	8	8	35	33	4	10	9	17	32	51
20 Bury	46	11	7	5	46	26	1	6	16	17	41	49
21 Lincoln City	46	7	9	7	33	34	3	7	13	22	43	46
22 CARDIFF CITY	46	7	5	11	22	29	5	4	14	31	54	45
23 Wolverhampton Wan.	46	6	6	11	29	47	5	4	14	28	51	43
24 Swansea City	46	9	6	8	27	27	2	4	17	16	60	43

1986/87 Division 4

1 Northampton Town	46	20	2	1	56	20	10	7	6	47	33	99
2 Preston North End	46	16	4	3	36	18	10	8	5	36	29	90
3 Southend United	46	14	4	5	43	27	11	1	11	25	28	80
4 Wolverhampton Wan.	46	12	3	8	36	24	12	4	7	33	26	79
5 Colchester United	46	15	3	5	41	20	6	4	13	23	36	70
6 Aldershot	46	13	5	5	40	22	7	5	11	24	35	70
7 Leyton Orient	46	15	2	6	40	25	5	7	11	24	36	69
8 Scunthorpe United	46	15	3	5	52	27	3	9	11	21	30	66
9 Wrexham	46	8	13	2	38	24	7	7	9	32	27	65
10 Peterborough Utd.	46	10	7	6	29	21	7	7	9	28	29	65
11 Cambridge United	46	12	6	5	37	23	5	5	13	23	39	62
12 Swansea City	46	13	3	7	31	21	4	8	11	25	40	62
13 CARDIFF CITY	46	6	12	5	24	18	9	4	10	24	32	61
14 Exeter City	46	11	10	2	37	17	0	13	10	16	32	56
15 Halifax Town	46	10	5	8	32	32	5	5	13	27	42	55
16 Hereford United	46	10	6	7	33	23	4	5	14	27	38	53
17 Crewe Alexandra	46	8	9	6	38	35	5	5	13	32	37	53
18 Hartlepool United	46	6	11	6	24	30	5	7	11	20	35	51
19 Stockport County	46	9	6	8	25	27	4	6	13	15	42	51
20 Tranmere Rovers	46	6	10	7	32	37	5	7	11	22	35	50
21 Rochdale	46	8	8	7	31	30	3	9	11	23	43	50
22 Burnley	46	9	7	7	31	35	3	6	14	22	39	49
23 Torquay United	46	8	8	7	28	29	2	10	11	28	43	48
24 Lincoln City	46	8	7	8	30	27	4	5	14	15	38	48

1987/88 Division 4

1 Wolverhampton Wan.	46	15	3	5	47	19	12	6	5	35	24	90
2 CARDIFF CITY	46	15	6	2	39	14	9	7	7	27	27	85
3 Bolton Wanderers	46	15	6	2	42	12	7	6	10	24	30	78
4 Scunthorpe United	46	14	5	4	42	20	6	12	5	34	31	77
5 Torquay United	46	10	7	6	34	16	11	7	5	32	25	77
6 Swansea City	46	9	7	7	35	28	11	3	9	27	28	70
7 Peterborough Utd.	46	10	5	8	28	26	10	5	8	24	27	70
8 Leyton Orient	46	13	4	6	55	27	6	8	9	30	36	69
9 Colchester United	46	10	5	8	23	22	9	5	9	24	29	67
10 Burnley	46	12	5	6	31	22	8	2	13	26	40	67
11 Wrexham	46	13	3	7	46	26	7	3	13	23	32	66
12 Scarborough	46	12	8	3	38	19	5	6	12	18	29	65
13 Darlington	46	13	6	4	39	25	5	5	13	32	44	65
14 Tranmere Rovers	46	14	2	7	43	20	5	7	11	18	33	64
15 Cambridge United	46	10	6	7	32	24	6	7	10	18	28	61
16 Hartlepool United	46	9	7	7	25	25	6	7	10	25	32	59
17 Crewe Alexandra	46	7	11	5	25	19	6	8	9	32	34	58
18 Halifax Town	46	11	7	5	37	25	3	7	13	17	34	55
19 Hereford United	46	8	7	8	25	27	6	5	12	16	32	54
20 Stockport County	46	7	7	9	26	26	5	8	10	18	32	51
21 Rochdale	46	5	9	9	28	34	6	6	11	19	42	48
22 Exeter City	46	8	6	9	33	29	3	7	13	20	39	46
23 Carlisle United	46	9	5	9	38	33	3	3	17	19	53	44
24 Newport County	46	4	5	14	19	36	2	2	19	16	69	25

1988/89 Division 3

1 Wolverhampton Wan.	46	18	4	1	61	19	8	10	5	35	30	92
2 Sheffield United	46	16	3	4	57	21	9	6	8	36	33	84
3 Port Vale	46	15	3	5	46	21	9	9	5	32	27	84
4 Fulham	46	12	7	4	42	28	10	2	11	27	39	75
5 Bristol Rovers	46	9	11	3	34	21	10	6	7	33	30	74
6 Preston North End	46	14	7	2	56	31	5	8	10	23	29	72
7 Brentford	46	14	5	4	36	21	4	9	10	30	40	68
8 Chester City	46	12	6	5	38	18	7	5	11	26	43	68
9 Notts County	46	11	7	5	37	22	7	6	10	27	32	67
10 Bolton Wanderers	46	12	8	3	42	23	4	8	11	16	31	64
11 Bristol City	46	10	3	10	32	25	8	6	9	21	30	63
12 Swansea City	46	11	8	4	33	22	4	8	11	18	31	61
13 Bury	46	11	7	5	27	22	5	6	12	28	45	61
14 Huddersfield Town	46	10	8	5	35	25	7	1	15	28	48	60
15 Mansfield Town	46	10	8	5	32	22	4	9	10	16	30	59
16 CARDIFF CITY	46	10	9	4	30	16	4	6	13	14	40	57
17 Wigan Athletic	46	9	5	9	28	22	5	9	9	27	31	56
18 Reading	46	10	6	7	37	29	5	5	13	31	43	56
19 Blackpool	46	10	6	7	36	29	4	7	12	20	30	55
20 Northampton Town	46	11	2	10	41	34	5	4	14	25	42	54
21 Southend United	46	10	9	4	33	26	3	6	14	23	49	54
22 Chesterfield	46	9	5	9	35	35	5	2	16	16	51	49
23 Gillingham	46	7	3	13	25	32	5	1	17	22	49	40
24 Aldershot	46	7	6	10	29	29	1	7	15	19	49	37

1989/90 Division 3

1 Bristol Rovers	46	15	8	0	43	14	11	7	5	28	21	93
2 Bristol City	46	15	5	3	40	16	12	5	6	36	24	91
3 Notts County	46	17	4	2	40	18	8	8	7	33	35	87
4 Tranmere Rovers	46	15	5	3	54	22	8	6	9	32	27	80
5 Bury	46	11	7	5	35	19	10	4	9	35	30	74
6 Bolton Wanderers	46	12	7	4	32	19	6	8	9	27	29	69
7 Birmingham City	46	10	7	6	33	19	8	5	10	27	40	66
8 Huddersfield Town	46	11	5	7	30	23	6	9	8	31	39	65
9 Rotherham United	46	12	6	5	48	28	5	7	11	23	34	64
10 Reading	46	10	9	4	33	21	5	10	8	24	32	64
11 Shrewsbury Town	46	10	9	4	38	24	6	6	11	21	30	63
12 Crewe Alexandra	46	10	8	5	32	24	5	9	9	24	29	62
13 Brentford	46	11	4	8	41	31	7	3	13	25	35	61
14 Leyton Orient	46	9	6	8	28	24	7	4	12	24	32	58
15 Mansfield Town	46	13	2	8	34	25	3	5	15	16	40	55
16 Chester City	46	11	7	5	30	23	2	8	13	13	32	54
17 Swansea City	46	10	6	7	25	27	4	6	13	20	36	54
18 Wigan Athletic	46	10	6	7	29	22	3	8	12	19	42	53
19 Preston North End	46	10	7	6	42	30	4	3	16	23	49	52
20 Fulham	46	8	8	7	33	27	4	7	12	22	39	51
21 CARDIFF CITY	46	6	9	8	30	35	6	5	12	21	35	50
22 Northampton Town	46	7	7	9	27	31	4	7	12	24	37	47
23 Blackpool	46	8	6	9	29	33	2	10	11	20	40	46
24 Walsall	46	6	8	9	23	30	3	6	14	17	42	41

1990/91 Division 4

1 Darlington	46	13	8	2	36	14	9	9	5	32	24	83
2 Stockport County	46	16	6	1	54	19	7	7	9	30	28	82
3 Hartlepool United	46	15	5	3	35	15	9	5	9	32	33	82
4 Peterborough Utd.	46	13	9	1	38	15	8	8	7	29	30	80
5 Blackpool	46	17	3	3	55	17	6	7	10	23	30	79
6 Burnley	46	17	5	1	46	16	6	5	12	24	35	79
7 Torquay United	46	14	7	2	37	13	4	11	8	27	34	72
8 Scunthorpe United	46	17	4	2	51	20	3	7	13	20	42	71
9 Scarborough	46	13	5	5	36	21	6	7	10	23	35	69
10 Northampton Town	46	14	5	4	34	21	4	8	11	23	37	67
11 Doncaster Rovers	46	12	5	6	36	22	5	9	9	20	24	65
12 Rochdale	46	10	9	4	29	22	5	8	10	21	31	62
13 CARDIFF CITY	46	10	6	7	26	23	5	9	9	17	31	60
14 Lincoln City	46	10	7	6	32	27	4	10	9	18	34	59
15 Gillingham	46	9	9	5	35	27	3	9	11	22	33	54
16 Walsall	46	7	12	4	25	17	5	5	13	23	34	53
17 Hereford United	46	9	10	4	32	19	4	4	15	21	39	53
18 Chesterfield	46	8	12	3	33	26	5	2	16	14	36	53
19 Maidstone United	46	9	5	9	42	34	4	7	12	24	37	51
20 Carlisle United	46	12	3	8	30	30	1	6	16	17	59	48
21 York City	46	8	6	9	21	23	3	7	13	24	34	46
22 Halifax Town	46	9	6	8	34	29	3	4	16	25	50	46
23 Aldershot	46	8	7	8	38	43	2	4	17	23	58	41
24 Wrexham	46	8	7	8	33	34	2	3	18	15	40	40

1991/92 Division 4

1	Burnley	42	14	4	3	42	16	11	4	6	37	27	83
2	Rotherham United	42	12	6	3	38	16	10	5	6	32	21	77
3	Mansfield Town	42	13	4	4	43	26	10	4	7	32	27	77
4	Blackpool	42	17	3	1	48	13	5	7	9	23	32	76
5	Scunthorpe United	42	14	5	2	39	18	7	4	10	25	41	72
6	Crewe Alexandra	42	12	6	3	33	20	8	4	9	33	31	70
7	Barnet	42	16	1	4	48	23	5	5	11	33	38	69
8	Rochdale	42	12	6	3	34	22	6	7	8	23	31	67
9	CARDIFF CITY	42	13	3	5	42	26	4	12	5	24	27	66
10	Lincoln City	42	9	5	7	21	24	8	6	7	29	20	62
11	Gillingham	42	12	5	4	41	19	3	7	11	22	34	57
12	Scarborough	42	12	5	4	39	28	3	7	11	25	40	57
13	Chesterfield	42	6	7	8	26	28	8	4	9	23	33	53
14	Wrexham	42	11	4	6	31	26	3	5	13	21	47	51
15	Walsall	42	5	10	6	28	26	7	3	11	20	32	49
16	Northampton Town	42	5	9	7	25	23	6	4	11	21	34	46
17	Hereford United	42	9	4	8	31	24	3	4	14	13	33	44
18	Maidstone United	42	6	9	6	24	22	2	9	10	21	34	42
19	York City	42	6	9	6	26	23	2	7	12	16	35	40
20	Halifax Town	42	7	5	9	23	35	3	3	15	11	40	38
21	Doncaster Rovers	42	6	2	13	21	35	3	6	12	19	30	35
22	Carlisle United	42	5	9	7	24	27	2	4	15	17	40	34

1992/93 (new Football League) Division 3

1	CARDIFF CITY	42	13	7	1	42	20	12	1	8	35	27	83
2	Wrexham	42	14	3	4	48	26	9	8	4	27	26	80
3	Barnet	42	16	4	1	45	19	7	6	8	21	29	79
4	York City	42	13	6	2	41	15	8	6	7	31	30	75
5	Walsall	42	11	6	4	42	31	11	1	9	34	30	73
6	Crewe Alexandra	42	13	3	5	47	23	8	4	9	28	33	70
7	Bury	42	10	7	4	36	19	8	2	11	27	36	63
8	Lincoln City	42	10	6	5	31	20	8	3	10	26	33	63
9	Shrewsbury Town	42	11	3	7	36	30	6	8	7	21	22	62
10	Colchester United	42	13	3	5	38	26	5	2	14	29	50	59
11	Rochdale	42	10	3	8	38	29	6	7	8	32	41	58
12	Chesterfield	42	11	3	7	32	28	4	8	9	27	35	56
13	Scarborough	42	7	7	7	32	30	8	2	11	34	41	54
14	Scunthorpe United	42	8	7	6	38	25	6	5	10	19	29	54
15	Darlington	42	5	6	10	23	31	7	8	6	25	22	50
16	Doncaster Rovers	42	6	5	10	22	28	5	9	7	20	29	47
17	Hereford United	42	7	9	5	31	27	3	6	12	16	33	45
18	Carlisle United	42	7	5	9	29	27	4	6	11	22	38	44
19	Torquay United	42	6	4	11	18	26	6	3	12	27	41	43
20	Northampton Town	42	6	5	10	19	28	5	3	13	29	46	41
21	Gillingham	42	9	4	8	32	28	0	9	12	16	36	40
22	Halifax Town	42	3	5	13	20	35	6	4	11	25	33	36

1993/94 Division 2

1	Reading	46	15	6	2	40	16	11	5	7	41	28	89
2	Port Vale	46	16	6	1	46	18	10	4	9	33	28	88
3	Plymouth Argyle	46	16	4	3	46	26	9	6	8	42	30	85
4	Stockport County	46	15	3	5	50	22	9	10	4	24	22	85
5	York City	46	12	7	4	33	13	9	5	9	31	27	75
6	Burnley	46	17	4	2	55	18	4	6	13	24	40	73
7	Bradford City	46	13	5	5	34	20	6	8	9	27	33	70
8	Bristol Rovers	46	10	8	5	33	26	10	2	11	27	33	70
9	Hull City	46	9	9	5	33	20	9	5	9	29	34	68
10	Cambridge United	46	11	5	7	38	29	8	4	11	41	44	66
11	Huddersfield Town	46	9	8	6	27	26	8	6	9	31	35	65
12	Wrexham	46	13	4	6	45	33	4	7	12	21	44	62
13	Swansea City	46	12	7	4	37	20	4	5	14	19	38	60
14	Brighton & Hove A.	46	10	7	6	38	29	5	7	11	22	38	59
15	Rotherham United	46	11	4	8	42	30	4	9	10	21	30	58
16	Brentford	46	7	10	6	30	28	6	9	8	27	27	58
17	Bournemouth	46	8	7	8	26	27	6	8	9	25	32	57
18	Leyton Orient	46	11	9	3	38	26	3	5	15	19	45	56
19	CARDIFF CITY	46	10	7	6	39	33	3	8	12	27	46	54
20	Blackpool	46	12	2	9	41	37	4	3	16	22	38	53
21	Fulham	46	7	6	10	20	23	7	4	12	30	40	52
22	Exeter City	46	8	7	8	38	37	3	5	15	14	46	45
23	Hartlepool United	46	8	3	12	28	40	1	6	16	13	47	36
24	Barnet	46	4	6	13	22	32	1	7	15	19	54	28

1994/95 Division 2

1	Birmingham City	46	15	6	2	53	18	10	8	5	31	19	89
2	Brentford	46	14	4	5	44	15	11	6	6	37	24	85
3	Crewe Alexandra	46	14	3	6	46	33	11	5	7	34	35	83
4	Bristol Rovers	46	15	7	1	48	20	7	9	7	22	20	82
5	Huddersfield Town	46	14	5	4	45	21	8	10	5	34	28	81
6	Wycombe Wanderers	46	13	7	3	36	19	8	8	7	24	27	78
7	Oxford United	46	13	6	4	30	18	8	6	9	36	34	75
8	Hull City	46	13	6	4	40	18	8	5	10	30	39	74
9	York City	46	13	4	6	37	21	8	5	10	30	30	72
10	Swansea City	46	10	8	5	23	13	9	6	8	34	32	71
11	Stockport County	46	12	3	8	40	29	7	5	11	23	31	65
12	Blackpool	46	11	4	8	40	36	7	6	10	24	34	64
13	Wrexham	46	10	7	6	38	27	6	8	9	27	37	63
14	Bradford City	46	8	6	9	29	32	8	6	9	28	32	60
15	Peterborough Utd.	46	7	11	5	26	29	7	7	9	28	40	60
16	Brighton & Hove A.	46	9	10	4	25	15	5	7	11	29	38	59
17	Rotherham United	46	12	6	5	36	26	2	8	13	21	35	56
18	Shrewsbury Town	46	9	9	5	34	27	4	5	14	20	35	53
19	Bournemouth	46	9	4	10	30	34	4	7	12	19	35	50
20	Cambridge United	46	8	9	6	33	28	3	6	14	19	41	48
21	Plymouth Argyle	46	7	6	10	22	36	5	4	14	23	47	46
22	CARDIFF CITY	46	5	6	12	25	31	4	5	14	21	43	38
23	Chester City	46	5	6	12	23	42	1	5	17	14	42	29
24	Leyton Orient	46	6	6	11	21	29	0	2	21	9	46	26

1995/96 Division 3

1	Preston North End	46	11	8	4	44	22	12	9	2	34	16	86
2	Gillingham	46	16	6	1	33	6	6	11	6	16	14	83
3	Bury	46	11	6	6	33	21	11	7	5	33	27	79
4	Plymouth Argyle	46	14	5	4	41	20	8	7	8	27	29	78
5	Darlington	46	10	6	7	30	21	10	12	1	30	21	78
6	Hereford United	46	13	5	5	40	22	7	9	7	25	25	74
7	Colchester United	46	13	7	3	37	22	5	11	7	24	29	72
8	Chester City	46	11	9	3	45	22	7	7	9	27	31	70
9	Barnet	46	13	6	4	40	19	5	10	8	25	26	70
10	Wigan Athletic	46	15	3	5	36	21	5	7	11	26	35	70
11	Northampton Town	46	9	10	4	32	22	9	3	11	19	22	67
12	Scunthorpe United	46	8	8	7	36	30	7	7	9	31	31	60
13	Doncaster Rovers	46	11	6	6	25	19	5	5	13	24	41	59
14	Exeter City	46	9	9	5	25	22	4	9	10	21	31	57
15	Rochdale	46	7	8	8	32	33	7	5	11	25	28	55
16	Cambridge United	46	8	8	7	34	30	6	4	13	27	41	54
17	Fulham	46	10	9	4	39	26	2	8	13	18	37	53
18	Lincoln City	46	8	7	8	32	26	5	7	11	25	47	53
19	Mansfield Town	46	6	10	7	25	29	5	10	8	29	35	53
20	Hartlepool United	46	8	9	6	30	24	4	4	15	17	43	49
21	Leyton Orient	46	11	4	8	29	22	1	7	15	15	41	47
22	CARDIFF CITY	46	8	6	9	24	22	3	6	14	17	42	45
23	Scarborough	46	5	11	7	22	28	3	5	15	17	41	40
24	Torquay United	46	4	9	10	17	36	1	5	17	13	48	29

1996/97 Division 3

1	Wigan Athletic	46	17	3	3	53	21	9	6	8	31	30	87
2	Fulham	46	13	5	5	41	20	12	7	4	31	18	87
3	Carlisle United	46	16	3	4	41	21	8	9	6	26	23	84
4	Northampton Town	46	14	4	5	43	17	6	8	9	24	27	72
5	Swansea City	46	13	5	5	37	20	8	3	12	25	38	71
6	Chester City	46	11	8	4	30	16	7	8	8	25	27	70
7	CARDIFF CITY	46	11	4	8	30	23	9	5	9	26	31	69
8	Colchester United	46	11	9	3	36	23	6	8	9	26	28	68
9	Lincoln City	46	10	8	5	35	25	8	4	11	35	44	66
10	Cambridge United	46	11	5	7	30	27	7	6	10	23	32	65
11	Mansfield Town	46	9	8	6	21	17	7	8	8	26	28	64
12	Scarborough	46	9	9	5	36	31	7	6	10	29	37	63
13	Scunthorpe United	46	11	3	9	36	33	7	6	10	23	29	63
14	Rochdale	46	10	6	7	34	24	4	10	9	24	34	58
15	Barnet	46	9	9	5	32	23	5	7	11	14	28	58
16	Leyton Orient	46	11	6	6	28	20	4	6	13	22	38	57
17	Hull City	46	9	8	6	29	26	4	10	9	15	24	57
18	Darlington	46	11	5	7	37	28	3	5	15	27	50	52
19	Doncaster Rovers	46	9	7	7	29	23	5	3	15	23	43	52
20	Hartlepool United	46	8	6	9	33	32	6	3	14	20	34	51
21	Torquay United	46	9	4	10	24	24	4	7	12	22	38	50
22	Exeter City	46	6	9	8	25	30	6	3	14	23	43	48
23	Brighton & Hove A.	46	12	6	5	41	27	1	4	18	12	43	47
24	Hereford United	46	6	8	9	26	25	5	6	12	24	40	47

1997/98 Division 3

1	Notts County	46	14	7	2	41	20	15	5	3	41	23	99
2	Macclesfield Town	46	19	4	0	40	11	4	9	10	23	33	82
3	Lincoln City	46	11	7	5	32	24	9	8	6	28	27	75
4	Colchester United	46	14	5	4	41	24	7	6	10	31	36	74
5	Torquay United	46	14	4	5	39	22	7	7	9	29	37	74
6	Scarborough	46	14	6	3	44	23	5	9	9	23	35	72
7	Barnet	46	10	8	5	35	22	9	5	9	26	29	70
8	Scunthorpe United	46	11	7	5	30	24	8	5	10	26	28	69
9	Rotherham United	46	10	9	4	41	30	6	10	7	26	31	67
10	Peterborough Utd.	46	13	6	4	37	16	5	7	11	26	35	67
11	Leyton Orient	46	14	5	4	40	20	5	7	11	22	27	66
12	Mansfield Town	46	11	9	3	42	26	5	8	10	22	29	65
13	Shrewsbury Town	46	12	3	8	35	28	4	10	9	26	34	61
14	Chester City	46	12	7	4	34	15	5	3	15	26	46	61
15	Exeter City	46	10	8	5	39	25	5	7	11	29	38	60
16	Cambridge United	46	11	8	4	39	27	3	10	10	24	30	60
17	Hartlepool United	46	10	12	1	40	22	2	11	10	21	31	59
18	Rochdale	46	15	3	5	43	15	2	4	17	13	40	58
19	Darlington	46	13	6	4	43	28	1	6	16	13	44	54
20	Swansea City	46	8	8	7	24	16	5	3	15	25	46	50
21	CARDIFF CITY	46	5	13	5	27	22	4	10	9	21	30	50
22	Hull City	46	10	6	7	36	32	1	2	20	20	51	41
23	Brighton & Hove A.	46	3	10	10	21	34	3	7	13	17	32	35
24	Doncaster Rovers	46	3	3	17	14	48	1	5	17	16	65	20

1998/99 Division 3

1	Brentford	46	16	5	2	45	18	10	2	11	34	38	85
2	Cambridge United	46	13	6	4	41	21	10	6	7	37	27	81
3	CARDIFF CITY	46	13	7	3	35	17	9	7	7	25	22	80
4	Scunthorpe United	46	14	3	6	42	28	8	5	10	27	30	74
5	Rotherham United	46	11	8	4	41	26	9	5	9	38	35	73
6	Leyton Orient	46	12	6	5	40	30	7	9	7	28	29	72
7	Swansea City	46	11	9	3	33	19	8	5	10	23	29	71
8	Mansfield Town	46	15	2	6	38	18	4	8	11	22	40	67
9	Peterborough Utd.	46	11	4	8	41	29	7	8	8	31	27	66
10	Halifax Town	46	10	8	5	33	25	7	7	9	25	31	66
11	Darlington	46	10	6	7	41	24	8	5	10	28	34	65
12	Exeter City	46	13	5	5	32	18	4	7	12	15	32	63
13	Plymouth Argyle	46	11	6	6	32	19	6	4	13	26	35	61
14	Chester City	46	6	12	5	28	30	7	6	10	29	36	57
15	Shrewsbury Town	46	11	6	6	36	29	3	8	12	16	34	56
16	Barnet	46	10	5	8	30	31	4	8	11	24	40	55
17	Brighton & Hove A.	46	8	3	12	25	35	8	4	11	24	31	55
18	Southend United	46	8	6	9	24	21	6	6	11	28	37	54
19	Rochdale	46	9	8	6	22	21	4	7	12	20	34	54
20	Torquay United	46	9	9	5	29	20	3	8	12	18	38	53
21	Hull City	46	8	5	10	25	28	6	6	11	19	34	53
22	Hartlepool United	46	8	7	8	33	27	5	5	13	19	38	51
23	Carlisle United	46	8	8	7	25	21	3	8	12	18	32	49
24	Scarborough	46	8	3	12	30	39	6	3	14	20	38	48

1999/2000 Division 2

		P	W	D	L	F	A	W	D	L	F	A	Pts
1	Preston North End	46	15	4	4	37	23	13	7	3	37	14	95
2	Burnley	46	16	3	4	42	23	9	10	4	27	24	88
3	Gillingham	46	16	3	4	46	21	9	7	7	33	27	85
4	Wigan Athletic	46	15	3	5	37	14	7	14	2	35	24	83
5	Millwall	46	14	7	2	41	18	9	6	8	35	32	82
6	Stoke City	46	13	7	3	37	18	10	6	7	31	24	82
7	Bristol Rovers	46	13	7	3	34	19	10	4	9	35	26	80
8	Notts County	46	9	6	8	32	27	9	5	9	29	28	65
9	Bristol City	46	7	14	2	31	18	8	5	10	28	39	64
10	Reading	46	10	9	4	28	18	6	5	12	29	45	62
11	Wrexham	46	9	6	8	23	24	8	5	10	29	37	62
12	Wycombe Wanderers	46	11	4	8	32	24	5	9	9	24	29	61
13	Luton Town	46	10	7	6	41	35	7	3	13	20	30	61
14	Oldham Athletic	46	8	5	10	27	28	8	7	8	23	27	60
15	Bury	46	8	10	5	38	33	5	8	10	23	31	57
16	Bournemouth	46	11	6	6	37	19	5	3	15	22	43	57
17	Brentford	46	8	6	9	27	31	5	7	11	20	30	52
18	Colchester United	46	9	4	10	36	40	5	6	12	23	42	52
19	Cambridge United	46	8	6	9	38	33	4	6	13	26	32	48
20	Oxford United	46	6	5	12	24	38	6	4	13	19	35	45
21	CARDIFF CITY	46	5	10	8	23	34	4	7	12	22	33	44
22	Blackpool	46	4	10	9	26	37	4	7	12	23	40	41
23	Scunthorpe United	46	4	6	13	16	34	5	6	12	24	40	39
24	Chesterfield	46	5	7	11	17	25	2	8	13	17	38	36

2000/01 Division 3

		P	W	D	L	F	A	W	D	L	F	A	Pts
1	Brighton & Hove A.	46	19	2	2	52	14	9	6	8	21	21	92
2	CARDIFF CITY	46	16	7	0	56	20	7	6	10	39	38	82
3	Chesterfield	46	16	5	2	46	14	9	9	5	33	28	80
4	Hartlepool United	46	12	8	3	40	23	9	6	8	31	31	77
5	Leyton Orient	46	13	7	3	31	18	7	8	8	28	33	75
6	Hull City	46	12	7	4	27	18	7	10	6	20	21	74
7	Blackpool	46	14	4	5	50	26	8	2	13	24	32	72
8	Rochdale	46	11	8	4	36	25	7	9	7	23	23	71
9	Cheltenham Town	46	12	5	6	37	27	6	9	8	22	25	68
10	Scunthorpe United	46	13	7	3	42	16	5	4	14	20	36	65
11	Southend United	46	10	8	5	29	23	5	10	8	26	30	63
12	Plymouth Argyle	46	13	5	5	33	17	2	8	13	21	44	58
13	Mansfield Town	46	12	7	4	40	26	3	6	14	24	46	58
14	Macclesfield Town	46	10	5	8	23	21	4	9	10	28	41	56
15	Shrewsbury Town	46	12	5	6	30	26	3	5	15	19	39	55
16	Kidderminster H.	46	10	6	7	29	27	3	8	12	18	34	53
17	York City	46	9	6	8	23	26	4	7	12	19	37	52
18	Lincoln City	46	9	9	5	36	28	3	6	14	22	38	51
19	Exeter City	46	9	9	6	22	20	4	5	14	18	38	50
20	Darlington	46	10	6	7	28	23	2	7	14	16	33	49
21	Torquay United	46	8	9	6	30	29	4	4	15	22	48	49
22	Carlisle United	46	8	8	7	26	26	3	7	13	16	39	48
23	Halifax Town	46	7	6	10	33	32	5	5	13	21	36	47
24	Barnet	46	9	8	6	44	29	3	1	19	23	52	45

2001/02 Division 2

		P	W	D	L	F	A	W	D	L	F	A	Pts
1	Brighton & Hove A.	46	17	5	1	42	16	8	10	5	24	26	90
2	Reading	46	12	7	4	36	20	11	8	4	34	23	84
3	Brentford	46	17	5	1	48	12	7	6	10	29	31	83
4	CARDIFF CITY	46	12	8	3	39	25	11	6	6	36	25	83
5	Stoke City	46	16	4	3	43	12	7	7	9	24	28	80
6	Huddersfield Town	46	13	7	3	35	19	8	8	7	30	28	78
7	Bristol City	46	13	6	4	38	21	8	4	11	30	32	73
8	Queen's Park Rgs.	46	11	10	2	35	18	8	4	11	25	31	71
9	Oldham Athletic	46	14	6	3	47	27	4	10	9	30	38	70
10	Wigan Athletic	46	9	6	8	36	23	7	10	6	30	28	64
11	Wycombe Wanderers	46	13	5	5	38	26	4	8	11	20	38	64
12	Tranmere Rovers	46	10	9	4	39	19	6	6	11	24	41	63
13	Swindon Town	46	10	7	6	26	21	5	7	11	20	35	59
14	Port Vale	46	11	6	6	35	24	5	4	14	16	38	58
15	Colchester United	46	9	6	8	35	33	6	6	11	30	43	57
16	Blackpool	46	8	9	6	39	31	6	5	12	27	38	56
17	Peterborough Utd.	46	11	5	7	46	26	4	5	14	18	33	55
18	Chesterfield	46	9	3	11	35	36	4	10	9	18	29	52
19	Notts County	46	8	7	8	28	29	5	4	14	31	42	50
20	Northampton Town	46	9	4	10	30	33	5	3	15	24	46	49
21	Bournemouth	46	9	4	10	36	33	1	10	12	20	38	44
22	Bury	46	6	9	8	26	32	5	2	16	17	43	44
23	Wrexham	46	7	7	9	29	32	4	3	16	27	57	43
24	Cambridge United	46	7	7	9	29	34	0	6	17	18	59	34

CARDIFF CITY MANAGERS

Fred Stewart	May 1911	May 1933
Bartley Wilson	May 1933	Feb 1934
Ben Watts-Jones	Feb 1934	April 1937
Bill Jennings	April 1937	Apr 1939
Cyril Spiers	April 1939	June 1946
Billy McCandless	June 1946	Nov 1947
Cyril Spiers	Nov 1947	May 1954
Trevor Morris	April 1954	July 1958
Bill Jones	Sept 1958	Sep 1962
George Swindin	Nov 1962	Apr 1964
Jimmy Scoular	June 1964	Nov 1973
Frank O'Farrell	Nov 1973	Apr 1974
Jimmy Andrews	May 1974	Nov 1978
Ritchie Morgan	Nov 1978	Nov 1981
Graham Williams	Nov 1981	Feb 1982
Len Ashurst	Mar 1982	Mar 1984
Jimmy Goodfellow	Mar 1984	Sep 1984
Alan Durban	Sep 1984	May 1986
Frank Burrows	May 1986	Aug 1989
Len Ashurst	Aug 1989	May 1991
Eddie May	July 1991	Nov 1994
Terry Yorath	Nov 1994	March 1995
Eddie May	March 1995	May 1995
Kenny Hibbitt	July 1995	Jan 1996
Phil Neal	Jan 1996	Oct 1996
Russell Osman	Nov 1996	Dec 1996
Kenny Hibbitt	Dec 1996	Feb 1998
Frank Burrows	Feb 1998	Jan 2000
Billy Ayre	Feb 2000	Aug 2000
Bobby Gould	Aug 2000	Oct 2000
Alan Cork	Oct 2000	Feb 2002
Lennie Lawrence	Feb 2002	

April 23 1927; Fred Keenor with the F.A. Cup

AFTERWORD BY THE AUTHOR

It was my acquisition in 1967 of a Cardiff City v. Tottenham Hotspur F.A. Cup match programme from February 1923 that sowed the seeds of this reference book. What was the result and the attendance, I wondered, for a game between what were then two of the country's leading clubs?

A visit to the reference library provided the answers from dusty bound-volumes of various newspapers. The report of the game made interesting reading, and over the next few years a weekly visit to the library enabled me to put together full details of each season, not just for Cardiff City but for the other Welsh clubs in the Football League, a task that I completed thirty years ago.

I also kept a match-by-match line-up record from then on, covering Cardiff City and the other clubs, including transfers in and out, managerial changes and other useful information on players etc. and that has been ongoing for the past thirty-two years. The ledger solves regular queries from my colleagues in the press and media, and has formed the major part of the research for this book.

Alongside the various written histories of the Club, plus the archive-photo series of publications, the "Definitive Cardiff City" will, I hope, be a useful reference and solve all the friendly arguments..."*They used to get 40,000 at every home game when they were in the First Division in the 1950s*" – a line I often hear from older supporters. But did they? – well, if you look at the appropriate season, the answers are there along with a great deal of other information.

Richard Shepherd
September 2002
